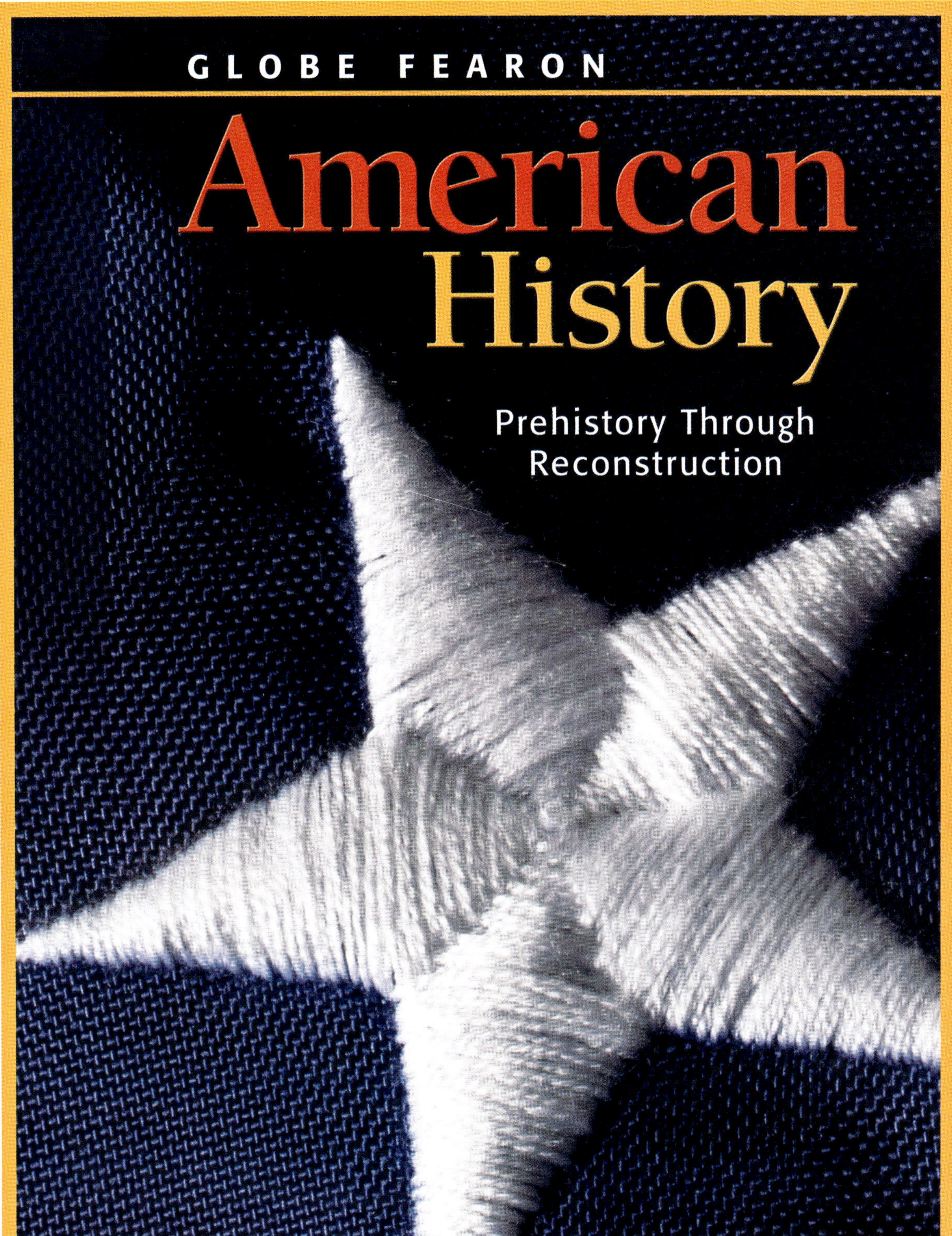

GLOBE FEARON
Pearson Learning Group

The following people have contributed to the development of this product:

Art & Design: Sharon Bozek, Sherri Hieber-Day, Jenifer Hixson, Salita Mehta, Elizabeth Nemeth, Jim O'Shea, Eileen Peters, Karolyn Wehner, Angel Weyant
Editorial: Linda Dorf, Elaine Fay, Alisa Loftus, Colleen Maguire, Jane Petlinski, Jennie Rakos, Tara Walters
Manufacturing: Nathan Kinney
Marketing: Katie Erezuma
Production: Lorraine Allen, Louis Campos, Karen Edmonds, Sue Levine, Karyn Mueller, Phyllis Rosinsky, Cindy Talocci
Publishing Operations: Travis Bailey, Kate Matracia

Acknowledgments appear on page R33, which constitutes an extension of this copyright page.

ISBN 0-13-024400-7

Printed in the United States of America
2 3 4 5 6 7 8 9 10 07 06 05

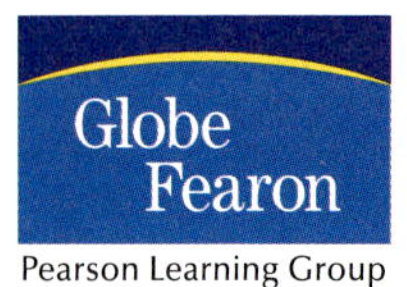

Pearson Learning Group

1-800-321-3106
www.pearsonlearning.com

Globe Fearon gratefully acknowledges the contributions of the following consultants and reviewers.

Content Consultants

Yong Chen, Ph.D.
Associate Professor, History and Asian American Studies
University of California, Irvine
Asian American studies

Frank De Varona, E.S.
Visiting Associate Professor
Florida International University
Miami, FL
Latino studies

Daniel J. Gelo, Ph.D.
Professor and Chair, Department of Anthropology
University of Texas at San Antonio
San Antonio, TX
Native American studies

Linda L. Greenow, Ph.D.
Chair, Department of Geography
S.U.N.Y. New Paltz
New Paltz, NY
Geography

Deborah Gray White, Ph.D.
Chair, Department of History
Rutgers University
New Brunswick, NJ
African American studies
Women's studies

Reviewers

Lawrence Broughton
Chairman, Social Studies Department
North Chicago Community High School
North Chicago, IL

Melvin Garrison
Social Studies Curriculum Specialist, K–12
Office of Curriculum Support
School District of Philadelphia
Philadelphia, PA

Flossie Baker Gautier
Social Studies Teacher
Bay High School
Panama City, FL

Floyd Kessler
Assistant Principal
Junior High School 190
Queens, NY

Charlotte Kresovich
Social Studies Teacher
School District of Philadelphia
Philadelphia, PA

Michael Mann
English and History Unified Curriculum Teacher
North Star Academy
Newark, NJ

Contents

Woolly mammoth (page 4)

John White (page 56)

Soldier's powderhorn (page 110)

Revolutionary War drum (page 164)

George Washington (page 244)

Cotton gin (page 323)

Alexis de Tocqueville (page 341)

Steam locomotive (page 372)

Slavery identification badge (page 378)

MAPS

CHARTS AND GRAPHS

Charts and Graphs Cont.

Build Your Skills

Past to Present

Connects topics in history to today

CONNECT History

Links history to other areas of study

Points of View

Presents two sides of important issues

They Made History

Highlights important people who made a difference

Primary Source Documents

Includes twelve key documents and speeches

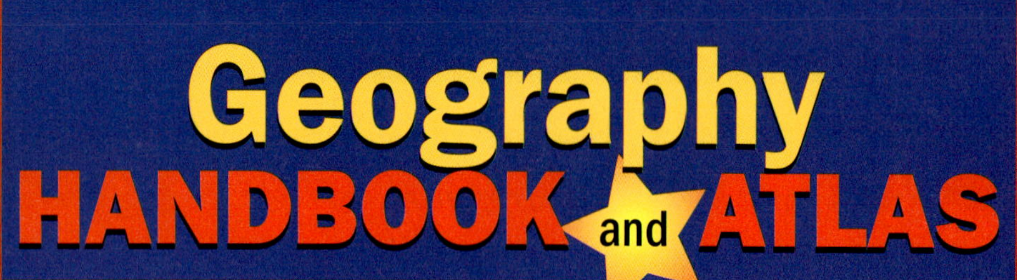

The Hubbard Glacier stretches into the sea near a cruise ship in Alaska.

Geography Handbook

Atlas

Why Study Geography?

A good place to begin your study of American history is with the study of geography. Geography is the study of the physical features of Earth and the people who live on it, including the relationship between people and their environment. Geography helps us to understand history by seeing how the characteristics of a place affect people and events.

Five Geography Themes

Geographers have developed five themes to show the connection between history and geography. These themes are location, place, region, movement, and human interaction.

Location Street signs in New York City

Location

When you study events in history, you need to know exactly where in the world they take place. The theme of location answers the question "Where is it?" To know precisely where a place is located, geographers have come up with a grid system of imaginary lines on maps. These are called lines of latitude and lines of longitude. You will learn more about this grid system on page GH7.

Sometimes, it is useful to know where an area is in relation to another area. For example, New York City is in the northeast corner of the United States, close to New Jersey and Connecticut. A specific location in New York City could be the intersection of 6th Avenue and West 52nd Street.

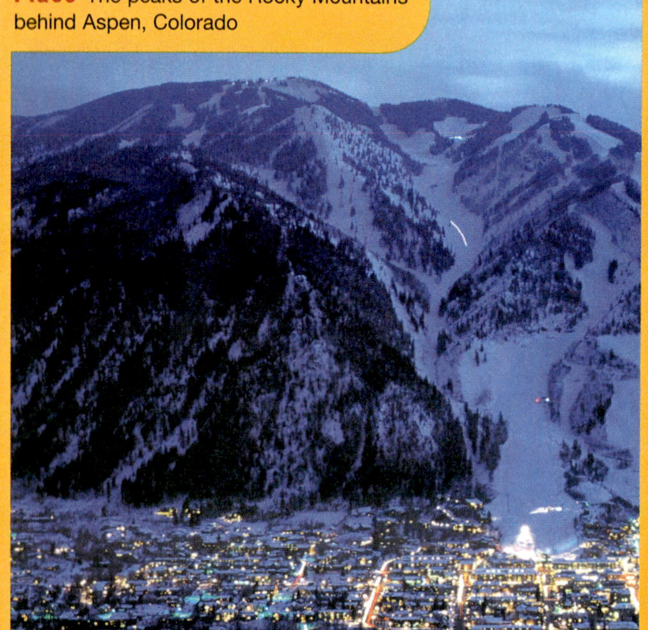

Place The peaks of the Rocky Mountains behind Aspen, Colorado

Place

Geographers help us to find out what a place is like. Every place on Earth has its own features that makes it different from every other place.

If you asked geographers to describe Aspen, Colorado, they would point out physical features such as rivers, hills, and mountains. They might also give its population, and describe the kind of buildings people have constructed there. So, a description of a place includes not only its geographical features, but also how people have shaped that place over time.

Region

Because the world is so vast, it is sometimes convenient to think about it in terms of regions. A region is an area that has similar features and characteristics. These can include similar landforms, the type of climate the region has, or even its own particular culture. For example, the Great Plains of the United States is a region because it is an area with a great deal of level land that is good for farming. The states in this region also share a similar climate that includes very cold winters.

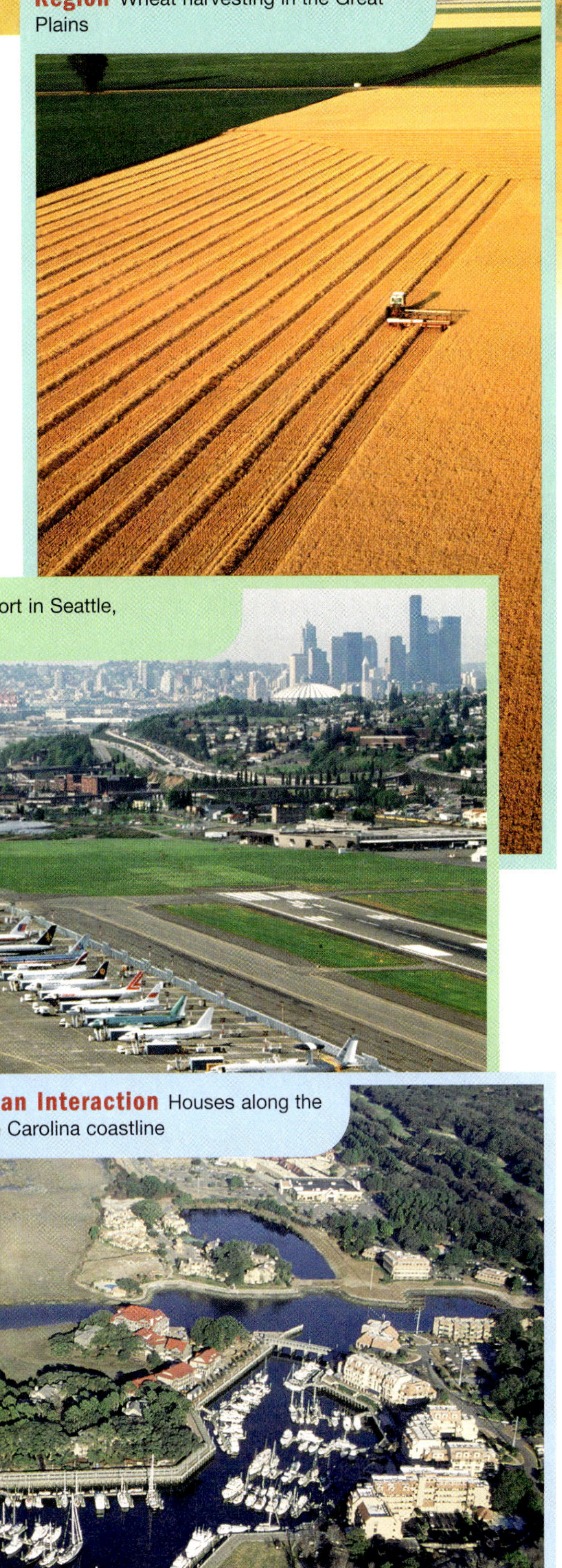

Region Wheat harvesting in the Great Plains

Movement Airport in Seattle, Washington

Human Interaction Houses along the North Carolina coastline

Movement

In early America, people moved around to hunt or gather food. Later, they traveled to explore, to conquer, and to gain riches. Some people left their homes to find good farmland, more space, or better jobs.

Today, movement has become a daily part of our lives. People use planes, trains, cars, buses, and subways to move from one place to another. Ships and planes crisscross the globe as goods and resources are exchanged among nations. When we study history, we look at the movement of people, ideas, and goods to understand the changes that have occurred.

Human Interaction

In the study of history, we look at the interaction between people and their surroundings. We might ask: How does the environment of a place affect how people live? The weather and resources of a place, for example, will determine how people use the land for business and recreation, as well as the types of houses people build. The North Carolina coast has been developed to allow people to take advantage of the water resources around them for business and leisure activities such as sailing and fishing.

Reading a Map

To understand geography, you need to know how to read a map and understand its parts.

Maps are drawings of places on Earth. To help you read maps, mapmakers—or cartographers—include certain elements on most maps they draw. These include the title, the key, the compass rose, the locator map, and the scale.

Many of the maps you see are general-purpose maps that give political or physical information. A political map shows boundaries as well as capital cities and major cities. A physical map shows natural features, such as rivers and oceans. Special-purpose maps show specific kinds of information. For example, a climate map is a special-purpose map that shows the temperature of a place or region.

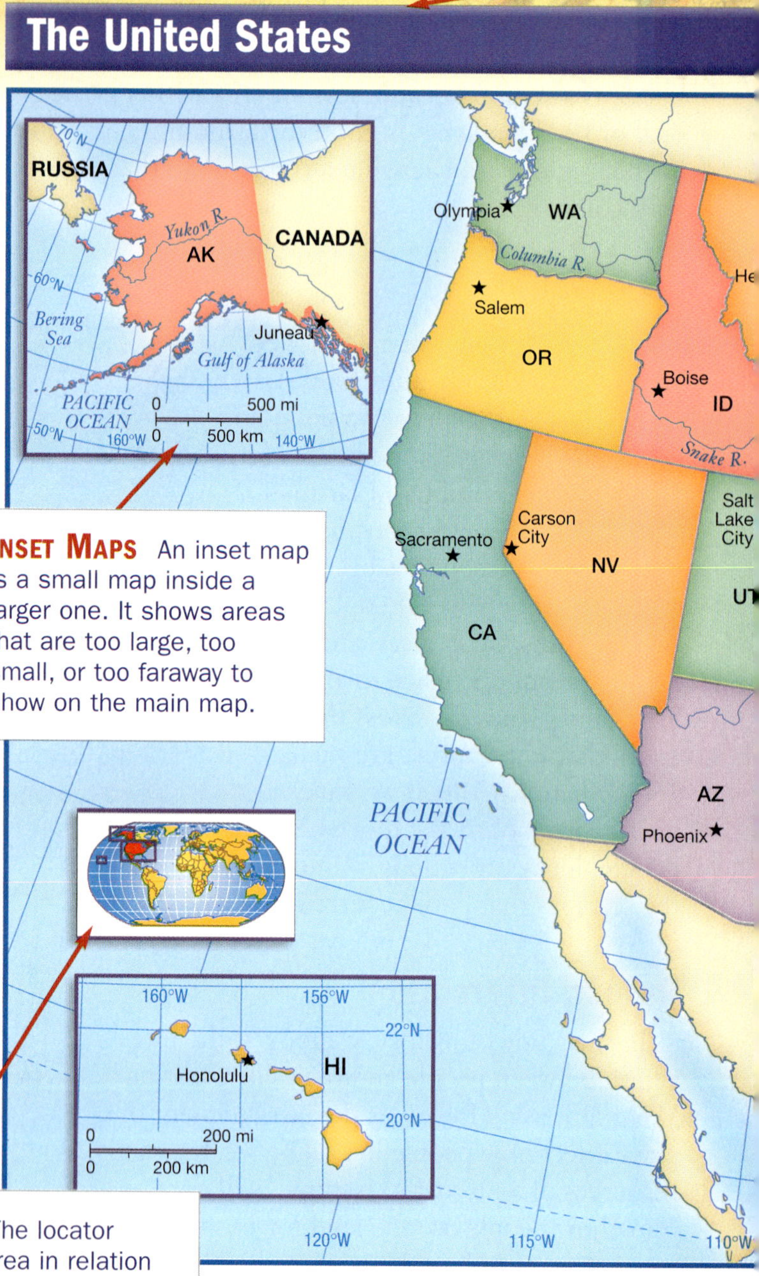

The United States

INSET MAPS An inset map is a small map inside a larger one. It shows areas that are too large, too small, or too faraway to show on the main map.

LOCATOR The locator shows an area in relation to a larger area. Here you can see where the United States is in relation to the world.

MAP TITLE The title tells the subject of the map and what kind of information can be found on the map.

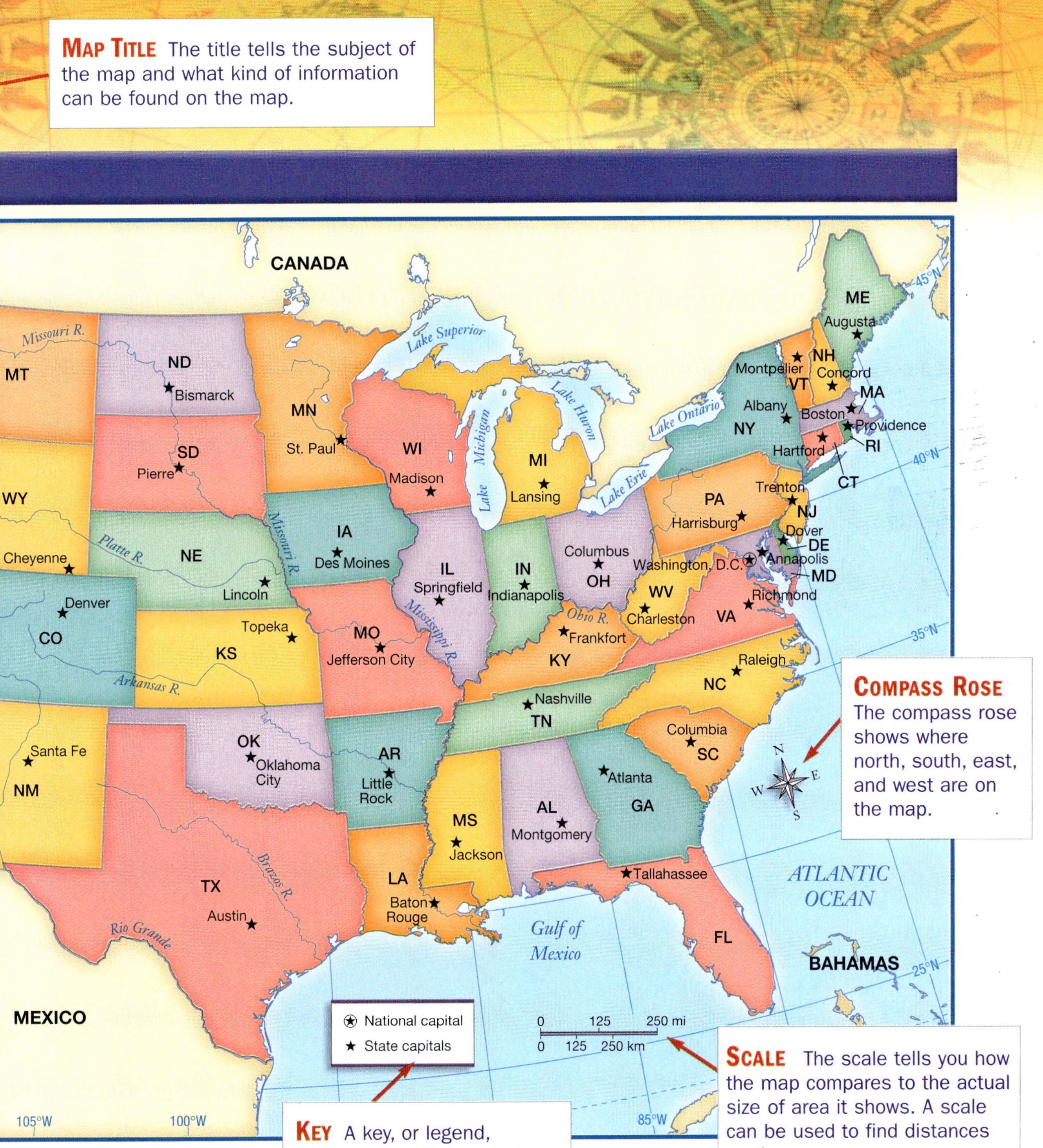

COMPASS ROSE The compass rose shows where north, south, east, and west are on the map.

KEY A key, or legend, explains what the symbols or colors on the map stand for.

SCALE The scale tells you how the map compares to the actual size of area it shows. A scale can be used to find distances on the map.

Latitude and Longitude

Mapmakers have created a special kind of grid system to help us find the exact location of any place on Earth.

Lines of Latitude

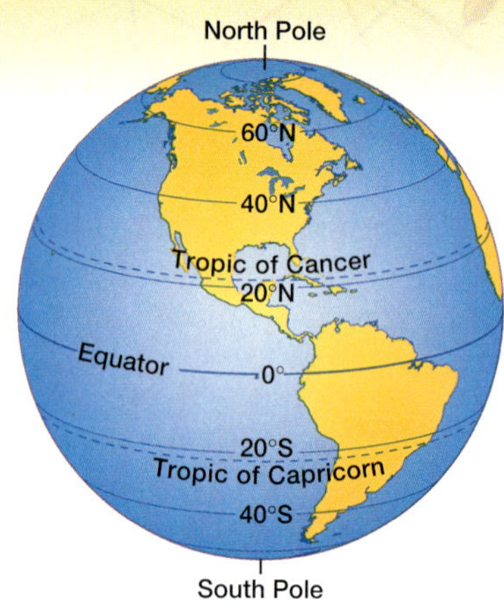

Latitude is the position of a place north and south of the equator. Lines of latitude run east to west around the globe. On the map, you can see that each line of latitude has a measurement in degrees (°).

The equator is an imaginary line that divides the earth into two halves, called hemispheres. The Northern Hemisphere lies north of the equator, and the Southern Hemisphere lies south of it.

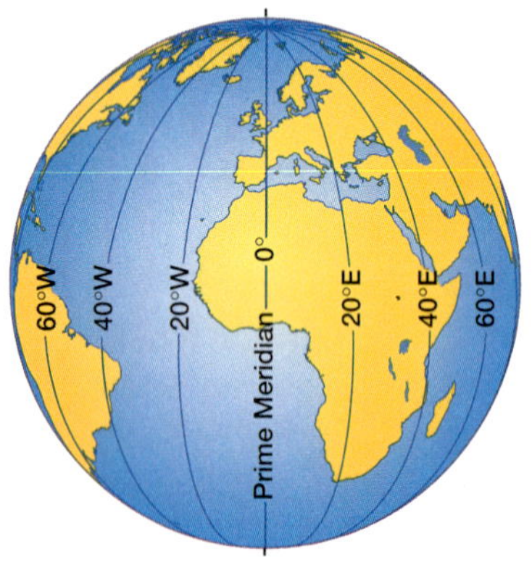

Lines of Longitude

Lines of longitude run from the North Pole to the South Pole. They are used to measure distance in degrees east and west of the prime meridian. On the map, you can see that each line of longitude has a measure in degrees (°).

The prime meridian is an imaginary line that also divides the earth into hemispheres. The half that lies west of the prime meridian is the Western Hemisphere. The half that lies to the east of the prime meridian is the Eastern Hemisphere.

Using Latitude and Longitude

Once you know the latitude and longitude of a place, you can locate it quickly on a map. The point at which lines of latitude and longitude meet is the grid address, or coordinates, of an exact location. For example, the city of New Orleans, Louisiana, is located at 30°N/90°W. This means that New Orleans is 30° north of the equator and 90° west of the prime meridian. Use the map to find the approximate coordinates of Philadelphia, Pennsylvania.

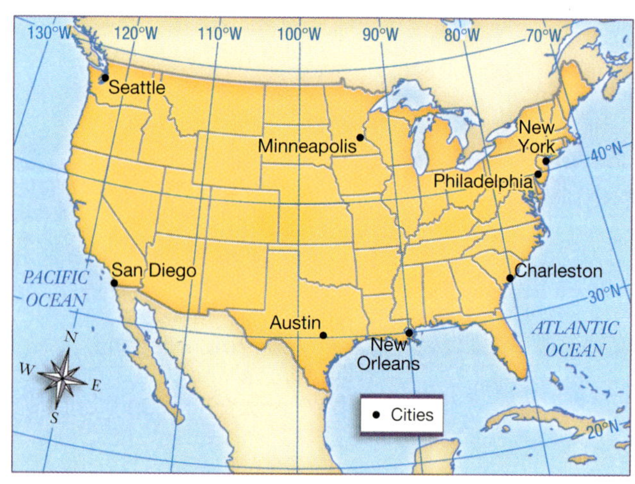

Map Projections

A map projection is a way of showing the round Earth on a flat surface.

To locate places, geographers use maps and globes. Because a globe is the same shape as the earth, it shows the sizes and shapes of the earth's features accurately. Even though a globe has this advantage, flat maps are more convenient. A flat map allows you to see all of the earth's surface at the same time. The disadvantage of a flat map is that it distorts how the earth really looks.

To solve this problem, mapmakers have developed different map projections. No map projection shows the earth correctly in every way. Some projections show the sizes of continents correctly but distort their shapes. Others show the correct shape of the landmasses but distort their sizes.

Mercator Projection

The Mercator projection shows the true shapes of landmasses, but distorts their sizes. On the Mercator projection, the actual curved lines of latitude and longitude are shown straight. Because the lines are straight, lands on either side of the equator must be stretched in size.

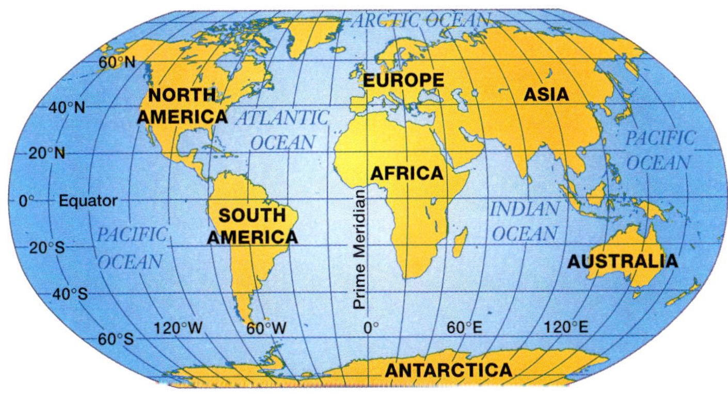

Robinson Projection

Today, many people use another kind of map projection called the Robinson projection. The lines of latitude and longitude are curved to show the curve of the earth's surface. The Robinson projection shows land and ocean sizes accurately, but the shapes of the land are slightly distorted.

Geography Dictionary

1. **Bay** a part of an ocean or lake that is partially enclosed by land
2. **Canyon** a narrow, deep valley with steep sides
3. **Delta** a triangular area of land formed from deposits at the mouth of a river
4. **Desert** a dry area where few plants grow
5. **Glacier** a large ice mass that moves slowly down a mountain or over land
6. **Harbor** a sheltered area of water where ships can anchor safely
7. **Island** an area of land completely surrounded by water
8. **Lake** a body of water that is almost completely surrounded by land
9. **Mountain peak** the very top part of a mountain
10. **Mountain range** a series of connected mountains
11. **Peninsula** a body of land jutting into a lake or ocean, surrounded on three sides by water
12. **Plain** an area of level land, usually at low elevation and often covered with grasses
13. **Plateau** a broad, flat area of land higher than the surrounding land
14. **River** a large natural flow of water that runs through the land
15. **Strait** a narrow strip of water connecting two larger bodies of water
16. **Swamp** an area of land that is saturated by water
17. **Valley** a long, low area of land that is between hills or mountains
18. **Volcano** an opening in the earth, usually raised, through which gases, lava, and hot ashes escape from the earth's interior

Atlas ★ The World

ARCTIC OCEAN
Arctic Circle
Europe
RUSSIA
KAZAKHSTAN
MONGOLIA
GEORGIA
ARMENIA
TURKEY
UZBEKISTAN
TURKMENISTAN
KYRGYZSTAN
TAJIKISTAN
AZERBAIJAN
SYRIA
LEBANON
IRAQ
IRAN
AFGHANISTAN
PAKISTAN
ISRAEL
JORDAN
KUWAIT
BAHRAIN
QATAR
UNITED ARAB EMIRATES
SAUDI ARABIA
OMAN
YEMEN
NEPAL
BHUTAN
CHINA
N. KOREA
S. KOREA
JAPAN
PACIFIC OCEAN
TAIWAN
Hong Kong
INDIA
MYANMAR (BURMA)
LAOS
BANGLADESH
THAILAND
VIETNAM
PHILIPPINES
CAMBODIA
BRUNEI
SRI LANKA
MALDIVES
MALAYSIA
SINGAPORE
INDONESIA
PAPUA NEW GUINEA
NORTHERN MARIANA ISLANDS
MARSHALL IS.
GUAM (U.S.)
FEDERATED STATES OF MICRONESIA
PALAU
KIRIBATI
NAURU
TUVALU
SOLOMON ISLANDS
VANUATU
FIJI
NEW CALEDONIA (FR.)
AUSTRALIA
NEW ZEALAND
INDIAN OCEAN
TUNISIA
LIBYA
EGYPT
West Africa
MALI
NIGER
CHAD
SUDAN
ERITREA
DJIBOUTI
ETHIOPIA
CENTRAL AFRICAN REP.
SOMALIA
CAMEROON
EQUATORIAL GUINEA
GABON
RWANDA
UGANDA
KENYA
DEM. REP. OF THE CONGO
CONGO
BURUNDI
TANZANIA
CABINDA (ANGOLA)
ANGOLA
SEYCHELLES
COMOROS
MALAWI
ZAMBIA
MADAGASCAR
NAMIBIA
ZIMBABWE
BOTSWANA
MAURITIUS
MOZAMBIQUE
SWAZILAND
RÉUNION (FR.)
SOUTH AFRICA
LESOTHO
ANTARCTICA
Europe
1 LUXEMBOURG
2 LIECHTENSTEIN
3 SAN MARINO
4 BOSNIA AND HERZEGOVINA
5 MACEDONIA
6 SWITZERLAND
7 CZECH REPUBLIC
8 YUGOSLAVIA
0 250 500 mi
0 250 500 km
Arctic Circle
SWEDEN
FINLAND
NORWAY
RUSSIA
ESTONIA
LATVIA
North Sea
DENMARK
Baltic Sea
LITHUANIA
IRELAND
UNITED KINGDOM
NETHERLANDS
RUSSIA
BELARUS
POLAND
GERMANY
BELGIUM
UKRAINE
SLOVAKIA
ATLANTIC OCEAN
Bay of Biscay
FRANCE
AUSTRIA
HUNGARY
MOLDOVA
SLOVENIA
CROATIA
ROMANIA
ANDORRA
Black Sea
PORTUGAL
SPAIN
MONACO
ITALY
Adriatic Sea
BULGARIA
ALBANIA
TURKEY
GREECE
Mediterranean Sea
AFRICA

North America

South America

Europe

National capitals
National boundaries
0
250
500 mi
0
250
500 km
N
S
E
W
Reykjavik
ICELAND
Arctic Circle
60°N
50°N
40°N
10°W
0°
10°E
20°E
30°E
Norwegian Sea
North Sea
Baltic Sea
ATLANTIC OCEAN
Bay of Biscay
Strait of Gibraltar
Adriatic Sea
Aegean Sea
Mediterranean Sea
Black Sea
NORWAY
Oslo
SWEDEN
Stockholm
FINLAND
Helsinki
RUSSIA
Moscow
Tallinn
ESTONIA
Riga
LATVIA
LITHUANIA
Vilnius
RUSSIA
Minsk
BELARUS
IRELAND
Dublin
UNITED KINGDOM
London
DENMARK
Copenhagen
NETHERLANDS
Amsterdam
Berlin
GERMANY
Warsaw
POLAND
Brussels
BELGIUM
Luxembourg
Paris
FRANCE
Prague
SLOVAKIA
Bratislava
Vienna
AUSTRIA
Budapest
HUNGARY
Kiev
UKRAINE
MOLDOVA
Chisinau
ROMANIA
Bucharest
Bern
SLOVENIA
Ljubljana
Zagreb
CROATIA
Sarajevo
Belgrade
BULGARIA
Sofia
Skopje
Tiranë
ALBANIA
GREECE
Athens
ASIA
ANDORRA
Monte Carlo
MONACO
PORTUGAL
Lisbon
Madrid
SPAIN
Rome
ITALY
Valletta
MALTA
AFRICA
1 LUXEMBOURG
2 LIECHTENSTEIN
3 SAN MARINO
4 BOSNIA AND HERZEGOVINA
5 MACEDONIA
6 SWITZERLAND
7 CZECH REPUBLIC
8 YUGOSLAVIA

Africa

EUROPE
ASIA
Strait of Gibraltar
Mediterranean Sea
Red Sea
Gulf of Aden
ATLANTIC OCEAN
INDIAN OCEAN
Tropic of Cancer
Tropic of Capricorn
Nile
Blue Nile
White Nile
Niger
Congo
Zambezi
Orange
L. Chad
L. Turkana
L. Victoria
L. Tanganyika
L. Malawi
MOROCCO
Rabat
ALGERIA
Algiers
TUNISIA
Tunis
LIBYA
Tripoli
EGYPT
Cairo
WESTERN SAHARA (MOROCCO)
MAURITANIA
Nouakchott
MALI
Bamako
NIGER
Niamey
CHAD
N'Djamena
SUDAN
Khartoum
ERITREA
Asmara
DJIBOUTI
Djibouti
ETHIOPIA
Addis Ababa
SOMALIA
Mogadishu
Dakar
Banjul
Bissau
GUINEA
Conakry
Freetown
Monrovia
Yamoussoukro
Ouagadougou
Accra
Lomé
Porto Novo
NIGERIA
Abuja
CAMEROON
Yaoundé
Malabo
CENTRAL AFRICAN REPUBLIC
Bangui
SÃO TOMÉ AND PRÍNCIPE
São Tomé
Libreville
GABON
REP. OF THE CONGO
Brazzaville
Kinshasa
DEM. REP. OF THE CONGO
Cabinda (ANGOLA)
UGANDA
Kampala
KENYA
Nairobi
Kigali
Bujumbura
TANZANIA
Dar-es-Salaam
SEYCHELLES
Victoria
COMOROS
Moroni
Luanda
ANGOLA
ZAMBIA
Lusaka
Lilongwe
Harare
ZIMBABWE
MOZAMBIQUE
MADAGASCAR
Antananarivo
Port Louis
MAURITIUS
Réunion (FR.)
NAMIBIA
Windhoek
BOTSWANA
Gaborone
Pretoria
Maputo
Mbabane
SWAZILAND
Maseru
SOUTH AFRICA
LESOTHO
N
E
S
W
40°N
30°N
20°N
10°N
0°
10°S
30°S
40°S
20°W
10°W
0°
10°E
20°E
30°E
40°E
50°E
60° E
1 BURKINA FASO
2 THE GAMBIA
3 SENEGAL
4 GUINEA-BISSAU
5 SIERRA LEONE
6 LIBERIA
7 CÔTE D'IVOIRE
8 GHANA
9 TOGO
10 BENIN
11 EQUATORIAL GUINEA
12 RWANDA
13 BURUNDI
14 MALAWI
National capitals
National boundaries
0 350 700 mi
0 350 700 km

Asia and The Middle East

The United States

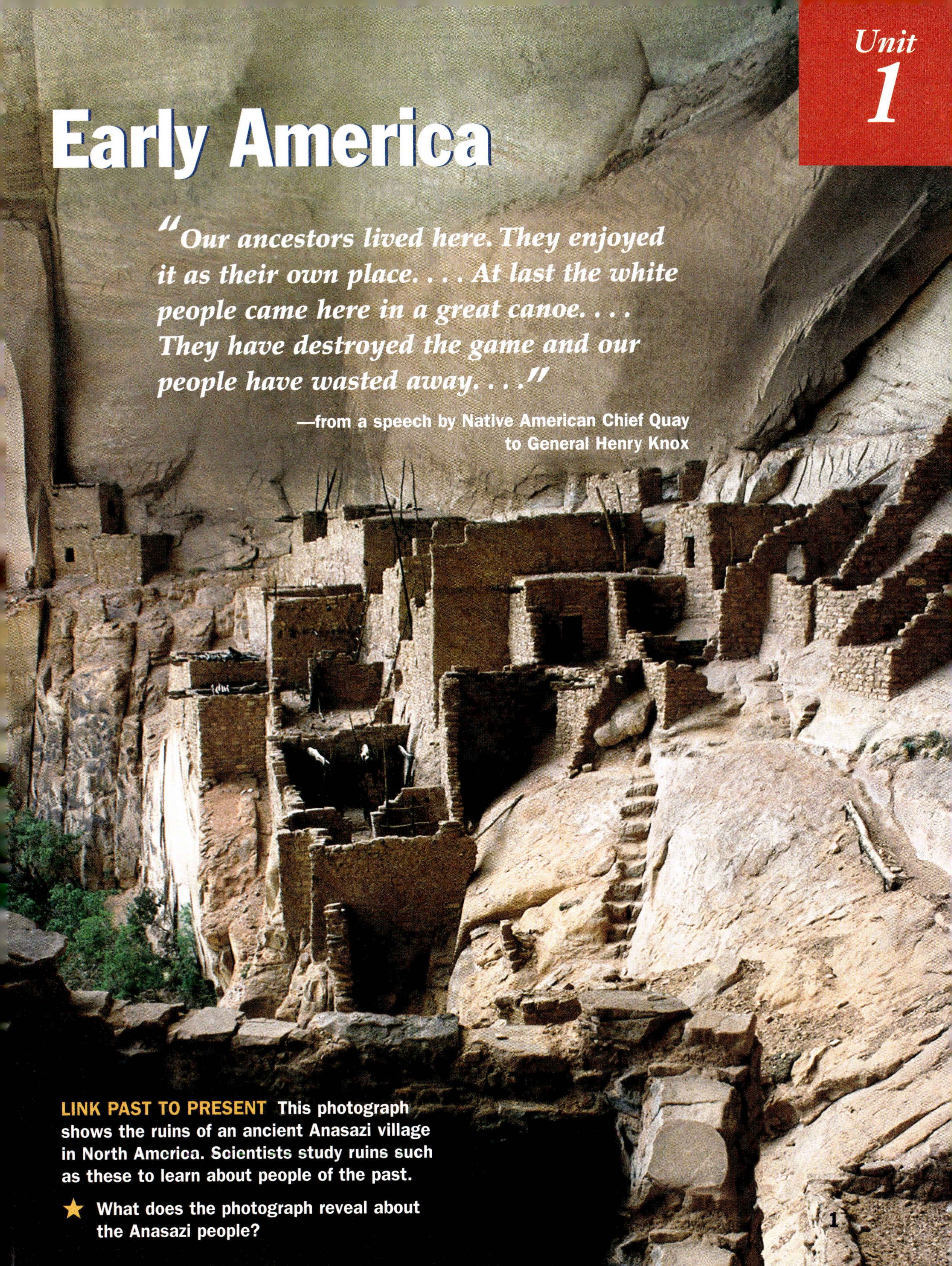

Unit 1

Early America

"Our ancestors lived here. They enjoyed it as their own place. . . . At last the white people came here in a great canoe. . . . They have destroyed the game and our people have wasted away. . . ."

—from a speech by Native American Chief Quay to General Henry Knox

LINK PAST TO PRESENT This photograph shows the ruins of an ancient Anasazi village in North America. Scientists study ruins such as these to learn about people of the past.

★ What does the photograph reveal about the Anasazi people?

CHAPTER 1

The First Americans
Prehistory–1570

I. Early Peoples
II. Civilizations in the Americas
III. Native Americans

The first people came to North America thousands of years ago. Who were these people? How did they get here, and where did they live? Scientists called archaeologists try to find the answers to these questions and many more. They study clues from the past. One scientist, Richard Leakey, said of the science of archaeology:

> "Litter of the past is the basis of archaeology. The coins, the pottery, the textiles and the buildings of bygone eras offer us clues as to how our [early ancestors] behaved . . . what they believed in and what was important to them."

The tools, weapons, and even bones left behind by the first Americans tell an interesting story. Their story is where our own history begins.

Anasazi pot

Events in the Americas (15,000 — 10,000 — 5000 — B.C.)

- **25,000 B.C.–12,000 B.C.** People cross a land bridge from Asia.
- **5000 B.C.** Agriculture develops in Mexico.
- **1300 B.C.** Olmec civilization begins.
- **300 B.C.** Hohokams grow corn in North America.

World Events (15,000 — 10,000 — 5000)

- **8000 B.C.** Agriculture develops in Asia.
- **2500 B.C.** Great Pyramids are built in Egypt.

VIEW HISTORY This photograph shows archaeologists digging up the remains of an ancient Anasazi village in northwestern New Mexico. Careful digging techniques give archaeologists a lot of information about a group of people. For example, the Anasazi made decorated pots (left), which they used in their everyday lives.

★ **What do the photograph and the pot tell about how the Anasazi made use of materials in their surroundings?**

Get Organized

VENN DIAGRAM

When you compare and contrast, you look at ways in which things are the same and different. Use a Venn diagram as you read Chapter 1. List differences between nomads and farmers in the outside sections of the circles. List similarities between the two groups in the overlapped section of the circles.

NOMADS
- Moved often in search of food
- Spent most of their time searching for food

Lived in the Americas

- Set up communities
- Developed skills such as making pottery and weaving

FARMERS

A.D. 100 Adena-Hopewell peoples thrive.

A.D. 200 Maya civilization flourishes.

A.D. 1200 Incas begin building an empire.

A.D. 1350 Aztec Empire develops.

A.D. 1570 Iroquois League is formed.

A.D. ➡ 500 1000 1500

A.D. 64 Part of Rome is destroyed by fire.

A.D. 300 African kingdom of Ghana grows.

A.D. 1000 Vikings begin exploring North America.

I Early Peoples

Terms to Know

nomad a person who moves about in search of food

migrate to move from one place to another

natural resource something provided by nature that is useful to people

agriculture the art or science of raising crops

culture all of a group's arts, beliefs, and ways of doing things

Main Ideas

A. The first people to live in the Americas were hunters from Asia.

B. Native Americans hunted, gathered wild plants and berries, and farmed, using different resources in different regions.

C. Native Americans lived in family and community groups.

MAKE GENERALIZATIONS
A generalization is a broad statement based on many separate facts. As you read this section, ask yourself the following question: What generalizations can be made about the first Americans?

A. From Asia to the Americas

Who were the first Americans? Most scientists believe that the first people to live in the Americas walked there from Asia.

Land Bridge From Asia

More than 30,000 years ago, Earth was in the grip of the last Ice Age. Temperatures had dropped so low that some winter snow did not melt even in the summer months. Huge glaciers called ice sheets covered most northern regions of the globe.

Creatures such as this woolly mammoth lived in North America during the Ice Age.

With so much water frozen into ice and snow, the level of the oceans dropped. The oceans were much lower than they are today. Because of the lower water levels, a land bridge surfaced in the Bering Sea. This bridge, sometimes called the Bering Land Bridge, linked the continent of Asia with the continent of North America. About one thousand miles wide, the Bering Land Bridge allowed hunters, who roamed the area in search of food, to cross from Asia into North America.

These hunters were **nomads**, people who move constantly in search of food. They followed and hunted herds of animals, such as woolly mammoths and mastodons. The children of these hunters were the first Native Americans because they were the first to be born in the Americas.

Today, their descendants are also known as Native Americans.

Scientists have discovered new evidence that suggests people may have traveled to North America even before nomads crossed the Bering Land Bridge. These people may have traveled by boat along the west coast of the continent. New theories about the first Americans continue to develop as more information is gathered by archaeologists. For now, most historians continue to hold to the theory that nomads crossed the Bering Land Bridge from Asia to North America.

Map Check

MOVEMENT In what directions did nomads travel to reach the Americas?

Spreading Throughout the Americas

Over a period of several thousand years, the nomads **migrated**, or moved, throughout the continent they had discovered. They spread south and east across North America to Central and South America.

About 12,000 years ago, the climate on Earth began warming. The Ice Age was ending, and the glaciers began to melt. As a result, the Bering Sea rose and covered the land bridge between Asia and North America. Other changes on Earth came as well: Large lakes formed by the glaciers drained and were replaced by rich soils. Plants and animals of the forests that had been forced southward by the glaciers returned to many northern areas.

In North and South America, many of the largest animals died. Climate changes and hunting by humans probably led to the disappearance of these animals from Earth.

 **Why did the first people come to the Americas from Asia?**

B. The Land and the People

As Native Americans spread across North, Central, and South America, they discovered a land of great variety. From tall mountains to plentiful rivers and dense forests, they adapted to this land with new ways of living.

Ancient tools were made from stone, bone, or wood.

Natural Resources

Throughout North and South America, the land differs. The Americas also have a variety of climates and **natural resources**, or things provided by nature that can be useful to people. Such resources include rivers, minerals, and soil. The land areas, or regions, were used by Native Americans in different ways. For example, Native Americans living on the Pacific Coast in the northern part of the North American continent ate fish and hunted whales, walruses, and seals. In the dry areas of the Southwest, people hunted birds, wild rabbits, and lizards. They also gathered seeds and nuts and dug up roots for food. Much of the eastern part of the continent was covered with forests. In the East, people ate deer, squirrels, and birds, along with seeds and berries.

In places where food was plentiful, such as along rivers, communities developed and grew. In the Northwest, salmon from the Columbia River in the present-day state of Washington provided a large, steady supply of food. Groups of people often spent several weeks together harvesting fish from the river.

In other places, such as the Great Basin in present-day Utah and Colorado, food was harder to find. People spent much of their time traveling in search of it, and conflicts often arose over food supplies.

Native Americans used natural resources for more than food. They sharpened stone called flint to make tools and weapons. They used tree limbs and shells to dig roots. They wove many kinds of grasses into clothing, as well as into nets to catch fish.

Spotlight on Geography

If you look closely at a globe of Earth, you'll see that it is divided by a major line of latitude, called the equator, and a major line of longitude, called the prime meridian.

The equator divides Earth into a Northern Hemisphere and a Southern Hemisphere. The prime meridian divides Earth into a Western Hemisphere and an Eastern Hemisphere. North America and South America are in the Western Hemisphere.

Learning to Farm

Around 5000 B.C., people in present-day Mexico started planting seeds to grow maize, or corn. In this way, **agriculture**, or the raising of food, began in the Western Hemisphere. Later, people also grew squash, beans, and peppers.

Slowly, knowledge of agriculture spread to other places. Sometime after 1500 B.C., farming began in what is now the southwestern United States.

Agriculture changed the way people lived. People no longer had to travel as much to find food. Permanent communities could be established, and their populations grew. Some people began working full time at making tools or trading with other groups. In some places, such as Mexico, people built large cities.

★ **When and where did people first begin to raise crops in the Americas?**

Native Americans spread nets across a portion of a river or lake to catch fish.

C. Everyday Life in Early America

Among Native American groups, both men and women had responsibilities to their families and to their community. In some communities, men and women shared the same jobs. In others, there was a clear division of labor.

Men and Women at Work

In most nonfarming communities, men and women performed different jobs. Men hunted and fished. Women worked closer to home, gathering wild plants and caring for children. Both might trap small animals, dig roots, and pick berries. Both might make tools such as fishhooks and needles from bone. Other larger tools, such as clubs and axes, were fashioned of wood and stone. Nonfarming communities were usually small because the people in them picked up their belongings and moved in order to find food.

In farming communities, there was usually an adequate supply of food. The fairly constant food supply meant that the community experienced a more permanent existence in a single location. Women were often responsible for raising crops. However, in some groups men shared in the work of clearing the land and helping with the harvest.

Community Life in Early America

Most Native American communities were made up of extended families. These families included fathers, mothers, and children, as well as grandparents, aunts, uncles, and cousins.

Small hunting and gathering groups had several families, with between 15 and 50 members. Large villages included more families and might have had up to several hundred residents.

Religion, or spirituality, was an important part of Native American life. Although Native American religions were varied, all of them were related to the natural world. Native Americans believed that everything in nature—including trees, animals, stones, and the sun and moon—had a special spirit or power.

Religious ceremonies served many purposes—for example, a ceremony might celebrate success in hunting or the harvest, or seek to bring rain after a dry period. People looked to religious leaders for help, especially in times of hardship.

The **culture**, or way of life, of these early Americans helped them succeed in their new land. In addition, as they hunted, gathered, or raised crops, their religious beliefs and ceremonies helped bind people to each other and to the world around them.

What were the roles of Native American men and women who lived in nonfarming communities?

Review History

A. How did the first people arrive in North America?

B. How did early Native Americans use the resources of the land where they lived?

C. What was life like in early Native American farming communities?

Define Terms to Know

Provide a definition for each of the following terms. **nomad, migrate, natural resource, agriculture, culture**

Critical Thinking

Why was the development of agriculture important in human history?

Write About History

Think about what life must have been like for someone living in North America around 2000 B.C. Write a journal entry describing an average day.

Get Organized

VENN DIAGRAM

Use a Venn diagram to compare and contrast the differences between farming and nonfarming communities.

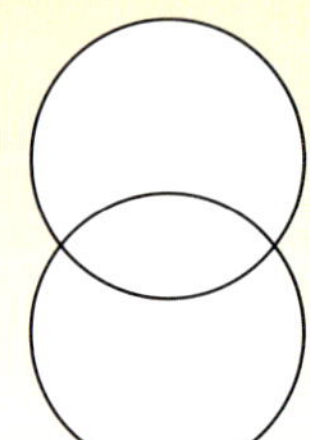

Build Your Skills

Social Studies Skill

READ A TIMELINE

Most days, you probably spend some time thinking about the order of different events. For example, on your way to school you might think about all the classes you will attend, as well as club or sports activities you might have scheduled for after school.

A timeline can help you remember events in chronological order, or time order. It is a visual tool that lists events in the order in which they have happened or will happen. It also shows the length of time between events.

Timelines can be very useful when you are studying history. They help you focus on a specific period by highlighting key events and putting them in order. You can also look for relationships among the events.

Here's How

Follow these steps to read a timeline.

1. Notice the period covered by a timeline. The earliest date is on the left. The latest date is on the right.
2. Like a ruler, a timeline is divided into equal units. These units, or intervals, may represent any block of time. Some timelines are divided into sections showing many years. Others are divided into sections of months or days.
3. Read the events from left to right. Notice the length of time between events.

Here's Why

You have just read about some events in the early history of the Americas. A timeline like the one below could help you compare what was happening in different regions.

Practice the Skill

Answer the questions below by reading the timeline on this page.

1. How might the first event listed on the timeline be related to the second event?
2. How many years passed between the farming of maize in Mexico and the establishment of farming villages in South America?

Extend the Skill

Create a timeline of the school year. Put at least five school events that are important to you on the timeline.

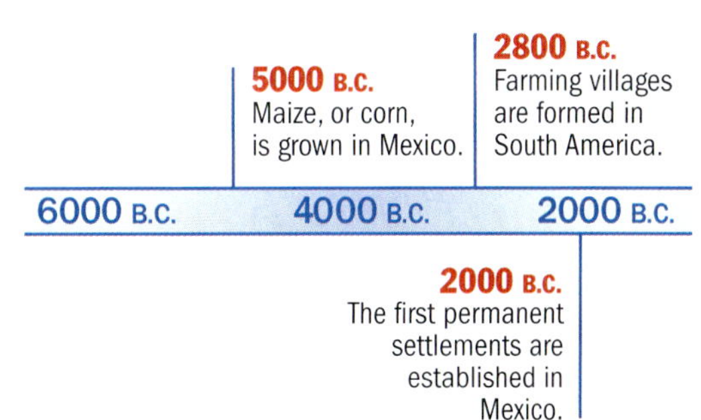

Apply the Skill

In this book you will see timelines that have different levels, or layers. Each level lists important dates for different topics. Look for relationships between events as you read these timelines.

II Civilizations in the Americas

Terms to Know

civilization a well-developed way of life of a people in one place and time

empire a large land area and population controlled by a single ruler or group

irrigate to supply water to dry land for growing crops

drought a long period without rainfall

pueblo an apartment-like adobe dwelling; Spanish word for village

Main Ideas

A. Powerful empires rose and fell in Mexico and in Central and South America.

B. Complex ways of life existed in North America long before Europeans arrived.

SUMMARIZE

When you summarize, you include only the most important points and leave out the details. As you read this section, concentrate on the main points. Then, pause to summarize what you have learned.

A. Peoples of the Americas

The early peoples of the Americas slowly developed into social groups. Over time, people in some of these groups built cities and fought for control over their territories. They eventually created complex societies that continue to amaze us today.

Olmecs and the Rise of Civilizations

The discovery of agriculture in the Americas led to the growth of large and powerful **civilizations**. A civilization is an advanced way of life developed by a particular group of people. Several civilizations existed in the mild climate of Mexico's central valley. Millions of people lived there in small farming villages.

The Olmecs were among the first people to thrive on Mexico's Gulf Coast. The Olmec civilization lasted from about 1200 B.C. until 400 or 300 B.C. The Olmecs built cities with huge pyramid-shaped temples. They also invented calendars and writing systems and practiced a complex religion that involved human sacrifice.

The Olmecs carved many giant stone heads like this one.

The Maya

The Maya began settling in Central America as early as 1500 B.C. By A.D. 200, they had developed cities of sky-high temples, palaces, and open courtyards. Maya temples and palaces were often carved with beautiful symbols from Maya writing. They also invented a ball game called *pok-a-tok*.

This Maya pyramid, El Castillo, was built in Chichén Itzá. People still visit the pyramid today.

The Maya recorded their writing on paper made from the inner bark of fig trees. Few of their books have survived. However, the symbols that have been translated reveal a great deal about Maya culture.

The Maya worshiped nature gods, such as the gods of the sun, moon, rain, and corn. Priests organized ceremonies to honor the gods. When opposing Maya rulers waged war against each other, they sacrificed their captives to the gods as part of one ceremony.

The Maya were expert farmers and scientists. They grew many fruits and vegetables, as well as cotton and cacao, which was used to make chocolate. They mapped the stars and used the stars' movements to keep track of planting and harvesting cycles. Because of these studies, they were able to work out a very accurate calendar. In mathematics, the Maya developed the use of a symbol for the number zero.

Over a period of hundreds of years, the Maya had indeed created an **empire**, or a large area controlled by one ruler or group. It was one of the greatest of the early American cultures. The descendants of the Maya still live in Mexico and Central America.

The Toltecs

About A.D. 900, as the Maya Empire was fading, another group arrived in Mexico from the north and took over the Maya lands. The Toltecs built great temples and huge sculptures. They used copper and gold to create jewelry and weapons.

The Toltec Empire was based on warfare. At its height, it reached from the Gulf Coast into Central America. Around A.D. 1200, however, the Toltecs' power crumbled under attacks by nomads

Map Check

LOCATION Which empire was bordered by a mountain chain?

The Aztecs

The Aztecs, also called the Mexica, came to the Valley of Mexico around the same time as the Toltec Empire was declining, about A.D. 1200. The Aztec peoples also came from the north. They were looking for a permanent home, and after years of wandering, they settled in the valley.

For many years, the Aztecs lived like most other people in the valley, in small independent villages. Then, about A.D. 1350, they combined forces with two other groups and began conquering their neighbors. Although the Aztecs did not have a large army, they were fierce fighters. They soon overpowered all the people in the valley.

The Aztecs demanded payment of goods from the villages they conquered. This payment could be farm products, such as corn, or gold and silver. With these riches, the Aztecs built a huge empire.

Their capital city, Tenochtitlán, was built in the middle of a lake. At first it covered two islands. As the population grew, the Aztecs expanded the islands using layers of mud. They grew crops on the islands, as well as in mountainous areas and dry regions. Causeways, an early type of walkway, connected the islands to the mainland. Tenochtitlán featured huge open courtyards called plazas and stone temples that resembled pyramids with steps. When a Spanish explorer saw the city for the first time, he wrote,

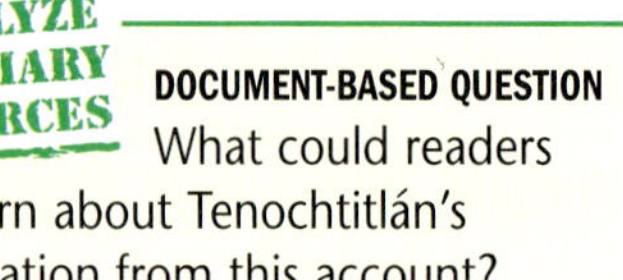

ANALYZE PRIMARY SOURCES

DOCUMENT-BASED QUESTION What could readers learn about Tenochtitlán's location from this account?

> "When we saw all those . . . great towns and temples and buildings rising from the water, all made of stone, it seemed like an enchanted vision."

The Aztecs controlled almost all of the areas where the Olmecs, Maya, and Toltecs had once lived. It is estimated that the Aztecs ruled millions of people from the Gulf of Mexico to the Pacific Ocean. Their ruler had great power and was treated almost like a god. Only the coming of Europeans early in the 1500s threatened the power of the Aztecs.

The Incas

Machu Picchu is northwest of Cuzco, in the Andes Mountains.

Farther south along the Andes Mountains in South America, the Inca Empire developed around A.D. 1200. The center of the empire was the city of Cuzco, high in the mountains of present-day Peru.

Over hundreds of years, the Inca Empire grew to an area of almost half a million square miles. The Incas ruled more than nine million people, mostly by conquering neighboring lands.

To link the distant parts of the empire, an army of workers built more than 14,000 miles of roads. Some of the roads crossed deep mountain gorges on suspension, or hanging, bridges. The roads were used primarily for government business and the military. Along the roads, the Incas also transported farm products, such as potatoes, cotton, and wool, to the cities. Gold and silver were brought to the cities from mines deep in the mountains.

In addition to roads, the Incas built structures of massive blocks of stone that fit tightly together. Today, the Inca city of Machu Picchu contains ruins of walls, roads, and buildings that show the skill of the Inca architects and builders of long ago.

 **How were the Maya and the Inca civilizations alike?**

B. North American Civilizations

North American civilizations were not empires ruled by a powerful, single ruler. Rather, they were united by a shared way of life. Many of these civilizations had disappeared by the time the Europeans arrived, for reasons that are not well understood.

The Adena–Hopewell People

More than 2,000 years ago, people called the Adenas began to live in the Ohio River valley of North America. The Adenas lived in large villages and found food by hunting and gathering.

About 100 B.C., the Adenas developed into the Hopewell culture. Throughout the Illinois and Ohio valleys, they built earthen mounds for religious ceremonies and burial sites. Because of this practice, the Adena-Hopewells became known as mound builders.

Adena-Hopewell burial mounds contain ancient objects that tell us how the people lived. For example, some mounds contained grizzly bear teeth. From this evidence we know that the people traded with groups in the Rocky Mountains. Other mounds held ornaments made of shells from the southeast coast.

The Great Serpent Mound in southeastern Ohio was built by the Adena-Hopewell or Mississippian peoples.

The Adena-Hopewell civilization reached its height at about A.D. 100. Then, sometime around A.D. 400 the civilization declined, probably due to food shortages resulting from a lack of rainfall. The Adena-Hopewell people abandoned their large villages.

The Mississippians

Another civilization developed in the Mississippi River valley of southeastern North America around A.D. 800. Like the Adena-Hopewells, the Mississippians were mound builders. They were also the first people in the eastern region to use agriculture on a large scale.

The Mississippian civilization stretched north from present-day Louisiana to Minnesota and as far east as South Carolina. The people lived in large towns or trading centers. Most towns contained a huge ceremonial pyramid-shaped mound surrounded by other large burial mounds.

The largest town was Cahokia, located near present-day St. Louis, Missouri, on the Mississippi River. The city served as the people's main trading and religious center. Sometime after A.D. 1300, the Mississippian civilization began to decline, probably because of food shortages caused by climate changes, or attacks by newcomers. By the time European explorers arrived at Cahokia in the mid-1600s, only a few dwellings and a small number of people remained.

Spotlight on Culture

Archaeologists study artifacts, or objects that remain behind after a civilization is gone. Archaeologists began studying the ruins of Cahokia in the 1920s. Among the artifacts found at Cahokia is a stone blade that was fastened on a pole and used as a hoe—a big improvement over a digging stick.

Farming of the Southwest

For many years, the first peoples living in the deserts of the American Southwest were hunters and gatherers. In addition to catching small animals, they collected nuts, roots, and seeds. Then, about 300 B.C., one of these groups, the Hohokams, began growing corn. To do this, they had to **irrigate**, or bring water to the dry desert lands. Sometime later, another group called the Anasazis began farming north of this area.

The Anasazis developed a culture that influenced many other groups in the Southwest. They built large multiple dwellings that were like apartment buildings. Some dwellings were built on high flat areas, while others were built into the desert cliffs of present-day Arizona, New Mexico, Colorado, and Utah. The buildings were made of stone and sun-dried clay, called adobe.

About A.D. 1300, the Anasazis abandoned their villages. Although no one knows for certain, they may have left because of a severe **drought**, or time of little rainfall.

Many years later, when Spanish explorers saw the large apartment-style houses, they called them **pueblos**. The word *pueblo* is the Spanish word for "village." The Pueblo Native Americans who live in the Southwest today are descendants of the Anasazis.

How were the mound builders' settlements different from those of the Anasazis?

Review History

A. What were the major achievements of the Maya, Aztecs, and Incas?

B. How were the North American civilizations different from the civilizations of Central America and Mexico?

Define Terms to Know

Provide a definition for each of the following terms.
civilization, empire, irrigate, drought, pueblo

Critical Thinking

How do the achievements of the early civilizations in the Americas affect us today?

Write About Geography

Write a paragraph describing the locations and physical geography, or geographical features, of the civilizations you have read about.

Get Organized

VENN DIAGRAM

Select two civilizations that you have read about in this section, such as the Aztecs and Incas. Use a Venn diagram to compare and contrast their ways of living.

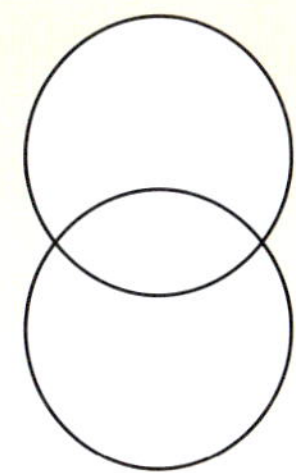

III Native Americans

Terms to Know

clan a small unit of related Native American families that may be known by a common symbol, such as a bear or turtle

dry farming a method of farming that makes use of all the water available in a dry land

Main Ideas

A. Native Americans established farming communities in the Northeast and Southeast.

B. Groups in the Great Plains and the Southwest adapted to the dry conditions of the area.

C. Native Americans in the North and West relied on fishing, hunting, and trade.

CAUSE AND EFFECT
When something happens, we often ask why. In other words, we look for a *cause* for what happened. The result is the *effect*. As you read this section, look for examples of cause and effect.

A. Eastern Peoples

Eventually, the large population centers of the Adena-Hopewell and Mississippian civilizations were abandoned. Native Americans lived in smaller groups throughout the lands north of Mexico. In the Northeast and Southeast, many Native Americans lived at least part of the year in farming communities.

The Algonquins

In the Northeastern Woodlands, many Native Americans belonged to the Algonquin or Iroquois language groups. The Algonquins were a large group of about 50 distinct cultures. All the Algonquins spoke related languages. Algonquin communities were based on family units. Extended families lived together in one house.

Many eastern Algonquin groups hunted, fished, and farmed. The forest provided them with abundant natural resources. They built their houses out of thin saplings that were bent to form a wooden frame and then covered with sheets of bark. They made canoes out of birch bark or hollowed-out logs, and carved bowls and spoons out of wood. With bows and arrows or stone-tipped spears, the Algonquins hunted deer, moose, bear, and smaller animals. Woodland shrubs provided blueberries and other berries.

Do You Remember?
In Section I, you learned that Native Americans along the Pacific Coast and in the Southwest also relied on natural resources for survival.

The Algonquins cut and burned trees to fertilize the soil. In clearings created by the burning, they planted beans, corn, and squash. Every few years, as the soil became less productive, the people moved to new areas.

The Iroquois

Five groups, or nations, belonged to the Iroquois. They were the Mohawks, Cayugas, Oneidas, Onondagas, and Senecas. All of them lived in present-day New York State. For years, they fought constantly.

Perhaps around 1570, the five nations united to create the Iroquois League. They agreed not to fight among themselves and to unite to fight common enemies. Members declared:

> "Our strength shall be in union, our way the way of . . . peace. . . . Be of strong mind, O chiefs. Carry no anger and hold no grudges."

ANALYZE PRIMARY SOURCES

DOCUMENT-BASED QUESTION Why would members of the Iroquois League remind each other to "carry no anger"?

Like the Algonquins, the Iroquois lived in farming communities. They grew many kinds of corn, beans, and squash—crops they called the "sacred three sisters." The Iroquois built large houses, called longhouses, in which several families lived. These buildings had wooden frames and a thick covering of grass.

The Southeast

The Cherokees, Creeks, Choctaws, Chickasaws, and Caddos were among the groups who lived in the Southeastern Woodlands. Some groups, such as the Cherokees, lived in small related groups called **clans**. Most villages in this region were surrounded by high wooden fences that helped in the defense against attacks by other groups. Other villages included temples where religious ceremonies were held. Some southeastern peoples, such as the Caddos, built burial mounds like the Adena-Hopewells.

Like groups in the Northeastern Woodlands, the peoples of the Southeastern Woodlands hunted and farmed to feed themselves. Their main crops were corn, beans, and squash. The warm climate provided a long growing season. Thus, these people were able to produce plenty of food and support large communities. Southeastern Woodland communities were well-established by the time Europeans arrived in the 1500s.

Native Americans of the Southeast were skilled crafters. They created clay pots and bowls and wove mats and carpets out of grasses or bark. In addition, they made jewelry from shells and bone. Many of these items were used as trade goods with people who lived farther west.

This drawing shows a Native American village in the Southeast during the 1580s.

★ **What did Native Americans of the Northeastern Woodlands and the Southeastern Woodlands have in common?**

B. Peoples of the Plains and the Southwest

West of the Mississippi River, the landscape changed. Woodlands gave way to grassy plains and desert. Native Americans who lived in these regions adapted to their surroundings.

The Plains Peoples

In the central grasslands, or Great Plains, lived groups such as the Arapahos, Cheyennes, Comanches, and Crows. The Dakotas and other groups migrated from the East to the Plains. Many peoples of the Plains moved often, following great herds of buffalo.

Plains peoples hunted the buffalo for more than food. Some buffalo skins were used to cover shelters, called tipis, while others were made into clothing. The people melted the fat of the buffalo and used it to waterproof shelters and moccasins. They also shaped buffalo bones into tools, utensils, and weapons.

Between the Rocky Mountains and the Pacific Coast ranges is a dry region known as the Great Basin. The Great Basin stretches from present-day Idaho into Nevada, Utah, and California. Groups such as the Paiutes and Shoshones lived there. They relied on small mammals, insects, lizards, and certain plants for food.

Pueblo Culture of the Southwest

The Southwest region—including parts of present-day Arizona, Colorado, Mexico, New Mexico, and Utah—was dry and barren. Native Americans of the Southwest had to learn to grow crops on this dry land.

One of the earliest Native American groups to inhabit the Southwest was the Anasazi. By the time Europeans arrived in the 1500s, another group who were descendants of the Anasazi lived there as well. They were the Pueblos.

The Pueblos were skilled at making many crafts, including decorated pottery.

The Pueblos included groups such as the Hopis and the Zunis. Their villages were made up of apartment-like dwellings constructed of adobe. Most Pueblo groups practiced **dry farming**, using all the water available in their dry land. For example, they planted crops in ditches where rainwater collected. The Zunis, however, built dams and waterways to bring water to their fields. In addition to food crops, Hopis raised cotton, and Hopi men wove cloth for their own use and for trade.

 **How did the people of the Great Plains, the Great Basin, and the southwestern region adapt to their surroundings?**

C. Native Americans in the North and West

Native American groups lived in the Far North region of North America and along the Pacific Northwest Coast and large rivers in the Northwest. They developed trade networks across the region.

The Far North and West

The Inuit (sometimes called Eskimos) and Aleuts lived in the northern regions of present-day Canada and Alaska. They were hunters and fishers who followed herds of caribou, a type of large deer. The Inuit were the first Native Americans to hunt with bows and arrows.

Along the Pacific Coast, Inuit and Aleuts hunted seals, walruses, otters, and whales for food. They also used the skins of these animals for clothing. These people were expert boat builders and sailors.

In winter, some Inuit groups built snow houses called igloos. They used sleds pulled by a person or a dog team to carry heavy loads over snow and ice. Some groups moved between coastal and inland areas so they could take advantage of both kinds of land and natural resources.

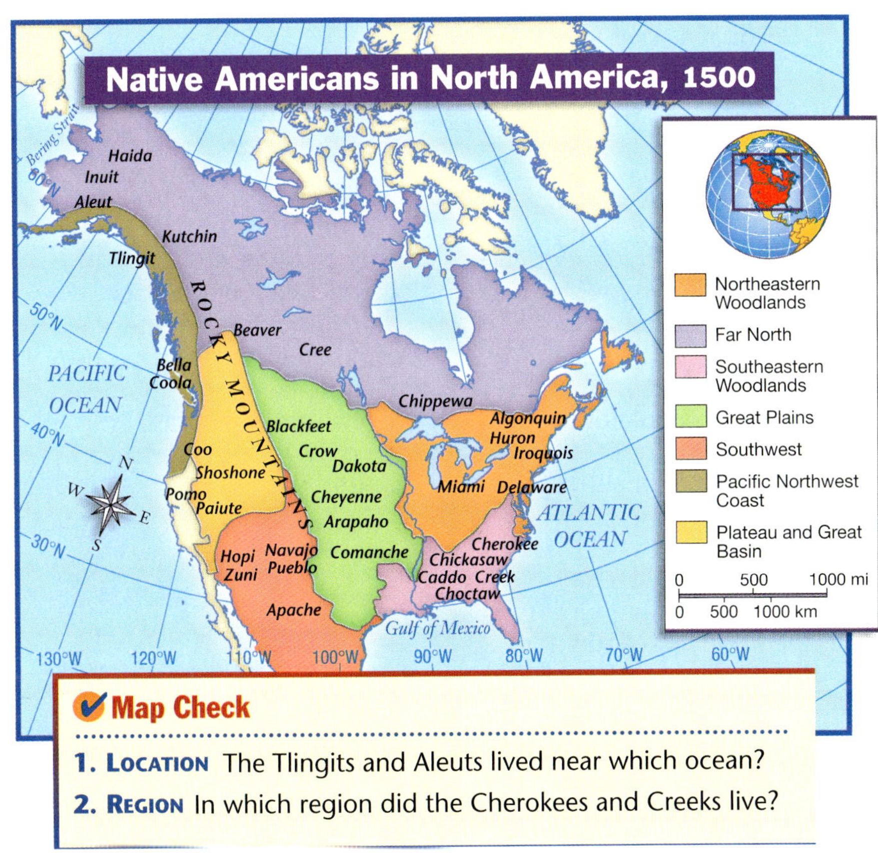

Map Check

1. **LOCATION** The Tlingits and Aleuts lived near which ocean?
2. **REGION** In which region did the Cherokees and Creeks live?

Coastal Fishing Cultures

Native Americans of the Pacific Northwest Coast and the coast areas of the Far North included groups such as the Tlingits, Haidas, and Aleuts. Water played a major role in their activities.

Fishing was an important part of their lives, so Native Americans of these regions built their villages near the mouths of rivers or near the coastline. They constructed their houses of wooden planks, using the rich resources of the northwest forests. Wood was also used to make boats and beautiful carved objects.

A variety of fish were plentiful in the region, but salmon was particularly abundant. Salmon swim from the ocean into rivers once each year to lay their eggs. This annual event created a dependable source of food. The salmon arrived in huge numbers, and people spread nets across the rivers to catch the fish.

After a large catch, Native Americans who lived near the Pacific Ocean dried the salmon on wooden racks in the sun. Fish preserved in this way could be eaten all year. In fall, people of the Pacific Coast regions traveled inland to hunt and to gather other foods. They took dried salmon with them to trade with other Native Americans for tools or clothing.

What common food source did the Native Americans in the North and West have?

Review History

A. How did Native Americans in the Northeast and Southeast live?

B. How was farming possible in the dry Southwest?

C. How did Native Americans of the North and West make use of natural resources?

Define Terms to Know

Provide a definition for each of the following terms.
clan, dry farming

Critical Thinking

Why did people of the North need to use all parts of the sea animals they hunted?

Write About Government

Think about the purpose of the Iroquois League. Write a short paragraph explaining how the formation of this league helped its members survive.

Get Organized

VENN DIAGRAM

The Native Americans of North America shared some common characteristics. Use a Venn diagram to compare and contrast the ways of living of two Native American groups.

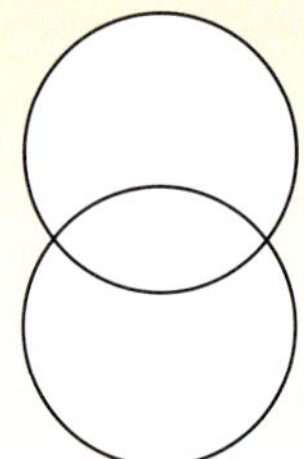

CONNECT History & Art

Native American Art

The earliest Native Americans were focused on survival. However, some early Americans used charcoal and berries to paint images on cave walls. Even nomadic groups decorated practical items, such as clothing.

As Native American settlements became permanent, people in different regions gained new skills. They made clay pots, baskets, or cloth. Most of the things they made were useful, but over time, many everyday objects became valued for their beauty as well. Native Americans also showed their creativity in making jewelry and objects for religious ceremonies.

WEAVINGS AND JEWELRY FROM THE ANDES In South America, the Incas took the art of weaving to a high level. They used wool from llamas and alpacas, which are camel-like animals that are also used as pack animals, to carry goods from place to place. Alpacas and llamas have bushy coats of wool that the Incas used to make sturdy, colorful cloth. Geometric designs in bright colors were popular. The Incas also made finely crafted ornaments of gold.

POTTERY FROM THE SOUTHWEST The people of the southwestern part of North America became expert pottery makers. Their pottery, used mainly for cooking, was often decorated with black and white zigzags and other designs. Later designs used orange and sometimes showed deer or birds. Today, Native American artists continue to make pottery with these traditional designs.

Critical Thinking

Answer the questions below. Then, complete the activity.

1. How did the Incas use alpacas and llamas to their best advantage?
2. Why do you think people took the time to make everyday objects beautiful?

Write About It

Go to the following Web site to view examples of Native American art: www.gfamericanhistory.com.

In a brief paragraph, describe one piece of art that interests you, and explain when and where it was made.

Native Americans developed distinct art forms, represented by this Inca statue of an alligator.

CHAPTER 1 Review

Chapter Summary

In your notebook, complete the following outline. Then, use your outline to write a brief summary of the chapter.

The First Americans

I. Early Peoples
  A. From Asia to the Americas
  B.
  C.
II. Civilizations in the Americas
  A.
  B.
III. Native Americans
  A.
  B.
  C.

Interpret the Timeline

Use the timeline on pages 2–3 to answer the following questions.

1. When and where did agriculture first develop in the Americas?
2. **Critical Thinking** What African civilization existed at about the same time as the Maya civilization?

Use Terms to Know

Select the term that best completes each sentence.

civilization **dry farming** **empire** **migrate** **nomad**

1. A person who crossed the land bridge from Asia to North America was a ________.
2. The well-developed way of life of the Maya is an example of a ________.
3. After crossing the Bering Land Bridge, Native Americans began to ________ south.
4. The Incas controlled an ________ of almost half a million square miles.
5. Most Pueblo groups lived in dry areas and used an agricultural method called ________.

Check Your Understanding

1. **Summarize** how Asians would have been able to walk to North America long ago.
2. **Give examples** of animals that were hunted by Native Americans in three different regions of North America.
3. **Describe** the building skills of the Incas.
4. **Explain** why the Adena-Hopewells and the Mississippians built mounds.
5. **Explain** how the Algonquins made use of wood for their daily needs.
6. **Summarize** the importance of the buffalo to many Plains peoples.

Critical Thinking

1. **Recognize Relationships** How did different lands and climates affect the lifestyle of early Native Americans?
2. **Analyze Primary Sources** Why do you think the Spanish explorer quoted on page 12 was so amazed at the sight of Tenochtitlán?
3. **Analyze Primary Sources** What does the drawing of a southeastern Native American village on page 17 tell you about how these people lived?

Put Your Skills to Work

READ A TIMELINE

You have learned that a timeline can help you understand the order of events in history. It can also help you tell how many years there were between events.

Use the timeline below to answer the following questions.

1. When and where did the Maya civilization flourish?
2. Did the Mississippian civilization develop before or after the Adena-Hopewell civilization began?

100 Adena-Hopewell civilization thrives in North America.

800 Mississippian civilization develops in North America.

A.D. 100 — 300 — 500 — 700 — 900

200 Maya civilization flourishes in Central America.

900 Toltec civilization is formed in Mexico.

In Your Own Words

JOURNAL WRITING

If you were an archaeologist studying the Great Serpent Mound shown on page 14, what questions might you have about this mound? How would you find the answers to your questions? Make a list of questions. Then, add a few notes about how you might take your investigation further.

Net Work

INTERNET ACTIVITY

Working with a group of classmates, use the Internet as a resource to create a museum display about the people of the Mississippi River valley. Include maps, models, diagrams, and drawings or photographs of artifacts. Include a brief description of each object or visual. Share your display with the class.

For help in starting this activity, visit the following Web site: www.gfamericanhistory.com.

Look Ahead

In the next chapter, learn about West African civilizations and the first European explorers to reach the Americas.

CHAPTER 2

Early Exploration 1000–1535

I. West African Trading Kingdoms
II. Early European Expeditions
III. Major Voyages to the Americas

In the 1400s, some people still believed that Earth was flat. They thought that if you sailed too far in one direction, you would fall off its edge. Christopher Columbus knew they were wrong. He knew Earth was actually round. After spending many years studying maps and explorers' journals, he decided that he could reach Asia by sailing westward around the globe. Columbus convinced the king and queen of Spain that his idea would work and set sail in 1492. As the long weeks at sea passed, his crew became restless. The sailors feared they would never see land again. Columbus wrote in his journal:

> "I am told by a few trusted men . . . that if I persist in going onward, the best course of action will be to throw me into the sea some night."

Columbus did persist, and he was rewarded. He was one of a handful of bold men who began to explore the world by sea in the late 1400s.

Early navigation tool

1000
Leif Ericson sails to North America.

Events in the Americas	1000	1100	1200
World Events	1000	1100	1200

1095
Religious wars called Crusades begin near Jerusalem.

1240
Empire of Ghana taken over by Muslim invaders.

VIEW HISTORY This painting by Edward Moran shows Columbus arriving in North America. Many explorers used an early navigation tool (left) to help find their location as they sailed the ocean.

★ **What do the painting and the navigation tool tell about the early voyages of exploration?**

Get Organized

TIMELINE

A timeline is used for putting events in order. Timelines can be read from bottom to top, like the one shown here, or from left to right, like the one at the bottom of the page. Use a timeline as you read Chapter 2 to record important events.

1500
1492 Columbus reaches the Americas.
1400
1325 Aztecs build Tenochtitlán.
1300
1295 Marco Polo publishes book on his journey to China.
1200

I West African Trading Kingdoms

Terms to Know

caravan a group of travelers with pack animals

tax money paid to a government

kinship family relationships

Main Ideas

A. African civilizations were influenced by geography and natural resources.

B. Three large trading kingdoms developed in West Africa.

C. Outside the trading centers, life in West Africa centered on family and farming.

Active Reading

MAIN IDEAS AND DETAILS

History is more than just facts or details. It is also about big ideas. As you read this section, ask yourself this question: What details support the main ideas?

A. The Riches of Africa

While different cultures developed in the Americas, other civilizations emerged on the African continent. The rich resources of Africa encouraged its inhabitants to trade with one another.

Land of Contrasts

Africa is the second-largest continent in the world. It takes up about one fifth of Earth's land surface. The location of the continent affects its different climates. The equator runs across the middle of Africa. Thick rain forests lie along the equator and receive more than 60 inches of rainfall each year.

North and south of the rain forests lie savannas. Savannas are areas covered with tall grasses and having few trees. The climate is mild, making savannas good for farming. The northern and southern parts of Africa contain deserts. These areas receive very little rainfall, and temperatures have been known to reach 136°F. The Sahara in northern Africa is the world's largest desert. The northern and southern coastal regions have mild, dry climates that are good for settlement and farming.

Spotlight on Geography

The northern region of Africa was not always a desert. Fossils found in the region indicate that the area was once swampy and damp and supported many types of large dinosaurs. The bones of some of the largest dinosaurs have been found in the deserts of North Africa.

Africa's Resources

Before 1400, two of the most important resources in Africa were gold and salt. Gold came from the forest and savanna regions in West Africa. Miners dug for gold or sifted through rivers to find it. Salt, considered as valuable as gold because it could preserve foods, was not found in West Africa. It was plentiful, however, in the Sahara. In one Saharan village, workers even used salt blocks to build their houses.

Africans in the west needed salt. Africans in the north wanted to trade the salt they had for gold. Trade routes were developed to exchange these resources.

The Trans-Sahara Route

Between 1000 and 1450, much of North Africa was ruled by Muslims, or people who follow the religion called Islam. The Muslims traded with people from West Africa, Europe, and Asia. As a result, North Africa became the crossroads of the world.

Resources gathered in West Africa, such as gold, were carried from the savannas of West Africa along the Trans-Sahara route to Muslim kingdoms in North Africa and the Middle East. **Caravans**, or groups of traders with pack animals, were used to transport these goods across the desert. In North Africa the gold was traded for salt and other goods. The merchants of the Muslim kingdoms then carried the West African goods to other parts of the world. Eventually, items such as farm products, ivory tusks from elephants, spices, and silk were traded along this route as well as gold and salt.

 **How did the resources in Africa lead to trade?**

Caravans with camels were used to transport goods across the Sahara.

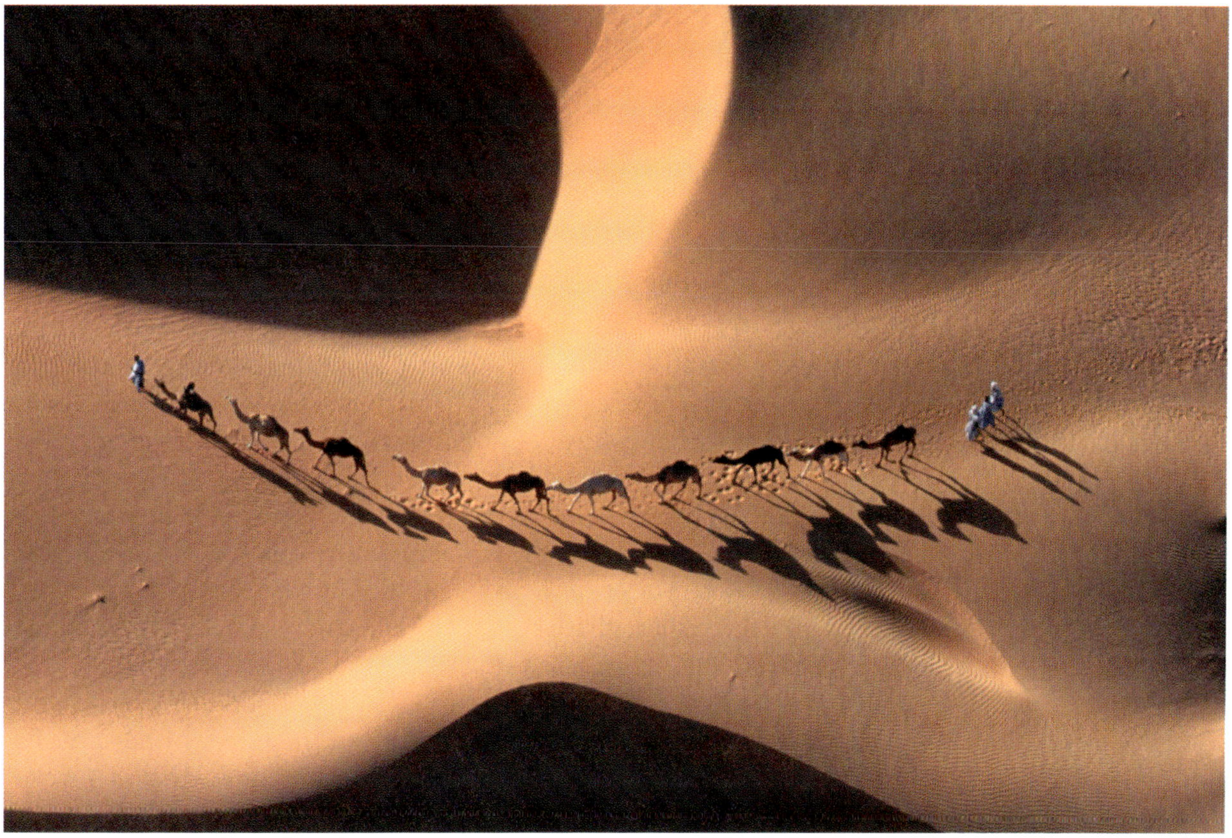

Map Check

LOCATION Which of the three West African kingdoms was the largest in land area?

B. West African Kingdoms

The trade routes across Africa led to the growth of three large trading empires. These were Ghana, Mali, and Songhai. All of these empires were located on the southern edge of the Sahara.

Ghana and Mali

The earliest known West African trading empire was Ghana, which existed from 700 to about 1240. Ghana began as a trading post. It was a stopping point for merchants from North Africa. These merchants traveled south to trade their salt for gold.

Ghana was controlled by a powerful ruler. He forced people to pay **taxes**, or payments to the government, on items they traded in his empire. As a result, the empire became very wealthy. Eventually, Ghana was taken over by Muslim invaders from North Africa.

By the 1200s, the empire of Mali emerged. The most famous ruler of Mali was a wealthy king named Mansa Musa. In the early 1300s, he made a journey from Mali to the Middle East, bringing large amounts of gold with him. His journey caused the spread of stories about the great wealth of Mali far beyond Africa. However, after Mansa Musa's death around 1332, the empire of Mali declined.

Songhai

Songhai was the largest and most powerful of the West African trading empires. By 1468, Songhai had taken control of the gold-salt trade and most of Mali, including the city of Timbuktu. The rulers of Songhai encouraged trade with Europe and Asia. Songhai traders crossed the Sahara to trade gold and ivory for salt, weapons, cloth, and horses.

The rulers of Songhai built many schools. Timbuktu became famous as a center of learning. Scholars from northern Africa and the Middle East came to study law, history, and religion. The Songhai empire existed until almost 1600.

The Coastal Kingdoms

South and west of the trading empires, smaller states developed along the coastline. These kingdoms included Senegambia, Benin, and Guinea. Many of the trade goods carried across the Sahara by merchants came from these coastal kingdoms. The people of Benin were best known for sculpture. They made detailed figures of bronze and ivory. Other coastal kingdoms traded gold and ivory.

 **What did Ghana, Mali, and Songhai have in common?**

C. West African Society

Outside of the trading centers, most West Africans were farmers. Farming had been practiced in West Africa for thousands of years before the great trading kingdoms developed.

This woman is selling peppers at a modern market in West Africa.

Farming in West Africa

The crops grown in West Africa varied with the land and climate. Grains, such as millet and sorghum, were the main crops on the savannas. The savannas also provided food and space for grazing animals such as cattle, goats, and sheep.

In the wetter, warmer coastal regions close to the equator, West African farmers grew yams, bananas, beans, peppers, and peas. They also raised goats, sheep, and chickens in forest clearings.

Farm villages were permanent or semipermanent. In coastal areas, villagers moved every few years to clear new plots of ground to farm. They used the slash-and-burn method to farm. Farmers would cut down trees and grasses and then burn them to clear a field. The ashes from the burning fertilized the soil.

Both men and women took part in farming and herding livestock. Farm products were traded in local markets, just as they are today.

Families and Communities

In West African communities, **kinship**, or relationships based on common ancestors, helped to define a person's role and importance. Kinship networks included parents, children, aunts, uncles, cousins, and grandparents. Many times, adopted family members were a part of the kinship network. Families in some areas were centered around the mother and her sisters. In other areas, they centered around the father and his brothers. Kinship influenced religion in West Africa as well. In many communities, West Africans believed that an ancestor's spirit could have an influence over their lives. As a result, they prayed to their ancestors for protection.

In the empires of West Africa, not everyone was free. These societies considered slavery a form of punishment for criminals and prisoners of war. Enslaved persons adopted new kinship patterns and were protected by the same laws as free people.

Most people did not remain enslaved for life. They served a term and were then free. Their children were not born into slavery. Slaves could inherit property, including their own slaves. This form of slavery changed after Europeans began to arrive in West Africa in the early 1400s.

What was life like for men and women in West African society?

Review History

A. Why was salt an important item for trade in West Africa?

B. What were the three large trading empires in West Africa?

C. How did kinship affect West African society?

Define Terms to Know

Provide a definition for each of the following terms.
caravan, tax, kinship

Critical Thinking

Why did the three great trading kingdoms develop along the edge of the Sahara?

Write About Geography

Write a paragraph explaining how the geography of Africa influenced trade.

Get Organized

TIMELINE

Think about three main events described in this section. Use a timeline like the one below to record these events. Make sure the date you enter at the top of the timeline is the latest, or most recent date.

Build Your Skills

Social Studies Skill

READ A HISTORICAL MAP

There are many different kinds of maps. Some give information about the physical features of a place, while others show population growth, agricultural products, or road and highway information. Other kinds of maps show information from the past. These maps are called historical maps.

Historical maps give specific information about an area and what took place there in the past. Some historical maps show boundaries, while others give information about wars and battles, or the movement of people from place to place over time. Look at the historical map below to see what information it shows.

Here's How

Follow these steps to read a historical map.

1. Look at the title of the map to find the topic and the time period of the map.
2. Look at the map key to learn the meanings of symbols on the map.
3. Read the labels to learn the names of the locations shown on the map.

Here's Why

You have just read about the early trading kingdoms of West Africa. Suppose you were asked to describe the trade routes within Africa. A historical map could help.

Practice the Skill

Study this map. Then, answer the following questions.

1. What general area does this map show?
2. What information is given in the map key?
3. What trade centers in Songhai are labeled?

Extend the Skill

Use the map to write two statements about trade in Africa.

Apply the Skill

As you read the rest of this chapter, look for other historical maps. Compare the maps with the information in the section.

II Early European Expeditions

Terms to Know

commerce the buying and selling of goods

navigate to control the direction of a boat or ship

astrolabe an instrument used to calculate the position of the stars

plantation a large farm requiring many workers

Main Ideas

A. European contact with Asia and Africa began during the Middle Ages.

B. Demand for Asian goods in Europe led to exploration.

C. Portugal led the way in exploring sea routes to expand trade.

Active Reading

PROBLEMS AND SOLUTIONS

People in the past often took actions to solve problems. Look for examples of problems that people faced. Ask yourself, How did they solve these problems?

A. Europe Looks Outward

The period from 476 until about 1300 is often called the Middle Ages. For much of this period, there were few advances in education or science. Europeans had little contact with the outside world. However, by about 1100, Europeans began to look outward to come into contact with new cultures.

Nobles made war with each other by having knights do battle on their behalf.

Europe in the Middle Ages

During the Middle Ages, Europe was divided into small territories ruled by wealthy nobles. These nobles defended their lands with armies that included knights, or mounted soldiers. These territories were often at war with each other. As a result of constant warring, people had little time for trade or exploration. In fact, western Europeans increasingly grew more isolated from the rest of the world.

Knowledge of the outside world was very limited. What people learned was usually from the Catholic Church, which was the primary religious institution in Europe at that time. As a result, life focused around the Church and religion. Only nobles and church officials received a formal education. The vast majority of people worked on farms. Throughout the Middle Ages, the power of the Catholic Church continued to grow.

As the years of the Middle Ages passed, Europe began to slowly change. People wanted to learn more about the world. Europe was ready for a dramatic change.

The Crusades

The leader of the Catholic Church was the pope, who lived in Rome, Italy. In 1095, Pope Urban II asked European nobles to help him. He wanted them to travel to the Middle East to the Muslim trading kingdoms. His goal was to drive the Muslims out of the Holy Land. The Holy Land was the region surrounding the city of Jerusalem. It was an important area to both Catholics and Muslims. The pope said,

> "O bravest of knights, descendants of unconquered ancestors, do not be weaker than they, but remember their courage . . . Set out on the road to the [Holy Land] . . . take the land from that wicked people, and make it your own."

DOCUMENT-BASED QUESTION How did Pope Urban II convince Europeans to travel to the Holy Land?

Catholic and Muslim people would spend much of the next 200 years fighting for control of this land. These religious wars were known as the Crusades.

Although the European Catholics did not regain the Holy Land, the Crusades brought changes to Europe. More people had traveled to distant lands. Europeans discovered new ideas, foods, and inventions. Europeans began to trade with Muslims, who had products from Africa and Asia. Crusaders returned home with silk and cotton cloth, spices such as pepper and ginger, and other treasures. These luxuries were soon in great demand in Europe.

Marco Polo

About the time of the last Crusade, an Italian merchant from Venice named Marco Polo traveled to China. He returned many years later with silks, spices, and stories about eastern Asia. Marco Polo's account of his journey was published in 1298. He told of his trip and the wealth of China. Soon after, many European nobles began planning similar adventures, hoping to bring back riches.

By the early 1300s, Europe was regularly receiving goods from China and India. Merchants often traveled across the long, overland route from Europe to eastern Asia called the Silk Road. These merchants brought back silks, spices, gunpowder, and other goods from China. From India, merchants returned with spices, tea, and fine fabrics. The route was dangerous because it passed through many different lands that included tall mountains and wide deserts. Merchants were exposed to bandits and a long journey.

Marco Polo, shown here in Asian clothing, inspired others to travel to Asia.

★ **How did the Crusades affect European trade?**

B. Trade With the East

As Europe began to hear news of the outside world, it also began to undergo political change. Throughout Europe, kings gained more power by uniting smaller kingdoms to form nations.

Seeking power and wealth for their countries, these rulers sponsored trade caravans to Asia. They also encouraged sea voyages to find new routes to India and China.

Muslim and Italian Merchants

In the 1300s and 1400s Italian and Muslim merchants controlled most trade with Asia. The Muslim merchants often bought their cargoes from traders in eastern Asia or India. The goods were then carried to the Middle East along the Silk Road. Rulers of lands along the Silk Road demanded money from traders who passed through their territories. To pay for the expense of this journey and still make money, the Muslim traders then sold the goods to Italian merchants for high prices.

The Italian merchants controlled all trade routes that crossed the Mediterranean Sea. They transported the goods by ship to the port cities of Genoa and Venice before carrying them overland to northern and western Europe. Then, so that they too could make money, they increased the prices of the goods again before selling them throughout Europe. People in Europe were willing to pay these high prices for desirable Asian goods, so trade increased and the merchants prospered.

The Need for a Sea Route

More frequent trade with Asia transformed Europe. Europeans began to use spices like ginger and nutmeg to preserve and flavor meats. Cinnamon was used not only to flavor food, but also as perfume. Silk was used to make beautiful and comfortable clothing. Gunpowder fueled weapons used in battles. The people in the nations of Europe demanded Asian goods.

By the mid-1300s, three new nations had emerged in Europe—Portugal, England, and France. Each of these nations wanted a larger share of the Asian trade. However, they could not remove the Italians who controlled much of the **commerce**, or trade, between the East and West. These three countries would have to find another way to get to Asia. Thus, they began to explore trade routes across the Atlantic Ocean.

★ **What were the problems with the land route from Europe to Asia?**

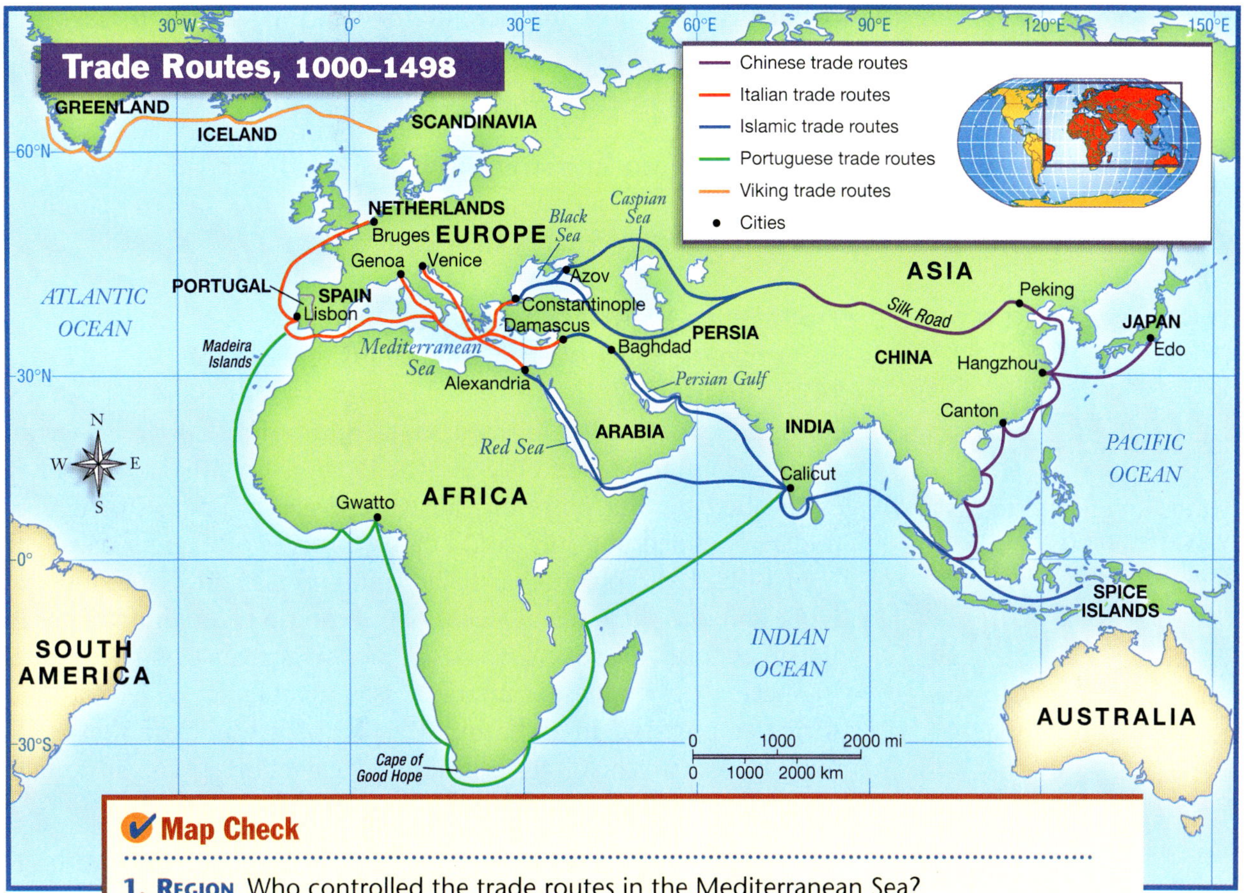

Trade Routes, 1000–1498

- Chinese trade routes
- Italian trade routes
- Islamic trade routes
- Portuguese trade routes
- Viking trade routes
- • Cities

Map Check

1. **REGION** Who controlled the trade routes in the Mediterranean Sea?
2. **LOCATION** What city in India is located along a trade route?

C. Portuguese Exploration

The Portuguese developed trade routes across the oceans. They became the first Europeans to trade by sea with West Africa and Asia.

Portugal Leads the Way

Henry, a prince in Portugal, wanted his nation to control Asian trade. To do this, Portuguese sailors needed better ships and tools to **navigate**, or travel across, the seas. In 1419, Prince Henry invited experts in geography, mathematics, and astronomy to come to his court in Portugal and share their knowledge.

Prince Henry also sponsored sea voyages along the west coast of Africa. He hoped Portuguese ships would be able to travel by water all the way to India. His determination to find the best ways to travel the ocean earned him the nickname "Prince Henry the Navigator."

The Portuguese used caravels like this one to travel the oceans.

Portuguese sailors used technology and inventions to seek out new water routes to Asia. They designed a ship built for sailing long distances, called a caravel. With the ability to sail into the wind and a good rudder for steering, it was built to travel long distances at sea. The compass was an instrument that showed sailors direction. The **astrolabe** was a tool that used the position of the stars to help measure a ship's distance from the equator.

Then & Now

Every four years, daring sailors in large yachts compete in an around-the-world race that takes them around the Cape of Good Hope. Just as Bartolomeu Dias did, they must deal with high winds and fierce storms and waves so high that they could swallow small buildings. One racer commented on the size of the waves. He said, "You go down the hill and hit bottom and then ride up the other side."

Trade With West Africa and Beyond

Portuguese sailors began exploring the west coast of Africa in 1415. First, they found the Madeira Islands west of Africa. Portuguese settlers established sugar **plantations**, or large farms, there. From the Madeira Islands, the Portuguese sailed south. They established trading posts on the African coast. There Portuguese traders obtained not only gold but also ivory, cloth, and slaves.

In 1488, Bartolomeu Dias sailed south around the Cape of Good Hope and into the Indian Ocean. No European before him had been able to conquer the strong winds and ocean currents along this route.

Another Portuguese captain, Vasco da Gama, sailed around Africa and arrived in India in 1498. Now, it was clear that a sea route to Asia was possible. This journey gave Portugal an advantage in the competition for trade with Asia among European nations.

What did the Portuguese obtain through trade with West Africa?

Review History

A. Why were Asian goods so valuable in Europe?

B. Why did Europeans want to find a sea route to Asia?

C. How did Portugal become the leader in trade with Asia?

Define Terms to Know

Provide a definition for each of the following terms.
commerce, navigate, astrolabe, plantation

Critical Thinking

How did the rise of new nations in Europe lead to overseas exploration?

Write About Culture

Marco Polo wrote about what he saw in Asia. Write a journal entry describing the riches of Asia as Marco Polo might have described them.

Get Organized

TIMELINE

In this section, you learned about events during the late Middle Ages in Europe. Copy the timeline below, and record at least four events from this period on it.

III Major Voyages to the Americas

Terms to Know

expedition a journey made for a specific purpose

colony a settlement in a distant land that is governed by another country

Main Ideas

A. Early Viking and Spanish explorers were the first Europeans to reach the Americas.

B. The search for a route to Asia drew European explorers to the Americas.

Active Reading

CLASSIFY

When you classify information, you put items into categories. As you read this section, classify the geographic regions explored by Europeans.

A. Europeans Reach the Americas

In the early 1400s, the Portuguese dominated sea travel. However, other countries wanted to find ocean routes to Asia. Some of the explorers from other European countries tried to sail west rather than east to reach Asia. Their voyages led to the European exploration of the Americas.

Competition From Spain

Portuguese success in trading with Africa inspired other nations to explore the seas. Portugal's main rival in overseas exploration was Spain. The country of Spain was formed in the 1460s by the union of two kingdoms. Queen Isabella and King Ferdinand wanted to make their nation one of the strongest in Europe.

To do this, they would have to develop trade routes to Asia. However, they had few able captains. This problem was solved when an Italian adventurer arrived in Spain. His name was Christopher Columbus. He offered to sail for Ferdinand and Isabella if they would provide ships and crews. He promised to make Spain wealthy by bringing gold back from his travels.

Christopher Columbus, like most informed people of his time, knew that the world was round. He also knew that Asia was east of Europe. He reasoned that there was another way to get to Asia—by sailing west. Columbus, however, miscalculated the size of the world, believing it to be much smaller. Also, he did not know that other continents lay to the west between Europe and Asia.

Christopher Columbus was one of the first European explorers to reach the Americas.

Spotlight on

Geography

Amerigo Vespucci, an Italian explorer, was one of the first people to realize that Columbus had not found an ocean route to Asia, but had reached two new continents. Between 1499 and 1504, Vespucci made at least two trips to the Americas. He wrote many letters describing the lands as a "new world." In 1507, a German mapmaker created a map of these lands and named the area America in honor of Amerigo Vespucci.

The Voyage West

Queen Isabella of Spain offered Columbus three ships and about 90 sailors. The ships were named the *Niña*, the *Pinta*, and the *Santa María*. On August 3, 1492, Christopher Columbus departed from Spain to begin his **expedition**, or journey.

Columbus first sailed to the Canary Islands. He left these islands on September 9, heading directly west. About a month later, land was sighted. On October 12, 1492, Columbus anchored off an island in the Caribbean Sea. He named the island San Salvador and claimed it for Spain.

Before Columbus

Columbus was not the first European to arrive in the Americas. Almost 500 years before his voyage, sailors from Scandinavia—today the countries of Norway, Sweden, and Denmark—under the command of Leif Ericson sailed to the shores of North America. These sailors were called Norsemen, or Vikings. European explorers of the 1400s had no knowledge of the earlier Norse voyages.

The Norse sailors probably arrived on the North American continent by chance. They encountered a land with grapevines. As a result, Ericson named it Vinland. The Vikings built fishing and trading villages on the shores of Vinland, but soon abandoned them. Based on artifacts that they recovered there, archaeologists now know that Vinland was in Newfoundland, in northeastern Canada.

Columbus in America

When Columbus landed on San Salvador, he believed that he was in Asia. Asian islands were known throughout Europe as "the Indies." So, when Columbus met the people who lived on the island, he named them Indians. These Native Americans called themselves Táino. They lived in villages and raised corn and yams. Columbus described them in his diary:

> "They willingly traded everything they owned. . . . They were well-built, with good bodies and handsome features. . . . They have no iron. Their spears are made of cane. . . . They would make fine servants."

ANALYZE PRIMARY SOURCES

DOCUMENT-BASED QUESTION How do you think Columbus viewed the Táino people?

Columbus's main interest was in finding gold. When he saw the gold earrings the Táino people wore, he demanded that they lead him to the source of the gold. Taking several Táinos to guide him, he sailed to another island he named Hispaniola, or "Little Spain." This island is present-day Haiti and the Dominican Republic.

Columbus found little gold in Hispaniola. However, when he returned to Spain, Columbus said that there were great gold mines to be found there. The search for gold would soon send other explorers to North and South America, including Vasco Núñez de Balboa who sailed for Spain in search of riches. Columbus, however, needed to earn money. Therefore, he took Táino people to Spain and sold them as slaves.

In 1493 Columbus returned to the Caribbean with 17 ships and about 1,500 people. His goal was to make Hispaniola a Spanish **colony**. A colony is a distant settlement ruled by another country.

Columbus made two more voyages to the Caribbean hoping to find gold. By the early 1500s, Columbus and other Spanish explorers had claimed the islands of present-day Puerto Rico, Jamaica, and Cuba. They did not, however, find large amounts of gold or a western sea route to Asia. That was left to Ferdinand Magellan, who also sailed for Spain. Between 1519 and 1522, his expedition became the first to circumnavigate, or sail completely around, the world. Magellan, however, did not survive the voyage.

 **Who were the first Europeans to reach North America?**

Some Early Portuguese and Spanish Explorations, 1488–1522

EXPLORER	COUNTRY REPRESENTED	YEAR	GOAL	ACCOMPLISHMENT
Bartolomeu Dias	Portugal	1487–1488	To find southern tip of Africa	Sailed around southern Africa into Indian Ocean
Christopher Columbus	Spain	1492–1504 (4 voyages)	To find western route to Asia	Explored West Indies and Central and South America
Vasco da Gama	Portugal	1497–1498	To sail around Africa to eastern Asia	Reached India
Vasco Núñez de Balboa	Spain	1513	To find gold	Crossed Isthmus of Panama and saw Pacific Ocean
Ferdinand Magellan	Spain	1519–1522	To find western route to Asia	First expedition to sail around the world

Chart Check

What goal did many explorers have in common?

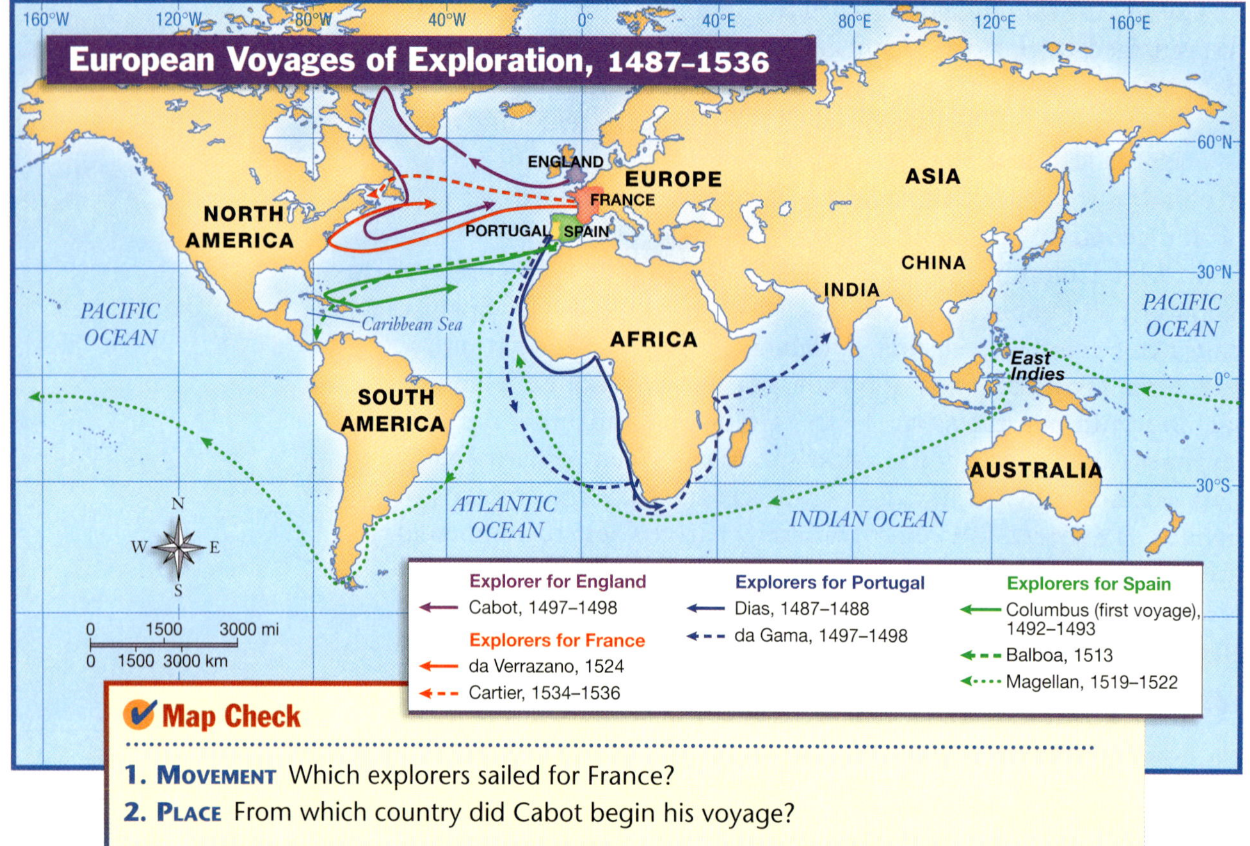

Map Check

1. **Movement** Which explorers sailed for France?
2. **Place** From which country did Cabot begin his voyage?

B. More Nations, More Explorations

News of Columbus's voyage sparked the interest of Europeans to find a western sea route to Asia. England and France were now eager to find their own western routes to the riches in Asia. Portugal, however, was in control of the eastern sea route around Africa. It sent out more explorers as well.

Cabral and Cabot

By 1494, Spain and Portugal were the two European nations exploring most of the world. In that year, they agreed to the Treaty of Tordesillas. This treaty drew an imaginary line north to south on the globe, through the Atlantic Ocean and what is today Brazil. Portugal claimed all lands east of the line, and Spain claimed all lands west.

After the treaty, Portugal sent out explorers. One of these, Pedro Cabral, traveled southwest across the Atlantic Ocean. He landed on the shore of present-day Brazil, in South America, and claimed the land for Portugal.

In 1497, a captain named John Cabot sailed from England westward across the North Atlantic Ocean. He landed near present-day Newfoundland, Canada. He returned to England certain that he had reached Asia. Cabot set out for a second voyage in 1498 but was lost at sea before he could return home.

French Exploration

French explorers also sailed to the Americas. The first of these explorers was an Italian working for the French named Giovanni da Verrazano. In 1524, he sailed from France to present-day South Carolina, then north to Nova Scotia and Newfoundland, Canada, before returning to France. Verrazano drew detailed maps of the entire North American coastline. These maps helped future explorers. One of the longest suspension bridges in the world is named after him. The Verrazano Narrows Bridge reaches from Brooklyn to Staten Island in New York City.

In 1534, Jacques Cartier traveled to the upper regions of the St. Lawrence River. Cartier tried to establish a French settlement along the St. Lawrence River in 1535, but the cold winter forced him to abandon this plan. For a time, Spain would be alone among Europe's nations in establishing colonies in the Americas.

Why did England, Portugal, and France send explorers west across the Atlantic Ocean?

Review History

A. Why did Christopher Columbus sail west?

B. What other European countries besides Spain were exploring routes to east Asia?

Define Terms to Know

Provide a definition for the following terms.
expedition, colony

Critical Thinking

Unlike Spain, England and France did not establish colonies on their first voyages to North America. What might account for this?

Write About History

If newspapers had existed in 1492, Christopher Columbus would have made the headlines. Write an article to tell readers in Spain about Columbus's first voyage.

Get Organized

TIMELINE

On a separate sheet of paper record some of the voyages and their dates made by the English, Portuguese, and French sailors after 1492.

PAST *to* PRESENT

Navigation

To find their way across oceans, early explorers used compasses, charts, and logs. These tools are still used today. Compasses are instruments that show navigators in what direction they are going. Charts are sea maps that show landmarks and paths in various directions. Logs are books in which captains record how far a ship has traveled and what occurred.

Early tools for calculating the position of ships on the sea were not very accurate. Ships could be miles off course without the captain knowing it. Today, radar, satellites, and computers help navigators determine the exact position of their ships.

Early navigators used maps and charts to help determine their location. These maps and charts were often not completely accurate. Today, much more precise charts are used by navigators.

A sextant is a tool used to find location by measuring the angle between the horizon and a star such as the sun. Using this information, sailors can determine their latitude.

2

Navigators today often use a Global Positioning System (GPS) to determine location. This system uses satellites to send signals to ships to determine location.

Today, navigation is much more precise due to advances in technology. Radar and compasses help sailors find their exact location in a very short time.

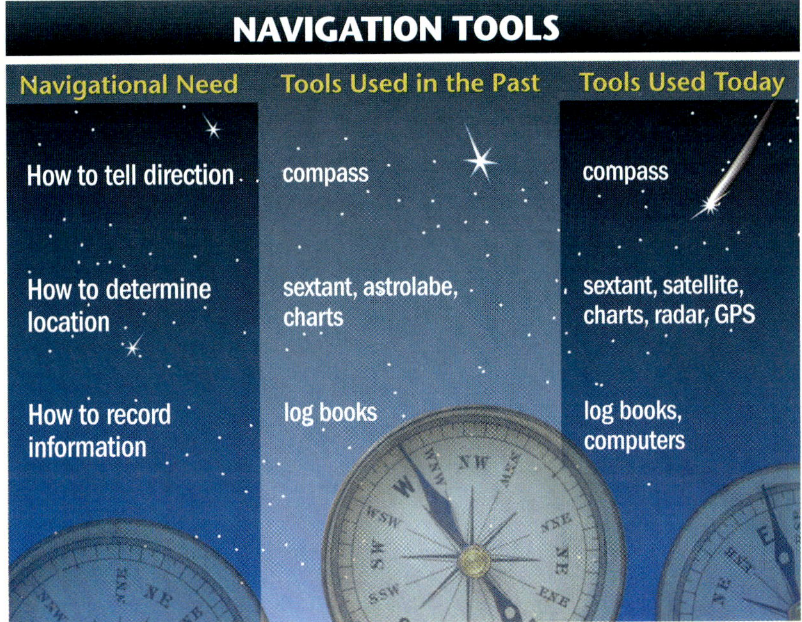

NAVIGATION TOOLS

Navigational Need	Tools Used in the Past	Tools Used Today
How to tell direction	compass	compass
How to determine location	sextant, astrolabe, charts	sextant, satellite, charts, radar, GPS
How to record information	log books	log books, computers

The chart above compares navigation tools used in the past to those used today.

Hands-On Activity

With a partner, conduct research on the Internet or in your school library to learn more about navigation tools. Make drawings, photocopies, or printouts of two navigation tools from the time of early explorers and two from today. Add captions to explain how these tools are used. To get started, you can go to: www.gfamericanhistory.com.

CHAPTER 2 Review

Chapter Summary

In your notebook, complete the following outline. Then, use your outline to write a brief summary of the chapter.

Early Exploration

I. West African Trading Kingdoms
   A. The Riches of Africa
   B.
   C.
II. Early European Expeditions
   A.
   B.
   C.
III. Major Voyages to the Americas
   A.
   B.

Interpret the Timeline

Use the timeline on pages 24–25 to answer the following questions.

1. How long after Columbus did John Cabot reach the Americas?
2. **Critical Thinking** Which event on the timeline shows Portugal's leadership in overseas exploration?

Use Terms to Know

Match each term with its definition.

a. caravan
b. colony
c. commerce
d. kinship
e. navigate
f. plantation
g. tax

1. to control the direction of a ship or boat
2. a settlement in a distant land that is governed by another country
3. money paid to a government
4. a large farm requiring many workers
5. a group of travelers with pack animals
6. a family relationship based on common ancestors
7. the buying and selling of goods

Check Your Understanding

1. **Identify** the location of the three large trading kingdoms of West Africa.
2. **Explain** why Mansa Musa's journey from Mali to the Middle East was important.
3. **Discuss** the effect Marco Polo's journey to China had on Europe.
4. **Identify** two navigation tools that helped the Portuguese become expert sailors.
5. **Explain** why Columbus called Native Americans "Indians."
6. **Identify** the reasons Spanish explorers traveled to North America.

Critical Thinking

1. **Make Inferences** Mansa Musa, the king of Mali, was respected by many people and nations. Based on your reading, why do you think Mansa Musa was so respected?
2. **Make Generalizations** In what ways did Europe change in the late Middle Ages?
3. **Analyze Primary Sources** Reread the quote on page 38. Why do you think Columbus thought the Táino would make good servants?

Put Your Skills to Work

READ A HISTORICAL MAP

You have learned that reading a historical map can help you understand events from the past. Use the map below that shows the voyage of Pedro Cabral to answer the following questions.

1. From which country did Cabral begin his expedition?
2. About how far south did Cabral go?

In Your Own Words

JOURNAL WRITING

Think of some examples of people today who are exploring unknown worlds. What drives these people to explore? How are they like or unlike the explorers from the late 1400s and early 1500s? Write a response to both of these questions in your journal.

Net Work

INTERNET ACTIVITY

Work with a group of your classmates. Use the Internet as a resource to create a visual presentation about the explorations of one European country mentioned in this chapter. Include a timeline listing the explorers from that country, a map showing their voyages, and a brief description of each explorer. Share your presentation with the class.

For help in starting this activity, visit the following Web site: www.gfamericanhistory.com.

Look Ahead

In the next chapter, learn how Spain established other colonies in the Americas.

CHAPTER 3

New Settlements in the Americas 1512–1682

I. **Spanish Conquest and Colonies**
II. **Other European Settlements**
III. **Slavery in the Americas**

Three English ships anchored off a small island in the James River, Virginia, in May 1607. The English settlers aboard the ships had just come to North America after a terribly long voyage. One of the leaders of the expedition, John Smith, noted,

> "We were at sea five months, where we both spent our victual [food] and lost the opportunity of the time and season to plant . . ."

The English settlers named their colony Jamestown after the king of England. Like others who had come to the Americas before them to start colonies, these English settlers would encounter many challenges.

English helmets

Events in the Americas

1512 Spanish colonists in the Caribbean import slaves from West Africa.

1521 Cortés conquers the Aztecs.

1533 Pizarro conquers the Incas.

1541 De Soto crosses the Mississippi River.

1565 St. Augustine is founded.

1590 Settlement of Roanoke fails.

1500 — 1540 — 1580

World Events

1514 Copernicus develops the theory of a sun-centered universe.

1558 Elizabeth I becomes queen of England.

1588 English defeat the Spanish Armada.

VIEW HISTORY This modern painting of the Jamestown colony is based on evidence found at the site by archaeologists. Objects dug up at the site, such as helmets (left), show that the colonists were prepared for danger.

★ **What evidence might archaeologists use to create a picture of the Jamestown settlement?**

Get Organized

KWL CHART

A KWL chart is used to organize what you know, what you want to know, and what you have learned. As you begin each section, fill in a chart with what you know and what you want to know. Then, at the end of each section, fill in what you have learned. Here is an example.

Know
Spain established colonies in the Americas.
Want to Know
Where were the Spanish colonies located?
Learned
The two largest colonies were in Mexico and South America.

1607 Jamestown, Virginia, is settled by English colonists.

1624 New Netherland is founded by the Dutch.

1682 Robert de La Salle claims Mississippi River valley for France.

1620 — 1660 — 1700

1620 — 1660 — 1700

1631 Mount Vesuvius erupts in Naples, Italy, killing more than 3,000 people.

1668 Spain recognizes Portugal's independence in the Treaty of Lisbon.

1690 An early form of the bicycle is invented.

I Spanish Conquest and Colonies

Terms to Know

conquistador the Spanish term for conqueror, or one who gains control by winning a war

encomienda system the system in which Native Americans were forced to work for Spanish landowners

mission a settlement established for religious work

Main Ideas

A. Spanish invaders conquered the Aztec and Inca Empires in the Americas and established colonies for Spain.

B. The search for gold led to Spanish explorations in North America.

Active Reading

POINTS OF VIEW

People often have different points of view. As you read this section, think about the viewpoints of the people described. Ask yourself: What explains each point of view?

A. Conquest of the Aztecs and the Incas

Christopher Columbus and others from Spain came to the Americas for different reasons. Some came for wealth, some to expand the Spanish Empire, and still others to spread the Christian religion. They did not, however, expect to find great civilizations in central Mexico and South America.

Cortés and the Aztecs

By 1500, the Aztecs were an advanced civilization. With an estimated population of more than 200,000 people, the Aztec capital, Tenochtitlán, was larger than any European capital at that time. It was also a city of great wealth.

In 1519, a Spanish explorer named Hernándo Cortés led a fleet of ships from Cuba to the east coast of the Gulf of Mexico. Rumors of gold had led him there. When the Aztec emperor Montezuma II learned of Cortés's arrival, he sent gifts to him and his men. Montezuma's lavish gifts aroused Cortés's interest, so he recruited a translator and led his men to Tenochtitlán. There, he was welcomed by Montezuma and provided with fine food and lodging. However, Cortés wished only to take the wealth of Tenochtitlán, so he took the emperor prisoner. Fierce fighting broke out between the Aztecs and the Spaniards.

The Aztecs drove the Spaniards from the city, but Montezuma was killed during the battle. Cortés attacked the capital for nearly three months. Although the Spaniards were few in number, they were too powerful for the Aztecs to resist.

This Aztec drawing shows Spaniards fighting with cannons and crossbows while the Aztecs fight with spears.

The Spaniards had several advantages over the Aztecs. First, they had stronger weapons, such as cannons, guns, and swords. The Aztecs had only bows and arrows and spears. Second, the Spaniards had horses. Fighters on horseback could easily overpower fighters on foot. Third, they received help from local people who did not like living under the harsh Aztec rule. In addition, many Aztecs died of smallpox—a disease brought by the Spaniards.

By 1521, the Aztec Empire had fallen. An Aztec account from that year records this defeat:

> "Broken spears lie in the roads; We have torn our hair in our grief. The houses are roofless now, and their walls are red with blood."

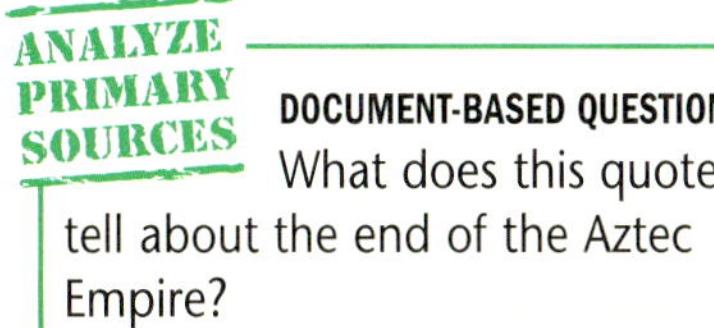

DOCUMENT-BASED QUESTION What does this quote tell about the end of the Aztec Empire?

The Spaniards quickly began building a new city on the ruins of Tenochtitlán which they called Mexico City. Mexico City would become the capital of the colony called New Spain. Soon after the conquest of the Aztecs, thousands of Spaniards arrived in New Spain.

Pizarro Conquers the Incas

The riches that Cortés found in Mexico prompted other **conquistadors**, or Spanish conquerors in the 1500s, to travel to the Americas. One of those conquistadors was Francisco Pizarro. In 1531, Pizarro led an expedition of 180 men to what is present-day Peru in South America.

Pizarro had heard rumors that a wealthy civilization existed in South America. When he arrived, he indeed found a great civilization—the Incas. Pizarro captured and killed the Inca ruler Atahualpa. He then went on to fight the Incas for control of their empire. However, without their leader the Incas were unable to fight the Spaniards effectively. By 1533, Pizarro and the Spaniards were in control of the Inca Empire. The wealth there was greater than that which Cortés had found in Mexico.

The encomienda system worked well for the Spaniards, but not for the Native Americans. Bartolomé de las Casas fought against the encomienda system.

Spanish Colonization in the Americas

Conquest was only the first step in building a Spanish Empire in the Americas. Spain also needed to encourage Spanish settlers to move to their newly conquered lands. Then, when settlers became established in an area, the next step was to convert the native people to Christianity. To accomplish both of these goals, Spain set up land and labor arrangements called encomiendas. Under the **encomienda system** a settler was given a large plot of land and a group of workers from the native population.

While the encomienda system worked well in attracting Spanish settlers, it was disastrous for the native people. They had their land taken away and eventually were enslaved by the Spaniards.

Spaniards and Native Americans

Many Spaniards became rich by conquering or enslaving the Native Americans, but others spoke out against such cruelty. One of these men was a priest by the name of Bartolomé de las Casas. Las Casas first came to the Americas in 1502, and was granted a large encomienda. Eventually, though, Las Casas decided that the encomienda system was wrong because it enslaved the native people.

Las Casas protested the mistreatment of Native Americans. His protests encouraged Spain to change some laws regarding the treatment of native people. For example, native people were to be cared for and protected in religious settlements called **missions**. Life in missions also helped to convert Native Americans to the Catholic religion. Another new law stated that farmworkers were to be paid wages, even though these wages would be very low.

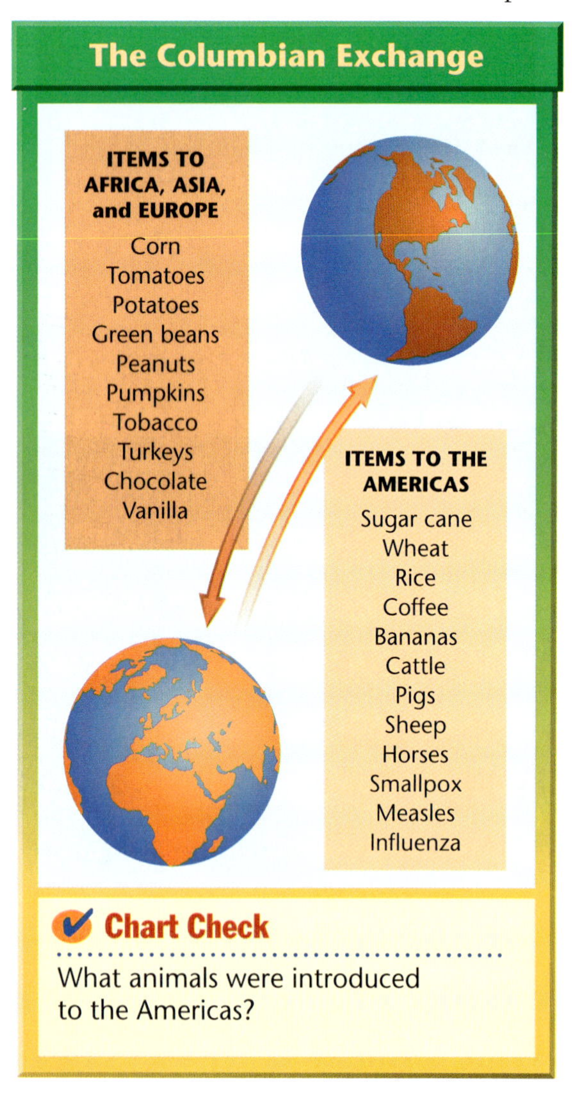

Chart Check

What animals were introduced to the Americas?

It was difficult, however, to enforce these laws thousands of miles away from Spain. As a result, most colonists in New Spain and other Spanish colonies in the Americas ignored the laws. They continued to force Native Americans to work on farms and ranches, and in silver mines. Many workers died from overwork. Others died from European diseases, such as smallpox and measles, to which they had no natural resistance. Within 100 years of being conquered by Spain, more than 90 percent of the Native Americans in Mexico had died from these diseases.

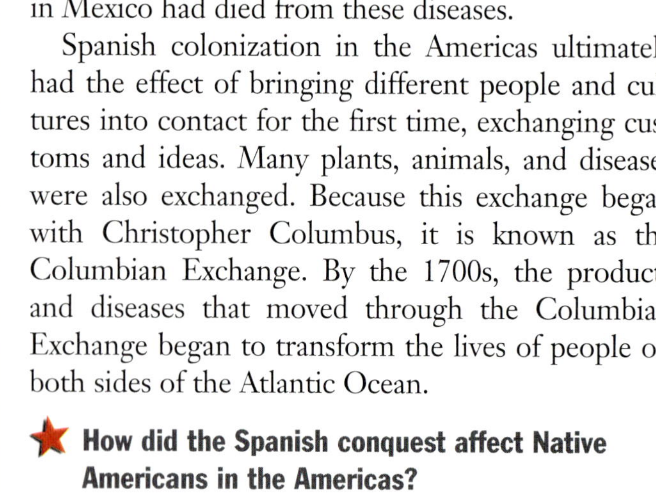

Spanish colonization in the Americas ultimately had the effect of bringing different people and cultures into contact for the first time, exchanging customs and ideas. Many plants, animals, and diseases were also exchanged. Because this exchange began with Christopher Columbus, it is known as the Columbian Exchange. By the 1700s, the products and diseases that moved through the Columbian Exchange began to transform the lives of people on both sides of the Atlantic Ocean.

★ **How did the Spanish conquest affect Native Americans in the Americas?**

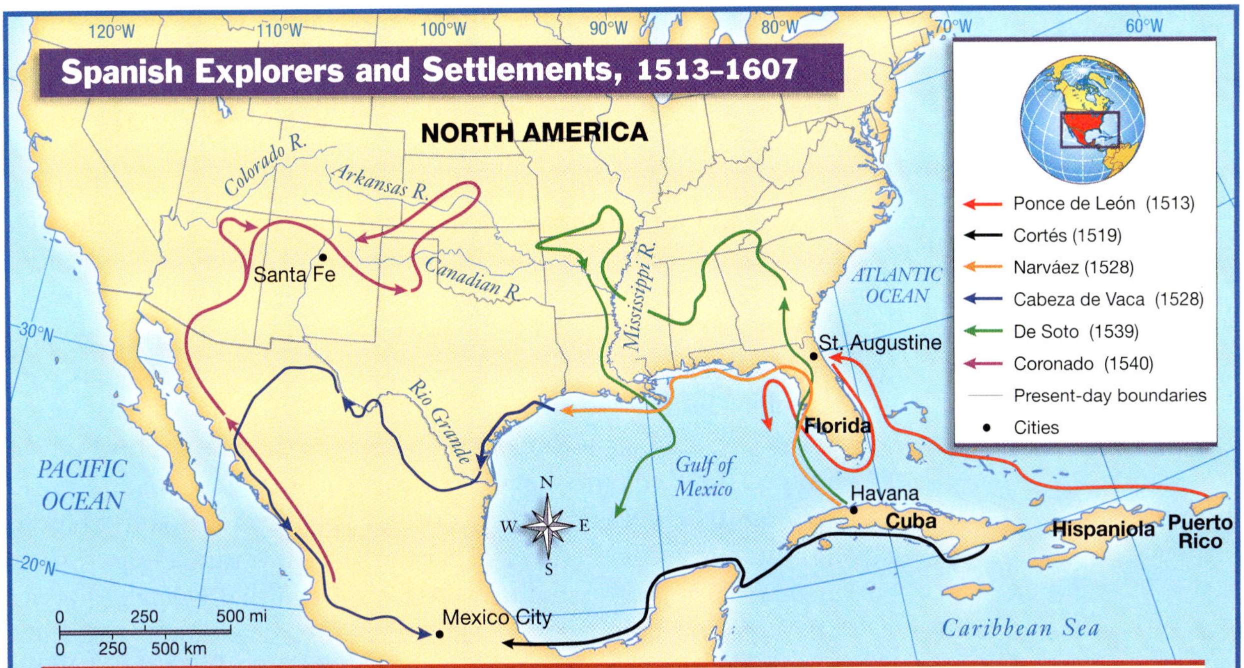

Spanish Explorers and Settlements, 1513–1607

Map Check

1. **PLACE** Which Spaniards began their explorations from Havana, Cuba?
2. **LOCATION** What river did Cabeza de Vaca cross in his exploration of 1528?

B. Exploring North America

Spanish conquistadors also searched the land north of New Spain for gold and silver. In this part of North America, however, they did not find what they were seeking.

Early Explorations

The first Spaniard to explore lands that are now part of the United States was Juan Ponce de León. In 1513, he left Puerto Rico to find a fountain that was rumored to give all who drank from it eternal youth. During his search, Ponce de León reached an unknown coast. He claimed this land for Spain, naming it *La Florida*. Ponce de Léon explored the area again in 1521 looking for gold but found only natives, who killed him with poisoned arrows.

In 1528, a Spanish explorer, Pánfilo de Narváez, landed near present-day Tampa, Florida, with a few hundred people. Later, nearly all of his crew were killed in a shipwreck off the coast of present-day Texas. Two of the ship's survivors were Alvar Nuñez Cabeza de Vaca and Esteban, a slave of African descent. Together, they spent six years walking across northern Mexico and the southern and southwestern regions of today's United States.

Juan Ponce de León was the first European to explore present-day Florida. He was looking for the legendary Fountain of Youth.

Then & Now

Coronado's expedition marked the beginning of Spanish influence in the American Southwest. Today, this region is home to many people of Spanish descent. This group includes people from Mexico and other Spanish-language regions.

De Soto and Coronado

When Cabeza de Vaca returned to Mexico, he told stories about wealth in North America. These stories convinced others to explore. In 1539, Hernándo de Soto and about 700 conquistadors landed in Florida and explored several present-day southern states. However, they did not find the treasure that they had hoped for. De Soto continued his journey, reaching the Mississippi River. There, he caught a fever and later died. His crew continued the journey.

At about the same time, Francisco Coronado explored what is now the west coast of Mexico, searching for seven cities with streets of gold. He traveled to present-day Arizona, New Mexico, Texas, Oklahoma, and Kansas. Coronado failed to find gold. However, he claimed the lands that he had traveled through for Spain.

Because gold was never discovered, Spanish rulers and explorers lost interest in North America for the next 100 years. Only two permanent Spanish settlements were founded in that period. One was St. Augustine, founded in Florida in 1565. It is the oldest permanent European-founded city in the United States. St. Augustine became the center of Spanish settlement in the northeast. As a result, Spain controlled Florida for more than two centuries. The other settlement, Santa Fe, was founded in 1610, in present day New Mexico.

 **Why did Spanish explorers lose interest in North America for some time after 1542?**

Review

Review History

A. Why did Spanish explorers come to the Americas?

B. What areas of southern North America did the conquistadors explore in the early to middle 1500s?

Define Terms to Know

Provide a definition for each of the following terms.
conquistador, encomienda system, mission

Critical Thinking

Explain the positive and negative effects of Spanish conquests in North America.

Write About History

When two civilizations clash, one civilization is often overpowered by the other. Write a paragraph explaining how the Spanish civilization overpowered the Aztec and Inca civilizations.

Get Organized

KWL CHART

At the beginning of this section, you started a KWL chart on Spanish settlements. Now complete the chart by filling in what you have learned in this section.

Know
Want to Know
Learned

Build Your Skills

Study Skill

IDENTIFY THE MAIN IDEA

Most of the information that you read is tied together by a main idea. The main idea is the subject or topic of the information. The details and facts within the information support the main idea. Sometimes the main idea is clearly stated. Other times, you have to figure it out for yourself.

When you read about history, you will find many facts. These facts support a main idea. You can look for main ideas in each paragraph. Sometimes a main idea is developed over several paragraphs.

Identifying the main idea will help you understand what you read and make connections between the facts. It will also make history more meaningful to you.

Here's How

Follow these steps to identify the main idea.

1. Read the heading or title of a section of text to learn the general topic.
2. Look for a topic sentence when you read a paragraph. A topic sentence states the main idea.
3. If there is no topic sentence, ask yourself, What are all of the sentences about?
4. Write or state the main idea.

Here's Why

You have just read about the Spanish conquest of the Aztecs. If you were asked to explain how the conquistadors were successful, knowing the main idea of the section would help you answer this question.

Practice the Skill

Read the paragraph to the right. Then, use the directions above to find the main idea. Write the main idea in your own words.

Extend the Skill

With a partner, reread a paragraph in Section I of this chapter. Talk about the main idea and state it in your own words.

Apply the Skill

As you read the remaining sections of this chapter, identify the main ideas. Identify the subject of each paragraph and each section. Then, use these main ideas to gain a better understanding of the chapter.

The Spaniards had several advantages over the Aztecs. First, they had stronger weapons, such as cannons, guns, and swords. The Aztecs had only bows and arrows and spears. Second, the Spaniards had horses. Fighters on horseback could easily overpower fighters on foot. Third, they received help from local people who did not like living under the harsh Aztec rule. In addition, many Aztecs died of smallpox —a disease brought by the Spaniards.

Main idea: ____________________

II Other European Settlements

Terms to Know

charter an official document in which rights are given by a government to a person or company

joint-stock company a group of investors who share both risk and profit

cash crop a crop that is grown to be sold rather than used by a farmer

Main Ideas

A. Dutch colonists settled along the Hudson River, and French colonists settled in eastern Canada.

B. The first English effort to colonize North America was a failure.

C. The first permanent English colony at Jamestown, Virginia, had a difficult beginning.

Active Reading

MAKE GENERALIZATIONS

When you generalize, you make broad statements that summarize many facts. Example: Most Spanish explorers were interested in finding gold. As you read this section, pause to generalize about what you have read.

A. French and Dutch Colonies in North America

Several European countries had explored North America. However, Spain was the only country to establish colonies in the Americas. By the 1600s, however, this situation began to change.

Henry Hudson and Dutch Settlement

In 1609, an English explorer named Henry Hudson sailed west. He was hired by Dutch merchants from the Netherlands to find a Northwest Passage, or a water route through North America to Asia.

When Hudson reached North America, he sailed into a river in present-day New York. Later, this river was named the Hudson River. Hudson claimed the land around the river for the Netherlands. In 1614, the Dutch began to build trading posts in the area. By 1624, Dutch traders founded the colony of New Netherland. This colony covered the Hudson River valley. New Amsterdam, the colony's largest settlement, was located on Manhattan Island. It was named after the city of Amsterdam in the Netherlands. There, the Dutch colonists prospered by trading with the Native Americans for furs.

Then & Now

When the Dutch settled on Manhattan Island, they built a wall to protect themselves from attack. In 1664, the Dutch, having too few soldiers to defend the wall, surrendered to the English. The area where the wall stood was named Wall Street by the English. Today, Wall Street is a center of world finance where many bankers and stockbrokers work.

French Settlements

After Giovanni da Verrazano and Jacques Cartier explored land in North America for France, other French explorers came to the area. In 1603, Samuel de Champlain sailed up the St. Lawrence River. On its banks, he founded Quebec in 1608. Like New Netherland, it was a trading colony based on the fur trade.

Over the next few years, Champlain continued to explore the area. He sailed all the way to the Great Lakes and claimed them for France. For all of his success, he is remembered as the "Father of New France."

In 1682, Robert de La Salle, explored the area from the Great Lakes to the mouth of the Mississippi River on the Gulf of Mexico. He claimed the entire Mississippi River valley for France. This area was named Louisiana in honor of King Louis XIV of France.

Do You Remember?
In Chapter 1, you learned where Native American groups lived in North America. Europeans encountered these native people as they explored the continent.

 **What kind of settlements did the Dutch and the French establish in North America?**

B. England Starts to Colonize

John Cabot had claimed much of the North Atlantic coast for England in 1497. The people of England were eager to colonize this new land. Before they could, however, the English government needed to settle affairs with Spain.

Tension Between England and Spain

Beginning in the mid-1500s, relations between England and Spain became tense. Spain was becoming rich from the gold and silver it found in the Americas. English leaders, including Queen Elizabeth I, envied Spain's wealth and worried about Spain's growing power.

By 1588, Spain was ready to invade England. Its rulers sent a huge fleet of ships, the Spanish Armada, to conquer England. However, England's smaller, faster ships, aided by a storm, defeated the Spanish Armada. England was now free to colonize North America.

In 1588, the English defeated the Spanish Armada.

John White found the letters *CRO* carved into a tree. To this day the fate of the settlers on Roanoke Island remains a mystery.

The Lost Colony

Queen Elizabeth gave Sir Walter Raleigh a **charter**, an official document, to start a colony in North America. In 1587, Raleigh sent 117 men, women, and children, led by John White, to settle his colony. On Roanoke Island off the coast of what is now North Carolina, they decided to make their home. After a month, White was forced to sail back to England for supplies.

White was delayed and did not return for three years. When he arrived, the colonists had vanished. The only clue he found was the letters *CRO* carved into a tree and the word *Croatoan* carved into a door post. Croatoan Island was about 100 miles from Roanoke, but bad weather kept White from searching there. The colonists were never seen again.

 **How did Queen Elizabeth support colonization in North America?**

C. Jamestown

The English did not give up on settling North America. They were determined to increase their wealth by starting colonies. This time, they were slightly more successful.

Starting Up a Colony

Sending expeditions to North America was costly and had a great risk of failure. To help solve these problems, English merchants organized **joint-stock companies**. In a joint-stock company, each owner pays a part of the cost of starting the company. In return, each person receives part of the profit the company makes. Joint-stock companies paid for English expeditions to establish colonies in North America.

In 1606, King James I of England issued a charter to the Virginia Company in London. The charter gave the company permission to send settlers to the Atlantic Coast of North America. The company's goal was to make a profit through trade or through mining gold.

In May 1607, three ships carrying over 100 people landed in present-day Virginia, along the Chesapeake Bay. They sailed into the James River. About 30 miles upstream, they founded a settlement called Jamestown in honor of their king.

The Jamestown Settlement

Jamestown was the first permanent English settlement in North America. It had problems from the beginning. The land was swampy and filled with mosquitoes. Little fresh drinking water was nearby. There were frequent conflicts with the local Native Americans—the Algonquins. The Algonquins viewed the English settlement as an invasion of their territory. Furthermore, most of the settlers did not bother to grow food for the colony. Most spent their time looking for gold, not farming. Yet no gold was found near Jamestown.

Without a hard-working man named John Smith, Jamestown might not have survived. Smith became the leader of the colony. To survive the first winter, he persuaded Powhatan, chief of the Algonquins, to trade corn with the colonists for other goods. When spring came, Smith ordered the colonists to plant crops, cut down trees, and catch fish so they could sustain themselves.

They Made History

Pocahontas 1595–1617

Pocahontas, whose given name was Matoaka, was the daughter of the Algonquin chief Powhatan. Pocahontas was a nickname meaning "frisky." According to legend, at age 12 she saved John Smith from being executed by her father. Years later, to help maintain peace with the Algonquins, colonist John Rolfe offered to marry the young woman. Rolfe, Pocahontas, and their infant son traveled to London in 1616. People there called her "Lady Rebecca." Near the end of her visit, at age 22, Pocahontas became ill with smallpox and died.

Pocahontas went to England with John Rolfe where she posed in European clothes for this painting.

Critical Thinking Why were the actions of Pocohantas important to the survival of the Jamestown colony?

In 1609, about 400 new settlers arrived, but they did not bring enough supplies. Then, John Smith had to return to England. The loss of his leadership coupled with the bitterly cold winter of 1609 caused serious food shortages and hunger for the colonists. In addition, relations had broken down between the colonists and the Algonquins, and they would not trade food with the starving colonists. Colonist George Percy later recalled "the starving time":

> "Our food was but a small can of barley, [soaked] in water, to five men a day . . . our men night and day groaning in every corner of the fort most pitiful to hear . . . some departing out of this world, many times three or four in a night."

ANALYZE PRIMARY SOURCES

DOCUMENT-BASED QUESTION According to this passage, what were conditions like in Jamestown?

By the spring of 1610, when more settlers arrived, only about 60 of the nearly 500 Jamestown residents were still alive.

After 1612, Jamestown's situation improved. In that year, the colonists began to grow tobacco. By 1619, tobacco had become the colony's most important **cash crop.** A cash crop is grown for sale rather than for a farmer's own use. Tobacco would remain important in the colony for more than 200 years. Soon, Virginia would become one of the most populous English colonies.

 **Why did the colonists nearly starve to death in the winter of 1609?**

Review History

A. Why were the Dutch and the French colonies important?

B. What happened to the colony of Roanoke?

C. What problems did the colonists at Jamestown have?

Define Terms to Know

Provide a definition for each of the following terms.
charter, joint-stock company, cash crop

Critical Thinking

Why do you think the colonists at Roanoke were never seen again? Explain your theory.

Write About Citizenship

Create a list of rules for the colonists living in Jamestown. The rules should make sure that people do their share of the work and are treated fairly.

Get Organized

KWL CHART

At the beginning of this section, you started a KWL chart on English settlements in North America. Now complete the chart by filling in what you have learned in this section.

Know
Want to Know
Learned

III Slavery in the Americas

Terms to Know

sanitation disposal of waste

indentured servant person who agrees to work for another for a certain period of time until a debt is paid

Main Ideas

A. European traders forced millions of West Africans to go to the Americas.

B. In the Caribbean and the Southern colonies in North America, African slaves were forced to work on plantations.

Active Reading

DRAW CONCLUSIONS
When you draw conclusions, you add up bits of information and make judgments about what these bits mean. As you read this section, draw conclusions about slavery in the 1500s.

A. The Colonial Slave Trade

Slavery was a part of all European colonies in the Americas. For a few years after Columbus landed on San Salvador, Spanish colonists enslaved native people. Soon, however, Africans made up the majority of the enslaved population of the Americas.

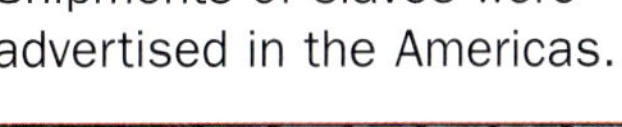

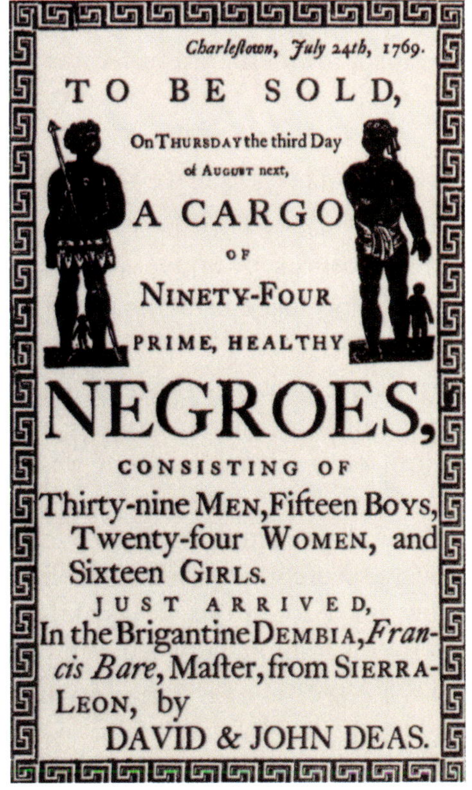

Shipments of slaves were advertised in the Americas.

Origins of African Slavery

Slavery existed in Africa and Europe long before Columbus sailed in 1492. In Africa, slaves had legal rights and could reach positions of power. Enslaved persons could become free by marrying into the family that they served. In addition, the children of slaves were free.

In contrast, the system of slavery that developed in the Americas was based on race. Enslaved persons, as well as their children, had little hope of regaining their freedom. One of the first groups of Europeans to enslave Africans was the Portuguese. It is believed that Portuguese sailors took slaves from West Africa as early as the 1430s. African rulers willingly sold slaves to Europeans.

African slaves taken by the Portuguese were not treated well. Some were shipped to Portuguese sugar plantations in Brazil and the Canary Islands. Once there they were forced to work long hours under harsh conditions in the fields. Sugar was more valuable to the Portuguese planters than were the lives of slaves. Portuguese planters worked their slaves hard because the costs of replacing them were small. This system of slavery would soon spread throughout the Americas.

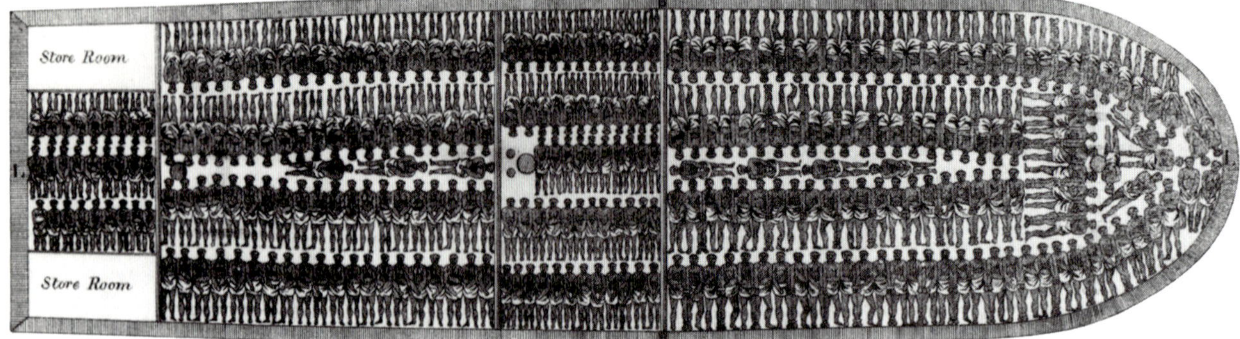

This diagram shows how enslaved Africans were forced to exist in crowded conditions on slave ships as they were transported across the Atlantic Ocean.

The Slave Trade

Most African slaves in the Americas were from West Africa. In the mid-1400s the Portuguese began trading with West African villages for large numbers of slaves. These slaves were sometimes traded for guns and ammunition, which were then used to capture more slaves. Other items that were exchanged included textiles, alcohol, and other finished goods. One village would raid another for the purpose of capturing more people to sell into slavery.

Once captured and sold to European traders, the terrified men and women faced miserable conditions. Usually they were chained at the neck and wrists and branded by the trading company that bought them. Then, they were loaded by canoe onto waiting slave ships. One English captain described the desperate attempts of some Africans to avoid being enslaved:

DOCUMENT-BASED QUESTION Why do you think West Africans might have risked death by jumping out of a slave ship?

> “The[y] are so wilful and loth [unwilling] to leave their own country, that they have often leap'd out of the canoes, boat and ship, into the sea, and kept under water till they were drowned, to avoid being taken up.”

Many captives were forced into dark cargo, or storage, areas in the lowest part of the ship. They had little air and almost no room to move. There was no **sanitation**, or way to dispose of waste. They were given very little food and water.

About 10 to 20 percent of the slaves died from sickness on a ship. Those who fought their captors were severely punished and sometimes killed. The rest endured a journey of four to six weeks in their cramped and filthy surroundings. In this fashion, between 7 and 10 million Africans were brought to the Americas.

What were the conditions on slave ships?

B. The Growth of Slavery

Spanish settlements on Caribbean islands, such as Cuba and Hispaniola, thrived because they produced sugar. At first, the Spaniards tried to use native people as laborers. Soon, however, African slaves became a part of Spanish America.

Native Americans and Slavery

Native Americans on the Caribbean islands had welcomed Columbus and other explorers from Spain. The Spaniards, however, viewed the Native Americans differently. They saw the Native Americans as a source of free labor.

The Spanish conquistadors forced the Native Americans to work in the sugar fields and gold mines. However, the population of Native Americans quickly declined due to overwork and disease. Within a few years, there were not enough Native Americans left to provide labor for the Spanish colonizers. Also, church officials had been protesting the cruel treatment of Native Americans. The Spaniards turned to a new source of workers—West Africa. As early as 1512, Spanish colonizers in the Caribbean began importing slaves from West Africa. While African slavery was first introduced in the islands in the Caribbean, it soon spread. African slavery became firmly established with the growth of sugar plantations.

Slavery in Other Caribbean Colonies

Spain and Portugal were not the only European nations to set up sugar colonies in the Caribbean. England, France, and the Netherlands started their own sugar colonies in the Caribbean and South America during the 1600s. All of these colonies eventually imported large numbers of African slaves as laborers.

The English Caribbean colonies were some of the largest producers of sugar. English plantation owners did not use slaves at first. Instead, they brought over **indentured servants** from England. Indentured servants are people who agree to work for a number of years to pay off a debt. In this case, the debt was the cost of their trip to the Americas.

Usually, after completing their obligation to work, indentured servants were given land in the colony. However, the number of indentured servants gradually decreased, and English plantation owners began to rely on African slaves for labor.

Africans to the Americas, 1451–1810

DESTINATION	NUMBER OF PEOPLE
Brazil	2,501,400
English colonies	2,013,000
French colonies	1,600,200
Spanish colonies	945,600
Dutch colonies	500,000

Chart Check

To which destination did the greatest number of Africans go?

African Slaves in the English Colonies

Some of the African slaves who were brought to the Americas were taken to the English colonies in North America. As the demand for laborers increased, more and more West Africans arrived in Virginia.

In 1619, the first African slaves brought to Virginia arrived in a Dutch ship. Most of these slaves came to Virginia from the Caribbean as field hands to plant, tend, and harvest tobacco.

For many years, there were relatively few enslaved people living in English North America. Originally, slaves worked side-by-side with indentured servants. However, with the increased farming of tobacco, and later cotton, there was a growing need for slave labor.

Landowners in Virginia and other Southern colonies gradually came to rely on slave labor to support their farming economy. Because these colonies depended on tobacco, and later rice, cotton, and indigo—a plant used to make blue dye—many workers were required to plant and harvest these crops. It proved more profitable for landowners to use slaves than to use indentured servants. Most indentured servants worked for a few years and then gained their freedom.

In what ways were indentured servants different from enslaved people?

Review History

A. Where and why was West African slavery introduced to the Americas?

B. Why did plantation owners in the Americas want to increase the number of slaves?

Define Terms to Know

Provide a definition for each of the following terms.
sanitation, indentured servant

Critical Thinking

For what reasons were people forced into slavery?

Write About History

Some people spoke out against slavery in the Americas. Write a persuasive essay addressed to early American colonists about the injustice of slavery.

Get Organized

KWL CHART

At the beginning of this section, you started a KWL chart on the beginning of slavery in the Americas. Now complete the chart by filling in what you have learned in this section.

Know
Want to Know
Learned

Points *of* View

The Slave Trade

The slave trade between Africa and the Americas began in the early 1500s. Portuguese traders had found that slaves could be purchased on the West African coast at a low cost. They soon began shipping these slaves to the Caribbean to raise sugar cane. Because most African workers came from well-developed agricultural societies, their farming skills made them desirable workers.

While most Europeans accepted the African slave trade, some did not. The passages below were written by a Spanish official living in the Caribbean and a leader of the Catholic Church living in Spain.

Shackles, such as these, were used to restrain slaves.

"There is an urgent need for Negro slaves . . . Let ships go there [Cape Verde] and bring away as many male and female Negroes as possible, newly imported and between the ages of fifteen to eighteen or twenty years. They will be made to adopt our customs in this island. . . .

The burden of work on the Indians will be eased and unlimited amounts of gold will be mined. This is the best land in the world for Negroes . . . and it is very rarely that one of these people die."

—Alonso de Zuazo, Spanish judge on Hispaniola (1518)

"[A] thousand acts of robbery and violence are committed in the course of bartering and carrying off Negroes from their country and bringing them to the Indies. . . . Since the Portuguese and Spaniards pay so much for a Negro, [the Africans] go out to hunt one another . . . as if they were deer. . . . And no one is horrified that these people are ill-treating and selling one another, because they are considered uncivilized and savage. . . . They embark four and five hundred of them in a boat. . . . The very stench is enough to kill most of them, and indeed, very many die."

—Brother Tomas de Mercado
Seville, Spain (1587)

DOCUMENT-BASED QUESTIONS

1. What is Alonso de Zuazo's point of view on the slave trade?
2. How does Brother Mercado's point of view on the slave trade differ from Zuazo's view?
3. **Critical Thinking** Why does Zuazo support using Africans as slaves?

CHAPTER 3 Review

Chapter Summary

In your notebook, complete the following outline. Then, use your outline to write a brief summary of the chapter.

New Settlements in the Americas

I. Spanish Conquest and Colonies
   A. Conquest of the Aztecs and the Incas
   B.
II. Other European Settlements
   A.
   B.
   C.
III. Slavery in the Americas
   A.
   B.

Interpret the Timeline

Use the timeline on pages 46–47 to answer the following questions.

1. In what year did Cortés conquer the Aztecs?
2. **Critical Thinking** After 1560, in what parts of the Americas were colonies being founded?

Use Terms to Know

Match each term with its definition.

a. cash crop
b. charter
c. conquistador
d. indentured servant
e. joint-stock company
f. mission

1. an official government document that gives rights to a person or company
2. a crop that is grown to be sold rather than used by a farmer
3. a settlement established by a church for religious work
4. Spanish term for a military leader who won land in the Americas for Spain
5. a group of investors who share both risk and profit
6. a person who agrees to work for another for a certain period of time until a debt is paid

Check Your Understanding

1. **Explain** how Cortés was able to defeat the Aztecs.
2. **Describe** the reasons for the Spanish exploration of North America.
3. **Identify** the areas of North America that were claimed by France.
4. **Summarize** what happened at the English colony of Roanoke.
5. **Explain** how slavery grew in the Caribbean islands.
6. **Describe** the kinds of work slaves were forced to do in the English colonies of North America.

Critical Thinking

1. **Analyze Primary Sources** Do you think the picture of the Spaniards fighting the Aztecs on page 48 was drawn during the battle? Explain.
2. **Analyze Information** How do the English experiences at Roanoke and Jamestown show how difficult it was to start new colonies?
3. **Analyze Primary Sources** What does the quote on page 60 suggest about West Africans' reaction to slavery?

Put Your Skills to Work

IDENTIFY THE MAIN IDEA

You have learned that identifying main ideas can help you tie facts together and understand what you read. Read the paragraph below. Identify the sentence, or sentences, that contain the main idea. Write the main idea in your own words.

> In 1588, Spain was ready to invade England. Its rulers sent a huge fleet of ships, the Spanish Armada to conquer England. However, England's smaller, faster ships, aided by a fierce storm, defeated the Spanish Armada. England was now free to colonize North America.
>
> Main idea: ______________________

In Your Own Words

JOURNAL WRITING

People who study history often ask, "What if?" They try to determine what life would have been like if events in the past had turned out differently. For example, what if England had lost the war with Spain? Would the United States be the same today? In your journal, answer this question or another "What if?" question based on events in this chapter.

Net Work

INTERNET ACTIVITY

Working with a partner, use the Internet as a resource to do one of the following tasks.

1. Create a scrapbook about Jamestown. Find pictures of artifacts to show how people lived, and include them in your scrapbook.
2. Draw a diagram of the Jamestown fort. Then, present your findings to the rest of the class.

For help in starting this activity, visit the following Web site: www.gfamericanhistory.com.

Look Ahead

In the next chapter, learn how other colonies in North America began.

Unit 1 Portfolio Project

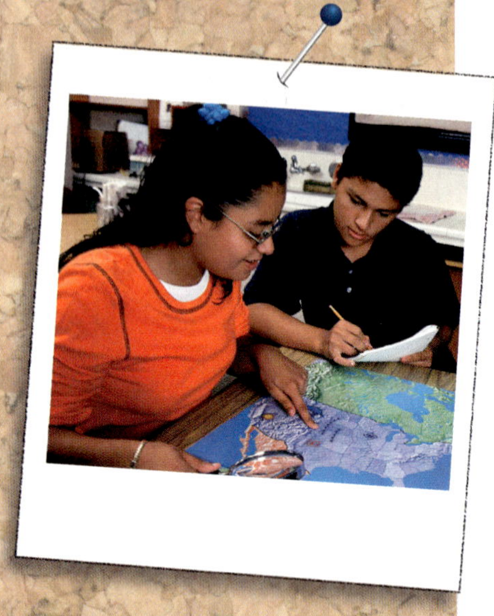

Mapmaking Contest

YOUR ASSIGNMENT

Historical maps contain a wealth of information about what happened in the past. In your class, form four teams of mapmakers. Each team will create a historical map for a different part of the world discussed in Unit 1.

PLANNING THE MAP

Choose Your Map As a team, choose a map topic from the following list. Each team in the class should choose a different topic.

Early Migration in North America
Empires in the Americas, 200–1500
West African Trading Kingdoms, 700–1600
European Voyages, 1400s–1600s

Research Use your library to gather information for your map. As you do this, think about ways to make your map informative.

Plan Your Map Decide what information you will include in your map. Also, think about questions such as these: How big will the map be? What tools will you use to draw the map? What items will you label on the map? What illustrations will you add? Assign tasks to each team member. You may refer to this Web site for ideas: www.gfamericanhistory.com.

MAKING AND SHARING THE MAP

Draw Some students may work on the map at different stages. For example, some might draw the outline. Others might add the important features or illustrations.

Review Check your map to make sure the information is accurate. Also, proofread all labels and make corrections.

Compare Display all the maps in one place. Share comments on the maps. Then, vote on the map that is most attractive and informative.

Multimedia Presentation

Create a video about the period, using historical maps. Have a narrator explain important points while a partner uses historical maps to point out details of the presentation. Do your filming and show your video to the class.

Unit 2

The American Colonies

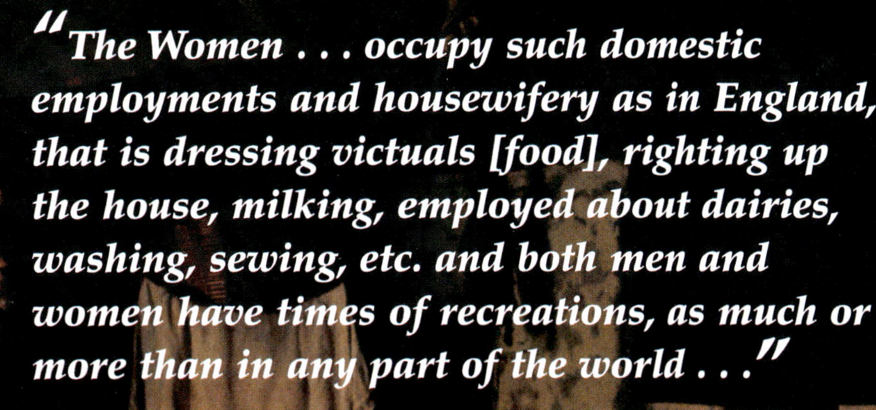

"The Women . . . occupy such domestic employments and housewifery as in England, that is dressing victuals [food], righting up the house, milking, employed about dairies, washing, sewing, etc. and both men and women have times of recreations, as much or more than in any part of the world . . ."

—from a description written in 1656 by John Hammond, a colonist from Maryland

LINK PAST TO PRESENT These women are re-enacting life in colonial America. Participating in a re-enactment can help people better understand what life was like in the past.

★ Judging by the photograph and the quotation, what was life like for women in the American colonies?

CHAPTER 4

Founding Colonial America 1607–1733

I. New England Colonies
II. Middle Colonies
III. Southern Colonies

Between 1630 and 1640, more than 20,000 people from England sailed to the American colonies. Here, they hoped to practice their religion in their own way—something they could not do in England. Just as important, they wanted to create a better society in which people of a community helped each other and lived proper and productive lives. John Winthrop, leader of the Massachusetts Bay Colony, hoped to set an example for others to follow. He told his followers,

> "We must consider that we shall be as a City upon a Hill. The eyes of all people are upon us, . . ."

These settlers were not the only people to seek a new home and freedom to practice their religion in North America. Catholics, Quakers, Jewish people, and other settlers also began new lives in colonial America.

A child's chair brought to North America

U.S. Events

- **1607** First English settlement at Jamestown begins.
- **1620** Mayflower Compact is signed.
- **1630** Puritans settle the Massachusetts Bay Colony.
- **1636** Rhode Island is settled.
- **1649** Toleration Act approved in Maryland.
- **1664** England takes over New Netherland.

1600 — 1620 — 1640 — 1660

World Events

- **1603** William Shakespeare's *Hamlet* is written.
- **1637** Foreigners are expelled from Japan.

VIEW HISTORY This painting shows the arrival of English settlers in America. Most early settlers from England risked everything, including their lives, to make this voyage. They could only bring their most valuable possessions on the journey, such as this child's chair (left).

★ **How does the artist capture the sense of danger and uncertainty that the settlers faced as they landed on the shores of America for the first time?**

Get Organized

MAIN IDEA/SUPPORTING DETAILS CHART

Seeing the connection between main ideas and supporting details can help you understand history. As you read Chapter 4, use a chart like the one below to link main ideas with the details that support them. List the main idea in the oval and the details in the boxes. Here is an example from this chapter.

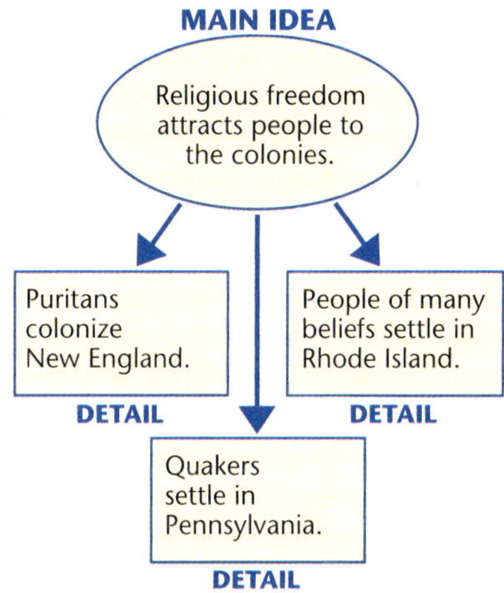

1676 Bacon's Rebellion takes place.

1700 Colony of Pennsylvania is third largest of English colonies.

1729 Carolina is split into North and South Carolina.

1733 Georgia, last of the 13 colonies, is settled.

1680 1700 1720 1740

1680 1700 1720 1740

1672 Charles II ends persecution of Catholics in England.

1689 English government enacts a Bill of Rights.

1707 Scotland joins England and Wales to become Great Britain.

1733 Industrial Revolution begins in Great Britain.

I New England Colonies

Terms to Know

Puritan a member of a religious group that wanted to simplify the practices of the Church of England

Separatist a Puritan who wished to break away, or separate, from the Church of England

persecute to punish or mistreat a person because of his or her beliefs

Pilgrim a religious traveler to a new land; a founder of Plymouth Colony

economy the way in which goods and services are produced and consumed in a community

Main Ideas

A. The desire for religious freedom brought early colonists to New England.

B. Puritans settled Massachusetts Bay Colony, and founded nearby colonies for religious freedom and other reasons.

C. New England colonists used the resources around them to develop the economy of the region.

Active Reading

PREVIEW

Previewing is a good way to prepare your mind for reading. To preview, read the headings that start the text and scan the photos and maps. Ask yourself the following question: Do the text and visuals follow a sequence?

A. Settlement at Plymouth

After Jamestown was founded, many people from England came to North America. Here, they hoped to settle in colonies where they could practice their religions freely. Most of these settlers had no idea what they would find when they finally reached their new home.

Religious Disagreement in Europe

The early 1600s was a time of religious unrest in England and the rest of Europe. This unrest had begun much earlier—in 1517—when a German priest named Martin Luther protested certain policies of the Roman Catholic Church. Luther believed that the Church had become damaged by too much wealth and power. Other religious leaders also broke from the Roman Catholic Church. They founded many new Christian churches. They were called Protestant churches because of their protest against the authority of the Roman Catholic Church. One of these new churches was the Church of England.

Some Protestants in England felt that the Church of England was too similar to the Catholic Church. They were called **Puritans**, because they wanted to purify the Protestant Church of its remaining Catholic practices. Other Puritans wished to break away completely, or separate from the Church of England. They were known as **Separatists**. Puritans were often **persecuted**, or mistreated, because of their beliefs. As a result, some decided to flee England. This was the beginning of the Great Migration, when Puritans left England to find religious freedom in other parts of the world.

Plymouth Colony

Some Separatists left England to settle in North America. In September 1620, a small group of colonists sailed for Virginia on the ship *Mayflower*. They called themselves **Pilgrims** because they were travelers headed for a new land for a religious reason.

After a stormy, nine-week voyage, the colonists sighted land. However, they were far north of Virginia. In fact, they had sighted present-day Cape Cod, Massachusetts. Before leaving their ship at Plymouth, the Pilgrims signed an agreement to make laws for their colony. This agreement was called the Mayflower Compact.

The Mayflower Compact was the first example of self-rule by colonists in the Americas.

Led by William Bradford, the colonists worked to establish their new home at Plymouth, but life in North America was hard. During the first winter, nearly half of the settlers died of disease, cold, and poor nutrition. Conditions improved the next year when Native Americans showed them how to plant corn and trap beavers. The Pilgrims celebrated in the fall of 1621 after harvesting their first crops. This celebration is what many people today think of as the first Thanksgiving.

You can read the Mayflower Compact on page R3.

 **What did the Pilgrims agree to in the Mayflower Compact?**

B. New England Expands

Other Puritans came to North America and formed the Massachusetts Bay Colony. However, some of these new settlers had different opinions about how their colony should operate. As a result, they branched out and started new colonies.

Massachusetts Bay

In 1629, a group of English merchants received a charter from King Charles I to start a fishing and lumbering colony near Plymouth, Massachusetts. They also wanted the colony to be a refuge, or safe place, for English Puritans. The merchants formed the Massachusetts Bay Company and attracted more than 1,000 people to journey with them to the colony.

In 1630, several ships arrived in New England. Under the leadership of John Winthrop, the Massachusetts Bay Colony grew to more than 11,000 people by 1640. The colonists founded several towns in Massachusetts, including Salem and Boston.

Then & Now

In 1630, John Winthrop spoke to the other Puritans before they landed at Salem, north of Plymouth. He told them that they were going to be part of a great dream. They would build "a City upon a Hill," a model community that others could look up to.

This idea has remained popular in the United States. Recent Presidents, including Ronald Reagan, have called the United States "a city upon a hill."

Not everyone in colonial Massachusetts was a Puritan, but all were required to follow Puritan rules. Those who did not were severely punished. In addition, only members of the Puritan-controlled church could vote.

Rhode Island

Roger Williams was one individual who disagreed with Puritan policies in the Massachusetts Bay Colony. Williams objected to the strong influence of the Puritan church on the colony's laws. He also believed that the colonists should pay Native Americans for the land they were taking.

In 1635, Williams and a few followers left Massachusetts Bay and founded the town of Providence. It became the first town in the colony of Rhode Island. Because religious freedom was promoted in Rhode Island, people of many beliefs, as well as those who disagreed with Puritan beliefs, settled in the new colony. Among these people was an outspoken colonist named Anne Hutchinson, whose beliefs had angered Puritan ministers in the Massachusetts Bay Colony.

They Made History

Anne Hutchinson 1591–1643

Anne Hutchinson was a Puritan who lived in Boston with her husband and children. She believed that leading a holy life was more important than attending church or praying. Others in Boston agreed with her, and she soon had many followers, including some men.

Hutchinson's ideas challenged and angered Puritan ministers and some political leaders who believed that her teachings were wrong. They were also angry that a woman was teaching men. In 1637, Puritan community leaders and ministers put Hutchinson on trial. They found her guilty of rebelling against the government and drove her out of the Massachusetts Bay Colony. As a result, she and her family resettled in Rhode Island, where religious freedom was allowed.

This statue of Anne Hutchinson stands in front of the Massachusetts State House.

Critical Thinking In what ways were Anne Hutchinson's beliefs challenging to Puritan ministers and some political leaders?

Connecticut

As the Massachusetts Bay Colony grew, many colonists began to look elsewhere for land to farm. Some colonists settled in present-day Connecticut. In 1636, a Puritan minister named Thomas Hooker led a small group of settlers from Boston to the Connecticut River valley. Here they found fertile soil to farm. Three years later, several towns agreed to form a government in which men who owned property were allowed to vote.

New Hampshire

Two merchants began the settlements of New Hampshire and Maine in 1629. Few people moved into these areas at first. Then, in 1638, John Wheelwright and others who agreed with Anne Hutchinson's ideas moved from Massachusetts to New Hampshire. Hoping to practice their own religious beliefs, they founded the town of Exeter.

New Hampshire became a separate colony in 1679. Maine, however, remained part of Massachusetts until 1820.

 **For what reasons did people leave the Massachusetts Bay Colony to establish other settlements in New England?**

C. Life in Early New England

The colonists in New England began a new way of life in which they made the most of the natural resources around them. They also faced some unexpected conflicts.

New England Resources

Farming was difficult in New England because of the rocky soil and short growing season. Some colonists became farmers, but farms were small. People generally raised only enough for their own needs.

Instead of farming, the **economy** of New England was dependent upon the area's forests and the nearby Atlantic Ocean. An economy is the way in which a community creates and uses goods and services. Lumber, fishing, whaling, and shipbuilding all became important industries. Shipping was important, too. Port cities, such as Boston, became key trade centers in New England.

Whaling off the Atlantic coast was dangerous work for men in small longboats.

Metacomet, also known as King Philip, is shown wearing traditional clothing and carrying a quiver of arrows.

The New England Town

Most people in New England lived in small, well-organized towns. Houses were located around a central green, or meadow. At the center of every village was a meetinghouse that served as both church and town hall. In these tightly-settled villages unity and proper Puritan behavior was promoted.

Fighting With Native Americans

As the Massachusetts Bay Colony expanded to the west, settlers pushed into Native American lands. Native American groups, such as the Pequots, found themselves competing with the newcomers for land and resources. Fighting broke out. Then, in 1637, a group of colonists attacked Pequot settlements along the Connecticut River, killing hundreds of native people.

In 1675, another bloody conflict took place as the Wampanoags, a Native American group, tried to stop English expansion. This conflict was called King Philip's War because the chief of the Wampanoag people, Metacomet, was known to the settlers as King Philip. After three years of fighting, the colonists defeated the Wampanoags. From then on, Native Americans generally retreated westward ahead of the advancing settlers.

What prevented English colonists and Native Americans from living together peacefully?

Review History

A. Why did Puritans and Separatists leave England to come to North America?

B. What were some reasons for founding colonies in New England?

C. How did the colonists use natural resources?

Define Terms to Know

Provide a definition for each of the following terms.
Puritan, Separatist, persecute, Pilgrim, economy

Critical Thinking

How did Puritan leaders respond to those who disagreed with them? Give an example.

Write About Geography

Write a paragraph that describes the layout of a typical New England town.

Get Organized

MAIN IDEA/SUPPORTING DETAILS CHART

Use a chart like the one below to show details that support each main idea in this section. For example, use this main idea: The Puritan influence was strong in New England.

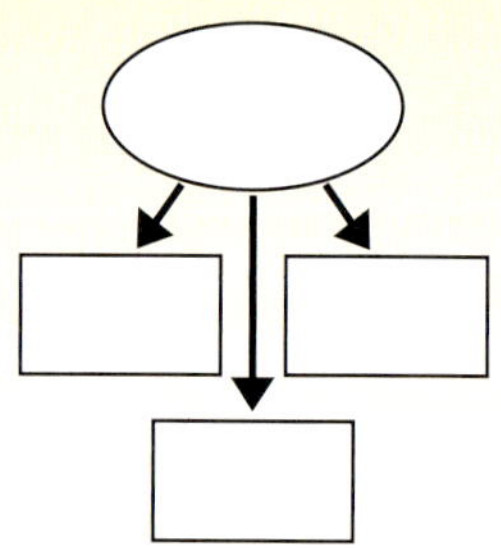

Build Your Skills

Social Studies Skill

INTERPRET A BAR GRAPH

Suppose students at your school sold boxes of oranges as a fundraiser. Afterward, you want to compare how many boxes were sold by each grade. A bar graph could help you. Bar graphs use a series of bars to show varying amounts of something. This "something" is called data. The length of each bar represents an amount, which allows you to make comparisons.

When you read about history, you will find information—such as population figures, war casualties, or types of work people do—presented in bar graphs.

Here's How

Follow these steps to read a bar graph.

1. Read the title of the graph to learn what information is being presented.
2. Read the labels at the side and bottom.
3. Notice where the bars stop in order to see what amounts they represent.
4. Compare the lengths of the bars on the graph to make comparisons.

Here's Why

You have just read about the settlement of New England colonies. If you had to write about population growth in the colonies, a bar graph could help.

Practice the Skill

Study the bar graph. Then, answer the questions that follow.

1. Which two colonies had the smallest populations in 1700?
2. Which colony's population grew the most between 1700 and 1740?

Extend the Skill

Draw two conclusions about the population of the New England colonies from the bar graph.

Apply the Skill

As you read the next section, interpret the bar graph of population growth for Pennsylvania.

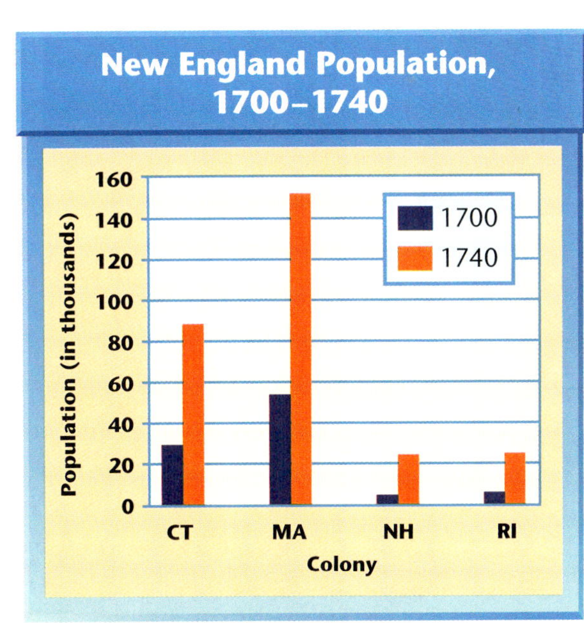

II Middle Colonies

Terms to Know

patroon a Dutch landowner in the colony of New Netherland

subsistence farming growing only enough crops to meet the needs of one household

proprietary colony a colony owned and managed by one or more individuals

Main Ideas

A. New York was founded from the Dutch colony of New Netherland.

B. New Jersey and Delaware, like other Middle colonies, were home to people from many European countries.

C. Pennsylvania was founded on the principle of religious freedom.

Active Reading

SUMMARIZE

When you summarize, you state only the main points and leave out details. As you read the chapter, pause after each *A., B.,* and *C.* section to summarize what you have read.

A. New Netherland Becomes New York

Since 1624, Dutch settlers in New Netherland had prospered as fur traders and farmers. By the mid-1600s, however, trouble was brewing. A war in Europe had erupted between England and the Netherlands. Trouble was brewing in another place as well. That place was the North American colony of New Netherland.

Taking New Netherland

Trouble in the colonies began when King Charles II of England granted his brother James a huge area of land between the Connecticut and Delaware rivers. Much of this land was already claimed by Dutch settlers who lived in the Hudson River valley. This area was the colony of New Netherland, whose capital was New Amsterdam.

James, whose title was the Duke of York, decided to claim this land for England. In 1664, he sent a fleet of ships to New Netherland. The armed ships arrived at the shores of New Amsterdam. Because the colony was not prepared for battle, Dutch governor Peter Stuyvesant was forced to surrender. Afterward, both the town and the larger colony were renamed New York in honor of the Duke of York.

The English fleet went on to capture Swedish settlements along the Delaware River. Swedish settlers had come to the Delaware area as early as 1638. In fact, they were the first settlers to build log cabins in North America. The Duke of York had set his sights on these thriving settlements, and by September 1664, all of New Netherland, including the Swedish settlements, was under English control.

Peter Stuyvesant was the Dutch governor of New Netherland in 1664.

Life in New York

Although the Dutch government lost control of its colony, the people already living there did not experience much change. Dutch landowners, called **patroons**, were allowed to keep their lands under the new government. The Duke of York granted other large pieces of land to English friends and supporters.

Most people in New York practiced **subsistence farming**, the growing of just enough crops and livestock to meet their everyday needs. Other colonists traded with Native Americans for beaver skins, which were made into a popular type of hat in Europe.

New York was not dominated by a single religious group. Instead, it attracted settlers of different religions from many countries. Eventually, people of English background outnumbered Dutch people in New York. French Protestants, called Huguenots, were also drawn to the colony, as were people from the countries of Sweden, Finland, and Germany.

The Iroquois and Delaware Indians had enjoyed good relations with the Dutch in New Netherland. When the English took over the colony, these good relations continued—at least for a while.

 **New York was settled by people from which European nations?**

B. New Jersey and Delaware

Two other colonies were founded in the middle section of the Atlantic coast. Though settlers had lived there for many years, it was not until England took control that their populations grew.

New Jersey

When the English took over New Netherland, the Duke of York granted the land from the Hudson River south to the Delaware River to two of his friends, John Berkeley and George Carteret. These two men called their colony New Jersey after the English Island of Jersey.

The colony's rich soils attracted many colonists—including farmers from New England as well as newcomers from Germany and Ireland. They joined the Swedes, Finns, and Dutch who already lived there.

Delaware

The Delaware River valley was originally settled by people from Sweden. The Dutch took over this tiny colony for a brief time until the English captured its main settlement as part of their conquest of New Netherland.

 **What attracted colonists to New Jersey?**

Spotlight on Culture

The colony of Delaware was originally started by Swedes who built a fort along the Delaware River. This fort, called Fort Christina, was located near what is now Wilmington, Delaware.

Swedes and Finns in the colony of New Sweden hoped to control all the Dutch ships using the river. New Sweden was taken over by New Netherland before that ever happened.

C. Religious Freedom in Pennsylvania

Pennsylvania was part of the group of colonies that became known as the Middle colonies. Unlike New York, New Jersey, and Delaware, however, Pennsylvania was founded as a religious refuge.

Then & Now

During the 1720s and 1730s, many colonists in Pennsylvania belonged to a religious group known as the Amish. Amish came to Pennsylvania for religious freedom.

Many Amish people still live in southeastern Pennsylvania. Most still farm successfully, much as their ancestors did in the 1700s, without electricity or modern equipment. Lancaster County, Pennsylvania, is known as Amish Country and is one of the most popular tourist spots in the state.

A Refuge for Quakers

Quakers were a religious group in England who believed in equality and peace. They held simple, quiet religious services without ministers. Because of their beliefs, Quakers refused to serve in the military or pay taxes to support the Church of England. For these actions, they were arrested, fined, or even hanged for their disobedience.

William Penn was a young Quaker lawyer who believed that the Quakers must leave England. He asked King Charles II to grant the Quakers a safe home in North America. The king owed money to Penn's family so, as payment, King Charles granted Penn a large piece of land in North America. William Penn became the proprietor, or owner, of the colony. Because the colony was owned and managed by a person or group, it was an example of a **proprietary colony**. The colony was named Pennsylvania for William Penn's father. Pennsylvania means "Penn's woods."

A Colony Based on Brotherhood

William Penn's dream was to make his colony a place where people of all nationalities and religions could live in harmony. Penn guaranteed freedom of religion to everyone who lived there.

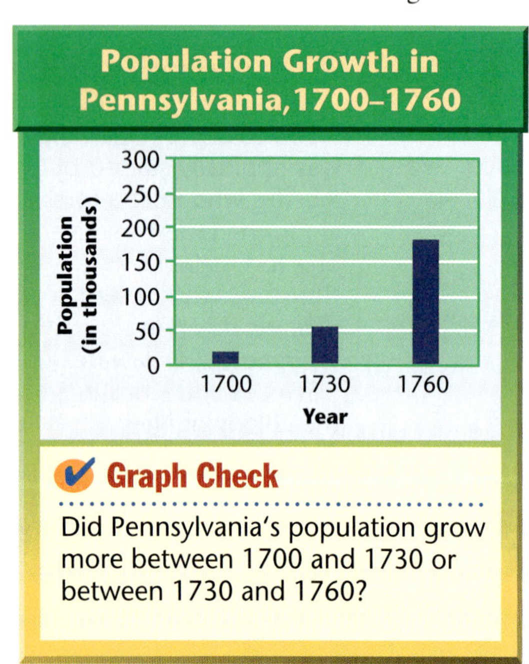

Many Quakers streamed into the colony, but others came, too. Penn printed advertisements for his colony in Dutch, French, German, and English. He attracted thousands of eager settlers, who were drawn to Pennsylvania's mild climate and fertile soils. These settlers came from Germany, Holland, Switzerland, Scotland, and Ireland.

Pennsylvania grew rapidly. By 1700, just 19 years after its founding, it was the third largest and wealthiest of the English colonies. Like other Middle colonies, Pennsylvania had a long growing season. Common crops included fruits, vegetables, and grains—especially corn, wheat, and rye. Within the colony, Penn created the most thoroughly planned city in North America. The city's design included wide streets, parks, gardens, and public buildings centered around a town square. Penn's model city was called Philadelphia, or the "City of Brotherly Love."

William Penn established peaceful relations with Native Americans. He is shown here making an agreement with the Delawares.

Working With Native Americans

Maintaining good relations in the region with Native Americans, known as the Delawares, was part of Penn's plan to preserve harmony. In a letter to the Delaware chiefs, Penn wrote that he hoped they could always live together as neighbors and friends.

Penn did not believe in taking land that did not belong to him, so he purchased land from the Native Americans. As a result, Pennsylvania was able to avoid the violent conflicts with native peoples that occurred in other colonies.

 **Why did the colony of Pennsylvania grow quickly?**

Review History

A. How did the colony of New York begin?
B. From what countries did settlers in New Jersey and Delaware come?
C. Why did William Penn welcome people besides Quakers to Pennsylvania?

Define Terms to Know

Provide a definition for each of the following terms.
patroon, subsistence farming, proprietary colony

Critical Thinking

How did Quaker beliefs affect policies in the colony of Pennsylvania?

Write About Economics

Write a paragraph that explains how the economy of the Middle colonies was different from that of the New England colonies.

Get Organized

MAIN IDEA/SUPPORTING DETAILS CHART

Use a chart like the one below to link supporting details with a main idea in this section. For example, use this main idea: The Middle colonies drew people from many European countries.

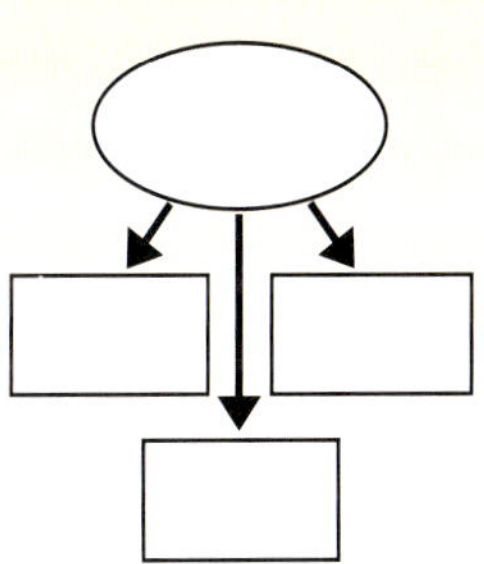

III Southern Colonies

Terms to Know

immigration the act of coming into a country to live there

royal colony a colony directly under the rule of a king or queen

backcountry an area inhabited by few people and far from more settled areas

debtor a person who owes money

Main Ideas

A. The climate and natural resources of Virginia and Maryland attracted many settlers.

B. Competition for land increased conflicts in the Chesapeake region.

C. South Carolina and Georgia developed farming economies that eventually depended on slavery.

Active Reading

CAUSE AND EFFECT

A cause is something that triggers, or leads to, another event. That event is the effect. As you read this section, look for examples of cause and effect.

A. The Chesapeake Colonies

The first English settlers in North America had chosen the Chesapeake Bay area for their settlement. They had made a wise decision, for the area had a mild climate, rich soil, and numerous natural resources. Many other settlers soon followed.

Virginia

The idea for a colony in Virginia first began when the Virginia Company of London received permission to build a new colony in North America. The first English settlement of the new colony was at Jamestown in 1607. After hard times during the early years, it grew quickly after 1612. In that year, John Rolfe introduced a type of tobacco that thrived in the humid Chesapeake climate. Tobacco became the chief crop of Virginia and nearby colonies. Because Virginia's climate and land were ideal for large-scale farming, the colony attracted many settlers.

In the beginning, the Virginia Company had allowed only company stockholders to buy land. In 1618, the company changed its policy to increase **immigration**, or settlement by people from other countries. As a result of this change in policy, any male settler who was the head of a household could now own land. The more family members who came with him, the more land he could acquire. This enabled some colonists in Virginia to establish large farms called plantations.

Most colonists who arrived in Virginia in the 1600s were indentured servants. They were usually poor young men from England. After the 1670s, African slaves were brought to southern plantations, where they harvested the profitable crops of tobacco and cotton.

While tobacco helped make the colony of Virginia wealthy, King James I of England had already written against it,

> "A custom loathsome to the eye, hateful to the nose, harmful to the brain, and dangerous to the lungs."

ANALYZE PRIMARY SOURCES **DOCUMENT-BASED QUESTION** In what ways did James I think that smoking tobacco was harmful?

In addition to tobacco, King James found something else about Virginia to dislike—its government. Virginia had a lawmaking body, made up of elected male landowners, called the House of Burgesses. The king was concerned that this body might gain too much power. As a result, in 1624, he made Virginia a **royal colony**, by placing it directly under his own control.

Maryland

In 1632, another colony took root in the Chesapeake Bay area. Years earlier in England, George Calvert, also known as Lord Baltimore, had become a Roman Catholic. Because Catholics were persecuted in England, Baltimore wanted to build a colony where Catholics could live and worship in peace. The king of England granted Baltimore 10 million acres of land along the Chesapeake Bay in North America.

After Lord Baltimore's death, his son Cecil took over the territory. St. Mary's, a settlement on the Potomac River, became the colony of Maryland.

As more settlers arrived, Protestants began to outnumber Catholics in Maryland. To protect the Catholics, the second Lord Baltimore approved the Toleration Act of 1649. This law set up religious toleration, or acceptance of all Christians, in Maryland. It was an important step toward true religious freedom in the colonies.

Lord Baltimore, as proprietor of the colony, granted large sections of land to his friends and business associates. As in Virginia, the most powerful men in Maryland were wealthy landowners.

 **Why was the colony of Maryland founded?**

Map Check

LOCATION What geographic feature do 12 of the 13 colonies share?

B. Colonial Conflict

Tobacco crops made Virginia and Maryland wealthy colonies, but increased the demand for land, which led to conflict.

Native Americans Resist

As tobacco profits grew, more settlers came to Virginia and moved onto Native American lands. The Powhatans, who were natives of the region, were determined to halt the settlers' progress. In 1622, they attacked several settlements. The colonists then attacked Powhatan villages. After years of fighting, the Powhatans retreated west into the **backcountry**, or the least settled part of the region.

The Thirteen Colonies, 1607–1732

COLONY	FOUNDER	DATE OF CHARTER	REASONS FOR FOUNDING
Plymouth[1]	William Bradford	1620	Religious freedom
Massachusetts Bay[1]	John Winthrop	1630	Religious freedom
New Hampshire	John Mason	1623	Trade, religious freedom
Rhode Island	Roger Williams	1636	Religious freedom
Connecticut	Thomas Hooker	1636	Separate Puritan settlement; political freedom
New York	Peter Minuit, James, Duke of York	1624	Trade and land
New Jersey	John Berkeley, George Carteret	1664	Trade and land
Pennsylvania	William Penn	1681	Establish a Quaker colony; religious, political freedom
Delaware	Peter Minuit, Swedish settlers	1638	Trade and land
Virginia (Jamestown)	John Smith	1607	Trade and land
Maryland	Cecil Calvert (second Lord Baltimore)	1632	Establish a Roman Catholic settlement
North Carolina	Eight English businessmen	1663	Trade and land
South Carolina	Eight English businessmen	1663	Trade and land
Georgia	James Oglethorpe	1733	Home for debtors

NEW ENGLAND — MIDDLE COLONIES — SOUTHERN COLONIES

[1] Plymouth and Massachusetts Bay combined into one colony, 1691.

Chart Check

What were the most common reasons that colonies were founded?

Tidewater Versus Backcountry

By the 1680s, most of the best land along the rivers and bays, called the Tidewater, was already claimed. Therefore, latecomers to Virginia and Maryland, as well as freed indentured servants, settled farther west onto Indian lands in the Appalachian Mountains. Here, they carved out small farms, growing crops without the need for slave labor. They resented taxes and other laws that favored the wealthy coastal plantation owners.

As farmers moved westward, they often clashed with Native Americans. In 1676, Nathaniel Bacon, a settler in western Virginia, formed a rebel band to lead raids on Native Americans and take their land. When the government did not provide the help he wanted, Bacon marched to Jamestown, Virginia's capital, and burned the town. Bacon's Rebellion lasted only a short time. When Bacon died suddenly, the revolt fell apart. This uprising, however, highlighted the conflict between settlers and Native Americans and between wealthy landowners and poorer citizens.

 **Why were some settlers unhappy with the government of Virginia?**

Nathaniel Bacon and other settlers burned Virginia's capital to protest the treatment of backcountry farmers.

C. The Carolinas and Georgia

Three more colonies developed south of Virginia—North Carolina, South Carolina, and Georgia. The colony of Georgia marked the southern boundary of English settlement.

The Carolinas

Settlement of the land between Virginia and Florida, which was called Carolina, began in 1663. Many of Carolina's first settlers were English plantation owners from the Caribbean colonies of Barbados and Jamaica. When they moved to Carolina, they brought enslaved workers from their plantations with them.

The colonists settled in the southern coastal region of the colony. In 1680, they relocated their settlement, Charles Town, to the site of Charleston today. Their main crops were rice, indigo, and tobacco. All of these crops were raised on large plantations using slave labor.

In the northern part of the colony, most of the settlers were poor farmers from Virginia. They distrusted the wealthy landowners who were settling the southern coast. Eventually, these small farmers insisted that Carolina be divided. In 1729, the colony was split into North Carolina and South Carolina.

Georgia

Georgia was the last of the English colonies to be settled. It began when a man named James Oglethorpe approached King George II with an unusual idea. He wanted to start a colony for **debtors**, or people who owed money. At the time, people in England, or Great Britain as it came to be known in 1707, were often sent to prison for not paying their debts. Oglethorpe wanted to offer these debtors a second chance. He stated,

ANALYZE PRIMARY SOURCES
DOCUMENT-BASED QUESTION Do you think Oglethorpe's words proved true?

> "In America, there are enough fertile lands . . . to feed [subsist] all the . . . poor in England. . . ."

The king was not very interested in helping poor people. However, he was concerned about the nearby Spaniards in Florida. He wanted to provide some protection to the other British colonies, so he agreed to Oglethorpe's plan.

In 1733, colonists built a fort and town at the mouth of the Savannah River. Oglethorpe set strict rules for running the colony—named Georgia after Great Britain's king—including a ban on slavery. As a result, the colony grew slowly at first. By the 1750s, these rules were lifted. Georgia then began to develop a farming economy based on slave labor, similar to that of South Carolina.

 **What was unusual about the founding of Georgia?**

Review History

A. Why was tobacco growing successful in the Chesapeake Bay area?

B. What conflicts developed in Maryland and Virginia? Why?

C. Why did the colony of Carolina split in 1729?

Define Terms to Know

Provide a definition for each of the following terms.
immigration, royal colony, backcountry, debtor

Critical Thinking

Why would plantation owners in coastal Virginia have more influence on the colony's government than backcountry farmers would?

Write About History

Explain the importance of the Toleration Act for all the colonies.

Get Organized

MAIN IDEA/SUPPORTING DETAILS CHART
Use a chart like the one below to link details with main ideas in this section. For example, use this main idea: Slavery took root in the Southern colonies.

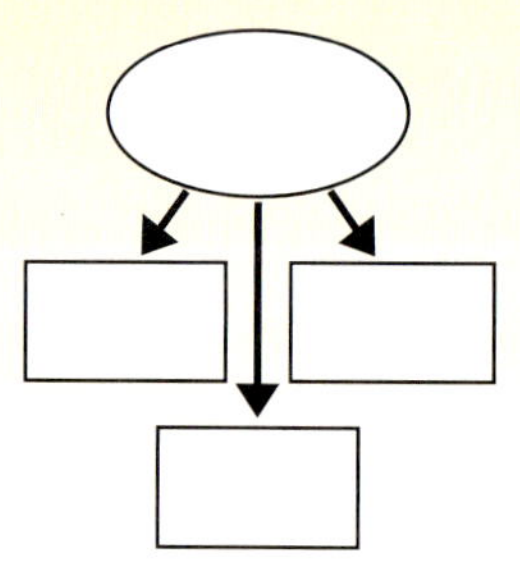

Points of View

St. Luke's Church in Virginia

Religious Tolerance

Most Americans today accept the idea that people have the right to follow any religion they choose. Early colonists, however, held different views. The Puritans of New England, for example, did not tolerate, or accept, other religious groups. People who disagreed with the official religion in their communities were called religious dissenters. Roger Williams and Anne Hutchinson were dissenters. They were forced to move from the Massachusetts Bay Colony to Rhode Island, a colony that embraced the idea of religious tolerance. The following passages, written during the early colonization of North America, express the opposing views held by the colonists.

"I dare . . . proclaim to the world, in the name of our colony, that all [people of other beliefs], shall have free liberty to keep away from us, and . . . be gone as fast as they can, the sooner the better. [We seek] to preserve unity of spirit, faith, and ordinances [laws], to be all like minded . . . and by no means to permit [differing religious] opinions."

—From Nathaniel Ward, *The Simple Cobbler of Aggawam*, 1647

"[F]or the more quiet and peaceable government of this province and the better to preserve mutual love and amity [friendship] amongst the inhabitants . . . Be it therefore . . . enacted . . . that no person or persons whatsoever within this province . . . professing to believe in Jesus Christ shall from henceforth be any ways troubled, molested [hurt] . . . nor any way compelled [forced] to the belief or exercise of any other religion against his or her consent."

—From *Maryland Act of Toleration*, 1649

DOCUMENT-BASED QUESTIONS

1. In the first passage, why is the writer against religious tolerance?
2. In the second passage, what reasons are presented by the writer in favor of some religious tolerance?
3. **Critical Thinking** Does anything surprise you about the Puritan's point of view on religious tolerance in the first passage? Why?

CHAPTER 4 Review

Chapter Summary

In your notebook, complete the following outline. Then, use your outline to write a brief summary of the chapter.

Founding Colonial America

I. New England Colonies
   A. Settlement at Plymouth
   B.
   C.

II. Middle Colonies
   A.
   B.
   C.

III. Southern Colonies
   A.
   B.
   C.

Interpret the Timeline

Use the timeline on pages 68–69 to answer the following questions.

1. Which occurred first, the signing of the Mayflower Compact or the English takeover of New Netherland?
2. **Critical Thinking** Which events in North America and the world show a concern for religious freedom?

Use Terms to Know

Select the term that best completes each sentence.

backcountry **royal colony**
persecuted **subsistence farming**
proprietary colony

1. In England, Puritans and Separatists were ________, or mistreated, because of their beliefs.
2. Latecomers to Virginia and Maryland began farming in the ________, or less settled area.
3. Because it was owned and managed by one individual, Georgia was a ________.
4. In North Carolina, some farmers engaged in ________, raising only enough food for their own use.
5. The king of England made Virginia a ________, so that it would be directly under his control.

Check Your Understanding

1. **Describe** the purpose of the Mayflower Compact.
2. **Identify** Roger Williams and what he accomplished.
3. **Discuss** how people in the colony of New York made a living.
4. **Identify** the reasons people chose to settle in Pennsylvania.
5. **Compare and contrast** the founding of two southern colonies.
6. **Identify** the reason that Nathaniel Bacon led a rebellion against Virginia's government.

Critical Thinking

1. **Analyze Primary Sources** Do you think that the remarks made by King James I on page 81 about smoking tobacco had a negative effect on the colonists?
2. **Analyze Primary Sources** Do you think debtors trusted James Oglethorpe's opinion of American land as he described it on page 84? Why?
3. **Recognize Relationships** How did settlers in some colonies create the same problems that they had faced in England?

Put Your Skills to Work

INTERPRET A BAR GRAPH

You have learned that interpreting a bar graph can help you compare numerical information. Review the graph below about population growth in four southern colonies. Then, answer the following questions.

1. Which colony had the largest population in 1700?
2. Which colonies had almost the same population in 1740?

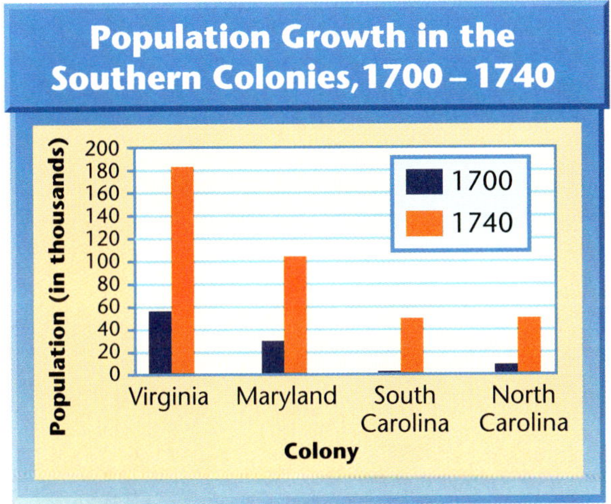

In Your Own Words

JOURNAL WRITING

Anne Hutchinson and Roger Williams stood up for their beliefs. They did so even though many others disapproved of their views. Write a journal entry about a belief that is important to you.

Net Work

INTERNET ACTIVITY

Working with a group of classmates, use the Internet as a resource to create a report about life in early colonial America. First, choose a focus for your report. For example, you might write about the Pilgrims at Plymouth, Native Americans in New York, Quaker settlers in Pennsylvania, or Catholic settlers in Maryland. Include information about everyday life. Also, include at least one primary source in your report.

For help in starting this activity, visit the following Web site: www.gfamericanhistory.com.

Look Ahead

In the next chapter, learn more about life in the 13 American colonies.

CHAPTER 5

The Thirteen Colonies 1650–1775

I. The Colonial Economy
II. Life in the Colonies
III. Slavery in the Colonies

During the 1700s, the eastern coast of North America became a populated, thriving land. People moved to the colonies from Great Britain and other European countries. Families grew, and colonists built more settlements. As a result, the landscape of North America changed. Cities developed. Farms spread out across the land. J. Hector St. John de Crèvecoeur, a colonist who had come from France, described the setting in colonial America:

> "Here [a British citizen] beholds fair cities, substantial villages, extensive fields, an immense country filled with decent houses, good roads, orchards, meadows, and bridges, where one hundred years ago all was wild, woody, and uncultivated!"

In addition to building cities and roads, the colonists built a new life. What was life like for these early Americans? How did they adapt to their new home?

Butter churn

1650 Acts of Trade and Navigation, limiting colonial trade, begin.

1693 College of William and Mary is founded in Virginia.

U.S. Events	1650	1675	1700
World Events	1650	1675	1700

1665 First issue of the *London Gazette* is printed.

1690 John Locke publishes his *Essay Concerning Human Understanding.*

VIEW HISTORY This illustration shows what Philadelphia, Pennsylvania, looked like in 1702, when a vast countryside stretched beyond the city. Most colonists lived and worked in the country. There they used butter churns similar to the one pictured (left) to turn cream into butter.

★ **What elements of colonial life are shown in the illustration?**

Get Organized

VENN DIAGRAM

Using a Venn diagram is a good way to compare and contrast two things. Use a Venn diagram as you read Chapter 5. List similarities in the space where the circles overlap. List differences in the outside part of each circle. Here is an example from this chapter.

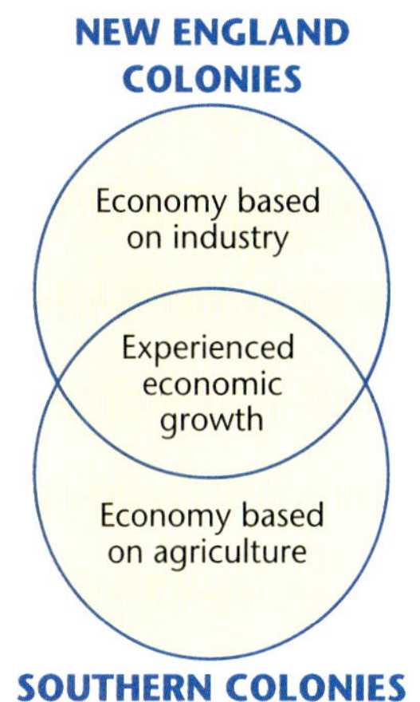

1725 | **1750** | **1775**

1734 Great Awakening begins in Massachusetts.

1735 Zenger trial is an early step toward freedom of the press.

1739 Stono Rebellion is put down.

1750 Population of the colonies tops 1 million.

1769 Dartmouth College in New Hampshire is founded.

1775 Population of the colonists is about 2.5 million. Number of enslaved people is about 250,000.

1725 | **1750** | **1775**

1725 Catherine the Great becomes ruler of Russia.

1729 Methodists begin meeting in Great Britain.

1740 Freedom of press and worship are introduced in Germany.

1754 First woman doctor graduates from a German university.

I The Colonial Economy

Terms to Know

barter to exchange one product or service for another

mercantile system an economic system that stresses increasing national wealth by selling more than buying in foreign trade

export to sell goods to another country

import to buy goods from another country

Main Ideas

A. Geography influenced the types of agriculture found in each of the three regions of the colonies.

B. Regional natural resources affected the growth of trade, industry, and cities.

C. The English government took steps to control the colonies' foreign trade in order to increase England's wealth.

GENERALIZE

To generalize is to make a broad statement that takes into account many related details. Example: Geography influences a nation's economy. As you read this section, pause from time to time to generalize about what you have read.

Spotlight on Geography

Many New England towns near the Atlantic Ocean were founded as fishing villages. Fishing is still a vital business in New England.

In 1991, the *Andrea Gail* sailed from Gloucester harbor in Massachusetts. After fishing for two weeks, the ship was struck by a storm, which has been called the storm of the century, and sank. All of the crew members were lost at sea. The story was told in both a book and a film.

A. Farming in the Colonies

Despite difficult beginnings, the 13 English colonies in North America continued to grow. Villages, towns, and cities developed. In 1700, the colonial population was about 250,000. By 1750, it had topped 1 million. Settlers came from European countries such as England, Germany, France, and Sweden. During this time, the colonists developed their own way of life and learned to make the most of the natural resources around them. They **bartered**, or exchanged one good or service for another, to obtain products that they could not produce themselves. Farming, which made use of the land, became an important part of life in each of the three regions of the English colonies—the New England colonies, the Middle colonies, and the Southern colonies.

Small Farms in New England

In the New England colonies—Massachusetts, New Hampshire, Connecticut, and Rhode Island—farming was difficult. The land was generally hilly, and the soil was rocky. Winters were long and cold, which shortened the growing season. In addition, thick forests covered much of the land. Trees had to be cleared before crops could be planted. Because of these conditions, farms in the region remained small.

Most New England farmers grew some combination of corn, wheat, and barley. They also raised cattle, pigs, or sheep. Most families did not produce any surplus, or extra, food.

Rich Land in the Middle Colonies

In the Middle colonies—Pennsylvania, New York, New Jersey, and Delaware—family farms were larger. A milder climate meant a longer growing season in the extremely rich soil of this area. Also, the land was more level, and much of it had already been cleared by Native Americans. Farmers in this region grew grains and raised livestock. The Middle colonies were known as the bread colonies.

Plantations in the Southern Colonies

Many people in the Southern colonies—Maryland, Virginia, North Carolina, South Carolina, and Georgia—had small family farms. However, others owned large plantations. The broad coastal plain of the region, combined with a mild climate and fertile soils, provided an ideal setting for growing several crops. In Maryland and Virginia, plantations usually grew tobacco. Farther south, in South Carolina and Georgia, rice and indigo were the most common crops.

The strong demand in Europe for tobacco and other southern crops encouraged plantation owners to enlarge their farms. Because of the great size of the plantations, a large number of workers was needed. By the 1700s, enslaved Africans made up most of this work-force. Slavery was a major difference between the economy of the Southern colonies and the economies of those farther north.

 **What was agriculture like in the Middle colonies?**

Large plantations like this one developed in the Southern colonies.

B. The Rise of Colonial Industries

Natural resources in the three regions led to the development of different industries. This industrial development combined with the large population increase led to the growth of towns and cities.

Spotlight on History

In 1707, Scotland joined England and Wales to become Great Britain, or Britain.

New England Industries

People in New England found an abundance of natural resources in the cold waters of the North Atlantic Ocean. The sea teemed with fish. Sea captains braved the dangerous weather and currents off Newfoundland and Nova Scotia to fill their ships with fish.

Another industry that used the natural resources of New England was the lumber industry. New England colonists learned that lumber from the abundant forests brought high prices in Great Britain because large trees were not plentiful there. In the colonies, wood was used to build ships, houses, and furniture. Because shipbuilding and fishing were important economic activities, many New England colonists lived and worked in cities or small towns near ports. The shipbuilding industry thrived in port cities such as Boston, Massachusetts, and Newport, Rhode Island. Shipbuilding helped to make fishing and whaling successful.

Map Check

Region In what area was lumber abundant?

Iron and Furs in the Middle Colonies

Pennsylvania and New York became two of the fastest growing colonies. In the Middle colonies, good relations with Native Americans helped the colonists develop a fur trade with Europe. This region also had several iron furnaces. They were used to melt iron ore into bars that could then be shaped into pots and tools. Both the fur trade and the making of iron products helped to diversify, or vary, the economy of the Middle colonies.

Industries in the Southern Colonies

North Carolina made products that were sold to British and colonial shipbuilders and sailors. The most important product was tar, which was used to waterproof ships. Tar was made from a sticky substance found in the wood of pine trees. Another industry that developed in the Southern colonies was cotton. Cotton, which grows on cotton plants, can be made into cloth. In busy southern port cities, such as Charleston, South Carolina, cotton was shipped to Great Britain to be made into clothing.

The Growth of Cities and Towns

The many colonial industries contributed to the growth of cities and towns. Port cities developed rapidly because the colonial economy depended on shipping and trade. People in port cities such as New York City, Boston, Philadelphia, and Charleston saw hundreds of ships entering and leaving the ports.

Other people who worked in towns and cities throughout the colonies had specialized skills. These crafts people included shoemakers, barrelmakers, potters, printers, and blacksmiths, who made items such as horseshoes from iron. These crafts people made the everyday items that the colonists needed.

There were no factories in colonial towns. Most manufacturing, or making of goods, took place in homes. For example, cloth was woven by women and girls working at home. They spun thread from cotton, wool, or linen and wove it into fabric on large wooden looms.

 **How did people who were not farmers support themselves and their families?**

A colonial woman uses a spinning wheel to make thread.

C. Controlling Colonial Trade

In the beginning, the English colonies in North America had many foreign trading partners. They traded with Dutch, French, and Spanish colonies in the West Indies and Africa. They also traded with other European countries.

England, however, did not want to see the wealth of the colonies going to its rivals. It had established the North American colonies to make England rich.

The Mercantile System

Like other countries in Europe in the 1600s, England had an economy based on the **mercantile system**. Under this system, a nation could become wealthy through trade. A country wanted to **export**, or sell, more products than it **imported**, or bought.

The colonies were an important part of England's mercantile system. They produced raw materials such as lumber, iron, and cotton and shipped them to England. This busy overseas trade made many colonial merchants and shipowners wealthy. The raw materials were made into finished products, such as furniture, tools, and clothing, which were then shipped to the colonies and to other parts of the world. Colonists were expected to buy finished products from England rather than manufacture their own. England did not want the colonists making their own finished products, because England would sell less of its products and make less money.

Shipbuilding was a large industry, particularly in the New England colonies.

Navigation Acts

To control colonial trade, the English government passed a series of laws beginning in 1650. The Acts of Trade and Navigation were enacted over more than a one-hundred-year period. Many are named Navigation Acts. The following are some of the limits these laws placed on colonial commerce:

1. All goods shipped to and from the colonies had to be carried on English or colonial ships.
2. Important colonial goods that England did not produce such as tobacco and cotton could be shipped only to England.
3. Ships from other European countries had to stop in England first so that England could collect taxes on their cargo.

Some colonial merchants and shippers followed the laws. They understood that they were English citizens, and they wanted to obey the laws of their government. Also, the laws meant more business for colonial shipbuilders. Other colonists disliked the Navigation Acts because they believed the taxes favored English merchants. In addition, the taxes raised the prices that colonists had to pay for European goods. Some merchants turned to smuggling, or trading goods illegally with other countries. The Navigation Acts produced the first tensions between England and the colonies.

 **Why were colonies important to the English economy?**

Review History

A. How did geography affect farming in each of the three colonial regions?

B. What natural resources helped to create jobs in the New England and Middle colonies?

C. How did the Navigation Acts limit the colonies' trade with other countries?

Define Terms to Know

Provide a definition for each of the following terms.
barter, mercantile system, export, import

Critical Thinking

Why was trade with England and other countries important to the colonists?

Write About Economics

Write a report that explains how different colonial viewpoints regarding the Navigation Acts may affect relations between England and the colonies.

Get Organized

VENN DIAGRAM

Think about things you might compare and contrast in this section. Use a Venn diagram to show similarities and differences. For example, how was farming in the New England and Middle colonies alike and different?

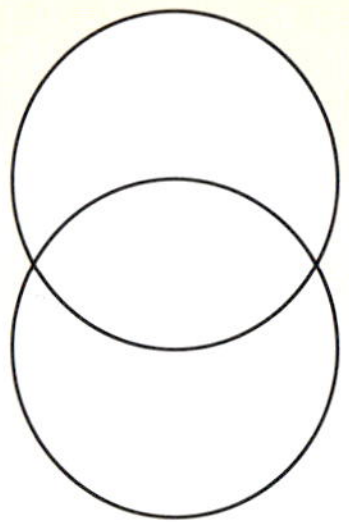

Build Your Skills

Study Skill

TAKE NOTES AND OUTLINE

You have just been given an assignment to write a report. You go to a library and find books on your topic. Then what? How do you gather and record the facts you need in a way that makes sense?

When you research, you use sources such as books, magazines, newspapers, and the Internet. To make the best use of these sources, you need to take notes and then organize your notes in an outline before you write the report.

Here's How

Follow these steps for notetaking and outlining.

1. As you read, record each main idea on a separate notecard or sheet of paper.
2. Under each main idea, add important details in your own words.
3. Organize your cards or sheets of paper into groups of information having the same main idea.
4. Create an outline. Label main ideas with Roman numerals, subtopics with capital letters, and supporting details with Arabic numbers.

Here's Why

You have just read about colonial economy. Suppose you needed to write an essay on the economy in New England. Taking notes and outlining could help you to write an informative essay and save you time.

Practice the Skill

Copy the outline on a sheet of paper. Complete the outline using the information in Section I.

Extend the Skill

Create outlines for the economies of the Middle and Southern colonies. Then, use all three outlines to write a brief essay about the economies of the 13 colonies.

Apply the Skill

As you read the remaining sections of this chapter, take notes and outline what you have read. Then, use your notes to review the information in this chapter.

Topic: New England's Economy

I. Nonfarming activities
   A. Fishing
      1. Caught many fish
      2.
   B. Lumber related activities
      1. Shipbuilding
      2.

II. Farming
   A.
      1.
      2.
   B.
      1.
      2.

II Life in the Colonies

Terms to Know

apprentice a person who works to learn a specific skill

libel a false statement made in writing about someone

Main Ideas

A. Families contributed in many ways to life in the colonies.

B. Colonial society was shaped by the Enlightenment, schools, and newspapers.

C. The Great Awakening was a religious movement that encouraged self-reliance and equality.

MAKE INFERENCES
When you make an inference, you use reason to draw your own conclusion from the facts. As you read this section, make several inferences about the lives of women in the colonies.

A. Colonial Social Structure

Although work was important to the success of the American colonies, prosperity depended upon strong colonial families. Like Great Britain, the colonies' social structure included many classes.

Colonial Society

For many colonists, life in America was better than the life they had left behind in Europe. By the early 1700s, towns and cities were growing, farms prospered, and trade increased. All of these developments helped both the upper class of society—clergy, ship merchants, great landowners—and the lower classes of society. Near the bottom of society were indentured servants, poor farmers, and later, enslaved persons.

Family Life

Family and religion were important to the colonists. Farm families, especially those living on smaller farms, needed to work together. Sons helped fathers clear and plant the fields, and daughters helped mothers cook, sew, and tend to young children. Most colonial families took religion very seriously. They turned to their ministers for guidance in how to conduct their everyday lives.

Women played a vital role in the economy. They made products such as soap and cloth at home. In towns, some women assisted their husbands in the family business, working as shopkeepers, innkeepers, and printers.

Then & Now

In the 1700s, people living in the colonies often died from diseases because there were no cures or medicines for those diseases at the time. Today, most American children are vaccinated against many diseases at a young age to prevent the occurrence of the diseases.

Despite their role in the economy and in society, married colonial women had few legal rights. After marrying, a woman had to give her husband control of her property. She could not own a business without her husband's permission. She also could not vote or serve on juries. Most colonial girls and young women were not even allowed to attend school.

Colonial women made soap for their families.

Colonial women usually shared in the day-to-day farm chores. In addition, they performed household tasks such as cooking and washing, and they raised the family's children. Children were supervised strictly. Both boys and girls shared in the family work. Girls helped with the housework. Boys worked the fields and tended the livestock. Some boys worked as **apprentices** to learn a trade and later went into business for themselves. An apprentice is someone who works with a master craftsperson for a period of time to gain a specific skill.

 **How were married women's legal rights limited in the colonies?**

B. Colonial Society

In the 1700s, the colonists began to move away from British ways of life. British ideas and traditions had strongly influenced the colonists, but new ideas and practices began to develop that set the colonists apart from the people of Great Britain.

The Enlightenment in America

In the late 1600s, a new way of thinking about human beings was taking hold in Europe. Leaders of the movement, such as John Locke, pointed out that human beings had the ability to reason. These philosophers, or thinkers, believed that through reasoning, people could gain knowledge; and through knowledge, people could understand the world and improve society. The spread of these ideas was known as the Enlightenment. Many Enlightenment philosophers became involved in scientific studies and experiments, searching for new inventions and practical knowledge. They wanted to discover how the physical universe worked.

By the early 1700s, a similar wave of interest in science and learning took place among educated citizens in colonial America. Some prominent New Englanders, such as John Winthrop Jr., studied astronomy. Others experimented in chemistry. Still others, such as John Bartram, gathered plants from all over eastern North America and cataloged them.

Benjamin Franklin studied electricity.

By far the most famous philosopher of the Enlightenment movement in the American colonies was Benjamin Franklin. He conducted amazing experiments with electricity, invented a practical iron stove for heating rooms, started a library in Philadelphia, and helped to spread Enlightenment ideas.

Colonial Education

Education was an important part of the culture in colonial America. From the beginning, education was a high priority in New England. The Puritans set up both primary and secondary schools in their towns. The main goal of these schools was to teach the students to be good Christians.

Because fewer towns existed in the South and settlers were more spread out, schools were harder to establish. However, both public and private schools did exist in the Southern colonies. Yet throughout the colonies, farm work demanded much more of a boy's time than school did.

The colonists also established schools for higher learning. The first colleges in the colonies were founded for the purpose of training young men to become ministers. The Puritans founded Harvard College in Massachusetts in 1636. The College of William and Mary in Virginia, founded in 1693, was the first college in the Southern colonies. The first secular, or nonreligious, college was the University of Pennsylvania. It was established in 1754 in Philadelphia with the help of Benjamin Franklin.

Then & Now

During the 1700s, Williamsburg became the center of commerce, education, and government for the colony of Virginia. At one end of the main street stood the colonial capitol. At the other end was the College of William and Mary. Today, Colonial Williamsburg is a place where people can see how Americans lived during the 1700s.

Newspapers and the Power of the Press

Newspapers were important to colonial society for spreading information. By 1746, there were 15 newspapers in the British colonies. They printed articles about events in Europe, local news, and letters from readers. These newspapers were tightly controlled by the British government. In fact, British law kept newspaper editors from printing articles that spoke badly of the government.

This situation changed in 1735. John Peter Zenger, a young German settler, was hired to start a New York City newspaper. He printed several articles attacking the New York governor's dishonesty and greed. Zenger was put on trial for **libel**, or making false written statements that hurt a person's reputation. The jury decided that Zenger had printed truthful criticisms and let him go. Zenger's trial was an early step toward freedom of the press in America.

What basic belief did Enlightenment philosophers hold?

C. Religion in the Colonies

In the early 1700s, many different Protestant religions were flourishing. However, by 1730, there was concern that colonists were not as enthusiastic about religion as they had been. The colonists no longer felt uncertain about starting new colonies. They may have felt less dependent on religion and their churches. Then, in the mid-1700s, religion again became an important part of colonial life.

The Great Awakening

As the colonies grew and became more prosperous, many young men attended college not to become ministers, but to prepare for nonreligious professions. This situation alarmed many ministers. They were concerned that colonists were not placing enough emphasis on religion in their lives.

From the 1730s to the 1760s, ministers of many faiths began to try to wake up people's religious feelings. The New England minister Jonathan Edwards was an early leader in this movement, known as the Great Awakening. In one of his sermons, Edwards compared the listener to a spider hung over a fire:

> "Oh sinner! Consider the fearful danger you are in! It is a great furnace of wrath, a wide and bottomless pit, full of the fire of wrath. . . . You hang by a slender thread."

ANALYZE PRIMARY SOURCES

DOCUMENT-BASED QUESTION What was Jonathan Edwards trying to get colonists to do by telling them God was angry with them?

Another popular preacher during the Great Awakening was George Whitefield. He traveled throughout the colonies, delivering powerful sermons outdoors to thousands of people.

Colonists flocked to hear the powerful sermons of George Whitefield and other preachers during the Great Awakening.

This picture shows the Dartmouth College shield. Dartmouth was founded by a minister of the Congregationalist Church in 1769.

Effects of the Great Awakening

The Great Awakening had important and long-lasting effects. Many people converted to, or joined, a religion for the first time. Religious groups such as the Congregationalists and Presbyterians attracted new members.

The Great Awakening movement helped people see all religions as equally important and promoted religious tolerance. It also helped to unify the colonies because people everywhere took part in it.

Another effect of the Great Awakening was the founding of new colleges. Religious groups founded six colleges between 1746 and 1769, including Princeton, Dartmouth, and Rutgers. Although these colleges were founded by specific religious groups, students of all religions attended them.

Perhaps most importantly, the Great Awakening made people feel they could rely on themselves. They realized that they could interpret the Bible for themselves instead of being dependent on the spiritual teachings of preachers. Ordinary people began to decide for themselves what to believe and how to worship. This new confidence in the power of the individual would eventually spill over into politics. The idea of self-government, with equal rights for people at all social levels, began to seem natural to Americans.

 **How did preachers during the Great Awakening draw people back to religion?**

Review History

A. What jobs did women perform in the colonies?

B. How did educated colonists respond to the Enlightenment movement?

C. How did the Great Awakening affect the way colonists viewed themselves and their society?

Define Terms to Know

Provide a definition for each of the following terms.
apprentice, libel

Critical Thinking

Why did educated people in the colonies welcome the spirit of the Enlightenment?

Write About History

You live in one of the colonies with your family. Write a paragraph describing a typical day. Explain what you do and what other members of your family do.

Get Organized

VENN DIAGRAM

Use a Venn diagram to compare and contrast the work done by girls and boys in colonial families.

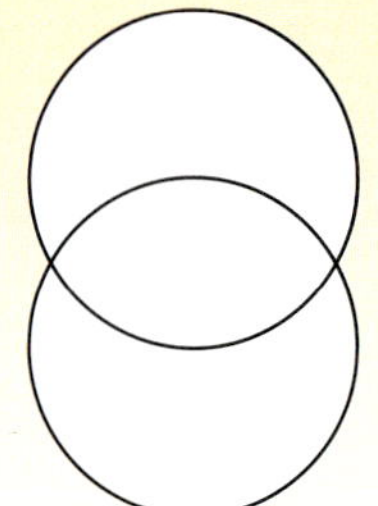

III Slavery in the Colonies

Terms to Know

overseer a person who is in charge of enslaved people

slave code a set of laws that limited the activities of enslaved people

Main Ideas

A. Africans were brought to North America from West Africa and then sold into slavery.

B. Enslavement of Africans existed in all of the colonies although not all Africans in the colonies were slaves.

Active Reading

POINTS OF VIEW

People living at different times often have different points of view. As you read this section, contrast views of slavery in the past with views of it today.

A. Slavery Takes Root

The growth of the plantation system in the Southern colonies resulted in an increased number of enslaved people who were used as laborers. Large numbers of enslaved people were forcibly taken from West Africa to the colonies. The horrifying voyage was just the beginning of the harsh life that enslaved Africans would face.

The Number of African Slaves Increases

The first few Africans who arrived at Jamestown were indentured servants. Like other indentured servants, they worked for a specified number of years and then they were free. However, by the mid-1600s, most Africans arrived in the colonies as enslaved people and remained so.

As the number of colonists grew, so did the number of enslaved people. By 1775, about 2.5 million colonists lived in the British colonies, compared to 250,000 in 1700. This increase in population also affected the number of enslaved people in the colonies. In 1700, only about 25,000 enslaved Africans lived in North America. By 1760, the number had increased to 250,000—ten times as many.

Do You Remember?

In Chapter 3, you learned about the crowded and filthy conditions on the ships that carried enslaved Africans across the Atlantic Ocean.

The Middle Passage

Most Africans were brought to the colonies in trading ships. They were thought of by the slave traders as cargo, or freight, like other trade goods. The colonies used several different trade routes to ship goods. One of these routes went straight from the colonies to Britain and directly back again.

Spotlight on *Culture*

On the islands off the coast of South Carolina, Africans developed a unique language called Gullah. It blended English and several African languages. Through this language, many African words, such as *goober* (peanut) and *gumbo* (okra, or a stew made with okra), passed into the English language.

However, the trade route used to transport enslaved Africans took a different course. This route went from the North American colonies, to West Africa, then to the West Indies, and finally back to the colonies. Because the trade route had three separate parts that together formed the shape of a triangle, it has been called triangular trade.

On the first part of the route, ships went from New England to Africa. There, products such as rum (made from West Indian sugar) and iron goods were traded for enslaved Africans. On the second part of the route, called the Middle Passage, the ships sailed back across the Atlantic Ocean to the West Indies. There, some enslaved Africans were traded for molasses and sugar. The ships then sailed on to the colonies, carrying these goods and the remaining enslaved Africans.

Many enslaved people died on the Middle Passage because of the horrifying conditions on board. Those who completed the voyage to the Americas were sold to plantation owners or other slave traders. This was another terrifying experience for African people.

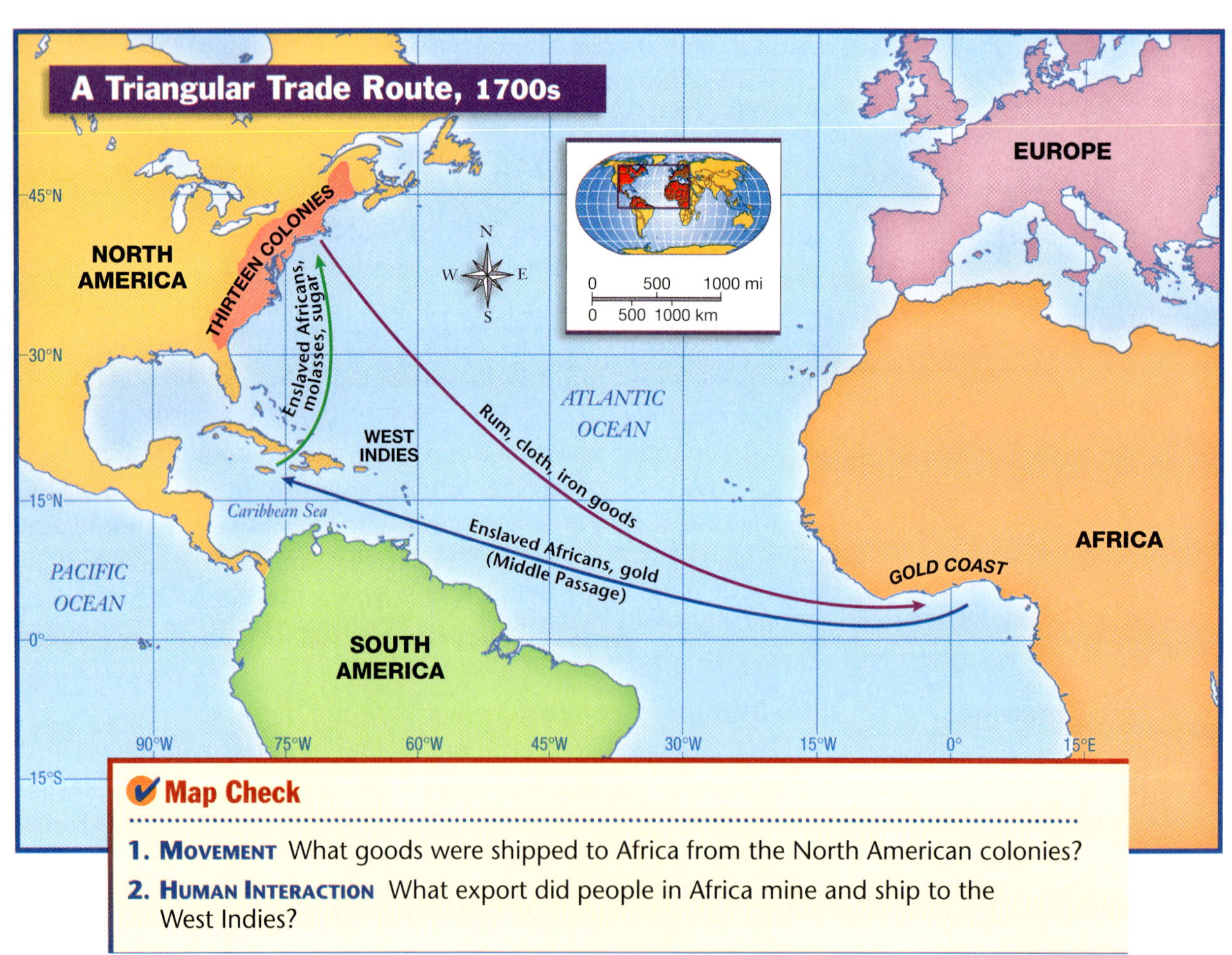

Map Check

1. **Movement** What goods were shipped to Africa from the North American colonies?
2. **Human Interaction** What export did people in Africa mine and ship to the West Indies?

Olaudah Equiano, a Nigerian captured when he was 11, described the event this way:

> On a signal given . . . the buyers rush at once into the yard where the slaves are confined, and make choice of that parcel they like best. . . . In this manner, without scruple [care], are relations and friends separated, most of them never to see each other again.

DOCUMENT-BASED QUESTION
According to Olaudah Equiano, why was a slave sale especially painful for Africans?

What was the Middle Passage?

B. Africans in the Colonies

The vast majority of enslaved Africans lived on plantations in the Southern colonies. However, slavery existed in all of the British colonies. Throughout the colonies, there lived free Africans as well.

Free Africans

Not all Africans in North America were enslaved. There were small numbers of free Africans in nearly every colony. Some had gained their freedom by escaping from their owners. Others were the children or grandchildren of indentured servants who had worked for a specified number of years and then were free.

Most free Africans lived in cities and worked as independent crafts people. For the most part, they could not vote, but some did own land. Free Africans were few in number and widely separated. Thus, they did not develop a distinct culture.

Enslaved Africans

In the Southern colonies, dozens to hundreds of Africans worked on large tobacco and rice plantations. Most were fieldworkers, but some became household workers or developed skills that included carpentry and weaving. Fieldworkers, both men and women, typically worked from sunrise to sunset, often in groups under an **overseer**, or a boss hired by the plantation owner. If overseers chose to, they could beat and threaten enslaved people to make them work harder. Household workers generally received better treatment.

Africans in the Colonies, 1690–1750

YEAR	NEW ENGLAND COLONIES	MIDDLE COLONIES	SOUTHERN COLONIES
1690	905	2,472	13,307
1700	1,680	3,361	22,476
1710	2,585	6,218	36,063
1720	3,956	10,825	54,058
1730	6,118	11,683	73,220
1740	8,541	16,452	125,031
1750	10,982	20,736	204,702

Chart Check

In 1750, how many more Africans lived in the Southern colonies than in the New England colonies?

In this painting, some enslaved people in South Carolina are performing a West African dance.

On plantations, enslaved Africans lived together in their own buildings. They tried to rebuild the large kinship groups they had known in West Africa by forming families and making friends. However, at any time, a mother, father, or child might be sold to a new owner. Plantation slaves also developed their own unique culture, blending elements of African religion, music, language, and customs with the European traditions of the slaveholders.

In the New England and Middle colonies, enslaved Africans made up only a small percentage of the total population. The majority of enslaved people lived in large cities such as Philadelphia, Boston, and Newport. They worked as household servants, crafts people, shopkeepers, and general laborers. Enslaved people in rural areas almost always worked as field hands alongside their owners. Slaveholders in these colonies usually kept only one or two enslaved people.

Slave Codes

All of the British colonies made **slave codes** part of their laws. These codes refused basic rights to enslaved Africans, who were not allowed to give evidence in court, run a business, hold property, or gather in public. They could not even marry without permission from the slaveholder. Enslaved people also were not allowed to attend school or learn to read and write.

Under the slave codes, the children of enslaved Africans were considered enslaved as well. A person could actually be born into slavery. This fact made slavery in America very different from the kind of slavery found in Africa. The belief of many white people that African people were inferior reinforced these rigid laws. Owners saw their enslaved workers as property, not as persons.

Silent Resistance

Enslaved people were closely watched by their overseers. Furthermore, any show of force, such as striking an overseer, was severely punished. Thus, few enslaved workers openly rebelled.

Many enslaved workers found indirect ways to oppose slavery. They would work slowly on purpose, pretend to be ill, or break tools. More active resisters destroyed crops and burned barns.

Rebellion

Occasionally, enslaved people organized revolts against their owners. The largest slave uprising, known as the Stono Rebellion, took place around Stono River near Charleston, South Carolina, in 1739. About 20 enslaved people stole guns and gunpowder from a supply store and killed two storekeepers. Then, they marched south hoping to find freedom in Spanish Florida. Along the way, about 80 other enslaved people joined them. They continued killing people as they made their way through South Carolina.

A group of South Carolina plantation owners chased and caught them. Fighting broke out, and people on both sides were killed. Most of the enslaved people who managed to escape were later captured and executed for taking part in the uprising.

 **How were the activities of enslaved Africans limited?**

Review History

A. What happened to West Africans after they were brought to North America?

B. How was slavery in the Southern colonies different from slavery in the other colonies?

Define Terms to Know

Provide a definition for each of the following terms.
overseer, slave code

Critical Thinking

How might life be difficult even for free Africans?

Write About Culture

In what ways did enslaved Africans try to maintain their African culture?

Get Organized

VENN DIAGRAM

Use a Venn diagram to respond to this question: How did Africans live in the Southern colonies and the other colonies?

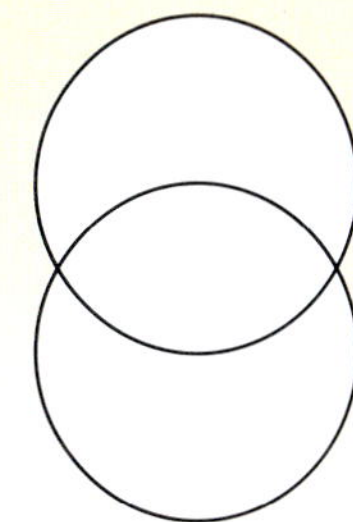

PAST *to* PRESENT

Education

In the 1700s, not all children attended school. Those who did studied only reading, writing, and math. Girls usually left school after a short time if they were allowed to attend at all. A few boys continued on to high school or college.

Colonial schools could be noisy places. Books, paper, pens, and ink were scarce items, so students recited their lessons out loud. Classrooms did not have maps or boards. Students wrote on bark or slate rather than on paper.

Today, state laws require all children to attend school until age 16. Most young people graduate from high school, and one in two finishes college.

Children were not required to attend school in the 1700s. However, some children did go to school. Some colonial boys even continued their education through high school or college.

Traditionally, hornbooks, like this one, had the alphabet or other simple lessons for students.

Most students in the 1700s had few books, writing materials, maps, and other resources with which to learn. Today, students and teachers in the United States often use computers in their classrooms to work with educational software programs and access the Internet for information.

There were no dictionaries in the early 1700s, and even educated people spelled the same word in different ways. This chart shows how colonial spellings often differed from the spellings used today for the same words.

Hands-on Activity

Conduct research to answer one of the following questions about education in the 1700s. What were classrooms like? What kind of clothing did students wear to school? What kinds of rules did they follow? Then, give an oral presentation or create a poster to present the results of your research to others. To get started, you can go to: www.gfamericanhistory.com.

CHAPTER 5 Review

Chapter Summary

In your notebook, complete the following outline. Then, use your outline to write a brief summary of the chapter.

The Thirteen Colonies

I. The Colonial Economy
   A. Farming in the Colonies
   B.
   C.

II. Life in the Colonies
   A.
   B.
   C.

III. Slavery in the Colonies
   A.
   B.

Interpret the Timeline

Use the timeline on pages 88–89 to answer the following questions.

1. In what year was the Zenger trial held?
2. **Critical Thinking** Which events show evidence of educational advances in Europe and the colonies?

Use Terms to Know

Match each term with its definition.

a. apprentice	**d. import**	**g. overseer**
b. barter	**e. libel**	**h. slave code**
c. export	**f. mercantile system**	

1. to exchange one product or service for another
2. a person who is in charge of enslaved people
3. to sell goods to another country
4. a person who works to learn a specific skill
5. to buy goods from another country
6. an economic system that stresses increasing national wealth by selling more than buying in foreign trade
7. a set of laws that limited the activities of enslaved people
8. a false statement made in writing about someone

Check Your Understanding

1. **Identify** three products that were made in the colonies.
2. **Explain** how the mercantile system might make a nation wealthy.
3. **Discuss** the roles of family members in the colonies.
4. **Summarize** the effect of the Great Awakening on religion in the colonies.
5. **Explain** how a distinct culture developed among enslaved Africans on southern plantations.
6. **Identify** two examples of resistance by enslaved people.

Critical Thinking

1. **Draw Conclusions** How did differences in geography affect the development of unique cultures in the New England, Middle, and Southern colonies?
2. **Analyze Primary Sources** What words in the quotation by Jonathan Edwards on page 99 made the sermon emotional?
3. **Analyze Primary Sources** According to the quotation by Olaudah Equiano on page 103, how did slave owners choose which African slaves they would buy?

Put Your Skills to Work

TAKE NOTES AND OUTLINE

You have learned that taking notes and outlining can help you gather and organize information. Reread the section "Africans in the Colonies" on pages 103–104. Take notes on this section using notecards or separate sheets of paper. Then, organize your notes, copy the following outline, and complete the outline by adding subtopics and important details.

Topic: Africans in the Colonies
I. Free Africans
  A. Freedom
    1. Escaped from owners
    2.
  B. Their lives and work
    1. Lived mostly in cities
    2.
II. Enslaved Africans
  A.
    1.
    2.
  B.
    1.
    2.

In Your Own Words

JOURNAL WRITING

People agree that slavery is unjust and cruel. Those who lived through it knew this best. Slavery also had an impact on those who were not enslaved. Write a journal entry about how slavery is damaging to society as a whole.

Net Work

INTERNET ACTIVITY

Working with a partner, use the Internet as a resource to write a report on life in colonial America. Find information about how the colonists lived, what activities they did, and how they dressed. Then, write a first-person account of colonial life as if you were a colonist. Include illustrations and photographs that you find to show what life was like.

For help in starting this activity, visit the following Web site: www.gfamericanhistory.com.

Look Ahead

In the next chapter, learn how Great Britain, with the help of the colonists, gained control of North America.

CHAPTER 6

Roots of Rebellion 1689–1763

I. England's Colonial Rule
II. Conflict With the French
III. The French and Indian War

In the mid-1700s, the colonies were caught up in a war between Great Britain and France. It was fought on the North American continent. Land, resources, and control of a continent were at stake. Native Americans played a crucial role in this struggle. With most of the fighting taking place in the regions west of the colonies, both the British and the French governments needed support from Native Americans in order to succeed. In this war, the colonists fought alongside British soldiers. A British writer for a Maryland newspaper thought the colonies might not succeed:

> "The French . . . will easily over-run the [colonies], because each [colony] considers itself as independent of the Rest . . . to unite 13 [colonies] which fill an extent of 1,600 miles is not easy."

The war, however, did help to unite the colonies. Afterward, the colonies would begin to think about standing on their own.

A soldier's powderhorn

U.S. Events

1689 King William's War begins.

1696 Board of Trade established to supervise colonial trade.

1702 Queen Anne's War begins.

1680 — 1700 — 1720

World Events

1689 English Bill of Rights is adopted.

1707 Scotland joins England and Wales to become Great Britain.

VIEW HISTORY This colored engraving shows British troops storming the French colonial city of Quebec in 1759. During the French and Indian War, soldiers kept their gunpowder dry by carrying it in a powderhorn (left).

★ **How are the soldiers approaching the city in this picture?**

Get Organized

FIVE *Ws* CHART

A Five *Ws* chart can help you better understand vital information about events by answering the questions of *Who* was involved, *What* the event was about, *Where* it occurred, *When* it happened, and *Why* it occurred. Here is an example from this chapter.

Who?	William and Mary
What?	Accepted English Bill of Rights
Where?	London, England
When?	1689
Why?	In order to gain power, William and Mary agreed to limit their own power as monarchs.

1744 King George's War begins.

1754 Colonists meet in Albany, New York. French and Indian War begins.

1763 British take control of New France.

1740 1760 1780

1740 1760 1780

1748 French philosopher Montesquieu writes about separation of powers in government.

1756 Seven Year's War begins in Europe.

1760 George III becomes King of England.

1762 Six-year-old Mozart begins grand tour of Europe.

I England's Colonial Rule

Terms to Know

monarch a ruler

Parliament the British law-making branch of government

assembly an elected group that makes laws

Main Ideas

A. Through the Glorious Revolution and the English Bill of Rights, English citizens gained more power to govern themselves.

B. All the colonial governments had a governor, a council, and an assembly.

C. Colonists had many rights and freedoms, but some of them were limited.

COMPARE

By comparing two items, you find ways in which they are similar, or alike. As you read this section, ask yourself: How was colonial government like the government in Great Britain?

A. Changes in English Government

By the early 1700s, colonial America was developing a character of its own. It was strongly shaped by English ideas—especially ideas about government. Changes in England's government in the late 1600s gave people in England more say in how they were governed. After these changes, English colonists, too, wanted more control over their own affairs.

Limiting the Power of Rulers

England had been ruled by **monarchs**, or kings and queens, for many years. However, these rulers did not have total control of the government as monarchs did in other parts of Europe. The first document to limit the power of English monarchs was the Magna Carta, or Great Charter.

You can read the Magna Carta on page R2.

The Magna Carta, written in 1215, proclaimed that even a monarch was not above the law. The Magna Carta gave certain rights to nobles, including protection under the law. Slowly the rights granted by the Magna Carta to the nobility began to filter down to include most English citizens.

In addition to the limits imposed by the Magna Carta, another step was taken that further limited the power of English monarchs. In 1295, the **Parliament**, or English legislative body, met for the first time—nobles together with commoners. Parliament began to represent the people of England. Parliament eventually came into conflict with the English rulers.

The Glorious Revolution

In the late 1600s, Parliament and the king, James II, struggled against each other for more power. Some of the problems centered around religion. Most members of Parliament were Protestant, but James was a Roman Catholic. He wanted to create an all-Catholic government. Members of Parliament worried that James's son would carry on a Catholic government. They secretly plotted to overthrow the king.

Parliament invited James's daughter Mary, who was a Protestant, and her husband, William of Orange, to take the throne. James II fled to France, and William and Mary became the new English monarchs in 1689. This takeover was called the Glorious Revolution.

William and Mary, England's new rulers in 1689, agreed to limits on their power.

As part of their agreement with Parliament, William and Mary had to limit their powers as England's rulers. These limits were spelled out in the English Bill of Rights in 1689. It gave Parliament greater powers in governing England. William and Mary agreed that Parliament would have the right to pass laws, to tax citizens, and to approve the existence of a permanent army.

The Rights of English Citizens

The English Bill of Rights made Parliament more powerful than the monarch. For example, the monarch could no longer suspend Parliament's laws and only Parliament could approve taxation. In addition, people could approach the monarch about wrongs done to them without penalty.

In 1690, the English philosopher John Locke wrote about the rights of English citizens. Locke explained what he called the contract theory of government. He wrote:

> "Men being . . . by nature all free, equal, and independent, no one can . . . be subjected [be put under] to the political power of another, without his own consent."

DOCUMENT-BASED QUESTION According to Locke, what is needed before a person is given political power over others?

Locke believed that governments were formed because people allowed them to be formed. Governments made a contract with the people to protect certain natural rights, such as life, liberty, and property. If government did not protect these rights, then the contract was broken, and a new government could be put in place. Locke's ideas were well-known in the English colonies and influenced their ideas about government.

 **What documents limited the power of English monarchs?**

B. The Structure of Colonial Government

Government in the colonies was limited in power, just as it was in England. Each part of the government depended on another part for a portion of its power. The basic parts of government were similar throughout the 13 colonies.

Governors and Councils

The governor was head of the colonial government. In most colonies, the governor was appointed by the English king. In others, such as Maryland, Pennsylvania, and Delaware, the proprietor, or owner, of the colony chose a governor. In two colonies, Connecticut and Rhode Island, colonists elected their own governors. However, the king had the right to approve or reject all governors.

The governor's job was to make sure the colonists obeyed English laws as well as those of the colony. The governor also chose the members of the council and other officials, such as tax collectors.

Colonial governors ruled with the help of a council composed of wealthy men. Their approval was usually needed for the governor to enforce laws. Some councils also acted as the highest court of the colony. When colonists were accused of severe crimes, they were tried by a jury in most colonies. The jury was made up of free, white males from the community.

Structure of Colonial Government

ENGLISH MONARCH

GOVERNOR
- Appointed, approved, or rejected by English monarch
- Head of colonial government
- Had final approval on laws

COUNCIL
- Appointed by governor
- Approved laws
- Highest court in some colonies

ASSEMBLY
- Made laws
- Elected by colonists
- Held "power of the purse"
- Paid governor's salary

Chart Check

Whom did the governor have the power to appoint?

Making Laws

In addition to a governor and a council, each colony had a lawmaking body, usually called an **assembly**. The assembly was elected by and represented voters in each colony. Assemblies had many different names. In Virginia, the assembly was called the House of Burgesses; in Maryland, it was the House of Delegates; and in Massachusetts, it was the House of Representatives.

Colonial assemblies worked with the governor and council to make laws. However, there were many instances when the governor and assemblies clashed. During most of the 1600s, governors held much more power than colonial assemblies did. By the early 1700s, assemblies began to take more control as they won the right to make laws. Weak governors began to give way to the colonial assemblies.

★ **What powers did the governor of a colony have?**

C. Colonial Freedom and Its Limits

Even before the first assemblies were formed, early colonists were involved in governing themselves. In New England, villagers gathered in their meetinghouses to elect officials. They also made decisions about everything from road repair to appointing schoolmasters.

Colonists would often debate fiercely in meeting halls about local government decisions.

The Right to Vote

Voting was a basic right of English citizens and had been a part of colonial life from its earliest days. However, the right to vote was limited. In early New England, voting was limited by religion. In Massachusetts, for example, only Puritans could vote and take part in town meetings. Voting limits based on religion later disappeared, but others remained in place throughout the colonies.

The most common limits were based on race, gender, and property. In all colonies, women, Africans, and Native Americans were not allowed to vote. Only white males who owned property could vote in elections. They also were the only ones allowed to serve in colonial assemblies or hold other public offices.

The Habit of Self-Government

In the 1700s, colonial assemblies began to gain more power. They won the right to introduce laws and to discipline their members. Most importantly, they gained the power to decide how much money should be raised through taxes and how it should be spent. This power included deciding how much to pay governors, councilors, and other colonial officials.

Assemblies had the power to tax and provide money for government operations. This power was known as the "power of the purse." They used this power to take control away from colonial governors. By the mid-1700s, colonists throughout the 13 colonies looked to their elected assemblies rather than to their governors for leadership.

After 1689, England was engaged in several wars with European rivals. England's government relied on the American colonists for help and did not spend much time interfering with the affairs of the colonies. During this period, the colonies became accustomed to managing their own affairs. Self-government, or being able to make their own laws, became not so much a habit but a right that they now took for granted.

Ships were the main way to transport goods to and from the colonies.

Regulating Trade

Some of the most visible limits on colonial freedom affected trade. To enforce the Navigation Acts, customs officials were stationed in the colonies to collect taxes on imported goods. The English navy also enforced these trade rules.

Parliament passed another Navigation Act in 1696. This act gave customs officials new tools for enforcing trade laws. They could now search ships without notice if they thought merchants were smuggling goods. In addition, people accused of breaking trade laws would be tried in naval courts, not by colonial juries. To further regulate colonial trade, King William III—William of Orange—established the Board of Trade in the same year to supervise trade and investigate the enforcement of the Navigation Acts and other colonial affairs.

Many colonists ignored the new trade laws. Others complained but followed them. In the following years, English officials spent less effort enforcing colonial trade laws. They were more concerned about France's growing presence in North America.

 **What important power did colonial assemblies gain in the 1700s?**

Review

Review History

A. What rights did Parliament gain as a result of the Glorious Revolution?

B. How were colonial governments organized?

C. How was the right to vote limited in the colonies?

Define Terms to Know

Provide a definition for each of the following terms.
monarch, Parliament, assembly

Critical Thinking

How might life in the colonies have been different if all adults had had the right to vote?

Write About Government

Using the Magna Carta on page 771 and the text in this section, write a paragraph explaining the benefits won by the English from the Magna Carta.

Get Organized

FIVE *Ws* CHART

A Five *Ws* chart is a good way to understand important events. Complete a Five *Ws* chart for the topic of "Structure of Colonial Government."

Who?	
What?	
Where?	
When?	
Why?	

Build Your Skills

Critical Thinking

UNDERSTAND CAUSE AND EFFECT

You wake up, look at the clock and realize that you have overslept. Instantly, you ask yourself, What happened? When you look for connections between events, you are thinking about cause and effect. Maybe you forgot to set your alarm or you did not hear it go off. Both events are examples of causes. The effect is that you overslept and will have less time to get ready for school.

Historical events, too, are often linked by cause and effect. For example, Parliament passed the English Bill of Rights. It was a cause. The effect was that people in England enjoyed more rights that were protected by law.

Here's How

Follow these steps when you read to understand cause and effect.

1. Look for words and phrases that signal a cause, such as *while*, *because*, and *due to*.
2. Look for words that signal an effect, such as *therefore* and *as a result*.
3. Identify logical connections between an event and what came before or after.

Here's Why

Understanding cause and effect will allow you to understand that there are reasons why things happen—and there are consequences.

Practice the Skill

Copy the chart shown on the right on a sheet of paper. Read Section I again and look for cause-and-effect relationships. Fill in the missing parts of the chart.

Extend the Skill

Give an oral presentation explaining how more power was given to the lawmaking bodies in both England and the colonies.

Apply the Skill

As you read the rest of this chapter, think about the causes and effects of key events. For example, create a cause/effect chart showing events between the French and the English.

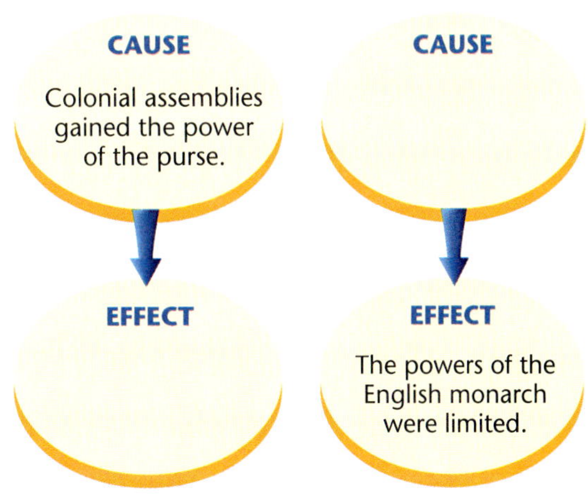

II Conflict With the French

Terms to Know

emigrate to leave one country to settle in another country

ally a nation, group, or people who are friendly with other people for a common goal

militia a group of citizen-soldiers who volunteer when needed

Main Ideas

A. New France was geographically large but had a small European population.

B. New France depended on Native Americans for trade.

C. Great Britain and France fought over land in North America, but these wars did not bring much change.

Active Reading

SUMMARIZE

Summarizing is a review of what you read. To summarize, you pick out important points and leave out most details. As you read this section, summarize relations between the French colonists and the Native Americans.

A. New France

As English colonists continued to settle the Atlantic coast, French settlers were also moving to North America. They settled in land north and west of the English colonies. New France, however, developed very differently from the English colonies.

French Settlement in North America

French settlers had been arriving in North America from the time Samuel de Champlain founded Quebec in 1608. France, however, was more interested in the fur trade than in settlement.

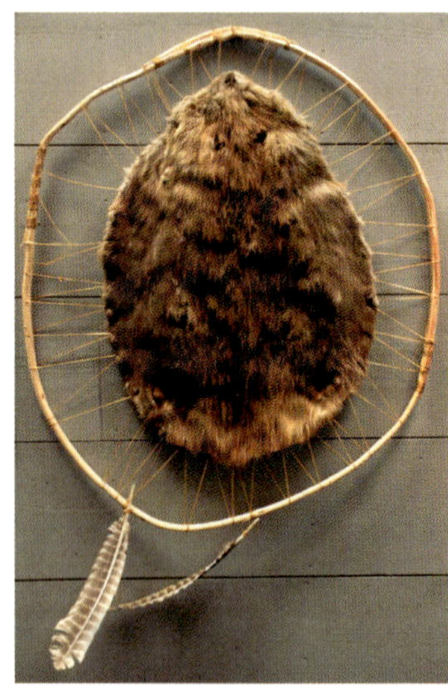

Beaver furs were one of the chief trade items in New France.

New France was made up of three distinct areas. First, there was the area called Acadia. This colony was located in present-day eastern Canada. Second, the area to the west of Acadia, which included the cities of Montreal and Quebec, was also a part of New France. Third, in the 1700s, other French colonists began to arrive in the region of Louisiana which was centered in the Mississippi River valley. The major settlements there included New Orleans, Mobile, and Biloxi.

New France never attracted as many settlers as the English colonies did. France was ruled by Catholic monarchs who did not want French non-Catholics to **emigrate**, or leave, to settle in New France. Starting in 1661, King Louis XIV encouraged French Catholics to move to New France. However, most French Catholics already owned land and were not persecuted. Therefore, they had little desire to move.

French non-Catholics who might have been willing to relocate were discouraged from doing so. By 1750, there were only about 70,000 French settlers in New France compared with about 1.5 million in the English colonies.

A Wilderness Empire

Although the population of New France was small, its land area was huge. Geographically, New France was much larger than all of the English colonies combined. French trappers and traders traveled great distances in their search for furs. They fanned out over the vast forested interior, or central portion, of the continent that lay between Canada and Louisiana.

The French trappers and traders were known as *coureurs de bois*, which is French for "runners of the woods." Of course, they did not run. They usually traveled in canoes made of birch bark wrapped over a frame or of a log that had been hollowed out by burning. Using these canoes, the *coureurs de bois* ventured deep into the continent.

The adventurous trappers and traders were not the only French people to roam the North American wilderness. Catholic missionaries traveled far from French centers such as Quebec, Montreal, and New Orleans. Their goal was to convert Native Americans to Catholicism. By the mid-1700s, French adventurers and missionaries had claimed a large territory for France. It covered much of what is now known as Canada, the Great Plains, the Great Lakes region, and the Missouri and Mississippi River valleys.

 **What areas in North America did the French settle?**

B. The French, English, and Native Americans

Most of the people who lived in French-claimed territory were Native Americans. For the most part, French traders, trappers, and missionaries all enjoyed good relationships with them.

Friendly Relations Develop

The French fur trade depended on good relations with Native Americans. From the earliest days of French exploration and settlement, the Hurons and Algonquins had been **allies**, or friends, of the French. Champlain helped them fight their long-time enemy, the Iroquois. As French trappers, traders, and missionaries moved into new areas, they formed similar relationships with other Native Americans.

Fur trappers and traders in New France often allied themselves with Native Americans.

The Iroquois and their warriors were one of the most powerful groups of Native Americans in colonial America.

The French trappers, traders, and missionaries who explored the wilderness lived among Native Americans. Many of them adopted Native American ways, and some trappers married Native American women. French traders wanted pelts, or animals skins, from Native American trappers. In return, they gave the Native Americans items that they were eager to have, such as iron kettles, blankets, and muskets. Friendly relations with Native Americans allowed New France to thrive as a colony even without a large French population.

The Iroquois and the English

The Iroquois League was one of the few Native American groups that did not ally themselves with the French colonists. In the 1600s, the Iroquois League was composed of five nations: the Mohawk, Oneida, Onondaga, Cayuga, and Seneca. Back in 1609, Samuel de Champlain had fought with Algonquins and Hurons against a group of Mohawk Iroquois. From that time, the Iroquois were unfriendly toward the French. The Iroquois turned to the Dutch, and later the English, to obtain trade goods. Eventually, the Iroquois defeated their rivals and became the most powerful Native American group in the region.

Conflicts with the Iroquois made French trade difficult. Most of the furs had to be taken to ports, such as Quebec, for shipment to France. Most routes to Quebec, however, passed near Iroquois lands. If the Iroquois attacked, the traders' valuable cargo might be lost. The only way to avoid this risk was to travel far to the north around Iroquois country.

Defending New France

English colonists also challenged France's fur trade. They trapped furs on Iroquois lands in what today is western Pennsylvania and Ohio, just as the French trappers did. This competition sometimes led to violence. English colonists attacked French trappers and raided small French settlements along the border between what is now Maine and Canada. In the South, Carolinians tried to convince English officials to stop French trappers from taking furs in the southern Appalachian Mountains.

Faced with these threats, French officials began to build a series of forts to defend their fur empire. The governor of New France explained the importance of defending the French settlements:

> "[Canada] alone is in a position to wage war against them [the English] in all their possessions on the Continent of America . . . and which, if means be not found to prevent it, will soon absorb . . . all the Colonies . . . of the Continent of America."

ANALYZE PRIMARY SOURCES

DOCUMENT-BASED QUESTION Why was what is now Canada an important location for a French settlement?

French forts served as military headquarters, missions, and trading posts. They were located near rich trapping grounds or important shipping points. Among the most important forts were Louisbourg, near the mouth of the St. Lawrence River, and Fort Frontenac, at the northeast end of Lake Ontario. These two outposts gave France control of the St. Lawrence River.

 **Why were the Iroquois generally unfriendly toward the French?**

Fort Louisbourg was one of many forts that provided protection to the fur trade in New France.

C. North American Colonial Wars

In the late 1600s, France, England, and Spain became caught up in a worldwide race for colonies and resources. They also struggled for power and territory in Europe. The result was a series of wars that lasted, on and off, for the next 74 years.

In these wars, France and England fought each other not only in Europe but also in North America. Each of these wars had its own name in the colonies.

King William's War

The first war between France and England began in 1689. This war was known as King William's War. In North America, the war was fought in Canada and New England as the French and their Native American allies fought the English for control of Hudson Bay. French troops raided English settlements in New England and New York, while **militias**, or groups of citizen-soldiers, from the English colonies attacked French Acadia.

Native Americans who were allied with France made raids against settlers in New England and New York. Meanwhile, the Iroquois fought with the English and attacked French trappers and traders. Neither side won the war. In 1697, the two sides agreed to stop fighting and returned all captured territory.

Colonial Wars in North America

WAR	DATE	RESULT
King William's War	1689–1697	No territory changed hands.
Queen Anne's War	1702–1713	England gained control of the French territories Newfoundland and Acadia.
King George's War	1744–1748	British colonists captured Louisbourg but gave it back to France.

Chart Check

Which colonial war had the most decisive result?

Queen Anne's War

In 1702, another war began, which lasted until 1713. This time, England fought both France and Spain. In the colonies, this conflict was known as Queen Anne's War. French troops and Native Americans repeatedly attacked New England colonists. Dozens of New Englanders were captured and taken to Canada as prisoners. Many villages were also destroyed. Meanwhile, English colonists in South Carolina fought with Spaniards and their Native American allies.

As a result of Queen Anne's War, England, or Great Britain as it came to be known in 1707, gained control of two large French territories—Newfoundland and Acadia. Acadia was later renamed Nova Scotia. For the next 31 years, no major conflicts broke out in North America. However, there were always conflicts in the wilderness over the fur trade.

King George's War

In 1739, Spain and Great Britain began fighting again over colonial trade. Five years later, in 1744, the French joined Spain in fighting the British. This conflict led to a third colonial war called King George's War.

During King George's War, colonists from New England captured the French fort at Louisbourg. Louisbourg was one of the most important French forts because it controlled access to the St. Lawrence River from the Atlantic Ocean. However, in the treaty that ended the war in 1748, Britain returned Louisbourg to the French. Many colonists were angered that hundreds of Americans had died for nothing.

After three wars for control of North America, the balance of power had not really changed. The treaty that ended King George's War was merely a way to give the combatants a chance to regain their strength. Great Britain still had its colonies along the Atlantic coast. France still claimed vast areas in the middle of the continent. Both countries still competed for furs in the regions that separated their colonies.

Fur trappers and traders depended on forts to protect them during their long marches through the wilderness.

What was the effect of the fighting between Great Britain and France in the colonies?

Review History

A. Why did New France have a small European population?

B. Why were the French able to develop good relations with Native Americans?

C. What was one cause of the fighting between Great Britain and France in North America?

Define Terms to Know

Provide a definition for each of the following terms.
emigrate, ally, militia

Critical Thinking

Why did conflicts between countries in Europe result in wars in North America?

Write About Geography

Write a short paragraph describing the French colonies in North America. Include details about size, geographic features, and population centers.

Get Organized

FIVE *Ws* CHART

A Five *Ws* chart is a good way to understand important events. Complete a Five *Ws* chart on "French Relations with Native Americans."

Who?	
What?	
Where?	
When?	
Why?	

III The French and Indian War

Terms to Know

representative a person selected to act and speak in place of others

ambush a surprise attack from a hidden position

cede to give up or surrender land

Main Ideas

A. Great Britain and France clashed over control of the Ohio River valley.

B. Both American colonists and the British army helped defeat French forces in the French and Indian War.

C. When the war ended, Great Britain gained control of all French territory in eastern North America.

SEQUENCE OF EVENTS
To understand a sequence of events, ask yourself what happened first, second, and so on. Use a numbered list or a chart to sequence events. As you read this section, list the sequence of events in the French and Indian War.

A. Conflict in the Ohio River Valley

After the end of King George's War, France and Great Britain fought over the Ohio River valley. This region to the west of the British colonies was rich in furs and rivers that could be used to transport them. Both countries claimed the region.

British Expansion

By the mid-1700s, the population of the British colonies in North America was growing rapidly. However, its land area was limited. To the east was the Atlantic Ocean, to the west, the Appalachian Mountains. As a result, colonists looked to cross the mountains and settle land even farther west.

During the 1740s, British fur traders began exploring and using lands west of the Appalachian Mountains, in the Ohio River valley. In 1749, King George II of Great Britain granted 200,000 acres of this region to a group of Virginia business owners who formed the Ohio Company. They planned to settle the Ohio River valley.

French Claims

France had long ago claimed this region. However, the Iroquois had kept French traders from using the Ohio River. This situation changed when the French made friends with the Miamis, Shawnees, and Eries who lived in the area in 1749. These Native American groups were rivals of the Iroquois. Now, French traders would have access to a key shipping route for pelts.

In 1753, French soldiers built Fort Le Boeuf east of Lake Erie. The French government now tried to officially claim the land. This attempt was a direct challenge to the British presence there. The governor of Virginia sent out a twenty-one-year-old militia officer named George Washington to warn the French that they were on British territory. Washington reported back that the French were determined to stay.

 **How did France show that it intended to remain in the Ohio River valley?**

Map Check

MOVEMENT How might a trader transport goods from Fort Frontenac to Fort Niagara?

B. The War Unfolds

The French claims worried powerful British merchants and their colonial partners. Together, they convinced the British government to send several thousand troops to North America to drive the French out. The French government responded by sending its own troops. The stage was set for a conflict. It would become the fourth and greatest colonial war in North America.

Albany Plan of Union

With war and the threat of a French takeover on the horizon, the colonists tried to join together. In 1754, **representatives** from all the northern colonies held a meeting in Albany, New York. Representatives are people selected to act for others.

The representatives were supposed to discuss making a treaty with the Iroquois. However, the topic was soon changed. Benjamin Franklin of Pennsylvania, who admired the union of the Iroquois nations, thought the colonies would be stronger if they united. He proposed the Albany Plan of Union. It called for a president appointed by the British king and an assembly made up of members from each colony. The assembly would have the power to lead military operations if war broke out, manage western settlement and Native American relations, and pass laws to raise taxes.

The Albany Plan of Union was the first attempt to unite the 13 colonies in a common cause. However, both the colonists and the British government rejected it. People in the colonies wanted to control their own taxes and military forces. The British government did not want a colonial assembly interfering with its powers.

Do You Remember?

In Chapter 5, you learned that Benjamin Franklin was the most famous philosopher of the Enlightenment movement in the colonies. He conducted experiments with electricity, invented a stove for heating rooms, and started a library in Philadelphia.

Battles in the Wilderness

In 1754, the war was beginning in the west. George Washington, with a militia force, was sent to remove the French troops. Washington, with little military experience, was soon forced to surrender after being swarmed by French soldiers and Native Americans.

The colonists soon received help from Britain. In 1755, a large force of British soldiers arrived in Virginia. They immediately moved west toward French territory.

The British soldiers in their bright red uniforms were easy targets for an **ambush**, or a surprise attack. In the woods, British forces lost to smaller forces of French troops with their Native American allies. Later, New Hampshire colonist Robert Rogers would use surprise attacks against French forces.

The French won most of the early battles of the war. However, after three years of fighting, the tide turned toward the British. The British allied themselves with the Iroquois who knew much of the area. The British used their navy to prevent supplies from arriving in New France. The British were also able to draw on the greater number of colonists in the British colonies to strengthen their armies. In 1759, 4,000 British troops captured the city of Quebec, and it became clear that British forces would win the war.

 **How were the British able to win the war?**

They Made History

Robert Rogers 1731–1795

Robert Rogers was the leader of a special colonial fighting force called Rogers' Rangers. A farmer and woodsman from New Hampshire, Rogers knew how to travel and fight in the dense forests of the wilderness. Rogers' Rangers took on the toughest challenges. In 1756, British officers asked Rogers to train others in his effective ambush method of warfare. He commanded nine companies of men, two of which had Native American commanders. Rogers' Rangers became famous for their bravery during the French and Indian War.

Robert Rogers commanded a specially trained fighting force during the French and Indian War.

Critical Thinking

What skills helped Rogers' Rangers fight in the French and Indian War?

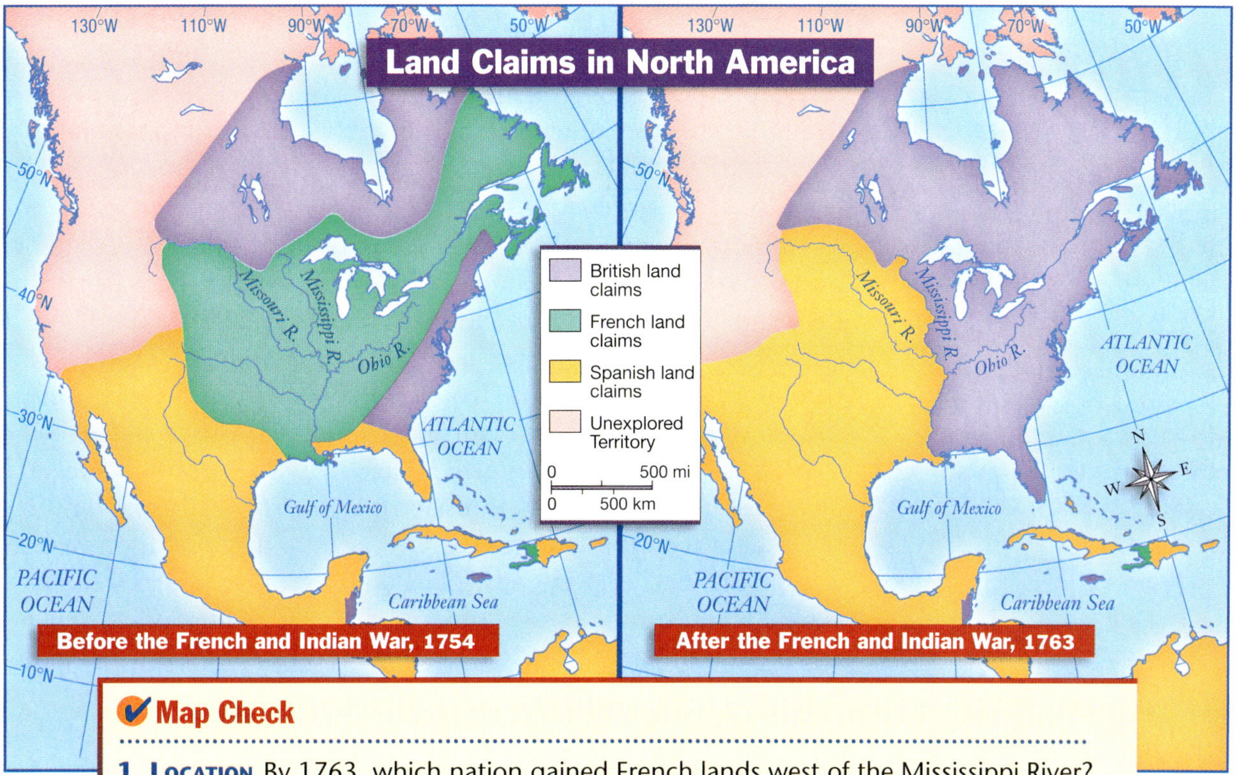

Land Claims in North America

British land claims
French land claims
Spanish land claims
Unexplored Territory

Before the French and Indian War, 1754

After the French and Indian War, 1763

Map Check

1. **Location** By 1763, which nation gained French lands west of the Mississippi River?
2. **Region** What river became the border between British and Spanish lands in North America after the war?

C. Effects of the War

The fall of Quebec was the most important British victory in the war. Fighting continued for another four years, as the British captured Montreal and other French settlements in New France. In 1762, Spain entered the war on the side of France, but the help arrived too late.

The Treaty of Paris

Spanish aid in the war did not have the effect France desired. The war officially ended with the Treaty of Paris in 1763. Under the treaty, France **ceded**, or gave up possession of, northern New France and all lands east of the Mississippi River to Britain. Spain, as an ally of France, was forced to give Florida to Great Britain. To get Spain to enter the war, France ceded all claims west of the Mississippi River, including New Orleans, to Spain.

North America was now divided between Great Britain and Spain, with the Mississippi River as the boundary. French military power in North America had come to an end. Great Britain was now in control of much of New France.

Even though Britain gained control of what is now Canada in the Treaty of Paris, many French citizens in Montreal and Quebec remained. Today, most residents of Quebec speak French. In fact, both French and English are the official languages of Canada.

Spotlight on History

After the French and Indian War, the power of the Iroquois would continue to weaken. Eventually, fighting with British colonists and diseases introduced from Europe would destroy the power and influence of the Iroquois.

The war was also a turning point for the British colonies. For the first time, they had acted together for a common cause and gained military experience. In addition, with the French gone, colonists would not be discouraged from moving west of the Appalachians.

Native Americans After the War

Without France in the area to act as a threat, colonists were now pushing outward into Iroquois territory in western New York and the Ohio River valley. In addition, Native American groups had made war against each other in order to control the fur trade. It was through these wars that the Iroquois gained their power. However, this power was weakened by diseases brought from Europe.

Native Americans recognized their declining position. Several groups found a leader in Pontiac of the Ottawa nation. Uniting several Native American groups, he began to make raids on British settlements in the spring of 1763. Pontiac's initial attacks were successful. He captured and destroyed 10 of 14 major posts that he attacked. By December 1763, colonial and British forces had gathered their strength and struck back, driving Pontiac west where he soon had to give in. Even though the British were successful, Pontiac's rebellion was a warning that they would have to take a greater hand in colonial government.

How did the French and Indian War affect Native Americans?

Review History

A. Why did France and Britain both want the lands of the Ohio River valley?

B. What was the Albany Plan of Union?

C. How did the map of North America change as a result of the French and Indian War?

Define Terms to Know

Provide a definition for each of the following terms.
representative, ambush, cede

Critical Thinking

What effect did the French and Indian War have on relations between Native Americans and colonists?

Write About History

Write a speech from a Native American or British colonist's point of view telling why you are involved in the French and Indian War.

Get Organized

FIVE *Ws* CHART

A Five *Ws* chart is a good way to understand important events. Complete a Five *Ws* chart on "The Beginning of the French and Indian War."

Who?	
What?	
Where?	
When?	
Why?	

CONNECT History & Literature

The French and Indian War in Fiction

At the time of the French and Indian War, a wilderness separated the North American colonies of Great Britain and France. Included in this area was the upper Hudson River valley in northern New York. This land is the setting of *The Last of the Mohicans*, James Fenimore Cooper's popular adventure novel about the war.

A WILDERNESS THEME James Fenimore Cooper was born in 1789, long after the French and Indian War had ended. Cooper, however, knew the woods and Native Americans firsthand because he had grown up in an unsettled area of New York.

The novel includes an actual event from the war—the French attack on Fort William Henry, and the British surrender. Cooper's aim, however, was not to create a realistic picture of the war. Instead, he wanted to call attention to the vanishing way of life in the wilderness through the main character of Hawkeye, a brave scout for the British, and his two close Native American friends.

AN ACTION-PACKED STORY Hawkeye's companions are Mohicans—Algonquin-speaking Native Americans. Together, they take on the job of escorting a British officer and two young women to Fort William Henry. They experience many adventures along the way as they try to fight off a fierce Huron named Magua, who wants to kidnap the young women.

Critical Thinking

Answer the questions below. Then, complete the activity.

1. Why did Cooper write *The Last of the Mohicans*?
2. Historical novels are very popular with readers of all ages. Why do you think they are so popular?

Write About It

Go to the following Web site to find the online text of *The Last of the Mohicans*: www.gfamericanhistory.com. Read Chapter 3 of the novel. This chapter introduces the characters Hawkeye and his Mohican friend Chingachgook. In a paragraph, describe one of the two characters.

This illustration by N.C. Wyeth reveals the action of *The Last of the Mohicans*.

CHAPTER 6 Review

Chapter Summary

In your notebook, complete the following outline. Then, use your outline to write a brief summary of the chapter.

Roots of Rebellion

I. England's Colonial Rule
  A. Changes in English Government
  B.
  C.
II. Conflict With the French
  A.
  B.
  C.
III. The French and Indian War
  A.
  B.
  C.

Interpret the Timeline

Use the timeline on pages 110–111 to answer the following questions.

1. What war in Europe began two years after the French and Indian War started?
2. **Critical Thinking** What events on the timeline show the development of democracy?

Use Terms to Know

Select the term that best completes each sentence.

ambush **emigrate** **representative**
cede **militia**

1. During the French and Indian War, an ________, or a surprise attack from a hidden position, was used against British troops.
2. France encouraged only Roman Catholics to ________, or leave, France to settle in North America.
3. Benjamin Franklin was a ________ to the meeting in Albany, New York.
4. The Treaty of Paris required France to ________, or give up, its eastern lands to Great Britain.
5. Instead of being professional soldiers, American colonists who fought served in a ________.

Check Your Understanding

1. **Discuss** the effect of the Magna Carta on English government.
2. **Explain** how American colonists developed the habit of self-government.
3. **Identify** the *coureurs de bois* and explain why they were important to the French economy.
4. **Discuss** why and where the French built forts in New France.
5. **Summarize** the main ideas in the Albany Plan of Union.
6. **Identify** the advantages of the French in the French and Indian War.

Critical Thinking

1. **Analyze Primary Sources** How might a colonial woman or an enslaved person respond to John Locke's quotation on page 113?
2. **Draw Conclusions** How were French relations with Native Americans helpful to their cause?
3. **Draw Conclusions** How would British leaders view the 13 colonies after the French and Indian War?

Put Your Skills to Work

UNDERSTAND CAUSE AND EFFECT

You learned that understanding cause and effect can help you identify the relationships between events in history.

Copy the following chart. Identify two cause-and-effect relationships that you read about in this chapter. Write the causes in the circles at the top and the effects in the circles on the bottom.

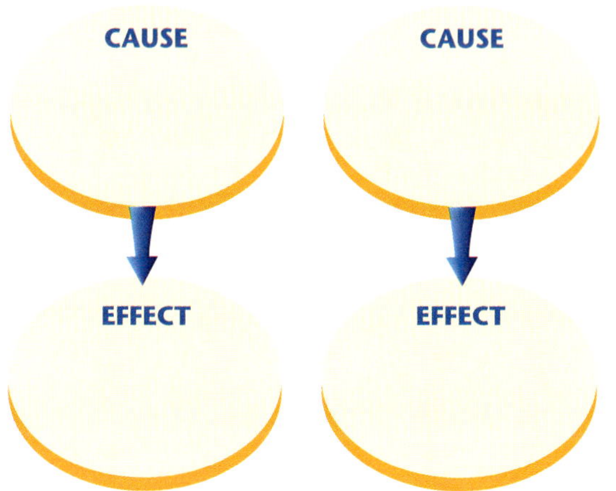

In Your Own Words

JOURNAL WRITING

The Magna Carta and the English Bill of Rights were agreements between the people and government. People often make agreements today. For example, two students working together on a project might agree to divide the work. Write a journal entry that describes a time you made an agreement. Include what was expected of you and what you received.

Net Work

INTERNET ACTIVITY

Both the French and the British built forts in North America during the period of conflict between France and Britain. Working with a partner, use the Internet as a resource to create a model or drawing of a fort. Include a short written description or list of important facts about your fort.

For help in starting this activity, visit the following Web site: www.gfamericanhistory.com.

Look Ahead

In the next chapter, learn about the colonies' changing relationship with Great Britain.

Unit 2 Portfolio Project

History Quiz Show

YOUR ASSIGNMENT

Quiz shows are a popular form of entertainment. Contestants enjoy displaying their knowledge. Viewers enjoy testing their wits against the person in the "hot seat." For this assignment, you will test your knowledge of American history as you design a history quiz show.

GETTING READY

Choose Your Content With a team of four to six students, select one chapter from the list below. The chapter will be the one for which you write questions.

Chapter 4 Founding Colonial America, 1607–1733
Chapter 5 The Thirteen Colonies, 1650–1775
Chapter 6 Roots of Rebellion, 1689–1763

Choose a Format Decide on a format for your show. To get ideas, think of popular quiz shows you know. For example, will you have players choose a category first? Will questions be displayed or simply read by an announcer? How much time will you allow for contestants to answer questions?

Write Questions Begin writing questions. Choose questions that can be answered in a word or phrase. Record each question on a separate card or slip of paper. Refer to this Web site for ideas: www.gfamericanhistory.com.

Review Questions Review and edit your questions. Make sure that each question is worded clearly and that each answer is correct.

THE SHOW BEGINS

Find Contestants Ask for volunteers from outside your team to serve as contestants.

Play Your Game Conduct your quiz show in front of the class. Keep score as you play to determine the winner of your game.

Multimedia Presentation

Turn your quiz show into a board game. Use a computer graphics program to design a game board with a path for players to follow. The only rule is that players must answer history questions correctly in order to advance along the path to the finish. Test your game, and then share it with others in the class.

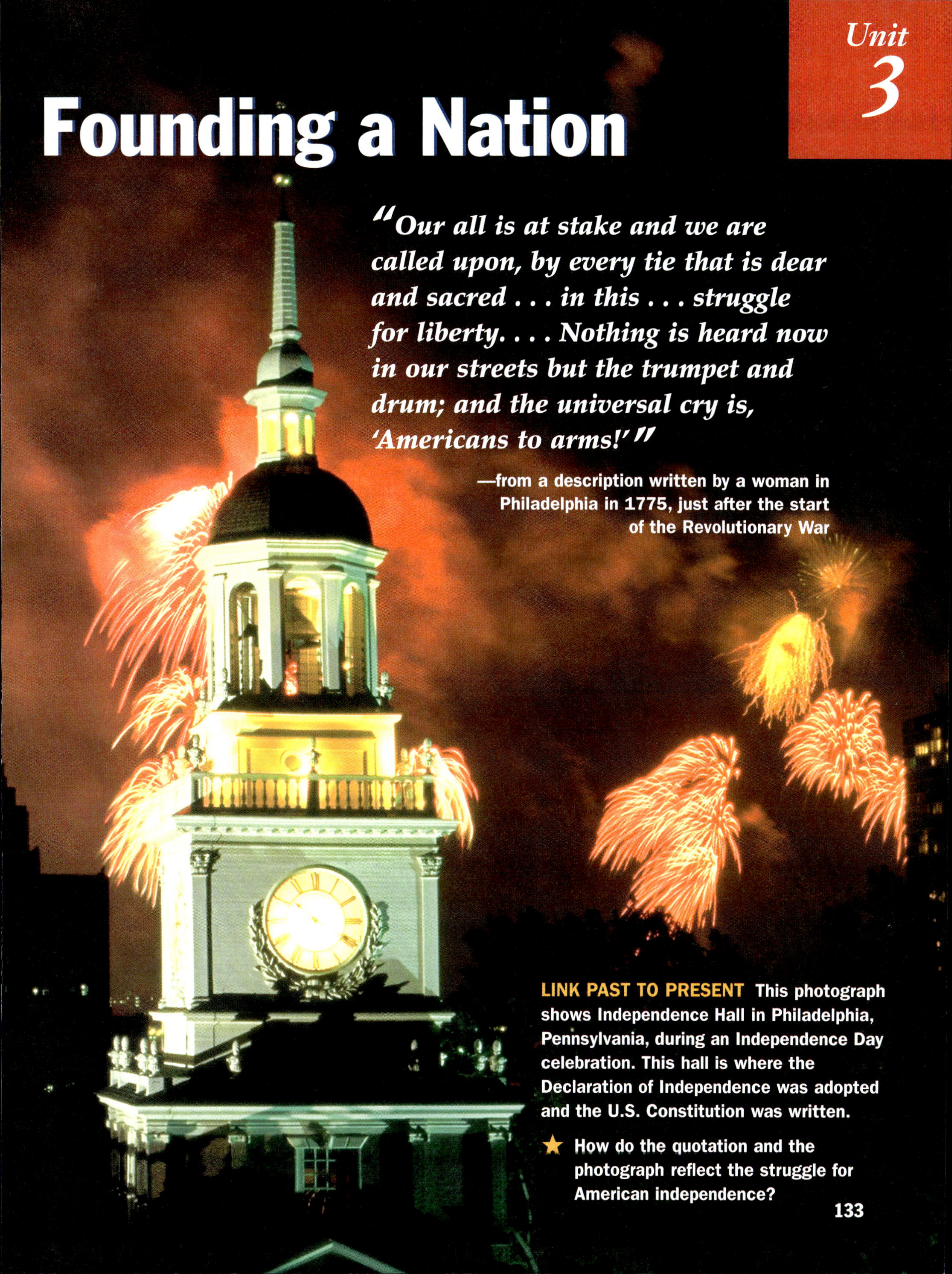

Unit 3

Founding a Nation

"Our all is at stake and we are called upon, by every tie that is dear and sacred . . . in this . . . struggle for liberty. . . . Nothing is heard now in our streets but the trumpet and drum; and the universal cry is, 'Americans to arms!'"

—from a description written by a woman in Philadelphia in 1775, just after the start of the Revolutionary War

LINK PAST TO PRESENT **This photograph shows Independence Hall in Philadelphia, Pennsylvania, during an Independence Day celebration. This hall is where the Declaration of Independence was adopted and the U.S. Constitution was written.**

★ **How do the quotation and the photograph reflect the struggle for American independence?**

CHAPTER 7

Road to Independence 1763–1776

I. **Resistance to British Taxes**
II. **Growing Tensions**
III. **A Declaration of Independence**

In 1763, few people in the American colonies wished to break their connection with Great Britain. Most of the two million colonists were proud to be British citizens. Then, the British government began to tax the colonies. Outraged, the colonists asked the following question: How could our government tax us without our consent? Because the colonists were not represented in Parliament, they had not voted for the taxes. Therefore, they argued, the taxes were illegal and unjust. Legislator John Adams of Massachusetts wrote in his diary:

> "The people have become more attentive to their liberties . . . and more determined to defend them."

With the onset of new taxes, the colonists now insisted on self-government.

Colonial lantern

U.S. Events

1763 British Parliament issues the Proclamation of 1763.

1764 Sugar Act requires colonists to pay taxes on imported sugar.

1765 Colonists riot in response to the Stamp Act.

1767 Parliament passes the Townshend Acts.

1758 | 1762 | 1766

World Events

1758 | 1762 | 1766

1762 British earl creates the sandwich.

1765 In Scotland, James Watt improves the design of the steam engine.

VIEW HISTORY The horseback riders are spreading the news that fighting between American and British troops had begun. The colonial lantern (left) lit the way for colonists carrying important messages at night.

★ **Why do you think the artist chose to paint a dark, cloudy sky in this picture?**

Get Organized

CAUSE-AND-EFFECT CHAIN

Recognizing the causes and effects of events can help you to better understand history. Use a cause-and-effect chain as you read Chapter 7. List each important event in a box. In the ovals, fill in a cause and an effect. Here is an example from this chapter.

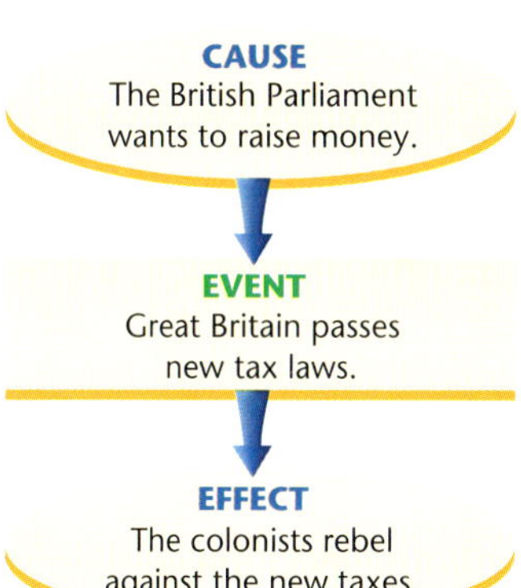

1770 Boston Massacre occurs.

1773 Boston Tea Party takes place.

1775 Revolutionary War starts at Lexington and Concord.

1776 Declaration of Independence is signed.

1770 — 1774 — 1778

1770 — 1774 — 1778

1770 James Cook discovers Botany Bay in Australia.

1771 First edition of the *Encyclopaedia Britannica* is published.

1774 Louis XVI becomes king of France.

1777 Antoine Lavoisier discovers that oxygen is needed to make fire.

I Resistance to British Taxes

Terms to Know

frontier the region just beyond a settled area

proclamation an official announcement

revenue money received by a government from taxes and other sources

boycott a protest in which people refuse to buy certain goods

repeal to take back or cancel

Main Ideas

A. Great Britain made efforts to control the colonies.

B. The British government placed taxes on the colonies in order to help pay for the costs of the French and Indian War.

C. The colonists protested the Stamp Act tax by demonstrating and refusing to buy British goods.

POINT OF VIEW

A point of view is a person's way of looking at something. As you read this section, think about how the colonial leaders' point of view differed from that of the British Parliament.

A. Controls After the War

When the French and Indian War ended, British leaders faced two problems. One was keeping order on the western edge of its colonies. The other was paying off the huge debt caused by the war. Great Britain looked to the colonies for help with both problems.

Proclamation of 1763

After the French and Indian War had ended, some colonists began moving west over the Appalachian Mountains into the **frontier**. The frontier was just beyond the area the colonists had already settled. The Native Americans who lived in this area felt that the colonists were taking over their lands. In 1763, British and colonial forces had joined together and successfully defended the settlements against the Native Americans led by Pontiac. The conflict had shown the colonists and the British government that the Native Americans would not willingly give up their land.

In order to limit future conflict between colonists and Native Americans, the British government decided to stop all colonial settlement west of the Appalachian Mountains. King George III issued a **proclamation**, or an official government announcement. The Proclamation of 1763 drew an imaginary line down the center of the mountains. Colonists were not allowed to move west of that line. Thousands of colonists had planned to move into this region.

Spotlight on *Geography*

The Appalachian Mountains stretch all the way from Canada to Alabama and cover 17 states. The Appalachian mountain system includes the White Mountains, Green Mountains, Berkshire Hills, Catskill Mountains, Allegheny Mountains, Blue Ridge Mountains, Cumberland Mountains, and Great Smoky Mountains.

The colonists, however, did not want to live under this law. They had fought the French for access to the Ohio River valley. Furthermore, many colonial charters had given colonies the right to lands in the Ohio River valley and beyond. Thus, in spite of the Proclamation, settlers continued to sweep across the mountains into the frontier. Many colonists felt that the British government was interfering too much with their rights. The Proclamation of 1763 aroused great resentment in the colonies.

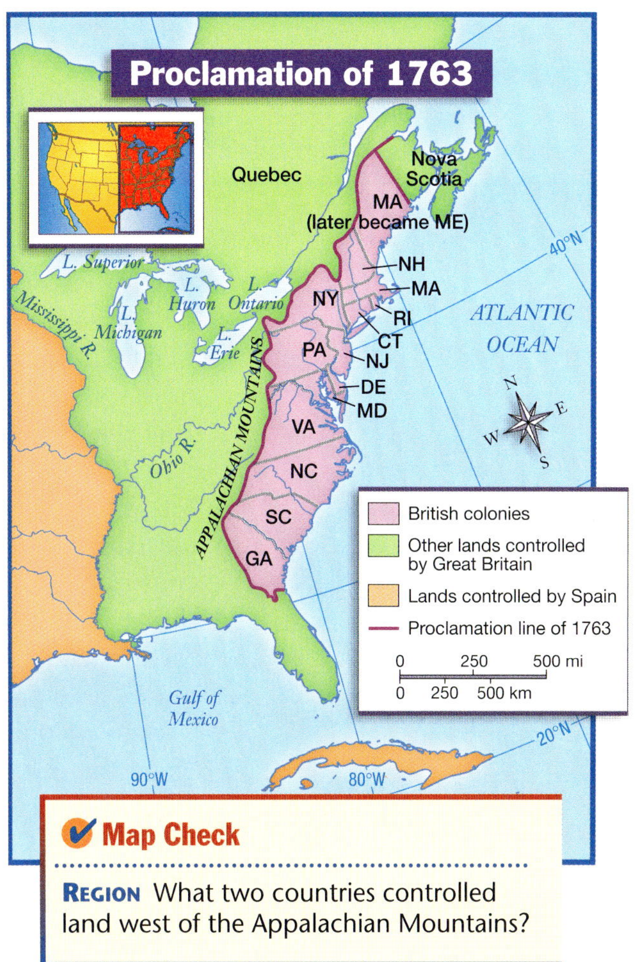

Map Check

REGION What two countries controlled land west of the Appalachian Mountains?

Quartering Act

After the French and Indian War, the British government decided to keep British troops in the American colonies to maintain order along the western edge of the colonies.

Providing food and shelter for these troops was expensive. In 1765, Parliament passed an act called the Quartering Act. This act forced the colonists to furnish quarters—food and shelter—to British soldiers. Also, colonial assemblies had to buy supplies for the troops.

Most colonial assemblies were unhappy about paying for the soldiers' food, supplies, and housing. The law was especially unpopular in New York, where most British troops were stationed. Some colonists suspected that British troops remained not to protect American colonists but to enforce British laws. When New York's assembly refused to follow the act, the British government suspended the assembly. However, the suspension was never carried out, since the New York assembly soon agreed to obey the act.

 **What was the purpose of the Proclamation of 1763?**

B. New Taxes

Years of war in North America with France and Spain had drained Great Britain's treasury. The country had borrowed large amounts of money to pay soldiers and ship supplies across the ocean. Keeping troops in the colonies after the war added to the debt.

The British government wanted the American colonies to pay a share of the debt. Parliament passed laws that would raise money by taxing the colonists.

Parliament Taxes the Colonists

The British government had passed a series of Navigation Acts beginning in the 1600s. These acts allowed Parliament to place taxes on goods sent to and from the American colonies for many years. These taxes were often used to control trade. As an example, Britain did not want the colonists to buy molasses, a sugary syrup, from the French West Indies. Therefore, Parliament passed a Navigation Act called the Molasses Act in 1733, which placed a high import tax on foreign molasses. This tax made molasses bought from British producers in the Indies cheaper than other molasses. As a result, the colonists began buying molasses only from the British producers.

In 1764, Parliament passed a Navigation Act called the Sugar Act. This law placed a tax on non-British imports of sugar, cloth, and coffee. Additionally, British ships were allowed to seize any ships carrying goods on which this import tax had not been paid. Unlike other taxes, this tax was used to raise money for the British government. The Sugar Act marked the first time Parliament had created a colonial tax just to bring in **revenue**, or money.

Many colonists insisted that Parliament had gone too far. It was taxing the colonies without their consent. They claimed that only the colonial assemblies could tax colonists in order to raise revenue.

The Stamp Act

Few colonists took a stand against the new taxes. The taxes affected only a few New England merchants who imported sugar. The Sugar Act, however, did not provide enough money to pay off Great Britain's debt.

In February 1765, Parliament passed the Stamp Act. It placed a tax on all printed items. Newspapers and many other items, including pamphlets and legal documents, had to have a stamp showing that the tax had been paid. The Stamp Act affected almost everyone in the colonies.

 **What were the Sugar Act and the Stamp Act?**

Stamps like this one were used to show that taxes had been paid on the printed item.

C. Reaction to British Taxation

A few colonists, such as James Otis of Massachusetts, spoke out against the Sugar Act. He pointed out that the colonists were not represented in Parliament. Therefore, Parliament did not have the right to tax them. He stressed the idea of no taxation without representation. After the Stamp Act was passed, more colonists took up this cry. On the day the Stamp Act went into effect, colonists showed their opposition by flying flags at half mast.

Protests in the Colonies

Colonists protested the Stamp Act by burning British tax stamps.

Printers, lawyers, merchants, and newspaper writers and editors were especially hurt by the Stamp Act. Many of them were influential people in a position to sway public opinion. During the spring and summer of 1765, these colonists worked to unite people against the Stamp Act. Patrick Henry, a member of the Virginia House of Burgesses, called the tax illegal and unjust. His heated statements were printed in newspapers across the colonies.

Soon the slogan "No taxation without representation" was heard throughout the colonies. In cities, especially in New England, groups calling themselves Sons of Liberty gathered beneath "Liberty Trees" to protest the Stamp Act. They organized demonstrations and burned piles of stamps. Some angry groups also threatened stamp tax collectors. The organizer and leader of the Sons of Liberty was Samuel Adams. He was a cousin of John Adams, who would later become the second President of the United States. Women joined the Daughters of Liberty to protest the Stamp Act.

Another form of protest was the **boycott**, in which colonists refused to buy British goods. New England merchants signed agreements with each other not to import British products. The boycott of products such as cloth and paper was effective because the British government lost the money that would have come from the taxes on the goods. Colonists passed out handbills, or small printed notices, carrying messages like this one:

> "It is desired that the Sons and Daughters of Liberty, would not buy any one thing of [William Jackson, importer], for in so doing they will bring disgrace upon themselves, and their posterity [future relatives], for ever and ever, Amen."

ANALYZE PRIMARY SOURCES

DOCUMENT-BASED QUESTION According to this handbill message, why should people not buy products from Great Britain?

Many women supported the boycotts. In place of British tea, they served tea made from homegrown herbs. Boycotting British tea was quite a sacrifice on the part of colonists because tea was such a popular drink. Instead of buying fabric from Britain, women made clothing from homespun cloth. The Daughters of Liberty even held cloth-spinning bees to encourage people to wear homemade fabrics.

In October 1765, delegates from nine colonies met in New York City to take action against the Stamp Act. This meeting was called the Stamp Act Congress. The delegates at the meeting recognized Britain's right to control colonial trade. However, they objected to Parliament's taxing the colonists without colonial representation in Parliament. In a letter to the British government, the delegates stated that only their own legislatures could tax them. They asked Parliament to **repeal**, or take back, the Stamp Act.

Then & Now

American colonists held boycotts in order to show that they disapproved of the Stamp Act.

Boycotts are still an effective type of protest today. For example, some people refuse to buy clothing made by companies that have illegal labor practices, such as paying below the minimum wage or hiring underage workers.

Repeal of the Stamp Act

The protests in the streets of the colonies got Parliament's attention. However, it was the boycotts that made Parliament take action. With fewer colonists buying British goods, tax money was being lost. British merchants were also losing business. They put pressure on leaders in Parliament to repeal the Stamp Act. Early in 1766, Parliament did just that.

Even though British lawmakers had backed down, they did not give up on the idea of taxing the American colonies. They quickly passed the Declaratory Act. This law stated that Parliament had the power to tax the colonists for any reason. Even though the Stamp Act was gone, the fight over taxation without representation would continue.

In what ways did colonists protest the Stamp Act?

Review History

A. How did the Proclamation of 1763 and the Quartering Act affect American colonists?

B. Why did Parliament decide to tax the colonies?

C. Why was the Stamp Act repealed?

Define Terms to Know

Provide a definition for each of the following terms.
frontier, proclamation, revenue, boycott, repeal

Critical Thinking

Do you think that Parliament's argument that the colonists should help pay for the French and Indian War was fair? Explain.

Write About Government

You are a colonist. Write a short letter to the editor of your city's newspaper stating your concerns about the Stamp Act.

Get Organized

CAUSE-AND-EFFECT CHAIN

Think about the main events in this section. Use a cause-and-effect chain to show the cause and effect of an event. For example, what was the cause and the effect of the Sugar Act or the Stamp Act?

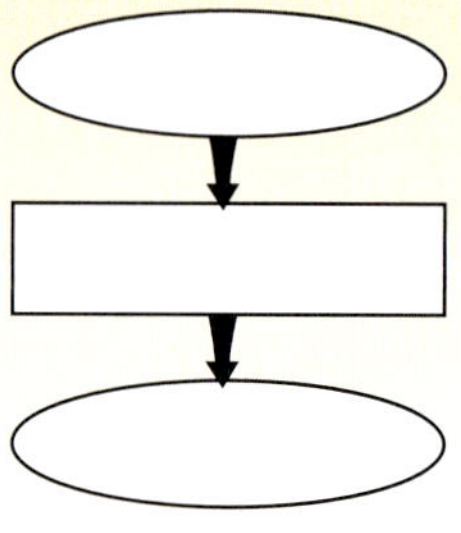

Build Your Skills

Social Studies Skill

READ TABLES AND CHARTS

Tables and charts are useful tools because they can present a large amount of information in a small and organized space. The material is sorted into columns and rows, so finding one piece of information is easy. Tables and charts also let you compare information in different categories. One common type of chart is a class schedule, which lists subjects, times, rooms, and teachers.

When you read about history, you will often come across tables and charts. Tables and charts may or may not have a title. The information may be sorted by place, date, event, or idea.

Here's How

Follow these steps to read a table or chart.

1. Read the title of the table or chart to find out the topic.

2. Read the headings to find out how the information is organized.

3. Study the information in the table or chart. Look for patterns or comparisons.

Here's Why

You have just read about laws passed by the British government that affected the colonies. Suppose you had to write a paragraph about the colonists' responses to these laws. Reading a table that showed their responses would help you.

Practice the Skill

Read the table. Then, answer the following questions.

1. What kinds of information are given in the table?

2. For which two acts was the response in the colonies the same?

3. How was the response to the Sugar Act different from the response to the Stamp Act?

DATE	ACTION BY PARLIAMENT	RESPONSE IN COLONIES
1763	Proclamation of 1763	Colonists ignore the boundary.
1764	Sugar Act	No widespread resistance
1765	Quartering Act	No widespread resistance
1765	Stamp Act	Riots, demand for repeal

Extend the Skill

Write a paragraph about the colonists' responses to the acts of Parliament listed in the table.

Apply the Skill

Study the charts and tables you find in the rest of the chapter, including in the Chapter Review. For example, read the table on page 146 of Section II. Compare and contrast the effects of the acts of Parliament on the colonies.

II Growing Tensions

Terms to Know

resolution a formal statement of opinion

massacre the brutal killing of a large number of people

Main Ideas

A. The Townshend Acts, which introduced new taxes on British goods shipped to the colonies, were resisted by the colonists.

B. Boston, Massachusetts, became the center of protest against British authority.

SEQUENCE OF EVENTS
By noticing the order in which events take place, you can better understand the information you read. As you read this section, keep track of the sequence, or order, of events.

A. More Taxes on the Colonists

In 1767, just a year after Parliament repealed the Stamp Act, it passed another set of taxes and rules. They were named the Townshend Acts, after the government official who helped to develop them. How would colonists react to these new laws?

The Townshend Acts

The Townshend Acts, like the Stamp Act, were passed in order to bring in money from the colonies. This money would be used to pay off Great Britain's war debt. These acts placed duties, or import taxes, on common products made in Britain and shipped to the colonies. Glass, paint, lead, paper, and tea were among the products that were taxed.

Tea was a popular drink among American colonists.

In addition, Parliament created a new police force, the Board of Customs Commissioners. This board strictly enforced trade laws and collected taxes. Parliament also set up new courts. In these courts, British judges, instead of colonial juries, decided the fate of colonists accused of breaking the trade laws. Colonists objected because the courts interfered with their right to govern themselves.

Many Forms of Protest

One well-known colonist, John Dickinson, wrote a series of newspaper essays called "Letters of a Pennsylvania Farmer." He argued that only colonial legislatures had the right to tax the colonists. These essays convinced many colonists to resist the new laws.

In Boston, Massachusetts, Samuel Adams and James Otis, leaders of the Sons of Liberty, led large demonstrations. Throughout the colonies, new boycotts began.

In 1768, customs officers in Boston seized a ship owned by local merchant John Hancock, who was accused of smuggling, or secretly importing goods without paying the import taxes. A group of angry Bostonians attacked the officers and forced them to leave. Parliament responded by sending troops to Boston. The troops were there to keep order and force the colonists to obey the laws.

In 1769, the colonial legislature in Virginia issued **resolutions**, or formal statements of opinion, stating that only it had the right to tax its citizens. In response to these resolutions, the British government ordered the assembly to be dissolved, or ended.

 **What taxes and laws did the Townshend Acts put into effect?**

B. Resistance in Boston

People in Boston resented having troops in their city controlling their activities. They felt that using an army in this way took away their basic liberties. To show their unhappiness, some Bostonians often annoyed and insulted the soldiers.

The Boston Massacre

On March 5, 1770, a crowd gathered at the headquarters of the customs officers. The colonists began teasing the British soldiers stationed there. Some colonists threw snowballs and rocks at the troops. Others called them names, such as "lobsterbacks," making fun of their long red jackets. There are conflicting reports about what happened next. One officer reported the following account:

> "One of the soldiers having received a severe blow with a stick, stepped a little on one side and instantly fired [his gun]. . . . On this a general attack was made on the men. . . . Instantly three or four of the soldiers fired, one after another, and directly after three more in the same confusion and hurry. The mob then ran away, except three unhappy men who instantly expired [died]."

Spotlight on Culture

In Boston, the Sons of Liberty were not the only people speaking out against unjust British laws. Although women were not encouraged to express their political views in public, Mercy Otis Warren was an exception.

Warren was the sister of James Otis, a leader of the Sons of Liberty. Her books and poems spoke out against British policies and encouraged people to think about the important issues of the day.

ANALYZE PRIMARY SOURCES

DOCUMENT-BASED QUESTION According to this account, what caused one of the soldiers to fire into the crowd?

This engraving of the Boston Massacre by colonist Paul Revere is a pro-colonial version of the event. The print was meant to encourage anti-British sentiment in the colonies.

In fact, five colonists were killed. One of them was Crispus Attucks, a runaway slave who worked as a sailor. This battle became known as the Boston Massacre. A **massacre** is the merciless killing of many people. Colonist Samuel Adams made sure that everybody heard about the Boston Massacre. His goal was to rally Americans to support the cause of liberty.

In 1772, Sam Adams called on Bostonians to form the Committee of Correspondence. Through letters and pamphlets, the committee kept people in Massachusetts informed about British actions in Boston. The letters also suggested ways of dealing with these actions. Similar committees sprang up in other colonies. This communication network played a key role in uniting the colonies against Great Britain.

The Boston Tea Party

Soon after the Boston Massacre, Parliament repealed most of the Townshend taxes. Only the tax on tea remained. Then, in 1773, Parliament passed the Tea Act. This act made it much cheaper for colonists to buy tea directly from the British East India Company than from colonial merchants.

The Tea Act angered colonial merchants because they would lose business. It also angered colonial consumers. Colonists everywhere joined in a tea boycott.

In November 1773, ships loaded with British tea arrived in New York, Philadelphia, and Boston. The colonists refused to unload it. In New York and Philadelphia, the ships were forced to return to Great Britain. In Boston, after the British governor there refused to let the ships leave the harbor, some colonists went a step further. On the night of December 16, 1773, members of the Sons of Liberty went aboard the ships that held the tea. Dressed as Mohawk Indians in order to disguise themselves, they threw more than 300 chests of tea into the harbor. The Boston Tea Party, as it became known, outraged British officials. Many colonists were upset as well. They felt that the Sons of Liberty had gone too far by destroying British goods.

The Boston Tea Party was one of the most daring protests made by the colonists.

The Intolerable Acts

The British government was determined to see that Boston's rebellious spirit did not spread to other colonies. Early in 1774, Parliament passed a series of laws called the Coercive Acts. *Coercive* means "forceful or threatening." These laws were meant to punish the people of Boston.

They Made History

Samuel Adams 1722–1803

Samuel Adams was one of the first American leaders to assert that independence should be the goal of the colonies. Adams was an extremely skillful organizer. He took a leading role in planning the Stamp Act protests and the Boston Tea Party. He worked hard to see that people who were in favor of independence were elected to colonial legislatures. He also wrote countless newspaper letters and essays that fanned the flames of protest. Many people in Boston and elsewhere in the colonies believed that Adams's ideas were dangerous to the colonies. However, his tireless efforts eventually convinced many colonists to support the cause of freedom.

Samuel Adams was one of the first colonial leaders in the fight for independence.

Critical Thinking What other skills besides organizational skills do you think Samuel Adams possessed?

Effects of Parliament Acts

ACT	EFFECT
Sugar Act (1764)	Placed tax on non-British imports of sugar, cloth, and coffee
Stamp Act (1765)	Placed tax on all printed items
Townshend Acts (1767)	Placed tax on imports of glass, paint, paper, lead, and tea from Britain
Intolerable Acts (1774)	Closed the port of Boston to trade; forbade town meetings in Massachusetts without approval
Quebec Act (1774)	Made western lands north of the Ohio River a part of the British colony of Quebec

Chart Check

Which act increased the price colonists paid for newspapers?

In the colonies, these laws were known as the Intolerable Acts, which did the following:

1. They closed the port of Boston to trade until the colony paid for the destroyed tea. This law hurt Boston's economy.
2. They forbade town meetings in Massachusetts without approval.
3. They let British officials located in Massachusetts, who were accused of crimes, be tried in Britain or in other colonies.
4. They established a new Quartering Act, after the original one had expired in 1770.

The Intolerable Acts were meant to be a warning to other colonies, but they only sparked new protests. In addition, many colonial assemblies passed resolutions in support of Massachusetts.

In June 1774, Parliament also passed the Quebec Act, which gave western lands north of the Ohio River to the British colony of Quebec. This law sealed off those western lands from further settlement by American colonists.

What was the reason for the Boston Tea Party?

Review

Review History

A. What forms of resistance did the Townshend Acts bring about?
B. How did the Boston Massacre affect other colonies?

Define Terms to Know

Provide a definition for each of the following terms.
resolution, massacre

Critical Thinking

Which part of the Intolerable Acts do you think was the most severe for the colonists?

Write About History

Write a paragraph expressing your opinion of the colonists' stand against the Tea Act.

Get Organized

CAUSE-AND-EFFECT CHAIN

Think about the main events in this section. Use a cause-and-effect chain to show the cause and effect of an event. For example, what was a cause and an effect of the Boston Massacre or the Boston Tea Party?

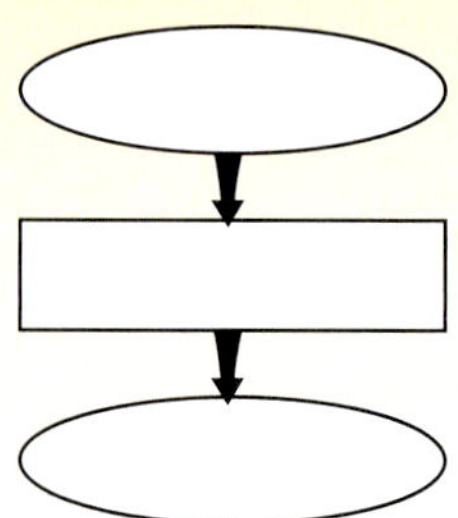

III A Declaration of Independence

Terms to Know

petition a formal written request

minuteman a member of the colonial militia

Patriot a person who supported independence from Great Britain

traitor a person who acts against his or her country

declaration a formal statement

Main Ideas

A. At the First Continental Congress, the colonies joined together against British authority.

B. The battles of Lexington and Concord started a war with Great Britain.

C. After attempts to settle differences with Great Britain, the colonists finally chose independence.

ARGUMENTS AND EVIDENCE

The colonists' decision to become independent from Great Britain was not made lightly. As you read this section, ask yourself: What arguments and evidence, or facts, did the colonists use to make their decision?

A. The Colonists Unite

People from the other colonies sympathized with colonists in Massachusetts and were angry with the British government for what it had done. The Committees of Correspondence quickly spread the news about the Intolerable Acts. In September 1774, colonial leaders called for a meeting in Philadelphia, Pennsylvania, to discuss what to do next.

The First Continental Congress

The meeting, called the Continental Congress, included delegates from all of the colonies except Georgia. Among the delegates were Samuel Adams and John Adams of Massachusetts and George Washington and Patrick Henry of Virginia. The goal of the meeting was to decide how the colonists should respond to the Intolerable Acts. One idea was a plan of union similar to the one offered many years before by Benjamin Franklin. The delegates discussed but rejected this idea. After several weeks, they agreed to send a **petition**, or written request, to the British government.

Do You Remember?

In Chapter 6, you learned that Benjamin Franklin proposed the Albany Plan of Union in 1754, but colonists and the British government rejected it. Franklin thought that the colonies would be stronger if they united.

An Appeal to the King

In the petition, the delegates explained that the colonies had disobeyed British laws because they felt that Parliament had been taxing them illegally. The delegates also demanded that the Intolerable Acts be repealed. They decided they would stop buying or selling all British products if Parliament did not repeal the laws.

George III, king of Great Britain

Another concern was that British troops in Boston might attack the colonies. To prepare for a possible war, the delegates urged the colonies to prepare their militias for battle. Then, the delegates agreed to meet again, if necessary, the following spring.

Most colonists still thought of themselves as loyal subjects of the British king. They felt that their quarrel was not with George III but with Parliament. Thus, the delegates addressed their petition to King George. They hoped that he would see their point of view.

★ **What was the main goal of the Continental Congress?**

B. The Crisis Deepens

In London, George III was not pleased with the petition from the Continental Congress. He demanded that Parliament stop all colonial resistance. However, throughout the colonies, people were calling for freedom. In March 1775, Patrick Henry, a delegate at the Continental Congress and a member of the Virginia House of Burgesses, addressed the other Virginia house members: "I know not what course others may take; but as for me, give me liberty or give me death!" The stage was set for war.

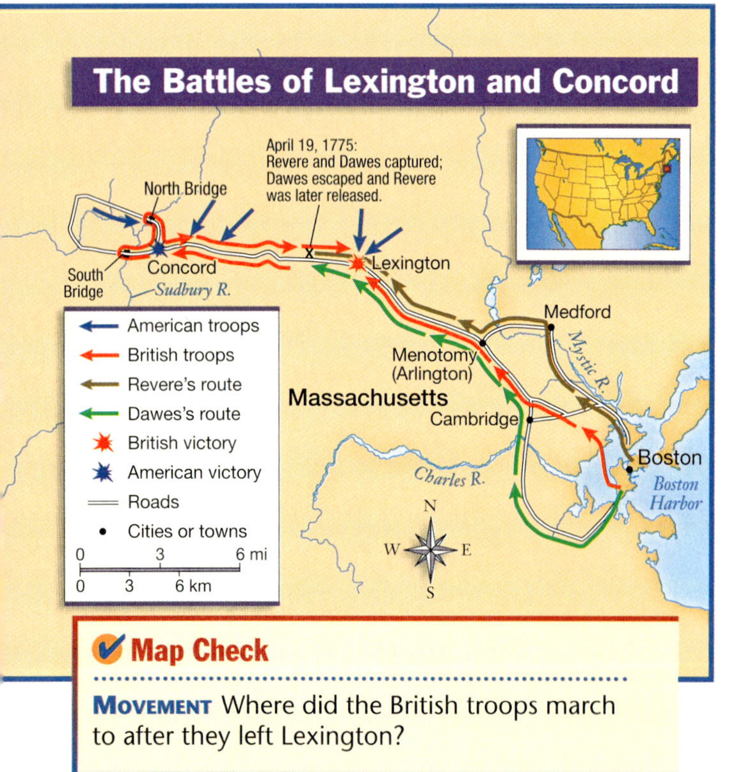

Map Check

MOVEMENT Where did the British troops march to after they left Lexington?

Lexington and Concord

In Massachusetts, people had been preparing for war. Members of the militia had been training and gathering weapons and gunpowder. They called themselves **minutemen** because they hoped to be ready in a minute's notice.

As the minutemen trained, the number of British soldiers in Boston grew to 4,000. On the night of April 18, 1775, British General Thomas Gage ordered about 700 soldiers to march to Concord, a small town northwest of Boston, and seize American military supplies there.

Two riders on horseback, Paul Revere and William Dawes, set out to alert people in Concord and Lexington, a town on the road to Concord, that British soldiers were on the way. These riders warned, "The British are coming!" Revere and Dawes were captured by a British patrol between Lexington and Concord, but Dr. Samuel Prescott carried the message to Concord. By the next morning, about 70 minutemen were ready and waiting at Lexington when the British troops arrived.

The British commander demanded that the minutemen leave. As they began to do so, a shot rang out. Immediately, British soldiers fired into the crowd of minutemen. Eight were killed, and ten more were wounded.

The British troops then marched on to Concord. Outside of town, a second battle took place. This time, 14 British soldiers were killed, and the British troops retreated.

As the British troops made their way back to Boston, they encountered more minutemen who fired at them. In all, the British lost more than 250 men, and the colonists lost almost 100 men. The incidents at Lexington and Concord were the first battles in a war with Great Britain. The events of April 19, 1775, are still recalled each year in Massachusetts and Maine on Patriot's Day. A **Patriot** was a person who supported independence from Great Britain.

The Battle of Bunker Hill

After the battles of Lexington and Concord, British forces remained in Boston. Then, on June 17, 1775, the first major battle of the war took place. Colonial soldiers positioned themselves on Bunker Hill and Breed's Hill, outside of Boston. This location allowed them to overlook the city and prepare for an attack.

The British soldiers attacked Breed's Hill. The British charged twice, and twice the Americans pushed them back. The colonists had no ammunition to waste, so one of the American commanders cried out, "Don't fire until you see the whites of their eyes!" The colonists followed the order, firing only when the British soldiers came close. By the third attack, the Americans had run out of gunpowder and could only throw rocks at their attackers.

The British won what is called the Battle of Bunker Hill, although it was fought on Breed's Hill. However, they had lost many more soldiers than the Americans had. One British officer remarked after the battle, "A few such victories will ruin our army." The American soldiers were mostly farmers and merchants, among whom were free Africans. The Battle of Bunker Hill convinced many Americans that they did stand a chance against the British army.

★ **What happened at the Battle of Bunker Hill?**

Colonial soldiers fought British soldiers at the Battle of Bunker Hill.

C. The Choice of Independence

The Second Continental Congress met in Philadelphia on May 10, 1775. Many of the same delegates from the First Continental Congress returned. Among the new delegates were Thomas Jefferson of Virginia and Benjamin Franklin of Pennsylvania. John Hancock of Massachusetts was selected as president of the Congress.

Thomas Paine's words in *Common Sense* convinced many people that the American colonies should break free from Great Britain.

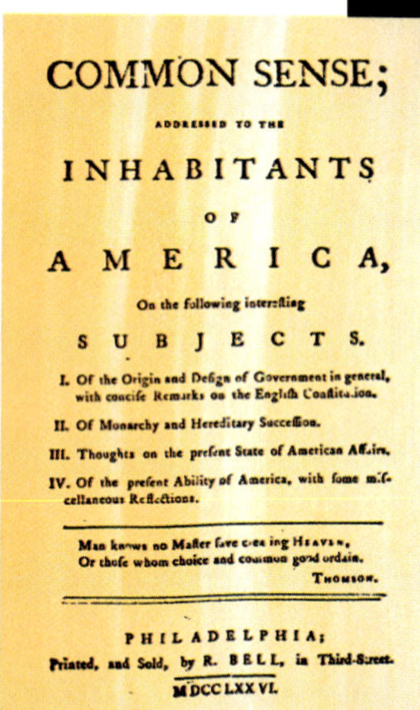

COMMON SENSE;

ADDRESSED TO THE

INHABITANTS

OF

AMERICA,

On the following interesting

SUBJECTS.

I. Of the Origin and Design of Government in general, with concise Remarks on the English Constitution.

II. Of Monarchy and Hereditary Succession.

III. Thoughts on the present State of American Affairs.

IV. Of the present Ability of America, with some miscellaneous Reflections.

Man knows no Master save creating Heaven,
Or those whom choice and common good ordain.
Thomson.

PHILADELPHIA;
Printed, and Sold, by R. BELL, in Third-Street.
MDCCLXXVI.

The Second Continental Congress

The Congress took steps for the defense of the colonies. It set up the Continental Army to fight against Britain. The delegates named George Washington of Virginia as the army's commander in chief.

The delegates decided to send another petition to King George. Known as the Olive Branch Petition, this document stated that the colonies were still loyal to the king. They pleaded with him to stop the fighting so that an agreement could be reached. However, they told King George that they would fight for their rights if necessary.

King George ignored the petition. He said that the colonists were **traitors**, or people who act against their country. He sent more troops to America to put down the colonists' rebellion.

Common Sense

By January 1776, more colonists were beginning to support the idea of independence from Great Britain. They felt that it was their only choice. These feelings were strengthened by a pamphlet called *Common Sense*, written by Thomas Paine, a magazine editor from Philadelphia.

Paine argued that declaring independence from Great Britain was common sense. He claimed that King George, like many other kings throughout history, had become a tyrant, or unjust ruler. He said,

> "O ye that love mankind! Ye that dare oppose, not only the tyranny, but the tyrant, stand forth!"

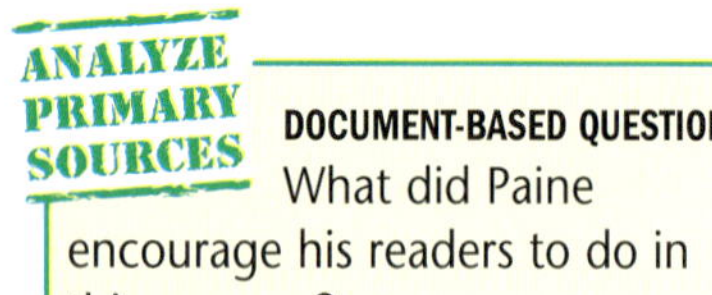

DOCUMENT-BASED QUESTION What did Paine encourage his readers to do in this passage?

Common Sense was read by hundreds of thousands of colonists. It helped many Americans to see the importance of fighting in order to achieve independence. They realized that they were not only fighting to protect their rights as British citizens; they were also fighting for liberty.

Declaring Independence

On June 7, 1776, Richard Henry Lee of Virginia made a bold proposal to the Second Continental Congress. He stated, "These United Colonies are, and of right ought to be, free and independent states." The delegates debated the idea for weeks. Finally, they agreed. They would declare their independence from Great Britain.

Thomas Jefferson was asked to draft a **declaration**, or formal statement, justifying independence. He drew on the ideas of English philosopher John Locke when writing the Declaration of Independence. He wrote the first draft in two to three days. The delegates worked carefully on the wording of the declaration. One of the most important ideas in this document is that people have natural rights, or rights as human beings, such as "life, liberty, and the pursuit of happiness."

You can read the Declaration of Independence on pages 157–161.

On July 4, 1776, most of the members of the Continental Congress approved and signed the Declaration of Independence. Four days later, a printed copy of the Declaration was read aloud to a cheering crowd in Philadelphia as the Liberty Bell was rung. The Declaration of Independence is still considered one of the most stirring statements in defense of liberty ever written. Every year on July 4, also called Independence Day, Americans celebrate the beginning of the country's independence.

 **How did King George respond to the Olive Branch Petition?**

Review History

A. What actions did the colonies take at the First Continental Congress?

B. How did fighting between Britain and the colonies begin?

C. Why did the colonists finally decide to declare independence from Great Britain?

Define Terms to Know

Provide a definition for each of the following terms.
petition, minuteman, Patriot, traitor, declaration

Critical Thinking

Why do you think that it took the delegates so long to declare independence from Great Britain?

Write About Government

From the point of view of a delegate at the Second Continental Congress, write a speech explaining the pros and cons of declaring independence.

Get Organized

CAUSE-AND-EFFECT CHAIN

Think about the main events in this section. Use a cause-and-effect chain to show the cause and effect of an event. For example, what was a cause and an effect of the colonists' decision to declare independence?

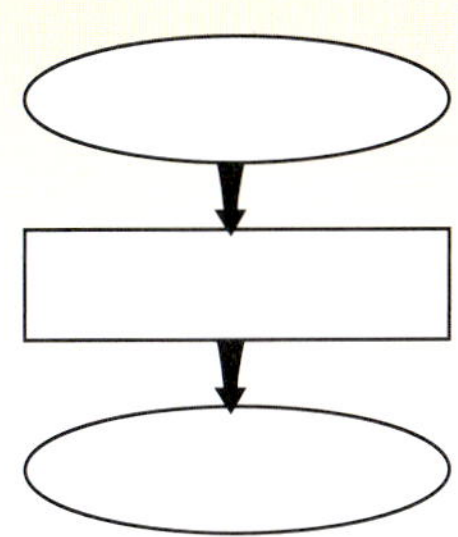

PAST *to* PRESENT

Medicine

At the same time that colonists were fighting for independence, they were also fighting such diseases as malaria and yellow fever. In the mid-to-late 1700s, little was known about the causes and treatments of most diseases. Few doctors had medical degrees. Deadly diseases spread rapidly through entire towns and cities. To fight diseases, doctors used treatments such as bloodletting, leeching, and even cutting off limbs.

The field of medicine became more scientific in the 1800s. Not until the 1900s, however, were drugs found to effectively fight major diseases. Today, new drugs and technologies are leading to constant improvements in medicine.

1 In the 1700s, bloodletting (above), or cutting skin to let blood come out, was supposed to remove "bad blood."

2 Leeching (below) was another method for drawing blood. Leeches, a type of worm that removes blood, were placed on the skin. Leeching was often harmful and could cause death.

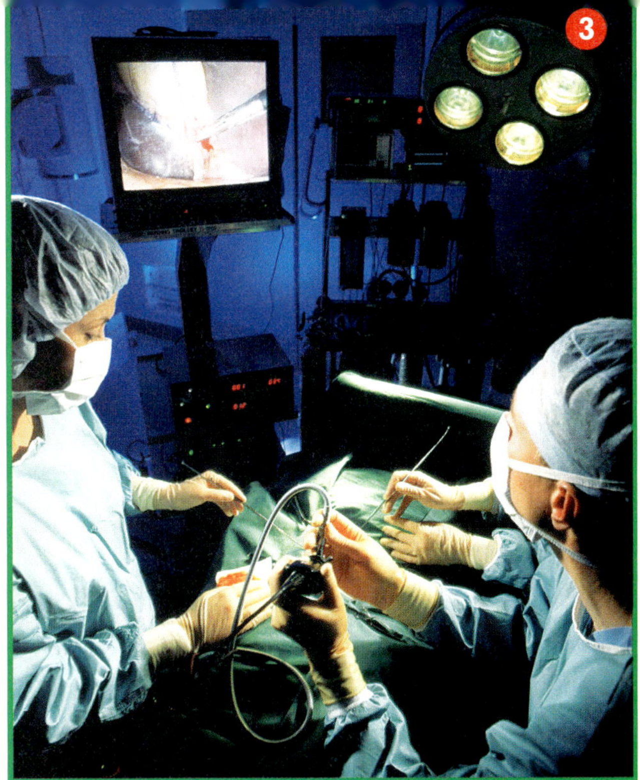

Today, the field of medicine has progressed greatly. This surgeon is using an optical-fiber viewing tube to see inside the body.

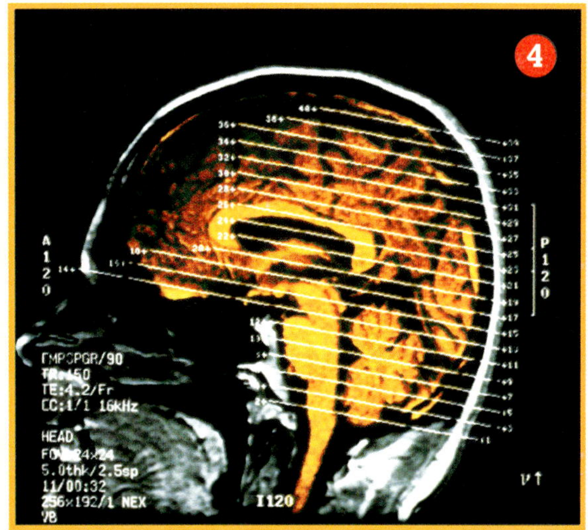

The development of magnetic resonance imaging (MRI) allows doctors to view images of any part of the human body from any angle without performing surgery.

Disease	Effects	Treatment	
		1700s	Today
Smallpox	Red spots (pocks) on the skin that leave scars; fever; death	Placing tiny bit of serum from an infected pock under skin of a healthy person, using a quill	Vaccine
Typhus	Chills, fever, headache, crust on tongue, dark red rash, death	Bloodletting	Experimental vaccine
Malaria	Chills and high fever, death	Drinking quinine made from the bark of a South American tree	Drugs such as chloroquine; no vaccine available yet
Yellow fever	Vomiting, yellowish color to skin, fever, death	Chewing garlic, sprinkling vinegar in a bowl, holding tobacco in the mouth	Vaccine

This chart lists some diseases, their effects, and treatments used in the 1700s and today.

Hands-on Activity

Diseases such as cancer and heart disease are a problem in today's society. How are these diseases treated? How might they be prevented? Make a poster to inform others about a disease that has not yet been cured. Include its cause, its symptoms, and its prevention or treatment. Use resources found on www.gfamericanhistory.com.

CHAPTER 7 Review

Chapter Summary

In your notebook, complete the following outline. Then, use your outline to write a brief summary of the chapter.

Road to Independence

I. Resistance to British Taxes
  A. Controls After the War
  B.
  C.
II. Growing Tensions
  A.
  B.
III. A Declaration of Independence
  A.
  B.
  C.

Interpret the Timeline

Use the timeline on pages 134–135 to answer the following questions.

1. How long after the Boston Tea Party did the colonies declare independence?
2. **Critical Thinking** Which events involve the colonists' reaction to British authority?

Use Terms to Know

Select the term that best completes each sentence.

boycott	petition	resolution
declaration	repeal	revenue

1. The British government taxed the colonists to raise ________.
2. The colonists began a ________ of British products to protest the Stamp Act.
3. The colonists wanted the British government to ________ the Intolerable Acts.
4. The colonists sent a ________ to King George III, asking him to stop the fighting in the colonies.
5. Thomas Jefferson drafted a ________ containing the colonists' reasons for independence from Great Britain.
6. A colonial ________ stated that only a colonial legislature had the right to tax its citizens.

Check Your Understanding

1. **Explain** why Parliament passed the Sugar Act and the Stamp Act.
2. **Summarize** the slogan "No taxation without representation."
3. **Identify** two important examples of colonial resistance that took place in Boston.
4. **Discuss** how the Intolerable Acts tightened control of colonists in Boston.
5. **Describe** the role of minutemen in the colonies' struggle with Great Britain.
6. **Explain** how Thomas Paine's pamphlet *Common Sense* influenced many Americans.

Critical Thinking

1. **Analyze Primary Sources** Do you think that the handbill message on page 139 was effective? Explain.
2. **Analyze Primary Sources** Do you think that the account by a British officer on page 143 is a reliable description of the event? Explain.
3. **Draw Conclusions** Do you think that the colonists' break from Great Britain could have been avoided? Explain.

Put Your Skills to Work

READ TABLES AND CHARTS

You have learned that reading tables and charts can help you to locate and compare information. Read the table below. It does not have a title, but some charts and tables do. Then, answer the following questions.

1. What was the role of Samuel Adams in the independence movement?
2. Which people listed in the table were authors?

NAME	ROLE
Samuel Adams	Leader of the Boston Sons of Liberty
John Hancock	President of the Second Continental Congress
Patrick Henry	Virginia legislator who spoke out against the Stamp Act
Thomas Jefferson	Primary author of the Declaration of Independence
Thomas Paine	Author of *Common Sense*
Mercy Otis Warren	Author of political plays, essays, and poems

In Your Own Words

JOURNAL WRITING

You have read about many events that led to the writing of the Declaration of Independence. Which event(s) would convince you to support independence? Write a journal entry that answers this question. Be sure to give reasons for your choice.

Net Work

INTERNET ACTIVITY

Working with a partner, use the Internet as a resource to research one or more of the delegates at the Second Continental Congress, such as Benjamin Franklin, Thomas Jefferson, and John Adams. Then, use your research to help you write a short report about the delegate or delegates you researched.

For help in starting this activity, visit the following Web site: www.gfamericanhistory.com.

Look Ahead

In the next chapter, learn about the colonies' war with Great Britain.

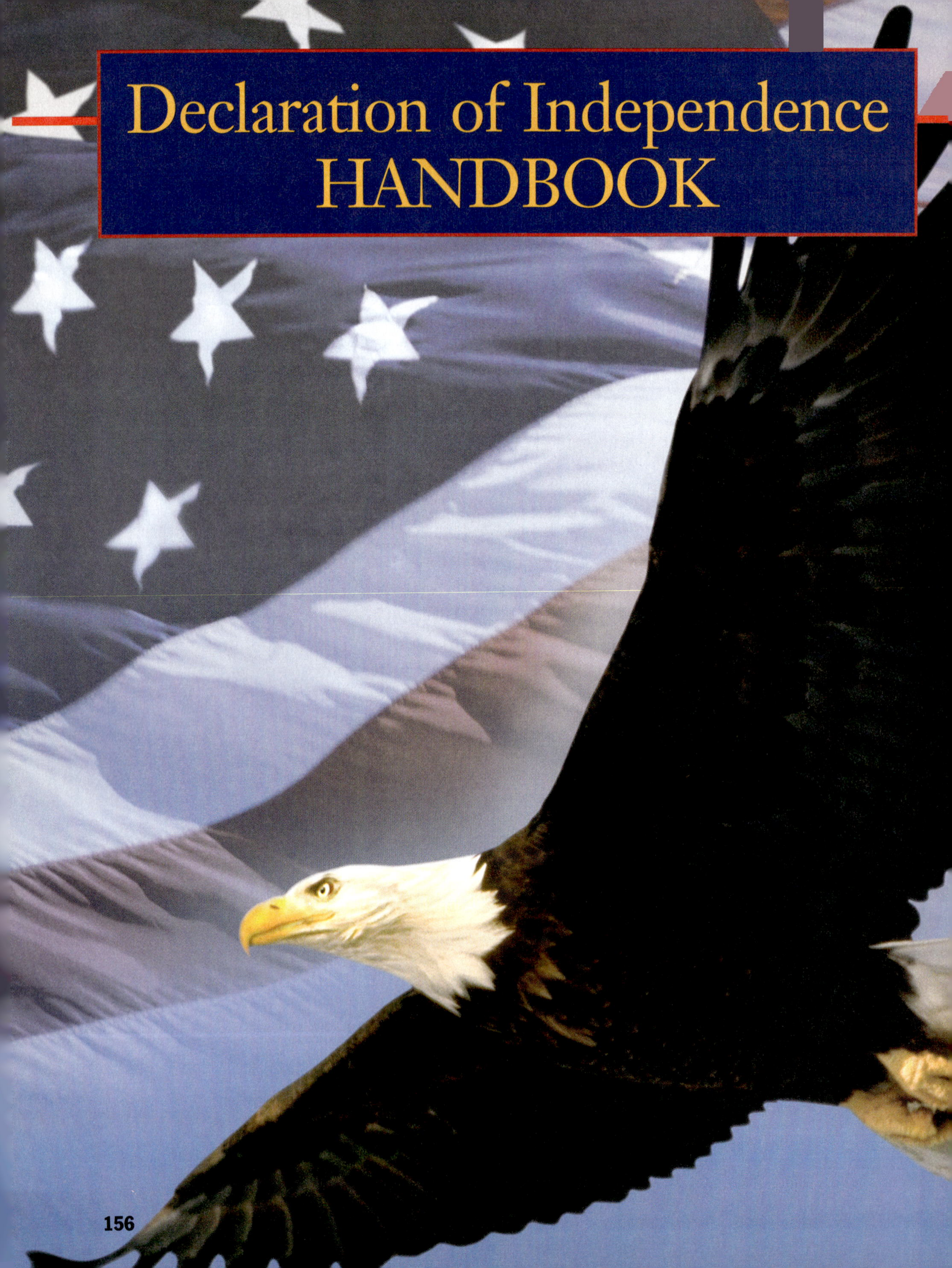

Declaration of Independence HANDBOOK

Document Dictionary

endowed provided

unalienable unable to be taken away

prudence care

The text of the Declaration of Independence, using modern spelling, punctuation, and capitalization appears on the following pages. The titles in red and notes in the margin have been added to help you understand the document.

Declaration of Independence

Action of the Second Continental Congress, July 4, 1776

Preamble

When in the course of human events, it becomes necessary for one people to dissolve the political bands which have connected them with another, and to assume among the powers of the earth, the separate and equal station to which the laws of nature and of nature's God entitle them, a decent respect to the opinions of mankind requires that they should declare the causes which impel them to the separation.

A New Theory of Government

We hold these truths to be self-evident, that all men are created equal, that they are **endowed** by their Creator with certain **unalienable** rights, that among these are life, liberty, and the pursuit of happiness. That to secure these rights, governments are instituted among men, deriving their just powers from the consent of the governed, that whenever any form of government becomes destructive of these ends, it is the right of the people to alter or to abolish it, and to institute new government, laying its foundation on such principles, and organizing its powers in such form, as to them shall seem most likely to effect their safety and happiness. **Prudence**, indeed, will dictate that governments long established should not be changed for light and transient causes; and accordingly all experience hath shown, that mankind are more disposed to suffer, while evils are sufferable, than to right themselves by abolishing the forms to which they are accustomed. But when a long train of abuses and

The Main Idea

A New Theory of Government

The colonists believed that humans are created equal and have equal rights to life, liberty, and the pursuit of happiness. Governments are formed to protect these rights. When a government threatens or takes away these rights, then the people have the right to change or do away with that government.

usurpations, pursuing invariably the same object, evinces a design to reduce them under absolute **despotism**, it is their right, it is their duty, to throw off such government, and to provide new guards for their future security.

Such has been the patient sufferance of these colonies; and such is now the necessity which constrains them to alter their former systems of government. The history of the present king of Great Britain is a history of repeated injuries and usurpations, all having in direct object the establishment of an absolute tyranny over these states. To prove this, let facts be submitted to a candid world.

Abuses by King George III

He has refused his **assent** to laws, the most wholesome and necessary for the public good.

He has forbidden his governors to pass laws of immediate and pressing importance, unless suspended in their operation till his assent should be obtained; and when so suspended, he has utterly neglected to attend to them.

He has refused to pass other laws for the accommodation of large districts of people, unless those people would **relinquish** the right of representation in the legislature, a right inestimable to them, and formidable to tyrants only.

He has called together legislative bodies at places unusual, uncomfortable, and distant from the depository of their public records, for the sole purpose of fatiguing them into compliance with his measures.

He has **dissolved** representative houses repeatedly, for opposing with manly firmness his invasions on the rights of the people.

He has refused for a long time, after such dissolutions, to cause others to be elected; whereby the legislative powers, incapable of **annihilation**, have returned to the people at large for their exercise; the state remaining in the meantime exposed to all the dangers of invasion from without, and **convulsions** within.

He has endeavored to prevent the population of these states; for

Document Dictionary

usurpation taking power and rights unjustly

despotism rule by a tyrant with unlimited power

assent agreement

relinquish give up

dissolved broken up

annihilation destruction

convulsion a disturbance or riot

The Main Idea

Abuses by King George III

This part of the Declaration lists offenses by the British king and Parliament against the colonies. This list explains why the colonists wanted to be free from Britain. It includes some of the following:

- ignoring laws that the colonies needed
- refusing to set up courts in the colonies
- refusing to let settlers move west
- housing troops in colonists' homes
- blocking trade with other countries

that purpose obstructing the laws for naturalization of foreigners; refusing to pass others to encourage their migrations hither, and raising the conditions of new appropriations of lands.

He has obstructed the administration of justice, by refusing his assent to laws for establishing judiciary powers.

He has made judges dependent on his will alone, for the tenure of their offices, and the amount and payment of their salaries.

He has erected a multitude of new offices, and sent hither swarms of officers to harass our people, and eat out their substance.

He has kept among us, in times of peace, standing armies, without the consent of our legislatures.

He has affected to render the military independent of and superior to the civil power.

He has combined with others to subject us to a jurisdiction foreign to our constitution, and unacknowledged by our laws; giving his assent to their acts of pretended legislation:

For quartering large bodies of armed troops among us;

For protecting them, by a mock trial, from punishment for any murders which they should commit on the inhabitants of these states;

For cutting off our trade with all parts of the world;

For imposing taxes on us without our consent;

For depriving us, in many cases, of the benefits of trial by jury;

For transporting us beyond seas to be tried for pretended offenses;

For abolishing the free system of English laws in a neighbouring province, establishing therein an arbitrary government, and enlarging its boundaries, so as to render it at once an example and fit instrument for introducing the same absolute rule into these colonies;

For taking away our charters, abolishing our most valuable laws, and altering fundamentally the forms of our governments;

For suspending our own legislatures, and declaring themselves invested with power to legislate for us in all cases whatsoever.

Acts of War Against the Colonies

He has **abdicated** government here, by declaring us out of his protection and waging war against us.

He has plundered our seas, ravaged our coasts, burnt our towns, and destroyed the lives of our people.

He is, at this time, transporting large armies of foreign mercenaries to compleat the works of death, desolation, and tyranny, already begun with circumstances of cruelty and **perfidy**, scarcely paralleled in the most barbarous ages, and totally unworthy the head of a civilized nation.

He has **constrained** our fellow citizens taken captive on the high seas to bear arms against their country, to become the executioners of their friends and brethren, or to fall themselves by their hands.

He has excited domestic **insurrections** amongst us, and has endeavored to bring on the inhabitants of our frontiers, the merciless Indian savages, whose known rule of warfare, is an undistinguished destruction, of all ages, sexes, and conditions.

Taking Action

In every stage of these oppressions we have petitioned for **redress** in the most humble terms: Our repeated petitions have been answered only by repeated injury. A prince, whose character is thus marked by every act which may define a tyrant, is unfit to be the ruler of a free people.

Nor have we been wanting in attentions to our British brethren. We have warned them from time to time of attempts by their legislature to extend an **unwarrantable** jurisdiction over us. We have reminded them of the circumstances of our emigration and settlement here. We have appealed to their native justice and **magnanimity**, and we have conjured them by the ties of our common kindred to disavow these usurpations,

Document Dictionary

abdicated given up
perfidy dishonesty
constrained forced
insurrection rebellion
redress relief
unwarrantable unforgivable
magnanimity kindness
consanguinity close relationship
levy make

The Main Idea

Acts of War Against the Colonies

The colonists provided examples of how the British committed acts of war against the colonies:

- attacking ships and ports
- burning their towns
- kidnapping American sailors and forcing them to fight against the colonies
- urging people to rebel against colonial governments

The Main Idea

Taking Action

The American colonists asked the king and British citizens for justice, but they received only unfair treatment. The Declaration states boldly that a king who allows this abuse is not fit to rule a free country.

which, would inevitably interrupt our connections and correspondence. They too have been deaf to the voice of justice and of **consanguinity**. We must, therefore, acquiesce in the necessity, which denounces our separation, and hold them, as we hold the rest of mankind, enemies in war, in peace, friends.

A Proclamation of Independence

We, therefore, the representatives of the United States of America, in General Congress, assembled, appealing to the Supreme Judge of the world for the rectitude of our intentions, do, in the name, and by authority of the good people of these colonies, solemnly publish and declare, that these united colonies are, and of right ought to be, free and independent states; that they are absolved from all allegiance to the British Crown, and that all political connection between them and the state of Great Britain, is and ought to be totally dissolved; and that as free and independent states, they have full power to **levy** war, conclude peace, contract alliances, establish commerce, and to do all other acts and things which independent states may of right do. And for the support of this declaration, with a firm reliance on the protection of Divine Providence, we mutually pledge to each other our lives, our fortunes, and our sacred honor.

Signed by John Hancock of Massachusetts, President of the Congress, and by the fifty-five other Representatives of the thirteen United States of America.

The Main Idea

A Proclamation of Independence

The final paragraph was a formal declaration of independence. It states that the colonies are free, and should be free, from the control of Britain and should have all the rights of an independent nation. These rights include the rights to

- make war and peace.
- create treaties with other nations.
- regulate trade.

DOCUMENT-BASED QUESTIONS

1. What is the purpose of the Declaration of Independence as stated in the Preamble?
2. According to the Declaration, when are people allowed to change their government?
3. How were the colonists' unalienable rights taken away by King George III?
4. How do you think the signers of the Declaration felt about making a formal declaration of independence from Britain?
5. How did the British citizens react when the American colonists asked them for help?
6. **Critical Thinking** In what ways would declaring formal independence benefit the American colonies?

CHAPTER 8

The Revolutionary War 1776–1783

I. The Early Years of War
II. The War Expands
III. An Independent Nation

By the winter of 1777–1778, the Americans had lost several key battles in the war against Great Britain. George Washington's troops were camped at Valley Forge, Pennsylvania. There, they faced a cold and snowy winter living in tents and unheated huts without enough clothing, blankets, or food. Dr. Albigence Waldo, a surgeon at Valley Forge, wrote in his diary:

> "Dec 14th Poor food—hard lodging—cold weather—fatigue —nasty clothes—nasty cookery—vomit half my time . . . I can't endure it—why are we sent here to starve and freeze."

Washington begged the Second Continental Congress to send supplies, but none came. He spoke to his troops, telling them that future generations depended on their courage. Though hungry and cold, the men began to train. By spring they were ready to fight again.

Washington's army cot

U.S. Events

1776
Americans win at Trenton, New Jersey.
Second Continental Congress adopts Declaration of Independence.

1777
British take Philadelphia, Pennsylvania.
Burgoyne surrenders at Saratoga.

1777–1778
American army winters at Valley Forge.

1778
France enters the Revolutionary War on the American side.

1778–1779
Fighting occurs in western lands.

	1776	1777	1778	1779
U.S. Events	1776	1777	1778	1779
World Events	1776	1777	1778	1779

World Events

1776
Adam Smith publishes free-market theory of economics.

1779
Spain declares war on Great Britain.

VIEW HISTORY This painting by William B.T. Trego shows Commander in Chief George Washington reviewing his troops at Valley Forge, Pennsylvania. Washington slept on an army cot (left) during the hard winter at Valley Forge.

★ **How would you describe the soldiers in this scene?**

Get Organized

CHART

Classifying information can help you understand what you have read. Classifying means putting information into categories. Use a chart as you read Chapter 8. List categories at the top. Add details for each category. Here is an example using this chapter.

Patriot Forces	British Forces
Untrained at first	Well-trained
Familiar with land; fighting for home and family	Outnumbered Patriot forces at first
Included African Americans, Hispanics, some women	Included some Loyalists and Native Americans

1780
British capture Charleston, South Carolina.
Benedict Arnold switches sides to join the British.

1781
French and American forces defeat British at Yorktown, Virginia.
British General Cornwallis surrenders at Yorktown.

1783
Treaty of Paris ends the Revolutionary War.
Washington resigns from the Continental army.

1780 1781 1782 1783

1780 1781 1782 1783

1781
Religious freedom for Christians is granted by Joseph II in Austria.

1783
Montgolfier brothers' hot-air balloon lifts from the ground near Paris.

I The Early Years of War

Terms to Know

Loyalist a person who remained loyal to the British government

mercenary a hired soldier

casualty a person wounded, captured, missing, or killed in battle

Main Ideas

A. While many Americans supported the War for Independence, many remained loyal to Great Britain.

B. After some early setbacks, American troops, under George Washington's leadership, began to achieve some victories.

C. The Continental army suffered from a lack of money and supplies.

Active Reading

DRAW CONCLUSIONS
Drawing a conclusion is like "connecting the dots" to see a picture. Separate facts are given, but you must connect them to form an overall idea. As you read this section, draw conclusions from the information.

A. Choosing Sides

The Revolutionary War was fully underway by the summer of 1776. In this war—sometimes called the War for Independence or the American Revolution—the British soldiers fought for their king. The American soldiers fought for their independence from Great Britain. Sometimes, American families and neighborhoods were divided by loyalties to different sides.

Patriots and Loyalists

The volunteers who fought in the early battles in Massachusetts called themselves Patriots. This term was used to describe Americans who favored independence from Britain. Those who opposed independence and remained loyal to Britain were called **Loyalists**. As many as 40 percent of Americans were Patriots. About 20 percent were Loyalists. The rest took neither side.

A Revolutionary War drum and fife

The Patriot Forces

Many Patriots decided to enlist in, or sign up for, the Continental army. The Second Continental Congress had created the army to fight the British. It had chosen George Washington as commander in chief and had asked that all colonies supply soldiers. To help build the army, Congress offered money and land to those who enlisted.

By the fall of 1776, Washington had a force of almost 20,000 untrained soldiers. Many served only the minimum term of six months, at which time they returned to their home colony.

The Patriot forces were badly outnumbered by the British army at first. However, the American army had some advantages. The Americans were familiar with the land and they were passionate about the cause of freedom. The Americans also had excellent leaders, especially in George Washington. Devoted to his duties, Washington returned home only once during the war. In the most difficult times of the war, respect for Washington kept many soldiers fighting.

The Patriot cause drew support from a wide group of Americans. African Americans—freemen and freed slaves—fought in the North and East. Hispanic troops fought in western battles in the Mississippi River valley and the Gulf of Mexico.

Patriot women also played a role in the Revolutionary War. Many sent food and sewed uniforms for soldiers. Others traveled with the Continental army as nurses and cooks. A few even took part in battles. At home, women often took over the roles of their absent husbands, fathers, and brothers. Women worked in the fields on farms and made decisions in family businesses.

Do You Remember?
In Chapter 7, you learned how many colonial women supported protests against unfair taxation by the British. They served home-grown herb tea and wore clothing of homemade fabrics instead of buying and using British products.

The British Forces

The British army was well-trained and well-armed. In addition, the British navy controlled the seas, moving troops and supplies easily to American ports. The British believed that they could quickly stamp out the American rebellion.

During the war, almost all colonial governors and officials remained loyal to Britain. Some merchants with close ties to Britain supported the British as well. Colonial Loyalists sometimes fought on the British side. However, many were put in prison or had their property taken away by Patriot authorities. As a result, some 100,000 Loyalists fled the colonies during the war.

Most Native American groups fought on the British side in the war. They feared that if the colonists won independence, further migration westward would force them off their lands.

★ **How did African Americans, Hispanics, and women take part in the war?**

African American men joined the fight for American independence.

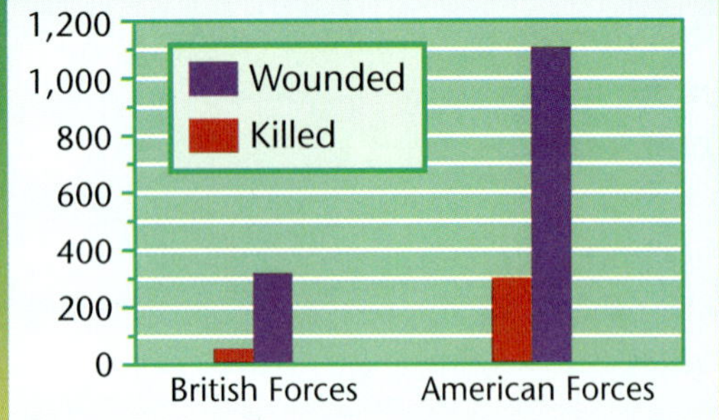

Soldiers Wounded and Killed, Battle of Brooklyn Heights, NY

Graph Check

Approximately how many more American soldiers were wounded during the battle than were British soldiers?

B. Early Setbacks, Small Victories

General Washington's army included volunteers who had fought at Lexington, Concord, and Bunker Hill. These soldiers, however, had little experience or military training.

Retreat From New York

On July 2, 1776, as the Second Continental Congress was adopting the Declaration of Independence, British troops landed in New York City. General William Howe was in command. His army of 32,000 soldiers was the largest army Britain had assembled in the 1700s. The British army included a large number of **mercenaries**, or hired soldiers, from Germany. These soldiers were known as Hessians because many of them came from the German state of Hesse.

Washington had less than two-thirds the number of soldiers that Howe had. When the two armies first met at Brooklyn Heights, on Long Island, New York, the Americans were badly beaten. The British captured New York City. Then, as the Americans retreated, first north, then south, the British chased them. In December 1776, Washington and his troops fled as far west as Pennsylvania. There, they set up camp on the Delaware River, across from Trenton, New Jersey.

Washington's early defeats left many colonists feeling that the fight for independence was a lost cause. Some soldiers became so discouraged that they left the army and went home.

Rallying the Americans

Among those who stayed with Washington was the young writer Thomas Paine, author of *Common Sense*. Sensing the mood of despair among the soldiers, he wrote an essay titled "The Crisis," which began,

> "These are the times that try men's souls: The summer soldier and the sunshine Patriot will, in this crisis, shrink from the service of his country; but he that stands it now deserves the love and thanks of man and woman."

ANALYZE PRIMARY SOURCES

DOCUMENT-BASED QUESTION Based on this quote, what might Paine think of a soldier who went home after his six-month term was up?

Washington and his officers read these words to their soldiers. The spirit of the troops improved, but they desperately needed a victory to show colonial supporters that they could win.

Crossing the Delaware

In search of a victory, Washington turned his attention to Trenton, New Jersey, which was held by Hessian troops. On Christmas night, 1776, Washington and 2,400 soldiers rowed small boats across the Delaware River. The Hessians would be celebrating the Christmas holiday, and Washington hoped to surprise them.

This plan worked. The Americans easily took Trenton, with only five **casualties**, or dead and wounded, on their side. Washington then moved on to capture nearby Princeton, New Jersey. These victories gave Americans hope that the war might be won. Cheered by the turn of events, many of the soldiers decided to rejoin the army.

★ **In the early days of war, why did colonists become discouraged?**

Washington's crossing of the Delaware River has become one of the lasting images of the Revolutionary War. In 1999, when the U.S. Mint began issuing quarters for each state, New Jersey's quarter was produced with the scene of Washington's crossing on one side of the coin.

C. Problems for the Continental Army

Washington had restored Patriot confidence in the army. Keeping the army together through the winter proved more difficult.

A Declining Fighting Force

Washington and his troops spent the first few months of 1777 in Morristown, New Jersey. The soldiers needed food and supplies. Congress, however, did not have the money to take care of the soldiers' needs because it had no power to collect taxes.

Washington and his troops crossed the Delaware River on December 25, 1776, to launch a surprise attack on Hessian soldiers the next morning.

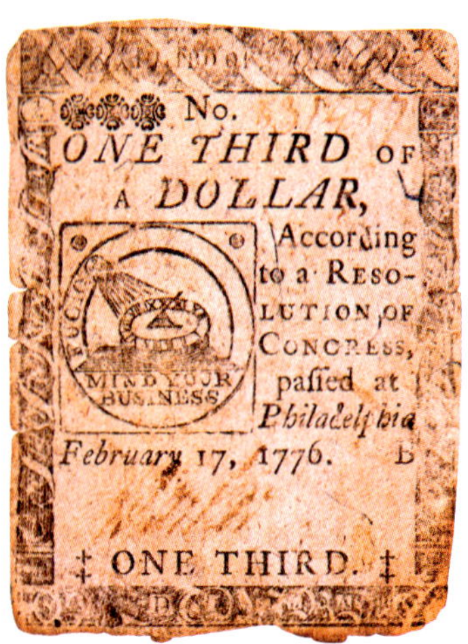

Colonists were not sure if the paper money issued by the Continental Congress would have any value after the war.

As the weather turned colder, many soldiers left the army. Soon, only about 1,000 remained. This number was far short of what Washington would need to fight in the spring. To keep his remaining troops alive, he sent soldiers into the countryside around Morristown. Here, the soldiers were often given food by local farmers.

Financing the Revolution

A lack of money was one of the biggest problems the Patriots faced. To address this problem, the Second Continental Congress approved the printing of $250 million in dollar bills called Continentals. Many people, however, would not take the Continentals. If Britain won the war, the American money would be worthless.

The problem of keeping troops in the army was even greater. To boost the number of enlistees, or people who joined the army of their own free will, Congress offered the colonists a bonus. If a soldier enlisted for three years, or until the end of the war, he would receive $20 and 100 to 200 acres of land.

By spring 1777, the Continental army had recovered. The troops that had stayed through the winter had regained their strength. Meanwhile, many others, attracted by the new offer of money and land, poured into camp. When Washington left Morristown that spring, he commanded about 9,000 troops.

How did the Second Continental Congress address the problem of paying for the war?

Review History

A. How did the Revolutionary War force Americans to choose sides?

B. How did the battles of Trenton and Princeton affect Americans?

C. Why did Washington have difficulty keeping soldiers in the army?

Define Terms to Know

Provide a definition for each of the following terms.
Loyalist, mercenary, casualty

Critical Thinking

How might the early years of the war have gone differently if more Americans had sided with the Patriots?

Write About History

Write a paragraph defending Washington's plan to launch a surprise attack on the Hessians at Trenton.

Get Organized

CHART

Think about ways to classify information in this section. For example, you might make a chart about the Continental army that contains these categories: *Problems, Solutions*.

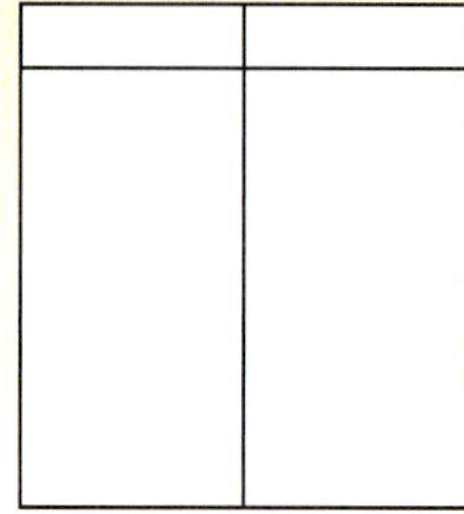

Build Your Skills

Social Studies Skill

READ A MILITARY MAP

You will often see a military map when you read about war. Military maps show the location of battles. They also show the routes traveled by troops as they moved toward their enemy or retreated from their enemy. Additional details, such as dates of battles or names of military leaders, may also be given.

When you study history, you often read descriptions of battles and wars. These descriptions become much clearer when you can refer to a map as you read. The map helps you get a clear picture of where the action took place.

Here's How

Follow these steps to read a military map.

1. Read the title to find out the topic of the map.
2. Study the map key. It shows the meanings of the symbols used on the map.
3. Notice the lines or arrows that show the movement of the troops. Locate important places on these routes.
4. Look for other information on the map such as names, dates, and battle sites.

Here's Why

You have just read about some of the early battles of the Revolutionary War. Reading a military map helps you picture where these battles took place.

Practice the Skill

Study the map at the right. Then, answer the following questions.

1. Who won the battle at White Plains, New York?
2. Where did Washington's troops go after Trenton, New Jersey?

Extend the Skill

Using this map, write about the movements of George Washington's troops in the early years of the war.

Apply the Skill

Study the military maps in the rest of the chapter by looking for troop movements and other details.

II The War Expands

Terms to Know

siege a long, drawn-out attack

garrison a place where troops are stationed and weapons and ammunition are stored

Main Ideas

A. While Washington's troops wintered at Valley Forge, Americans won the battle of Saratoga, and the French promised to help the colonists.

B. In western lands, Native Americans fought on the side of the British, but the Americans won most of the battles.

C. In 1778, the focus of the war shifted to the South.

Active Reading

SEQUENCE OF EVENTS

Sequencing events means putting them in one-two-three order. As you read about events during the Revolutionary War, think about what happened first, second, third, and so on.

A. The Tide Turns

The American victories in New Jersey forced Britain to come up with a plan for defeating the colonists. The British army hoped to capture the Hudson River valley. By doing so, it would cut off rebellious New England from the rest of the colonies. Then, British troops could march south and defeat the Southern colonies.

An Attack on Philadelphia

The plan called for two British forces from Canada to march south toward Albany, New York. General John Burgoyne would lead one group from Quebec. Another British force would be led by Lieutenant Colonel Barry St. Leger. A third British force, led by General William Howe, would march north from New York City.

Instead, General Howe decided to attack Philadelphia, Pennsylvania, the seat of the colonial government. By taking the city, Howe planned to deal a heavy blow to the Patriots. Therefore, he loaded his army onto ships and sailed south into Chesapeake Bay, landing in Maryland. As Howe moved toward Philadelphia, George Washington and his army marched to Philadelphia's defense.

The two armies clashed on September 11, 1777, at Brandywine Creek, south of Philadelphia. The British forces quickly overpowered the Americans. On September 26, Howe's troops marched into Philadelphia. Washington tried to drive them out, but failed. Finally, the American army retreated to nearby Valley Forge, Pennsylvania.

General William Howe was commander in chief of British forces in America until 1778.

Washington's soldiers huddled around fires at Valley Forge camp.

Valley Forge

The winter of 1777–1778 at Valley Forge was one of the hardest times for the Continental army. The soldiers suffered throughout this second miserable winter of the war. For weeks they lived on firecake, a thin biscuit of flour and water cooked over a campfire. One soldier wrote about the lack of food in his journal. He wrote that there was only firecake and water for breakfast, lunch, and dinner.

Besides hunger, the soldiers faced other problems. They had no blankets or warm clothing to protect them from the freezing cold and snow. They shivered in uniforms that were little more than rags, and barefoot soldiers left tracks of blood in the snow as they walked. Weak and hungry, many soldiers died of poor nutrition and disease.

Washington again was forced to send groups to get food from local farmers. By March 1778, supplies taken from nearby farms had improved the health of the soldiers. The promise of extra pay and bonuses helped, too. New soldiers joined the army at Valley Forge.

Saratoga

While Washington and his troops had struggled to defend Philadelphia, British forces under General Burgoyne and St. Leger had moved south toward Albany, New York. St. Leger's forces were overcome at Oriskany by a brilliant young officer named Benedict Arnold. Arnold chased St. Leger west from Oriskany to Fort Ontario. Meanwhile, Burgoyne's troops reclaimed the fort at Ticonderoga, New York. As Burgoyne marched farther south, however, militias traveled from all across New England to oppose him. Burgoyne decided to retreat to Saratoga to await reinforcements, or

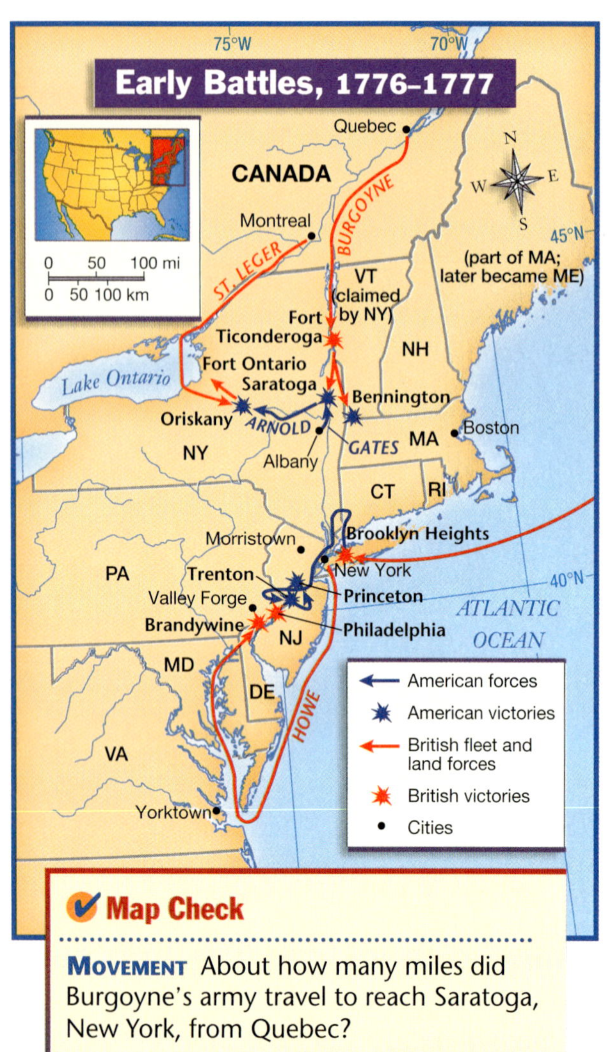

Map Check

MOVEMENT About how many miles did Burgoyne's army travel to reach Saratoga, New York, from Quebec?

additional troops. Howe's decision to go to Philadelphia, however, had left Burgoyne alone.

A troop of Continental soldiers led by General Horatio Gates and Benedict Arnold surrounded Burgoyne at Saratoga. The British forces were badly outnumbered. After a **siege**, or prolonged attack, Burgoyne surrendered on October 17, 1777. The 5,700 British soldiers captured in the battle were imprisoned in Virginia, and Burgoyne was sent home to Great Britain.

An Alliance With France

The victory at Saratoga marked the turning point in the Revolutionary War. When the people of France learned of Burgoyne's surrender, they rejoiced. France and Great Britain were long-time enemies. The French now believed that the colonists might actually win the war.

In February 1778, leaders in France and the United States signed two treaties that set up a plan for France to send supplies and troops to help the Americans win the war. France became the first country to recognize and sign a treaty with the new nation—the United States of America.

★ **What were some of the hardships American soldiers faced at Valley Forge?**

B. The War in the West and at Sea

Not all the fighting of the Revolutionary War took place in the 13 original colonies. Other battles raged farther west in the British territory that had once been controlled by France.

George Rogers Clark

Since the beginning of the war, Native American allies of the British had been attacking frontier settlements. In July 1778, George Rogers Clark, a frontiersman and militia leader, and about 175 volunteers captured a British **garrison**, or military post, at the old French town of Kaskaskia in present-day Illinois. Then, Clark moved north and captured Cahokia, also in present-day Illinois. In a final sweep eastward, he took the British post at Vincennes, in present-day Indiana. Clark's efforts ended the raids on western settlements. He dealt a damaging blow to British and Native American hopes in the West.

Naval Battles

Although most battles were fought on land, Congress had funded a Continental navy to fight the war at sea. The most famous sea battle occurred in September 1779. At that time, John Paul Jones, a commander in the Continental navy, attacked a British warship that was protecting a group of merchant ships off the coast of Great Britain. The group scattered, but the two warships remained and battled side by side. When asked to surrender, Jones replied, "I have not yet begun to fight." Finally, the British commander surrendered. Jones's victory over the powerful British navy inspired many Americans, and he became a national hero.

John Paul Jones's ship, the *Bonhomme Richard*, defeated the British warship *Serapis*.

Battles With Native Americans

The Iroquois often raided settlements in New York and Pennsylvania. Their leader, Joseph Brant, was a Mohawk and one of Britain's greatest allies. In 1779, General Washington sent 4,000 troops to stop the Iroquois raids. The troops burned Seneca and Cayuga villages and destroyed crops, ending the power of the Iroquois League.

At about the same time, in the territory of Kentucky, Daniel Boone and other settlers fought the British and their Shawnee allies for control of the region. For the next several years, the settlers fought to maintain Patriot control of Kentucky.

 **How did the fighting in the West affect Native Americans?**

Joseph Brant, chief of the Iroquois during the Revolutionary War, allied with the British.

C. The War in the South

Beginning in 1778, the war shifted to the South where there were many Loyalists. The British planned to use sea power and the support of Loyalists to win key battles. However, they did not forsee having to fight Patriots in the backcountry.

Savannah and Charleston

In November 1778, British troops arrived by ship in Savannah, Georgia. They quickly captured the city. Next, the British forces marched north to Charleston, South Carolina, burning houses, barns, and crops along the way. At Charleston, the British were joined by more troops led by General Charles Cornwallis. In February 1780, the combined army attacked Charleston while a large force of American soldiers tried to defend the city.

The British navy controlled the waters near Charleston, and no supplies could get through to the Americans by land or sea. On May 12, 1780, the American general Benjamin Lincoln was forced to surrender his entire army of 5,500 troops to the British. The defeat at Charleston was the greatest American loss of the war.

The War in the Backcountry

Horatio Gates, the hero of Saratoga, had been sent south by the Continental Congress. His mission was to stop the British forces from sweeping through the Carolinas. However, Gates proved to be unsuccessful. By mid-August 1780, Cornwallis had almost total control of South Carolina.

Then, on October 7, at King's Mountain, South Carolina, a band of Patriots surrounded and defeated part of Cornwallis's army. Meanwhile, Washington sent his most skilled commander, General Nathanael Greene, to the region. On January 17, 1781, Greene led the Americans to a small victory at Cowpens, South Carolina.

Beginning in March 1781, General Greene and his troops fought repeatedly with Cornwallis and the British forces. Greene's strategy was to wear out the enemy by fighting for a short while and then retreating. Eventually, Cornwallis lost so many soldiers that he decided to leave the Carolinas and head north to Virginia.

 **Why did the war shift to the South in 1778?**

Review History

A. What did France decide to do after the Battle of Saratoga?

B. How did George Rogers Clark and Daniel Boone affect the war in the West?

C. What successes did the Americans have in the backcountry of the Carolinas?

Define Terms to Know

Provide a definition for each of the following terms.
siege, garrison

Critical Thinking

Why do you think British leaders thought they would find support in the South?

Write About History

Write a dialogue between two soldiers stationed at Valley Forge during the winter of 1777–1778.

Get Organized

CHART

Create a chart to classify information about the battles in the West and the South. For example, you might use the following categories in your chart: *location, outcome.*

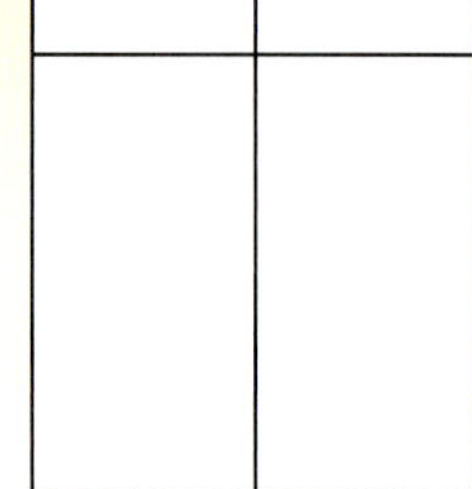

Points of View

Independence From Great Britain

The start of the war did not stop the debate over independence. In newspapers, pamphlets, and daily conversations, people discussed the pros and cons of separating from Great Britain.

Some people debated whether trade would improve or become worse if the colonies chose independence. Others questioned whether the British government had treated the colonies unfairly. Once fighting began, many felt it would be impossible to have a close relationship with Great Britain. Others held out hope. The following passages are from two pamphlets written at the beginning of the war.

British crown

"But Britain is the parent country say some. Then the more shame upon her conduct. Even brutes do not devour their young. . . . [D]ependence on Great Britain tends directly to involve this Continent in European wars and quarrels. As Europe is our market for trade, we ought to form no partial connection with any part of it. . . . [T]he business of it [this Continent] will soon be too weighty and intricate to be managed . . . by a power so distant from us, and so very ignorant of us. . . . "

—Thomas Paine, 1776

"It is time to lay aside those animosities [hatreds] which have pushed on Britons to shed the blood of Britons. . . . By a reconciliation, with Great Britain, peace . . . will be restored. . . . Agriculture, commerce, and industry would resume their wonted [usual] vigor. . . . [O]ur trade would still have the protection of the greatest naval power in the world. . . . While connected with Great Britain, we have bounty on almost every article of exportation; and we may be better supplied with goods by her than we could elsewhere. . . . "

—Charles Inglis, 1776

DOCUMENT-BASED QUESTIONS

1. From Paine's point of view, what are two points in favor of independence?
2. According to Inglis, what are two points in favor of reconciliation?
3. **Critical Thinking** Which argument on each side do you think is the strongest? Why?

III An Independent Nation

Terms to Know

civilian a person who is not a member of the military

inflation a sharp increase in the price of goods and services

republic a government that receives its power from the people, who elect its leaders

Main Ideas

A. Victory at Yorktown, Virginia, by American and French forces ensured the end of the Revolutionary War.

B. After the war ended, in the Treaty of Paris, Great Britain recognized the United States as an independent nation.

C. The United States was a new republic with high goals and a number of problems to solve.

MAIN IDEAS AND DETAILS

Main ideas are broad statements that take into account several or many facts. Details are statements that support the main idea. As you read this section, look for main ideas and the details that support them.

A. Final Victory

In Virginia, the goal of British general Cornwallis was to close off supply routes to the Carolinas. Cornwallis commanded thousands of British soldiers. He reasoned that the Patriots had only a small fighting force in Virginia, so there would probably not be much of a fight.

A Patriot Turns Traitor

In 1780, George Washington placed Benedict Arnold in command of West Point, a fort on the Hudson River. Arnold was one of Washington's finest generals, and his future in the American army looked bright. However, Arnold did not feel his talents had been amply recognized. So, in exchange for a large sum of money, Arnold turned traitor—he agreed to turn over West Point to the British.

The plot was discovered in time, but Arnold escaped. To the shock of Patriots everywhere, Arnold then switched sides and joined the British forces in September 1780.

Strategies for Battle

Now, as Cornwallis was marching from Richmond, Virginia, he joined forces with Arnold. Cornwallis, Arnold, and their soldiers camped in Yorktown, Virginia, near the coast of the Chesapeake Bay. There they waited for British ships to bring new supplies and more troops.

Meanwhile, American and French forces were moving toward Yorktown by land and sea. A fleet of 24 French warships was sailing for Chesapeake Bay. At the same time, American forces under General Anthony Wayne and French troops commanded by the Marquis de Lafayette were marching east toward Yorktown.

Map Check

MOVEMENT Which two British generals commanded forces at Yorktown, Virginia?

The Battle of Yorktown

George Washington, who had been planning to attack New York, sensed an opportunity. American and French forces could trap Cornwallis at Yorktown. Washington and the French Count de Rochambeau marched their soldiers south to join the American and French troops already camped outside Yorktown.

On September 5, 1781, British ships carrying supplies and troops to Cornwallis entered Chesapeake Bay. The French fleet stopped them before they could reach Yorktown. Now, Cornwallis was surrounded by more than 16,000 enemy soldiers—he was outnumbered two to one.

On October 9, the American and French forces began firing on Cornwallis and his troops. Because the British troops were outnumbered and low on supplies, Cornwallis realized that he could not win the battle. He tried to sneak his troops out of Yorktown, but bad weather prevented his escape. Cornwallis was forced to surrender on October 19, 1781, four years after the American victory at Saratoga. In a letter to General Howe, commander of the British forces in North America, Cornwallis wrote,

> "I . . . inform your Excellency that I have been forced to give up the posts of York and Gloucester, and to surrender the troops under my command . . . as prisoners of war to the combined forces of America and France."

ANALYZE PRIMARY SOURCES

DOCUMENT-BASED QUESTION How do you think the British king reacted when he heard of the surrender of Cornwallis?

After the surrender of Cornwallis, the British troops were marched out of Yorktown. The siege of Yorktown was over, and so was the Revolutionary War. Although fighting continued for many months in the backcountry, the victory at Yorktown ensured American independence.

★ **Why was the French fleet important in the victory at Yorktown?**

This unfinished painting by Benjamin West shows the men present at the signing of the Treaty of Paris. From left to right are John Jay, John Adams, Benjamin Franklin, and two others.

B. The War Ends

King George III of Great Britain did not want to end the war. However, the British government could no longer afford to keep fighting. Britain was also at war with France and Spain, who were allied with each other. As a result, Britain and the United States worked out a peace treaty, and the United States of America became an independent nation.

The Treaty of Paris

John Adams of Massachusetts, Benjamin Franklin of Pennsylvania, and John Jay of New York traveled to Paris to negotiate, or work out, the terms of a peace treaty. On September 3, 1783, the United States and Great Britain signed the Treaty of Paris. This agreement included the following conditions:

1. Great Britain recognized the United States of America as an independent nation.
2. The western boundary of the United States was the Mississippi River.
3. The northern boundary was the Great Lakes, and the southern boundary was Spanish Florida. However, exact boundaries were to be worked out at a later time.
4. Americans would have the right to fish in the North Atlantic Ocean off the coast of British Canada.
5. Debts owed to British merchants should be paid, and rights and property that had been taken from Loyalists during the war should be restored.

Reasons for the American Victory

How were the Americans able to gain their independence from the most powerful empire in the world? How was it possible for them to defeat the British army? At the start of the Revolutionary War, many people thought the Americans had no chance for victory. After all, the colonists had no army, and they were just beginning to form a government.

As the war progressed, however, the Americans were able to make use of a number of advantages. First, the Americans were fighting on their own ground. They knew the countryside, and they could choose the best routes and the best positions for their troops. Second, they could obtain reinforcements of soldiers and supplies more easily than the British. American soldiers could find supplies locally, while the British often waited months for supplies to arrive by sea.

Third, the Americans had the aid of several foreign nations, especially France. Without French loans, ships, and soldiers, the Americans may not have won the war.

Fourth, George Washington's leadership inspired his troops and gave many Americans the hope that they could win. British leaders, on the other hand, often failed in their strategy, in their communications, and sometimes even in their dedication to winning.

The biggest advantage in the war was probably the Americans' determination to be free. Their strong desire for liberty meant that even after terrible winters and humiliating defeats in battle, they could continue fighting until the war was won.

 **Why did the Americans win the war?**

Spotlight on History

In 1776, the number of soldiers in the Continental army may have been fewer than 20,000. However, by the end of the Revolutionary War, more than 200,000 Americans had served in the Continental army. More than 160,000 had served in the militias.

C. A New Nation

After the war, most of the men and women who had taken part in the fight for independence returned home. Even George Washington, the leader of the Continental army, returned to his plantation in Virginia. Americans now faced the task of making their new, independent nation work.

Americans pulled down a statue of King George III to show that they were no longer under British rule.

Washington's Farewell

On December 4, 1783, General George Washington, commander in chief of the Continental army, gathered his officers together in New York City for a farewell dinner. He told his friends and fellow soldiers:

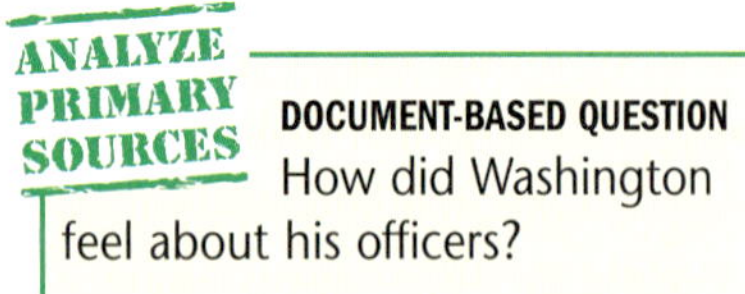

DOCUMENT-BASED QUESTION How did Washington feel about his officers?

> "With a heart full of love and gratitude, I now take leave of you. I most devoutly wish that your latter days may be as prosperous and happy as your former ones have been glorious and honorable."

Washington's farewell was unique. He invited each officer to come and take him by the hand. As the officers responded, there was much sorrow and weeping.

Afterward, Washington left for Annapolis, Maryland, where the Second Continental Congress was meeting. Before the Congress, he officially resigned from the army. Then, he returned home to Mount Vernon, Virginia. Washington did not seek to increase his power over others. Instead, he chose to leave the military and become a **civilian**, or a nonmilitary citizen. To many Americans, Washington seemed to be the model of a new kind of citizen.

George Washington's triumphant return to New York in 1783 signaled the beginning of a new, independent United States.

Problems After the War

Although they were free of British rule, the people of the United States faced some serious problems. For one thing, British troops remained for many years in the wilderness areas of present-day Ohio and Michigan. Also, Spanish Florida became the home of many outlaws, runaway slaves, and Native Americans who often raided settlements across the Georgia border.

More pressing was the problem of building confidence in the new government. Continentals, the money that Congress had ordered to be printed during the war, now needed to be backed with gold. Congress, however, had no gold. Because trade had almost stopped during the war, the amount of incoming money had dropped.

Although plenty of paper money was available, it had very little value. As a result, prices skyrocketed. For example, a bushel of wheat that sold for $1 in 1777 cost $80 in 1779. This steep rise in the price of goods is called **inflation**. When inflation occurs, people feel "poorer" because they cannot buy as much with their money.

High Goals For a New Nation

The Declaration of Independence set a high goal for the new nation of the United States. Its opening words had stated that "all men are created equal." However, in the late 1700s, *all men* really meant "all white men who could vote." The War for Independence did not really change the lives of women, African Americans, and others who had lived with inequality all their lives.

During the Revolutionary War and after, some women spoke out on their position in society. One such woman was Mercy Otis Warren, who, besides being a well-known writer and poet, often voiced her views about politics and women's role in society.

The Revolutionary War did not bring many benefits to African Americans either. Some slaves in the South were freed by the British army. However, the war did not end slavery. Many of the men who had signed the Declaration, including Thomas Jefferson, owned slaves and continued to do so after the war. For African Americans, equality was far from being a reality.

Still, the United States was the first nation to be founded on the ideal and goal of equal rights. It was also a **republic,** a nation in which the citizens, rather than monarchs or nobles, held supreme power. As such, the nation became a model for many countries around the world.

★ **What economic problem did the United States face after the war?**

Spotlight on History

After helping the Americans win the Revolutionary War, the French faced their own revolution in 1789. Many people in France felt that the king limited their freedom. They wanted more rights.

French citizens staged a revolt against the king in 1789 and created a *Declaration of the Rights of Man and of the Citizen.* In 1792, France set up a republic. In 1793, King Louis XVI and his family were killed.

Review

Review History

A. How did American and French forces defeat the British army at Yorktown?

B. What were the most important terms of the Treaty of Paris?

C. What was unique about the new republic of the United States?

Define Terms to Know

Provide a definition for each of the following terms.
civilian, inflation, republic

Critical Thinking

What concerns for the future do you think members of the Continental Congress might have had at the end of the war?

Write About History

Write a paragraph about how the alliance with France helped Americans win the war.

Get Organized

CHART

Create a chart to classify information about the outcomes of the Revolutionary War. For example, you might use the following categories in your chart: *positive outcomes, negative outcomes.*

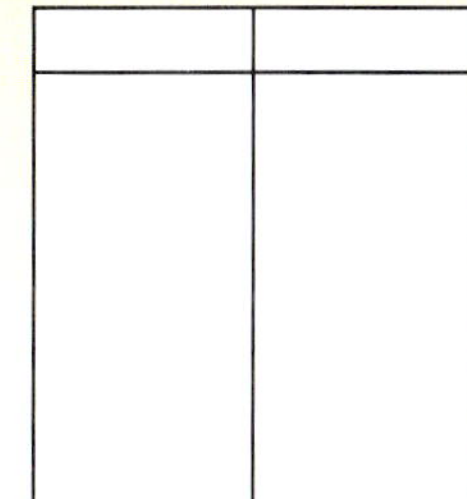

CHAPTER 8 Review

Chapter Summary

In your notebook, complete the following outline. Then, use your outline to write a brief summary of the chapter.

The Revolutionary War

I. The Early Years of War
   A. Choosing Sides
   B.
   C.
II. The War Expands
   A.
   B.
   C.
III. An Independent Nation
   A.
   B.
   C.

Interpret the Timeline

Use the timeline on pages 162–163 to answer the following questions.

1. Where did the British surrender to the Americans take place?
2. **Critical Thinking** How important were the French to the outcome of the Revolutionary War?

Use Terms to Know

Select the term that best completes each sentence.

casualty	**republic**
inflation	**siege**
Loyalist	

1. A person who sided with Great Britain during the Revolutionary War was a ________.
2. A person who was killed or wounded in the Revolutionary War was a ________.
3. The ________ at Saratoga ended in a victory for the Americans.
4. After the war, the colonists decided to set up a new kind of government called a ________.
5. Sharply rising prices, or ________, became a serious problem for the new nation.

Check Your Understanding

1. **Discuss** the advantages and disadvantages that the Patriot forces had in the war.
2. **Explain** what happened to Loyalists during the war.
3. **Explain** why the Battle of Saratoga was a turning point in the war.
4. **Identify** military leaders who fought for the Patriots during the war in the South and the West.
5. **Explain** the significance of the Treaty of Paris to the United States.
6. **Summarize** the impact of the war on the lives of women and African Americans.

Critical Thinking

1. **Analyze Primary Sources** Why do you think Paine's message on page 166 was effective in rallying Patriots?
2. **Make Inferences** Why did France agree to help the American colonists in their fight for independence?
3. **Analyze Primary Sources** Judging from his farewell address, part of which is quoted on page 180, how do you think George Washington felt at the end of the war?

Put Your Skills to Work

READ A MILITARY MAP

You have learned that reading a military map can help you follow the progress of a war. Military maps often show the location of battles and the movement of troops in those battles.

Answer the following questions about the map below.

1. How would you describe the British route to Saratoga?
2. Which side won the battles of Saratoga and Bennington?

In Your Own Words

JOURNAL WRITING

The American colonists declared independence because they felt that they were being treated unfairly. They defended their rights and stood up for their beliefs. In your journal, write about a time when you stood up for something you believed in.

Net Work

INTERNET ACTIVITY

Working with a group of classmates, use the Internet as a resource to create a report on one of the major battles of the Revolutionary War. Find information about the troops, the military leaders, and the outcome of the battle. Then, write a brief account of the events that took place. Use maps of the battle site as well as charts and graphs to serve as visual aids for your report. Then, present your report to the class.

For help in starting this activity, visit the following Web site: www.gfamericanhistory.com.

Look Ahead

In the next chapter, learn how American leaders created a government for the new nation.

CHAPTER 9

Forming a Government 1777–1791

I. The First Government
II. Problems in the New Nation
III. The U.S. Constitution and the Bill of Rights

The British army surrendered to General George Washington at Yorktown in 1781. Americans breathed a huge sigh of relief. The last important battle in their war for independence was over. However, many felt that an even more difficult challenge lay ahead. What kind of government would the new nation have? Some people could not imagine a government without kings and queens. One of these was Colonel Lewis Nicola. Nicola wrote a letter to George Washington. He urged the general to declare himself king. Washington refused. He replied,

> "... you could not have found a person to whom your schemes were more disagreeable."

Washington believed that the United States of America needed a new kind of government—one in which the people, not kings, ruled. Which form would this government take?

Continental Congress money

1777 Second Continental Congress adopts the Articles of Confederation.

1781 Articles of Confederation are ratified.

1784 Spain closes the Mississippi River to American ships.

U.S. Events: 1775 — 1779 — 1783

Presidential Term Begins

World Events: 1775 — 1779 — 1783

1778 Hawaiian Islands are discovered and named the Sandwich Islands.

1782 Beethoven's first works are published.

VIEW HISTORY In this painting, George Washington watches as delegates sign the Constitution on September 17, 1787. Economic hardships in the United States, including a drop in the value of money (left), led leaders to create the U.S. Constitution.

★ **How do you think the delegates felt as they signed the Constitution?**

Get Organized

CAUSE-AND-EFFECT CHAIN

Recognizing the causes and effects of events helps you to understand history. Use a cause-and-effect chain as you read this chapter. List an important event in the box. In the ovals, fill in a cause and an effect. Here is an example from this chapter.

CAUSE
The central government is too weak.

EVENT
The Constitutional Convention

EFFECT
The U.S. Constitution is written.

1787
Northwest Ordinance is passed.
Shays's Rebellion occurs.
Delegates write a new constitution in Philadelphia.

1788
U.S. Constitution is ratified.

1791
Bill of Rights is added to the Constitution.

1787 — 1791 — 1795

1789 George Washington

1787 — 1791 — 1795

1788–1789
King George III suffers from temporary insanity.

1789
French Revolution begins.

1792
France abolishes the monarchy.

I The First Government

Terms to Know

constitution the basic laws and plan of a nation's government

confederation a union of countries or states for a common purpose

sovereignty the power of self-government

ratify to approve

Main Ideas

A. During the Revolutionary War, new state governments replaced British rule.

B. The Articles of Confederation created the first government for the newly independent United States.

Active Reading

COMPARE AND CONTRAST

Comparing and contrasting items can help you to understand how they are the same and different. As you read this section, compare and contrast the powers of the states and the federal government.

A. Replacing British Rule

Each state established its own government during the Revolutionary War. At the same time, leaders began forming a new national government. Americans knew they wanted a republic, but they were uncertain about how to make their ideas work.

Organizing New State Governments

During the Revolutionary War, 11 states rewrote their colonial charters to form state governments. Connecticut and Rhode Island decided to adopt their colonial charters as state **constitutions**, or plans for government. These new state governments replaced the old colonial system put in place by the British. States chose new governors. They also elected representatives to new assemblies.

Americans used their new state governments to protect the basic rights and freedoms of the people. All of the new state constitutions included a section, known as a bill of rights, that described the basic rights of citizens. These rights included freedom of speech, religion, and the press.

Each state constitution was different in many ways. For example, some northern states ended slavery. Other states, especially those in the South, passed laws to protect slavery. Voting rights also differed. Many states, including North Carolina, allowed free African American men to vote. New Jersey's constitution, written in 1776, gave women who owned property the right to vote.

Above all, Americans wanted to make sure that certain freedoms were guaranteed to them. This idea would later become a foundation of the American government.

For Thomas Jefferson, governor of Virginia during the Revolutionary War, individual freedoms were very important. He wrote the Virginia Statute for Religious Freedom, which became law in 1786. This law allowed the citizens of Virginia the right to worship in any way they chose. Other states followed Virginia's example. Near the end of his life, Jefferson considered this Virginia law a greater accomplishment than serving as President of the United States.

Jefferson believed strongly that people should be free to think and feel the way they wanted. He believed it was not the duty of the government to tell people what to think. He thought the government's main duty should be to prevent people from hurting others.

Creating a Federal Government

While the Revolutionary War was being fought, the Second Continental Congress took steps to create a federal government, or a national government made up of all the states. The Congress realized that a framework was needed for the new government in order to unite the states. However, delegates disagreed on the type of government they should have. The Congress appointed a committee to create a plan.

The committee could have created a monarchy, or rule by a king or queen. However, because Great Britain was a monarchy, many delegates rejected that idea. Instead, they decided to create a republic. A republic is a form of government in which citizens elect their leaders.

All property owners in New Jersey—including women—could vote after the state constitution was passed in 1776.

U.S. Government Under the Articles of Confederation

WEAKNESSES	STRENGTHS
No president to enforce laws made by Congress	Included representatives from every state
No court system	Issued currency
No power to tax the states to raise money	Owned land, which it could sell to raise money
Required 13 votes to change the Articles of Confederation	Maintained armed forces
Small states and large states each had one vote	Conducted foreign affairs and signed treaties

Chart Check

How was the government under the Articles of Confederation able to pay its debts?

Now, the committee faced the question of how much power the federal government should have. Many Americans wanted a weak federal government. They felt more loyalty toward their state than to the nation. Others, however, wanted to create a strong, unified government.

★ **Why was the creation of new state governments important?**

B. The Articles of Confederation

After five months of debate, members of the Continental Congress chose to give more power to the states and less to the federal government. They had decided that they did not want a strong national government controlling them. After all, they were fighting a war to escape the powerful British government.

What the Articles Said

The members of the Second Continental Congress decided to create a **confederation,** or a union of the states. A committee was appointed to write a constitution. On November 15, 1777, the Congress approved its plan known as the Articles of Confederation. This document listed the powers of the federal government and the powers of the states in the new United States of America.

The Articles of Confederation created a federal government made up only of a congress. They did not allow for a president or king to enforce the laws. The Articles also did not establish a court system. Some of the strengths and weaknesses of the new government under the Articles of Confederation are listed in the chart on this page.

One goal of the Articles of Confederation was to reserve most powers for the states. The states would govern their own affairs and remain separate from one another. The federal government was meant to be only "a firm league of friendship" among the states.

According to the Articles of Confederation, each state kept its full **sovereignty**, or control of its own affairs. By agreeing to the Articles, the states promised to help each other defend their freedom. However, in case of war, each state had to provide its own soldiers and choose its own leaders.

Even though Congress was the head of the federal government, it had very limited powers. It could make agreements with foreign governments and could resolve disagreements among the states. It was charged with paying the costs of the United States government. However, it did not have the authority to collect money for these expenses through taxes.

States could send from two to seven delegates to Congress, but each state had only one vote. As a result, small states had as much power as larger ones. Congress could pass laws only with the agreement of the delegates of 9 out of 13 states. Thus, any five states could block action by Congress. Also, no changes could be made in the Articles of Confederation unless all the states agreed.

Approving the Articles

Before the Articles of Confederation could take effect, all 13 states had to **ratify**, or approve the document. By May 5, 1779, 46 delegates from 12 states had signed their names to the Articles of Confederation. Their states had accepted the new agreement.

However, a disagreement about states' claims to land between the Appalachian Mountains and the Mississippi River delayed the ratification process. Some small states were concerned that Virginia, Massachusetts, New York, and several other large states claimed too much of this land. They thought that the western land should belong to the United States. The states that had claimed the territories disagreed. They wanted to sell the land to settlers in order to pay off debts from the Revolutionary War.

The state of Maryland refused to ratify the Articles of Confederation until all of the states ceded, or gave up, their claims to western land. In 1780, New York was the first state to agree to Maryland's demands. The ownership of the land was transferred to the national government. Maryland was satisfied that New York had set a good example for the rest of the states.

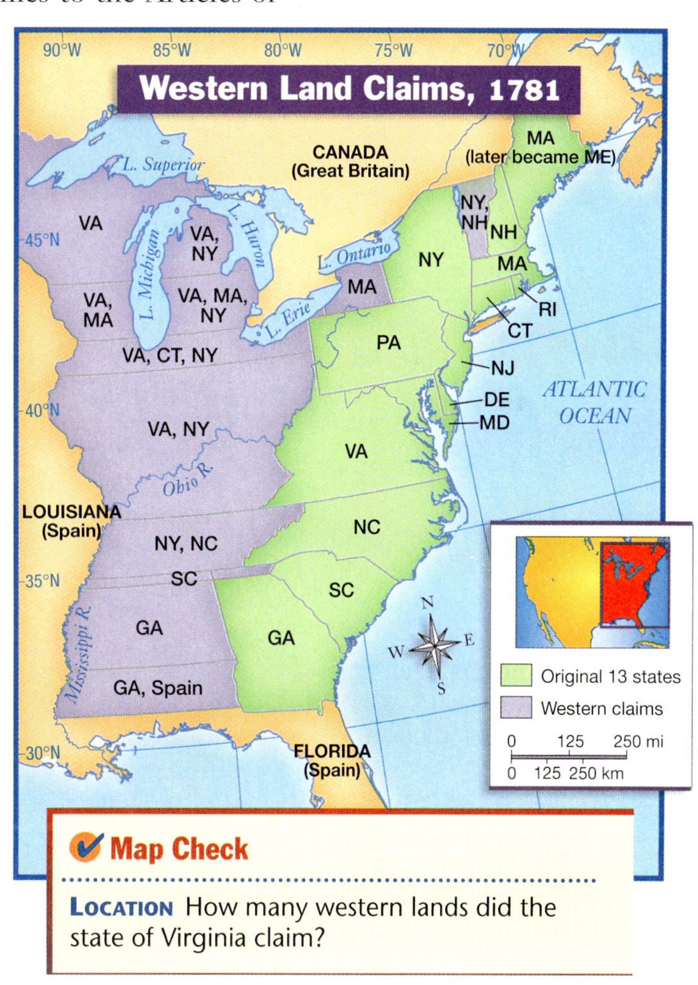

Map Check

LOCATION How many western lands did the state of Virginia claim?

In March 1781, Maryland became the last of the 13 states to ratify the Articles of Confederation. The Articles of Confederation officially became the first U.S. constitution on March 1, 1781. In its first three articles, the document stressed that the new government was, above all else, a union of independent states.

> "ARTICLE I. The stile [name] of this confederacy shall be 'The United States of America.'
>
> ARTICLE II. Each state retains its sovereignty, freedom, and independence, and every power, jurisdiction [limits of power] and right, which is not by this confederation expressly given to the United States in Congress assembled.
>
> ARTICLE III. The said states hereby . . . enter in a firm league of friendship with each other for their common defense, the security of their liberties and their mutual and general welfare. . . ."

DOCUMENT-BASED QUESTION According to this document, in what ways are the states "united"?

The new country finally had a plan for its federal government, and the states still retained their power. Would this system work?

 **When did the last state ratify the Articles of Confederation?**

I Review

Review History

A. How did the new state governments try to protect certain freedoms?

B. How was power divided between the federal government and the states under the Articles of Confederation?

Define Terms to Know

Provide a definition for each of the following terms.
constitution, confederation, sovereignty, ratify

Critical Thinking

Why were some Americans opposed to a strong federal government?

Write About History

After the Articles of Confederation were written, they had to be ratified by all 13 states. Write a speech persuading the states to approve the Articles of Confederation.

Get Organized

CAUSE-AND-EFFECT CHAIN
Think about the main events in this section. Use a cause-and-effect chain to link these events together. For example, what was a cause and an effect of the writing of the Articles of Confederation?

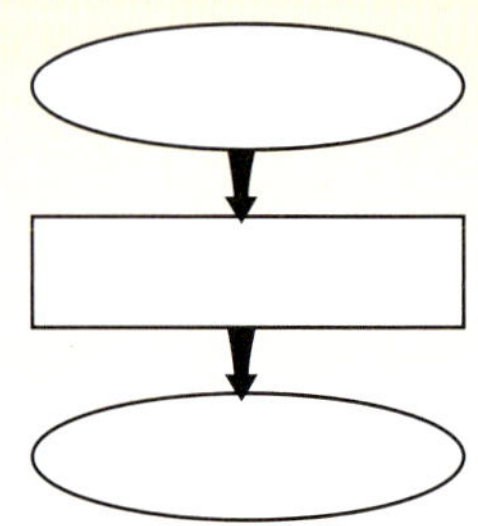

Build Your Skills

Critical Thinking

MAKE A FLOWCHART

Have you ever made popcorn in a microwave oven? You must perform the steps in a certain order. For example, you cannot open the bag and eat the popcorn before you pop it! Think about the steps you follow to make microwave popcorn. The order in which events happen is their sequence.

One way to understand the sequence of events is to make a flowchart. A flowchart shows the order of events.

Making a flowchart can help you to understand the order of the important events you read about. For example, making a flowchart of the events leading up to the creation of the Articles of Confederation can help you to better understand Section I.

Here's How

Follow these steps to make a flowchart of historical events.

1. Decide the first and last events in your flowchart.
2. Identify the events you want to add to the chart. Look for words such as *soon, before, later, after, then, while, first,* and *last* that can tell you when an event happened.
3. Make a chart like the one on this page.

Here's Why

You have just read about how the 13 states created a new government. You want to organize the events you read about to understand them better. Making a flowchart would help you to place the events in a logical order.

Practice the Skill

Read Section I again. Then, add events in the boxes to complete the chart.

Extend the Skill

Think about something you know how to do well. Create a flowchart to show the steps you take to do this activity. Make sure the flowchart shows the correct sequence of the steps.

Apply the Skill

As you read the remaining sections of this chapter, think of ways you can use flowcharts to understand the sequence of important events. Use your flowchart as a study tool.

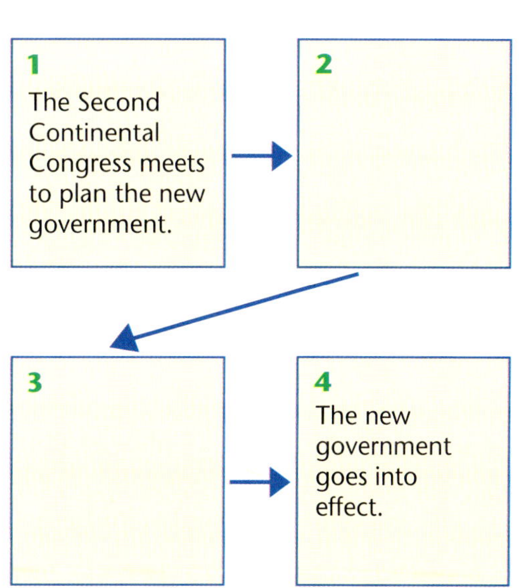

II Problems in the New Nation

Terms to Know

ordinance a law

public domain land owned by the government

arsenal a building used to store weapons and ammunition

Main Ideas

A. The federal government under the Articles of Confederation was unable to solve problems with foreign nations.

B. Congress planned and encouraged the settlement of the western territory.

C. An economic crisis led to protests and demands for a more effective form of government.

MAKE GENERALIZATIONS When you make generalizations, you examine details in order to state a main, or overall, idea. As you read this section, make a generalization about why people were dissatisfied with the Articles of Confederation.

A. Foreign Relations Problems

The federal government created by the Articles of Confederation was unable to deal successfully with many serious problems. One of these problems was foreign relations with Great Britain and Spain.

Tensions Continue With Great Britain

The 1783 Treaty of Paris gave Americans independence from Great Britain. However, other issues were left unsettled. British troops refused to leave their forts in areas south of the Great Lakes. Great Britain decided to keep these soldiers in the forts until Americans paid debts owed to British merchants. The British also wanted the Americans to return property taken from people who had supported Great Britain during the Revolutionary War.

Congress did not have the power to make American citizens pay these debts. The issue was left up to the state governments, but the states refused to repay anyone. Because of this disagreement, Great Britain closed its ports to American ships. The British also banned American merchants from trading in Canada. The fragile economy of the United States suffered.

A Border Dispute With Spain

Spain had been an ally of the United States for a time during the Revolutionary War. However, at the end of the war, the United States found itself in a border dispute with Spain.

In 1784, Spain had territory west of the Mississippi that it wanted to protect from U.S. expansion. Therefore, it closed the lower Mississippi River and the port of New Orleans, Louisiana, to American shipping. Western farmers were furious because they used the river to bring their goods to markets in the East.

American officials were anxious to resolve the problem. Spanish officials were also interested in a resolution because they wanted to establish a trade relationship with the new United States. John Jay, the American Secretary of Foreign Affairs, negotiated a treaty to settle the dispute. In the treaty, both countries agreed to open trade relations. In return, a border was set between Georgia and Spanish Florida. Also, Spain was allowed to maintain control of the Mississippi River.

The treaty was brought to Congress for approval. However, southern leaders were outraged that the treaty allowed Spain to continue to control access to the Mississippi River. American ships could not enter the river from the south. Five southern states voted against the treaty, so it was not approved. The failure of Congress to approve this treaty was another example of the weakness of the federal government under the Articles of Confederation.

 **Why did Great Britain refuse to remove its soldiers from forts near the Great Lakes?**

B. Settling the West

Another problem that faced the federal government involved the western territory of the United States. This land had been given to the federal government by the states in the 1780s. What should the government do with it? Congress decided to encourage people to move to the territory. The plans for developing the area were explained in three land **ordinances**, or regulations. In general, Congress was successful in settling the western territory.

Some adventurous Americans traveled to the unsettled western territory.

Land Ordinances of 1784 and 1785

The Ordinance of 1784 suggested that the United States would not keep colonies, as Great Britain and other European countries had done. Instead, the United States would add to the number of independent states in the country. When a territory had as many people as the smallest state in the country, it could apply for statehood.

The Ordinance of 1785 described the transfer of land owned by the government to private owners.

Public, or government-owned, land was called the **public domain**. Surveyors, people who measure and make maps of land, laid out the land in townships. Each township was six miles by six miles. Then, the townships were divided into 36 sections that were one square mile each. One section in every township was set aside for public schools. Four additional sections were kept for Revolutionary War veterans to live on.

When an area had been surveyed, the land could be sold for $640 per section. Many sections were then divided into smaller areas for sale to individuals.

The Northwest Ordinance of 1787

The Northwest Ordinance of 1787 created the Northwest Territory. This area was all the land north of the Ohio River and east of the Mississippi River. Several states had to give up their claims to this land before the Articles of Confederation were ratified. During the next 60 years, the states of Ohio, Indiana, Illinois, Michigan, and Wisconsin, and part of Minnesota, were created from it.

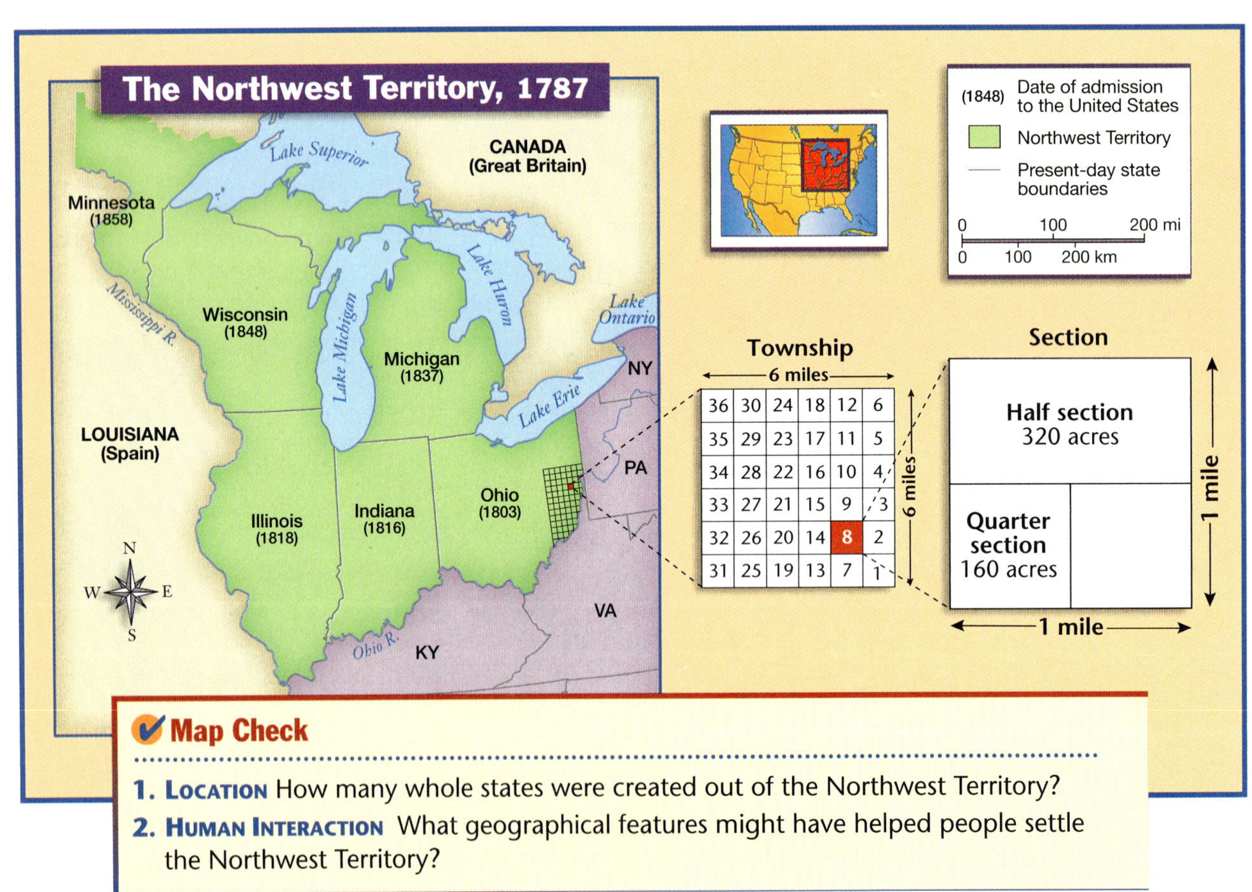

36	30	24	18	12	6
35	29	23	17	11	5
34	28	22	16	10	4
33	27	21	15	9	3
32	26	20	14	8	2
31	25	19	13	7	1

Map Check

1. **Location** How many whole states were created out of the Northwest Territory?
2. **Human Interaction** What geographical features might have helped people settle the Northwest Territory?

The ordinance also included several laws for the Northwest Territory. One law outlawed slavery in the territory and in any states created from it. The ordinance also strongly supported education in the new territories. Part of the ordinance read,

> "Religion, morality, and knowledge being necessary to good government and the happiness of mankind, schools and the means of education shall forever be encouraged."

ANALYZE PRIMARY SOURCES **DOCUMENT-BASED QUESTION** Why did the writers of the Northwest Ordinance think education was important?

 **What was the Northwest Ordinance?**

C. Financial Hardships

The government had successfully managed its western territory, but it was not so successful in other areas. Serious economic problems existed in the new nation. Congress could not solve these problems because it had limited powers. As a result, American citizens became upset with the way the country was governed.

A Shaky Economy

The United States suffered an economic crisis during the 1780s. The crisis had several causes. After the Revolutionary War, Congress was unable to pay back money that Americans had loaned to the Second Continental Congress. Congress also borrowed money from foreign countries to operate the government. This new borrowing increased the debt, or the amount of money the government owed to others. At first, Congress was able to pay back part of the foreign debt. It used money that it had received from the states. Yet, as the economy grew worse, states sent less money to Congress.

Do You Remember?
In Chapter 8, you learned that the Continental Congress borrowed money and printed its own paper money to pay for the war. The paper money, called Continentals, was not backed by gold because Congress had no gold.

The economy was also hurt by barriers to trade that the states had created. The states placed taxes on goods imported from other states. They also taxed goods traveling through their state. These taxes discouraged trade between the states and slowed the economy. Soon, citizens of all the states felt the effects of the failing economy.

Shays's Rebellion

The economic problems led some people to rebel against the government. In Massachusetts, the state government had raised taxes to pay off its debt. If people could not pay their taxes, they would lose their land. However, the taxes were so high that many people owed more money than they could earn in an entire year. A group of farmers became angry about this increase in taxes.

Daniel Shays and rebel farmers attacked an arsenal in Massachusetts in 1787.

The farmers asked the Massachusetts State government to lower their taxes. When the government ignored their request, a rebellion broke out. The rebellion was led by Daniel Shays, who had served as a captain during the Revolutionary War. In September 1786, the rebel farmers forced the courts to close so that judges could no longer seize their land.

Shays and his followers also wanted the government to print more paper money. They thought that having more money in circulation would make it easier for people who owed money to pay their loans back. However, the printing of more money would also decrease the value of the money. Banks did not like this idea.

In January 1787, Shays and more than 1,000 men attacked a federal **arsenal**, or a place where weapons are stored. The members of the militia in the arsenal quickly stopped the attack and ended the rebellion. The uprising frightened state and national leaders. George Washington said that people like Shays were a danger to the United States.

The problems in the United States led many citizens to question the Articles of Confederation. They began to ask, Does our country need a new kind of government? Should it have the power to solve the problems we face?

 **How did the states' trade barriers hurt the U.S. economy?**

II Review

Review History

A. What were two problems that the United States had with foreign countries?

B. How did Congress encourage settlement of the western territory?

C. Why did farmers rebel in 1786?

Define Terms to Know

Provide a definition for each of the following terms.
ordinance, public domain, arsenal

Critical Thinking

How did the weak federal government cause problems for Americans?

Write About Government

Congress was unable to solve the problems that faced the nation. Write a letter suggesting some changes that Congress could make to the Articles of Confederation to make it more effective.

Get Organized

CAUSE-AND-EFFECT CHAIN

Think about the main events in this section. Use a cause-and-effect chain to link these events together. For example, what were some causes and effects of the weak U.S. economy during the 1780s?

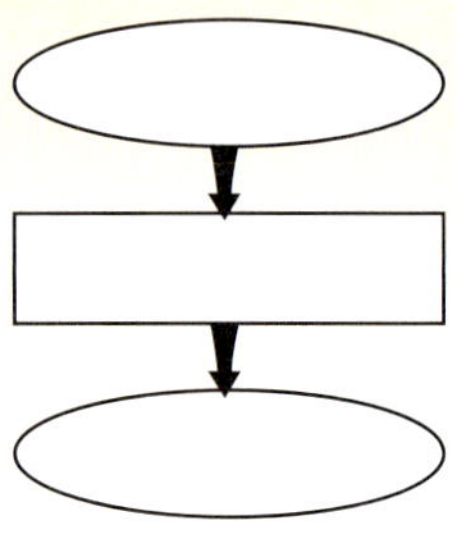

CONNECT History & Government

Creating the Post Office

Millions of people use the United States Postal Service every day. They communicate by sending and receiving mail. Most of the time, the mail takes only a few days to arrive.

The postal system was very different in the early years of the United States. Letters could take weeks or months to arrive. Postal riders traveled by day and night on horseback, using lanterns to light their way.

CALLING MR. FRANKLIN In 1775, the Continental Congress decided to start a national postal system. The leaders of the United States knew that a good communication system was needed if the nation was going to survive and grow. Benjamin Franklin was asked to serve as the first postmaster. Franklin was a printer, businessperson, author, scientist, and patriot. He had also been the postmaster in Philadelphia. He worked quickly to organize the postal system.

FASTER AND MORE RELIABLE MAIL Franklin made several changes to the existing colonial postal system. He created a simple and accurate way to manage the bookkeeping accounts. He also built new roads so that the mail could be carried faster. These roads were known as post roads. In addition, he increased the frequency of mail deliveries. Previously, mail had been delivered only twice during the winter. Franklin ordered that it be delivered every week.

Since Franklin's time the U.S. Postal Service has grown into the largest postal system in the world. It delivers more than 200 billion pieces of mail every year—almost half of all the mail in the world! It sells postal products like stamps at 38,000 places nationwide.

Critical Thinking

Answer the questions below. Then, complete the activity.

1. Why was creating a postal system so important for the Continental Congress?
2. In what ways did the postal service improve daily life in the United States?

Write About It

Working in a small group, go to the following Web site to learn more about the history of the U.S. Postal Service. Then, prepare a "Did You Know?" display about the post office. www.gfamericanhistory.com.

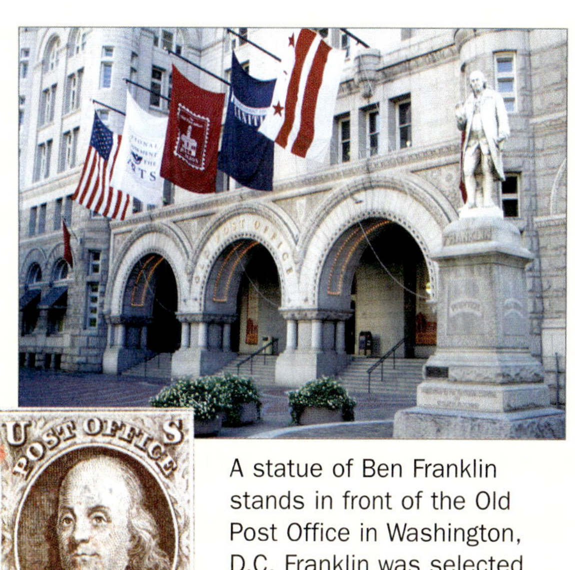

A statue of Ben Franklin stands in front of the Old Post Office in Washington, D.C. Franklin was selected for one of the first postage stamps issued (left).

III The U.S. Constitution and the Bill of Rights

Terms to Know

legislative branch the lawmaking branch of the federal government

executive branch the law-enforcing branch of the federal government

judicial branch the law-interpreting branch of the federal government

electoral college a group of people from each state who perform the official duty of electing the President and Vice President

checks and balances a system to keep one part of a government from becoming stronger than other parts

veto to reject a law

amendment a change or an addition

Main Ideas

A. Calls for a more effective government led to the Philadelphia Constitutional Convention in 1787.

B. A new U.S. Constitution was written.

C. The U.S. Constitution created a strong federal government and protected the individual rights of Americans.

Active Reading

PROBLEMS AND SOLUTIONS

The first step in solving a problem is to identify what the problem is. As you read this section, ask yourself: What problems arose during the writing of the new Constitution?

A. Steps Toward a New Constitution

The government created by the Articles of Confederation was too weak. In 1786, the same year that farmers in Massachusetts began their rebellion, some of the most important men in the country worked together to find a way to strengthen the government.

The Annapolis Convention

After only six years under the Articles of Confederation, many Americans believed they had created a government too weak to be effective. Business owners wanted a stronger economy and fewer trade barriers. Veterans of the Revolutionary War wanted to be paid for their service in the army. Farmers wanted the government to stop increasing taxes and seizing land.

Some people, such as Alexander Hamilton, an officer during the Revolutionary War, and George Washington, decided the nation needed a much stronger federal government. Others, such as Thomas Jefferson and Patrick Henry, were worried. They feared that a strong federal government might take away citizens' individual freedoms.

In 1786, citizens from Virginia and Maryland invited representatives from all the states to a convention, or meeting, in Annapolis, Maryland. Only five states sent delegations, but important decisions were made about the concerns of the nation. Delegates, including Alexander Hamilton of New York and James Madison of Virginia, agreed that the Articles of Confederation did not provide an effective government. They asked all the states to send delegates to a constitutional convention in Philadelphia, Pennsylvania.

The Constitutional Convention

In May 1787, 55 delegates from 12 states met in the State House in Philadelphia. Only Rhode Island refused to send representatives. The goal of this meeting was to improve the Articles of Confederation. The delegates hoped to create a stronger federal government that could solve the problems of the country.

The delegates of the Philadelphia Constitutional Convention came to be known as the Founding Fathers. Almost all of them had attended college. Most of them owned a great deal of property and had served in state legislatures or Congress. There were no women, Native Americans, or African Americans at the Convention.

Many of the Founding Fathers were well known. Everyone trusted and admired George Washington, so he was quickly and unanimously chosen to preside over the Convention. James Madison kept a detailed diary of the Convention. Other important members of the Convention were Gouverneur Morris of Pennsylvania, Alexander Hamilton, and Benjamin Franklin. Two important national leaders, Thomas Jefferson and John Adams, were not present. Jefferson was serving the country as ambassador to France. Adams was ambassador to Great Britain.

★ **What happened at the Annapolis Convention?**

The State House of Pennsylvania, now known as Independence Hall, was built in 1732. The Liberty Bell once hung in the bell tower.

Spotlight on

Government

The delegates to the Constitutional Convention suffered through miserable conditions for 17 weeks as they wrote the Constitution. They met during one of the hottest summers in years.

Temperatures soared in the meeting room, because the windows had been boarded shut for secrecy. In addition, the men wore heavy jackets and powdered wigs, as was the fashion in 1787.

B. Planning a New Government

One of the delegates' first decisions was to keep their discussions secret. Then, the delegates discussed their ideas for a new government. They soon realized that they needed to do much more than revise the Articles of Confederation. They needed to write a whole new constitution. However, their ideas differed greatly. Northern and southern states disagreed. Large and small states disagreed. Unless they found a plan that everyone could agree on, the new nation's future seemed unclear.

Debates and Decisions

One disagreement centered on representation in the **legislative branch**, or lawmaking branch, called Congress. Some delegates wanted all the states to have one vote. The Articles of Confederation used this system. Other delegates believed that representation should be tied to the number of people in a state.

James Madison and Edmund Randolph, both from Virginia, suggested that Congress have two houses, or parts. The number of representatives in both houses would be based on the population of each state. Therefore, larger states would receive more votes than smaller states. This was known as the Virginia, or Large-State, Plan.

William Paterson of New Jersey had a different idea. His plan called for equal representation for all states in a one-house Congress. The largest and smallest states would have the same number of representatives. This plan favored the smaller states. It was known as the New Jersey, or Small-State, Plan.

These two plans were alike in one way: In addition to the legislative branch, both also called for two new branches of government. The **executive branch** would enforce laws. The **judicial branch** would interpret laws and set up courts.

A plan proposed by Roger Sherman of Connecticut helped the delegates reach an agreement. His plan called for two houses in the legislative branch. States would be represented equally with two members in the upper house, known as the Senate. In the lower house, called the House of Representatives, the number of members from each state would depend on the state's population. States with more people would have more representatives in the lower house. In addition, both houses would have to agree on all legislation.

In July, the delegates agreed to Sherman's plan. It became known as the Great Compromise. A compromise is an agreement in which both sides trade off demands.

The delegates disagreed on another important issue. When counting the population of a state, how would enslaved people be counted for the purposes of taxation and representation in Congress?

The delegates eventually decided that for every five enslaved people, three would be counted. This decision was known as the Three-Fifths Compromise. In addition, the delegates agreed that slavery would be protected. Congress could not interfere with the importation of African slaves for 20 years.

John Locke

The Framework of the New Government

The completed Constitution created a framework for the government. It included ideas about government from several sources: The delegates used an idea from a seventeenth-century Englishman, John Locke, that stated that people should be able to remove a government that does not protect their rights. They also included the French philosopher Montesquieu's belief that certain freedoms should be granted to all people.

The Constitution contained seven articles. These articles set up the three branches of government and identified the duties of each branch. The articles also set up a federal system, which is made of a national government and state governments. The Constitution explained which powers belong to the national government and which powers belong to the individual states.

The Constitution contained rules for elections. People elect members of Congress directly by voting for a candidate. The President and Vice President are elected through a different system, which uses a group of people called the **electoral college**. This group is made up of electors. The number of electors for each state is equal to the number of that state's senators and representatives in Congress. When citizens vote, they are actually picking electors who then vote for a candidate. Electors are expected to vote for the candidate who wins the popular election, or the election in which ordinary citizens vote, in their state. The candidate with the most electoral votes wins the election.

You can read the Constitution of the United States on pages 214–239.

Checks and Balances

The Constitution included many **checks and balances**. These duties and rules were designed to keep one part of government from becoming stronger than any other part. For example, Congress passes laws, but the President can **veto**, or refuse to enact, them. In addition, the Supreme Court can decide whether or not a law is constitutional. The President appoints federal officials, but the Senate has to approve them. The President is commander in chief of the army, but only Congress can declare war. Most acts of one branch require the approval or cooperation of another branch of government.

 **What decisions did the delegates make concerning slavery?**

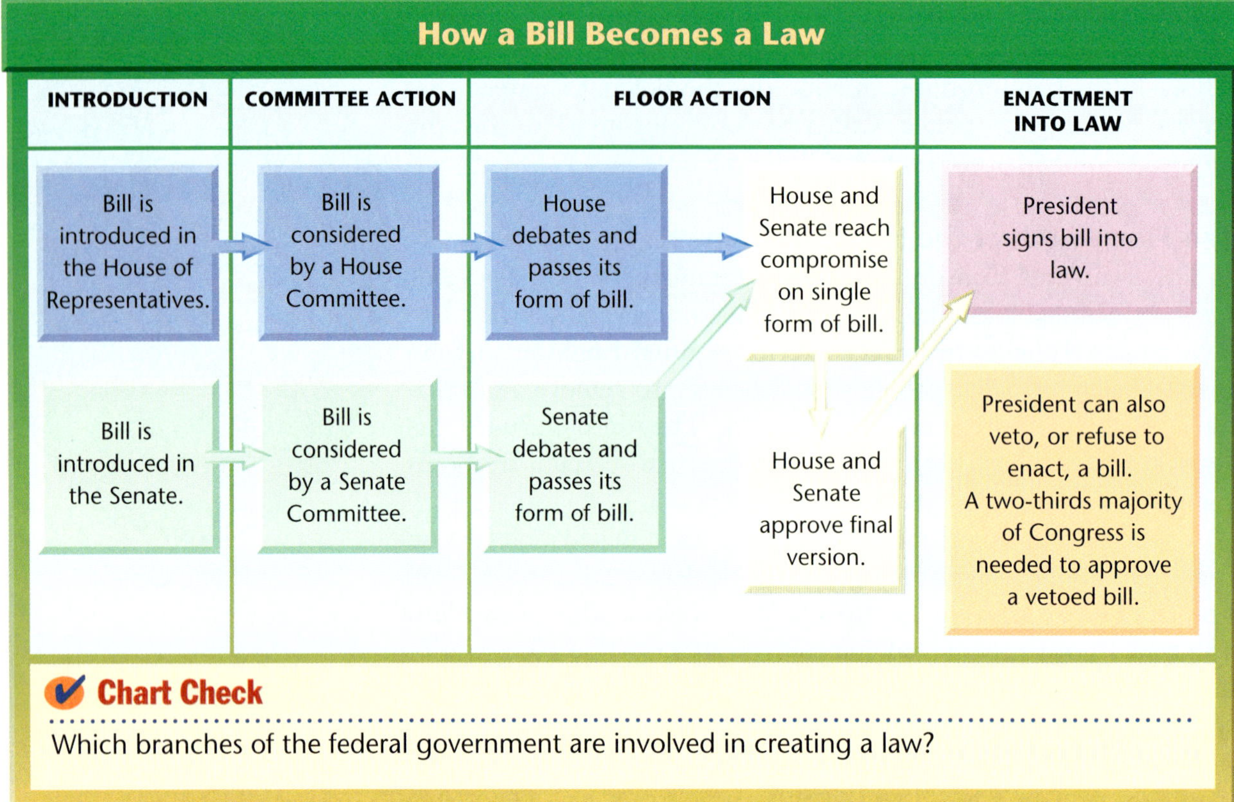

C. Approving the New Constitution

The Constitutional Convention delegates signed the U.S. Constitution on September 17, 1787. Before it went into effect, the Constitution had to be ratified by at least nine states.

Federalists and Antifederalists

Americans had different opinions of the Constitution. Those who supported it called themselves Federalists because they wanted a strong federal government. Federalists included Alexander Hamilton, George Washington, John Jay, James Madison, and John Adams.

People who opposed the Constitution were called Antifederalists. They did not want the federal government to have too much power. Instead, they wanted more power for the states. Patrick Henry and John Hancock were both Antifederalists.

Federalists James Madison, Alexander Hamilton, and John Jay wrote 185 famous essays, known as *The Federalist Papers*. These essays were printed in New York state newspapers between October 1787 and August 1788. The essays explained the Constitution and urged people to support it.

Ratification and the Bill of Rights

Delaware was the first state to ratify the Constitution. New Jersey, Pennsylvania, Georgia, and others soon followed. In June 1788, New Hampshire became the ninth state to ratify the Constitution. The new government was approved. However, the support of key states, including New York, Massachusetts, and Virginia, had not been won. Their approval was important to the success of the new government.

People in New York, Massachusetts, and Virginia worried that the Constitution gave the federal government too much power. To win the support of these states, Federalists promised to add **amendments**, or additions, to the Constitution. These amendments would guarantee individual rights. With this promise, these three states ratified the Constitution.

Ten amendments were added to the Constitution in 1791. They are known as the Bill of Rights. They protect individual rights, such as the freedom of religion, speech, and assembly. They were based on the Virginia Declaration of Rights, which was adopted in 1776.

Excitement ran high as the new nation set off on its journey. However, people were fearful of the many challenges that still lay ahead. It would be the responsibility of all citizens to help the new government succeed.

 **Why is the Bill of Rights an important part of the Constitution?**

The first ten amendments, known as the Bill of Rights, showed that the Constitution could be changed when needed. The Constitution has been amended only 27 times in more than 200 years. The last amendment was added in 1992. It addressed changes in the salaries of senators and representatives.

You can read the Bill of Rights on page 229.

Review History

A. What was the original purpose of the Philadelphia Convention?

B. In what ways did the Founding Fathers compromise on the structure of the U.S. government?

C. How did the Bill of Rights help gain approval for the Constitution?

Define Terms to Know

Provide a definition for each of the following terms.
legislative branch, executive branch, judicial branch, electoral college, checks and balances, veto, amendment

Critical Thinking

Why do you think a system of checks and balances was included in the Constitution?

Write About Citizenship

Write a newspaper editorial about the Founding Fathers' decision to keep their discussions secret.

Get Organized

CAUSE-AND-EFFECT CHAIN

Think about the main events in this section. Use a cause-and-effect chain to link these events together. For example, what were some causes and effects of many Americans' desire to protect individual freedoms?

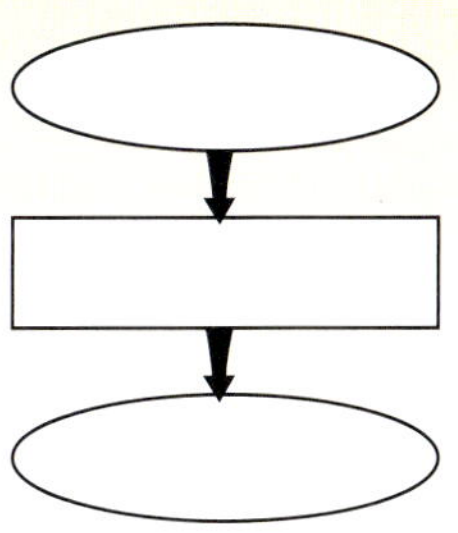

CHAPTER 9 Review

Chapter Summary

In your notebook, complete the following outline. Then, use your outline to write a brief summary of the chapter.

Forming a Government

I. The First Government
  A. Replacing British Rule
  B.
II. Problems in the New Nation
  A.
  B.
  C.
III. The U.S. Constitution and the Bill of Rights
  A.
  B.
  C.

Interpret the Timeline

Use the timeline on pages 184–185 to answer the following questions.

1. How long after the Articles of Confederation were ratified was the Constitution ratified?
2. **Critical Thinking** Which world events show that another country may have been influenced by the growth of democracy in the United States?

Use Terms to Know

Select the term that best completes each sentence.

amendment	**ratify**
constitution	**sovereignty**
ordinance	

1. Under the Articles of Confederation, the states kept their full ______.
2. Congress passed an ______ that created the Northwest Territory.
3. The Articles of Confederation were replaced with a new ______.
4. Nine states had to ______ the Constitution before it could take effect.
5. An addition to the Constitution is an ______.

Check Your Understanding

1. **Explain** how the Virginia State government increased individual freedom for citizens.
2. **Identify** two duties of the federal government under the Articles of Confederation.
3. **Summarize** the reasons for Shays's Rebellion.
4. **Describe** the problems that the nation faced under the Articles of Confederation.
5. **Compare** the Virginia Plan and the New Jersey Plan.
6. **Explain** why some states delayed ratification of the Constitution.

Critical Thinking

1. **Compare and Contrast** In what ways were the Articles of Confederation and the U.S. Constitution alike? In what ways were they different?
2. **Analyze Points of View** How did the opinions of the delegates from small states and large states differ on the topic of representation in Congress?
3. **Evaluate** How did the federal government become stronger under the Constitution?

Put Your Skills to Work

MAKE A FLOWCHART

You have learned that making a flowchart can help you to understand a sequence of events. A flowchart can also help you to identify causes and effects and find relationships among events.

Copy the following chart. Fill in the boxes with events from this chapter that link the events described in the first and last boxes.

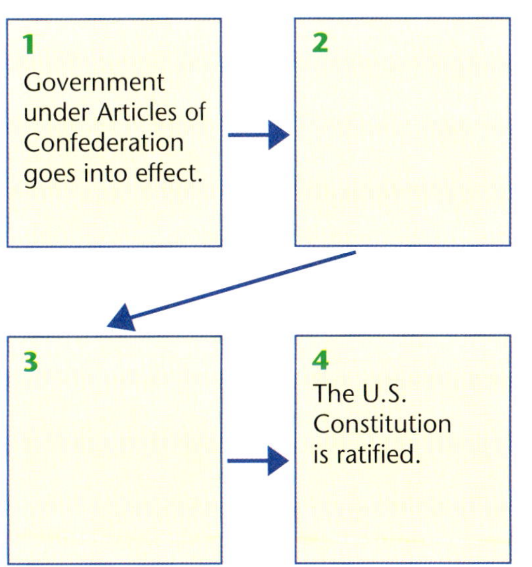

In Your Own Words

JOURNAL WRITING

The delegates to the Constitutional Convention in Philadelphia had to compromise on many issues. Write about a time when you and a friend agreed to compromise about something.

Net Work

INTERNET ACTIVITY

Working with a group of classmates, use the Internet as a resource to put together a short biography of one of the Founding Fathers. People you might choose include George Washington, James Madison, Gouverneur Morris, Alexander Hamilton, and Benjamin Franklin. Summarize the key events in your subject's life. Include an illustration of your subject and a famous quotation from that person. Compile a class anthology called *They Wrote the Constitution.*

For help in starting this activity, visit the following Web site: www.gfamericanhistory.com.

Look Ahead

In the next chapter, read about the early years of the new government.

Constitution HANDBOOK

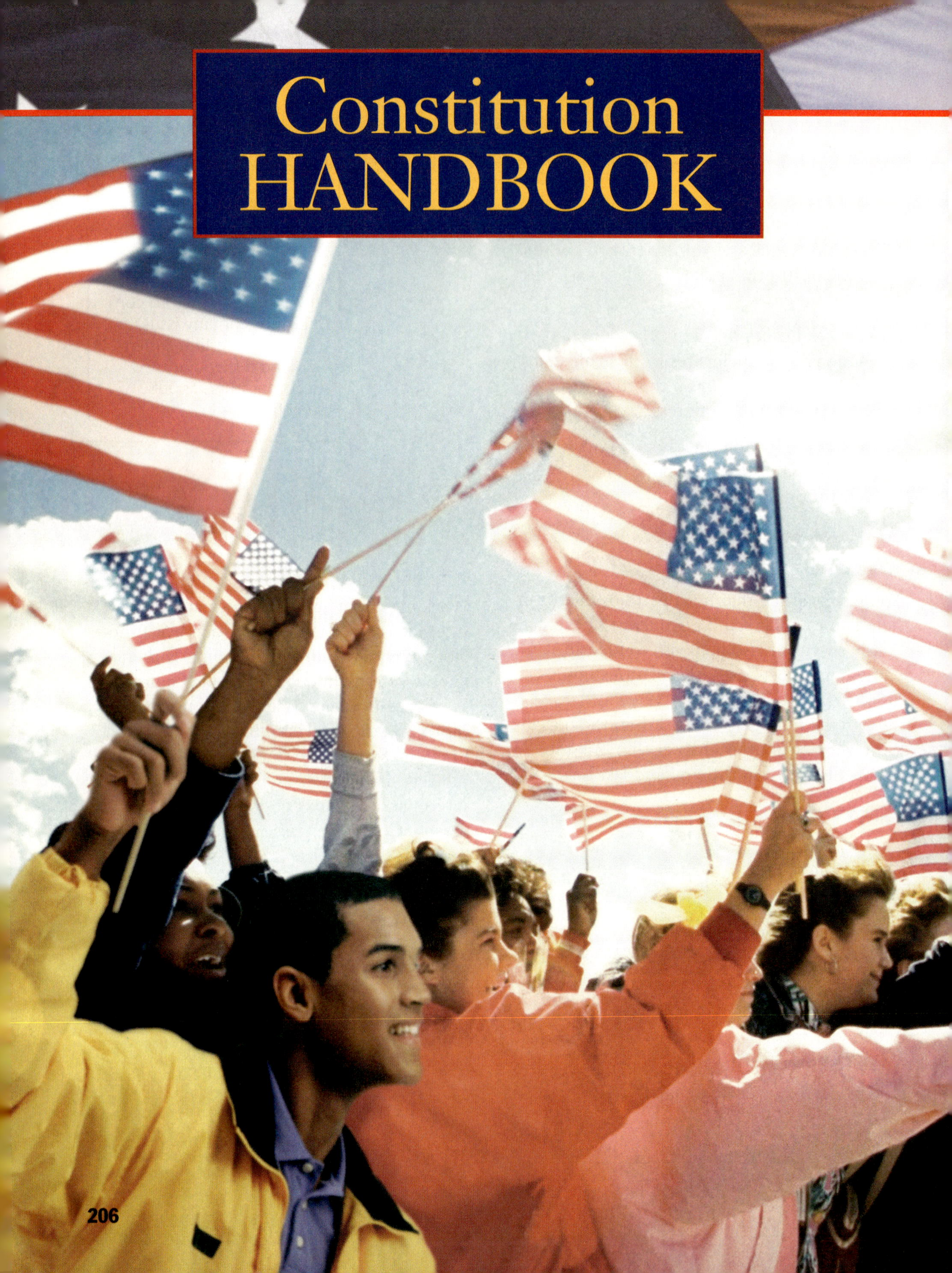

What the Constitution Is

More than 200 years after it was written, the Constitution still provides the rules by which the people of the United States live together. The Founding Fathers of the Constitution constructed a document flexible enough to be used in today's world. The newspapers and magazines that you read are free to print the news because freedom of speech and the press are protected in the Constitution. Even the right to have clubs and sports teams is guaranteed in the Constitution.

Contents

Goals of the Constitution

The Founding Fathers of the Constitution wanted to create a single, united nation with a fair government and a fair system of laws. Their goals are stated in the Preamble, or beginning, of the Constitution:

> “. . . to form a more perfect union, establish justice, insure domestic tranquility, provide for the common defense, promote the general welfare, and secure the blessing of liberty to ourselves . . .”

Principles of the Constitution

The Founding Fathers of our nation, as well as most colonists, opposed the harsh rule of the British king. They wanted a government that was fairer and less cruel. However, the weaknesses of the Articles of Confederation made them realize that a strong national government was necessary to run a country.

The Founders faced many questions:

- How could they create a government that was strong but that still allowed its citizens the liberty for which they had fought so hard?
- How could they make sure that the country was well led but that power would not fall into the hands of a few?
- How could power be balanced between the people who made the rules and those who had to live by them?

Their solutions can be found in the basic principles of the Constitution: popular sovereignty, federalism, limited government, separation of powers, and checks and balances.

Popular Sovereignty

The opening words of the Constitution, "We the people of the United States," express the principle of popular sovereignty. In a government based on popular sovereignty, the people rule. The citizens have the right to elect the people who make the laws and other decisions for them.

Federalism

The Founding Fathers wanted to create a strong national government. They also wanted to give the state governments some authority. The principle of federalism divides power between the federal government and the state governments. The federal government deals with national issues. The state governments have the power to make decisions on local matters. Some powers are shared by the federal and the state governments. The chart below shows how some of the powers are shared under federalism.

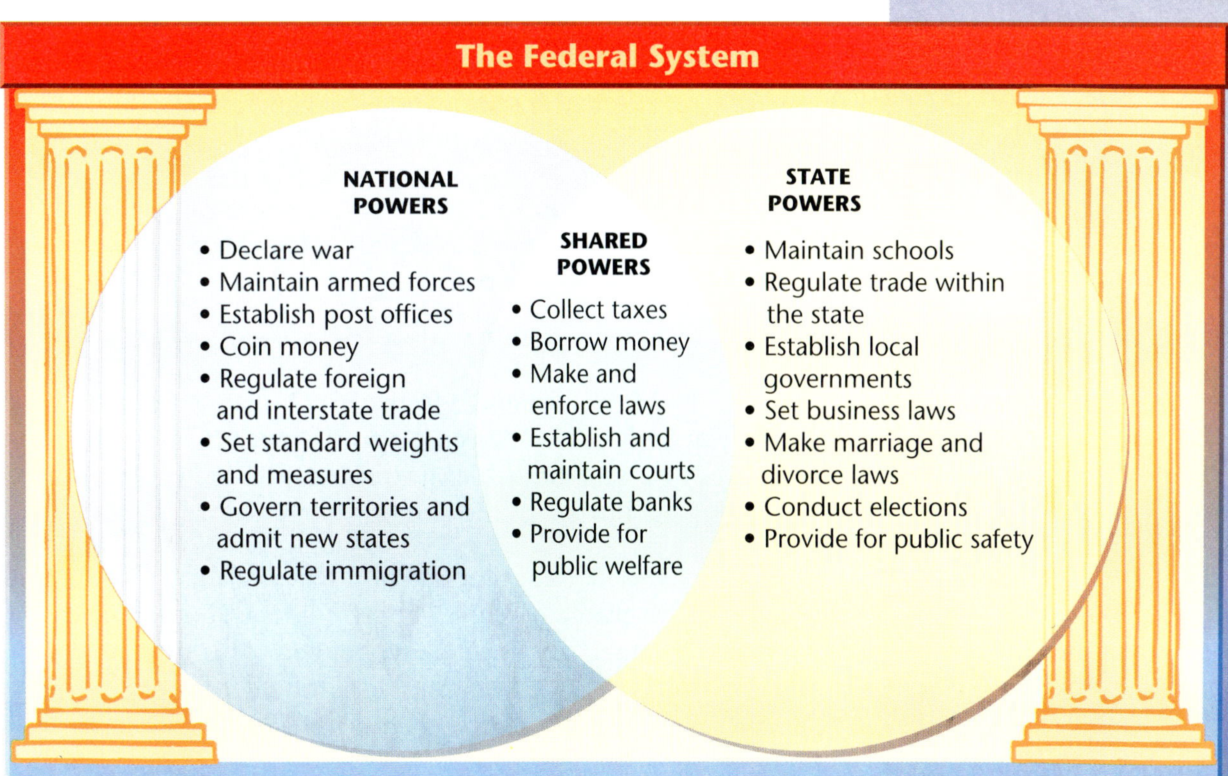

Limited Government

The Founding Fathers of the Constitution remembered the harsh rule of the British king and feared misuse of power. They wanted to prevent the government from using its power to give one group special advantages. They also wanted to make sure that no group's rights could be taken away. Article I of the Constitution defines the powers that the government has and the powers that it does not have.

The Bill of Rights states the most important limit on government. It guarantees that the federal government may not take away the individual freedoms of the people.

Limited government is also known as "rule of the law." In the U.S. government, everyone—whether citizens or powerful leaders—must obey the law.

Separation of Powers

The Constitution divides the federal government into three branches: the legislative, the executive, and the judicial. Each branch of government has its own powers and its own duties. No one branch has more power than another. This division of the federal government is known as the separation of powers.

Articles I, II, and III of the U.S. Constitution state how the powers are divided among the three branches.

Checks and Balances

The Founding Fathers wanted to be certain that no branch of government could abuse power. To do so, they set up a system that makes sure each branch of government has powers that limit and control the powers of the two other branches.

This control is called a system of checks and balances. The three branches of government keep a "check" on one another, making sure that a "balance" of power is maintained. This system helps make sure that the three branches work together fairly. The following chart shows how the checks and balances work.

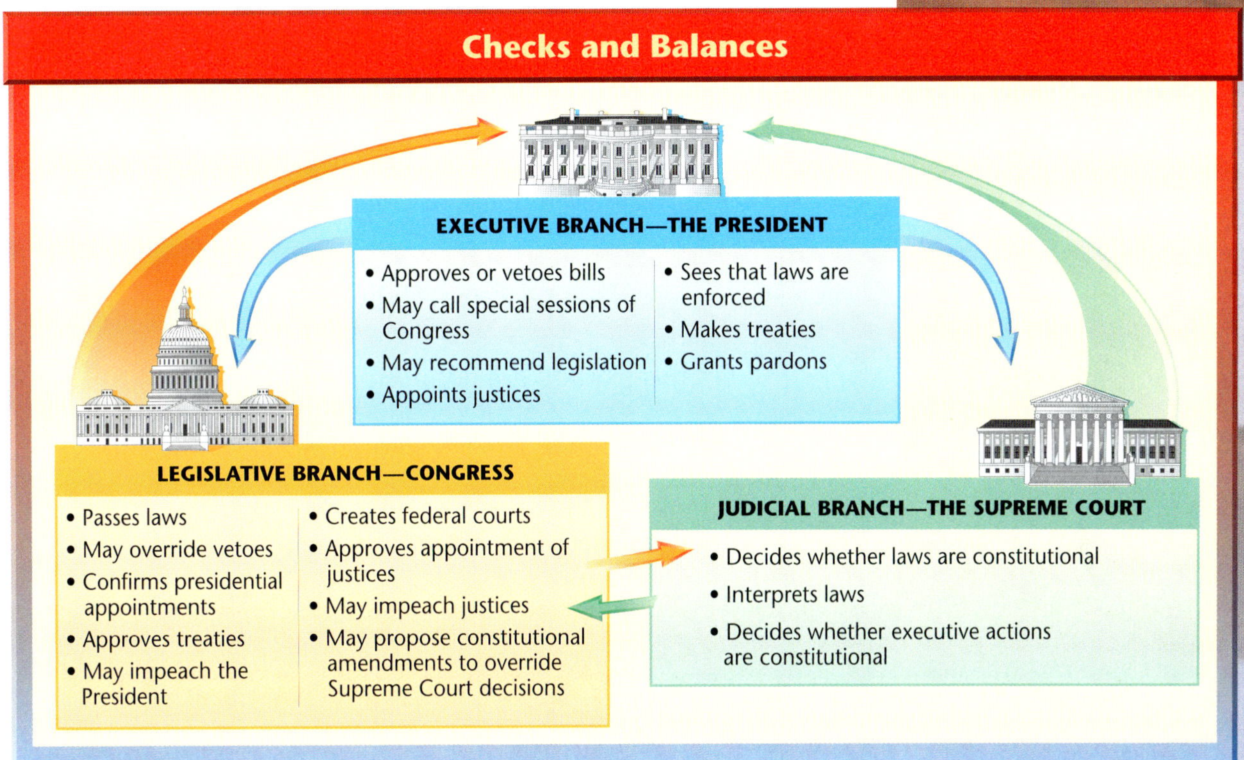

A Living Document

When the Constitution was written, only white men over age 21 who owned property were allowed to vote in national elections. Today, citizens over the age of 18 are permitted to vote. How did this change come about?

The Founding Fathers of the Constitution realized that the United States would grow and change. They realized that the Constitution would have to change to meet new circumstances and challenges. That is why it is called a "living document."

The Founding Fathers outlined a process by which amendments, or written changes, could be added to the Constitution. However, the amendment process was set up to be difficult in order to discourage minor or frequent changes.

How to Amend the Constitution

There are two steps to amending the Constitution. The first step is proposing the amendment. An amendment to the Constitution can be proposed in two ways:

- Two-thirds of each house of Congress can vote for the amendment.
- Two-thirds of the state legislatures can ask for Congress to call a special convention to suggest the amendment. So far, this method has not been used.

The second step is ratifying, or approving, the amendment. All amendments must be agreed to by the states.

The chart below shows how the amendment process works.

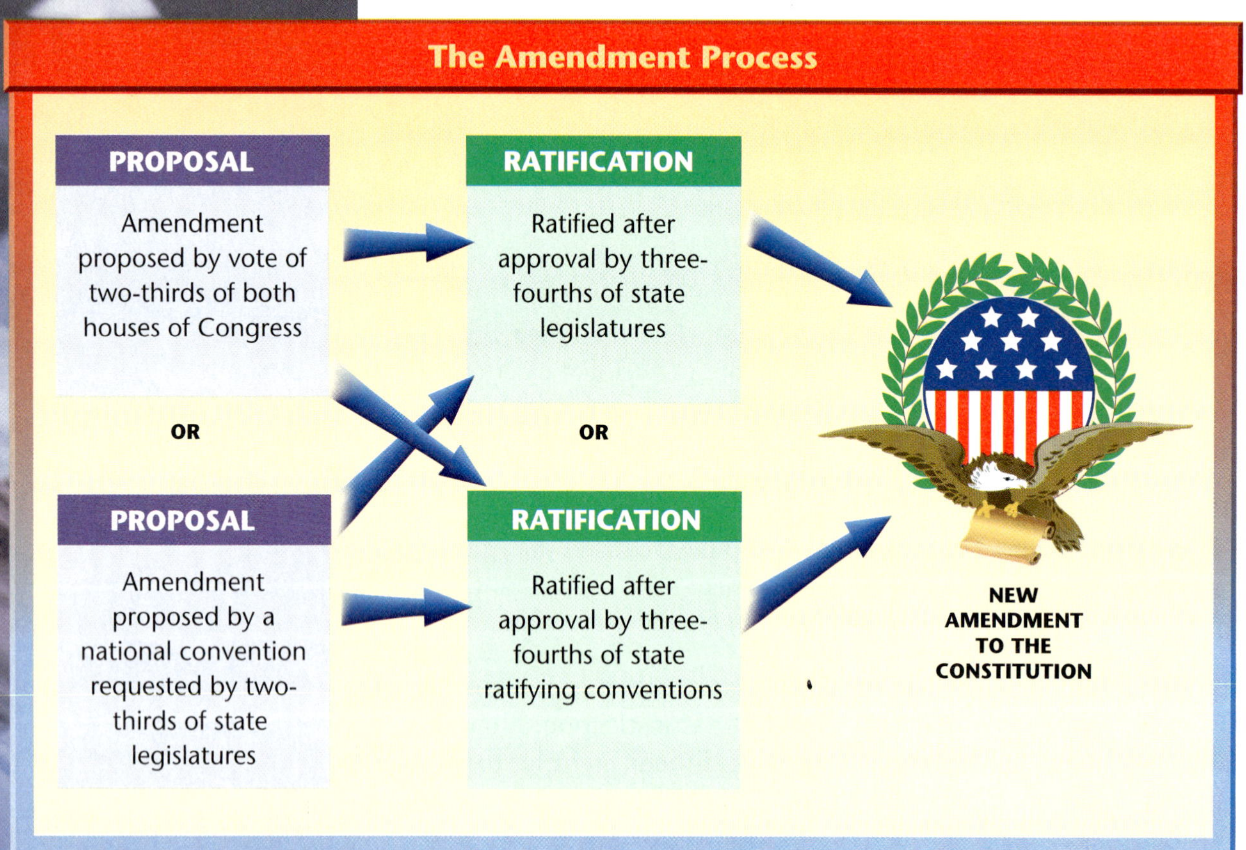

Citizenship

As a citizen of the United States, you are entitled to all the rights in the U.S. Constitution. A democratic society also needs its citizens to carry out certain duties and responsibilities in order to run smoothly.

Duties

Duties are actions required by law. Here are some duties to keep in mind:

- It is each person's duty to obey the law and to respect everyone's rights equally.
- Americans also have a duty to pay taxes. The federal government uses tax money to build roads and bridges, maintain the armed forces, support education, and provide health insurance for the elderly.
- Another duty of citizens is to defend their country. Eighteen-year-old males must register with the federal government in case the nation may need to call on them for military service.

Responsibilities

A healthy democracy depends on its citizens to accept certain responsibilities in their communities. Here are some responsibilities to keep in mind:

- Become well informed. Know what is happening in your community, your state, your country, and the world.
- Know your rights. You cannot protect your rights unless you know what they are. You can get information about your rights from books and from government publications.
- Vote. All American citizens can vote when they are 18 years of age. Voting is probably your most important responsibility as a citizen. When you vote, you choose people to represent you in government. You exercise your right of self-government—the very principle upon which the United States was founded.

The text of the Constitution, using modern spelling, punctuation, and capitalization, appears on the following pages. Portions which no longer apply or have been changed are crossed out. The titles in bold and notes in the margin have been added to help you understand the document.

The Constitution
of the United States of America

Preamble

We the people of the United States, in order to form a more perfect Union, establish justice, insure domestic **tranquility**, provide for the common defense, promote the general welfare, and secure the blessings of liberty to ourselves and our **posterity**, do **ordain** and establish this Constitution for the United States of America.

Article I. The Legislative Branch

Section 1. Congress All legislative powers herein granted shall be **vested** in a Congress of the United States, which shall consist of a Senate and House of Representatives.

Section 2. House of Representatives

1. ELECTIONS The House of Representatives shall be composed of members chosen every second year by the people of the several states, and the electors in each state shall have the qualifications **requisite** for electors of the most numerous branch of the state legislature.

2. QUALIFICATIONS No person shall be a representative who shall not have attained to the age of twenty-five years, and been seven years a citizen of the United States, and who shall not, when elected, be an inhabitant of that state in which he shall be chosen.

3. NUMBER OF REPRESENTATIVES Representatives ~~and direct taxes~~ shall be apportioned among the several states which may be included within this Union, according to their respective numbers, ~~which shall be determined by adding to the whole number of free persons, including those bound to service for a term of years, and excluding Indians not taxed, three-fifths of all other persons.~~ The actual **enumeration** shall be made within three years after the first meeting of the Congress of the United States, and within

Document Dictionary

tranquility peace

posterity future generations

ordain to establish by law

vested held completely

requisite required

enumeration an official count, such as a census

impeachment the constitutional process of accusing the President or other high officials of a crime

The Main Idea

Section 2. House of Representatives

States must hold elections for the House of Representatives every two years.

A representative must

- be at least 25 years old.
- have been a citizen of the United States for seven years.
- be a resident of the state that elects the representative.

The total number of representatives in the House is limited to 435.

every subsequent term of ten years, in such manner as they shall by law direct. The number of representatives shall not exceed one for every thirty thousand, but each state shall have at least one representative; ~~and until such enumeration shall be made, the state of New Hampshire shall be entitled to choose 3, Massachusetts 8, Rhode Island and Providence Plantations 1, Connecticut 5, New York 6, New Jersey 4, Pennsylvania 8, Delaware 1, Maryland 6, Virginia 10, North Carolina 5, South Carolina 5, and Georgia 3.~~

4. VACANCIES When vacancies happen in the representation of any state, the executive authority thereof shall issue writs of election to fill such vacancies.

5. OFFICERS AND IMPEACHMENT The House of Representatives shall choose their speaker and other officers; and shall have the sole power of **impeachment**.

Section 3. The Senate

1. NUMBER OF SENATORS The Senate of the United States shall be composed of two senators from each state, ~~chosen by the legislature thereof,~~ for six years; and each senator shall have one vote.

2. CLASSIFYING TERMS Immediately after they shall be assembled in consequence of the first election, they shall be divided as equally as may be into three classes. ~~The seats of the senators of the first class shall be vacated at the expiration of the second year, of the second class at the expiration of the fourth year, and of the third class at the expiration of the sixth year,~~ so that one-third may be chosen every second year; ~~and if vacancies happen by resignation, or otherwise, during the recess of the legislature of any state, the executive thereof may make temporary appointments until the next meeting of the legislature, which shall then fill such vacancies.~~

3. QUALIFICATIONS No person shall be a senator who shall not have attained to the age of thirty years, and been nine years a citizen of the United States, and who shall not, when elected, be an inhabitant of that state for which he shall be chosen.

The Main Idea

Section 3. The Senate

Senators are elected every six years. The Founding Fathers of the Constitution made Senate terms longer than House terms to make the Senate more stable.

A Senator must

- be at least 30 years old.
- have been a citizen of the United States for nine years.
- live in the state he or she will represent.

Document Dictionary

pro tempore for the time being

concurrence agreement

indictment accusation

quorum the minimum number of members who must be present in order to conduct business

adjourn stop a meeting

felony a serious crime

breach break

emolument a payment

The Main Idea

Section 4. Congressional Elections and Meetings

Each state makes its own rules about electing senators and representatives. However, Congress may change these rules at any time. The Constitution requires the Congress to meet at least once a year.

The Main Idea

Section 5. Rules and Procedures

Each house is responsible for overseeing its elections, determining its rules, and punishing its members for violation of such rules. Each house must keep a record of its proceedings and votes so that people know how their representatives voted on bills.

4. ROLE OF VICE PRESIDENT The Vice President of the United States shall be President of the Senate, but shall have no vote, unless they be equally divided.

5. OFFICERS The Senate shall choose their other officers, and also a president **pro tempore**, in the absence of the Vice President, or when he shall exercise the office of President of the United States.

6. IMPEACHMENT TRIALS The Senate shall have the sole power to try all impeachments. When sitting for that purpose, they shall be on oath or affirmation. When the President of the United States is tried, the Chief Justice shall preside: And no person shall be convicted without the **concurrence** of two-thirds of the members present.

7. PUNISHMENT FOR IMPEACHMENT Judgment in cases of impeachment shall not extend further than to removal from office, and disqualification to hold and enjoy any office of honor, trust, or profit under the United States; but the party convicted shall nevertheless be liable and subject to **indictment**, trial, judgment, and punishment, according to law.

Section 4. Congressional Elections and Meetings

1. REGULATIONS The times, places, and manner of holding elections for senators and representatives, shall be prescribed in each state by the legislature thereof; but the Congress may at any time by law make or alter such regulations, except as to the places of choosing senators.

2. SESSIONS The Congress shall assemble at least once in every year, ~~and such meeting shall be on the first Monday in December, unless they shall by law appoint a different day.~~

Section 5. Rules and Procedures

1. QUORUM Each house shall be the judge of the elections, returns, and qualifications of its own members, and a majority of each shall constitute a **quorum** to do business; but a smaller number may **adjourn** from day to day, and may be authorized to compel the attendance of absent members, in such manner, and under such penalties as each house may provide.

2. RULES AND CONDUCT Each house may determine the rules of its proceedings, punish its members for disorderly behavior, and, with the concurrence of two-thirds, expel a member.

3. RECORD KEEPING Each house shall keep a journal of its proceedings, and from time to time publish the same, excepting such parts as may in their judgment require secrecy; and the yeas and nays of the members of either house on any question shall, at the desire of one-fifth of those present, be entered on the journal.

4. ADJOURNMENT Neither house, during the session of Congress, shall, without the consent of the other, adjourn for more than three days, nor to any other place than that in which the two houses shall be sitting.

Section 6. Payment and Privileges

1. SALARY The senators and representatives shall receive a compensation for their services, to be ascertained by law, and paid out of the treasury of the United States. They shall in all cases, except treason, **felony**, and **breach** of the peace, be privileged from arrest during their attendance at the session of their respective houses, and in going to and returning from the same; and for any speech or debate in either house, they shall not be questioned in any other place.

2. RESTRICTIONS No senator or representative shall, during the time for which he was elected, be appointed to any civil office under the authority of the United States, which shall have been created, or the **emoluments** whereof shall have been increased during such time; and no person holding any office under the United States, shall be a member of either house during his continuance in office.

Section 7. How a Bill Becomes a Law

1. TAX BILLS All bills for raising revenue shall originate in the House of Representatives; but the Senate may propose or concur with amendments as on other bills.

The Main Idea

Section 6. Payment and Privileges

Members of Congress are paid by the federal government. Congressional immunity protects members from punishment for anything said in Congress. This protection allows the members to speak freely. However, it does not protect them from arrest for criminal offenses.

The Main Idea

Section 7. How a Bill Becomes a Law

All taxation bills must start in the House of Representatives. Bills have to be passed by both houses of Congress.

Document Dictionary

debt money, goods, or services owed to another person or group

counterfeiting to make an imitation of

tribunal court

The Main Idea

Section 8. Powers of Congress

The powers and duties of Congress are listed here. They are specific powers that include the right to

- tax.
- borrow money.
- regulate trade.
- coin money.
- set up post offices.
- declare war.
- raise an army and a navy.

2. APPROVING A BILL Every bill which shall have passed the House of Representatives and the Senate, shall, before it become a law, be presented to the President of the United States; if he approve he shall sign it, but if not he shall return it, with his objections to that house in which it shall have originated, who shall enter the objections at large on their journal, and proceed to reconsider it. If after such reconsideration two-thirds of that house shall agree to pass the bill, it shall be sent, together with the objections, to the other house, by which it shall likewise be reconsidered, and if approved by two-thirds of that house, it shall become a law. But in all such cases the votes of both houses shall be determined by yeas and nays, and the names of the persons voting for and against the bill shall be entered on the journal of each house respectively. If any bill shall not be returned by the President within ten days (Sundays excepted) after it shall have been presented to him, the same shall be law, in like manner as if he had signed it, unless the Congress by their adjournment prevent its return, in which case it shall not be a law.

3. ROLE OF THE PRESIDENT Every order, resolution, or vote to which the concurrence of the Senate and House of Representatives may be necessary (except on a question of adjournment) shall be presented to the President of the United States; and before the same shall take effect, shall be approved by him, or being disapproved by him, shall be repassed by two-thirds of the Senate and House of Representatives, according to the rules and limitations prescribed in the case of a bill.

Section 8. Powers of Congress

1. TAXATION The Congress shall have the power to lay and collect taxes, duties, imposts, and excises, to pay the **debts** and provide for the common defense and general welfare of the United States; but all duties, imposts, and excises shall be uniform throughout the United States;

2. BORROW MONEY To borrow money on the credit of the United States;

3. TRADE To regulate commerce with foreign nations, and among the several states, and with the Indian tribes;

4. NATURALIZATION, BANKRUPTCY To establish a uniform rule of naturalization, and uniform laws on the subject of bankruptcies throughout the United States;

5. MONEY To coin money, regulate the value thereof, and of foreign coin, and fix the standard of weights and measures;

6. COUNTERFEITING To provide for the punishment of **counterfeiting** the securities and current coin of the United States;

7. POST OFFICES To establish post offices and post roads;

8. COPYRIGHTS AND PATENTS To promote the progress of science and useful arts, by securing for limited times to authors and inventors the exclusive right to their respective writings and discoveries;

9. FEDERAL COURTS To constitute **tribunals** inferior to the Supreme Court;

10. INTERNATIONAL LAW To define and punish piracies and felonies committed on the high seas, and offenses against the law of nations;

11. WAR To declare war, ~~grant letters of marque and reprisal,~~ and make rules concerning captures on land and water;

12. ARMY To raise and support armies, but no appropriation of money to that use shall be for a longer term than two years;

13. NAVY To provide and maintain a navy;

14. RULES FOR ARMED FORCES To make rules for the government and regulation of the land and naval forces;

15. MILITIA To provide for calling forth the militia to execute the laws of the Union, suppress insurrections and repel invasions;

16. RULES FOR MILITIA To provide for organizing, arming, and disciplining the militia, and for governing such part of them as may be employed in the service of the United States, reserving to the states respectively, the appointment of the officers, and the authority of training the militia according to the discipline prescribed by Congress;

Document Dictionary

attainder to punish a person without a trial

ex post facto law a law that punishes a person for an action that was legal when the action was performed

tender money

duty of tonnage charge per ton

The Main Idea

Section 9. Powers Denied to Congress

Congress does not have the powers listed in this section. This clause reflects the Founding Fathers' fear of creating a government that was too powerful. Congress cannot

- set a direct tax on people unless it is in proportion to the total population.
- tax goods sent from one state to another or from a state to another country.
- favor one state over another in making trade laws.

17. DISTRICT OF COLUMBIA To exercise exclusive legislation in all cases whatsoever, over such district (not exceeding ten miles square) as may, by cession of particular states, and the acceptance of Congress, become the seat of the government of the United States, and to exercise like authority over all places purchased by the consent of the legislature of the state in which the same shall be, for the erection of forts, magazines, arsenals, dockyards, and other needful buildings; and

18. ELASTIC CLAUSE To make all laws which shall be necessary and proper for carrying into execution the foregoing powers, and all other powers vested by this Constitution in the government of the United States, or in any department or officer thereof.

Section 9. Powers Denied to Congress

1. SLAVERY ~~The migration or importation of such persons as any of the states now existing shall think proper to admit, shall not be prohibited by the Congress prior to the year one thousand eight hundred and eight, but a tax or duty may be imposed on such importation, not exceeding ten dollars for each person.~~

2. HABEAS CORPUS The privilege of the writ of habeas corpus shall not be suspended, unless when in cases of rebellion or invasion the public safety may require it.

3. ILLEGAL PUNISHMENT No bill of **attainder** or **ex post facto law** shall be passed.

4. DIRECT TAX No capitation, ~~or other direct,~~ tax shall be laid, unless in proportion to the census or enumeration herein before directed to be taken.

5. EXPORT TAXES No tax or duty shall be laid on articles exported from any state.

6. TRADE PREFERENCES No preference shall be given by any regulation of commerce or revenue to the ports of one state over those of another; nor shall vessels bound to, or from, one state, be obliged to enter, clear, or pay duties in another.

7. SPENDING PUBLIC MONEY No money shall be drawn from the treasury, but in consequence of appropriations made by law; and a regular statement and account of the receipts and expenditures of all public money shall be published from time to time.

8. TITLES OF NOBILITY No title of nobility shall be granted by the United States; and no person holding any office of profit or trust under them, shall, without the consent of the Congress, accept of any present, emolument, office, or title, of any kind whatever, from any king, prince, or foreign state.

Section 10. Powers Denied to the States

1. RESTRICTIONS No state shall enter into any treaty, alliance, or confederation; grant letters of marque and reprisal; coin money; emit bills of credit; make anything but gold and silver coin as **tender** in payment of debts; pass any bill of attainder, ex post facto law, or law impairing the obligation of contracts, or grant any title of nobility.

2. IMPORT AND EXPORT TAXES No state shall, without the consent of the Congress, lay any imposts or duties on imports or exports, except what may be absolutely necessary for executing its inspection laws; and the net produce of all duties and imposts, laid by any state on imports or exports, shall be for the use of the treasury of the United States; and all such laws shall be subject to the revision and control of the Congress.

3. PEACETIME AND WAR RESTRAINTS No state shall, without the consent of Congress, lay any **duty of tonnage**, keep troops, or ships of war in time of peace, enter into any agreement or compact with another state, or with a foreign power, or engage in war, unless actually invaded, or in such imminent danger as will not admit of delay.

Article II. The Executive Branch

Section 1. The Presidency

1. TERMS OF OFFICE The executive power shall be vested in a President of the United States of America. He shall hold his office during the term of four years, and, together with the Vice President, chosen for the same term, be elected, as follows:

The Main Idea

Section 10. Powers Denied to the States

The Founding Fathers of the Constitution understood the dangers of a powerful federal government, but they also wanted to prevent the 13 states from acting like independent nations. The states may not assume any of the powers that are specifically given to Congress. These powers include the right to

- make treaties with other nations.
- coin money.
- declare war.
- tax trade.

The Main Idea

Section 1. The Presidency

Article II of the Constitution gives the President "executive power." This power includes the right to enforce the laws of the U.S. government. The first clause sets the term of office at four years.

A President must

- have been born in the United States.
- be at least 35 years old.
- have lived in the United States for at least 14 years.

Document Dictionary

natural-born citizen a citizen born in the United States to parents who are U.S. citizens but who live in another country

affirmation a statement declaring that something is true

2. ELECTORAL COLLEGE Each state shall appoint, in such manner as the legislature thereof may direct, a number of electors, equal to the whole number of senators and representatives to which the state may be entitled in the Congress; but no senator or representative, or person holding an office of trust or profit under the United States, shall be appointed an elector.

3. FORMER METHOD OF ELECTING PRESIDENT ~~The electors shall meet in their respective states, and vote by ballot for two persons, of whom one at least shall not be an inhabitant of the same state with themselves. And they shall make a list of all the persons voted for, and of the number of votes for each; which list they shall sign and certify, and transmit sealed to the seat of the government of the United States, directed to the president of the Senate. The president of the Senate shall, in the presence of the Senate and House of Representatives, open all the certificates, and the votes shall them be counted. The person having the greatest number of votes shall be the President, if such number be a majority of the whole number of electors appointed; and if there be more than one who have such majority, and have an equal number of votes, then the House of Representatives shall immediately choose by ballot one of them for President; and if no person have a majority, then from the five highest on the list the said House shall in like manner choose the President. But in choosing the President, the votes shall be taken by states, the representation from each state having one vote; a quorum for this purpose shall consist of a member or members from two-thirds of the states, and a majority of all the states shall be necessary to a choice. In every case, after the choice of the President, the person having the greatest number of votes of the electors shall be the Vice President. But if there should remain two or more who have equal votes, the Senate shall choose from them by ballot the Vice President.~~

4. TIME OF ELECTIONS The Congress may determine the time of choosing the electors, and the day on which they shall give their votes; which day shall be the same throughout the United States.

5. REQUIREMENTS FOR PRESIDENT No person except a **natural-born citizen,** or a citizen of the United States, at the time of the adoption of this Constitution, shall be eligible to the office of President; neither shall any person be eligible to that office who shall not have attained to the age of thirty-five years, and been fourteen years a resident within the United States.

6. SUCCESSION In case of the removal of the President from office, or of his death, resignation, or inability to discharge the powers and duties of the said office, the same shall devolve on the Vice President, and the Congress may by law provide for the case of removal, death, resignation or inability, both of the President and Vice President, declaring what officer shall then act as President, and such officer shall act accordingly, until the disability be removed, or a President shall be elected.

7. SALARY The President shall, at stated times, receive for his services, a compensation, which shall neither be increased nor diminished during the period for which he shall have been elected, and he shall not receive within that period any other emolument from the United States, or any of them.

8. OATH OF OFFICE Before he enter on the execution of his office, he shall take the following oath or **affirmation**: "I do solemnly swear (or affirm) that I will faithfully execute the office of President of the United States, and will to the best of my ability, preserve, protect, and defend the Constitution of the United States."

Section 2. Powers of the President

1. MILITARY POWERS The President shall be commander in chief of the Army and Navy of the United States, and of the militia of the several states, when called into the actual service of the United States; he may require the opinion, in writing, of the principal officer in each of the executive departments, upon any subject relating to the duties of their respective offices, and he shall have power to grant reprieves and pardons for offenses against the United States, except in cases of impeachment.

2. CHECKS AND BALANCES He shall have power, by and with the advice and consent of the Senate, to make treaties, provided two-thirds of the senators present concur; and he shall nominate, and by and with the advice and consent of the Senate, shall appoint

The Main Idea

Section 2. Powers of the President

This section gives the President the power to

- command the nation's armed forces.
- obtain information from the head of each executive.
- grant pardons for federal offenses.
- make treaties and appoint government officials with the advice and consent of the Senate.

ambassadors, other public ministers and consuls, judges of the Supreme Court, and all other officers of the United States, whose appointments are not herein otherwise provided for, and which shall be established by law; but the Congress may by law vest the appointment of such inferior officers, as they think proper, in the President alone, in the courts of law, or in the heads of departments.

3. FILLING VACANCIES The President shall have power to fill up all vacancies that may happen during the recess of the Senate, by granting commissions which shall expire at the end of their next session.

Section 3. Presidential Duties He shall from time to time give to the Congress information of the state of the Union, and recommend to their consideration such measures as he shall judge necessary and expedient; he may, on extraordinary occasions, convene both houses, or either of them, and in case of disagreement between them, with respect to the time of adjournment, he may adjourn them to such time as he shall think proper; he shall receive ambassadors and other public ministers; he shall take care that the laws be faithfully executed, and shall commission all the officers of the United States.

Section 4. Impeachment The President, Vice President, and all civil officers of the United States, shall be removed from office on impeachment for, and conviction of, treason, bribery, or other high crimes and **misdemeanors.**

Article III. The Judicial Branch

Section 1. The Court System The judicial power of the United States, shall be vested in one Supreme Court, and in such inferior courts as the Congress may from time to time ordain and establish. The judges, both of the Supreme and inferior courts, shall hold their offices during good behavior, and shall, at stated times, receive for their services, a compensation, which shall not be diminished during their continuance in office.

Document Dictionary

misdemeanor a minor violation of the law

equity fairness

consul a government official who looks after our government's interests in other countries

admiralty officials in charge of the navy

levying starting or waging

The Main Idea

Section 3. Presidential Duties

The President shall deliver a state of the Union message to Congress shortly after the beginning of each congressional session. In this message, the President can suggest laws that should be made. The President must see that laws are executed.

The Main Idea

Section 1. The Court System

The Supreme Court is the nation's highest court. Its judges are appointed by the President, with the approval of the Senate, and they may hold office for life. Congress has the power to establish other federal courts.

Section 2. Authority of the Courts

1. FEDERAL COURTS AND JUDGES The judicial power shall extend to all cases, in law and **equity**, arising under this Constitution, the laws of the United States, and treaties made, or which shall be made, under their authority; to all cases affecting ambassadors, other public ministers and **consuls**; to all cases of **admiralty** and maritime jurisdiction; to controversies to which the United States shall be a party; to controversies between two or more states; ~~between a state and citizens of another state;~~ between citizens of different states; between citizens of the same state claiming lands under grants of different states, and between a state, or the citizens thereof, and foreign states, ~~citizens or subjects~~.

2. SUPREME COURT In all cases affecting ambassadors, other public ministers and consuls, and those in which a state shall be party, the Supreme Court shall have original jurisdiction. In all the other cases before mentioned, the Supreme Court shall have appellate jurisdiction, both as to law and fact, with such exceptions, and under such regulations as the Congress shall make.

3. TRIAL BY JURY The trial of all crimes, except in cases of impeachment, shall be by jury; and such trial shall be held in the state where the said crimes shall have been committed; but when not committed within any state, the trial shall be at such place or places as the Congress may by law have directed.

The Main Idea

Section 2. Authority of the Courts

Federal courts handle certain kinds of cases. Only a few are handled directly by the Supreme Court. The judgment of the Supreme Court is final.

Section 3. Treason

1. DEFINITION Treason against the United States, shall consist only in **levying** war against them, or in adhering to their enemies, giving them aid and comfort. No person shall be convicted of treason unless on the testimony of two witnesses to the same overt act, or on confession in open court.

2. PUNISHMENT The Congress shall have power to declare the punishment of treason, but no attainder of treason shall work corruption of blood, or forfeiture except during the life of the person attainted.

The Main Idea

Section 3. Treason

Treason is a serious act of disloyalty against the United States. It is the only crime defined in the Constitution.

Document Dictionary

immunity legal protection

construed interpreted

Article IV. Relations Among the States

Section 1. State Acts and Records Full faith and credit shall be given in each state to the public acts, records, and judicial proceedings of every other state. And the Congress may by general laws prescribe the manner in which such acts, records, and proceedings shall be proved, and the effect thereof.

The Main Idea

Section 2. Rights of Citizens

A citizen of one state must be given the same rights as a citizen of another state when visiting that other state. The governor of a state has the power to send someone accused of a crime in another state back to that other state for trial.

Section 2. Rights of Citizens

1. CITIZENSHIP The citizens of each state shall be entitled to all privileges and **immunities** of citizens in the several states.

2. CRIMINAL JURISDICTION A person charged in any state with treason, felony, or other crime, who shall flee from justice, and be found in another state, shall on demand of the executive authority of the state from which he fled, be delivered up, to be removed to the state having jurisdiction of the crime.

3. FUGITIVE SLAVES ~~No person held to service or labor in one state, under the laws thereof, escaping into another, shall, in consequence of any law or regulation therein, be discharged from such service or labor, but shall be delivered up on claim of the party to whom such service or labor may be due.~~

The Main Idea

Section 3. New States

Only Congress can admit new states to the Union.

Section 3. New States

1. ADMISSION New states may be admitted by the Congress into this Union; but no new state shall be formed or erected within the jurisdiction of any other state; nor any state be formed by the junction of two or more states, or parts of states, without the consent of the legislatures of the states concerned as well as of the Congress.

2. CONGRESSIONAL AUTHORITY The Congress shall have power to dispose of and make all needful rules and regulations respecting the territory of other property belonging to the United States; and nothing in this Constitution shall be so **construed** as to prejudice any claims of the United States, or of any particular state.

The Main Idea

Section 4. Guarantees to the States

The U.S. government will protect all states from enemies and help the states deal with rebellion or local violence.

Section 4. Guarantees to the States The United States shall guarantee to every state in this Union a republican form of government, and shall protect each of them against invasion; and on application of the legislature, or of the executive (when the legislature cannot be convened) against domestic violence.

Article V. Amending the Constitution

The Congress, whenever two-thirds of both houses shall deem it necessary, shall propose amendments to this Constitution, or, on the application of the legislatures of two-thirds of the several states, shall call a convention for proposing amendments, which, in either case, shall be valid to all intents and purposes, as part of this Constitution, when ratified by the legislatures of three-fourths of the several states, or by conventions in three-fourths thereof, as the one or the other mode of ratification may be proposed by the Congress; provided that ~~no amendment which may be made prior to the year one thousand eight hundred and eight shall in any manner affect the first and fourth clauses in the ninth section of the first article;~~ and that no state, without its consent, shall be deprived of its equal suffrage in the Senate.

The Main Idea

Article V. Amending the Constitution

These procedures are necessary to amend, or change, the Constitution. The process is very difficult. Since 1789, only 33 amendments have been proposed, and 27 have been ratified. There are two ways of proposing an amendment:

- by a two-thirds vote in Congress
- by a national convention called by Congress at the request of two-thirds of the individual state legislatures

Article VI. National Debts and Ratification

Section 1. Debts All debts contracted and engagements entered into, before the adoption of this Constitution, shall be as valid against the United States under this Constitution, as under the Confederation.

Section 2. Supreme Law This Constitution, and the laws of the United States which shall be made in pursuance thereof; and all treaties made, or which shall be made, under the authority of the United States, shall be the supreme law of the land; and the judges in every state shall be bound thereby, anything in the constitution or laws of any state to the contrary notwithstanding.

Section 3. Loyalty to the Constitution The senators and representatives before mentioned, and the members of the several state legislatures, and all executive and judicial officers, both of the United States and of the several states, shall be bound by oath or affirmation, to support this Constitution; but no religious test shall ever be required as a qualification to any office or public trust under the United States.

The Main Idea

Article VI. National Debts and Ratification

The Constitution is the highest law of the land. All national and state lawmakers must support the Constitution.

Document Dictionary
abridging limiting or restricting
redress correction

The Main Idea

Article VII. Ratification of the Constitution

The last article says that the Constitution was to become law when 9 of 13 states approved it. The members of the Constitutional Convention present on September 17, 1787, witnessed and signed the Constitution.

Article VII. Ratification of the Constitution

The ratification of the conventions of nine states, shall be sufficient for the establishment of this Constitution between the states so ratifying the same.

Done in convention by the unanimous consent of the states present the seventeenth day of September in the year of our Lord one thousand seven hundred and eighty-seven and of the independence of the United States of America the twelfth. In witness whereof, we have hereunto subscribed our names,

George Washington—*President and deputy from Virginia*

New Hampshire
John Langdon
Nicholas Gilman

Massachusetts
Nathaniel Gorham
Rufus King

Connecticut
William Samuel Johnson
Roger Sherman

New York
Alexander Hamilton

New Jersey
William Livingston
David Brearley
William Paterson
Jonathan Dayton

Pennsylvania
Benjamin Franklin
Thomas Mifflin
Robert Morris
George Clymer
Thomas FitzSimons
Jared Ingersoll
James Wilson
Gouverneur Morris

Delaware
George Read
Gunning Bedford, Jr.
John Dickinson
Richard Bassett
Jacob Broom

Maryland
James McHenry
Daniel of St. Thomas Jenifer
Daniel Carroll

Virginia
John Blair
James Madison, Jr.

North Carolina
William Blount
Richard Dobbs Spaight
Hugh Williamson

South Carolina
John Rutledge
Charles Cotesworth Pinckney
Charles Pinckney
Pierce Butler

Georgia
William Few
Abraham Baldwin

Amendments to the Constitution

Amendment 1. Religious and Political Freedom

Ratified December 15, 1791

Congress shall make no law respecting an establishment of religion, or prohibiting the free exercise thereof; or **abridging** the freedom of speech, or of the press; or the right of the people peaceably to assemble, and to petition the government for a **redress** of grievances.

Amendment 2. Right to Keep Arms

Ratified December 15, 1791

A well-regulated militia, being necessary to the security of a free state, the right of the people to keep and bear arms, shall not be infringed.

Amendment 3. Housing of Soldiers

Ratified December 15, 1791

No soldier shall, in time of peace, be quartered in any house, without the consent of the owner; nor in time of war, but in a manner to be prescribed by law.

Amendment 4. Search and Arrest Warrant

Ratified December 15, 1791

The right of the people to be secure in their persons, houses, papers, and effects, against unreasonable searches and seizures, shall not be violated; and no warrants shall issue, but upon probable cause, supported by oath or affirmation, and particularly describing the place to be searched, and the persons or things to be seized.

Amendment 5. Rights of Accused Persons

Ratified December 15, 1791

No person shall be held to answer for a capital, or otherwise infamous crime, unless on a presentment or indictment of a grand jury, except in cases arising in the land or naval forces, or in the militia, when in actual service in time of war or public danger; nor shall any person be subject for the same offense to be twice put in jeopardy of life or limb; nor shall be compelled in any criminal

The Main Idea

Amendments 1–10. The Bill of Rights

The first ten amendments, which became part of the Constitution in 1791, are known as the Bill of Rights. They protect the basic freedoms of the American people.

The Main Idea

Amendment 4. Search and Arrest Warrant

This amendment protects people's privacy and safety. A law officer cannot search a person or a person's home unless a judge has issued a valid search warrant.

Document Dictionary

common law a law based on past decisions by judges

bail money that an accused person provides to the court as a guarantee that he or she will be present for a trial

The Main Idea

Amendment 6. Rights to a Fair Trial

Persons accused of serious crimes have the right to a speedy and public trial. They must be told of what they are accused. They have the right to have a lawyer and to see and question those who accuse them.

The Main Idea

Amendment 10. Powers Reserved to the States

This amendment limits federal powers. It states that powers not given to the federal government and not denied to the states belong to the states or to the people who live in them.

case to be a witness against himself; nor be deprived of life, liberty, or property, without due process of law; nor shall private property be taken for public use, without just compensation.

Amendment 6. Rights to a Fair Trial

Ratified December 15, 1791

In all criminal prosecutions, the accused shall enjoy the right to a speedy and public trial, by an impartial jury of the state and district wherein the crime shall have been committed, which district shall have been previously ascertained by law, and to be informed of the nature and cause of the accusation; to be confronted with the witnesses against him; to have compulsory process for obtaining witnesses in his favor, and to have the assistance of counsel for his defense.

Amendment 7. Rights in Civil Cases

Ratified December 15, 1791

In suits at **common law**, where the value in controversy shall exceed twenty dollars, the right of trial by jury shall be preserved; and no fact tried by a jury, shall be otherwise reexamined in any court of the United States, than according to the rules of the common law.

Amendment 8. Limits on Bails, Fines, and Punishments

Ratified December 15, 1791

Excessive **bail** shall not be required, nor excessive fines imposed, nor cruel and unusual punishments inflicted.

Amendment 9. Rights Retained by the People

Ratified December 15, 1971

The enumeration in the Constitution of certain rights shall not be construed to deny or disparage others retained by the people.

Amendment 10. Powers Reserved to the States

Ratified December 15, 1971

The powers not delegated to the United States by the Constitution, nor prohibited by it to the states, are reserved to the states respectively, or to the people.

Amendment 11. Lawsuits Against States

Ratified February 7, 1795

The judicial power of United States shall not be construed to extend to any suit in law or equity, commenced or prosecuted against one of the United States by citizens of another state, or by citizens or subjects of any foreign state.

Amendment 12. Election of the President and Vice President

Ratified June 15, 1804

The electors shall meet in their respective states and vote by ballot for President and Vice President, one of whom, at least, shall not be an inhabitant of the same state with themselves; they shall name in their ballots the person voted for as President, and in distinct ballots the person voted for as Vice President, and they shall make distinct lists of all persons voted for as President, and of all persons voted for as Vice President; and of the number of votes for each, which lists they shall sign and certify, and transmit sealed to the seat of the government of the United States, directed to the President of the Senate; the President of the Senate shall, in the presence of the Senate and House of Representatives, open all the certificates and the votes shall then be counted; the person having the greatest number of votes for President, shall be the President, if such number be a majority of the whole number of electors appointed; and if no person have such majority, then from the persons having the highest numbers not exceeding three on the list of those voted for as President, the House of Representatives shall choose immediately, by ballot, the President. But in choosing the President, the votes shall be taken by states, the representation from each state having one vote; a quorum for this purpose shall consist of a member or members from two-thirds of the states, and a majority of all the states shall be necessary to a choice. And if the House of Representatives shall not choose a President whenever the right of choice shall devolve upon them, ~~before the fourth day of March next following,~~ then the Vice President shall act as President, as in the case of the

The Main Idea

Amendment 12. Election of the President and Vice President

Electors vote for the President and Vice President separately. An elector is a person chosen by the state legislature to elect the President and Vice President.

Document Dictionary

previous condition of servitude people who were formerly enslaved

The Main Idea

Amendment 14. Rights of Citizens

People who are born in the United States or who are granted citizenship are U.S. citizens. They are also citizens of the states in which they live. States may not make laws that overrule the rights given to citizens by the U.S. Constitution. States may not take away a person's life, freedom, or property unfairly. They must treat all people equally under the law.

death or other constitutional disability of the President. The person having the greatest number of votes as Vice President, shall be the Vice President, if such number be a majority of the whole number of electors appointed, and if no person have a majority, then from the two highest numbers on the list, the Senate shall choose the Vice President; a quorum for the purpose shall consist of two-thirds of the whole number of senators, and a majority of the whole number shall be necessary to a choice. But no person constitutionally ineligible to the office of President shall be eligible to that of Vice President of the United States.

Amendment 13. Abolition of Slavery

Ratified December 6, 1865

SECTION 1. Neither slavery nor involuntary servitude, except as a punishment for crime whereof the party shall have been duly convicted, shall exist within the United States, or any place subject to their jurisdiction.

SECTION 2. Congress shall have power to enforce this article by appropriate legislation.

Amendment 14. Rights of Citizens

Ratified July 9, 1868

SECTION 1. All persons born or naturalized in the United States, and subject to the jurisdiction thereof, are citizens of the United States and of the state wherein they reside. No state shall make or enforce any law which shall abridge the privileges or immunities of citizens of the United States; nor shall any state deprive any person of life, liberty, or property, without due process of law; nor deny to any person within its jurisdiction the equal protection of the laws.

SECTION 2. Representatives shall be apportioned among the several states according to their respective numbers, counting the whole number of persons in each state, ~~excluding Indians not taxed.~~ But when the right to vote at any election for the choice of electors for President and Vice President of the United States, representatives in Congress, the executive and judicial officers of a state, or the members of the legislature thereof, is denied to any of the ~~male~~ inhabitants of such state, ~~being twenty-one years of age,~~ and citizens of the United States, or in any way abridged, except for participation in rebellion, or other crime, the basis of representation therein shall be reduced in the proportion which the number of such male citizens shall bear to the whole number of ~~male~~ citizens ~~twenty-one years of age~~ in such state.

SECTION 3. No person shall be a senator or representative in Congress, or elector of President and Vice President, or hold any office, civil or military, under the United States, or under any state, who, having previously taken an oath, as a member of Congress, or as an officer of the United States, or as a member of any state legislature, or as an executive or judicial officer of any state, to support the Constitution of the United States, shall have engaged in insurrection or rebellion against the same, or given aid or comfort to the enemies thereof. But Congress may by a vote of two-thirds of each house, remove such disability.

SECTION 4. The validity of the public debt of the Untied States, authorized by law, including debts incurred for payment of pensions and bounties for services in suppressing insurrection or rebellion, shall not be questioned. But neither the United States nor any state shall assume or pay any debt or obligation incurred in aid of insurrection or rebellion against the United States, or any claim for the loss or emancipation of any slave, but all such debts, obligations, and claims shall be held illegal and void.

SECTION 5. The Congress shall have power to enforce, by appropriate legislation, the provisions of this article.

Amendment 15. African American Suffrage

Ratified February 3, 1870

SECTION 1. The right of citizens of the United States to vote shall not be denied or abridged by the United States or by any state on account of race, color, or **previous condition of servitude**.

SECTION 2. The Congress shall have power to enforce this article by appropriate legislation.

Document Dictionary

apportionment division and distribution

The Main Idea

Amendment 16. Income Tax

Congress has the power to collect taxes on its citizens based on their personal incomes rather than on the number of people living in a state.

The Main Idea

Amendment 17. Direct Election of Senators

Senators are elected directly by the voters and not by state legislatures. This is to make senators more responsible to the people they represent.

Amendment 16. Income Tax

Ratified February 3, 1913

The Congress shall have power to lay and collect taxes on incomes, from whatever source derived, without **apportionment** among the several states, and without regard to any census or enumeration.

Amendment 17. Direct Election of Senators

Ratified April 8, 1913

SECTION 1. The Senate of the United States shall be composed of two senators from each state, elected by the people thereof for six years; and each senator shall have one vote. The electors in each state shall have the qualifications requisite for electors of the most numerous branch of the state legislatures.

SECTION 2. When vacancies happen in the representation of any state in the Senate, the executive authority of such state shall issue writs of election to fill such vacancies: Provided, that the legislature of any state may empower the executive thereof to make temporary appointments until the people fill the vacancies by election as the legislature may direct.

SECTION 3. ~~This amendment shall not be so construed as to affect the election or term of any senator chosen before it becomes valid as part of the Constitution.~~

Amendment 18. Prohibition

Ratified January 16, 1919

SECTION 1. ~~After one year from the ratification of this article the manufacture, sale, or transportation of intoxicating liquors within, the importation thereof into, or the exportation thereof from the United States and all territory subject to the jurisdiction thereof for beverage purposes is hereby prohibited.~~

SECTION 2. ~~The Congress and the several states shall have concurrent power to enforce this article by appropriate legislation.~~

SECTION 3. ~~This article shall be inoperative unless it shall have been ratified as an amendment to the Constitution by the legislatures of the several states, as provided in the Constitution, within seven years from the date of the submission hereof to the states by the Congress.~~

Amendment 19. Women's Right to Vote

Ratified August 18, 1920

SECTION 1. The right of citizens of the United States to vote shall not be denied or abridged by the United States or by any state on account of sex.

SECTION 2. Congress shall have power to enforce this article by appropriate legislation.

Amendment 20. Terms of the President and Congress

Ratified January 23, 1933

SECTION 1. The terms of the President and Vice President shall end at noon on the 20th day of January, and the terms of senators and representatives at noon on the third day of January, of the year in which such terms would have ended if this article had not been ratified; and the terms of their successors shall then begin.

SECTION 2. The Congress shall assemble at least once in every year, and such meeting shall begin at noon on the third day of January, unless they shall by law appoint a different day.

SECTION 3. If, at the time fixed for the beginning of the term of the President, the President elect shall have died, the Vice President elect shall become President. If a President shall not have been chosen before the time fixed for the beginning of his term, or if the President elect shall have failed to qualify, then the Vice President elect shall act as President until a President shall have qualified; and the Congress may by law provide for the case wherein neither a President elect nor a Vice President elect shall have qualified, declaring who shall then act as President, or the manner in which one who is to act shall be selected, and such person shall act accordingly until a President or Vice President shall have qualified.

The Main Idea

Amendment 19. Women's Right to Vote

In 1920, women finally won the right to vote in both national and state elections. The struggle went on for almost 75 years before passage of the Nineteenth Amendment.

The Main Idea

Amendment 20. Terms of the President and Congress

Presidents start their new terms on January 20. Congress starts its new term on January 3.

Document Dictionary

inoperative not in force

primary an election in which registered members of a political party nominate candidates for office

SECTION 4. The Congress may by law provide for the case of the death of any of the persons from whom the House of Representatives may choose a President whenever the right of choice shall have devolved upon them, and for the case of the death of any of the persons from whom the Senate may choose a Vice President whenever the right of choice shall have devolved upon them.

SECTION 5. Sections 1 and 2 shall take effect on the 15th day of October following the ratification of this article.

SECTION 6. This article shall be **inoperative** unless it shall have been ratified as an amendment to the Constitution by the legislatures of three-fourths of the several states within seven years from the date of its submission.

The Main Idea

Amendment 21. Repeal of Prohibition

This amendment repealed the Eighteenth Amendment, which prohibited the manufacture, sale, and transportation of alcohol.

Amendment 21. Repeal of Prohibition

Ratified December 5, 1933

SECTION 1. The eighteenth article of amendment to the Constitution of the United States is hereby repealed.

SECTION 2. The transportation or importation into any state, territory, or possession of the United States for delivery or use therein of intoxicating liquors, in violation of the laws thereof, is hereby prohibited.

SECTION 3. This article shall be inoperative unless it shall have been ratified as an amendment to the Constitution by conventions in the several states, as provided in the Constitution, within seven years from the date of the submission hereof to the states by the Congress.

The Main Idea

Amendment 22. Limitation of Presidential Terms

A President is limited to two terms in office. Any President who serves less than two years of a previous President's term may be elected for two more terms.

Amendment 22. Limitation of Presidential Terms

Ratified February 27, 1951

SECTION 1. No person shall be elected to the office of President more than twice, and no person who has held the office of President, or acted as President, for more than two years of a term to which some other person was elected President shall be elected to the office of the President more than once. ~~But this article shall not apply to any person holding the office of President when this article was proposed by the Congress, and shall not prevent any person~~

~~who may be holding the office of President, or acting as President, during the term within which this article becomes operative from holding the office of President or acting as President during the remainder of such term.~~

SECTION 2. This article shall be inoperative unless it shall have been ratified as an amendment to the Constitution by the legislatures of three-fourths of the several states within seven years form the date of its submission to the states by the Congress.

Amendment 23. Presidential Electors in the District of Columbia

Ratified March 29, 1961

SECTION 1. The district constituting the seat of government of the United States shall appoint in such manner as the Congress may direct: A number of electors of President and Vice President equal to the whole number of senators and representatives in Congress to which the district would be entitled if it were a state, but in no event more than the least populous state; they shall be in addition to those appointed by the states, but they shall be considered, for the purposes of the election of President and Vice President, to be electors appointed by a state; and they shall meet in the district and perform such duties as provided by the twelfth article of amendment.

SECTION 2. The Congress shall have power to enforce this article by appropriate legislation.

The Main Idea

Amendment 23. Presidential Electors in the District of Columbia

By the time this amendment was ratified in 1960, more than 760,000 people lived in Washington, D.C. However, the Constitution had no provisions for allowing residents of the District of Columbia to vote in presidential elections. Now the District of Columbia has three electoral college votes.

Amendment 24. Abolition of Poll Taxes in National Elections

Ratified January 23, 1964

SECTION 1. The right of citizens of the United States to vote in any **primary** or other election for President or Vice President, for electors for President or Vice President, or for senator or representative in Congress, shall not be denied or abridged by the United States or any state by reason of failure to pay any poll tax or other tax.

SECTION 2. The Congress shall have power to enforce this article by appropriate legislation.

Document Dictionary

compensation payment for services

The Main Idea

Amendment 25. Presidential Disability and Succession

This amendment establishes procedures for how the U.S. government will continue to work if the President dies, resigns, or is temporarily disabled. This amendment also states that if a vacancy exists in the office of Vice President, the President nominates a Vice President, and a majority of both houses of Congress must approve the nominee.

Amendment 25. Presidential Disability and Succession

Ratified February 10, 1967

SECTION 1. In case of the removal of the President from office or of his death or resignation, the Vice President shall become President.

SECTION 2. Whenever there is a vacancy in the office of the Vice President, the President shall nominate a Vice President who shall take office upon confirmation by a majority vote of both houses of Congress.

SECTION 3. Whenever the President transmits to the President pro tempore of the Senate and the Speaker of the House of Representatives his written declaration that he is unable to discharge the powers and duties of his office, and until he transmits to them a written declaration to the contrary, such powers and duties shall be discharged by the Vice President as Acting President.

SECTION 4. Whenever the Vice President and a majority of either the principal officers of the executive departments or of such other body as Congress may by law provide, transmit to the President pro tempore of the Senate and the Speaker of the House of Representatives their written declaration that the President is unable to discharge the powers and duties of his office, the Vice President shall immediately assume the powers and duties of the office as Acting President. Thereafter, when the President transmits to the President pro tempore of the Senate and the Speaker of the House of Representatives his written declaration that no inability exists, he shall resume the powers and duties of his office unless the Vice President and a majority of either the principal officers of the executive department or of such other body as Congress may by law provide, transmit within four days to the President pro tempore of the Senate and the Speaker of the House of Representatives their written declaration that the President is unable to discharge the powers and duties of his office. Thereupon Congress shall decide the issue, assembling within forty-eight hours for that purpose if not in session. If the Congress, within twenty-one days after receipt of the latter written declaration, or, if

Congress is not in session within twenty-one days after Congress is required to assemble, determines by two-thirds vote of both houses that the President is unable to discharge the powers and duties of his office, the Vice President shall continue to discharge the same as Acting President; otherwise, the President shall resume the powers and duties of his office.

Amendment 26. Eighteen-Year-Old Vote

Ratified July 1, 1971

SECTION 1. The right of citizens of the United States, who are eighteen years of age or older, to vote shall not be denied or abridged by the United States or by any state on account of age.

SECTION 2. The Congress shall have power to enforce this article by appropriate legislation.

Amendment 27. Congressional Compensation

Ratified May 7, 1992

No law, varying the **compensation** for the services of the senators and representatives, shall take effect until an election of representatives shall have intervened.

The Main Idea

Amendment 27. Congressional Compensation

Congress may raise members' salaries, but the raise takes effect only after the next congressional elections. This delay allows voters to speak out on the proposed raises.

DOCUMENT-BASED QUESTIONS

1. What are three differences between the House of Representatives and the Senate?
2. Why do you think a person must have been born in the United States in order to be eligible to be President?
3. If a person charged with a crime flees to another state, what action is that state required to take?
4. How many states were needed to ratify the Constitution in order for it to take effect?
5. **Critical Thinking** How would you describe the impact of the Fourteenth, Fifteenth, and Sixteenth amendments on life in the United States?
6. **Critical Thinking** Which three amendments passed since 1800 do you think have had the most significant impact on American society today?

Unit 3 Portfolio Project

School Constitution

YOUR ASSIGNMENT

The Founding Fathers met in Philadelphia in 1787 to write a constitution for the new nation. They compromised to create a plan for the new government. If you were asked to write a constitution for your school government, what would you write?

THE CONVENTION

Decide on Articles First, meet as a class. Decide what articles you should include in your school constitution. What topics should the articles cover? For example, you may want articles explaining how the student council will be elected and what responsibilities it will have. Include a process for amending your constitution.

Divide Into Committees Next, form committees. Each committee will work on one article.

WRITE THE CONSTITUTION

Work in Committees Each committee should research and discuss the general area that its article will cover. Assign a different duty to each committee member. Refer to this Web site for ideas: www.gfamericanhistory.com.

Make a Draft After discussing different ideas, write a draft of your article.

Debate, Rewrite, and Adopt Your Article Like the Founding Fathers, you may find that there are disagreements about your article. In your committee, discuss these differences. Then, reach a compromise that all members can accept.

Adopt the Constitution Finally, present your finished article to the class convention. Discuss each article, suggesting and voting on changes if needed. Then, vote on adopting the completed constitution as a whole. Make a copy of your new constitution for each class member.

Multimedia Presentation

Make a video documentary called *The Writing of the School Constitution.* Include interviews with the "Founding Fathers and Mothers" of your constitution. Show committees in action and whole-class debates. Edit your documentary and screen it for the class.

Unit 4

Building the Republic

"You have, with a great expense of blood and treasure, rescued yourselves . . . from the domination of Europe. Perfect the good work you have begun."

—from *The History of the American Revolution*, by Dr. David Ramsay, published in 1789

LINK PAST TO PRESENT The USS *Constitution* was launched in Boston Harbor in 1797. Today, the *Constitution* and a museum dedicated to preserving the ship's history are located in Boston.

★ How does the quotation reflect the difficulties of the new nation?

CHAPTER 10

A Government for a New Nation 1789–1800

I. **George Washington as President**
II. **Early Challenges**
III. **The Presidency of John Adams**

After leading the Constitutional Convention, George Washington told colleagues that he looked forward to a life of peace and contentment on his Virginia plantation, Mount Vernon. In 1789, however, the country called upon his services once again. Washington could not refuse the offer to become the nation's first President. With a heavy heart, he wrote to his friend Henry Knox:

> "[S]o unwilling am I, in the evening of a life nearly consumed in public cares, to quit a peaceful abode for an ocean of difficulties."

Washington made the long journey from Virginia to New York. Along the way, he was hailed as a hero by the American people.

George Washington's telescope

U.S. Events

1789 George Washington is elected as the first President of the United States.

1790 First U.S. census is taken.

1791 National bank opens.

1792 Washington is re-elected.

U.S. Events	1785	1790
Presidential Term Begins		1789 George Washington
World Events	1785	1790

World Events

1789 French Revolution begins.

1791 Mozart conducts the first performance of *The Magic Flute* in Austria.

1792 Denmark becomes the first country to ban slave trade.

VIEW HISTORY This painting, *A View of Mount Vernon*, shows George Washington's Virginia home of 45 years. Today, the plantation receives more than 1 million visitors each year, where people may view objects such as a telescope (left) that Washington used.

★ **What does this painting tell you about Mount Vernon?**

Get Organized

FLOWCHART

The order in which events happen is called their sequence. Making a flowchart can help you understand the sequence of the important events you read about. Use a flowchart as you read Chapter 10. List important events in the order in which they occur. Here is an example from this chapter.

1. Washington becomes the first President. →
2. He chooses a Cabinet to advise him. →
3. Jefferson and Hamilton develop different ideas. →
4. Political parties develop around their ideas.

1794 Whiskey Rebellion takes place. Battle of Fallen Timbers occurs.

1795 Treaty of Greenville is signed. Jay's Treaty is passed. Pinckney's Treaty is passed.

1797 XYZ Affair occurs.

1798 Alien and Sedition Acts are passed.

1799 George Washington dies.

1795 — 1800

1797 John Adams

1795 — 1800

1793 French king and queen are executed during the French Revolution. France outlaws slavery in Haiti.

1796 Spain joins France in a war against Great Britain.

1799 Napoleon becomes dictator of France.

I George Washington as President

Terms to Know

inauguration a formal ceremony to induct an elected official into office

census an official population count

Cabinet a group of people chosen by the President to give advice

precedent an example for the future

unconstitutional something that goes against the U.S. Constitution

tariff a tax on imported goods

Main Ideas

A. George Washington and other members of the government had a great responsibility to the new nation.

B. President Washington and the members of Congress took steps to put the new government into action.

C. Alexander Hamilton proposed a plan to rescue the nation's economy.

Active Reading

SUMMARIZE

One good way to review what you have learned is to summarize, or present the most important information in a shortened form. As you read this section, try to summarize the most important information in a few sentences.

A. Welcome, Mr. President

George Washington and the men who formed the new U.S. government in 1789 had a difficult task. They were the first to hold these jobs. They had to learn their duties without examples to follow. They also knew that they would be models for the people who held these posts after them.

The First Election

In the first presidential election, in 1789, George Washington of Virginia was unanimously elected as the nation's leader. He had no opponent. Washington was well qualified to be the first President. He had been a military commander in the Revolutionary War, and had led the Constitutional Convention in Philadelphia in 1787. He was also popular and respected by Americans. John Adams of Massachusetts became the first Vice President.

George Washington traveled eight days from Virginia to New York City for his inauguration.

George Washington's **inauguration** as the first President of the United States took place on April 30, 1789. An inauguration is the induction of an elected official into office. Washington, clothed in a plain brown suit, stood on the balcony of Federal Hall in New York City as a large crowd watched. New York City served as the first capital of the United States until 1790. Then, Philadelphia became a temporary capital from 1790 to 1800, while a permanent national capital was being designed.

As Washington took the oath as the first person to be sworn in as President, people wondered: Can the new nation live up to its great promise?

> "I do solemnly swear that I will faithfully execute the office of President of the United States, and will to the best of my ability preserve, protect, and defend the Constitution of the United States, so help me God."

DOCUMENT-BASED QUESTION What promises does a new President make?

After taking the oath of office, President Washington went back to the Senate chamber and gave a short speech. In his inaugural address, he spoke of the importance of representative government. A witness, William Maclay, later wrote in his diary that the President trembled as he read his speech. The new President had led soldiers into battle. He had suffered with them in freezing weather at Valley Forge. Yet, even a brave soldier could tremble at the uncertain future that lay ahead of him and his country.

The American people were also a little unsure. The idea of a President was so new in the 1780s that no one was certain how he should be addressed. Almost every other country was ruled by kings, queens, or other royal figures. People addressed royalty as "Your Excellency" or "Your Majesty." Titles like these were too grand for George Washington. Americans decided to use a simpler title—Mr. President.

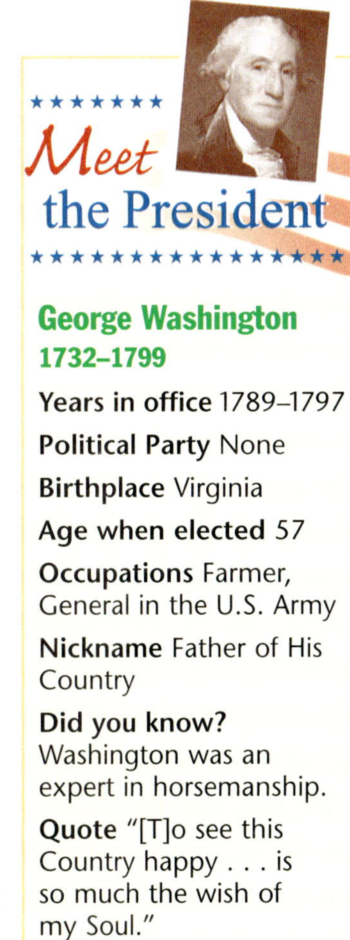

Meet the President

George Washington
1732–1799

Years in office 1789–1797

Political Party None

Birthplace Virginia

Age when elected 57

Occupations Farmer, General in the U.S. Army

Nickname Father of His Country

Did you know? Washington was an expert in horsemanship.

Quote "[T]o see this Country happy . . . is so much the wish of my Soul."

Building Unity

In 1790, the U.S. government counted all of the country's citizens—almost 4 million—in the first U.S. **census** taken. Every 10 years since then the United States counts its number of citizens. It was important that Americans feel a sense of loyalty to their new nation. Washington was from Virginia. Adams was from Massachusetts. The first two capitals were New York City and Philadelphia. All of the states felt included in the new government.

To create a feeling of unity among all people and emphasize that he was President of the whole country, Washington toured states throughout the new nation. Creating a feeling of unity among all the people of the United States would be one of President Washington's most important duties. Also ahead were the tasks of building a strong government and economy.

★ **What special challenge did the members of the country's new government face?**

B. Organizing the New Government

To help him solve the many problems facing the new country, Washington chose a **Cabinet**, or group of advisors. Together with the President and Vice President, the Cabinet is part of the executive branch of government.

The first Congress established three Cabinet positions. They were Secretary of State, Secretary of the Treasury, and Secretary of War. It also created two other positions, Attorney General and Postmaster General, that later became Cabinet positions. The number of Cabinet positions has increased over the years.

The President's Advisors

President Washington chose his Cabinet members wisely. Thomas Jefferson of Virginia was the first Secretary of State. He advised the President on how to deal with foreign countries. Alexander Hamilton of New York was Secretary of the Treasury. He looked after the country's economy. Henry Knox of Massachusetts, Washington's friend from the days of the Revolutionary War, was Secretary of War. Knox was responsible for the army and navy. Edmund Randolph of Virginia was Attorney General. He gave Washington advice on the country's laws. The fact that these men were from different states also helped unify the country. Washington set a **precedent**, or practice that would be followed in the future, of asking his Cabinet members to help him make decisions on national issues.

Congress Defines Its Powers

Congress, the legislative branch of government, also had to determine what its job was. The Constitution gave Congress the power to tax, print money, make laws about business, establish post offices, and declare war. Representatives wondered what else the Congress could do.

One paragraph in the Constitution gave Congress the power to "make all laws which shall be necessary and proper for carrying into execution the foregoing powers." Senators and representatives asked themselves: What does this sentence mean? How far can we go to make new laws? This part of the Constitution is called the "elastic clause" because its meaning can be stretched like a rubber band. This clause allows Congress to stretch its power to pass laws it finds necessary. Very soon, it would become the center of an important argument about the country's future. However, the framework of the Constitution has enabled the U.S. government to remain strong through difficult times.

Spotlight on Culture

Over the years, George Washington has become closely connected to two well-known stories. One story tells of Washington chopping down a cherry tree. The other claims that Washington had false teeth made of wood.

Neither of these stories is true. The cherry tree incident was completely made up. Although Washington did wear false teeth, they were not made of wood. They were most likely made out of bone or ivory. However, it is true that when Washington died, he had only one real tooth left in his mouth.

The Court System

The Constitution created a Supreme Court but did not state how many justices, or judges, there should be. Congress passed the Judiciary Act of 1789 to organize the court system of the United States. This law created a chief justice and five associate justices of the Supreme Court. It also formed 13 district courts—one for each state—and three circuit courts of appeal. These courts are known as lower courts because their decisions can be reviewed by the Supreme Court. Since the Judiciary Act was passed, the number of associate justices and district courts has changed, but the court system today has the same framework as in 1789.

The Supreme Court has an especially important job. It settles disagreements over the meaning of laws passed by Congress and state legislatures. If the Supreme Court believes that a law goes against the Constitution, it can declare the law **unconstitutional**. A law passed by Congress that is declared unconstitutional does not remain a law. President Washington chose John Jay of New York as the first chief justice of the Supreme Court.

Do You Remember?

In Chapter 9, you learned that John Jay was one of the authors of *The Federalist Papers*, together with Alexander Hamilton and James Madison. These essays urged people to support the new Constitution.

 **What did President Washington and Congress do first?**

C. Hamilton's Economic Plans

One of the biggest problems that the new government faced was the failing economy. Alexander Hamilton, Secretary of the Treasury, offered solutions to the country's financial problems.

Hamilton's Proposals

Hamilton believed the economy would improve if the government would pay off all of its debt. He also believed that other countries would then feel encouraged to trade with the United States and, as a result, the U.S. economy would improve.

To raise the money to pay these debts, Hamilton said the United States should issue bonds, or certificates of debt. He also proposed creating **tariffs**, or taxes on goods brought into the country. Finally, Hamilton suggested creating a national bank. He argued that the bank would provide a place for the government to keep money. Until this time, each state had issued its own currency, or paper money. A national bank would circulate money that could be used throughout the country.

The Bank of the United States opened in Philadelphia in 1791.

Congress Approves Hamilton's Plans

President Washington favored Hamilton's proposals. However, some leaders, including Thomas Jefferson and James Madison, disagreed with Hamilton's ideas. After much debate, Congress adopted the proposals, and Hamilton's plans went into effect.

The two sides did compromise on one issue. Southern states were upset about having to give money to the government in order to repay debts. They had already repaid most of their debts. In return for their support, people in the North agreed to have the country's permanent capital located in a city in the South. The new site was chosen by President Washington in 1790. It was located in an area near Mount Vernon. The site was on land in Maryland and Virginia that lay on both sides of the Potomac River.

Benjamin Banneker

Washington hired French architect Pierre L'Enfant to design the capital. Later, L'Enfant left the project and took the plans. Benjamin Banneker, a mathematician who had been born into a free African family in Maryland, served on the planning committee. He was able to reproduce from memory L'Enfant's plans for the national capital.

Within a few years, it was decided that the national capital would be called Washington, in honor of the President. The capital is on federal land that is named the District of Columbia, commonly called D.C. The name of the national capital is Washington, D.C.

 **What economic solutions did Alexander Hamilton propose?**

Review History

A. Why was Washington the clear choice to be the first President?

B. What is the job of the Cabinet?

C. What compromise was made concerning the location of the nation's permanent capital?

Define Terms to Know

Provide a definition for each of the following terms.
inauguration, census, Cabinet, precedent, unconstitutional, tariff

Critical Thinking

Why was building unity an important goal for President Washington?

Write About Citizenship

Think about what it would have been like to be in the crowd as George Washington took the oath of office. Write a postcard to a friend describing your feelings.

Get Organized

FLOWCHART

Think about the main events in this section. Use a flowchart to show the sequence of these events. Start with the election of George Washington as the first President.

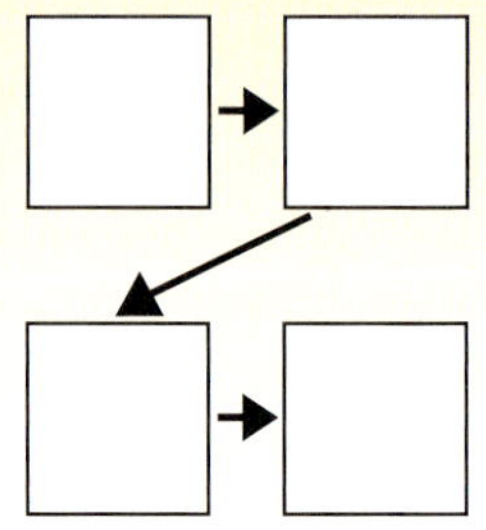

Build Your Skills

Social Studies Skill

USE PRIMARY AND SECONDARY SOURCES

When you want to find information, you go to a source. For example, if you want to find someone's telephone number, your source would be the telephone book.

Two main types of sources are used in history—primary and secondary sources. Primary sources are firsthand accounts of events created by people who were present at the events. They include letters, speeches, autobiographies, newspaper articles, and photographs.

Secondary sources are materials written or created after events. They are created by people who did not take part in the events. Secondary sources include history books, encyclopedia articles, and biographies. This textbook contains both primary and secondary sources.

Here's How

Follow these steps to use primary and secondary sources.

1. Determine what information you want.
2. Decide whether you should use a primary source or a secondary source. Do you need firsthand information or more general information?
3. Examine the information in your source. Does it meet your needs?

Here's Why

You can use primary sources to see history through the eyes of people who were at an event. You can use secondary sources to learn about descriptions of events and about basic facts.

Practice the Skill

Copy the chart on a sheet of paper. Decide which type of source you would use to answer the question on the chart. Fill in the chart. Explain why you chose that type of source.

QUESTION:	How did George Washington react to being elected President?
Which type of source would you use?	
Why?	

Extend the Skill

Think of one fact you would like to know about George Washington. Use the Internet or your school library to find a primary or secondary source containing that information.

Apply the Skill

As you read the remaining sections of this chapter, look for information in the sections and in the quotations provided. What type of information do these sources give you? Which sources are primary sources and which sources are secondary sources? How do you know?

II Early Challenges

Terms to Know

implied power a power that is not stated in the Constitution

Union the United States of America

neutral not taking one side or the other

impressment seizing someone and forcing that person into service for a country

Main Ideas

A. Differing views in the United States led to the emergence of political parties.

B. The United States faced and overcame new challenges on the western frontier.

C. President Washington's foreign policy tried to keep the United States isolated from other countries.

POINTS OF VIEW
Comparing different points of view can help you see both sides of an issue. As you read this section, keep a list comparing the points of view of two important figures, Alexander Hamilton and Thomas Jefferson.

A. The Rise of Political Parties

Alexander Hamilton and Thomas Jefferson had different opinions on the nation's economy. They also viewed the role of government differently. Some Americans sided with Hamilton, whereas others thought Jefferson was right.

Views on Government

Although President Washington had said he did not want to run for re-election in 1792, he later agreed to do so in the hope of uniting the country. Throughout Washington's first term, two of his Cabinet members, Alexander Hamilton and Thomas Jefferson, had opposing views of how the nation should be governed, as well as of other important issues.

For example, Jefferson had opposed Hamilton's economic plan. He felt that it gave the national government too much power. He wanted to leave as much power as possible to the state governments. Jefferson was concerned that a strong national government would take away the rights of the citizens.

Hamilton disagreed. He believed that the United States needed a strong national government in order to deal with the country's problems. The main purpose of having a strong national government, according to Hamilton, was to create the right conditions for the growth of business and industry. Hamilton believed that without business and industry, and the money they made, the United States had no hope of surviving.

Views on Industry

Jefferson and Hamilton also disagreed on the kind of future they saw for the country. Hamilton wanted the United States to become a great manufacturing and business power with large cities. Jefferson hoped it would remain a nation of small, independent farms and villages. Hamilton thought the wealthy and educated citizens should have the most power. He said,

> "All communities divide themselves into the few and the many. The first are the rich and well-born, the other the mass of the people. . . . The people are turbulent and changing; they seldom judge or determine right."

Jefferson disagreed. He believed that ordinary people, left to themselves, could prosper on their own and that government should provide guidelines that allowed them to run their own lives.

> "[A] wise and frugal Government, which shall restrain men from injuring one another, shall leave them otherwise free to regulate their own pursuits of industry and improvement."

ANALYZE PRIMARY SOURCES

DOCUMENT-BASED QUESTION Do you agree with Hamilton's or with Jefferson's statement regarding ordinary people? Why?

Interpretation of the Constitution

Another important issue that Hamilton and Jefferson could not agree on was how to interpret the Constitution. Hamilton's view is called a loose interpretation. He believed that Congress could pass laws on any subject unless it was strictly forbidden in the Constitution. His support for flexibility was based on the "elastic clause" of the Constitution. This clause gave Congress the power to pass laws that were "necessary and proper." Therefore, Congress could expand its power beyond that which was directly stated in the Constitution. These powers were known as **implied powers**. For example, Hamilton argued that Congress could create a national bank, because it was necessary for collecting taxes and regulating trade.

Alexander Hamilton

Thomas Jefferson

Jefferson believed the government was limited to only those powers stated in the Constitution. Because there was no mention of a national bank in the Constitution, he thought Congress did not have the power to create one. This view is called a strict interpretation.

Political Parties Form

Many people agreed with Hamilton's ideas of a strong national government and the importance of industry. These people formed a political party called the Federalist Party. A political party consists of a group of people holding similar views on policies a government should follow.

Jefferson and James Madison began a political party to oppose Hamilton's ideas. This party was known as the Democratic-Republican Party. People who supported this party wanted a limited national government and stronger state governments.

 **In which areas did the two political parties differ?**

B. Problems on the Western Frontier

Washington was re-elected in 1792. Different viewpoints on political issues were not the only concern in the United States during this time. Increased taxes angered some citizens. Also, conflicts with Native Americans in the Northwest Territory arose. Washington showed that the national government had the power to handle such problems.

The Whiskey Rebellion

In 1794, some farmers in western Pennsylvania became angry about the tax on whiskey—a tax that Congress passed to encourage Hamilton's plan for economic growth. These farmers grew the corn that was used to make the whiskey. Sometimes they even made the whiskey themselves. The tax would affect them the most by reducing their profits. The farmers refused to pay the tax.

In protest, an armed mob burned buildings and threatened to attack Pittsburgh, Pennsylvania. In addition, federal tax collectors who attempted to collect the tax were chased away. In one instance, a group of angry farmers attacked one collector. They covered him with tar and feathers and then set his house on fire. These actions were known as the Whiskey Rebellion.

Then & Now

In the early days of political parties in the United States, Federalist and Democratic-Republicans disagreed on economic issues, foreign policy, and the interpretation of the Constitution. The two major parties today, the Democratic and Republican parties, also hold different views on issues such as healthcare, the economy, and tax reform.

Differences Between the First Two U.S. Political Parties

FEDERALIST	DEMOCRATIC-REPUBLICAN
Strong national government	Strong state governments
Industry based on manufacturing and business	Industry based on independent farmers
Loose interpretation of the Constitution	Strict interpretation of the Constitution
National bank	Opposed to a national bank

✔ Chart Check

Which party supported a strict interpretation of the Constitution?

Rebellious farmers opposed to the whiskey tax tar and feather a tax collector.

President Washington feared that the Whiskey Rebellion would lead to more trouble. Under the new Constitution, the President had the power to force citizens to obey the law. With Hamilton's urging, Washington ordered an army of 13,000 soldiers into western Pennsylvania in 1794 to stamp out the rebellion. When the army approached Pittsburgh, the leaders of the rebellion fled. Some were arrested, but none were found guilty. Washington's action showed Americans that the national government would use its power to enforce laws.

Tensions With Native Americans

Shawnee, Chippewa, Iroquois, Ottawa, and other Native American groups lived in the Northwest Territory, which was the land north of the Ohio River and east of the Mississippi River. These groups did not believe that the U.S. government had any control over them. They also became upset by settlers who moved onto their lands. As a result, fighting often broke out between the Native Americans and the settlers. President Washington felt that these northwest lands were important to the growth of the United States. He sent troops to settle the conflict.

Do You Remember?
In Chapter 9, you learned that the Northwest Ordinance of 1787 created the Northwest Territory.

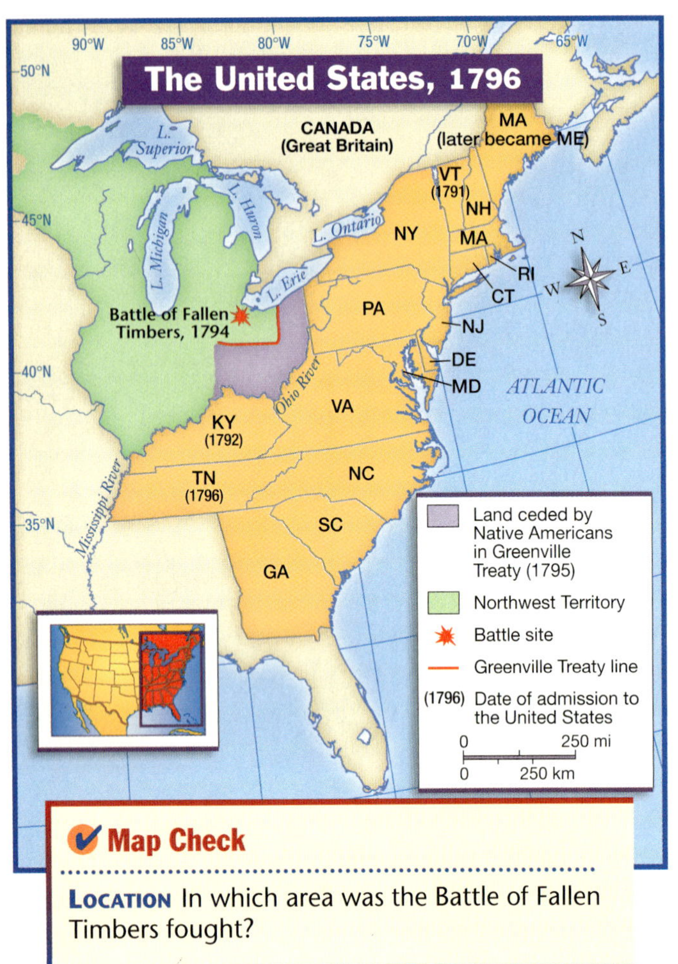

Map Check

LOCATION In which area was the Battle of Fallen Timbers fought?

In 1794, General "Mad" Anthony Wayne led an army to stop Native American raids on settlers. He defeated the Native Americans at the Battle of Fallen Timbers near present-day Toledo, Ohio. The next year, the Native Americans were forced to sign the Treaty of Greenville. They agreed to leave most of what would become the state of Ohio and parts of what would become the states of Indiana, Illinois, and Michigan. This treaty opened the area to more settlers.

New States Join the Union

President Washington's approach to these problems proved that the national government was strong. The addition of new states to the **Union**, or the United States of America, also increased the strength of the nation. Vermont became the fourteenth state in 1791. Kentucky joined the Union in 1792. In 1796, Tennessee became the sixteenth state in the Union. Each new state enlarged and strengthened the United States.

★ **What effect did Washington's response to the Whiskey Rebellion have?**

C. Washington's Foreign Policy

In foreign affairs, President Washington followed a policy of remaining **neutral**, or not taking sides. He believed that getting involved in other countries' disputes would be harmful to the United States. Nevertheless, staying neutral was not easy.

Revolution in France

In 1789, the same year the Constitution was adopted, a revolution began in France. Revolutionaries overthrew King Louis XVI and proclaimed France a republic. France asked the United States to help defend its new government against Great Britain and other European countries.

Hamilton and Jefferson disagreed on this issue. Hamilton advised President Washington to remain neutral. Jefferson thought French democracy was much like American democracy. He advised President Washington to support France. Washington agreed with Hamilton and declared that the United States would remain neutral.

Conflict With Great Britain

A second problem involved Great Britain. Great Britain was at war with France, so the British navy was seizing American ships that were trading with France. The British also forced captured American sailors to work for the British navy. This practice was known as **impressment**.

Washington tried to avoid going to war with Britain by sending Chief Justice John Jay to speak with British officials in 1794. Jay returned from Britain the next year with an agreement known as Jay's Treaty. In it, the British agreed to leave their forts south of the Great Lakes and establish a border between the United States and British Canada. The United States agreed that Great Britain could seize cargo ships bound for France. The United States also agreed to pay debts owed to British merchants. Jay's Treaty was very unpopular in most areas of the United States.

Opening the Mississippi River

Another treaty opened up the Mississippi River to American shipping. Thomas Pinckney negotiated this treaty with Spain in 1795. In Pinckney's Treaty, Spain agreed that Americans could use the Mississippi River to reach the port of New Orleans and the Gulf of Mexico. The agreement also created a boundary between the state of Georgia and Spanish Florida.

Why did Washington try to remain neutral in foreign affairs?

Review

Review History

A. How did political parties begin in the United States?

B. How did the federal government extend its power over the western frontier during this period?

C. What were the results of Washington's neutral policy in foreign affairs?

Define Terms to Know

Provide a definition for each of the following terms.
implied power, Union, neutral, impressment

Critical Thinking

Compare and contrast the views of Hamilton and Jefferson on interpreting the U.S. Constitution.

Write About Geography

Write an article about the importance of settling northwest lands in the late 1700s. Explain how these territories are important to the growth of the United States.

Get Organized

FLOWCHART

Think about the rise of political parties discussed in this section. Use a flowchart to show a sequence of events describing this rise. Begin with the appointments of Hamilton and Jefferson to the Cabinet.

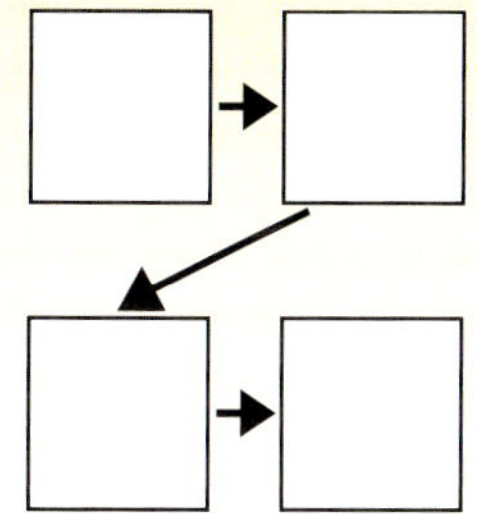

III The Presidency of John Adams

Terms to Know

alliance an agreement between two or more people, groups, or nations to cooperate with one another

immigrant a person who moves into a country from another country

nullify to cancel

Main Ideas

A. The election of 1796 strengthened political parties.

B. President John Adams faced serious challenges in both foreign and domestic affairs.

Active Reading

CAUSE AND EFFECT

A historical event may have one or more causes and effects. As you read this section, identify the causes and effects of events.

A. John Adams Becomes President

As the presidential election of 1796 drew nearer, Americans were anxious. The only President they had ever known had decided to retire. Washington had served his country for almost 25 years. Now, Americans had to decide who would take his place.

The Election of 1796

In 1796, presidential candidates ran as party members instead of as individuals for the first time in the nation's history. President Washington favored his Vice President, John Adams of Massachusetts. The Federalists followed Washington's wishes and nominated, or chose, John Adams. They chose Thomas Pinckney of South Carolina as the vice presidential candidate.

The Democratic-Republicans, the party led by Thomas Jefferson and James Madison, chose Jefferson as their presidential candidate. Aaron Burr of New York was chosen as the vice presidential candidate of the Democratic-Republicans. This was the first time in the country's history that two people ran for each of the nation's highest offices.

John Adams was elected the nation's second President in 1796.

Adams received the most number of votes by the electors—the people chosen by state voters to select the President and Vice President. In the election of 1796, electors were also selected by the state legislatures and by other methods. According to the Constitution, the candidate with the most electoral votes would become President. The person who came in second would be Vice President. As a result, Adams became President. Jefferson received the second-highest number of votes. He became Vice President, even though he was not of the same party as Adams.

Washington Says Good-Bye

In September 1796, George Washington issued his Farewell Address. First, he warned citizens against joining political parties. He feared political parties would destroy American unity. Second, he urged Americans to remain neutral in foreign affairs and avoid **alliances**, or agreements, with other countries. He added,

> "The great rule of conduct for us in regard to foreign nations is, in extending our commercial relations, to have with them as little political connection as possible. So far as we have already formed engagements let them be fulfilled with perfect good faith. Here let us stop."

ANALYZE PRIMARY SOURCES **DOCUMENT-BASED QUESTION** Why did Washington fear political involvement with foreign countries?

After his presidency, Washington hoped he could finally lead a quiet life at Mount Vernon. However, Washington died only two years after his retirement. At his funeral, General Henry Lee said that Washington was "first in war, first in peace, and first in the hearts of his countrymen."

 **How was the election of 1796 different from earlier elections?**

They Made History

Abigail Adams 1744–1818

Abigail Adams, wife of President John Adams, was a strong supporter of all people's rights. She believed that women had the right to a formal education. Like most other women of her time who did receive an education, Adams was educated at home. However, the desire to learn led her to study poetry, drama, history, and other subjects. She became one of the best-read women of her time. She often expressed her views and ideas to her husband. She urged him to promote the rights of all people. John Adams relied on his wife's advice and support during his career. While he was President, he wrote, "I never wanted your advice and assistance more in my life."

Abigail Adams, wife of President John Adams, advised her husband during his presidency.

Critical Thinking How did Abigail Adams use her position to promote her views?

B. Troubles at Home and Abroad

Problems greeted President Adams as soon as he took office in 1797. Disagreements with France brought the United States to the brink of war.

Spotlight on Government

The XYZ Affair angered President Adams and many Americans. The Democratic-Republican Party, which had supported France in the past, did not condemn France's actions. As a result, the Federalist Party was seen as the party of patriotism. Many Americans voted for Federalist candidates in the 1798 congressional elections.

The XYZ Affair

The French were angry that in Jay's Treaty the United States permitted Britain to seize cargo bound for France. In return, the French began stopping American ships bound for Great Britain. Adams sent three Americans to France in late 1797 to negotiate with the French foreign minister. Three French officials asked for a bribe, or secret payment, for themselves before they would even speak to the Americans. These officials were referred to as *X*, *Y*, and *Z* in the United States. The Americans refused to pay the bribe.

Congress prepared for war. President Adams cut off trade with France. Over the next two years, French and American ships fought each other. Because war was never declared, this fighting is known as the "undeclared war." In 1800, the French agreed to end the undeclared war. Adams's tough response in the XYZ Affair showed Europeans that the new United States would not be pushed around.

Democratic-Republicans spoke out against Adams's policy regarding France. In response, Federalists passed the Sedition Act in 1798. This act stated that the government could jail or fine anyone who criticized a member of Congress, the President, or any other U.S. government official. The Democratic-Republicans said the law was unconstitutional because it restricted their right to free speech.

This engraving from 1798 illustrates an actual fight between two members of Congress. Democratic-Republican Matthew Lyon is being attacked by Federalist Roger Griswold, who is using a stick.

Federal Laws and States' Reactions

Two other laws passed by Federalists in 1798 also tried to weaken the Democratic-Republicans. Federalists believed that most new **immigrants**, or people who move into a country from another country, were likely to vote for the Democratic-Republicans. The Alien Acts increased the waiting period from 5 years to 14 years before aliens could become citizens of the United States and have the right to vote. Aliens are people who are not yet citizens of the country in which they live. Also, the President could send away any alien who was not a citizen and whom the President considered a danger to the United States.

Jefferson led an effort to oppose these laws. He arranged for the Kentucky legislature to declare the laws to be of "no force" in the state. James Madison had a similar act passed in Virginia. These actions were the first examples of an important idea: States could overrule the federal government if they disagreed with laws passed by Congress. By overruling a federal law, the states **nullified**, or cancelled, the law. The belief that individual states have the power to overrule federal law is known as states' rights.

A serious conflict over states' rights was avoided when Adams was not re-elected in 1800. However, within 30 years, the issue of states' rights would become hotly debated again.

 **Why did the Federalists pass the Alien and Sedition Acts?**

Review History

A. What was the outcome of the election of 1796?

B. What caused the XYZ Affair?

Define Terms to Know

Provide a definition for each of the following terms.
alliance, immigrant, nullify

Critical Thinking

Should the government have the right to silence people who criticize it?

Write About Government

Write an article that supports the political views of either the Federalists or the Democratic-Republicans. Choose one issue, and give reasons why you agree with that party's view.

Get Organized

FLOWCHART

Use a flowchart to show the sequence of events that contributed to conflicts between the two parties. Begin with President Washington's selection of John Adams to follow him as President.

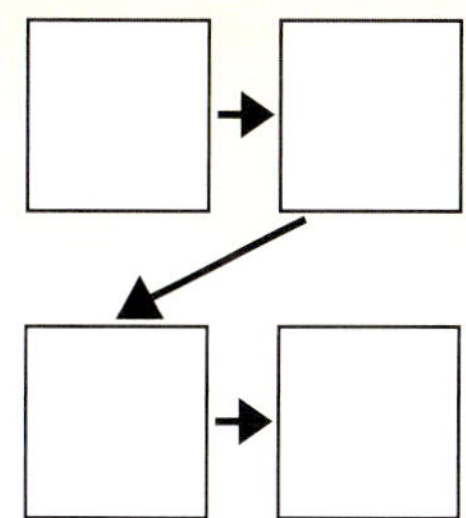

PAST *to* PRESENT

Presidential Elections

American politics began with the inauguration of George Washington as the nation's first President. He was elected unanimously—he had no opponent. During Washington's presidency, two of his Cabinet members—Alexander Hamilton and Thomas Jefferson—disagreed about government policy. This disagreement contributed to the rise of political parties.

By the election of 1796, presidential candidates were selected by their parties. Adams and Jefferson did not campaign for that election. The campaigning was done mostly by newspaper writers and editors. Today, presidential candidates promote themselves by distributing election buttons, displaying banners, and speaking at rallies. Under today's political-party system, representatives from each state, called delegates, attend national conventions every four years to choose their party's candidate.

George Washington was sworn in as the nation's first President at Federal Hall in New York City in 1789.

There were no campaign items for John Adams. However, once he was elected President, his name and image appeared on everyday objects, such as this piece of pottery.

3

Americans vote every four years for a President of the United States. At the 2000 Republican National Convention, delegates chose George W. Bush as the Republican candidate. He won the 2000 election after a close race against Al Gore, the Democratic candidate and Vice President.

4 Items such as these campaign buttons from George W. Bush's and Al Gore's campaigns in 2000 show support for a particular candidate and political party.

Two U.S. Political Parties

Party	Democratic	Republican
Year	1828	1854
Symbol	donkey	elephant
Nickname	no nickname	Grand Old Party (G.O.P.)
Number of Presidents Since Party Began	14	18
First Elected President	Andrew Jackson	Abraham Lincoln
Party Quote	"Opportunity to every American, and responsibility from every American."	"We believe that freedom comes from opportunity; from opportunity comes growth; and from growth comes progress and prosperity."

This chart provides some general information about the Democratic and Republican parties.

Hands-on Activity

Prepare a class debate about a school dress code. The team supporting the dress code are the Federalists. The team opposing the dress code are the Democratic-Republicans. Select the party that you would support and explain your opinion. Use the Internet and other resources to learn more about debating and dress codes. To get started, go to: www.gfamericanhistory.com.

CHAPTER 10 Review

Chapter Summary

In your notebook, complete the following outline. Then, use your outline to write a brief summary of the chapter.

A Government for a New Nation

I. George Washington as President
   A. Welcome, Mr. President
   B.
   C.

II. Early Challenges
   A.
   B.
   C.

III. The Presidency of John Adams
   A.
   B.

Interpret the Timeline

Use the timeline on pages 242–243 to answer the following questions.

1. What were two U.S. events that occurred during President Washington's first term?
2. **Critical Thinking** Which world events might have led to more immigrants coming to the United States?

Use Terms to Know

Match each term with its definition.

a. alliance	d. immigrant	g. tariff
b. Cabinet	e. impressment	h. unconstitutional
c. census	f. neutral	i. Union

1. a group of people chosen by the President to give advice
2. a person who moves into a country from another country
3. a tax on imported goods
4. not taking one side or the other
5. something that goes against the U.S. Constitution
6. seizing someone and forcing that person into service for a country
7. an official population count
8. an agreement between two or more people, groups, or nations to cooperate with one another
9. the United States of America

Check Your Understanding

1. **Explain** how President Washington helped to build loyalty and unity in the country.
2. **Discuss** the role of the Supreme Court.
3. **Summarize** the differences between the ideas of Hamilton and Jefferson.
4. **Describe** Washington's foreign policy.
5. **Summarize** the two main points of Washington's Farewell Address.
6. **Identify** the challenges President Adams faced and how he addressed them.

Critical Thinking

1. **Analyze Primary Sources** According to the presidential oath found on page 245, what kinds of actions can a President take to "preserve, protect, and defend" the Constitution?
2. **Analyze Primary Sources** Whose ideas, Hamilton's or Jefferson's, found in the quotations on page 251, do you feel better describe our country today? Explain.
3. **Evaluate** Do you agree with George Washington that political parties are a danger to American unity? Give reasons for your answer.

Put Your Skills to Work

USE PRIMARY AND SECONDARY SOURCES

You have learned that using both primary and secondary sources can add to your understanding of history.

Copy the chart on a sheet of paper. Then, choose one example of each type of source from this chapter. Fill in the chart by identifying the type of source and what information the source gives.

TYPE OF SOURCE	INFORMATION

In Your Own Words

JOURNAL WRITING

Being the first person to do something is never easy. George Washington faced a tremendous challenge in being the first President. In your journal, write about a challenge you have faced and the outcome. What did you learn from the challenge?

Net Work

INTERNET ACTIVITY

Working with a partner, use the Internet to find primary sources in history. Locate a primary source historical document that concerns an event or person discussed in this chapter. Download the document you choose. Then, present it to the class. Explain the document's importance. Provide background on the event or person that is the subject of the document.

For help in starting this activity, visit the following Web site: www.gfamericanhistory.com.

Look Ahead

In the next chapter, learn how an important decision doubled the size of the new country.

CHAPTER 11

An Era of Expansion 1800–1815

I. Jefferson as President
II. The Louisiana Purchase
III. The War of 1812

When Americans looked at a map of their country in early 1803, they saw the 13 original states. They also saw vast unsettled areas to the west and southwest. Beyond their homes lay the unknown: dense forests, arid deserts, great rivers, and mighty mountains.

All of this would soon change. Almost overnight, the United States would nearly double in size because of the purchase of land from France. Robert Livingston, one of the men who arranged the purchase of the new land, knew something great had just happened. He said,

> "We have lived long, but this is the noblest work of our whole lives. . . . From this day the United States take their place among the powers of the first rank. . . . The instruments which we have just signed . . . prepare ages of happiness for innumerable generations of human creatures."

Peace medal

U.S. Events

1803 United States buys Louisiana Territory. Supreme Court hears *Marbury* v. *Madison.*

1804 Lewis and Clark begin their journey. Aaron Burr kills Alexander Hamilton in a duel.

1806 Lewis and Clark return to St. Louis.

U.S. Events	**1800**	**1805**
Presidential Term Begins	1801 Thomas Jefferson	
World Events	**1800**	**1805**

World Events

1800 Spain surrenders the Louisiana Territory to France.

1804 Santo Domingo wins independence from France.

1806 British blockade French ports.

VIEW HISTORY This painting by Albert Bierstadt shows a mountain landscape inhabited by Native Americans in the nineteenth century. Westward explorers gave peace medals (left) to Native Americans they met during their travels.

★ **Do you think this painting is an accurate picture of the American West beyond the Mississippi River? Why or why not?**

Get Organized

PROBLEM/SOLUTION CHART

Throughout history, people have faced problems and searched for solutions. Use a problem/solution chart as you read Chapter 11. In the first oval, write a problem faced by the people you read about. In the second oval, write the solution they found. Here is an example from this chapter.

PROBLEM

The election of 1800 ended in a tie.

SOLUTION

The Twelfth Amendment is adopted.

1807 Embargo Act is passed.

1811 Battle of Tippecanoe Creek occurs.

1812 War of 1812 begins.

1814 Washington, D.C., is burned by the British.

1815 War of 1812 ends.

1810 — **1815**

1809 James Madison

1810 — **1815**

1812 Napoleon invades Russia with 600,000 men.

1815 Napoleon is defeated at Waterloo.

I Jefferson as President

Terms to Know

radical someone who favors extreme social or economic changes

judicial review a court review to determine whether a law is constitutional

Main Ideas

A. The election of 1800 was marked by confusion and produced an unusual tie.

B. Thomas Jefferson implemented popular changes during his presidency.

C. The case of *Marbury* v. *Madison* created a new role for the Supreme Court.

Active Reading

COMPARE AND CONTRAST
Comparing and contrasting two ideas or actions can help you understand how they are different and alike. As you read this section, ask yourself: How did President Jefferson's ideas compare with the ideas of President Adams?

A. The Election of 1800

President John Adams ran for re-election in 1800 against his Vice President, Thomas Jefferson. During Adams's presidency the Federalists had passed laws that angered many Americans. As a result, this election was a bitter one. Each party argued that the other was a threat to the Constitution.

Adams Versus Jefferson

The Federalist Party nominated John Adams again for President and C. C. Pinckney of South Carolina for Vice President. The Democratic-Republicans nominated Vice President Thomas Jefferson for President and Aaron Burr of New York for Vice President. Federalists told voters that Jefferson was a dangerous **radical**, or someone who favored extreme change in order to solve the country's problems. Democratic-Republicans fought back by saying that Adams wanted to become "King of America."

A mug used during Jefferson's time

A Confusing Election

When the electoral votes were counted, Jefferson had defeated Adams, 73 to 65. It was clear that Adams had lost the election of 1800. Yet, there was still a problem for Jefferson: Under the Constitution, members of the electoral college voted for President and Vice President without specifying which office was to be filled by which candidate. The two Democratic-Republican candidates, Jefferson and Burr, had received the same number of votes. The House of Representatives had to break the tie and decide which man would become President.

The House voted 35 times, but the tie held. Finally, Jefferson gained the help of an unlikely friend, Alexander Hamilton. Hamilton disliked Burr more than he disliked Jefferson. So he persuaded some of his supporters to choose Jefferson. As a result, Jefferson became the third President, while Burr became Vice President. Because of this confusing election, the Twelfth Amendment to the Constitution was ratified in time for the next election. It required electors to vote separately for President and Vice President.

 **What role did Alexander Hamilton play in the election of 1800?**

B. A New President, a New Direction

Thomas Jefferson took the oath of office on March 4, 1801. He spoke these words to his fellow Americans:

> "Let us . . . fellow citizens, unite with one heart and one mind. . . . We are all Republicans; we are all Federalists."

DOCUMENT-BASED QUESTION What do you think Jefferson meant when he said, "We are all Republicans; we are all Federalists"?

Jefferson's View of Government

President Jefferson believed in a weaker central government and stronger, more independent state governments. He hoped that ordinary citizens would take a bigger role in public affairs. Jefferson wanted more cooperation with Congress and better trade relations with other countries. He also did away with much of the formality of the earlier Presidents. He walked to his inauguration instead of riding in a grand coach. He met the foreign minister from Great Britain while dressed in slippers and comfortable clothes. On special occasions, he opened the White House to anyone who wanted to see him.

Jefferson persuaded Congress to take away taxes on some items produced in the United States. He also thought that the government was spending too much money. The President's supporters in Congress reduced spending by decreasing the size of the army and navy. The army went from about 4,000 troops to about 2,500 troops. The number of ships in the navy was also greatly reduced.

Jefferson's election marked the first time in U.S. history that the political party in power changed. The new President placed Democratic-Republicans in government jobs formerly held by Federalists. Jefferson's actions began a trend that continues today whenever a President of a different political party is elected.

Jefferson believed that if the government left people alone, they would create more wealth and achieve a better society. His political opponents, the Federalists, disagreed. They felt that strong government leadership was needed to direct the country's economy.

Thomas Jefferson
1743–1826

Years in office 1801–1809

Political Party Democratic-Republican

Birthplace Virginia

Age when elected 57

Occupations Farmer, Governor of Virginia, Minister to France

Did you know? Jefferson and John Adams died on the same day, July 4, 1826, fifty years after the signing of the Declaration of Independence.

Washington, D.C., looked very different in Jefferson's time.

In the election of 1804, Jefferson was once again the Democratic-Republican candidate for President. George Clinton of New York was his running mate, or vice presidential candidate. Jefferson's Federalist opponent for President was C. C. Pinckney. Because Jefferson's policies as President had been popular with most Americans, he won re-election easily.

Spotlight on Government

Today, Thomas Jefferson is regarded as one of the most influential Presidents in U.S. history. In fact, his image appears on the nickel and the two dollar bill. The Jefferson Memorial in Washington, D.C., was dedicated in 1943 on the anniversary of his birth. Jefferson was even chosen as one of the four Presidents to be included on Mount Rushmore.

Burr Versus Hamilton

Some members of the Federalist Party were upset with Jefferson's policies. They had a secret plan to withdraw the New England states from the United States and create a separate country. However, in order to succeed, they needed New York State to join them. So, in 1804, they offered to support Aaron Burr in his campaign to be governor of New York if he supported their plan. Burr refused their support.

After hearing rumors of the Federalists' plot, Alexander Hamilton accused Burr of treason, or betrayal. Burr lost the election for governor, mostly because Alexander Hamilton opposed him. Then, Burr challenged Hamilton to a duel. A duel is a potentially deadly fight with pistols to settle a quarrel between two people. Hamilton accepted the challenge. On July 11, 1804, the two men met in Weehawken, New Jersey. They exchanged shots, and Hamilton was severely wounded. He died the next day.

★ **How did Jefferson reduce government spending?**

C. A Stronger Role for the Supreme Court

The power of the Supreme Court grew in the early 1800s. The Court's new power was based on **judicial review**. Judicial review is the process by which the Supreme Court studies a law to decide if it is constitutional. The role of the Supreme Court in the national government was strengthened after this power was used for the first time.

Marbury v. *Madison*

The Chief Justice of the Supreme Court was John Marshall. He had been Secretary of State under President Adams. One of Adams's last official acts was to appoint Marshall, a Federalist, Chief Justice. Even though Marshall was highly respected by many, including Jefferson, he and President Jefferson disagreed on many issues. One of these issues was Marshall's decision, in 1803, to hear a legal case called *Marbury* v. *Madison.*

During the last days of his presidency, John Adams had appointed dozens of Federalists, including William Marbury, to federal judgeships created by the Judiciary Act of 1801. President Jefferson and many Democratic-Republicans called these men "midnight judges" because Adams had filled their positions just before he left office. Jefferson refused to allow his Secretary of State, James Madison, to give Marbury the official papers that would make him a judge. Marbury sued, or brought a legal case against, Madison.

This painting by Samuel F. B. Morse shows the old House of Representatives meeting room. In the early 1800s, the Supreme Court borrowed space in this room for hearings.

John Marshall

After studying the facts of the case, Chief Justice Marshall made a ruling. The Judiciary Act of 1789 required the Supreme Court to decide cases involving federal officials. However, Marshall ruled that the Judiciary Act of 1789 was unconstitutional, or in violation of the Constitution. He found that the Constitution did not give the Supreme Court the right to decide cases involving federal officials. Therefore, the Court did not have the authority to force Madison to give Marbury the judgeship.

Judicial Review

Chief Justice Marshall's ruling in 1803 established the important principle of judicial review that is still in effect today. The Supreme Court reviews laws and the actions of Congress and the President to make sure they do not violate the U.S. Constitution. If the Supreme Court finds that laws and actions go against the Constitution, it can then declare them unconstitutional. This process of judicial review is an important part of the system of checks and balances.

John Marshall served as Chief Justice until his death in 1835. During his long career, he decided many important cases. The Court's actions during the Marshall years became the model for all Supreme Courts to follow.

 **What is judicial review?**

Review

Review History

A. Why was the election of 1800 a confusing one?

B. How did Jefferson's ideas about government and the economy differ from his opponents' ideas?

C. How did *Marbury* v. *Madison* establish the idea of judicial review?

Define Terms to Know

Provide a definition for each of the following terms.
radical, judicial review

Critical Thinking

Do you think that Jefferson's desire that ordinary people take a bigger part in government was a good one? Why or why not?

Write About Government

Democratic-Republicans and Federalists had different views on the role of government. Write an editorial defending one point of view.

Get Organized

PROBLEM/SOLUTION CHART

Use a problem/solution chart to examine the problems faced by the people you read about in Section I. For example, what problem did Chief Justice Marshall deal with and what was the solution?

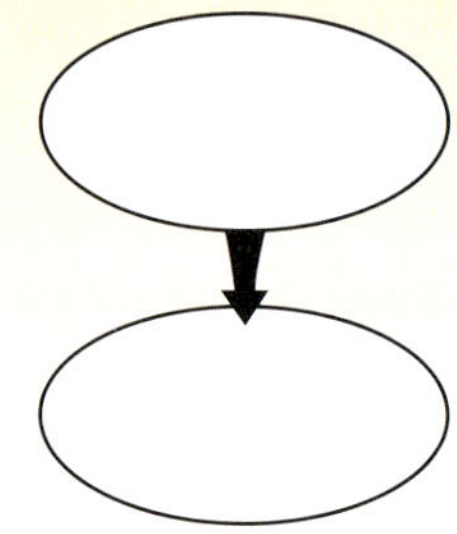

Build Your Skills

Social Studies Skill

INTERPRET POLITICAL CARTOONS

Political cartoons are drawings that express a point of view. Their subject can be a political issue or a current event. Artists who draw political cartoons often use humor and exaggeration to show their opinion. Their goal is to influence people's views about important events. Some political cartoons express a positive point of view. Many, however, are opposed to a policy, a person, or an event.

When you read about history, political cartoons can be a primary source of information. They reflect the thoughts and the feelings of some people who lived during the time period you are studying. For example, you might need to write an essay about Thomas Jefferson. Looking at a political cartoon from that time period might help you understand the opinions of some people who lived at that time.

Here's How

Follow these steps to analyze a political cartoon.

1. Identify the subject of the cartoon.
2. Examine labels, words, and titles to understand the cartoonist's message.
3. Look for symbols in the cartoon and decide what they stand for.
4. Draw conclusions about the artist's point of view on the subject.

Here's Why

You have just read about Thomas Jefferson's presidency. The following cartoon is about Jefferson. It shows him fighting with the American eagle for a copy of the Constitution.

Practice the Skill

Explain the message of the cartoon on the right. Be as specific as you can. Decide which political party might have agreed with it. Refer to events and ideas you read about in Section I.

Extend the Skill

Find a current political cartoon in a newspaper or a magazine. Bring the cartoon to class and share it with your classmates.

Apply the Skill

Use the skills you have practiced to analyze the political cartoon in Section II.

This cartoon about Jefferson was drawn around 1800.

II The Louisiana Purchase

Terms to Know

tribute money paid for protection

embargo an order stopping trade with another country

Main Ideas

A. President Thomas Jefferson faced problems with Barbary pirates and Great Britain.

B. President Jefferson bought the vast Louisiana Territory from France.

C. Meriwether Lewis and William Clark explored the Louisiana Territory.

SEQUENCE OF EVENTS
The order in which events happen is their sequence. As you read this section, ask yourself the following question: What is the sequence of events that led to the Louisiana Purchase?

A. Troubles Across the Ocean

Thomas Jefferson, like John Adams before him, wanted to follow George Washington's advice to avoid conflicts with foreign countries. However, avoiding conflicts was not easy to do. One problem—with the Barbary States of Morocco, Algiers, Tunis, and Tripoli—actually led to war.

The Pirates of the Mediterranean

The Barbary States were located along the coast of North Africa. Pirates from these states raided ships in the Mediterranean Sea to steal cargo and kidnap passengers for ransom. Some countries, including the United States, paid money, called a **tribute**, so that the pirates would not raid their ships.

After Jefferson became President, the pirates asked for more money from the United States. Jefferson refused to pay. In May 1801, the pasha, or ruler, of Tripoli ordered his soldiers to chop down a pole that held an American flag. This act was his way of declaring war. In response, Jefferson sent warships to the Mediterranean.

In 1803, the USS *Philadelphia* was captured by the pirates and its crew was held hostage. A 25-year-old navy lieutenant named Stephen Decatur sneaked onto the captured ship and destroyed it to prevent the pirates from using it. The USS *Constitution* then bombarded Tripoli. Finally, in 1805, the United States negotiated a peace treaty in which it agreed to pay the pasha $60,000 to rescue the captured Americans. It was not until 1816 that the United States stopped paying tribute to the other Barbary States.

Problems With Great Britain

President Jefferson faced other problems. Great Britain was at war with France. So, Great Britain tried to cut off U.S. trade with France. The French military, led by Napoleon Bonaparte, then tried to cut off U.S. trade with Great Britain. Jefferson believed that international law gave the United States the right to trade with any nation it wished.

British ships began seizing cargo and sailors from American ships. This practice of impressment involved forcing American sailors to serve on British warships. In 1807, a British ship stopped a U.S. Navy ship, the USS *Chesapeake*, off the coast of Virginia. Angry Americans called for war. Instead, the President ordered all British warships to leave U.S. waters. In addition, Congress passed the Embargo Act of 1807. An **embargo** is an order that ends all trade relations with another country. This act ordered U.S. ship owners to stop trading with European countries.

 **Why was the Embargo Act of 1807 important?**

B. The Louisiana Purchase

President Jefferson was also facing problems at home. France had taken control of New Orleans, Louisiana, and the Mississippi River. These locations were important to trade in the United States.

In this cartoon, King George III, ruler of Great Britain (left), and Napoleon I, emperor of France (right), attack each other with sticks. They empty Thomas Jefferson's pockets at the same time.

ANALYZE PRIMARY SOURCES

DOCUMENT-BASED QUESTION What does this cartoon suggest about America's place in the war between Britain and France?

France Gains Control of New Orleans

Spain had given France the Louisiana Territory in 1800. This area included all of the land between the Mississippi River and the Rocky Mountains. In 1802, France also took over the important port of New Orleans. Even though U.S. ships had use of the river, Jefferson became worried that France would shut down U.S. trade on the river and in New Orleans. In 1803, Jefferson sent his Secretary of State, James Monroe, to Paris to join the U.S. ambassador, Robert Livingston. Their mission was to buy the port of New Orleans for up to $10 million. Jefferson knew that the country that controlled New Orleans also controlled the Mississippi River.

Napoleon Bonaparte was also worried—but for different reasons. France's war with Great Britain was growing and Napoleon wanted to focus all of his energies on the war. However, on the Caribbean island of Santo Domingo a revolution was brewing. Under the command of François Toussaint L'Ouverture, the enslaved people who lived there began a revolt to gain their independence from France. Napoleon's troops had trouble stopping the revolt. The French troops would not be able to leave the island to defend Louisiana if the Americans or the British decided to take it by force.

Toussaint L'Ouverture fought in Santo Domingo, now Haiti and the Dominican Republic, for independence from France.

A Deal Is Made

When Monroe and Livingston arrived in France to buy New Orleans, they received a surprise invitation. The French finance minister, Charles de Talleyrand, asked Monroe: "How much will you give for the whole of Louisiana?"

Napoleon realized that if he sold the Louisiana Territory to the United States he could use the money to pay for the war with Great Britain. He could also avoid conflict with the United States. In April 1803, a deal known as the Louisiana Purchase was made. The United States would buy New Orleans and all of the Louisiana Territory for 60 million francs, or about $15 million. That is only about four cents an acre! When Monroe and Livingston signed the treaty on April 30, 1803, the area of the United States doubled.

When Jefferson learned how much land Monroe and Livingston had bought, he asked himself if the President had the power to buy new lands. Jefferson was concerned because the Constitution did not mention buying territory, and he believed in a strict interpretation of the Constitution. However, he found a way to justify the purchase. The Constitution gave the President the power to negotiate treaties.

★ Why did Napoleon decide to sell the Louisiana Territory?

Then & Now

Because it was once owned by France, the state of Louisiana is different in many ways from the other 49 states. Many Louisianans still speak a form of French. Also, many towns and cities in Louisiana have French names. Finally, the state's system of law is based on Napoleon's system rather than an English system.

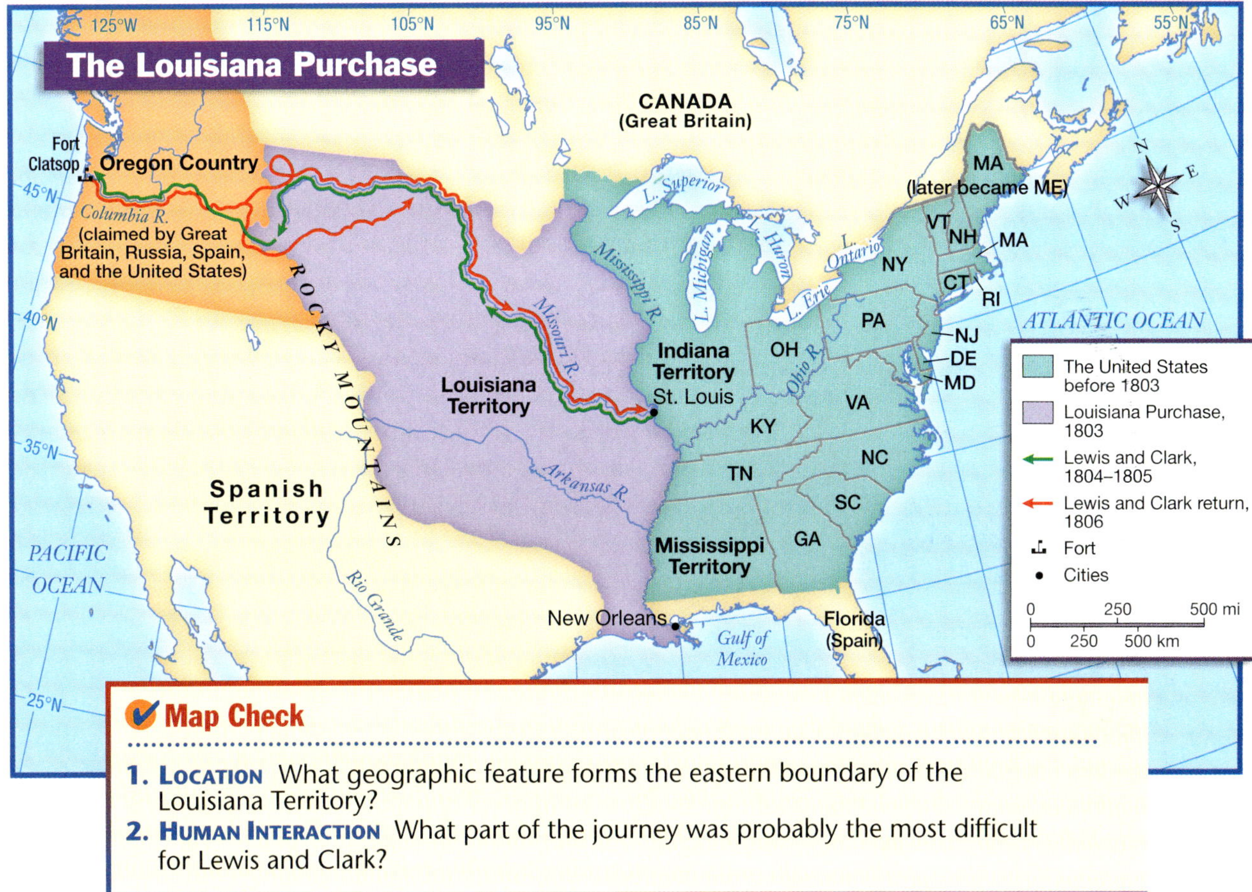

Map Check

1. **LOCATION** What geographic feature forms the eastern boundary of the Louisiana Territory?
2. **HUMAN INTERACTION** What part of the journey was probably the most difficult for Lewis and Clark?

C. Exploring the Louisiana Territory

The United States now stretched all the way to the Rocky Mountains. However, most Americans did not even know what these lands looked like. President Jefferson looked for someone willing to explore this great, unknown territory.

The Lewis and Clark Expedition

President Jefferson decided to send a team of explorers to survey the new land. He chose his personal secretary, Meriwether Lewis, and an army officer, William Clark, to lead the expedition. These men would travel up the Missouri River to explore the northern part of the territory. Jefferson hoped that they would find a water route linking the Mississippi River to the Pacific Ocean. This route would provide the new western lands with access to markets in the east. Jefferson also instructed them to make notes about "the soil and face of the country, its growth and vegetable production . . . the animals . . . mineral production . . . climate . . . winds . . . [and] times of appearance of particular birds, reptiles, or insects."

Lewis and Clark and a group of more than 40 others gathered in St. Louis, where the Missouri River flows into the Mississippi River. They left St. Louis on May 14, 1804.

Lewis and Clark's expedition followed the Missouri River to present-day central North Dakota. The explorers traveled by foot, horse, canoe, and a type of shallow riverboat known as a keelboat.

Lewis and Clark spent the first winter at Fort Mandan near present-day Bismarck, North Dakota. There they hired a French-Canadian fur trader, Toussaint Charbonneau, and his Shoshone wife, Sacagawea, to act as their guides. In the spring, they continued on through the Rocky Mountains. Then, they followed the Columbia River to the Pacific Ocean, at the border of the present-day states of Washington and Oregon. When Clark first saw the Pacific Ocean on November 7, 1805, he proclaimed:

> "Ocean in view! O! the joy!"

ANALYZE PRIMARY SOURCES

DOCUMENT-BASED QUESTION Why was Clark so excited to reach the Pacific Ocean?

They Made History

Sacagawea 1788–1812

Sacagawea was a Shoshone Native American born around 1788. She was kidnapped as a young child by another Native American group. Later she was sold as a slave to a French-Canadian trader named Toussaint Charbonneau and became his wife. Lewis and Clark hired Charbonneau as a guide and interpreter and agreed to let Sacagawea and her young son join them. Along the way, Sacagawea acted as an interpreter when they met other Native Americans. When they met a group of Shoshones, Sacagawea realized that the chief was her brother. She helped the travelers get the food and horses that they needed to continue their journey. Many memorials have been dedicated to Sacagawea for her contributions to American history.

Sacagawea helped Lewis and Clark travel through the Rocky Mountains. The U.S. Mint issued a golden dollar (left) with Sacagawea's image in 2000.

Critical Thinking How was Sacagawea able to help Lewis and Clark in ways that Charbonneau could not?

The Explorers Return Home

A page from William Clark's journal with a drawing of a bird, called a sage grouse.

The Lewis and Clark expedition reached the Pacific Ocean in November 1805. They built Fort Clatsop near the mouth of the Columbia River in present-day Oregon. Lewis and Clark planned to sail home on a ship. Months passed, however, so the group decided to return overland. Splitting up for part of the return trip, Lewis and Clark arrived in St. Louis again in September 1806. They had traveled about 8,000 miles in almost two-and-a-half years.

The expedition had actually traveled far beyond the border of the Louisiana Territory in its search for a water route to the Pacific. It even established a U.S. claim to Oregon. Lewis and Clark took careful notes of what they saw. They created many maps and brought back plant samples for President Jefferson. The explorers also brought back a prairie dog and a magpie for the President. Americans found the stories of Lewis and Clark's journey exciting. They had proved that people could travel overland to the Pacific Ocean. Soon, many others would want to follow in their footsteps.

Another explorer of the new territory was Zebulon Pike. With a small group, he followed the Arkansas River to present-day Colorado. There, he saw a great mountain that is known today as Pikes Peak. In 1807, Pike took his expedition into Spanish-owned lands. He was captured by Spanish cavalry and accused of spying. He eventually returned to the United States and told tales of his journey.

 **How did Lewis and Clark record what they saw on their expedition?**

Review History

A. What was similar about the U.S. conflicts with Tripoli and with Great Britain?

B. How did President Jefferson go against one of his principles in order to buy land?

C. What was the purpose of Lewis and Clark's journey?

Define Terms to Know

Provide a definition for each of the following terms.
tribute, embargo

Critical Thinking

In what way did Toussaint L'Ouverture's revolt help the United States?

Write About Geography

William Clark recorded what he saw in a journal. Create a journal entry describing your town. In addition to notes, you may include maps and drawings.

Get Organized

PROBLEM/SOLUTION CHART

Use a problem/solution chart to understand the problems faced by the people you read about in this section. For example, what problem did the purchase of vast, unknown lands in Louisiana create, and what was the solution?

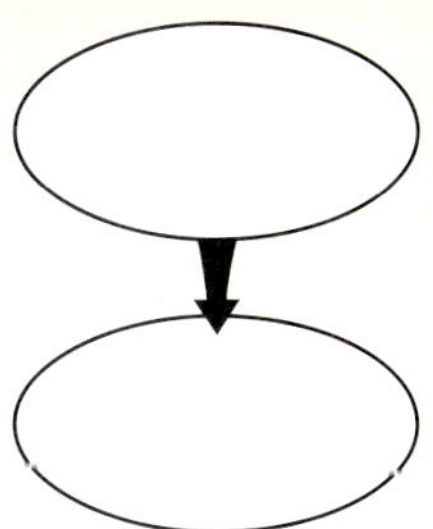

III The War of 1812

Terms to Know

anthem a song of praise

nationalism pride in one's country

Main Ideas

A. Fighting between Great Britain and France, along with troubles on the frontier, drew the United States closer to war.

B. The War of 1812 ended without a victory, but the United States did achieve some important successes.

C. Pride in the United States increased after the War of 1812.

Active Reading

PREDICT

Did you ever predict the ending of a movie or book? When you predict, you look for clues to future events. As you read this section, ask yourself the following question: What will be the result of the War of 1812?

A. Causes of the War

War raged in Europe throughout most of the period between 1793 and 1815. At the same time, tensions increased between Great Britain and the United States.

Battlefield Europe

Both France and Great Britain needed war supplies, food, and other materials from the United States. U.S. merchants became rich supplying both sides. However, tensions grew as Britain tried to prevent U.S. ships from supplying France. In turn, the French tried to keep American goods from reaching Britain.

President Jefferson's Embargo Act of 1807 cut off trade relations with Europe. Merchants in the United States suddenly lost business. Farmers could not sell their crops, and workers lost their jobs. Because of the unpopular embargo, smuggling was common. Americans demanded that the act be repealed. They were granted their wish in early 1809. Congress passed a law allowing U.S. ships to trade with any country except Great Britain or France.

Then & Now

James Madison, like Jefferson before him, tried to use trade to affect the foreign policy of other nations. He directed his trade policies against Britain and France.

In recent years, the United Nations, led by the United States, has used similar policies. It placed sanctions, or restrictions, on trade with Yugoslavia during the Balkan wars of the 1990s.

Troubles in the West

Conflicts in the West led to increased tensions between the United States and Great Britain. In the Northwest, the British continued to help Native Americans raid U.S. settlements. A Shawnee leader, named Tecumseh, joined several Native American peoples together.

Then, he led attacks against the settlers. His goal was to drive all settlers out of the Northwest Territory. He issued a warning:

> "You are continually driving the red people [from their land] when at last you will drive them into the [ocean]. . . . You ought to know what you are doing with the Indians. . . . It is a very bad thing and we do not like it."

DOCUMENT-BASED QUESTION What do you think Tecumseh is threatening to do in this statement?

President Madison sent General William Henry Harrison to fight against Tecumseh and his forces. In 1811, after Tecumseh left his headquarters to meet with Native Americans in the South, Harrison won a victory at the Battle of Tippecanoe Creek in present-day Indiana. When Tecumseh returned, his village was in ruins.

Tecumseh, chief of the Shawnees, fought against the western expansion of U.S. settlements.

The War Hawks

Americans' anger at the British grew. British ships continued practicing impressment. President Madison wanted to avoid war, but others wanted to fight. A group in Congress, called the War Hawks, raised their voices. Among their leaders were Henry Clay of Kentucky and John C. Calhoun of South Carolina. They hoped that winning a war against Great Britain would allow the United States to add more territory for its settlers by gaining control of Canada. They also hoped to push Spain, a British ally, out of Florida. Finally, in June 1812, Madison gave in to the War Hawks' pressure. The second war against Great Britain, called the War of 1812, began.

 **Why did Tecumseh and his forces attack settlers?**

B. Fighting the War of 1812

For most of the war, the British government was more concerned with battling the French. However, when Napoleon was defeated, Great Britain turned its attention to the United States.

Early Battles

While Britain and France fought in Europe, several battles took place in the United States. In 1813, Captain Oliver Hazard Perry defeated a fleet of British ships at the Battle of Lake Erie. American troops also unsuccessfully tried to invade Canada through Detroit, Michigan. Shortly after, Major General Andrew Jackson defeated the Creeks, Britain's allies, in present-day Alabama.

In April 1814, the British defeated the French in Europe. The capture of Napoleon allowed Great Britain to concentrate on the war in the United States.

The British Invasion

British troops planned a three-part invasion of the United States. One attack on New York, originating in Canada, was beaten back at the Battle of Plattsburg in September 1814. Another attack in the summer of 1814 was aimed at Washington, D.C., and Baltimore, Maryland.

The British forces captured the capital and burned some government buildings, including the White House and the Capitol. President Madison and the government had to flee from the city. First Lady Dolley Madison refused to leave until several national treasures were saved. Among these valuables was a large portrait of George Washington.

After attacking Washington, D.C., the British fleet sailed to Baltimore. It bombarded Fort McHenry near the city's harbor. Despite an intense attack off and on throughout the night, the fort was not destroyed. An American lawyer who was visiting one of the attacking ships was thrilled to see that the fort's flag still flew. The lawyer, an amateur poet named Francis Scott Key, wrote a poem to celebrate the moment. It was later called "The Star-Spangled Banner" and became the country's national **anthem**, or song.

The third British attack was at New Orleans. Major General Andrew Jackson led a force of army troops to defend the city. These troops were made up of pirates, Native Americans, state militia, and free African Americans. In 1815, Jackson's army defeated the British, and Jackson became a national hero.

Parts of Washington, D.C., were set on fire after British troops attacked the city.

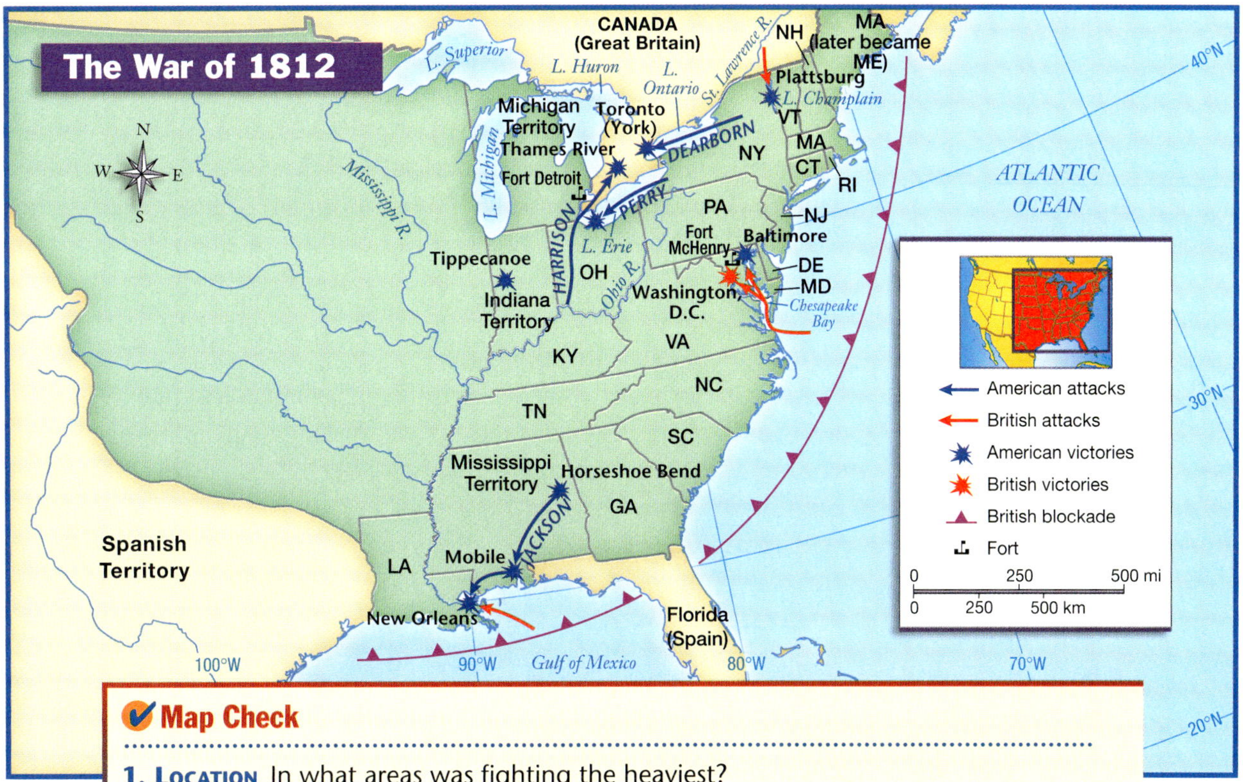

The War of 1812

CANADA (Great Britain)
L. Superior
L. Huron
L. Ontario
St. Lawrence R.
L. Michigan
Michigan Territory
Toronto (York)
Thames River
Fort Detroit
Mississippi R.
DEARBORN
PERRY
HARRISON
L. Erie
Ohio R.
Tippecanoe
Indiana Territory
OH
KY
TN
PA
NY
NH
MA (later became ME)
Plattsburg
L. Champlain
VT
MA
CT
RI
NJ
Fort McHenry
Baltimore
DE
MD
Washington, D.C.
Chesapeake Bay
VA
NC
SC
GA
Mississippi Territory
Horseshoe Bend
JACKSON
LA
Mobile
New Orleans
Spanish Territory
Florida (Spain)
Gulf of Mexico
ATLANTIC OCEAN
100°W
90°W
80°W
70°W
40°N
30°N
20°N

American attacks
British attacks
American victories
British victories
British blockade
Fort
0 250 500 mi
0 250 500 km

Map Check

1. **Location** In what areas was fighting the heaviest?
2. **Location** Approximately how long was the British blockade?

Negotiating the Peace

In December 1814, the British agreed to an end to the war. The great victory at the Battle of New Orleans actually came after peace talks had already ended the war. News traveled slowly in the early 1800s, and not everyone had learned that the war had ended. Great Britain was tired of war, as was the United States. Neither side seemed hopeful of winning. The Treaty of Ghent ended the war without bringing any changes at all. Great Britain and the United States kept the lands they held before the war. American and British merchants began trading goods again.

 **How did the defeat of Napoleon affect the War of 1812?**

C. Results of the War

The United States did not win or lose the War of 1812. Yet, the war did bring about some important changes. Americans took pride in their country's successes. The country had proven once again that it could stand on its own against Great Britain. Some people even called the war the Second War for Independence.

New American Heroes

Americans also realized that the country needed a strong government to withstand threats from abroad. Several new heroes had emerged from the conflict. Among these were military leaders General William Henry Harrison and Major General Andrew Jackson. Jackson became the most popular military hero since George Washington. Like Washington before them, Jackson and Harrison would one day hold the nation's highest office.

Growth of Nationalism

Most importantly, the country experienced a new sense of **nationalism** after the War of 1812. Nationalism is pride in one's country. The new nationalism led to a desire to keep expanding the boundaries of the United States.

African Americans, too, could take pride in their contributions to the war. Approximately 10 to 20 percent of U.S. sailors on the Great Lakes were African American. Their role in the war strengthened their claims for full citizenship.

Another positive result of the war occurred in Europe. The end of the war against Napoleon marked a turning point. Europe entered a period of peace that would last almost 100 years. As a result, the United States could begin to focus on its own development. The nation was about to enter a time of tremendous growth.

 **Who became a hero because of his victories in the War of 1812?**

Review History

A. How did the Embargo Act of 1807 hurt the United States?

B. What was the British plan to win the War of 1812?

C. In what ways were the results of the War of 1812 positive for the United States?

Define Terms to Know

Provide a definition for each of the following terms.
anthem, nationalism

Critical Thinking

Do you think that the United States could have avoided war with Great Britain? Why or why not?

Write About History

Write a newspaper article announcing the end of the War of 1812. Explain the results of the war from an American point of view.

Get Organized

PROBLEM/SOLUTION CHART

Think about the problems you read about in this section. Use a problem/solution chart to link a problem with its solution. For example, what problem did merchants face in 1807 and what was the solution?

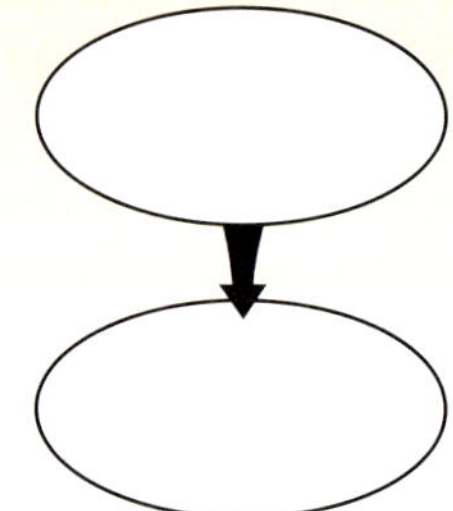

CONNECT History & Music

"The Star-Spangled Banner"

Almost all Americans know the words to the national anthem, "The Star-Spangled Banner." However, do you know the story of how the song was written?

ATTACK ON FORT McHENRY In 1814, the British army and navy headed north to Baltimore, Maryland, after attacking Washington, D.C. Fort McHenry guarded Baltimore's harbor. A huge American flag flew over the fort.

Before the attack on Baltimore began, the British admiral had a visitor, a young Washington lawyer named Francis Scott Key. He had come to ask for the release of Dr. William Beanes, an American doctor. Key and Beanes had to stay on the ship until after the attack.

"BOMBS BURSTING IN AIR" The bombardment began on September 13, 1814. An anxious Key watched the attack throughout the day and night. He feared the fort would fall under the tremendous storm of cannonballs. However, when dawn arrived the next morning, Key saw that a flag still flew over the fort.

A POEM Key was so overcome with joy that the attack had failed that he scribbled out a poem to celebrate. He called the poem "The Defense of Fort McHenry." Later, it was set to the tune of a well-known English song. Key's song became very popular, and soon it had a new name, "The Star-Spangled Banner." In 1931, Congress made it the national anthem.

Critical Thinking

Answer the questions below. Then, complete the activity.

1. Why did Francis Scott Key write his poem?
2. Do you think "The Star-Spangled Banner" makes a good national anthem? Why or why not?

Write About It

"The Star-Spangled Banner" describes a moment in American history. Key's poem also gave the American flag its name. Prepare a presentation about the history of the American flag. Then, share your presentation with the class. Go to the following Web site to begin your search: www.gfamericanhistory.com.

This painting of the attack on Fort McHenry shows "the bombs bursting in air" that Key depicted in his poem.

CHAPTER 11 Review

Chapter Summary

In your notebook, complete the following outline. Then, use your outline to write a brief summary of the chapter.

An Era of Expansion

I. Jefferson as President
  A. The Election of 1800
  B.
  C.
II. The Louisiana Purchase
  A.
  B.
  C.
III. The War of 1812
  A.
  B.
  C.

Interpret the Timeline

Use the timeline on pages 264–265 to answer the following questions.

1. How long did the War of 1812 last?
2. **Critical Thinking** What world event shows the weakening of European control in the Western Hemisphere?

Use Terms to Know

Match each term with its definition.

a. embargo
b. judicial review
c. nationalism
d. radical
e. tribute

1. pride in one's country
2. money paid for protection
3. a court review to determine if something is constitutional
4. an order to stop trade with another country
5. someone who favors extreme measures

Check Your Understanding

1. **Summarize** how Jefferson's political ideals differed from those of Adams.
2. **Discuss** John Marshall's contributions to the judicial branch of government during the early 1800s.
3. **Describe** how the United States doubled in size in 1803.
4. **Identify** two foreign threats to American security in the early 1800s.
5. **Summarize** the reasons for tension between the United States and Great Britain in the early 1800s.
6. **Explain** several results of the War of 1812.

Critical Thinking

1. **Analyze Primary Sources** In his inaugural address on page 267, Jefferson urged Americans to unite with one heart and mind. Do you think that people with different political opinions are bad for a country? Explain.
2. **Synthesize Information** In what ways did Lewis and Clark's expedition help western settlers?
3. **Make Inferences** Why do you think that neither Great Britain nor the United States was able to win a victory in the War of 1812?

Put Your Skills to Work

INTERPRET POLITICAL CARTOONS

Political cartoons are drawings that express a point of view. Artists who draw them use humor and exaggeration to influence people's opinions.

Study the following political cartoon. It shows a turtle, representing Jefferson's embargo. On a sheet of paper, answer the following questions.

1. What symbols are used in the cartoon?
2. What does Ograbme spell backwards?
3. What is the meaning of the cartoon?

A Jefferson-era cartoon

In Your Own Words

JOURNAL WRITING

Some Americans living in 1803 must have felt both excitement and fear about how gaining the Louisiana Territory would affect the rest of the country. Write a journal entry that describes a time when you felt both excited and a little frightened about something new that was happening.

Net Work

INTERNET ACTIVITY

Thomas Jefferson had many interests in addition to politics. These ranged from architecture to inventing new farming techniques. Working with a group of classmates, create a bulletin board about the life and accomplishments of the third President of the United States. Display your bulletin board in the classroom.

For help in starting this activity, visit the following Web site: www.gfamericanhistory.com.

Look Ahead

In the next chapter, learn how the United States continued to expand.

CHAPTER 12

The Nation Grows 1810–1842

I. The Rise of Nationalism
II. Jacksonian Democracy
III. U.S. Policies Toward Native Americans

The winds of change were blowing across the United States in the late 1820s. Americans were proud of their young country, and for the first time, a man born into poverty had been elected President. Andrew Jackson was wildly popular, and his victory in the 1828 presidential election was seen as a victory for the common people. After his inauguration, he held a party at the White House to celebrate. An eyewitness described the mayhem. She wrote,

> "But what a scene we did witness! . . . [A] rabble, a mob, of boys, . . . women, children scrambling, fighting, romping. . . . But it was the people's day, and the people's President, and the people would rule."

Ballot box

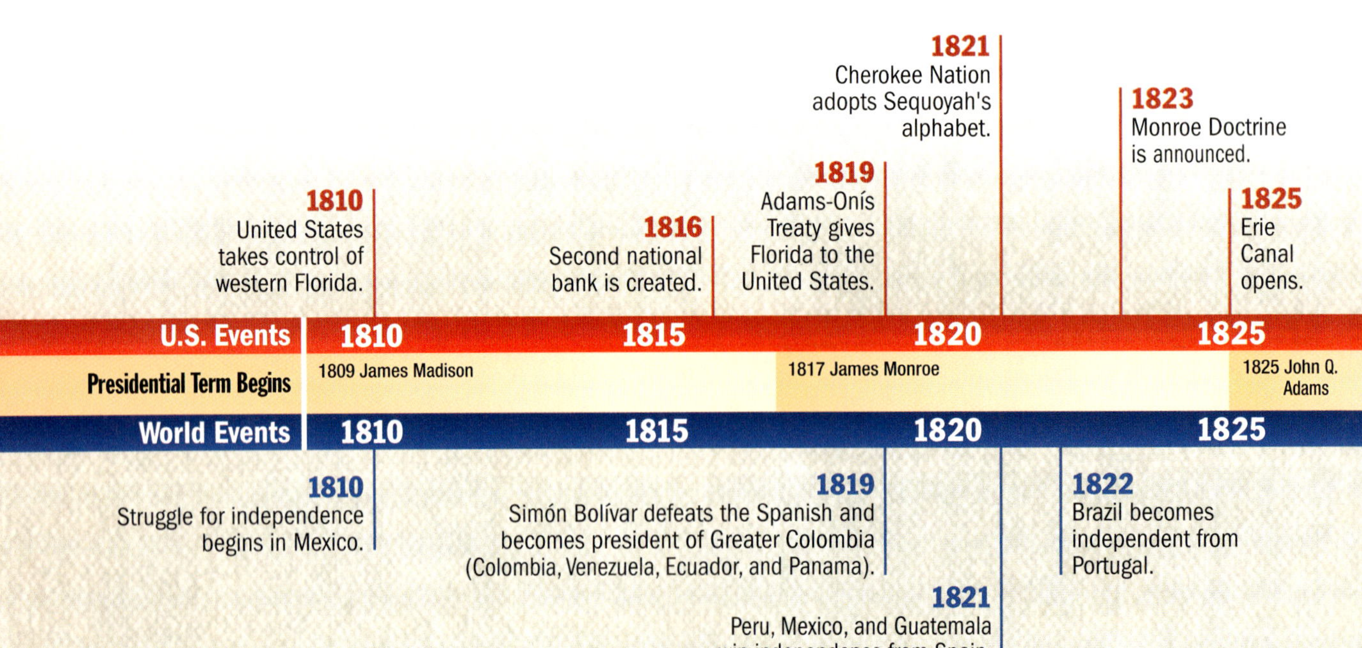

VIEW HISTORY Americans became more interested and involved in politics in the 1820s and 1830s. This painting shows voters on election day in Philadelphia, Pennsylvania. Voters placed their ballots in boxes like this one (left).

★ **What details in the painting show that the people thought of election day as a holiday and a time for celebration?**

Get Organized

VENN DIAGRAM

A Venn diagram helps you compare two items. Use a Venn diagram as you read Chapter 12. Begin by labeling each circle. Write the ways in which the items are different in the outside parts of each circle. Then, write the ways in which they are alike in the overlapping area. Here is an example from this chapter.

McCULLOCH v. MARYLAND

- About the 2nd National Bank
- States could not interfere

(Overlap)

- Followed Hamilton's interpretation
- Expanded federal goverment

- About shipping rights
- Government control of interstate trade

GIBBONS v. OGDEN

1830 Indian Removal Act is passed.

1834 Whig Party is formed. Bureau of Indian Affairs is created.

1837 U.S. economy weakens during Panic of 1837.

1838 Cherokee Trail of Tears begins.

1842 Seminole Wars end.

1830 — 1835 — 1840 — 1845

1829 Andrew Jackson

1837 Martin Van Buren

1841 William H. Harrison

1841 John Tyler

1830 — 1835 — 1840 — 1845

1830 Venezuela and Ecuador become independent republics.

1835 Juan de Rosas becomes dictator of Argentina.

1840 Pedro II is declared emperor of Brazil. Rafael Carrera becomes dictator of Guatemala.

I The Rise of Nationalism

Terms to Know

canal a waterway dug across land for ships to travel through

doctrine a set of beliefs or principles

Main Ideas

A. Changes in the United States after the War of 1812 included new tariffs and improved transportation.

B. Americans felt satisfaction with life in the United States, and the country experienced growing nationalism.

C. The United States strengthened its position in the Western Hemisphere.

IDENTIFY RELATIONSHIPS

You can identify a relationship between two time periods by connecting, or relating, similar events in each period. As you read this section, look for relationships between the "Era of Good Feelings" and today.

A. Plans for Improvement

At the end of the War of 1812, Americans were feeling a strong sense of nationalism, or pride in their nation. They were proud of their country's accomplishments in the war. During this time, many Americans focused on improvements in the United States.

The American System

Speaker of the House Henry Clay of Kentucky had a great dream for the United States. He wanted the country to become self-sufficient, or able to provide everything it needed for itself. Clay feared that the United States depended too much on foreign goods. So, he proposed a plan to Congress. This plan became known as the American System. It included three main points:

1. Tariffs, or protective taxes, should be placed on foreign goods. Clay believed that mills in New England would grow stronger if foreign goods became more expensive. A tariff was passed in 1816. It raised the price of imported goods and encouraged Americans to buy products made in the United States.
2. The government should form a new national bank to serve as the nation's central financial system. In 1816, the second Bank of the United States was created. It issued money, kept the nation's savings, and helped control the financial system.
3. The federal government should focus on improving transportation in the United States. The state governments began improving transportation systems.

Do You Remember?

In Chapter 10, you learned that Alexander Hamilton supported the formation of the first Bank of the United States.

Canals and Railroads

Many improvements were made to transportation in the United States. Steamboats began to navigate the nation's rivers. **Canals** were also built. A canal is a waterway dug across a section of land. Mule-led barges and small boats were able to move through these canals, transporting goods from one part of the country to another. One of the most important canals was the Erie Canal in New York. It opened in 1825 and connected the Hudson River to Buffalo, New York, a city on Lake Erie.

Another important advance in transportation was the railroad. Construction of the first major railroad line, the Baltimore and Ohio, began in 1828.

These developments tied the country together and helped Americans spread westward. Between 1812 and 1819, five newly formed states joined the union. They were Louisiana, Indiana, Mississippi, Illinois, and Alabama.

 **What was the goal of the American System?**

The National Road began in Cumberland, Maryland. Thousands of settlers used this road to reach land in the West.

James Monroe
1758–1831

Years in office 1817–1825

Political Party Democratic-Republican

Birthplace Virginia

Age when elected 58

Occupations Lawyer, Soldier, Ambassador

Did you know? While Monroe was President, Congress limited the number of stripes on the U.S. flag to thirteen, one for each original colony.

Quote "We lack many things, but we possess the most precious of all—liberty!"

B. The Era of Good Feelings

As feelings of nationalism spread, the country became more united. Confidence in the national government grew, and political disagreements disappeared for a while.

A New President

James Monroe easily won the election of 1816 to become President. Like Washington, Jefferson, and Madison, he was a Virginian and he was a gentleman-farmer. Monroe was so popular that he won all but one electoral vote in the election four years later.

The Federalist Party did not even nominate anyone to run against Monroe in the 1820 election. In fact, the Federalist Party no longer really existed. Many Federalists had joined the Democratic-Republican Party. The two-party system temporarily disappeared in American politics, and nationalism increased even more.

The sense of satisfaction among the American people during this time was very strong. Because of this, this period of time has become known as the "Era of Good Feelings." A newspaper reporter wrote at the time, "Never before, perhaps, since the institution of civil government, did the same harmony, the same absence of party spirit, the same national feeling [fill] a community."

The Supreme Court

The Supreme Court under Chief Justice John Marshall helped to increase nationalism and gave the government additional powers. Two of Marshall's most important decisions were made in the cases of *McCulloch* v. *Maryland* and *Gibbons* v. *Ogden*.

The case of *McCulloch* v. *Maryland* concerned the second national Bank of the United States. The state of Maryland wanted to tax the branch of the national bank in Baltimore. In 1819, the Supreme Court ruled that the states could not interfere with the bank because it had been created by the federal government. In the other important case, *Gibbons* v. *Ogden*, a debate arose in New York and New Jersey over shipping rights on the Hudson River. Marshall ruled in 1824 that only the federal government had the right to control trade between states.

In this case, Marshall followed Alexander Hamilton's idea of a loose interpretation of the Constitution. Marshall's rulings expanded the power of the federal government. His interpretations applied the Constitution to more and more areas.

How did the election of 1820 reflect the growing feeling of nationalism?

C. Nationalism and Foreign Policy

Foreign affairs soon captured the attention of Americans. Many eyes turned south, toward Florida.

Spain Loses Its Territory

In 1810, the United States took control of the western part of Florida, a Spanish territory. Spain protested, but it had been weakened by wars in Europe. It was also having trouble with its South American colonies.

Secretary of State John Quincy Adams negotiated with Spain about the rest of Florida. Discussions went nowhere. Then, in 1818, President Monroe ordered General Andrew Jackson to stop the Seminole people in Florida from raiding U.S. territory. However, Jackson decided instead to seize two Spanish forts.

Spain realized it was too weak to hold on to Florida. In 1819, the Adams-Onís Treaty was signed. Spain gave Florida to the United States for $5 million. The treaty also established the border between the Louisiana Territory and Spanish territory in the Southwest.

Within a few years, Spain lost almost all of its empire in the Americas. By 1824, it controlled only Cuba and Puerto Rico.

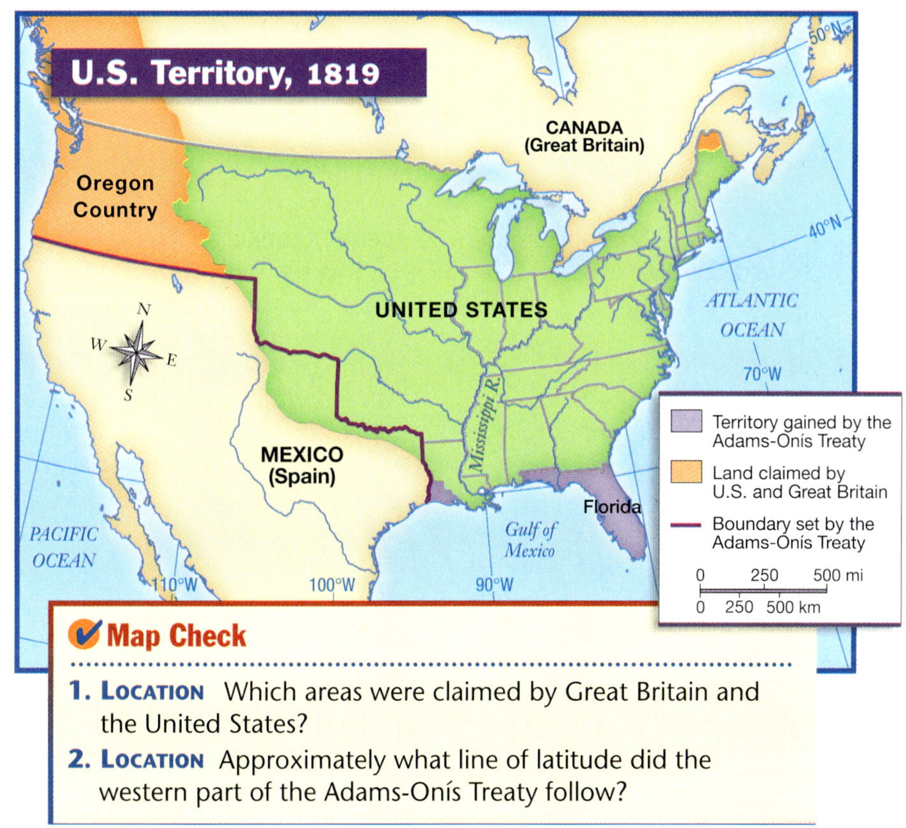

Map Check

1. **Location** Which areas were claimed by Great Britain and the United States?
2. **Location** Approximately what line of latitude did the western part of the Adams-Onís Treaty follow?

The Western Hemisphere was the focus of the Monroe Doctrine. It includes North and South America.

The Monroe Doctrine

Many Americans, including President Monroe and John Quincy Adams, were concerned that other European nations might take advantage of Spain's weakness. Nations such as France and Russia might try to increase their territory in the Western Hemisphere. In December 1823, Monroe announced a new foreign policy during his annual address to Congress. It became known as the Monroe Doctrine. A **doctrine** is a statement of beliefs. The Monroe Doctrine had three important parts:

1. The United States would not permit European countries to start or take over more colonies in the Western Hemisphere.
2. The United States would regard interference in the affairs of any country in the Western Hemisphere as a threat to the United States itself. The United States would oppose attempts to restore newly independent countries to the Spanish Empire.
3. The United States would not interfere with European nations or with existing colonies in the Western Hemisphere.

You can read the Monroe Doctrine on pages R3–R4.

At first, many European governments ignored the Monroe Doctrine. However, in time, the Monroe Doctrine became a basic principle of American foreign policy. It established goals for the United States and a clear message to its allies and enemies abroad.

 **How did the United States gain Florida?**

Review History

A. What part did transportation play in the American System?

B. How did Supreme Court rulings during this period affect relations between the states and the federal government?

C. Why was the Monroe Doctrine proposed?

Define Terms to Know

Provide a definition for each of the following terms.
canal, doctrine

Critical Thinking

What caused the increased feelings of nationalism in the United States?

Write About History

Write a newspaper editorial about the Monroe Doctrine from a European point of view.

Get Organized

VENN DIAGRAM

In this section you read about canals and railroads. Use a Venn diagram to compare these types of transportation.

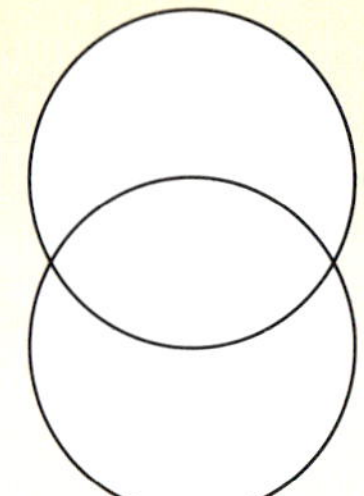

Build Your Skills

Critical Thinking

DRAW CONCLUSIONS

When you draw conclusions, you make judgments based on the information you have learned. For example, if you wake up in the morning and see that the sidewalk is wet, what conclusion can you draw? You would probably conclude that it rained during the night, based on previous experiences and your knowledge of weather.

Drawing the right conclusion from information is not always easy. With practice, however, you can gain confidence that the conclusions you draw are correct.

When you read about history, you must draw conclusions from the information you are given. Sometimes, the information will not tell you what conclusion to draw. In that case, you have to put your own skills to work.

Here's How

Follow these steps to draw conclusions when reading history.

1. Think about how what you read relates to what you already know about the subject.
2. Find details that support or oppose what you know.
3. Draw a conclusion by making a summary statement about the information you have read.

Here's Why

You have just read about the Monroe Doctrine. Suppose you had to write an essay about how this doctrine changed the role of the United States in the Western Hemisphere. You would need to draw a conclusion from the information you read.

Practice the Skill

Copy the detail/conclusion chart on a sheet of paper. Reread Section I. Then, draw a conclusion about the Monroe Doctrine.

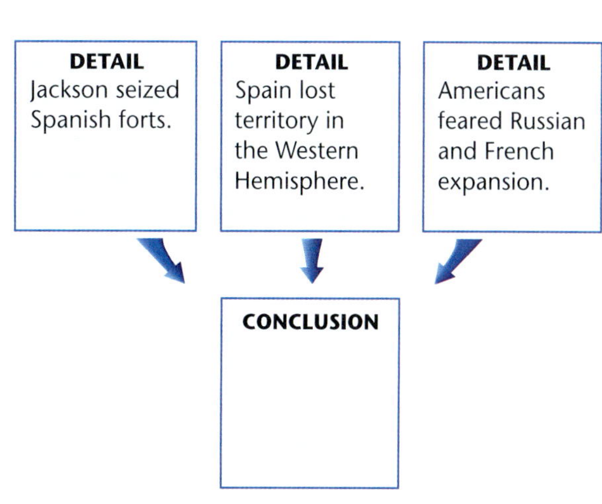

Extend the Skill

Write a paragraph about how the Monroe Doctrine changed the role of the United States in foreign affairs.

Apply the Skill

As you read the remaining sections of this chapter, draw conclusions about some of the important events.

II Jacksonian Democracy

Terms to Know

spoils system government appointments of friends by the winning party of an election

"kitchen cabinet" unofficial advisors to the President

sectionalism concern for the interests of a certain region or area

Main Ideas

A. Andrew Jackson was the first man born into poverty to serve as President.

B. Jackson's policies gave ordinary people more power in government.

C. Jackson's policies divided the nation over the Bank War and the Nullification Crisis.

SUMMARIZE

When you summarize, you form a general statement that sums up the information you have read. As you read this section, summarize ways that Andrew Jackson changed American political life.

A. A Man of the People

The first six Presidents were well-educated, land-owning gentlemen from established families in Virginia and Massachusetts. Andrew Jackson represented a new type of President.

The Election of 1824

There were four candidates for President in 1824. One of them was James Monroe's Secretary of State, John Quincy Adams. He was the son of the second President, John Adams. Another was Kentuckian Henry Clay, Speaker of the House and creator of the American System. The third candidate was William Crawford of Georgia. The fourth was Andrew Jackson. Jackson was a favorite son, or a favored candidate, of the people of Tennessee. Jackson had little formal education, yet he became a wealthy lawyer, political leader, and war hero. He was best known, however, as a spokesperson for democratic causes and ordinary people.

In the election, Jackson won the most popular votes and the most electoral votes. However, he did not win a majority, or more than half, of the electoral votes. According to the U.S. Constitution, when this event happens, the election must be decided by the House of Representatives. The choice was among the three candidates with the most electoral votes, which left Clay out.

Henry Clay convinced many representatives in the House to vote for John Quincy Adams. As a result, Adams became President. Adams then appointed Clay Secretary of State. This appointment angered Jackson and his supporters. They called it a corrupt bargain.

Poster from the 1824 election

Jackson declared, "Corruption, and intrigues at Washington . . . defeated the will of the people." Jackson quickly announced that he would be a candidate again in the 1828 election.

Andrew Jackson's Comeback

As President, John Quincy Adams supported a strong national government, tariff protection, and the building of new roads and canals. He also stressed the importance of education, scientific research, and exploration of the West. However, Adams, like his father, was an unpopular President. Many Americans thought he was proud, cold, and insensitive. In addition, he wanted to end slavery. This proposal was opposed by many Southerners who were also supporters of Jackson. Although Adams ran for re-election in 1828, he refused to campaign for himself, voicing instead that if the country needed him it would ask for his service.

The Election of 1824

CANDIDATE	POPULAR VOTES	ELECTORAL VOTES
Jackson	153,544	99
Adams	108,740	84
Crawford	46,618	41
Clay	47,136	37

Chart Check

How many electoral votes did Jackson need to win in order to have a majority, or more than 50 percent?

Andrew Jackson defeated Adams in the election of 1828. When the election was over, ordinary people who supported Jackson gathered in Washington, D.C., to celebrate the election of their hero.

Who won the most popular votes in the 1824 election?

B. Changes in American Politics

President Jackson made many important changes in American politics. These changes reflected his idea that all citizens should have more power in the government. Many of these changes are still in effect today.

Jackson Rewards His Allies

During Jackson's term, the Democratic-Republican Party of Thomas Jefferson and James Madison split. Supporters of John Quincy Adams and Henry Clay formed a new party, the National Republicans. Jackson's party became known as the Democratic Party. Jackson supported the party and used his power to reward his followers. He felt that offering jobs to his allies would attract more people to politics. He also believed that government was improved when ordinary citizens participated. He removed his opponents from political jobs and replaced them with his supporters. These government jobs became known as the "spoils of office," and the practice of filling positions with political supporters is called the **spoils system**. It is still followed today.

Spotlight on Government

Jackson wanted the government to be open to every American citizen. He often held public parties in the White House. Thousands of people joined these parties. His inauguration party was attended by so many people that it got out of control. The new President was forced to escape from the White House.

Meet the President

Andrew Jackson
1767–1845

Years in office 1829–1837

Political Party Democrat

Birthplace South Carolina

Age when elected 61

Occupations Lawyer, Soldier

Nickname Old Hickory

Did you know? Andrew Jackson was not good at spelling. He said, "It's a poor mind that can think of only one way to spell a word."

Quote "Let the people rule."

President Jackson did not fully trust many of his official advisors. Instead, Jackson depended on advice from a group of friends, newspaper editors, and political supporters. This group met often with the President at the White House. Jackson's enemies made fun of this group by calling them the "**kitchen cabinet**." However, most Presidents since Jackson have relied on similar groups of friends for advice and support.

Democratic Reforms

Jackson also changed the way Americans nominate candidates for President. Before Jackson's presidency, candidates were chosen by small groups of leaders in closed meetings. Voters had no say in choosing those candidates. Jackson helped to develop the convention system. A political convention is a large, open meeting of a political party to make decisions, such as choosing candidates. Jackson liked the idea because it allowed him to assemble party members from around the country. Today, all major political parties nominate presidential candidates at conventions.

Why did Jackson approve of the spoils system?

C. Sectionalism and States' Rights

Two difficult challenges arose during Jackson's presidency. These problems created tensions between the states. Nationalism was being replaced by **sectionalism**, or the concern primarily for a particular region.

The Bank War

One issue that divided the states was the national Bank of the United States. Jackson opposed the bank. He felt it had too much power over the nation's economy. Like many people from western states, he also believed that the bank was run in ways that favored rich people and Easterners.

Henry Clay supported the bank. Clay and his supporters convinced the head of the bank, Nicholas Biddle, to apply early to renew the bank's charter, or legal permit to operate. They knew Jackson would oppose the charter. They hoped his opposition would turn Americans against Jackson. In 1832, with Clay's support, Congress passed a bill to recharter the bank. As predicted, Jackson vetoed it. He said,

> "The bank is trying to kill me, but I will kill it."

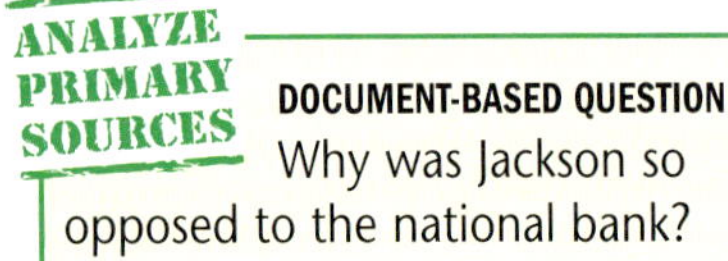

DOCUMENT-BASED QUESTION Why was Jackson so opposed to the national bank?

Clay, Biddle, and the National Republicans were surprised to find that most Americans supported Jackson. Because of his veto, the national bank's charter was not renewed. In a final effort to put the bank out of business, Jackson stopped depositing government money in the Bank of the United States. Instead, he placed federal money in smaller state banks. Weakened by this loss, the bank went out of business in 1836.

The Nullification Crisis

Beginning in 1789, the government helped American industries by creating a tariff. The tariff made imported goods more expensive than American-made products. In 1828, Congress raised the tariff even higher. This tariff hurt farmers in the South. They had to pay higher prices for manufactured goods but still had to sell their cotton at low prices. Opponents of the tariff called it the Tariff of Abominations. An abomination is something hateful.

John Calhoun of South Carolina was Jackson's Vice President, but he also was the spokesperson for the South. Calhoun made a radical suggestion. South Carolina should nullify, or cancel, the federal law creating the tariff. Calhoun claimed that a state could nullify any federal law it opposed. He gained the support of many Southerners.

To frighten Calhoun and his supporters, President Jackson asked Congress to pass the Force Bill. This bill would give the President the right to use troops to enforce the law. Calhoun was so angry that he quit as Vice President. Other leaders from South Carolina even threatened to leave the Union. Finally, a compromise was reached. The tariff was reduced to satisfy southern concerns, and the Force Bill was passed to satisfy Jackson.

The Nullification Crisis stirred up the old argument of states' rights. Many people, like Calhoun, believed that the states should have power over the federal government. Others believed the federal government should make the final decisions for the country. This debate led to an increase in sectionalism. Many Americans began focusing on what was good for their state or region instead of on what was good for the whole country.

This South Carolina woman is sewing an emblem to her hat to show her support of Calhoun's nullification plan.

The Whig Party

The rise of sectionalism, together with the bank war and the Nullification Crisis, caused Jackson's opponents to form a new political party in 1834. This party was known as the Whig Party.

Members of the Whig Party held different views on many issues, but they all agreed on one thing: Jackson and the Democrats must be defeated. They supported the idea of a strong legislative branch and a weak President. Jackson's enemies, including Henry Clay and John Calhoun, thought that he ruled more like a king than a President. The Whigs took their name from a political party in Great Britain that opposed the king. In using this name, members of the Whig Party showed that they did not support an American President who they felt ruled like a king.

ANALYZE PRIMARY SOURCES **DOCUMENT-BASED QUESTION** Why did the artist show Jackson standing on a copy of the Constitution?

Jackson's political enemies accused him of acting like a dictator or king. In fact, Jackson's opponents often called him King Andrew I.

The End of Jackson's Presidency

Jackson's battle with the national bank helped push the nation into economic hard times. When the Bank of the United States closed in 1836, there was no longer a central bank issuing bank notes. To keep the government's treasury strong, President Jackson issued an order called the "Specie Circular." It said the United States would accept only specie, or coins, of gold and silver as payment for public land.

A year later, during the Panic of 1837, economic conditions grew worse. Prices for farm goods fell. Without a national bank, it was difficult to restore economic health. Many Americans blamed these problems on Martin Van Buren, who followed Jackson as President. The economy continued to suffer for the next five years.

Even though he made many enemies, Andrew Jackson was one of the most popular Presidents in U.S. history. The years of his presidency are often called "The Age of Jackson." This is because he was strong-willed and not afraid to use the power of his office to fight for what he thought was best for the country. Jackson's role in strengthening the power of the presidency is probably what he is best known for. His policies also led to greater democracy in the United States. They brought more people into the nation's political life.

★ **How did Jackson's opponents respond to his strong leadership?**

Spotlight on Culture

Have you ever wondered where the term *OK* comes from? It is one of the most widely understood terms in the world. There are several theories for the beginning of this term.

One of these theories involves Martin Van Buren, the eighth U.S. President. Van Buren's nickname was Old Kinderhook. Kinderhook was the name of his hometown in New York. His supporters wore buttons with the letters *OK* to show their admiration for Van Buren.

Review History

A. Why did the 1824 election upset Andrew Jackson?

B. How did Jackson change the way presidential candidates are chosen by political parties?

C. How did the Bank War and the Nullification Crisis increase sectionalism?

Define Terms to Know

Provide a definition for each of the following terms.
spoils system, "kitchen cabinet," sectionalism

Critical Thinking

President Jackson was known as a "man of the people." However, many thought he acted more like a king. What caused these two views?

Write About Government

Do Americans today like their President to be someone just like them? Write a position paper supporting your opinion.

Get Organized

VENN DIAGRAM

In this section you read about two of the country's Presidents. Use details from this section to compare John Quincy Adams and Andrew Jackson.

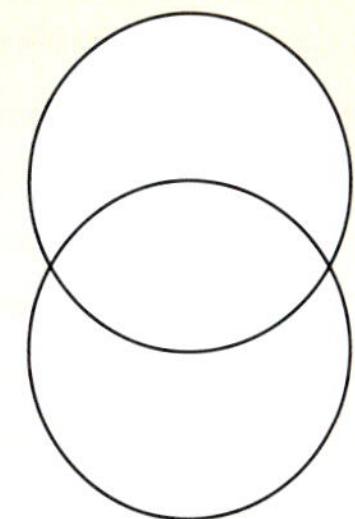

III U.S. Policies Toward Native Americans

Terms to Know

environment the social, cultural, and natural conditions that influence a community

relocate to move a person or group of people

Main Ideas

A. Federal government policies in the 1820s and 1830s forced Native Americans to move to reserved land west of the Mississippi River.

B. Some Native Americans in the South resisted moving to these lands and suffered great hardship.

POINTS OF VIEW
Comparing different points of view about an event can help you see issues more clearly. As you read this section, compare the different points of view about the removal of Native Americans.

A. Moving Native Americans

During the 1820s and 1830s, the U.S. government focused on its Native American policies. However, the conflict between the government and the Native Americans was not new. In fact, problems had existed since colonists first settled in North America.

Early U.S. Policies

Most English settlers saw Native Americans as part of the **environment**. The environment includes the people, landscape, and other factors that a community lives with. Some, especially Quakers, dealt fairly with native peoples. However, most colonists did not recognize land ownership or other rights of the Native Americans. Many Native Americans died as a result of wars and diseases brought by European settlers. Others were forced to move west.

A Crow dwelling made from buffalo skins

After the Revolutionary War, the U.S. government adopted various official policies toward Native Americans. President Washington agreed to use only treaties, or formal agreements, as a way to obtain land from Native Americans. However, in truth, Native Americans were often tricked or forced into giving up their lands.

In 1803, Thomas Jefferson bought the Louisiana Territory from France. At that time, he considered removing all of the Native Americans living east of the Mississippi River. Starting in 1804, small groups of Delawares, Kickapoos, and Cherokees were encouraged to move west of the Mississippi River.

Settlements on Native American Lands

By the time Jackson took office, more than 125,000 Native Americans still lived on land east of the Mississippi River. However, an increasing number of settlers began moving into this area. Native Americans fought against settlers who attempted to take their land. This caused tensions between settlers and Native Americans to increase.

Many Americans wanted the government to **relocate** the Native Americans, or force them to move, to the Great Plains. This flat central region of the United States began just west of the Mississippi River. Most Americans did not think the Great Plains area was suitable for farms. However, the Great Plains did have wild game. Buffalo, deer, antelope, and other animals could provide enough food for Native Americans.

In 1825, Secretary of War John Calhoun proposed a plan for relocation. He suggested that lands west of the state of Missouri and the Arkansas Territory be set aside forever for Native Americans. President Monroe accepted Calhoun's proposal as one of the last acts of his administration. During the presidency of John Quincy Adams, relocation continued even though Adams sympathized with Native Americans.

When Andrew Jackson became President in 1829, he followed a harsher policy. Jackson had won fame leading the Tennessee militia against Native Americans. Because he supported relocating Native Americans, some people considered Jackson to be an enemy of Native Americans. Others believed that moving these groups was meant to preserve the Native American way of life.

This painting by George Catlin shows Native Americans hunting buffalo on the Great Plains.

The Indian Removal Act of 1830

President Jackson and other political leaders wanted to open up the land that stretched from present-day Georgia to the Mississippi River for farming. With Jackson's support, Congress passed the Indian Removal Act in 1830. The act ordered Native Americans to give up their lands east of the Mississippi River in exchange for land west of the river. The area they were given, now mostly in Oklahoma, was known as Indian Territory. Supporters of this act argued that it protected Native Americans from the pressure of increased white settlement.

The Bureau of Indian Affairs was created in 1824 to organize and run the resettlement to Indian Territory. The Bureau created schools and offered help in starting farms. It also restricted white settlers from moving into the area reserved for Native Americans. By 1840, most Native Americans had moved from areas east of the Mississippi River to Indian Terrirory.

★ **Why did many Americans think the Great Plains should become the new home of Native Americans?**

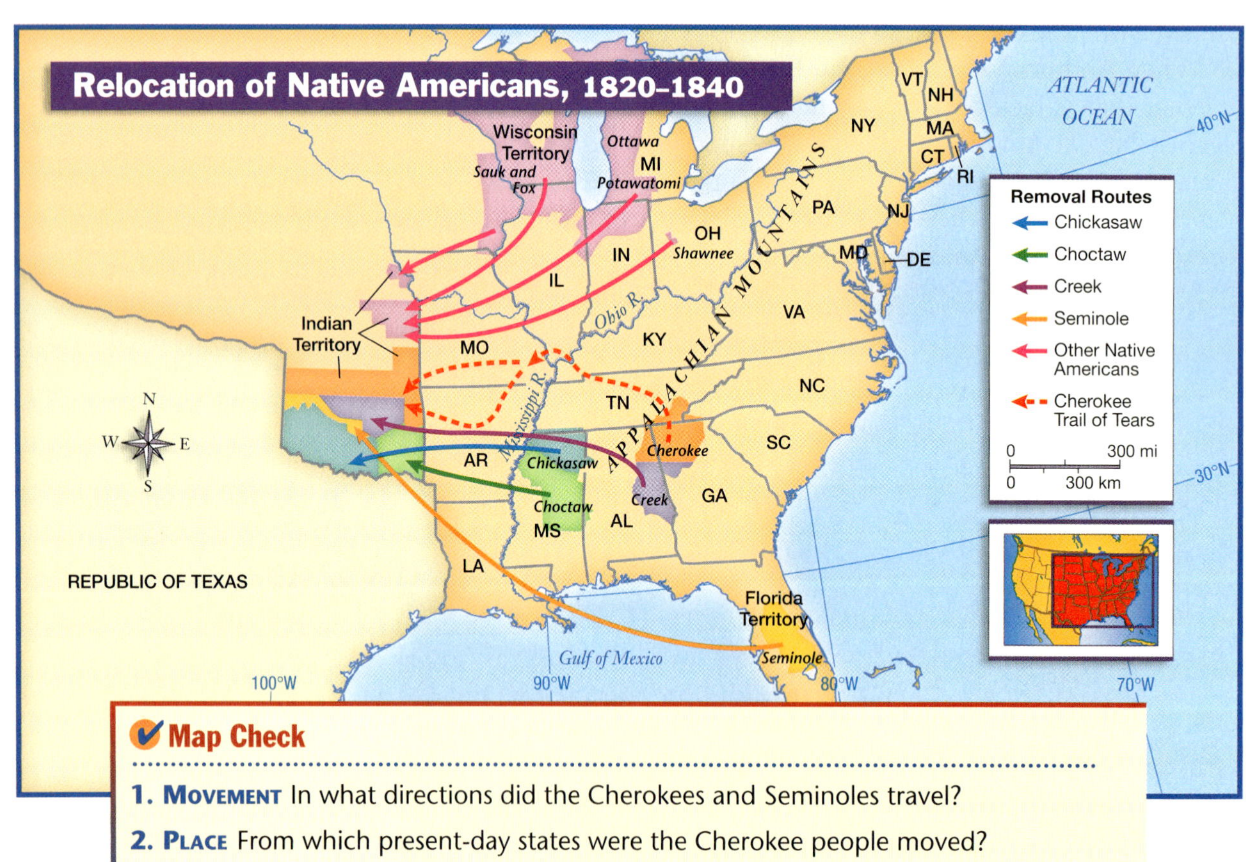

✔ Map Check

1. **Movement** In what directions did the Cherokees and Seminoles travel?
2. **Place** From which present-day states were the Cherokee people moved?

In 1838, more than 15,000 Cherokees were forced to set out on the Trail of Tears—a journey of hardship and death—to a new home in the West.

B. Tears and Bullets

Some Native Americans left for new homes in the West without resistance. Others were forced to make the journey. Still others turned to the Supreme Court for aid. In the end, however, almost all Native Americans were relocated to new homes in the West.

The Trail of Tears

Trouble began for the Cherokee people in Georgia during the 1820s. The Georgia state legislature tried to force the Cherokees to give up control of their land. Gold had been discovered there, so miners wanted access to the land. In 1835, some Cherokees signed the Treaty of New Echota in which they surrendered their lands. Most Cherokees, however, did not agree with this treaty. They wrote a letter of protest to the U.S. government.

The Cherokees went to court to defend their right to remain on their lands. They won the case. John Marshall and the Supreme Court ruled that the state of Georgia could not force the Cherokee people to move. However, President Jackson ignored the Supreme Court's decision. He sent soldiers to force the Cherokees to leave. The state of Georgia then seized their farms, homes, and businesses.

More than 15,000 Cherokee men, women, and children were forced by the U.S. Army to gather in camps in 1838. From there they marched 800 miles west to Indian Territory. The harsh journey was made worse by the cruelty of the soldiers. Their march became known as the Trail of Tears because of the hardships that the Cherokees suffered. Thousands of Cherokee people died from exposure to harsh weather, hunger, and disease.

Then & Now

Today, the Cherokees are one of the largest Native American groups. Almost 70,000 live in eastern Oklahoma, where the Trail of Tears led them. About 12,000 still live in the Smoky Mountain area, centered around the North Carolina town of Cherokee. These Cherokees are the descendants of about 1,000 who were able to avoid removal in the 1830s.

You can read the Appeal of the Cherokee Nation on page R4.

Different Reactions to Relocation

Many Native Americans in northern states moved so often that they sometimes had little attachment to specific homes. The Chippewas moved into Wisconsin and Minnesota. The Sauk and Foxes, Winnebagos, and Potawatomies relocated to Iowa. The Kickapoos, Delawares, Shawnees, Ottawas, Kaskaskias, Peorias, Miamis, and Iroquois accepted lands west of Missouri. Their feelings were expressed by Opothleyoholo, a Creek leader, in 1835: "[T]he white man has taken possession, and has every advantage over us; it is impossible for the red and white man to live together."

Native Americans who lived in southern states resisted removal. The Cherokees, Creeks, Chickasaws, Choctaws, and Seminoles—known as the Five Civilized Tribes—had adopted many features of the new American culture. Many were educated and had developed farms and homes they did not want to leave.

The Seminoles in Florida went to war in 1835, aided by runaway slaves. After seven years, hundreds of the Seminole people and 1,500 U.S. Army soldiers had died. Thousands of Seminoles were captured and moved to Indian Territory. Yet, the U.S. Army could not defeat the Seminoles, so it gave up trying. Some Seminoles chose to move to Indian Terrirory, but others stayed in Florida. By the 1850s, they were one of only a few groups that remained east of the Mississippi River.

What was the Trail of Tears?

Spotlight on Culture

In 1821, a Cherokee man named Sequoyah finished creating a written alphabet for the Cherokee language. It contained 85 characters that each represented a sound. Soon, thousands of Cherokees had learned it. By 1828, a Cherokee language newspaper, *The Cherokee Phoenix*, was published.

Review History

A. What was the Indian Removal Act of 1830?

B. Why did some Native American groups offer little resistance to relocation?

Define Terms to Know

Provide a definition for each of the following terms.
environment, relocate

Critical Thinking

Why do you think the U.S. Army was unable to defeat the Seminole people?

Write About History

Native American groups reacted to relocation in different ways. In a paragraph, compare two reactions.

Get Organized

VENN DIAGRAM

In this section you read about U.S. government policies toward Native Americans. Use details from this section to compare President Washington's and President Jackson's policies.

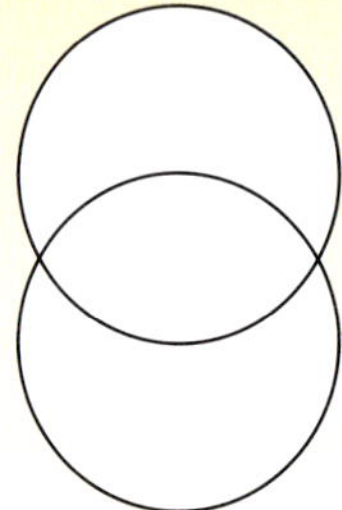

Points of View

Relocation of Native Americans

American settlers wanted more land in the 1820s and 1830s. Native Americans lived on the land that these settlers wanted, as they had for centuries. However, each group had different ideas about how the land should be used. Settlers wanted to carve farms out of the forests and mines out of the mountains. They wanted to build towns and villages. Many Native Americans lived a life of hunting and fishing. For this kind of life, they needed open areas of wilderness.

The following selections present two different views on the relocation of Native Americans from the Southeast.

A Native American canoe race

"It gives me pleasure to announce . . . that the . . . removal of the Indians . . . is approaching to a happy [end]. . . . [We] could not wish to see this continent restored to the conditions in which it was found by our forefathers. What good man would prefer a country covered with forests and [wandered] by a few thousand savages to our extensive Republic, studded with cities, towns, and prosperous farms . . ."

–Andrew Jackson, *Message to Congress,* December 8, 1830

"The Cherokees were happy and prosperous under . . . the government of the United States, and from the [helping] hand extended over them, they made rapid advances in civilization, morals and in the arts and sciences. Little did they anticipate, that when taught to think and feel as the American citizen, and to have with him a common interest, they were . . . forced to return to the savage life, and to seek a new home in the wilds of the far west, and that without their consent. . . ."

–from *Memorial and Protest of the Cherokee Nation,* 1836

ANALYZE PRIMARY SOURCES

DOCUMENT-BASED QUESTIONS

1. What reason does Jackson give to support removal of Native Americans?
2. How does the Cherokee writer describe the Cherokees' life before their removal to the West?
3. **Critical Thinking** Why does the Cherokee writer feel the United States has not been fair to his people?

CHAPTER 12 Review

Chapter Summary

In your notebook, complete the following outline. Then, use your outline to write a brief summary of the chapter.

The Nation Grows

I. The Rise of Nationalism
  A. Plans for Improvement
  B.
  C.

II. Jacksonian Democracy
  A.
  B.
  C.

III. U.S. Policies Toward Native Americans
  A.
  B.

Interpret the Timeline

Use the timeline on pages 286–287 to answer the following questions.

1. Who was President at the time of the passage of the Indian Removal Act?
2. **Critical Thinking** Which world events show that Spain was losing colonies in the Western Hemisphere?

Use Terms to Know

Select the term that best completes each sentence.

canal
doctrine
relocate
sectionalism
spoils system

1. A famous ________ connected the Hudson River to Buffalo, New York.
2. The practice of filling political jobs with supporters is called the ________.
3. President Monroe expressed his beliefs about foreign affairs in a ________.
4. The U.S. government began to ________ Native Americans to the West.
5. Disagreements between the states led to increased feelings of ________.

Check Your Understanding

1. **Identify** events that show the country experienced a growth of nationalism after the War of 1812.
2. **Summarize** the ideas contained in the Monroe Doctrine.
3. **Describe** two changes that Andrew Jackson made to American political life in the 1820s and 1830s.
4. **Explain** the idea of nullification.
5. **Discuss** U.S. government policies toward Native Americans during the 1820s and the 1830s.
6. **Explain** why the Five Civilized Tribes resisted removal more strongly than other Native American groups did.

Critical Thinking

1. **Evaluate** Do you think the nationalism in the United States in the 1820s was good for American citizens? Give reasons to support your answer.
2. **Analyze Primary Sources** What can you tell from the cartoon on page 298 about why Jackson's opponents felt he was acting like a king?
3. **Analyze Primary Sources** Based on the quote on page 304, why do you think Opothleyoholo felt that white people had an advantage over Native Americans?

Put Your Skills to Work

DRAW CONCLUSIONS

You have learned how to use details to draw conclusions based on the information you read.

Copy the chart below onto a sheet of paper. Add details to draw a conclusion about the relocation of the Cherokee people. Then, write your conclusion in the box on the bottom.

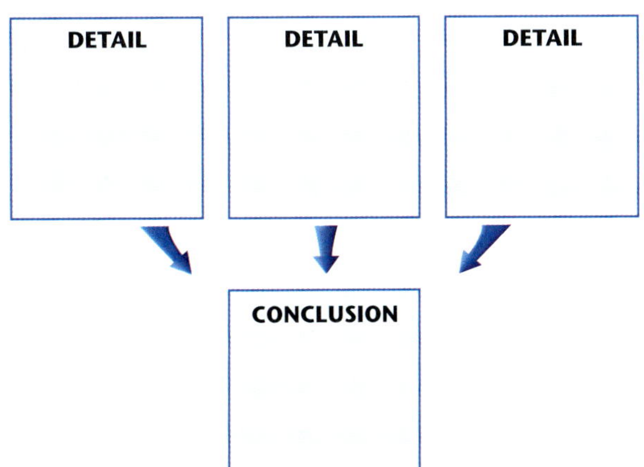

In Your Own Words

JOURNAL WRITING

President Jackson valued the advice of his friends. They helped him to make important decisions about running the country. Write a journal entry about a time when your friends helped you to make a decision. Was their advice helpful?

Net Work

INTERNET ACTIVITY

Working with a group of classmates, research and prepare a presentation about the Erie Canal. Include maps, drawings, photos of important sites today, songs about the canal, tall tales or stories, and information about life aboard the canal boats. Share your presentation with the class.

For help in starting this activity, visit the following Web site: www.gfamericanhistory.com.

Look Ahead

In the next chapter, learn how life was different in the North and in the South.

Unit 4 Portfolio Project

History Talk Show

YOUR ASSIGNMENT

Today, you can watch political talk shows on almost every television channel. Most shows have a host and special guests. Sometimes, the talk show can be very lively. As a class, create and present a series of political talk shows about American history.

PLAN YOUR SHOW

Get Started Each group should select a different chapter from this unit.

Set up the Show As a group, choose a name for your show. Assign roles. Each show will need a host and special guests. Choose your guests from the people discussed in your chapter. Some members of the group can become directors, researchers, or audience members.

Invite Guests Plan to have four or five guests on the show. For example, if your group chooses to do a talk show about Chapter 11, you might decide to invite Thomas Jefferson, Alexander Hamilton, Aaron Burr, James Madison, and Napoleon.

WRITE YOUR TALK SHOW

Research Your Role After you have assigned roles, reread the chapter to find information about the characters. Some group members will have to answer questions as they fill the roles of these characters. If you are the host or an audience member, you will need questions to ask the guests. You may also want to find additional information about a character or the time period your show covers. You may refer to this Web site for ideas: www.gfamericanhistory.com.

Present the Show Put your show on the air. "Televise" your show for the class. If you want, you can have other class members ask questions. Try to make your show as interesting and entertaining as you can. Remind group members to stay in the roles they have been assigned when asking and answering questions.

Multimedia Presentation

Turn your history talk show into a video presentation. Create a set for the show. Design costumes for the special guests and host. Choose theme music. Present "commercials" for products of the time period. Use video equipment to tape your show. Then, show your videotape to the class.

Unit 5

The Nation Expands

"... We came twenty miles without stopping and then camped for the night. We are near a fine spring of most excellent water. ... How glad we all are to have plenty of clear cold water to wash away the dust."

—from a diary written by Sarah Raymond, a teenage girl who traveled west with her family in 1865

LINK PAST TO PRESENT This photograph shows a re-enactment of a wagon train. Settlers traveled in covered wagons such as these as they moved west.

★ How does the transportation of today compare with the transportation used by western settlers in 1865?

CHAPTER 13

Life in the North and the South 1789–1860

I. The Industrial Revolution
II. Cotton Is King
III. The Slave System

In the early 1800s, regions of the United States were developing differently. In the North, factories were built and large cities grew. In the South, however, another way of life took hold. It was based on the work of enslaved African Americans. These workers could be bought and sold at slave auctions.

Josiah Henson was one enslaved African American. He escaped to Canada, where he became a Christian minister. In his autobiography, he wrote about being sold in 1795. He was five years old.

> “My brothers and sisters were bid off first, and one by one, while my mother, paralyzed with grief, held me by the hand. Then I was offered. . . .”

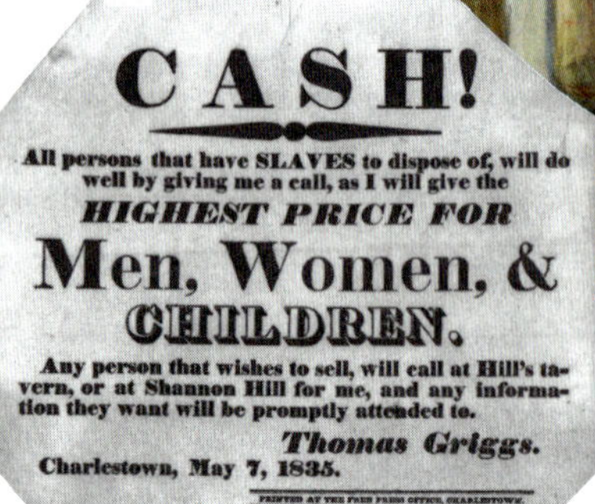

An 1835 advertisement offering cash for slaves

U.S. Events

- **1793** Eli Whitney invents the cotton gin.
- **1807** Robert Fulton sails the *Clermont*.
- **1808** Importation of enslaved Africans is banned.

Presidential Term Begins

- 1789 George Washington
- 1797 John Adams
- 1801 Thomas Jefferson
- 1809 James Madison
- 1817 James Monroe

1790 | 1800 | 1810 | 1820

World Events

- **1796** James Watt builds a steam engine for use in factories.
- **1802** British child-labor laws set 12 hours as maximum workday.

VIEW HISTORY Enslaved men, women, and children were sold at auctions like the one shown in this painting. Buyers and sellers of enslaved African Americans advertised with posters and in local newspapers (left).

★ **In what ways did slave auctions affect families?**

Get Organized

DETAIL/CONCLUSION CHART

When you draw conclusions, you make judgments based on information you know. Use the following diagram to draw conclusions as you read Chapter 13. Write details in the boxes. Then draw a conclusion based on the details. Here is an example from this chapter.

DETAIL
Machines were invented in Great Britain to make cloth.

CONCLUSION
The Industrial Revolution changed industry in the United States.

DETAIL
Samuel Slater brought machine designs to the U.S.

1822 Denmark Vesey leads revolt in South Carolina.

1830 Baltimore and Ohio Railroad begins operations.

1831 Nat Turner leads a rebellion in Virginia.
Cyrus McCormick builds mechanical reaper.

1844 Samuel Morse introduces the telegraph.

1860 Approximately four million enslaved African Americans live in the South.

1830 **1840** **1850** **1860**

1825 John Q. Adams | 1829 Andrew Jackson | 1837 Martin Van Buren | 1841 W. Harrison | 1841 John Tyler | 1845 James Polk

1830 **1840** **1850** **1860**

1834 Slavery is abolished in British Empire.

1837 Victoria becomes queen of Great Britain.

1844 First YMCA is founded in London.

I The Industrial Revolution

Terms to Know

factory a building with workers and machines in which manufacturing takes place

textile cloth

interchangeable parts identical parts that can be substituted for each other

mass production the making of many items in a short period of time

Main Ideas

A. The Industrial Revolution changed the way Americans manufactured goods.

B. Eli Whitney's inventions improved manufacturing.

C. The early 1800s was a time of improvements in transportation, daily life, and communication.

SEQUENCE OF EVENTS
The sequence of events is the order in which they happen. One event happens first, then another, then another. As you read this section, make a list of the sequence of events that led to the rise of manufacturing in the North.

A. New Ideas, New Machines

A new method of producing manufactured goods was developed in the United States in the 1790s. This development introduced a period of dramatic change called the Industrial Revolution, in which factories and machines replaced simple tools.

The Industrial Revolution in the United States

Before the Revolutionary War, most American colonists earned their living by farming. Some workers, such as storekeepers and blacksmiths, lived in towns. They sold goods that farmers could not produce for themselves. Often workers produced goods, such as shoes, in their homes. There were no **factories**, or buildings in which large groups of workers and machines manufacture goods. This way of life changed when the Industrial Revolution reached the United States.

Blacksmiths formed iron into useful items like horseshoes.

The Industrial Revolution began in Great Britain in the late 1700s. Special machines, powered by steam engines or water power, were invented for the **textile**, or cloth, industry. The process of making cloth had two steps: spinning, or making thread from cotton or wool, and weaving, or combining the threads into cloth.

The new machines allowed the British factories to spin and weave cloth at amazing speeds. Britain wanted to keep these new methods a secret, so that other countries could not profit from them. As a result, the British passed laws to prevent the export of their machines and to stop textile workers from leaving Great Britain.

In New England factories, women wove cloth on large machines called looms.

In the United States, the New England states were developing their own textile industry by the 1790s. American investors offered rewards to people who would help them build textile factories. In 1789, Samuel Slater, a young British textile mechanic, slipped out of Great Britain and came to the United States. Slater went to work for Moses Brown, an investor in Pawtucket, Rhode Island. Using only his memory of British textile mills, Slater designed and built a cotton-spinning machine. He then helped Brown build a textile factory on the Blackstone River.

This textile factory started the American Industrial Revolution. It also helped make New England the first manufacturing region in the United States. The cities of the Northeast soon became the country's trade and industrial centers.

The Lowell Factory System

The number of American factories quickly increased during the War of 1812. The war kept British imports from entering the United States. Another reason for the growth of U.S. industry was the Tariff of 1816, which made foreign goods more expensive. Americans began making more and more of their own goods.

A Boston merchant named Francis Lowell was an industrial pioneer. He had the idea that one factory could include all the steps needed to make a product. This method would save time and increase profits. Lowell built a giant textile factory in Waltham, Massachusetts, near Boston. Workers labored long hours spinning and weaving thread to make cloth.

Lowell also established a new labor system. He hired young, unmarried women, usually the daughters of farmers, to work in the factory. They made more money than they earned through farm labor. The women lived together in dormitories. The company offered religious instruction, education, and entertainment. It even encouraged workers to produce their own magazine. The British author Charles Dickens described the workers after a visit:

> "They were healthy in appearance, many of them remarkably so. . . . I cannot recall one young face that gave me a painful impression . . . no face bore an unhealthy or an unhappy look."

DOCUMENT-BASED QUESTION Do you think Dickens's descriptions were accurate? Why or why not?

Who was Samuel Slater?

B. Improvements in Manufacturing

Another person who changed manufacturing in the United States was Eli Whitney of Connecticut. He came up with the idea of **interchangeable parts**, or identical parts that can replace each other. His idea changed the way goods were manufactured.

Interchangeable Parts

Do You Remember?
In Chapter 10, you learned that French and American ships battled each other from 1798 to 1800 in the "undeclared war."

During the undeclared war between the United States and France in the 1790s, there were not enough muskets in the United States. Muskets were produced by skilled workers, and no two muskets were alike. Each part was made to fit and work in a single weapon. If a musket broke, it had to be repaired by a skilled worker who made a new part especially for that gun.

Eli Whitney wondered: What if each musket was exactly the same? What if all of the parts were made by machine so that they could be identical? Then, if a part broke, it could be replaced by a part from the factory. He designed machinery to make the musket parts according to a pattern. Each part could fit in any gun. Therefore, the parts did not have to be made by a highly skilled worker. Muskets were then cheaper, faster, and easier to produce.

Whitney's idea of interchangeable parts was soon applied to clocks, sewing machines, and other products. Today all **mass production**, or manufacturing on a large scale, is based on this idea.

Reasons for Northern Industrial Growth

Industrial growth was mostly centered in northern states. There were several reasons why this was so.

1. The southern economy was based on agriculture. Southerners produced cotton and other crops, which they then sold to people in the northern states and foreign countries.
2. The North had a larger population and more factory workers.
3. The North had better transportation systems.
4. The banking system in the North was more developed.
5. Immigrants from Europe came to the North and fueled the labor supply.

★ **What contribution did Eli Whitney make to the industrial development of the United States?**

A sewing machine from the early 1800s

C. Advances During the Industrial Revolution

The early 1800s was a time of tremendous creativity in the United States. Americans found ways to improve transportation, communication, and everyday tasks.

Better Transportation

Changes in industry resulted in the need for better transportation. Factories required raw materials to make their products. Then, these final products had to be shipped to different parts of the country. Henry Clay's American System created new canals, roads, and railroads. As transportation systems improved, costs for moving goods were lowered. Goods could be moved farther for less money.

In the early 1800s, new roads and turnpikes made moving goods and people easier. Turnpikes were roads that were privately owned. They were built by people who figured that they could make money by charging people who used their roads. Every ten miles or so, the road's owners would collect a toll, or fee. They did this by placing a pike, or pole, across the road. The pike would be turned when the toll was paid. This is how the *turnpike* got its name.

Canals, or waterways dug by people, linked the East coast with the Great Lakes. Railroads connected some cities. The first steam-operated railway for passengers and freight, the Baltimore and Ohio Railroad, began operating in 1830.

Improvements in transportation helped the American economy grow in the early 1800s. The same is true today. In the 1950s and 1960s the interstate highway system was built with federal money. Today trucks carry products throughout the country on these highways.

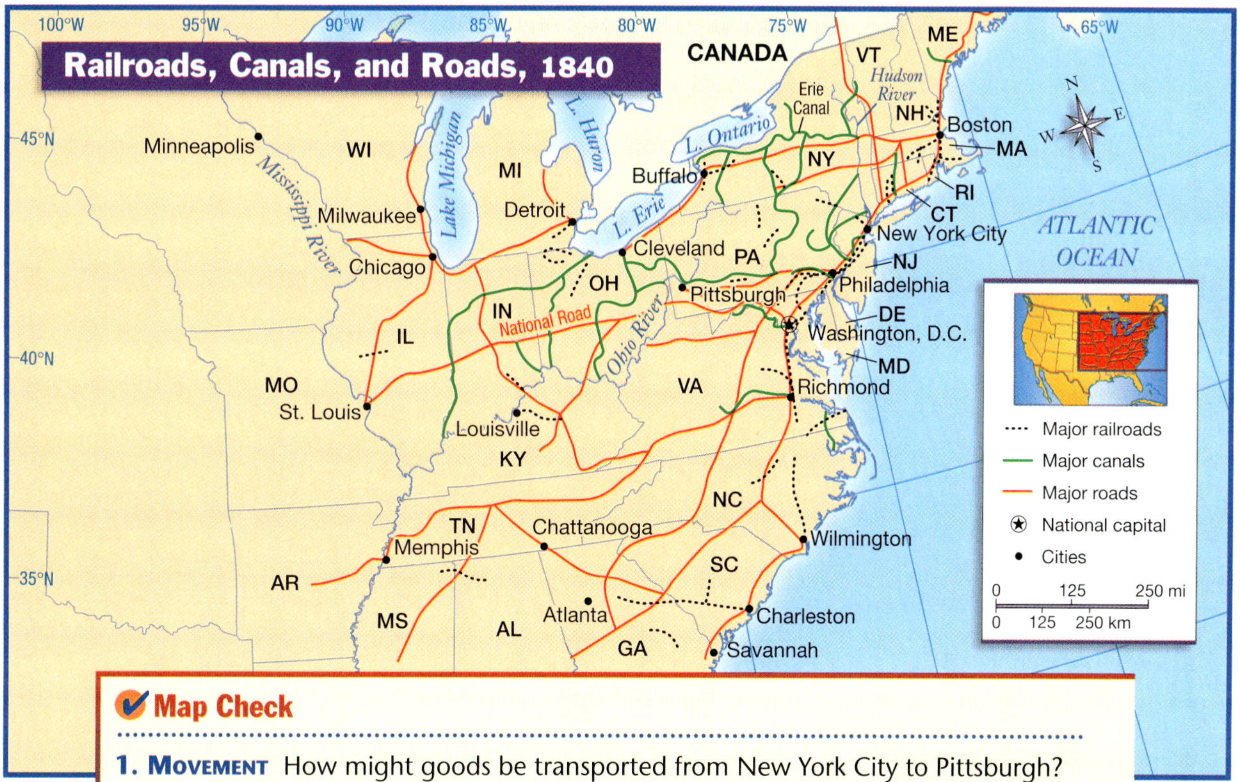

Railroads, Canals, and Roads, 1840

Map Check

1. **Movement** How might goods be transported from New York City to Pittsburgh?
2. **Human Interaction** Were more roads or canals built in the United States by 1840?

McCormick advertised his reaper in colorful brochures.

These improvements in transportation led to new inventions. In 1807, Robert Fulton sailed the *Clermont*, the first successful steam-powered boat, on the Hudson River against the current from New York City to Albany. He made the trip in less time than a horse-drawn wagon could and he carried a larger cargo. Beginning in the 1840s, long, sleek clipper ships crossed the oceans more quickly than other ships.

New Inventions

The Industrial Revolution was fueled by many new inventions. Some of these helped farmers. The mechanical reaper was invented by Cyrus McCormick in 1831. It replaced the slow method of harvesting crops by hand. John Deere's lightweight steel plow, invented in 1837, helped farmers plow the hard soil of the Great Plains.

Another invention made communication faster and easier. The first practical telegraph was developed by Samuel F. B. Morse and was completed in 1844. The telegraph sent electric pulses that were used to code letters and words. Messages sent by wire could travel instantly from one place to another.

How did transportation improve in the early 1800s?

Review History

A. How did the Industrial Revolution change the way Americans worked?

B. In what ways did interchangeable parts encourage industry to grow?

C. In what ways did changes in industry affect transportation?

Define Terms to Know

Provide a definition for each of the following terms.
factory, textile, interchangeable parts, mass production

Critical Thinking

Describe the impact of the Industrial Revolution on the textile industry.

Write About Economics

Francis Lowell's textile factory was one of the largest in the world when it was built. Why do you think people wanted to work at his factory?

Get Organized

DETAIL/CONCLUSION CHART

In this section, you learned about mass production. Use details from the section to draw a conclusion about this type of manufacturing.

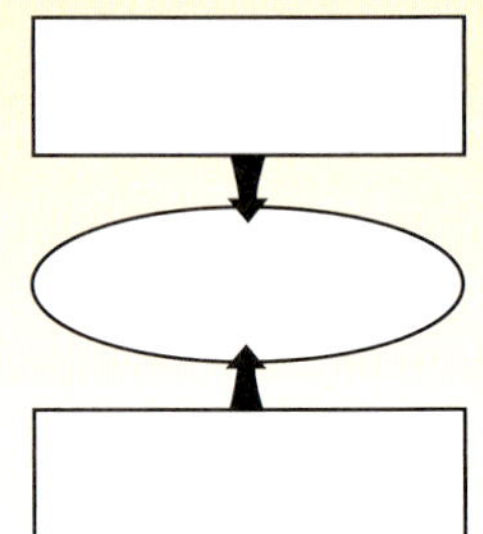

Build Your Skills

Social Studies Skill

USE A CIRCLE GRAPH

Circle graphs are used to show and compare percentages. They look similar to a pie that has been cut into pieces. In fact, circle graphs are sometimes called pie charts. Each "slice" represents the percentage of one item. By looking at the graph, you can see all the parts that make up the whole.

When you read about history, you will often find numbers that compare parts to a whole. A circle graph might show how urban and rural groups make up a state's total population. Each "slice" would represent one group. The circle graph would show what part of the total population is made up by each group. It would also show how the urban and rural groups compare in size with each other.

Here's How

Follow these steps to use a circle graph.

1. Read the title of the graph and the labels to find out what information the graph contains.
2. Study the graph to compare the different parts. Look at how each part relates to another and to the whole.
3. Draw conclusions about the graph.

Here's Why

Suppose you had to explain how the Industrial Revolution affected the workforce in the United States. You could use a circle graph to study the percentage of different types of jobs in the country.

Practice the Skill

Look at the circle graph on the right. Then, answer the following questions.

1. What does the whole circle represent?
2. What do the parts of the circle represent?
3. What conclusions can you draw about jobs in the United States in 1810?

Extend the Skill

Look in current newspapers or magazines to find a circle graph. Bring the circle graph to school and explain it to your classmates.

Apply the Skill

In Section III, you will read about people in the South. Show the population of free and enslaved persons by 1860 on a circle graph.

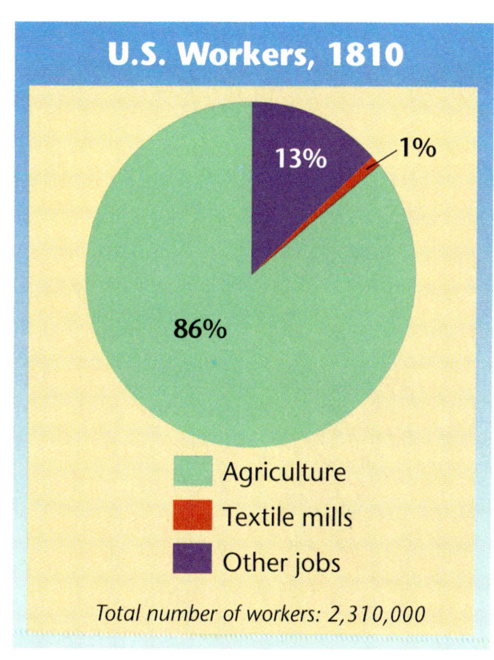

II Cotton Is King

Terms to Know

cotton gin a machine that removes seeds from cotton fibers

planter a person who owns and operates a plantation

Main Ideas

A. Eli Whitney's invention helped increase cotton production in the South.

B. Cotton played a major role in the economy of the United States.

C. Profits from cotton expanded the plantation system in the South.

CAUSE AND EFFECT
Often in history, one event caused another to happen. The second event is the effect, or result. As you read this chapter, ask yourself the following question: What were some effects of the invention of the cotton gin?

A. Eli Whitney's Invention

Cotton had been grown in the South as a cash crop since the late 1600s. When spun and woven, cotton made very comfortable clothing. However, the fluffy white cotton contained sticky green seeds that had to be removed before the cotton could be used. For years, people dreamed of building a machine to remove the seeds from raw cotton.

Beginnings of Cotton Farming in the United States

The first American cotton crops were harvested on farms located on southern islands just off the Atlantic coast. An easy-to-clean cotton, called long-staple cotton, grew well near the coast, but it could not be grown farther inland. Cotton growers soon learned that a different kind of cotton, called short-staple cotton, would grow inland. However, its seeds were hard to remove. The cotton fibers had to be separated from the seeds by hand.

A farmer could plant and harvest a lot of short-staple cotton. However, it took a worker a whole day to remove the seeds from just one pound of cotton. As a result, a great deal of time and effort were needed to produce only a small amount of cotton. This made southern cotton very expensive. The process of cleaning cotton also put an enormous strain on workers' hands and backs. Many farmers began to think that cotton would never be more than a minor crop in the South.

Cotton plant

Eli Whitney Makes a Difference

In 1792, Eli Whitney, the inventor who came up with the idea of interchangeable parts, took a job as a teacher on a cotton plantation near Savannah, Georgia. He had just graduated from Yale College in his home state of Connecticut. Whitney learned from the manager of the plantation about the problem of cleaning cotton.

Soon, Whitney began to think about solutions to the problem. He studied older machines designed to clean cotton. They did not work very well because they ground the seeds into the cotton fiber. In 1793, Whitney improved on these machines by placing a wooden cylinder covered in metal spikes into a box full of cotton. A worker used a hand crank to turn the cylinder. The spikes then hooked onto the fibers and pulled them through narrow slots through which the seeds could not pass. Whitney's machine could clean 10 pounds of short-staple cotton a day. Larger models were soon cleaning 1,000 pounds a day! With this machine, one person could do the work of hundreds working by hand.

Whitney called his machine a **cotton gin**, which was short for *cotton engine*. The cotton gin was so simple that anyone could build one. In a very short time, these machines appeared all across the South. Although the cotton gin was extremely popular, Whitney himself never earned much money from his widely-copied invention. Whitney soon returned to the North, where he put his idea of interchangeable parts to work in a factory.

 **Why was cotton difficult to clean by hand?**

Eli Whitney (top) tackled the tough problem of separating seeds from cotton. He invented the cotton gin (left).

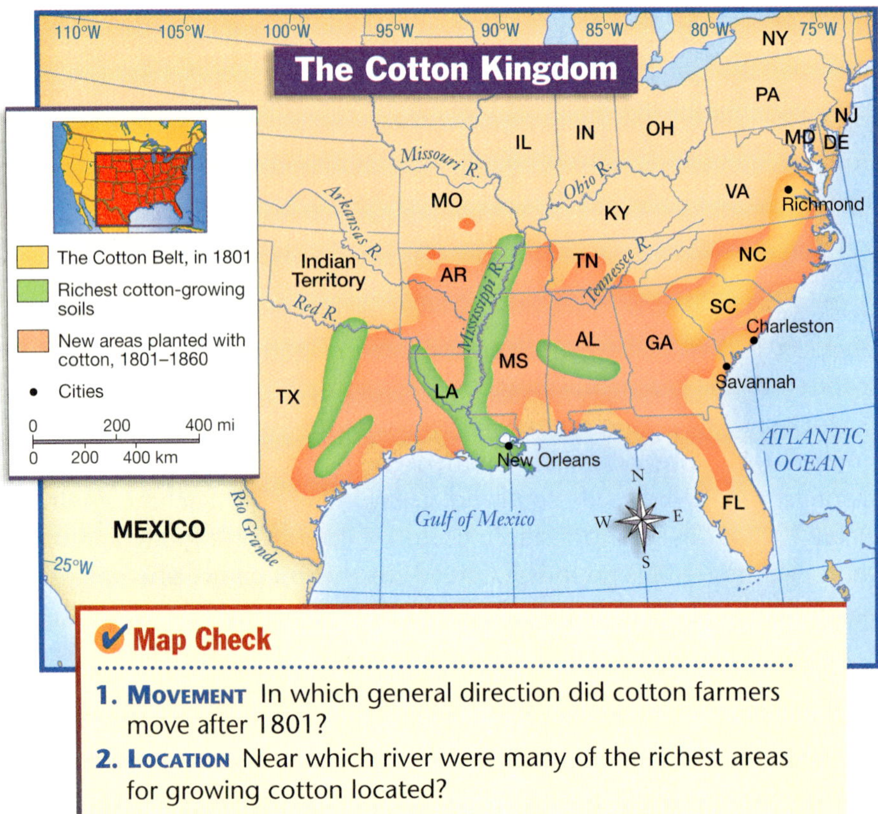

✔ Map Check

1. **Movement** In which general direction did cotton farmers move after 1801?
2. **Location** Near which river were many of the richest areas for growing cotton located?

B. The Cotton Industry

With the cotton gin available, many farmers in the South decided that they should grow cotton. They wanted to share in the huge profits that could be earned from this cash crop. The new cotton mills in the North wanted more and more southern cotton. So did the mills of Great Britain. Cotton growing spread west as far as Texas and north into Virginia. This large area in the South became known as the Cotton Kingdom.

Growth of the Cotton Kingdom

The large amounts of money to be made in cotton had important effects on the South. In the coastal states of South Carolina and Georgia, cotton became the primary crop. As Native Americans were removed from the Southeast to the West, **planters**, owners of large farms called plantations, moved into the lands that had belonged to the Native American groups. These planters were looking for newer, better cotton-growing lands. By the 1830s, cotton was the major cash crop in Alabama, Mississippi, Louisiana, Georgia, and Texas. By the 1850s, cotton was king in the South.

Do You Remember?
In Chapter 12, you learned how Native Americans were forced to leave their homes in the Southeast and move to lands west of the Mississippi River.

The southern cotton crops were important to the entire nation. The textile industry in the New England states developed rapidly because the South could supply it with more and more cotton. Railroads carried cotton bales to northern mills. Each huge cotton bale weighed up to 500 pounds. By 1860, the South produced almost 4 million bales every year. The graph on this page shows the growth of cotton production in the South.

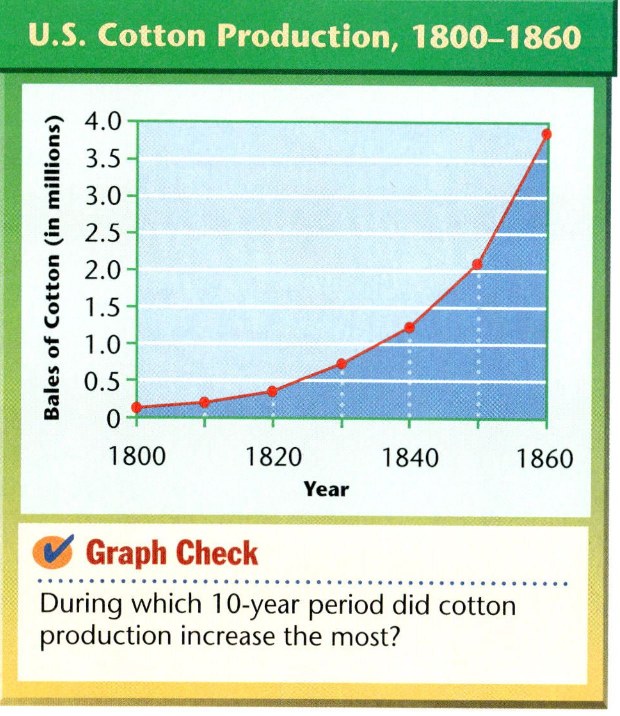

A Tariff Divides the Nation

Cotton became one of the main exports of the United States, especially to Great Britain. Great Britain needed American cotton for its own textile industry. So ships carried American cotton across the Atlantic Ocean.

Southerners also depended on imports from Great Britain, so they were unhappy with the U.S. tariff policy. The high tariff that protected factories in the North raised the prices of goods Southerners bought from other countries. Northerners argued that the high tariff was needed to allow U.S. industries to grow. However, Southerners did not accept this argument. All they knew was that the supplies they bought cost more. A serious conflict between the North and the South started to grow.

 **How did cotton encourage westward expansion?**

C. The Plantation System

The huge profits from cotton led to the expansion of the plantation system in the South. This system created a lifestyle that was very different from the way people lived in other parts of the country.

Beginnings of the Plantation System

In colonial Virginia, the first plantations produced tobacco. In South Carolina, planters grew rice and indigo. In Louisiana, sugar cane was grown on plantations. After the invention of the cotton gin, most plantation owners in the lower southern states began growing cotton. Large planters built cotton gins that were powered by mules or horses, rather than by a hand crank. Even small farmers could afford a cotton gin, so farms of all sizes grew cotton.

Planters

A planter was actually a business owner. He was responsible for producing and selling the cotton from his land. He bought supplies. He usually owned more than 20 slaves and set the schedule for planting, growing, picking, and selling the cotton. Very few Southerners could be considered planters. Only a small percentage of white slave owners in the South could afford to own more than 20 slaves. Most southern farmers owned fewer than 10 enslaved workers.

The planter often had the help of an overseer, an employee who watched over and directed workers. Most of the workers on the plantation were slaves. If the planter was married, he expected his wife to manage the household. As planters grew richer, they sometimes built a large house for their families.

Social life for plantation owners was limited because plantations were far apart from each other and from towns. Visiting friends brought news and a break from daily tasks. Younger children were educated at home. Older boys were often sent to boarding schools in nearby towns or in the North.

Mostly, life on plantations focused on the work of raising cotton. To raise more cotton, more workers were needed. Many people in the South thought that without slavery, the plantation system would have collapsed.

 **Who were the overseers?**

Review History

A. How did the invention of the cotton gin lead to the growth of cotton farming in the South?

B. Why did tensions grow between the North and the South?

C. What were the responsibilities of planters?

Define Terms to Know

Provide a definition for each of the following terms.
cotton gin, planter

Critical Thinking

Why was it risky for farmers to depend heavily on just one cash crop?

Write About History

Suppose you lived on a small farm in the South in 1793. You have just seen a demonstration of Eli Whitney's cotton gin. Write a letter to a friend describing what you saw and how you think it will alter life on your farm.

Get Organized

DETAIL/CONCLUSION CHART

In this section, you learned about the cotton gin. Use details from this section to draw a conclusion about this farm machine.

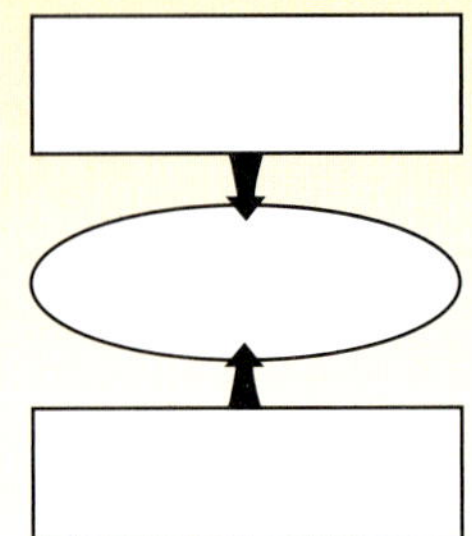

CONNECT History & Economics

The Cotton Gin: Supply and Demand

In this chapter, you read how the invention of the cotton gin by Eli Whitney changed the American economy. The rise in the amount of cotton produced in the South and the need for it in the textile mills of the North is an example of "supply and demand." Supply and demand is an important idea in economics, the study of money, goods, and services.

HOW SUPPLY AND DEMAND WORKS The supply of an item means how much is available. If very few MP3 players are available for people to buy, the supply is low. If there are a lot of MP3 players around, the supply is high. The demand for something is based on how many people want an item. If everybody wants to buy a new MP3 player, demand for it is high. If few people want one, demand is low.

Supply and demand work together to determine the price of goods and services. If few products are available and many people want them, the price will go up. If there are many products and the demand for them is low, the price will go down.

SUPPLY AND DEMAND FOR COTTON The cotton gin could clean cotton 50 to 100 times faster than a person could and led to an increase in the supply of cotton. In other words, more cotton became available. Northern factories developed ways to weave cloth much faster than by hand. This ability, along with people's desire to buy cotton clothes, raised the demand for cotton.

Because both supply and demand for cotton were high, cotton growers and factory owners became rich. Plantations spread throughout the South, increasing supply. More mills were built in the North, raising demand.

Critical Thinking

Answer the following questions. Then, complete the activity.

1. How did the cotton gin affect the supply and demand for cotton?
2. The cotton gin was an invention that changed many people's lives. What recent invention do you think has changed the most lives? Explain your answer.

Write About It

Learn more about Eli Whitney and the cotton gin on the Internet. Write a short paragraph explaining how supply and demand worked against Whitney and caused him to lose millions of dollars in profits. Use this Web site for ideas: www.gfamericanhistory.com.

Cotton gin

III The Slave System

Terms to Know

spiritual an expressive religious song

Underground Railroad escape routes used by enslaved African Americans to reach freedom in the North

Main Ideas

A. Slavery was a major part of the social and economic system of the South.

B. Enslaved African Americans developed a distinct culture.

C. Some enslaved African Americans tried to escape from the South, and a few led armed revolts.

SUMMARIZE

When you summarize material, you restate the main idea in shorter form. As you read this section, summarize the daily life of an enslaved African American on a plantation in the South.

A. Slavery in the United States

Slavery had existed in North America since the early 1600s. However, the number of enslaved people in the United States declined for a while in the 1700s. The cotton gin and the development of the plantation system changed that trend.

King Cotton

Enslaved people lived in all of the original British colonies. However, most slaves lived in the South. By the time of the Revolutionary War, slavery had almost disappeared from the northern colonies. Religious groups in the northern colonies, such as the Quakers, had taken a strong stand against it.

When the United States gained its independence, about one-half million African Americans were living in slavery. Congress banned the importation of enslaved Africans in 1808. No more Africans could be brought to the South for sale after that year. Many Americans, including some Southerners, were ready to let the system of slavery come to an end.

The invention of the cotton gin changed ideas about slavery in the South. As cotton became the principle crop, it was called King Cotton. Because the cotton gin allowed farmers to produce more cotton, they planted bigger crops. As the use of Whitney's invention spread, cotton farmers found they needed more and more workers. The cotton had to be planted, raised, picked, cleaned, and shipped. Many thought that only slave labor could provide enough workers to satisfy King Cotton.

Slavery and the Law

By 1860, approximately 4 million enslaved African Americans lived in the South. This meant that one out of every three people in the South was an enslaved African American. About half of the slaves in the South worked on plantations. They were the workers who produced the cotton, tobacco, sugar cane, and other crops grown on the farms and plantations in the South. Some enslaved people lived in cities. They worked in factories, as house servants, or as craftspeople.

One fourth of southern white families owned slaves. However, almost all Southerners supported slavery. Poor white farmers who could not afford to own slaves knew that slavery supported the southern economy. It also established a social order in the South.

This social and economic order was enforced by slave codes. These laws, which had been in effect since the 1700s, protected the interests of slave owners. Slaves were denied the basic freedoms that all U.S. citizens enjoyed. Some laws made it illegal to teach an enslaved person to read or write. The purpose of these laws was to gain greater control over enslaved people.

Do You Remember?
In Chapter 5, you learned that slave codes in many states made it illegal for African Americans to own property or gather in public.

 **When did Congress ban the importation of enslaved Africans?**

Many enslaved African Americans in the South worked in the cotton fields of large plantations.

B. Life Under Slavery

The conditions of daily life for enslaved African Americans differed from region to region. However, for almost all of them, life consisted of hard, unpaid work from dawn to dusk.

Work for Enslaved People

Enslaved African Americans arose early for work. Some women did chores such as cooking, washing, and cleaning in the owner's house. Some men worked as blacksmiths, carpenters, painters, shoemakers, or at other jobs. Sometimes, slaveholders hired out their enslaved workers to work for mills or factories, to load ships, or to build canals, roads, or railroads.

Most enslaved African Americans, however, worked long hours in the fields. Men, women, and children older than ten did the back-breaking work of growing cotton, sugar cane, tobacco, and other crops. One enslaved person described a day in the fields:

ANALYZE PRIMARY SOURCES

DOCUMENT-BASED QUESTION In what ways did an enslaved person's workload probably affect his or her health?

> "The [field] hands are required to be in the cotton field as soon as it is light in the morning, and, with the exception of fifteen minutes, they are not permitted to be a moment idle until it is too dark to see."

The lack of freedom and the threat of punishment were facts of life for enslaved people. Slaveholders and overseers had the legal right to physically punish slaves. The cruelest ones used whips or forced slaves to work while wearing leg irons. Former slave Harry McMillan recalled one form of punishment he witnessed: "Sometimes they dug a hole like a well with a door on top. This they called a dungeon, keeping you in it two or three weeks or a month, or sometimes till you died in there."

Groups of enslaved people often lived together in small cabins on plantations.

Family Life and Culture

Most enslaved African Americans developed strong family ties. Although marriages were not recognized by the law, most African American men and women married and raised a family. On plantations, families often lived together for many years. However, slaves always faced the fear of being traded or sold away from their loved ones. Because of this, African Americans relied on large, extended families, including grandparents, aunts, and uncles, as well as close friends.

Enslaved African Americans lived in simple cabins, usually in family groups. These houses often included only one or two bedrooms and a kitchen. Children often slept on blankets on the floor while adults slept in beds they had made themselves. Clothing was made from coarse, cheap cloth and was often tattered.

The shared life of enslaved people led to a distinct African American culture. It included many African traditions as well as American influences. African Americans often expressed themselves through storytelling, dancing, and art. They passed on African folk tales and crafts through the generations.

Religion and music were especially important to enslaved African Americans. Plantation owners introduced their workers to Christianity. The workers learned stories from the Bible that often helped them bear their sufferings. Slaves expressed their beliefs through religious songs called **spirituals**. Many spirituals are about the promise of a better life to come.

 **Why were spirituals important to enslaved African Americans?**

C. Resistance to Slavery

Many African Americans were forced to endure a life of slavery. Some rebelled against it. Others tried to escape to be closer to family members that had been separated from them. Still others ran away hoping to find freedom.

The Underground Railroad

A secret network of escape routes, created in the 1830s by free African Americans, former slaves, and antislavery whites, helped runaways reach freedom. Though it was not a real railroad, the **Underground Railroad** had "tracks," "stations," and "conductors." The tracks were the secret routes along back roads and rivers that led to northern states or to other countries, such as Cuba, Mexico, Canada, or the Bahamas. The stations were houses, churches, caves, or other safe places where slaves could hide, rest, and get food. Along the way, people known as conductors helped and guided the runaways on their journey to freedom.

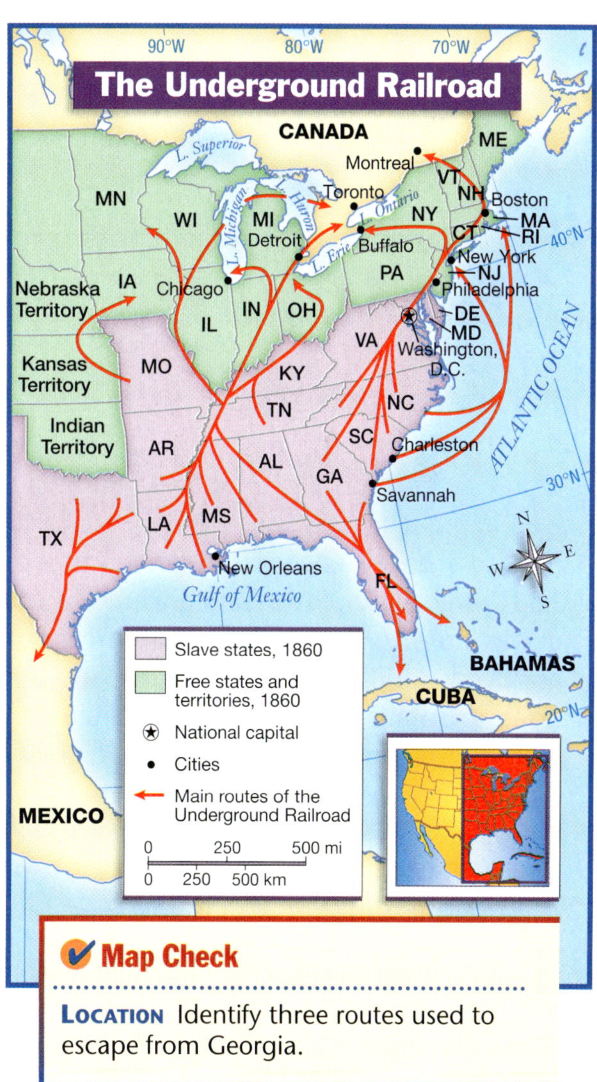

Map Check

LOCATION Identify three routes used to escape from Georgia.

Some of the conductors on the Underground Railroad were former slaves themselves. They had escaped and returned to the South to help others escape. Some people from the North who opposed slavery also worked in the Underground Railroad. Both the Northerners and the former enslaved African Americans who ran the Underground Railroad knew they were breaking the law. They were willing to risk great danger to battle slavery.

Enslaved African Americans sometimes used a special code that gave advice on how to escape from the South. One hidden message is contained in a song. Runaways were told to "follow the drinkin' gourd." The drinking gourd is the Big Dipper. Two stars in this constellation point to the North Star. Following the North Star would lead enslaved people north to freedom.

Slave Rebellions

A few enslaved African Americans took up arms to resist slavery. The best-known rebellion of enslaved African Americans against planters was known as Turner's Rebellion. It was led by Nat Turner in Virginia in 1831. This rebellion failed, and Turner was hanged.

They Made History

Nat Turner 1800–1831

Nat Turner was an enslaved African American who was born on a plantation in Virginia. Turner was a preacher. He believed that God wanted him to free all enslaved African Americans. In 1831, an eclipse of the sun convinced Turner that it was time to act. With a small group of other enslaved African Americans, he attacked and killed plantation owner Joseph Travis and the entire Travis family. His group was quickly joined by other enslaved African Americans. Within a day, Turner and his followers had killed more than 60 people. The authorities organized to capture them. Turner and his followers hid for six weeks. When he was finally captured, he was tried, convicted, and hanged.

The capture of Nat Turner ended the rebellion. His revolt led to stricter slave codes.

Draw Conclusions What might have caused slaves such as Nat Turner to stage revolts even though the chances of being caught were high?

One of the first rebellions was Gabriel's Uprising. A group of enslaved African Americans led by Gabriel Prosser tried to take over Richmond, Virginia, in 1800. They were defeated. Prosser, along with many of his followers, was executed.

In 1822, Denmark Vesey, a free African American man living in Charleston, South Carolina, also led a revolt. It, too, failed. Like Turner and Prosser, Vesey was hanged for his part in the rebellion.

An iron slave collar was sometimes used to make sure enslaved people could not escape.

Although these revolts were rare, planters and others in the South lived in fear of slave uprisings. After Turner's Rebellion, stricter slave codes were passed and harsher measures were taken to prevent more rebellions. For example, enslaved African Americans could no longer hunt with guns. They could not play bugles because it was feared that music could carry messages of rebellion. Night patrols were formed to prevent both the secret meetings of enslaved African Americans and their attempts to escape.

The South tightened its grip on the enslaved African Americans who grew its cotton and supported its way of life. However, storm clouds were forming to the North. More and more Americans felt that slavery could not continue to exist in a country devoted to freedom.

 **What was the Underground Railroad?**

Review History

A. In what ways did the cotton gin lead to a great increase in the number of enslaved African Americans in the South?

B. What was daily life like for slaves?

C. In what ways did some enslaved people resist slavery?

Define Terms to Know

Provide a definition for each of the following terms.
spiritual, Underground Railroad

Critical Thinking

Why did some Southerners who did not own slaves support the idea of slavery?

Write About Culture

The writer Ralph Waldo Emerson said, "If you put a chain around the neck of a slave, the other end fastens itself around your own." What did Emerson mean?

Get Organized

DETAIL/CONCLUSION CHART

Think about the ways that enslaved workers resisted slavery. Draw a conclusion about the Underground Railroad using this chart.

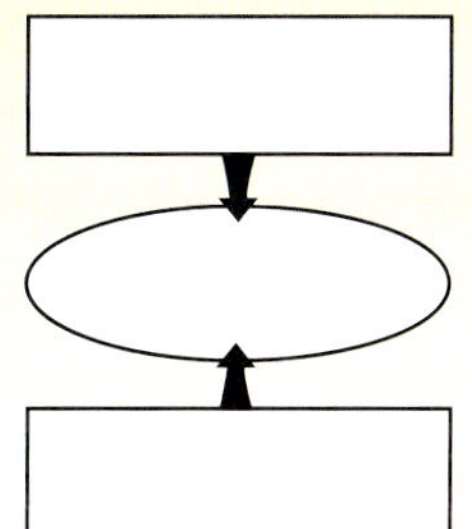

CHAPTER 13 Review

Chapter Summary

In your notebook, complete the following outline. Then, use your outline to write a brief summary of the chapter.

Life in the North and the South

I. The Industrial Revolution
  A. New Ideas, New Machines
  B.
  C.

II. Cotton Is King
  A.
  B.
  C.

III. The Slave System
  A.
  B.
  C.

Interpret the Timeline

Use the timeline on pages 310–311 to answer the following questions.

1. Which U.S. events had a direct effect on transportation?
2. **Critical Thinking** Which world events show that the world was becoming more industrialized during this period?

Use Terms to Know

For each term below, write a sentence that shows its meaning.

1. **cotton gin**
2. **factory**
3. **interchangeable parts**
4. **mass production**
5. **planter**
6. **spiritual**
7. **textile**
8. **Underground Railroad**

Check Your Understanding

1. **Discuss** two inventions that changed American life during the late 1700s and early 1800s.
2. **Identify** five reasons why the growth of manufacturing occurred mainly in the North.
3. **Summarize** the part that the cotton gin played in the growth of the Cotton Kingdom.
4. **Identify** three crops that were grown on plantations in the South.
5. **Describe** three aspects of the African American culture that developed in the South.
6. **Explain** how the economy of the South became dependent on slavery in the first half of the 1800s.

Critical Thinking

1. **Evaluate** How do interchangeable parts allow millions of Americans today to own personal computers?
2. **Analyze Primary Sources** Do you think the conditions of slavery described on page 326 discouraged slaves from running away?
3. **Recognize Relationships** How did Turner's Rebellion affect the lives of slaves who were not a part of the uprising?

Put Your Skills to Work

USE A CIRCLE GRAPH

You have learned that circle graphs are used to illustrate percentages. They let you see and compare the parts that make up a whole.

Look at the circle graphs below and study the information presented. Then, answer the following questions.

1. What was the percentage of cotton exports in 1800? in 1860?
2. What can you tell from the circle graphs about the importance of cotton exports to the U.S. economy?

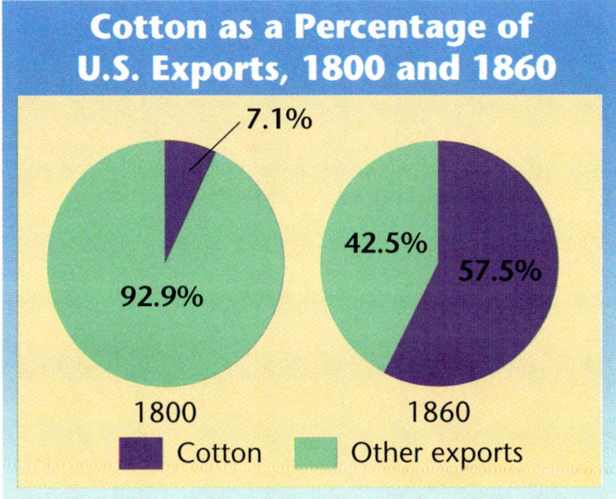

In Your Own Words

JOURNAL WRITING

Spirituals are religious songs that held great meaning for enslaved African Americans living on plantations in the South. Today many religious and nonreligious songs are meaningful to people. Write a journal entry about a song that is special in your life. Why does it have meaning for you?

Net Work

INTERNET ACTIVITY

Working with a group of classmates, use the Internet to make a documentary history of the beginnings of the Industrial Revolution in the United States. Include a timeline showing important events during the Industrial Revolution. Then, write short descriptions of important people during this time period. Also include illustrations of inventions or machines that were introduced during the Industrial Revolution. Share your documentary history with the class.

For help in starting this activity, visit the following Web site: www.gfamericanhistory.com.

Look Ahead

In the next chapter, learn how new ideas began to take hold of the country.

CHAPTER 14

The Spirit of Change 1800–1850

I. Cities and a Growing Population
II. New Ideas Take Shape
III. Reforming Society

During the first half of the 1800s, Americans began to look for ways that they could improve life in the United States. This reform effort was inspired by the belief that people are created equal and that they can govern themselves best. Ralph Waldo Emerson spoke of these new ideas in his essay "The American Scholar." He said,

> "We will walk on our own feet; we will work with our own hands; we will speak our own minds."

The reforms in the United States were widespread. Some were directed at life in the growing cities. Others focused on helping people in need. The most far-reaching reforms, however, dealt with equal rights for all people.

Fire mark

U.S. Events

1806 Noah Webster publishes the first American dictionary.

1821 Emma Willard establishes the Troy Female Seminary.

1825 Robert Owen starts the first nonreligious community in New Harmony, Indiana.

U.S. Events	1800	1810	1820
Presidential Term Begins	1801 Thomas Jefferson	1809 James Madison	1817 James Monroe; 1825 John Q. Adams
World Events	1800	1810	1820

World Events

1807 Great Britain prohibits slave trade with its colonies.

1821 Mexico becomes independent from Spain.

VIEW HISTORY This painting shows New York City during the first half of the 1800s. A city building often displayed a sign called a fire mark (left) to indicate which fire department would respond in case of a fire in that building.

★ **Judging from this picture, how was life in the 1800s different from life today?**

Get Organized

IDEA WEB

An idea web allows you to see the connection between topics and ideas or events. Use an idea web as you read Chapter 14. Write a topic in the center circle. Then, list related ideas or events in the outer circles. Here is an example from this chapter.

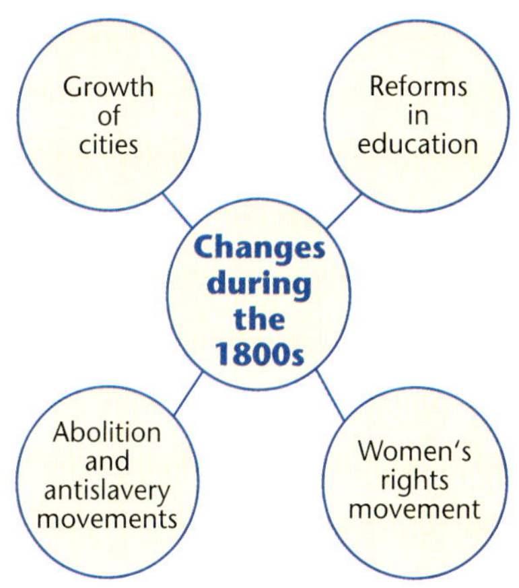

1830 Revolution starts in Germany.

1831 William Lloyd Garrison's newspaper, *The Liberator*, is founded.

1837 Horace Mann becomes the secretary of the Massachusetts Board of Education.

1839 First school district in New York is established.

1845 Failure of potato crops causes a food shortage in Ireland.

1847 Liberia is proclaimed an independent republic.

1848 Seneca Falls Convention meets to support women's rights.

1830 — 1840 — 1850

1829 Andrew Jackson; 1837 Martin Van Buren; 1841 William Harrison; 1841 John Tyler; 1845 James Polk; 1849 Zachary Taylor; 1850 Millard Fillmore

I Cities and a Growing Population

Terms to Know

rural having to do with the country

urban describing a city or city life

nativism the view that favors people born in a country over immigrants who come to that country

Main Ideas

A. The number of people moving to cities increased during the first half of the 1800s.

B. Immigration added to the population of American cities and caused feelings of resentment among some Americans.

C. The growth of cities brought changes in education.

CAUSE AND EFFECT
Recognizing cause and effect means seeing how one event causes another. As you read this section, look for examples of cause and effect. For example, what were some effects of the growing population of cities.

A. The Growth of Cities

In the first half of the 1800s, most Americans continued to live in **rural**, or country, areas. In growing numbers, however, people began moving to cities and towns to be near factories. The growth of cities led to several changes in the nation.

Americans Move to Cities

After 1800, the population of the United States increased greatly. In 1790, there were less than 4 million people in the entire country, not including the Native American population. By 1860, more than 30 million people lived in the United States.

Cities were becoming centers of growth in the 1800s. Only New York City, Philadelphia, Baltimore, and Boston had more than 20,000 people in 1800. By 1860, these cities each had grown to more than 100,000 people. Philadelphia alone had more than 500,000 people. Manhattan and Brooklyn—what later would be called Greater New York—had more than 1 million people.

Boston's Quincy Market building was designed in the early 1800s. The building, with its large columns, still stands today.

Exciting, Crowded, and Dirty

Cities were exciting places. Streets were bustling with wagons and carriages. There were department stores where one could buy almost anything. Buildings were tall—up to six stories high. Some hotels even had indoor plumbing, which was unusual at that time.

However, as the **urban**, or city, population grew, so did urban problems. Without enough housing for all the newcomers, cities became overcrowded. Many people lived in run-down buildings that had little light or air and poor sewage systems. Waste water and garbage were often dumped into the streets. The unclean conditions increased deaths from diseases. Fire was another problem in cities because most buildings were made of wood and were built close together.

 **How did cities change in the 1800s?**

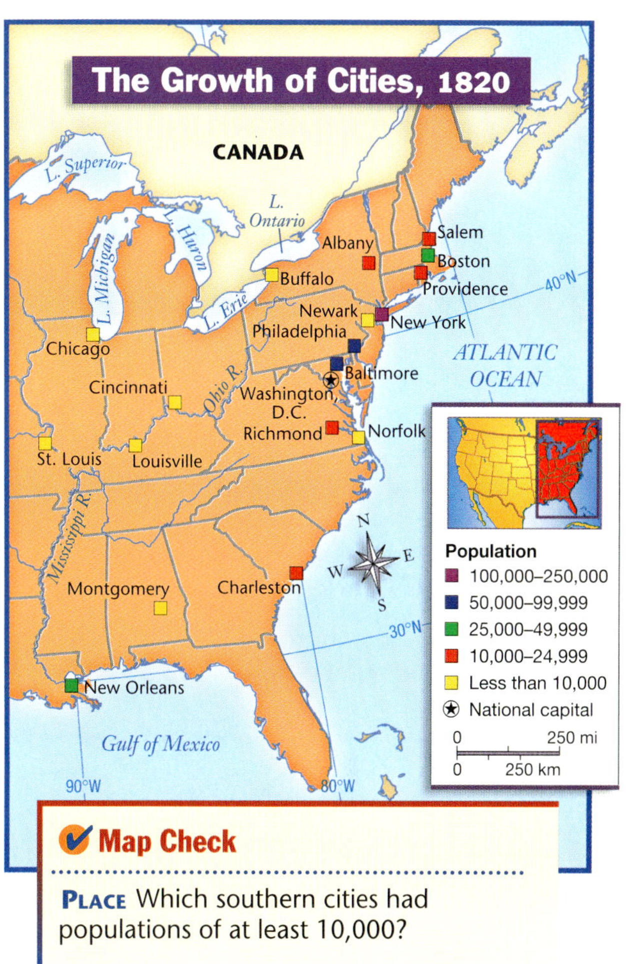

Map Check

PLACE Which southern cities had populations of at least 10,000?

B. Immigration Increases

Immigrants from foreign countries increased the population of the United States in the 1800s. This increase was particularly noticeable in the cities, where immigrants often settled. Immigrants enriched American life with new languages and customs, but the arrival of such a large number of people in a short period caused problems. Many Americans began to resent the growing number of immigrants.

Waves of Immigrants

Following the Revolutionary War, many people in other countries wanted to come to the United States. They were looking for jobs or for political or religious freedom. The U.S. government encouraged immigration. These new Americans could fill jobs created by the growing number of factories and businesses.

Beginning in the 1830s, the United States experienced a dramatic increase in immigration. More than 500,000 immigrants arrived in the 1830s. Another 1.4 million came in the 1840s, and 2.8 million more immigrated during the 1850s. People came from many countries, but the greatest numbers came from Ireland, Germany, and Great Britain.

Then & Now

Immigrants began coming to the United States in large numbers during the 1830s. Today, immigrants continue to enter the country at a rate that approaches nearly 1 million per year.

A Changing Culture

Thousands of people had moved to the United States during the colonial period in the 1700s. Because most came from Great Britain, British culture was adopted in the colonies. Most people spoke English and attended Protestant churches. They wore the same style of clothes and ate the same types of foods.

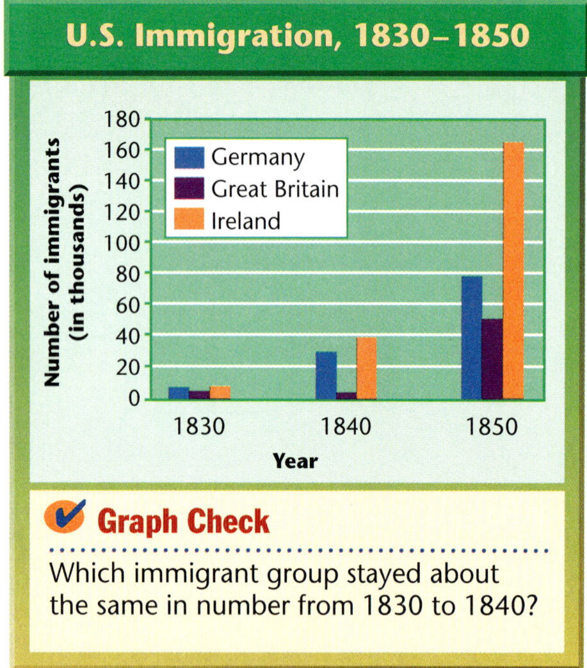

During the 1800s, neighborhoods of immigrants from various countries began to develop in cities. There, they could hear their native language, eat foods they were accustomed to, and worship in a church with people who held the same beliefs.

Irish people immigrated to the United States in large numbers because a disease known as blight destroyed their potato crops. This crop failure began in 1845 and caused a food shortage. Most Irish immigrants were too poor to buy land, so they lived in cities. Many young Irish women took jobs as maids, while men worked mostly in low-skilled jobs such as digging canals.

Many people from Germany moved to escape political and economic problems in their homeland. Revolutions broke out in Germany in 1830 and 1848, which caused people to flee. Because many Germans were crafts people, they also settled in cities where there were markets for their goods. They lived in neighborhoods with other Germans.

Each group of immigrants brought some part of its culture. One city could contain many separate cultures, because people from different countries created their own neighborhoods. As a result, a diversity, or a variety, of people from different cultures began to grow in the United States.

Reaction to Immigrants

Many Americans favored immigration because immigrants helped to settle the land and contributed to the country's growth. However, some American citizens disliked this new influence of other cultures in the United States. Increased immigration produced a negative reaction, known as **nativism**, among some Americans. This view favors people born in a country over immigrants to that country.

Nativism took many forms. Some native-born Americans resented immigrants because they felt that immigrants were taking jobs away from people who were born in the United States. Immigrants were also accused of bringing crime and disease to the cities.

Nativism led to the creation of the American Party in the 1840s. The American Party, which tried to limit immigration, began as a secret society. Members were told to say that they knew nothing about the party if they were asked, so it became known as the Know-Nothing Party.

Why did some Americans disapprove of immigration?

C. Reform in Education

Cities became centers of culture, with schools, theaters, clubs, churches, libraries, and museums that were either not available or not as widespread in rural areas. Cities offered many new opportunities. One of these opportunities was public education.

Public Education

Before the 1830s, free public education was not available, and children were not required to attend school. Most children who were educated either went to church schools or had private tutors. However, the growth of cities created a need for better education. In addition, many children no longer had to travel far to attend school because of the large number of children living in a small area.

Early schoolhouses had one room where children of all ages were taught.

Some people, such as Horace Mann, worked to create a public school system. He felt that taxes should support a public education system. In 1837, Mann became the first secretary of the Massachusetts Board of Education. He set the school year at six months and offered a variety of classes. Many people opposed the idea of public school. They did not want to pay taxes to educate other people's children. Mann responded,

> "I believe in the existence of a . . . natural law . . . which proves the *absolute right* of every human being that comes into the world to an education; and which, of course, proves the . . . duty of every government to see that the means of that education are provided for all."

ANALYZE PRIMARY SOURCES

DOCUMENT-BASED QUESTION According to Horace Mann, who is entitled to an education, and who should provide it?

Opposition to public education lessened. People realized that voters needed to be able to read and write to make intelligent decisions. Education was also seen as a way for people to better themselves, thus preventing poverty and reducing crime.

Horace Mann was a firm believer in public education and lectured in support of free public schools. In Connecticut, Henry Barnard led education reform. A law was passed in Pennsylvania requiring state support for schools. In 1839, Governor William H. Seward formed a system of school districts in New York. By the 1850s, most cities had tax-supported schools, although the South lagged behind in providing public education.

Limits on Education

Opportunities for African American children to attend school were limited. In the states that allowed slavery, it was against the law even to teach enslaved people how to read and write.

Although more children began to go to school in the 1850s, most attended for only a few years. They learned to read and write and do simple arithmetic. Secondary education, or schooling beyond grammar school, was far less common. By 1860, there were only about 300 public high schools, most of them in Massachusetts.

Mary Lyon raised $27,000 to start Mount Holyoke Female Seminary in South Hadley, Massachusetts.

Higher Education

New interest in education led to the founding of many small colleges. Several state-supported universities were also started, mainly in the southern and western areas of the country. One, the University of Virginia, was founded by Thomas Jefferson in 1819.

Most colleges or secondary schools did not admit women in the early 1800s. Emma Willard opened one of the first schools for women in 1821 in Troy, New York. It was named the Troy Female Seminary. Then, Mary Lyon founded Mount Holyoke in 1837, which also enrolled only women students. Oberlin College, opened in 1833 in Ohio, admitted both women and African Americans. It was the first college in the United States to admit men and women.

Why did opposition to public education lessen?

Review History

A. Why did people begin moving to cities?

B. Why did Irish and German immigrants tend to settle in cities?

C. What changes in education occurred during the first half of the 1800s?

Define Terms to Know

Provide a definition for each of the following terms.
rural, urban, nativism

Critical Thinking

Why did neighborhoods of people from the same country develop in U.S. cities?

Write About Culture

Write an editorial either in favor of or against tax-supported public education. Give reasons for your position.

Get Organized

IDEA WEB

Look back over Section I. Use an idea web to connect the information in the section. For example, what reforms were made in education during the first half of the 1800s?

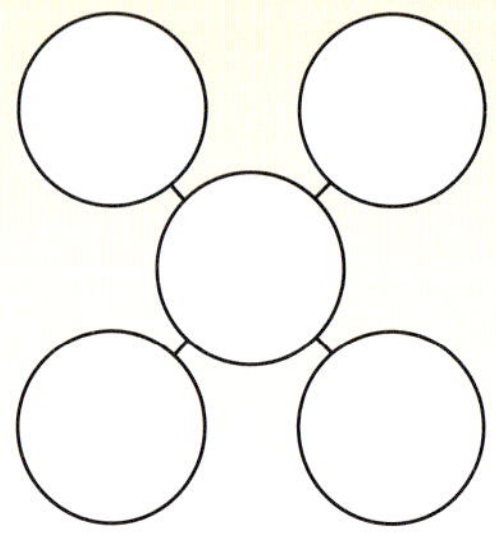

Build Your Skills

Critical Thinking

MAKE INFERENCES

You make inferences every day. Suppose you wake up in the morning during a week when the weather has been warm. You look outside and see that everyone is wearing a jacket. You can infer that the weather has turned cooler. Making inferences means using clues to understand things you have not been told.

When you read about history, you need to make inferences. The text will not always tell you everything. Sometimes it is necessary to use the facts you are given as clues to make inferences.

Here's How

Follow these steps to make inferences.

1. Gather facts as you read or listen to information.
2. Review what you already know about the topic from experience or from other information you have learned.
3. Use common sense and logic to make inferences based on what you have learned and what you already know.

Here's Why

You have just read that the growing numbers of immigrants created more diversity in the American culture. Suppose you had to write an essay on diversity in the United States during the first half of the 1800s. You could make inferences using the information in the text and your knowledge and experience of diverse cultures.

Practice the Skill

Copy the chart on a sheet of paper. Read Section I again and add facts from it to the first column. Fill in the second and third columns.

Facts From the Text	Facts From Your Experience	Inferences
People from many countries immigrated to the United States.	Different cultures exist around the world.	Immigrants brought new ideas and traditions to the United States.

Extend the Skill

Make inferences about the influence of diversity in the United States and write a paragraph about it.

Apply the Skill

As you read the remaining sections of this chapter, think about inferences you can make. For example, as you read Section II, you might make a chart with facts about new ideas in art, literature, science, and philosophy. Then, you can make inferences based on what you have read.

II New Ideas Take Shape

Terms to Know

utopia a perfect society

transcendentalism the belief that people learn truth and knowledge from their experiences with God and nature

individualism an emphasis on the value, rights, and power of the individual

Main Ideas

A. Americans began to read books written by American writers starting around the 1830s.

B. American literature emphasized the role of the individual and reflected American life.

C. Americans made advances in the arts and sciences.

Active Reading

DRAW CONCLUSIONS
When you draw conclusions, you make judgments based on the information you have learned. As you read this section, draw conclusions about nineteenth-century American art and literature.

A. Early Literature About Americans

By the 1830s, the growth of cities and of the population on the eastern coast was allowing some Americans to make writing a profession. This change occurred because of a growing audience of readers and a wider variety of American settings and themes to write about. During this period, European writers continued to record life in the United States too.

In the 1830s, Americans began reading more books written by American authors.

Early American Writing

During the time of the Revolutionary War and the early republic, many political essays were written in the United States. Benjamin Franklin wrote his autobiography in the late 1700s. However, the first significant works of creative literature were not produced until 1830 through 1850. These works of fiction featured American characters, scenes, and themes.

As late as 1830, almost 70 percent of the books read in the United States were written and published in Great Britain. By 1840, this number was only 30 percent. American readers relied less on foreign books as native-born writers began to write and publish more.

Europeans Write About American Life

European writers had a long tradition of writing about the Americas. In the sixteenth century, English writer Sir Thomas More used the Americas as the setting for a book titled *Utopia*. A **utopia** is a perfect society.

Later, visitors from various countries wrote about their experiences in the United States. Of these, Alexis de Tocqueville of France is probably the best known. Tocqueville was a politician and historian who lived in the first half of the nineteenth century. His best-known work was a book of four volumes that analyzed American politics and society. In *Democracy in America*, he praised Americans for their commitment to equality. At the same time, he warned that rule by the majority could limit individual expression.

 **What was Tocqueville's opinion of the United States?**

Alexis de Tocqueville studied the United States as a model of democracy. The illustration is a caricature, or a picture with exaggerated features.

B. American Literature Develops

Some of the most recognized writers of the 1830s and 1840s embraced **transcendentalism**. This philosophy emphasized the idea that knowledge and understanding come from sources other than what is experienced in the real world. Truth and knowledge come from a person's inner experiences with God and nature. Emphasis on the power, value, and rights of the individual is called **individualism**. Much of the early literature in the United States reflected this idea.

Transcendentalists

Ralph Waldo Emerson was a great believer in transcendentalism. He is perhaps best known for an essay titled "Self-Reliance." In this work, he argues that people must trust themselves above all else. Henry David Thoreau was also a transcendentalist. He lived at Walden Pond, near Emerson's farm in Massachusetts, for two years to learn lessons from nature. In his book *Walden*, Thoreau said,

> "I went to the woods because I wished to live deliberately, to front [want] only the essential facts of life, and see if I could not learn what it had to teach, and not, when I came to die, discover that I had not lived."

ANALYZE PRIMARY SOURCES

DOCUMENT-BASED QUESTION What do you think Thoreau means by "to live deliberately"?

Thoreau is also remembered for an essay in which he argued that citizens did not have to obey their government when it was wrong. Thoreau believed slavery was wrong and objected to Massachusetts being part of a country where slavery was permitted. Many American writers during this time spoke out against slavery.

The only known picture of Moby Dick drawn during Herman Melville's lifetime

Novels and Short Stories

American writers also wrote novels and short stories that reflected life in the United States. One of these writers was Washington Irving. Irving's famous *Sketch Book* included such classic stories as "Rip Van Winkle" and "The Legend of Sleepy Hollow." These stories are American versions of German folk tales. He also wrote one of the first biographies of George Washington.

James Fenimore Cooper captured the spirit of American democracy in a series of books called the Leatherstocking Tales. The most famous of those books were *The Last of the Mohicans* and *The Deerslayer*. Cooper's books were among the first truly American novels.

Authors Herman Melville and Nathaniel Hawthorne also contributed to American literature. Melville's famous book *Moby Dick* is a tale about a whaling captain who was set on revenge. Hawthorne's *The Scarlet Letter* takes place in a Puritan colonial village. Both of these novels became American classics.

In 1851, Harriet Beecher Stowe wrote a novel with a timely message. *Uncle Tom's Cabin* focused on the cruelty of slavery. It first appeared in an antislavery journal. Later, it was published as a book and was also made into a stage play. It remains an important influence in American culture today.

Spotlight on Culture

In 1806, the first truly American dictionary, with American pronunciation and style, was published by Noah Webster. For his second dictionary, *An American Dictionary of the English Language*, published in 1828, Webster learned 26 languages so that he could research the origins of American words.

Poetry

Henry Wadsworth Longfellow and Walt Whitman wrote poems that inspired Americans. Generations of schoolchildren learned Longfellow's "The Village Blacksmith." Whitman's best-known poems, collected in *Leaves of Grass*, were not widely popular during his lifetime but are considered important literature today.

The works of Edgar Allen Poe also became an important part of American literature. He fascinated people with his detective stories and horror stories. His poem "The Raven" is one of the most famous poems in American literature.

★ **What is transcendentalism?**

C. Advances in the Arts and Sciences

The existence of public education produced a more educated American society. During the first half of the nineteenth century, Americans achieved successes in the arts and sciences.

Arts in the United States

In the 1800s, a painting movement known as the Hudson River school developed in the New York area. Artists such as Thomas Cole, Asher B. Durand, and Thomas Doughty painted beautiful scenes from nature. These kinds of paintings are called landscapes. Many of them were scenes from the Hudson River valley, north of New York City. The artists painted American scenes in a distinctive style of their own.

This painting by Thomas Doughty is called *Hudson River Landscape.* The Hudson River school of painting had a style unique to the United States.

Whooping Crane by John J. Audubon is one of the many drawings of birds that he made during his lifetime.

The New York Philharmonic-Symphony Orchestra began performing in 1842. Foreign performers such as Jenny Lind, "The Swedish Nightingale," entertained American audiences. American composers were also popular. John Howard Payne composed "Home Sweet Home." Stephen C. Foster wrote popular songs such as "Oh! Susanna," "Camp Town Races," and "My Old Kentucky Home." Much of Foster's work was about southern plantation life even though he was born in Pennsylvania and lived in northern cities.

Advances in Science

In science, John J. Audubon published his beautiful drawings of birds in *The Birds of America*. Joseph Henry conducted experiments with electricity that made Samuel F. B. Morse's invention of the telegraph possible. Physician Crawford Long developed the use of ether as an anesthetic, or a drug that causes loss of feeling in parts of the body.

Scientists Louis Agassiz and Asa Gray made lasting contributions to the study of the natural world. Agassiz reformed natural science education in the United States with new teaching methods that he developed. Gray studied plants of the northern United States and wrote a book titled *Gray's Manual* that remains a standard reference on the subject today.

 **What was the Hudson River school?**

Review History

A. How did American literature begin to change in the 1830s?

B. How did American literature reflect American ideas and life?

C. What advances did Americans make in science during the first half of the 1800s?

Define Terms to Know

Provide a definition for each of the following terms.
utopia, transcendentalism, individualism

Critical Thinking

Would you expect transcendentalists to be more common in a city or in the country? Why?

Write About Culture

Think about the advances in American literature, painting, music, and science. Write a description about the one that makes the greatest impression on you and why.

Get Organized

IDEA WEB

Look back over Section II. Use an idea web to connect the information in the section. For example, what advances were made in the arts and sciences?

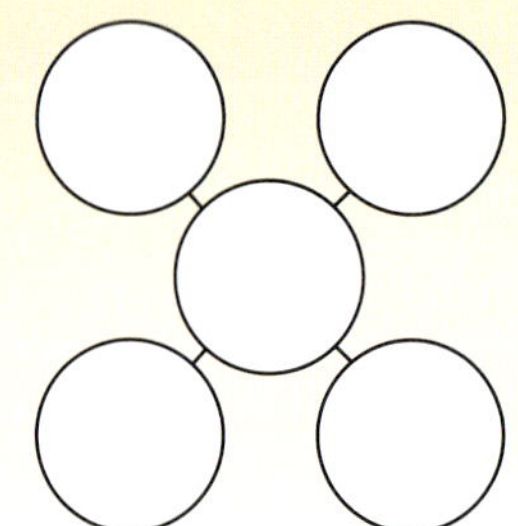

III Reforming Society

Terms to Know

revival a reawakening

reformer a person who wants to improve society

commune a community where people live and work together using shared resources

temperance a reform movement that was opposed to drinking alcohol

abolition the elimination of something, in this case slavery

Main Ideas

A. The spirit of reform dominated American life in the first half of the nineteenth century.

B. Ending slavery became the focus of reform beginning in the 1820s.

C. The fight for equal rights for women grew out of the struggle to end slavery.

Active Reading

SUPPORTING DETAILS
The main ideas of this section have already been identified. As you read this section, list the details that support these main ideas. For example, how did women fight for equal rights in the early nineteenth century?

A. The Spirit of Reform

From the 1820s onward, some Americans were filled with the spirit of reform. There was a belief that with hard work and good use of natural resources, the United States could be improved.

The Second Great Awakening

Many reforms stemmed from the Second Great Awakening that the United States experienced in the early 1800s. The movement began because religion seemed to be losing its influence. Preachers began the movement by calling for a **revival**, or reawakening, similar to the one of the 1700s. Charles G. Finney, a Congregational minister, and other preachers often spoke at outdoor gatherings called revival meetings. They urged people to live according to God's laws and to improve the society in which they lived.

Do You Remember?
In Chapter 5, you learned that the Great Awakening was a religious movement that focused on a return to religion in the American colonies.

New religious groups formed. William Miller of New York studied the Bible and concluded that Jesus would come sometime between March 21, 1843, and March 21, 1844, when the present world would end. The existing world did not end, but Miller's preaching to his followers about being ready for such an event led to the founding of the Seventh-Day Adventist Church by the mid-1800s.

Joseph Smith of New York founded the Church of Jesus Christ of Latter Day Saints. Members of this church, known as Mormons, believe in a present-day prophet. A prophet is a religious leader who is believed to be inspired by God. Mormons faced severe persecution. People outside their group felt threatened by their growing and independent community.

Inhumane conditions in the care of mentally-ill people, as pictured here, prompted Dorothea Dix to fight for reform.

Americans Strive to Improve

Many Americans thought social reforms would lead to a better life. Some **reformers** worked to improve the lives of people with mental and physical limitations. Thomas Gallaudet led the movement to provide education for hearing-impaired people. Samuel Gridley Howe worked to help people with limited or no eyesight.

Dorothea Dix fought for reform in the treatment of mentally-ill people. She dedicated herself to these reforms after visiting a prison. She reported that mentally-ill patients were kept in "cages, closets, cellars, stalls, pens!" As a result of her efforts, a number of states provided institutions in which mentally-ill people received better care.

Some reformers focused on conditions in prisons. They worked to eliminate brutal punishments such as whipping, to make prisons cleaner, and to separate first offenders from hardened criminals.

In 1825, Robert Owen founded a nonreligious **commune** where people lived and worked together. People in this community, and others like it, worked toward the common good. Owen, originally a cotton manufacturer in Britain, had become well-respected for providing decent conditions for his workers. Located in New Harmony, Indiana, the commune Owen started, as well as other communes, did not succeed mostly for economic reasons.

Still other reformers tried to correct basic problems in American society. The **temperance** movement worked to outlaw alcoholic beverages. In 1851, politician Neal Dow succeeded in passing a law that made it illegal to sell alcohol in the state of Maine. Over the next few years, several other states adopted similar laws.

★ **What general goal did nineteenth-century American reformers work toward?**

B. Reform and Slavery

The issue of slavery was a major topic of debate in the United States during the nineteenth century. The **abolition**, or elimination, of slavery dominated reform efforts beginning in the 1820s.

Abolition Versus Antislavery

Two different movements toward ending slavery existed—the abolition movement and the antislavery movement. Abolitionists were people who wanted slavery abolished immediately. They did not worry about what effects it would have. They believed slavery was so evil that it should be ended even though other problems might result. Many leaders of the abolitionist movement were Quakers. They believed that owning slaves went against Christian beliefs.

Antislavery groups also wanted slavery ended, but they recognized that the problem was not so simple. Slavery was legal, they argued, and a constitutional amendment would have to be passed to eliminate it. They also thought about how enslaved people would be affected. What would happen to them when slavery ended? Where would they live and work?

Both groups did agree on one thing. They felt strongly that slavery should not be allowed to expand to new territories. Some people from both groups also supported runaway slaves as they fled along the Underground Railroad to countries such as Canada, Cuba, and Mexico, where they could be completely free and without fear of being forcibly returned to slavery.

William Lloyd Garrison published his abolitionist views in his newspaper, *The Liberator*.

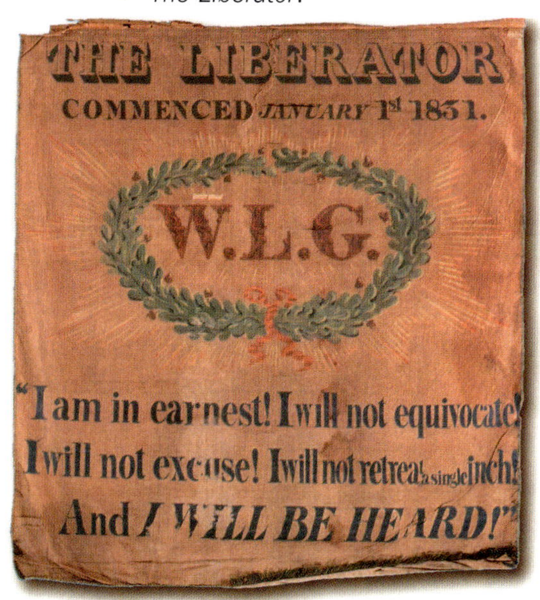

Abolitionist Writings

In 1831, William Lloyd Garrison founded an abolitionist newspaper, *The Liberator*, in Boston. Garrison and his followers wanted immediate freedom for all enslaved people in the United States. *The Liberator* became the main abolitionist newspaper in the country. In the first issue, Garrison showed how strongly he believed in the cause of abolition:

> "On this subject, I do not wish to think, or speak, or write with moderation. . . . I am in earnest! I will not equivocate! I will not excuse! I will not retreat a single inch! And *I WILL BE HEARD!*"

ANALYZE PRIMARY SOURCES

DOCUMENT-BASED QUESTION What feelings are portrayed in Garrison's statement?

Garrison was heard, and the abolition movement grew stronger. Other writers followed Garrison's lead. Editor and printer Elijah Lovejoy published antislavery essays. David Walker, a free African American, wrote an *Appeal . . . to the Colored Citizens of the World.* Walker wrote that enslaved people should fight for their freedom. Theodore Weld, a leader of the American Anti-Slavery Society, wrote *The Bible Against Slavery*. Fanny Kemble, noted actress and author, published her *Journal of a Residence on a Georgian Plantation.*

Leaders of the Abolitionist and Antislavery Movements

Frederick Douglass, a former enslaved person, became the best-known spokesperson for abolition. Charles Remond, a free African American, spoke eloquently against slavery. Robert Purvis, also a free African American, served on the board of the American Anti-Slavery Society. Sojourner Truth, a former enslaved person, traveled throughout the North and West speaking against slavery. All of these leaders forced many Americans to think about the injustice of slavery.

They Made History

Frederick Douglass 1818–1895

Frederick Douglass was named Frederick Bailey at birth. He was born into slavery in Maryland, in 1818. When he was eight years old, the slaveholder's wife taught him to read. In 1838, he escaped, changed his name to Frederick Douglass, and settled in Massachusetts. Inspired by William Lloyd Garrison, he became a traveling lecturer for the Massachusetts Anti-Slavery Society. Douglass spoke of the suffering endured by many people, including him. Despite his brilliance as a speaker, some people questioned his stories or how such a great speaker could have grown up as an enslaved person. In response, Douglass published an autobiography, *Narrative of the Life of Frederick Douglass*. He risked his freedom by publishing this book. With money raised by two friends, Douglass bought his freedom from his owner in 1846. Then, in 1848, he started his own antislavery newspaper, the *North Star*.

Frederick Douglass was a former enslaved person who became a leading spokesperson for abolition.

Critical Thinking Why was Frederick Douglass in danger of losing his freedom after publishing his autobiography?

The American Colonization Society

The American Colonization Society tried to solve the problem of what enslaved African Americans would do after slavery was ended. Members suggested that African Americans return to Africa. They even founded a settlement named Liberia on the coast of West Africa. It was to be a colony for formerly enslaved African Americans.

Some freed slaves did go to Liberia, but others chose to stay in the United States. The idea did not solve the problem of slavery in the United States.

 **What was the difference between the abolitionist movement and the antislavery movement?**

Elijah Lovejoy started the abolitionist newspaper *The Saint Louis Observer* in St. Louis, Missouri. This drawing shows Lovejoy's printing press being destroyed by an anti-abolitionist mob.

C. Women and Reform

Many women worked in antislavery efforts. The first woman to lead the antislavery movement was Sarah Grimké. In 1821, she left South Carolina and moved to Philadelphia because she could no longer stand to live with slavery. Her sister Angelina joined her in 1829. The Grimké sisters became antislavery spokespersons in 1837.

Women also worked in other areas of reform, especially education. The work many women did to gain equality for enslaved people led them to fight for their own equality.

Women's Role in Society

The role of women began to change in the first half of the nineteenth century. Women were still respected mainly as wives, mothers, and housekeepers. However, in the home, married women gained more power as decision makers. As women gained more power at home, some also turned their attention to the world outside. Those who had been working to end slavery started to look at their own unequal positions in society. They began to demand more rights.

Women had few of the rights that men did. Women were not allowed to vote. In a marriage, property was almost always owned by the husband, even if a woman had inherited property from her parents. Divorce was uncommon, but when it did occur, women usually did not receive custody of their children. They also did not receive any of the couple's property. In the early 1800s, women were not allowed to attend colleges or become doctors, ministers, or lawyers.

Spotlight on Culture

Mrs. Amelia Bloomer, a magazine publisher, made a piece of clothing popular. "Bloomers," named after her, were a kind of trousers that were gathered at the ankle. Bloomer wore the trousers under a shorter skirt than the long skirts that most women wore. Her fashion statement created quite a stir among both women and men.

A Movement for Women's Rights

Lucretia Mott and Elizabeth Cady Stanton launched a movement for equal rights for women in 1840. They worked to pass laws recognizing a woman's right to own property. Then, in 1848, Mott and Stanton held a women's rights convention in Seneca Falls, New York. Most of the 300 delegates to the convention were women, but some men, including Frederick Douglass, also attended. The delegates adopted a Declaration of Sentiments that demanded women's right to equality. It began with the words,

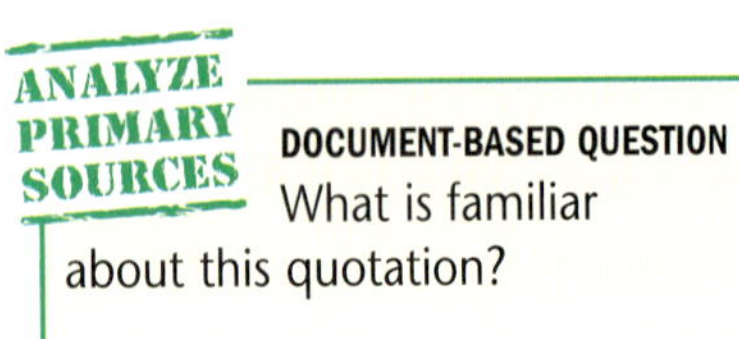

DOCUMENT-BASED QUESTION What is familiar about this quotation?

> "We hold these truths to be self-evident: that all men and women are created equal."

You can read the Declaration of Sentiments on page R5.

Women began to make some important strides in the long process toward equality. Dr. Elizabeth Blackwell became the first female doctor in the United States. Lucy Stone, who kept her maiden name after marriage, lectured for the rights of women. Susan B. Anthony worked to obtain women's right to vote. Women would not secure many of these rights until the next century, but the process had begun.

★ **What role did the antislavery movement play in women's struggle for equality?**

Review History

A. What were some ways Americans tried to improve society?

B. What was the goal of the abolitionist movement?

C. What were some of the rights women fought for in the first half of the nineteenth century?

Define Terms to Know

Provide a definition for each of the following terms.
revival, reformer, commune, temperance, abolition

Critical Thinking

The Declaration of Independence states that all men are created equal. What groups were not considered equal in the early 1800s?

Write About Citizenship

Write a paragraph explaining why one reformer's contributions in the first half of the 1800s were important.

Get Organized

IDEA WEB

Look back over Section III. Use an idea web to connect the information in the section. For example, what reforms were begun in the first half of the 1800s?

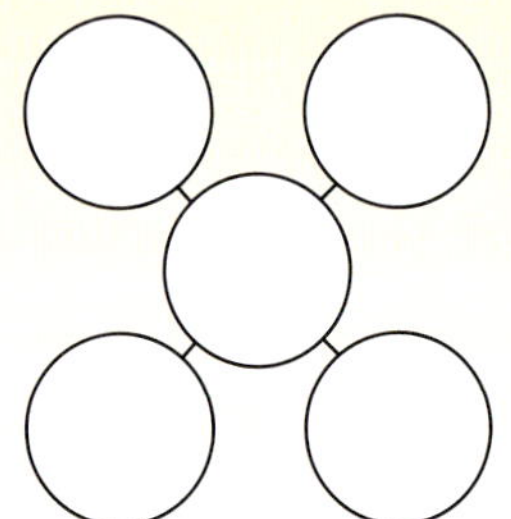

Points of View

The Fight for Women's Rights in the 1800s

In 1848, the Seneca Falls Convention marked the formal beginning of the women's rights movement. For years, women had been fighting for rights equal to men's. Women wanted to be allowed to own property and to vote.

In the late 1700s, some states had granted women the right to vote. However, by the early 1800s, women in all those states were no longer allowed to vote.

Newspapers printed views about the Seneca Falls Convention. There was praise, and there was criticism. The following passages are excerpts from newspaper reports of the convention.

Lucretia Mott and another woman were protected from an angry mob after a women's rights meeting.

"One of the most interesting events of the past week, was the holding of what is technically styled a Woman's Rights Convention, at Seneca Falls. . . . [I]n respect [with regard] to political rights, we hold woman to be justly entitled [given the right] to all we claim for man. We go farther, and express our conviction [strong belief] that all political rights which it is expedient [useful] for man to exercise, it is equally so for woman."

—From the *North Star*, 1848

"We are sorry to see that the women . . . are holding what they call 'Women's Rights Conventions.' . . . The women who attend these meetings, no doubt at the expense of their more appropriate duties . . . assert that it is wrong to deprive them of the privilege to become legislators, lawyers, doctors, divines, etc. etc. . . . Now it requires no argument to prove that this is all wrong."

—From *The Mechanic's Advocate*, 1848

DOCUMENT-BASED QUESTIONS

1. What is the point of view of the writer from the *North Star*?
2. What is the point of view of the writer from *The Mechanic's Advocate*?
3. **Critical Thinking** What does the writer for *The Mechanic's Advocate* probably think women should be doing instead of attending the convention?

CHAPTER 14 Review

Chapter Summary

In your notebook, complete the following outline. Then, use your outline to write a brief summary of the chapter.

The Spirit of Change

I. Cities and a Growing Population
  A. The Growth of Cities
  B.
  C.

II. New Ideas Take Shape
  A.
  B.
  C.

III. Reforming Society
  A.
  B.
  C.

Interpret the Timeline

Use the timeline on pages 332–333 to answer the following questions.

1. How many years after the newspaper *The Liberator* was founded did the Seneca Falls Convention meet?

2. **Critical Thinking** Which U.S. events show the development of public and higher education?

Use Terms to Know

Select the term that best completes each sentence.

abolition	**nativism**	**temperance**
commune	**reformer**	**utopia**

1. Distrusting someone who was born in another country is an example of ________.

2. A community where people live and work together for the common good is called a ________.

3. The ________ movement opposed the drinking of alcohol.

4. A perfect society is called a ________.

5. People who wanted all enslaved people to be freed immediately believed in _______.

6. A ________ worked to improve people's lives.

Check Your Understanding

1. **Discuss** the increase in immigration during the first half of the 1800s and the resulting rise in nativism.

2. **Summarize** the changes that took place in education during the first half of the nineteenth century.

3. **Identify** three American writers and three American artists from the first half of the nineteenth century.

4. **Discuss** three advances in science.

5. **Describe** the effect of the Second Great Awakening.

6. **Discuss** two issues that abolitionists and antislavery people agreed on.

Critical Thinking

1. **Analyze Primary Sources** What do you think Horace Mann meant by "a natural law" in the quotation on page 337?
2. **Analyze Primary Sources** According to the quotation on page 341, what did Thoreau hope to learn in his time at Walden Pond?
3. **Draw Conclusions** Why do you think the abolition movement found more support from people who lived in the North?

Put Your Skills to Work

MAKE INFERENCES

You have learned that you can make inferences from facts you read and from your own experiences. Making inferences can enrich your knowledge when you read history.

Copy the chart on a sheet of paper. In the first column, write some facts from this chapter. In the second column, list some things from your experience that relate to those facts. In the third column, make inferences based on the facts you learned and your experience.

Facts From the Text	Facts From Your Experience	Inferences

In Your Own Words

JOURNAL WRITING

Reformers of the nineteenth century were working to improve society in the United States. Write a description of your idea of a utopia. How would life be different in a perfect world? Describe the changes you would make, the kind of government there would be, and the rules people would have to follow.

Net Work

INTERNET ACTIVITY

Working with a group of classmates, use the Internet as a resource. Make a timeline showing the history of the African slave trade in the United States through the beginnings of the abolition movement. Include important events from the time of the first arrival of enslaved people to 1850. Find photographs, artwork, and quotations to illustrate your timeline.

For help in starting this activity, visit the following Web site: www.gfamericanhistory.com.

Look Ahead

In the next chapter, learn about the great push through the western frontier.

CHAPTER 15

Westward Expansion 1821–1853

I. Texas Wins Independence
II. War With Mexico and the Movement West
III. Settlement in California

Jesse Applegate took his place among the crowd of people, horses, and cows at Independence, Missouri. It was the spring of 1843, and he was about to travel west on the Oregon Trail. He wrote,

> "The migrating body numbered over 1,000 souls, with about 120 wagons, drawn by six ox teams, averaging about six yokes to the team, and several thousand loose horses and cattle. . . . No other race of men with the means at their command would undertake so great a journey. . . . They have undertaken to perform, with slow-moving oxen, a journey of 2,000 miles."

Like thousands of other pioneers, Jesse Applegate was seeking a new life in a new territory. The journey of these settlers helped the United States to expand westward.

Candlemaker and candlestick

U.S. Events

1821 Spain issues the first land grant to bring Americans to Texas.

1832–1833 Texas asks the Mexican government for separate statehood for Texas.

1836 Battle of the Alamo occurs. Texas gains its independence from Mexico.

	1820		1830
Presidential Term Begins	1821 James Monroe	1825 John Q. Adams	1829 Andrew Jackson

World Events

1821 Mexico gains its independence from Spain.

1830 Mexico forbids further American colonization in Texas.

1836 Napoleon III is exiled from France.

VIEW HISTORY Pioneers traveled in covered wagons as they made their way west. The journey usually took four to six months from the East Coast. Pioneers often carried a candlemaker and candlestick (left) to use as a source of light along the way.

★ **What hardships do you think the pioneers suffered as they traveled west?**

Get Organized

FIVE *Ws* CHART

When you read about history, you will usually see a lot of facts—dates, people, and events. Use the Five *Ws* (*Who? What? Where? When?* and *Why?*) to keep track of the facts as you read Chapter 15. For each important event, answer as many of these questions as you can. Here is an example from this chapter.

Who?	Stephen F. Austin
What?	Brought American settlers to Texas
Where?	Texas
When?	1820s
Why?	To increase the Texas population

1845 Texas is admitted to the United States.

1846 United States enters a war with Mexico.

1848 Gold is discovered in California. War with Mexico ends.

1850 California becomes the thirty-first state.

1853 United States buys land from Mexico in the Gadsden Purchase.

1840 | **1850**

1837 Martin Van Buren
1841 William H. Harrison
1841 John Tyler
1845 James K. Polk
1849 Zachary Taylor
1850 Millard Fillmore

1840 | **1850**

1840 Upper and Lower Canada are united.

1848 Revolutions occur throughout Europe. First submarine cable is laid across the English Channel from Great Britain to France.

I Texas Wins Independence

Terms to Know

empresario a person who received a contract to bring settlers to Texas in the 1800s

annexation the act of adding to or taking possession of

Main Ideas

A. Americans migrated to Texas in the 1800s in search of land and a new life.

B. Tensions between Texas settlers and Mexican leaders led to the Texas Revolution and independence.

C. After Texas gained its independence from Mexico, it joined the United States.

POINTS OF VIEW
When you compare points of view, you look at an issue from all sides involved. As you read this section, think about how the viewpoints of the Spanish and Mexican peoples and the American settlers in Texas differed.

A. The First Settlers in Texas

The search for cheap land and the promise of a new life drew settlers to the western territories in the 1800s. Many settled in Texas.

A Large Territory With Few People

Texas was part of the large territory in North America that belonged to Spain, but where few people lived. To attract more people to Texas, the Spaniards offered huge areas of land to **empresarios**, or people who promised to bring settlers to Texas.

Advertisements encouraged Americans to move to Texas.

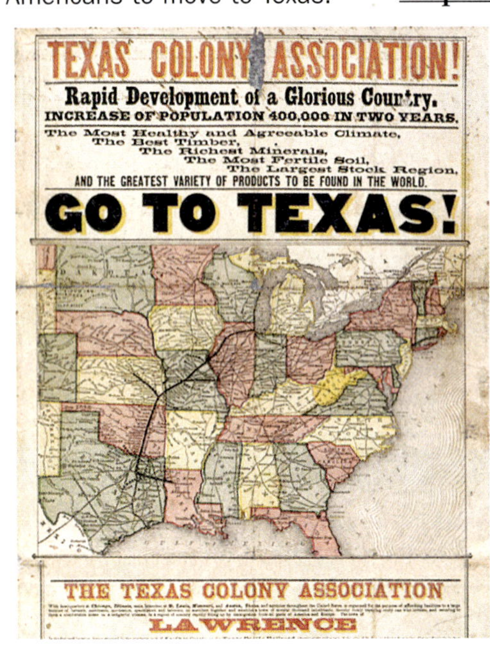

In 1821, the Spanish government gave Moses Austin the first land grant to bring American families to Texas. Austin died, but his son, Stephen F. Austin, took over the land grant and gathered 300 families to settle in Texas.

Americans Move to Texas

In 1821, Mexico won its independence from Spain. Texas now belonged to Mexico. Austin asked the new Mexican government to honor the contract he had with the Spanish government. Mexican leaders agreed as long as the settlers became Mexican citizens and joined the Roman Catholic Church. Each family was given 4,605 acres of land, at only a fraction of the cost of land in the United States. By 1835, nearly 30,000 Americans had settled in Texas.

B. The Texas Revolution

The growing number of American settlers and a clash of cultures led to conflicts. Soon, Texans were fighting a revolution of their own.

Tension Rises

Although the Texas settlers agreed to become Mexican citizens, many held on to their American culture. They resented Mexican customs and laws. Few settlers truly adopted the Catholic religion or even learned to speak Spanish. In addition, they had closer trade relations with the United States than with the rest of Mexico.

Mexican leaders worried that Texans were becoming too independent. They decided to take control. In 1830, the Mexican government passed a law that stopped American immigration to Texas and placed a high tax on goods imported from the United States. The law also encouraged more Mexicans and Europeans to settle in Texas. Mexican troops were sent into Texas to enforce this new law.

The new law and the growing number of Mexican soldiers upset Texas settlers. Many Tejanos, or Texans of Mexican descent, also became upset with the Mexican government. They felt that the government was taking away some of their rights as well.

Independence for Texas

In October 1832, the Texans held a convention at Stephen Austin's headquarters in San Felipe. Delegates wrote a petition to the Mexican government asking that Texas be made into a separate state within Mexico. Mexican officials denied their request.

In April 1833, delegates from Texas again asked for separate statehood. Stephen Austin personally delivered the request to Mexico City later in 1833. Then in January 1834, he was placed in prison for what Mexicans termed as rebelling against the government. After his release in July 1835, Texans decided that they must fight for their independence.

Stephen F. Austin was the first of nearly 30 empresarios who brought settlers to Texas. He is known as the Father of Texas.

In 1833, General Antonio López de Santa Anna became president of Mexico. Santa Anna was determined to control Texas and sent in more troops. Several conflicts took place between the Texans and the Mexican army. In 1835, fighting between the two groups broke out in Gonzales. This was the beginning of the Texas Revolution. Two months later, the Texans took over the city of San Antonio. On March 2, 1836, at another convention, Texas was declared to be independent of Mexico. With this declaration, the Republic of Texas was born. Sam Houston was appointed to lead the Texas army.

General Santa Anna was furious over the loss of San Antonio. Determined to take back the town, Santa Anna led the Mexican army to San Antonio in February 1836.

The Battle of the Alamo

A group of Texan soldiers stationed themselves in the chapel of the Mission San Antonio de Valero, also known as the Alamo, in San Antonio. For 13 days, the Texans, including Colonel William B. Travis, Jim Bowie, and Davy Crockett, fought off Santa Anna and nearly 1,800 Mexicans. On February 24, 1836, Travis sent the following message to the people of Texas and all Americans:

ANALYZE PRIMARY SOURCES

DOCUMENT-BASED QUESTION How did Travis's message predict what was to come?

> "I am besieged, by a thousand or more of the Mexicans under Santa Anna. . . . If this call is neglected, I am determined to sustain myself as long as possible & die like a soldier who never forgets what is due to his own honor & that of his country—Victory or Death."

Finally, on March 6, 1836, the Mexican troops rushed through the walls of the Alamo. All of the Texan troops—almost 190 men—were killed, including several Tejanos who had fought for Texas. The women and children, including Susanna Dickinson and her daughter, were spared.

They Made History

Susanna Dickinson 1814–1883

Susanna Dickinson was one of the few adult survivors of the Battle of the Alamo. She and her infant daughter, Angelina, left their home after the Battle of Gonzales to join her husband, Almaron Dickinson, in San Antonio. When Santa Anna's army approached the town, Dickinson and her daughter moved into the Alamo with the soldiers. Her husband and the other soldiers fought unsuccessfully against the Mexican army. Following the battle, Santa Anna released Dickinson with a letter of warning to Sam Houston. The warning stated that the Mexican army would chase all Texans out of Texas. Dickinson's account of the battle spread the news of the massacre at the Alamo throughout Texas.

Susanna Dickinson (left) witnessed the defeat of the Texan soldiers at the Alamo (above).

Critical Thinking How do you think Texans reacted to the news of the Battle of the Alamo?

Following the Battle of San Jacinto, the captured Santa Anna (wearing a blue shirt and white pants) stands in front of Sam Houston. Houston was wounded in the ankle during the battle.

Victory for Texas

Soon after the Battle of the Alamo, another battle took place at Goliad. The Texans were outnumbered and had to surrender. Santa Anna ordered that all the Texan soldiers be killed.

By the middle of March 1836, Sam Houston began gathering troops and heading east. Santa Anna and his army followed. Houston continued to retreat from the Mexican army so that he could train his men. After several weeks, the two armies met at the Battle of San Jacinto. During the battle, cries of "Remember the Alamo! Remember Goliad!" spurred Houston's army. The Texans defeated the Mexican army on April 21, 1836, and captured Santa Anna the next day. In a bargain for his life, Santa Anna agreed to give Texas its independence from Mexico.

 **What happened at the Battle of the Alamo?**

C. Texas Becomes a State

Texans formed the independent Republic of Texas in 1836. Most Texans, however, did not want Texas to remain an independent country. They wanted to join the United States.

The Republic of Texas

Sam Houston was elected president of the Republic of Texas in September 1836. Texas had many problems. The government had no money, and no other government recognized Texas as an independent republic. Texans also knew that Mexico could send troops at any time to challenge their independence. Houston tried to solve these problems by getting Texas admitted to the United States.

States Admitted to the United States, 1820 – 1850

YEAR ADMITTED	STATE	ORDER OF ENTRY
1820	Maine	23
1821	Missouri	24
1836	Arkansas	25
1837	Michigan	26
1845	Florida	27
1845	Texas	28
1846	Iowa	29
1848	Wisconsin	30
1850	California	31

 **Chart Check**

Which states were admitted to the United States during the 1840s?

Texas Joins the United States

The **annexation**, or addition, of Texas was debated in the United States from 1836 to 1845. When Texans voted in 1836 to elect their first president and approve the Texas Constitution, they also voted in favor of annexation. They felt Texas would prosper by being part of the United States. Some Americans wanted Texas to join the United States because it would expand the country. Others, however, did not want Texas added as a state because slavery was allowed there. If Texas joined the United States, the states that allowed slavery—the slaveholding states—would outnumber the free states—the states that did not allow slavery. As a result of this concern, Congress rejected the annexation of Texas.

As time passed, more people began to support the annexation of Texas. James Knox Polk of Tennessee won the presidential election of 1844 partly because he supported annexation. In 1845, Congress agreed to accept Texas as the twenty-eighth state of the Union.

 **Why did some Americans oppose the annexation of Texas?**

Review History

A. Why did so many Americans migrate to Texas beginning in the 1820s?

B. Why did Santa Anna agree to allow Texas to become independent?

C. Why did Texans want to join the United States?

Define Terms to Know

Provide a definition for each of the following terms.
empresario, annexation

Critical Thinking

Although Texas was part of Mexico, many Texans had closer ties to the United States. Why?

Write About History

Write an editorial explaining why Texas should or should not join the United States.

Get Organized

FIVE *W*s CHART

Review the information in this section. Use a Five *W*s chart to sort out the details. For example, who fought at the Alamo? Where was the battle? When did it take place? What happened? Why?

Who?	
What?	
Where?	
When?	
Why?	

Build Your Skills

Critical Thinking

DISTINGUISH FACT FROM OPINION

A fact is a statement that can be proven to be true. An opinion is somebody's belief; it cannot be proven. Suppose you hear a commercial for a new snack: "Only a hundred calories—and it tastes great!" Only the statement declaring that the snack contains 100 calories can be proven. This is a fact. Whether or not it tastes great is a matter of opinion.

When you read about history, it is important to be able to tell if you are reading a fact or an opinion.

Here's How

Follow these steps to distinguish fact from opinion.

1. Identify statements that can be proven to be true. Dates, names, and places are usually facts that can be proven.
2. Decide which statements are opinions. Phrases such as *I believe* or *I think* signal that a writer is giving an opinion.
3. What is the writer's purpose? Is the writer trying to convince you of something, or is the writer giving an account of what actually happened?

Here's Why

You have just read about the Battle of the Alamo and other events leading to independence for Texas. Suppose you had to write a factual account about one of these events. Separating the facts from the opinions would help you to write a factual account.

Practice the Skill

Read the passage that was written by a Mexican official in 1828 after visiting Texas. Decide which statements are facts and which are opinions. Then, on a sheet of paper, draw a two-column chart. List the facts in the first column and the opinions in the second column.

Extend the Skill

Write a paragraph that describes the state in which you live. Include both facts and opinions in your paragraph. Then, read your paragraph aloud to the class. Ask your classmates to identify which statements are facts and which are opinions.

> "As one covers the distance from Béjar to this town [Nacogdoches], he will note that Mexican influence is . . . diminished. . . . [T]he ratio of Mexicans to foreigners is one to ten. . . . It would cause you the same chagrin [sadness] that it has caused me to see the opinion that is held of our nation by these foreign colonists. . . . Texas could throw the whole nation into revolution."

Apply the Skill

As you read the remaining sections of this chapter, decide which statements are facts and which are opinions.

II War With Mexico and the Movement West

Terms to Know

Manifest Destiny the idea that the United States had the right to expand from the Atlantic Ocean to the Pacific Ocean

joint occupation the sharing of an area of land by two or more countries

mountain man a fur trapper or trader who went west to live in or near the mountains

Main Ideas

A. When Texas joined the United States, a war erupted between Mexico and the United States.

B. Americans wanted to expand the United States by occupying the Oregon Territory.

C. Settlers began to explore and develop western areas of the United States.

CAUSE AND EFFECT

When you recognize cause and effect, you see the relationship between events. As you read this section, look for the causes that led the United States to expand westward.

A. War With Mexico

Americans soon learned that the large area of Texas was not to be had without a price. Mexico and the United States both claimed Texas for themselves. A war would settle the issue.

Disagreements Between Mexico and the United States

Mexican president Santa Anna had agreed to the independence of Texas while he was held captive. The Mexican government, however, believed that Texas was still part of Mexico. The United States and Mexico argued over control of Texas. In addition, the United States claimed that the Texas border with Mexico was the Rio Grande. Mexico claimed that the border was the Nueces River.

The two countries also argued over California. President James Polk wanted to buy California from Mexico. Polk sent John Slidell to make a deal with the Mexican government. Slidell offered Mexico $5 million for New Mexico and $25 million for California. His offer was refused.

Spotlight on Geography

During the nineteenth century, the United States expanded its territory—usually by the purchase or annexation of lands. During this time, the United States also gained land as a result of war.

Fighting the War

President Polk decided to fight. He sent U.S. troops, led by General Zachary Taylor, to Texas. They camped along the Nueces River. Mexican troops stood along the Rio Grande. Polk then ordered the American soldiers to advance to the Rio Grande. Believing that the U.S. troops had invaded Mexican territory, the Mexican army crossed the Rio Grande, and the two armies clashed.

A declaration of war by the United States followed on May 13, 1846. President Polk said,

> "Mexico has . . . invaded our territory and shed American blood upon America's soil."

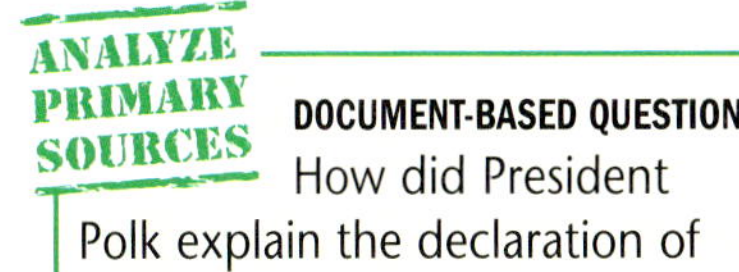

DOCUMENT-BASED QUESTION
How did President Polk explain the declaration of war on Mexico?

Taylor's soldiers defeated Santa Anna's Mexican troops in the Battle of Buena Vista, in 1847. General Winfield Scott's army then attacked Veracruz and captured Mexico City.

After several Mexican defeats, the two countries signed the Treaty of Guadalupe Hidalgo in 1848. Mexico withdrew its claim to Texas and ceded, or gave up land, a huge territory known as the Mexican Cession. In return, the United States paid Mexico $15 million. The United States gained nearly half of Mexico's territory, including Texas. California, Nevada, and Utah; most of Arizona; and parts of New Mexico, Colorado, and Wyoming were later created from this area. In 1853, the United States offered Mexico $10 million for the southern sections of present-day New Mexico and Arizona. This offer was known as the Gadsden Purchase.

★ **What were the key issues that led to the war with Mexico?**

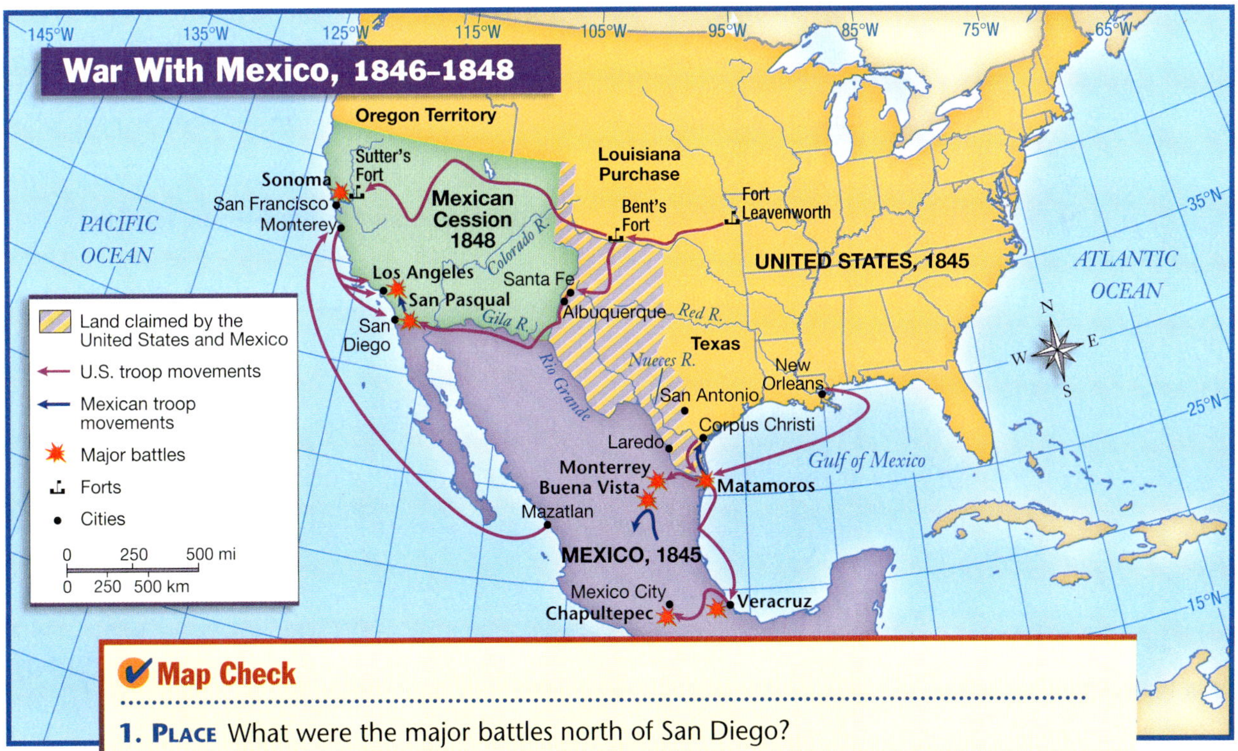

War With Mexico, 1846–1848

✔ Map Check

1. **PLACE** What were the major battles north of San Diego?
2. **MOVEMENT** How did the U.S. troops bypass the Mexican troops to reach Veracruz?

Spotlight on
Geography

The boundary, or border, between the United States and Canada, a country that Britain controlled, was clearly agreed upon. The border stretched from the Great Lakes to the Rocky Mountains.

However, west of the Rockies lay the Oregon Territory, which neither the United States nor Britain clearly controlled.

B. The Oregon Territory

During the war with Mexico, the United States was involved in a dispute with Great Britain. At issue was the Oregon Territory, which both countries claimed.

Manifest Destiny

Many people believed that it was the **Manifest Destiny** of the United States to expand to the Pacific Ocean. This idea led people to explore the West. In the 1840s, control of the Oregon Territory came into question between the United States and Great Britain. The idea of Manifest Destiny supported the U.S. claim to the territory.

The United States and Britain agreed on **joint occupation** of the Oregon Territory. Joint occupation meant that citizens of both countries could settle in the area.

Interest in Oregon Grows

The promise of rich land in Oregon attracted many Americans. Settlers followed the Oregon Trail for 2,000 miles from Independence, Missouri, to Fort Vancouver. Many died along the way from harsh weather or lack of food, but by 1845, more than 5,000 Americans lived in the Oregon Territory.

Knowing that war with Mexico was likely, President Polk wanted to avoid a war with Great Britain over the Oregon Territory. In 1846, the two countries agreed to split the territory. The dividing line was set at the forty-ninth parallel. The United States now included the lands of what are today Oregon, Washington, Idaho, and western Montana and Wyoming.

★ **What idea supported the U.S. claim to the Oregon Territory?**

This family of settlers lived and traveled daily in their covered wagon on their way out west in the 1800s.

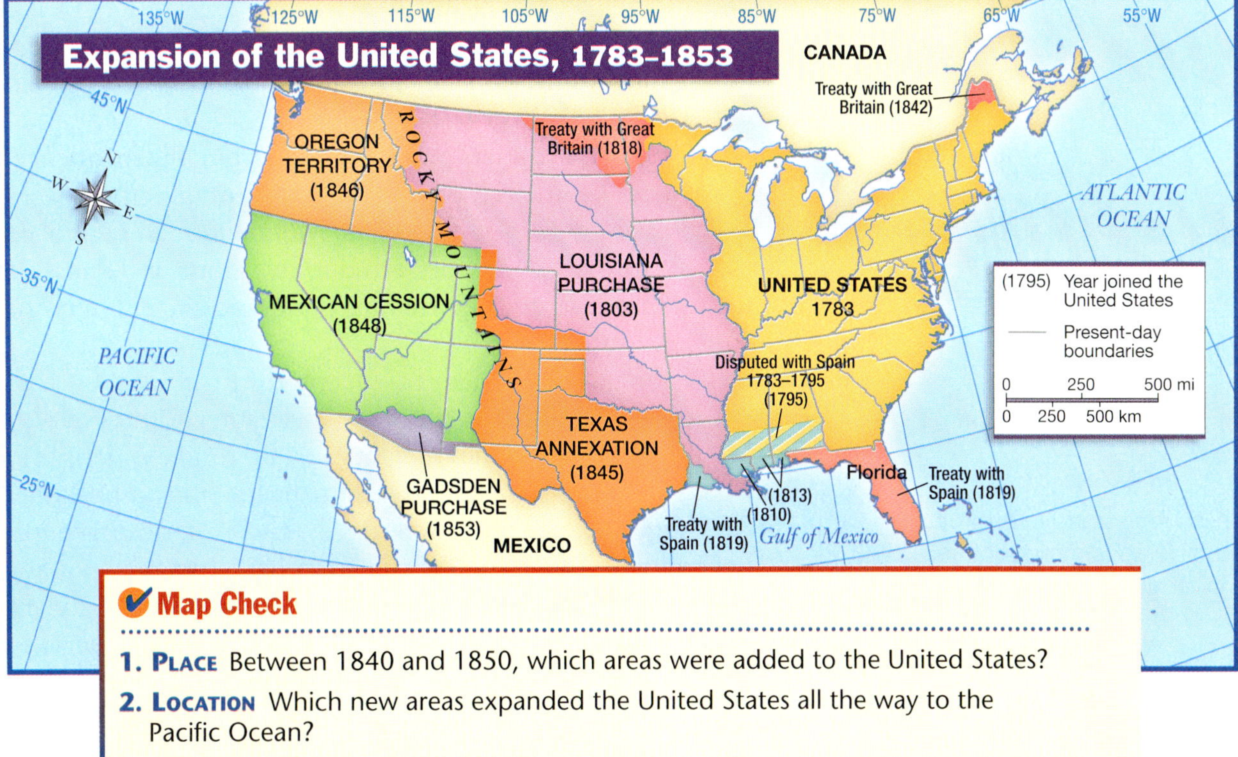

Map Check

1. **Place** Between 1840 and 1850, which areas were added to the United States?
2. **Location** Which new areas expanded the United States all the way to the Pacific Ocean?

C. Expansion in the West

Once the West was opened to settlement, people flooded into the new territories. Trails to the Northwest and the Southwest brought traders, trappers, and people seeking religious freedom.

The Mormons Settle in Utah

Members of the Church of Jesus Christ of Latter Day Saints, or Mormons, were looking for a place to live where they could practice their religion without persecution. In 1844, Joseph Smith, the founder of the religion, had been killed by an angry mob in Carthage, Illinois.

Brigham Young became the new Mormon leader. In 1846, Young led nearly 2,000 Mormons westward along the Oregon Trail. They suffered through a severe winter as they migrated to the Great Salt Lake valley in present-day Utah. Because this area was in Mexico, the Mormons felt they could practice their religion freely. From 1847 through 1848, thousands of Mormons moved west on what would be called the Mormon Trail. The northern half of Mexico, including Utah, was soon transferred to the United States in the Mexican Cession by the Treaty of Guadalupe Hidalgo. Young was appointed the first governor when the Utah Territory was organized in 1850.

Do You Remember?
In Chapter 14, you learned that members of the Church of Jesus Christ of Latter Day Saints, called Mormons, faced persecution.

African American Jim Beckwourth was a famous mountain man who, at one time, was also chief of the Crows.

Development of the Old Southwest

Santa Fe, in New Mexico, was the northernmost post of Mexico. In the 1800s, **mountain men**, or fur trappers and traders, pushed west of the Mississippi River to Santa Fe.

William Becknell, a trader, opened a trail from Independence, Missouri, to Santa Fe in 1821. Soon, the wagons of merchants were joined by increasing numbers of settlers. Mountain men also made the journey to the West. They preferred to live alone in the mountains but sometimes visited the trading posts to exchange furs for ammunition and supplies.

As with the Oregon Trail, many people traveling the Santa Fe Trail died on the journey. Some were overcome by weather. Others starved to death or died of thirst. Some were attacked by Native Americans.

The U.S. government made a treaty with the Sioux, Shoshone, Cheyenne, Arapaho, and other western Native American groups. The First Treaty of Fort Laramie, signed in 1851, assigned boundaries to each group. The boundaries were meant to decrease attacks on settlers, but the treaty was not very successful. Also, the U.S. Army could not patrol the entire length of the trails. When stopping for the night, members on a wagon train would often create a "fort" by arranging their wagons in the shape of a circle or a square and keeping people and livestock within it.

 **Why did Mormons migrate to the Great Salt Lake valley?**

Review History

A. What was agreed to in the Treaty of Guadalupe Hidalgo?

B. What arrangement did the United States have with Great Britain regarding the Oregon Territory?

C. Why did so many people die while migrating to the western territories?

Define Terms to Know

Provide a definition for each of the following terms.
Manifest Destiny, joint occupation, mountain man

Critical Thinking

In what ways were the disputes over Texas and the Oregon Territory alike? How were they different?

Write About Culture

You are a settler traveling on the Oregon Trail. Write a letter to a friend telling about the difficulties of your trip.

Get Organized

FIVE *W*s CHART

Review the information in this section. Use the Five *W*s chart to sort out the details. For example, who were the military leaders in the war with Mexico? What two countries fought in the war? Where? When? Why?

Who?	
What?	
Where?	
When?	
Why?	

III Settlement in California

Terms to Know

presidio a Spanish fort

prospector a person who looks for gold or other valuable ores

forty-niner a person who went to California in 1849 seeking gold

boomtown a mining camp that grew into a town almost overnight

Main Ideas

A. The Spaniards set up religious missions to introduce Christianity and a new way of life to Native Americans in California.

B. The gold rush brought thousands of settlers to California.

SEQUENCE OF EVENTS
As you read about history, it is important to understand the order in which events happen. As you read this section, pay attention to the sequence of events that led to California becoming the thirty-first state.

A. Early Spanish Settlements in California

Early Spanish conquerors in Central and South America found wealth in the earth. The land was rich with gold and silver. They spread north, into what is now California, in search of more.

Spanish Exploration

In the sixteenth century, Hernándo Cortés conquered the Aztecs and added Mexico to the Spanish Empire. He and the Spanish explorers were the first Europeans in California. Cortés established a colony on the Bay of La Paz in lower California in 1535. In 1542, Juan Rodríguez Cabrillo discovered San Diego Bay.

Spanish settlement of what is now southern California began in the 1700s. The Spaniards then continued to move north in California. They set up religious missions, whose goal it was to convert the Native Americans to Christianity. The missions were also meant to serve as supply and trading posts. In addition, the Spaniards built **presidios**, or forts, for protection. The first presidio was built in the present-day city of San Diego.

To encourage settlement, more than 800 land grants were issued. By 1824, Spain had built 21 missions, 4 presidios, and several small California towns.

Mission San Diego de Alcalá is the oldest of California's Spanish missions.

Mission San Luis Rey de Francia, a painting by Fannie Eliza Duvall

Spanish Missions

Spanish missions in northern California were operated by members of the Franciscan order of the Catholic Church. Nearly half of the missions were founded by Father Junipero Serra. Some of the more famous missions were in present-day San Diego, San Luis Obispo, San Francisco, San Juan Capistrano, Santa Barbara, San José, Santa Cruz, and San Fernando. The main task of the missionaries was to convert Native Americans to Christianity.

The missionaries also taught Native Americans to grow food, raise cattle and sheep, and make products from hides and furs of animals. This way of life was different from what Native Americans had known. They had been hunters and gatherers, not farmers, and some Native Americans did not want to change.

Life on a Mission

The focus of a mission was its church. However, a mission also included living quarters for priests and a few soldiers. The Native Americans lived in a separate area. Surrounding the missions were orchards, fields for crops, and pastures for livestock such as cattle and sheep. Native Americans were often forced to work in the fields and other parts of a mission. They provided much of the labor needed to build and run a mission.

The California missions were successful while under Spanish control. They thrived on producing crops, raising cattle, and trading furs. When Mexico gained its independence from Spain in 1821, Mexico took control of California. As more settlers arrived, the development of towns made the missions less necessary. Many of the Native Americans died from European diseases, difficult working conditions, and unhealthy living quarters. Many Native Americans who survived went back to their original way of life. As time passed, most of the missions were abandoned, and their land was given to settlers.

What effects did the Spanish missions have on Native Americans?

B. The California Gold Rush

The discovery of gold in California drew thousands of new settlers to California. Most came from the United States. However, the discovery of gold also attracted people from Canada, Mexico, and even as far away as Asia, Australia, and Europe.

The Discovery of Gold

On January 24, 1848, a carpenter named John Marshall made a discovery that would forever change California. Marshall was working for a Swiss settler named John Augustus Sutter who was having a sawmill built on his property in Coloma, near San Francisco. As he was working, Marshall noticed several shiny objects in the dirt. He realized that they were gold. Marshall told Sutter about the gold. The two men tried to keep the discovery to themselves. However, the news reached the eastern United States within several months. By June, thousands of Americans were making their way to California in search of gold.

That summer, R. B. Mason, a government official, reported that $50,000 in gold had been found daily. He said,

> "[T]here is more gold in the country drained by the Sacramento and San Joaquin rivers than will pay the cost of the present war with Mexico a hundred times over."

DOCUMENT-BASED QUESTION What effect do you think Mason's statement had on people?

People searched for gold along rivers and streams in northern California.

Then & Now

The population of California grew slowly until gold was discovered. After that, the population boomed, or increased rapidly. California's population boomed again in the 1990s with the growth of the computer industry in Silicon Valley. California currently has the largest population of any state in the United States.

Traveling to California

In the first month of 1849 alone, 61 ships, carrying about 50 **prospectors** each, left Boston, New York City, and other eastern ports for California. Prospectors are people who look for gold or other valuable ores. This flood of people continued for months. By the end of the year, more than 80,000 Americans had traveled to California in search of gold. Because so many came in 1849, the prospectors became known as **forty-niners**. By 1853, the gold rush had brought almost 250,000 people to the state.

Americans were not the only ones who moved to California. A California newspaper reported that about 50 Chinese immigrants lived in California at the beginning of 1849. Less than two years later, the newspaper reported that more than 4,000 Chinese people were living in California. Other prospectors came from as far away as Europe and Australia.

Most American prospectors traveled in wagon trains on an overland route that began in Independence, Missouri, and ended in Yuba County, California. Some prospectors made the journey by both land and water. These prospectors sailed on ships from the East Coast to the Central American country of Panama. There, they crossed by boat, on mules, or on foot before taking another ship to California.

California Boomtowns, 1850

Map Check

LOCATION What do you notice about the location of all the boomtowns?

The Search for Gold

When prospectors arrived, they needed only a few tools in order to look for gold. The most common tools were picks to loosen gravel from streambeds; shovels to scoop water, sand, and gravel; and tin pans to sift out the gold. Some people discovered nuggets, or large pieces, of gold. However, most found gold "sand," or small flakes of gold. Both were washed down streams from richer veins, or deposits of gold ore, located higher in the mountains.

The prospectors set up mining camps along these rivers. Here, they sifted through the riverbed soil looking for gold. As more people arrived, **boomtowns**, or towns that sprang up almost overnight, began to appear. However, many of these towns were abandoned when the gold ran out in the area.

Usually, a prospector would make a "strike," or find gold in a streambed. He would gather all he could by himself and sell it. Next, he would sell his claim to the land to a large company. The company would then bring in heavy equipment in order to harvest the richer veins of gold. Large companies made most of the money from gold mining.

While some prospectors did find gold, others were not so lucky. Searching for gold was often difficult. Many forty-niners gave up digging for gold and started businesses in towns or farms or ranches in the country.

California Becomes a State

In the Treaty of Guadalupe Hidalgo, signed in 1848, California was transferred from Mexico to the United States. The sudden rush of so many people created both a need for a stable government in California and enough people to request statehood. On November 13, 1849, Californians adopted a constitution and asked to be admitted to the United States. Because the constitution banned slavery, southern members of Congress blocked the admission of California for a time. Finally, California was admitted to the United States as the thirty-first state in September 1850. However, the struggle between slaveholding and free states was just beginning.

 **Why did the population of California increase so much in 1849?**

Spotlight on Culture

During the gold rush, Levi Strauss, a German immigrant, planned to sell tents to prospectors. However, when they were not interested in buying tents, Strauss decided to make pants out of the canvas used to make the tents. The sturdy pants caught on, and soon everyone wanted a pair. Strauss later substituted denim for the canvas and introduced the world to blue jeans.

Review History

A. Why did the Spaniards build missions in California?

B. What effects did the gold rush have in California?

Define Terms to Know

Provide a definition for each of the following terms.
presidio, prospector, forty-niner, boomtown

Critical Thinking

Besides the presence of gold mines, why do you think that the United States wanted to acquire California?

Write About Culture

It is 1849, and gold has been discovered in California. Write an advertisement that encourages people to go and find their fortune.

Get Organized

FIVE *Ws* CHART

Review the information in this section. Use the Five *Ws* chart to sort out the details. For example, who discovered gold in California? Where? When?

Who?	
What?	
Where?	
When?	
Why?	

PAST *to* PRESENT

Transportation

Travelers in the first half of the 1800s journeyed across the country in search of more land and gold in California. However, travel was slow. Railroads had not yet reached the West. People rode on horses or in covered wagons. Many walked. Their journey could take months to complete.

Today, speed and convenience are the main focus of transportation. People travel across the country by automobiles and trains within days and by airplanes within hours.

1 The prairie schooner got its name from pioneers who thought that, from a distance, the wagon's white cloth cover made it look like a ship sailing across the sea.

2 Steam locomotives like this one greatly increased the distance a person could travel in the mid-1800s.

By the end of the twentieth century, there were more than 125 million passenger cars registered in the United States.

4

This B-777 jet airliner carries nearly 400 passengers and cruises at more than 500 miles an hour.

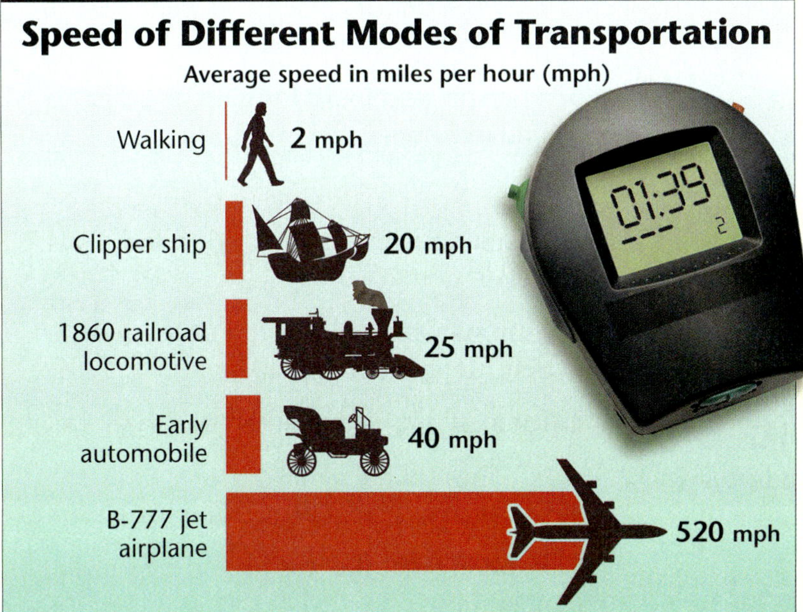

This table shows the average speeds of different kinds of transportation.

Hands-on Activity

How did the country move from covered wagons to jet airplanes? Who were the inventors who brought about changes in transportation? Research the major inventions in the history of transportation. Then, create a timeline that shows the dates and pictures of several inventions. To get started, go to: www.gfamericanhistory.com.

CHAPTER 15 Review

Chapter Summary

In your notebook, complete the following outline. Then, use your outline to write a brief summary of the chapter.

Westward Expansion

I. Texas Wins Independence
   A. The First Settlers in Texas
   B.
   C.

II. War With Mexico and the Movement West
   A.
   B.
   C.

III. Settlement in California
   A.
   B.

Interpret the Timeline

Use the timeline on pages 354–355 to answer the following questions.

1. How many years after Texas gained its independence was it admitted to the United States?
2. **Critical Thinking** Based on the events in the United States, what was a major theme of this period in American history?

Use Terms to Know

Match each term with its definition.

a. annexation
b. empresario
c. forty-niner
d. joint occupation
e. Manifest Destiny
f. mountain man
g. presidio
h. prospector

1. the idea that the United States had the right to expand from the Atlantic Ocean to the Pacific Ocean
2. a person who went to California in 1849 seeking gold
3. the sharing of an area of land by two or more countries
4. the act of adding to or taking possession of
5. a Spanish fort
6. a person who received a contract to bring settlers to Texas in the 1800s
7. a fur trapper or trader who went west to live in or near the mountains
8. a person who looks for gold or other valuable ores

Check Your Understanding

1. **Discuss** the events that led to the Texas Revolution.
2. **Summarize** the problems of the independent Republic of Texas.
3. **Identify** the causes of the war with Mexico.
4. **Summarize** the idea of Manifest Destiny.
5. **Explain** what life was like on a Spanish mission.
6. **Describe** the California gold rush.

Critical Thinking

1. **Analyze Primary Sources** Judging from his message found on page 358, how would you describe William Travis?
2. **Analyze Primary Sources** What would the Mexican government think of President Polk's statement on page 363?
3. **Make Inferences** How did the issue of slavery affect the admission of Texas and California to the United States?

Put Your Skills to Work

DISTINGUISH FACT FROM OPINION

You have learned that writers can use both facts and opinions in writing about history. Distinguishing fact from opinion can help you sort through the information you read.

Read the following passage by Richard Henry Dana in which he describes Spanish California in 1835. On a sheet of paper, draw a two-column chart. List the facts from the passage in the first column. List the opinions in the second column.

> "The bay of Monterey is very wide at the entrance . . . and the town lay directly before us, making a very pretty appearance; its houses being plastered, which gives a much better effect than those of Santa Barbara, which are of a mud-color. The red tiles, too, on the roofs contrasted well with the white plastered sides, and with the extreme greenness of the lawn."

In Your Own Words

JOURNAL WRITING

For 13 days, fewer than 190 men held off almost 2,000 Mexican soldiers at the Alamo. Write a journal entry about a time when you thought that the odds were against you. What was the situation? Why were the odds against you? What happened, and what did you learn from your experience?

Net Work

INTERNET ACTIVITY

Working with a group of classmates, use the Internet as a resource to create a poster showing what it was like to travel on the Oregon Trail in the 1840s. Include pictures and a map of the trail and the territories through which it ran. Describe what life was like on the trail and after arriving in Oregon. Share your project with the class when you are finished.

For help in starting this activity, visit the following Web site: www.gfamericanhistory.com.

Look Ahead

In the next chapter, learn about the events that led to a war between the slaveholding and free states.

Unit 5 Portfolio Project

A Stage Play

YOUR ASSIGNMENT

You are putting together a play in order to show what life was like in the United States during the first half of the 1800s. You want to accurately depict how Americans lived and worked about 200 years ago.

THE CASTING CALL

Choose Your Setting Each team will select a region of the country in which the play will be set. Choose from the following locations.

a large city in the North	a mining camp in California
a plantation in the South	the Oregon Trail

Plan Your Act After choosing your setting, decide who will be the characters in your play. Try to represent different groups of people in your setting. Assign each group member a different character.

Write the Script Write a short skit, giving each character lines to speak. Create an introduction, develop the plot, and write a conclusion to your play. Have each character speak about his or her life in the United States.

REHEARSAL

Character Study Search through textbooks, library books, the Internet, and other resources to find out how the people you will be portraying dressed and lived. Make and gather costumes and props. You may also refer to this Web site for ideas: www.gfamericanhistory.com.

Rehearse! Rehearse! Rehearse! Each person should memorize his or her lines in the play. Rehearse individually and as a group. Have a dress rehearsal before presenting the play to the class. Then, present your play.

Multimedia Presentation

Use a video camera to videotape your play. Use signs to display the title of the play and the names of the cast members. Then, act out the play as it is being recorded. When you are finished, edit the videotape to create a finished version. Show your videotape to other history classes.

Unit 6

A House Divided

"... General Sumner had a fight with the rebels this morning. He drove them towards the river, and then our gunboats opened on them, and they cut the rebels all to pieces. They ran and left everything behind them."

—from a letter by Christian Geisel, a Union soldier, in 1862

LINK PAST AND PRESENT Many people today re-enact historical events. In this photograph, people recreate a battle as it was fought in the Civil War.

★ What do the quotation and the photograph tell about how the Civil War was fought?

CHAPTER 16

The Road to War 1820–1861

I. The Question of Slavery in the West
II. Deepening Divisions Over Slavery
III. Challenges to Slavery
IV. Breaking Away From the Union

Solomon Northup worked on a cotton plantation in Louisiana. He described a typical day:

> "An hour before day light the horn is blown . . . the fears and labors of another day begin; and until its close there is no such thing as rest . . . "

By 1820, there were 1,530,000 people who, like Solomon Northup, were enslaved. The plantations they worked on were mainly in the South. Most plantation owners saw nothing wrong with forcing people to work without pay. Other Americans disagreed. They asked themselves the following questions: Wasn't our nation founded on the principles of freedom and liberty? How, then, can slavery be allowed? More and more, people would argue about whether slavery should continue.

Identification badges

1820 Missouri Compromise is proposed. Harriet Tubman is born about this year.

1836 Texas declares its independence.

U.S. Events	1815	1825	1835
Presidential Term Begins	1817 James Monroe	1825 John Quincy Adams	1829 Andrew Jackson
World Events	1815	1825	1835

1821 Peru, Mexico, and Guatemala win independence from Spain.

1825 First public railroad operates in England.

1833 Slavery is outlawed in British colonies.

VIEW HISTORY This painting by Eastman Johnson is called *A Ride for Liberty—The Fugitive Slaves*. In Charleston, South Carolina, African Americans were forced to wear badges (left).

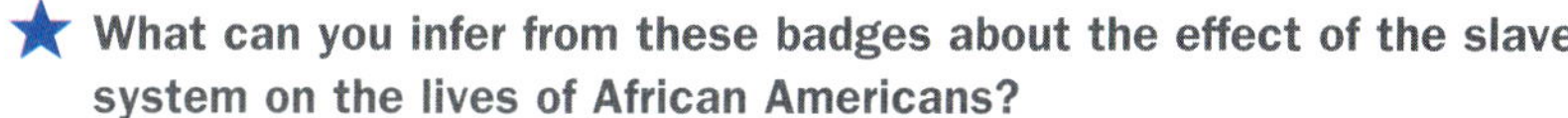

★ **What can you infer from these badges about the effect of the slave system on the lives of African Americans?**

Get Organized

CAUSE-AND-EFFECT CHAIN

Recognizing the causes and effects of events helps you to understand history. Use a cause-and-effect chain as you read this chapter. List each important event in the box. In the ovals, fill in a cause and an effect. Here is an example from this chapter.

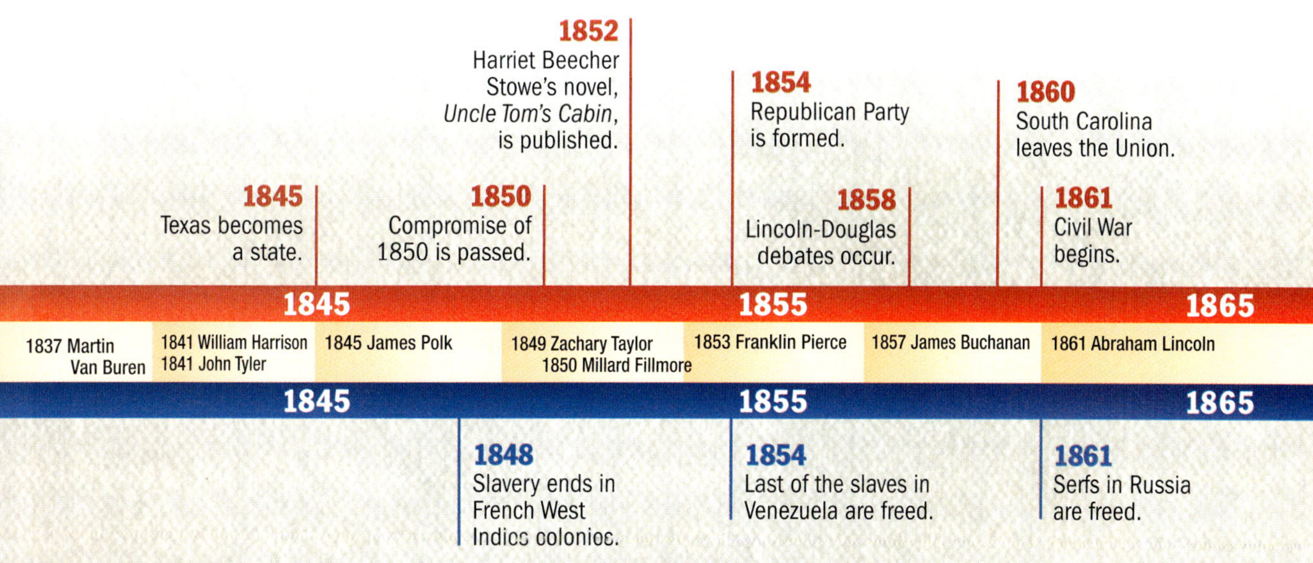

I The Question of Slavery in the West

Terms to Know

popular sovereignty control by the people

fugitive a person who has run away

secede to withdraw from or leave

Main Ideas

A. Congress approved the Missouri Compromise to keep a balance of power between free and slaveholding states.

B. The debate over slavery centered on new territories and states in the West.

C. The Compromise of 1850 was another attempt to satisfy both the North and the South.

Active Reading

PREDICT
When you predict, you use what you know to guess what might happen next. As you read this section, use the facts provided in order to predict how the issue of slavery would be settled in the new territories.

A. Slavery in an Expanding Nation

In the early 1800s, thousands of people moved to territories in the West. The question arose: When these territories join the Union—the United States—should they be slaveholding or free states? Differences of opinion between the North and the South would divide the country. Congress would have to decide.

Balance in the Senate

Many settlers from the South were slaveholders. They believed that the territories in the West should be admitted to the Union as slave states. Many people from the North wanted those territories to join as free states. They wanted slavery to be banned.

In 1819, there were 11 free states and 11 slaveholding states in the United States. Each state was represented by two senators. The power in the Senate between the North and the South, therefore, was evenly balanced. When Missouri asked to join the Union as a slaveholding state, this balance was threatened. Missouri's admission to the Union would give the South more power in the Senate.

An illustration for an anti-slavery publication

The Missouri Compromise

Leaders in Congress argued about Missouri's statehood for months. In 1820, Henry Clay from Kentucky, the Speaker of the House of Representatives, proposed a plan. It had the following three main points:

1. Missouri would join the Union as a slaveholding state. That would please the South.
2. Maine, which had also applied for statehood, would be admitted as a free state. That would please the North.
3. An imaginary line at latitude 36°30' would be drawn across the territory gained in the Louisiana Purchase. South of the line, slavery was permitted. North of the line, slavery was banned—except in Missouri.

Congress approved the plan called the Missouri Compromise. It was enacted in 1821. The plan kept the balance of power between the North and the South even in the Senate, as shown in the chart. For the time being, the question of slavery seemed settled.

Free and Slaveholding States

FREE	1821	SLAVEHOLDING
Maine		Missouri
Illinois		Alabama
Indiana		Mississippi
Ohio		Louisiana
Vermont		Tennessee
Rhode Island*		Kentucky
New York*		Virginia*
New Hampshire*		North Carolina*
Massachusetts*		South Carolina*
Connecticut*		Maryland*
New Jersey*		Georgia*
Pennsylvania*		Delaware*

* Original 13 States

Chart Check

How many of the original 13 states had banned slavery by 1821?

 **What was the purpose of the Missouri Compromise?**

B. More Lands, More Questions

The Missouri Compromise applied only to land that had been part of the Louisiana Purchase. The slavery debate was still to be settled in other territories.

Texas, California, and New Mexico

Texas applied for statehood after gaining its independence from Mexico in 1836. At the time, slavery was permitted in Texas. In 1845, after years of debate in Congress, Texas was admitted into the United States as a slaveholding state.

The issue of slavery remained a question in the land that was won from Mexico, including California and New Mexico. Great debates arose in Congress. In 1846, Representative David Wilmot of Pennsylvania called for a law that banned slavery in these lands. This bill, which never passed, was called the Wilmot Proviso.

In the Senate, John C. Calhoun of South Carolina believed, as did many Southerners, that government did not have the authority to ban slavery. He said that enslaved people were "property" that owners could take anywhere.

Other lawmakers, including Senator Stephen Douglas from Illinois, were more middle-of-the-road. They favored the idea of **popular sovereignty**, or letting the people of a territory decide. The people in a new territory could vote to settle the issue of slavery. The right to vote, however, was not extended to enslaved people.

Do You Remember?

In Chapter 15, you learned that the United States declared war on Mexico in 1846. After Mexico lost the war, it had to give up much of its land to the United States.

Then & Now

Third parties continue to play an important role in national politics. In the 2000 presidential election, the two leading candidates were Democrat Albert Gore Jr. and Republican George W. Bush. A third candidate, Ralph Nader of the Green Party, appealed to voters who were not satisfied with either major party. The Green Party stood for strong environmental protections and other reforms.

The Free-Soil Party

As the nation continued to debate the issue of slavery, sectionalism grew. Some Americans were more loyal to the North or to the South than they were to the entire country.

The leaders of the two major political parties—the Democrats and the Whigs—did not take a strong stand against slavery in the new territories. They did not want to lose the support of the South. This angered many voters. In 1848, some antislavery members of both parties formed the Free-Soil Party.

Free-Soilers, mainly Northerners, believed in the right of all citizens to control their own labor. They feared that slaves would take the place of paid workers, causing "free labor" to disappear. The party's motto was Free-Soil, Free Speech, Free Labor, Free Men. Its goal was to ban slavery in the new territories. Included in the party were abolitionists, who believed African Americans had a right to freedom.

In the presidential election of 1848, Zachary Taylor, a hero of the war in Mexico, was the Whig candidate. Lewis Cass, a senator from Michigan, was nominated by the Democrats. The Free-Soilers chose former President Martin Van Buren.

Zachary Taylor won the election by appealing to voters in both slaveholding states and free states. Although Taylor won, the Free-Soil Party received 10 percent of the popular vote and gained a number of seats in Congress. Slavery had become a major national issue.

 **Why did some Whigs and Democrats form a new political party?**

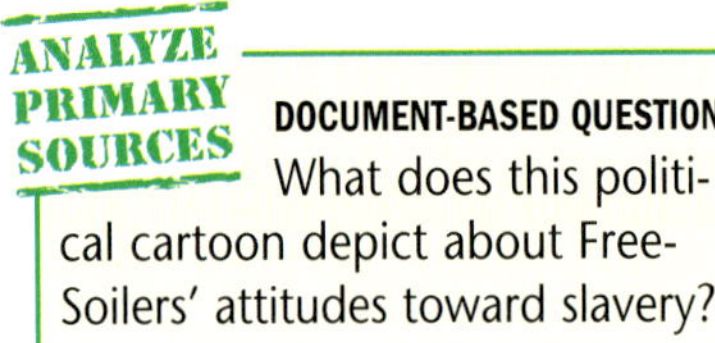

DOCUMENT-BASED QUESTION What does this political cartoon depict about Free-Soilers' attitudes toward slavery?

This political cartoon was published in the New York City newspaper *Harper's Weekly* in 1856.

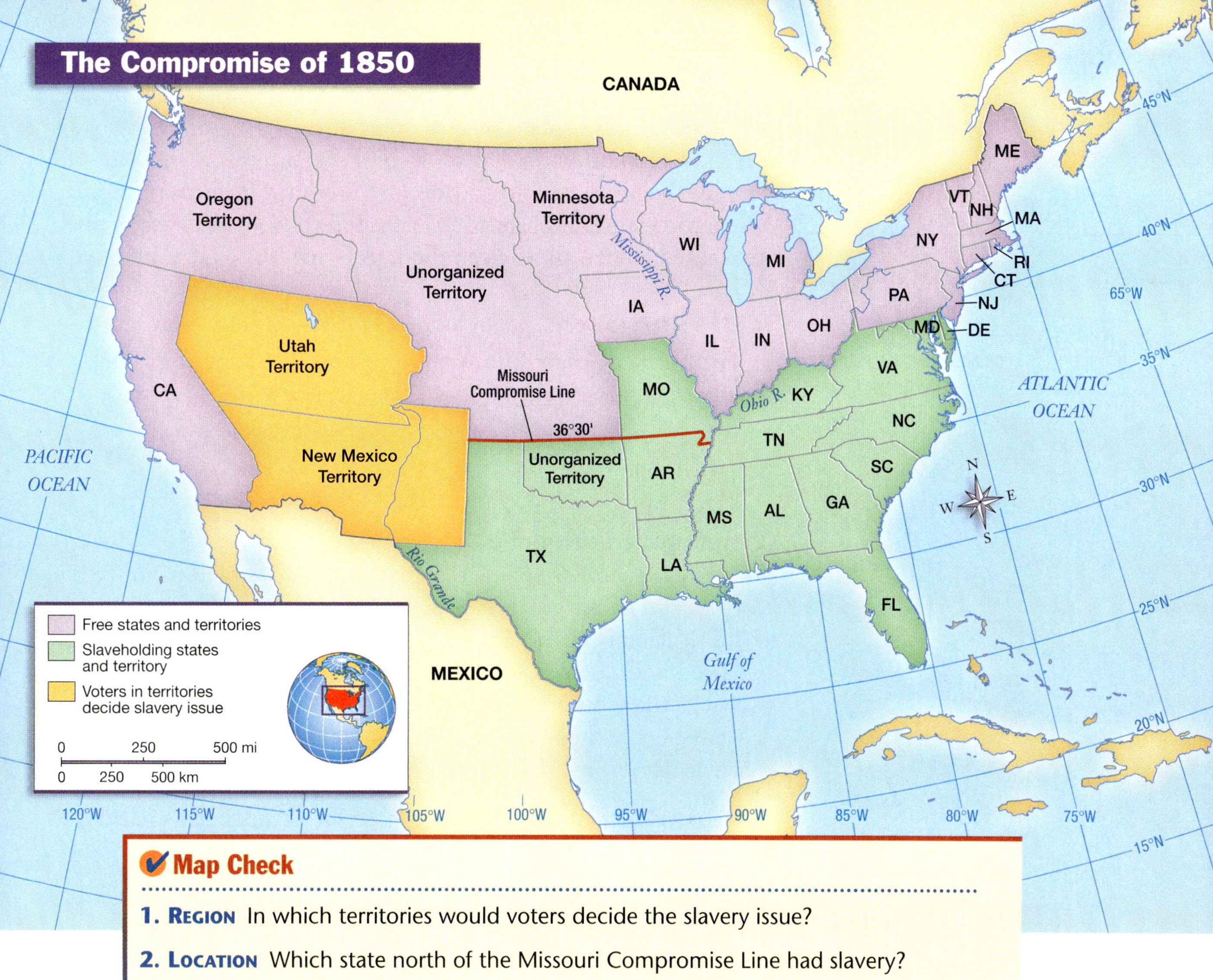

Map Check

1. **Region** In which territories would voters decide the slavery issue?
2. **Location** Which state north of the Missouri Compromise Line had slavery?

C. The Compromise of 1850

By 1849, there were 15 free states and 15 slaveholding states. When California asked to join the Union, the balance of power became a concern once again.

Clay, Calhoun, and Webster Debate

Henry Clay once more laid out a plan to satisfy both sides. In this plan, California would be admitted as a free state. Also, the slave trade would end in Washington, D.C. To please the South, Clay proposed a law that would help capture slaves who were **fugitives**, or runaways, who escaped to the North. The new law would force people in free states to help recapture escaped slaves. Finally, Clay proposed that popular sovereignty would decide the issue of slavery in the territories of Utah and New Mexico.

The plan was debated for eight months. Senator John C. Calhoun, too ill to address the Senate, asked another senator to read his speech. Calhoun warned that if southern interests were not respected, the South would **secede**, or withdraw, from the Union.

Senator Daniel Webster of Massachusetts defended Clay's plan. He wanted, above all, to keep the Union together. He said,

> "I wish to speak today not as a Massachusetts man, nor as a northern man, but as an American. . . . I speak for the preservation of the Union. . . . There can be no such thing as a peaceable secession. Peaceable secession is an utter impossibility."

ANALYZE PRIMARY SOURCES
DOCUMENT-BASED QUESTION What do you think Webster's opinion of sectionalism would be?

Compromise Is Reached

Finally, Senator Stephen Douglas proposed a plan to unify the North and the South. His idea was to divide Clay's plan into a series of bills. Members of Congress could vote for the bills they approved and not vote for the bills they opposed. The new laws, known as the Compromise of 1850, were passed by Congress.

Many people thought that the compromise would settle the issue of slavery. It did prevent a war—but for only ten years.

 **Why did Senator Henry Clay propose the Compromise of 1850?**

Review History

A. How did the Missouri Compromise keep the balance of power in the Senate?

B. Why were the debates in Congress centered on territories in the West?

C. How did the Compromise of 1850 satisfy the North and the South?

Define Terms to Know

Provide a definition for each of the following terms.
popular sovereignty, fugitive, secede

Critical Thinking

Why did tension between the North and the South increase despite compromises?

Write About History

Write an editorial about the debate in Congress leading to the Compromise of 1850. Use a northern or southern point of view.

Get Organized

CAUSE-AND-EFFECT CHAIN
Think about the main events in this section. Use your cause-and-effect chain to link these events together. For example, what were some causes and effects of the Compromise of 1850?

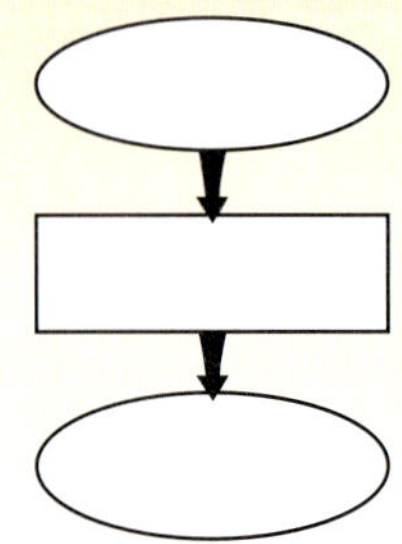

Build Your Skills

Critical Thinking

CLASSIFY INFORMATION

People often waste time looking for items. Classifying can save time and help people to remember where objects belong. Imagine trying to find a CD in a music store if the CDs were not classified by type of music and musical group. Think about how helpful it is to know exactly where to find the CD you want. Classifying means organizing items into categories that make sense.

When you read about history, you can classify information to help you find, examine, and remember it. It is helpful to classify information when you are reading, when you are studying for a test, or when you are preparing to write a paper. For example, you might choose to classify historical information by person, place, event, idea, or date.

Here's How

Follow these steps in order to classify historical information.

1. Identify the information that you want to classify.
2. Decide on the categories you will use to classify your information.
3. Make a chart of the information.

Here's Why

You have just read about the question of slavery in the West. Suppose you had to write an essay about the people who played important roles in the debate over slavery. Classifying would help you to organize the information and to write the essay.

Practice the Skill

Copy the chart on a sheet of paper. Read Section I again, and add names from it to Column 1. Fill in the second and third columns.

LEADER	STATE	CONTRIBUTION OR IDEA
Henry Clay	Kentucky	Missouri Compromise; Compromise of 1850
David Wilmot		
John C. Calhoun		

Extend the Skill

Write a brief essay about the leaders and their contributions that are listed in your chart.

Apply the Skill

As you read the remaining sections of this chapter, think of ways in which you can classify information. For example, as you read Section II, you might make a chart that contains the following categories: Issue or Event, Northern View, and Southern View. Use your chart as a study tool.

II Deepening Divisions Over Slavery

Terms to Know

extremist a person whose opinions are very different from those of most people

civil war a war between people of the same country

Main Ideas

A. The Fugitive Slave Law hardened northern attitudes against slavery.

B. The practice of popular sovereignty caused violence in Kansas.

C. The Dred Scott decision legalized slavery in the western territories.

Active Reading

CONTRAST POINTS OF VIEW

When you contrast points of view on an issue, you look at differences of opinion. As you read this section, contrast points of view on the Fugitive Slave Law and the Dred Scott case.

A. Changing Ideas in the North

Slavery no longer existed in the North. Therefore, many Northerners did not take a side in the slavery debate. Only a small number of people in the North were abolitionists. They continued to help enslaved people escape to freedom by using the Underground Railroad. Attitudes changed after the Compromise of 1850, when many Northerners realized that they must take one side or the other.

This advertisement offers a reward for the return of a fugitive slave.

$100 REWARD

Ran away from the subscriber, living near the Anacostia Bridge, on or about the 17th November, negro girl ELIZA. She calls herself Eliza Coursy. She is of the ordinary size, from 18 to 20 years old, of a chestnut or copper color. Eliza has some scars about her face, has been hired in Washington, and has acquaintances in Georgetown.

I will give fifty dollars if taken in the District or Maryland, and one hundred dollars if taken in any free State; but in either case she must be secured in jail so that I get her again.

JOHN. P. WARING.

Nov. 28, 1857.

The Fugitive Slave Law

One part of the Compromise of 1850 was the Fugitive Slave Law. The law required Northerners to help capture escaped slaves and return them to slaveholders in the South. People who broke the law could receive a six-month jail term and a $1,000 fine.

Before the Fugitive Slave Law went into effect, an enslaved person might escape to freedom along the Underground Railroad to free states. Now, there would be no escaping to safety anywhere in the United States. Even free African Americans might be rounded up in error and sent to slaveholders. If captured, African Americans were not even allowed to tell their story to a jury.

Many Northerners were upset about the law. It forced them to be part of the slave system even though they did not support it. In response, riots broke out in several northern cities.

Uncle Tom's Cabin

By 1852, it was impossible for Northerners to avoid the discussion of slavery. In that year, Harriet Beecher Stowe's novel *Uncle Tom's Cabin* was published. Stowe's book told the story of an enslaved African American named Uncle Tom who is at the mercy of the brutal slaveholder Simon Legree. This story reached millions of people, not only in book form, but also in stage presentations. *Uncle Tom's Cabin* helped people in many parts of the world understand that slavery was a human problem.

When *Uncle Tom's Cabin* appeared in 1852, it was a bestseller—with more than 300,000 copies sold in its first year. Many white Southerners complained that *Uncle Tom's Cabin* did not present a fair or accurate picture of the lives of enslaved African Americans. They argued that Stowe had seen little of slavery firsthand. They claimed that *Uncle Tom's Cabin* was filled with insults and lies. However, the book made many Americans ask if it was right for one human being to own another human being.

 **Why did some Northerners oppose the Fugitive Slave Law?**

They Made History

Harriet Tubman 1820–1913

Harriet Tubman was born into slavery in Maryland about 1820. When she was almost 30 years old, she feared that she might be sold away from her family, so she escaped to the North. There, Tubman joined the Underground Railroad's secret network of abolitionists who helped runaway slaves. Between 1850 and 1860, Tubman made 19 dangerous journeys to rescue family members and others. She led more than 300 enslaved African Americans to freedom in the United States and Canada. In fact, Tubman was so successful that southern slave catchers offered a reward of $40,000 for her capture!

Harriet Tubman
Black Heritage USA 13c

The photograph (above) shows Harriet Tubman, far left, with some of the people she helped escape. The stamp (left) of Harriet Tubman was issued in 1995.

Critical Thinking Why was Harriet Tubman so determined to help slaves escape to freedom?

Spotlight on Government

In 1858, after an angry debate over the fate of slavery in Kansas Territory, Republican Galusha Grow and Democrat Lawrence Keitt exchanged insults. This led to a full-scale brawl. Democrats and Republicans wrestled, and punches flew.

Suddenly, one man's wig fell onto the floor. He grabbed it quickly and put it on backward. The men who had been fighting moments before erupted into laughter, and the fight came to an end.

B. Kansas Becomes a Battleground

The Fugitive Slave Law and *Uncle Tom's Cabin* increased Northerners' opposition to slavery. Then, after the passage of the Kansas-Nebraska Act, the growing divide between Northerners and Southerners erupted into violence.

The Kansas-Nebraska Act

Senator Stephen Douglas of Illinois wanted to encourage people to settle in the West. In 1854, he sponsored the Kansas-Nebraska Act, which created the new territories of Kansas and Nebraska. In these territories, popular sovereignty would be used to determine the issue of slavery. The settlers would vote whether to allow slavery.

Both territories were north of latitude 36°30'. According to the Missouri Compromise, slavery was banned in territories north of this line. The Kansas-Nebraska Act would cancel the Missouri Compromise. Some Northerners felt betrayed by Douglas, a senator from a northern state.

Bleeding Kansas

Nebraska lay just west of Iowa, a free state. Kansas, which was farther south, bordered slaveholding Missouri. Because it was so close to other slaveholding states, Kansas soon became a battleground over the issue of slavery. The settlers' votes would decide whether Kansas would be a slaveholding territory or a free territory. Proslavery and antislavery settlers rushed to the area. Each side was determined to have the majority.

Just before the vote in 1855, thousands of proslavery Missouri residents, called "border ruffians," rode across the border into Kansas. These people were **extremists**, or people who held opinions not agreed on by the vast majority of people. A witness described the scene:

DOCUMENT-BASED QUESTION Why would people from Missouri come to Kansas to try to vote?

> "... before the polls were opened, some 300 to 400 Missourians and others were collected in the yard ... where the election would be held, armed with bowie-knives, revolvers, and clubs. They said they came to vote and whip the [Northerners]. ... Some said they came to fight."

The border ruffians voted illegally and helped to elect a proslavery government. In response, the antislavery settlers set up their own government. Kansas now had two different governments claiming authority. It became a territory in turmoil.

In May 1856, a group of border ruffians attacked Lawrence, Kansas, a town of many antislavery settlers. The border ruffians destroyed homes, businesses, and printing presses. The ruffians expected the people of Lawrence to fight back immediately, but they did not.

Three days later, however, a group of men—led by the abolitionist John Brown—dragged five proslavery men and boys from their homes and killed them. Proslavery forces struck back with more killings.

By late 1856, many people had died in the fighting in Kansas. This violence won the territory the grim nickname Bleeding Kansas. Some Americans called the fighting a **civil war**, or a war between people of the same country.

 **Why was there so much violence in Kansas?**

C. Attention Turns to the Capital

Soon after the fighting erupted in Kansas, many Americans turned their attention to Washington, D.C. There, the Supreme Court was hearing a case involving the freedom of Dred Scott.

The Dred Scott Case

In the 1830s, Dred Scott, an enslaved African American, was taken by his slaveholder from Missouri, a slaveholding state, to the free state of Illinois and then to the free territory of Wisconsin. In 1846, Scott and his wife, Harriet, sued for their freedom. He argued that once having lived in free areas, they were no longer slaves.

Dred and Harriet Scott sued for their freedom. The case eventually went to the Supreme Court.

Roger Taney wrote the Supreme Court decision that created further tension between slave-holding and free states.

In 1856, the nine justices of the U.S. Supreme Court heard the case. On March 6, 1857, Chief Justice Roger B. Taney announced the decision of the Court. The main parts of the decision were as follows:

1. Scott could not file a lawsuit because African Americans were not citizens.
2. The Constitution protects a citizen's right to own property. Slaves, considered property, could be taken anywhere by owners.
3. The U.S. Congress had no right to outlaw slavery in a territory. Therefore, the Missouri Compromise was unconstitutional.

Effects of the Dred Scott Case

The Dred Scott decision pleased many southern slaveholders. It meant that slavery was legal in all the territories. The decision gave white Southerners a right they had been demanding for years.

In the North, African Americans held meetings to criticize the ruling. White Northerners were also angered by the decision. Many of them had hoped that slavery would die out if it was not permitted in the territories. Now, slavery seemed likely to spread westward as the nation expanded.

 **What were three parts of the Supreme Court's decision in the Dred Scott case?**

Review History

A. Why did northern attitudes toward slavery change after the passage of the Fugitive Slave Law?

B. How did popular sovereignty lead to violence in Kansas?

C. How did the Dred Scott case answer the question of slavery in the West?

Define Terms to Know

Provide a definition for each of the following terms.
extremist, civil war

Critical Thinking

How do you think John Brown might have reacted to the Dred Scott decision?

Write About History

Write a paragraph about the Dred Scott decision in which you contrast two points of view.

Get Organized

CAUSE-AND-EFFECT CHAIN

Use your cause-and-effect chain to link the events of this section together. For example, what was one cause of changing attitudes toward slavery in the North? What was one effect?

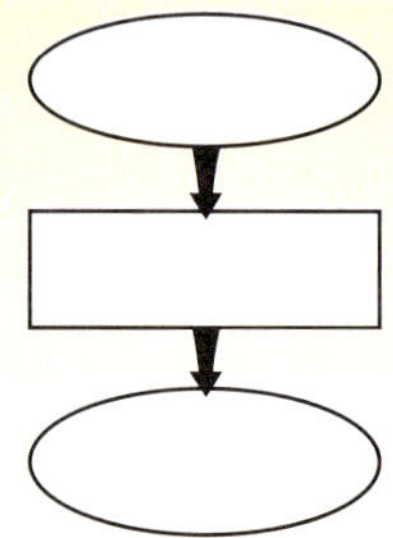

Points of View

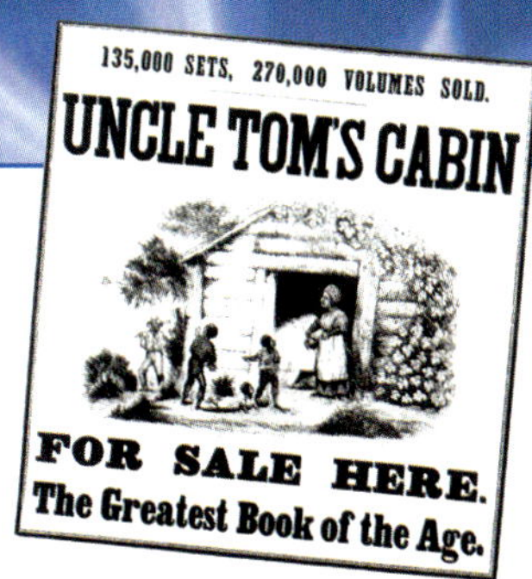

Advertisement for *Uncle Tom's Cabin*

Harriet Beecher Stowe and *Uncle Tom's Cabin*

Harriet Beecher Stowe (1811–1896) was the daughter of Lyman Beecher, a well-known Congregational minister and educator. In 1836, Harriet married Calvin Stowe. They had seven children.

Throughout much of her life, Stowe fought against slavery. In the 1830s and 1840s, the Stowe family helped slaves escape to freedom on the Underground Railroad. Stowe also taught formerly enslaved African American children in her family's school.

Stowe wrote a novel about the evils of slavery called *Uncle Tom's Cabin*. The book was published in 1852. The following passages are from book reviews of *Uncle Tom's Cabin*.

"... *Uncle Tom's Cabin* is an antislavery novel. It is a caricature [exaggeration] of slavery. It selects for description the most odious [distasteful] features of slavery–the escape and pursuit of fugitive slaves, the sale and separation of domestic slaves, the separation of husbands and wives, parents and children, brothers and sisters. It portrays the slaves of the story as more moral, intelligent, courageous, elegant and beautiful than their masters and mistresses. . . ."

—From *Southern Press Review,* 1852

"... *Uncle Tom's Cabin* . . . is stamped on every page with genius. . . . It proves that . . . Mrs. Stowe has the high ability of looking on both sides of one question. With feelings and principles equally opposed to slavery . . . she is yet able to paint the slaveholder. . . . with no touch of bigotry [prejudice]. . . . No southerner need be ashamed of the noble, kind and generous St. Clare [a slaveholder in the novel] or the angel-child, his daughter."

—From *Boston Morning Post,* 1852

DOCUMENT-BASED QUESTIONS

1. What is the point of view of the writer from the *Southern Press Review*?
2. What is the point of view of the writer from the *Boston Morning Post*?
3. **Critical Thinking** Examine how each review describes the characters in the novel who support slavery. What similarities and differences did you find between these two reviews?

III Challenges to Slavery

Terms to Know

emancipate to free

insurrection a rebellion against established authority

Main Ideas

A. The Republican Party was formed to block slavery's expansion in the West.

B. The debate over slavery sometimes erupted into violence.

C. The issue of slavery affected both Democrats and Republicans as they prepared for the 1860 election.

PROBLEM SOLVING

Efforts were made to find solutions to the country's problems before the Civil War erupted. As you read this section, identify problems between the North and the South. Then, identify solutions that were suggested to deal with those problems.

A. Founding a New Political Party

The issue of slavery continued to divide the two major political parties—the Democrats and the Whigs—in the early 1850s. Eventually, the Whig Party would disappear, destroyed by disagreements over slavery. A new party, the Republicans, would emerge.

Organizing the Republican Party

With the repeal of the Missouri Compromise, antislavery forces from the Democrats and the Whigs joined with Free-Soilers to form the Republican Party. Overall, the Republicans wanted to stop the expansion of slavery in new territories of the West. However, the party also included abolitionists who wanted to **emancipate**, or free, enslaved people throughout the country. Many Republicans wanted to give western lands to settlers free of charge. Many favored improvements such as railroads to help the economy grow.

The Republican Party was formed in 1854. In elections that year, party candidates won many seats in Congress, as well as several governorships in northern states.

Do You Remember?

In Chapter 14, you learned that the antislavery movement differed from the abolition movement. Abolitionists wanted an immediate end to slavery. Antislavery supporters took a more cautious approach. They wanted to work to end slavery slowly.

The Election of 1856

The Republican Party participated in a presidential election for the first time in 1856. The party's nominee for President was John C. Fremont. The Republicans clearly opposed the expansion of slavery into any territory. The Democrats nominated James Buchanan.

Although Fremont's name did not appear on ballots in any slave states, he carried the electoral votes in 11 free states. If he had won just one more state, Republicans would have won the election.

Southern Democrats realized how important they were to their party. Many wanted to ask the national party to support slavery in the next election. Northern Democrats realized that their party could not win in the North if it supported slavery.

 **Who came together to form the Republican Party?**

B. The Debate Over Slavery

By the 1850s, slavery was the main political issue in the country. Emotions intensified on both sides. A civil war between the North and the South was brewing, and there was no turning back.

The Sumner-Brooks Affair

In the Congress, feelings on both sides of the slavery issue ran high. In May 1856, violence broke out in the Senate following a speech by Charles Sumner of Massachusetts. In his speech the antislavery senator harshly criticized proslavery senators, especially Andrew Butler of South Carolina. Three days later, Representative Preston Brooks, a relative of Senator Butler, entered the Senate and struck Senator Sumner on the head with a gold-topped cane. Brooks continued beating Sumner until he was unconscious and bleeding.

Almost immediately, Sumner and Brooks became heroes in their regions. Brooks resigned from the House, was immediately reelected, and died soon after. Sumner, however, recovered slowly from the attack and eventually returned to the Senate.

Violence over the slavery issue broke out in the U.S. Congress. Here, Representative Brooks attacks Senator Sumner.

Abraham Lincoln and Stephen Douglas raced head to head in the 1858 Illinois Senate election. They would meet again in 1860 to battle for the White House.

The Lincoln-Douglas Debates

Stephen A. Douglas, a Democrat, wanted to run for President in 1860. First, he had to be re-elected to represent Illinois in the Senate. The Republicans chose Abraham Lincoln to run against Douglas in the Senate race. Lincoln was not as well known as Douglas.

Lincoln challenged Douglas to a series of public debates in different Illinois locations from August through October 1858. The debates gave voters a chance to compare the candidates' views on slavery in the territories.

During the debates, Lincoln spoke forcefully against permitting slavery in the territories. He said that the United States could not survive "half slave and half free." Douglas supported popular sovereignty, which was the right of territories to vote to allow or ban slavery within their borders. Neither man liked slavery, but they saw different ways of dealing with the issue.

The Republican Party opposed Douglas's position, but so did southern Democrats. Still, Douglas won the election and kept his Senate seat. On the other hand, Lincoln lost the election but gained a national reputation. Some Republicans began to think of this plain-speaking man as a possible presidential candidate.

John Brown at Harpers Ferry

After killing proslavery men in Kansas in 1856, John Brown left the territory. In 1859, he appeared in Virginia. Brown led a group of 18 to 21 followers, both African American and white, on a raid of the federal arsenal in Harpers Ferry. Weapons and ammunition were stored at the arsenal. Brown's plan was to give the weapons to enslaved African Americans to start a slave rebellion.

U.S. Marines led by Robert E. Lee surrounded Harpers Ferry. Ten of Brown's followers were killed, and Brown was captured. He and six other survivors were tried for treason and hanged. Treason is acting against your own country.

A hostage taken by Brown's group during the raid later wrote,

> "During the day and night I talked much with John Brown, and found him as brave as a man could be, and sensible upon all subjects except slavery. Upon that question he was a religious fanatic, and believed it was his duty to free the slaves, even if in doing so he lost his own life."

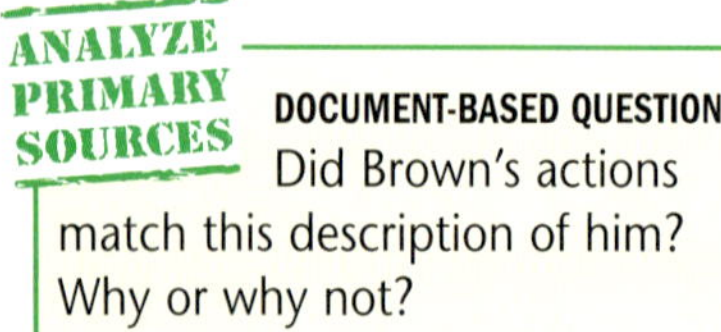

DOCUMENT-BASED QUESTION Did Brown's actions match this description of him? Why or why not?

Brown's raid symbolized Southerners' deepest fears—that this rebellion would lead to other slave **insurrections**, or uprisings. Southerners believed that northern abolitionists supported slave uprisings. This suspicion was confirmed when documents found at Harpers Ferry showed that Brown had received money from several wealthy Northerners.

★ How did the Lincoln-Douglas debates help Lincoln?

On October 18, 1859, John Brown (kneeling, at right) and his men were trapped by U.S. Marine fire at Harpers Ferry.

C. Choosing a Presidential Candidate

The Democratic Party was divided over the issue of slavery. This division weakened the party. In the coming election, Democrats would face not only a challenge from the Republican Party, but also internal challenges within their own party. The political parties prepared for a tough battle for the presidency.

The Democrats Divide

The Democratic Party met in Charleston, South Carolina, to select a presidential candidate for the election in 1860. The southern and northern Democrats were split over the issue of slavery. William L. Yancey, a delegate from Alabama, asked the party to support slavery in the territories. Stephen Douglas knew he could not win the presidential election in the North if his party supported the expansion of slavery. He used his influence to defeat Yancey's proposal, which was known as the Alabama Platform. As a result, Yancey and other southern delegates left the convention.

After the Southerners walked out, the remaining Democrats voted to hold another convention in six weeks in Baltimore, Maryland. There, Northern Democrats nominated Douglas for President. Douglas and his supporters believed in popular sovereignty for deciding the issue of slavery in the territories.

Southern Democrats held their own conventions in Richmond, Virginia, and in Baltimore. They nominated John C. Breckinridge of Kentucky for President. Breckinridge and his followers supported the Dred Scott decision. They believed slaveholders should be allowed to take their slaves into any territory.

Republicans Nominate Lincoln

The Republican delegates met in Chicago, Illinois, to nominate their presidential candidate. They knew that the split in the Democratic Party helped their chances for victory in the 1860 election. Four Republican candidates were nominated. One of them was Abraham Lincoln of Illinois. The other three candidates were better known nationally than Lincoln. However, Lincoln's supporters promised to give them jobs in his Cabinet if Lincoln was elected.

Senator William H. Seward was the leading candidate. He had become well known for his antislavery position and his talk about a conflict between the North and the South. Lincoln seemed more moderate in his views. Although he disliked slavery and promised to fight its spread, he had assured Southerners that he would not interfere with slavery in the South. Therefore, the Republican convention chose Lincoln because he seemed to be a safer choice than Seward.

To many white Southerners, however, Lincoln was a "black Republican" who wanted to end their way of life. Southerners threatened to secede if the Republicans won the election. To prevent secession, a third party formed. Known as the Constitutional-Union Party, it nominated John Bell of Tennessee. This party of southern Whigs and others tried to ignore the issue of slavery. It hoped to prevent a Republican majority in the electoral college.

 **Over what issue did the Democratic Party break apart in 1860?**

Review

Review History

A. Why was the Republican Party formed?

B. How did John Brown contribute to the violence that preceded the Civil War?

C. Who were the main candidates for President in 1860?

Define Terms to Know

Provide a definition for each of the following terms.
emancipate, insurrection

Critical Thinking

Why would the division of the Democratic Party help the Republican Party?

Write About Government

Write a speech as a delegate to the first Democratic convention in 1860. Your goal is to convince the party that it is necessary to remain united in order to defeat the Republicans.

Get Organized

CAUSE-AND-EFFECT CHAIN

You can use your cause-and-effect chain to see how one event in this section led to another. For example, what was a cause and an effect of the Lincoln-Douglas debates?

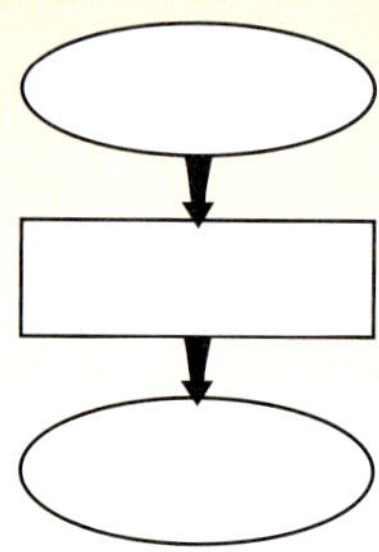

IV Breaking Away From the Union

Terms to Know

Confederacy the Confederate States of America, formed in 1861 by southern states that had seceded from the Union

line item veto a veto of a portion but not all of a proposed law

provisional temporary

Main Ideas

A. Some southern states seceded from the Union when Abraham Lincoln won the presidency.

B. Southern states that seceded formed the Confederate States of America.

C. Efforts to bring the seceded states back into the Union failed.

SEQUENCE OF EVENTS
Many events led to the Civil War. Understanding the order in which these events occurred will help you to make sense of this period. As you read this section, pay attention to the events that led to the battle at Fort Sumter.

Meet the President

Abraham Lincoln
1809–1865

Years in office 1861–1865

Political Party Republican

Birthplace Kentucky

Occupations Surveyor, Postmaster, Lawyer

Nickname Honest Abe

Did you know? Lincoln married Mary Todd In 1842. They had four sons. Only one, Robert, lived to adulthood.

Quote "I believe this government cannot endure, permanently half slave and half free."

A. Secession Splits the Nation

Southerners' worst fears came true in the election of 1860. Abraham Lincoln was elected President. Many feared that the institution of slavery was at risk.

The Election of 1860

Abraham Lincoln received only 40 percent of the popular vote. However, he earned a majority in the electoral college, which was enough to win the election. Lincoln won every free state except New Jersey, which was split between Stephen Douglas and Lincoln. John Breckinridge swept the South. John Bell took three slaveholding states between the North and the South: Kentucky, Virginia, and Tennessee. Stephen Douglas took three electoral votes in New Jersey and all the electoral votes of Missouri.

Secession in South Carolina

When the news of Lincoln's election reached South Carolina, the legislature called for a state convention to discuss leaving the Union. Delegates met in Charleston on December 20, 1860. All the delegates voted that "the union now subsisting [existing] between South Carolina and other States" was ended. The headline of the city's main newspaper, the *Charleston Mercury*, read "The Union Is Dissolved." *Union* usually refers to the entire United States. During the Civil War, however, the northern states were known as the Union, while the states that seceded were known as the **Confederacy**, or the Confederate States of America.

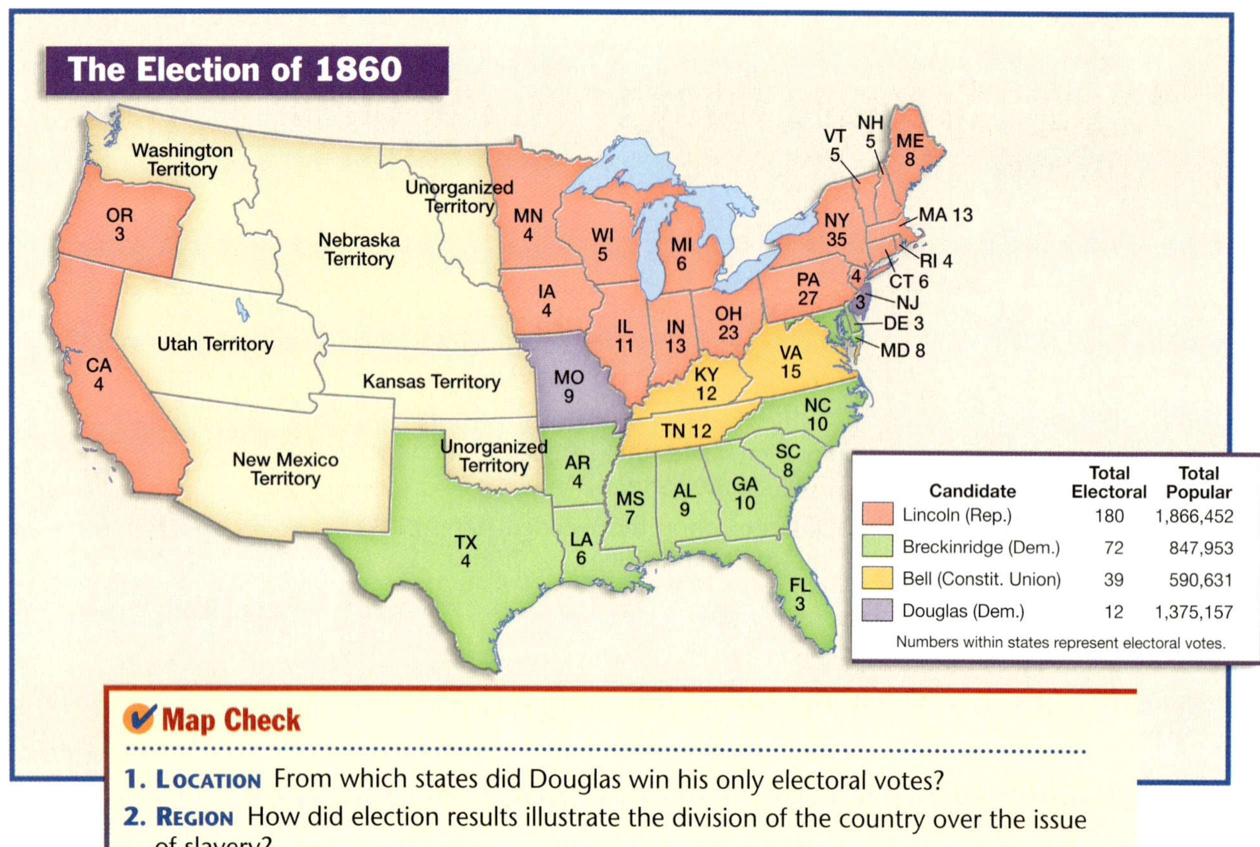

Map Check

1. **Location** From which states did Douglas win his only electoral votes?
2. **Region** How did election results illustrate the division of the country over the issue of slavery?

After South Carolina left the Union, many Americans still wanted to preserve it. Even in the South, some people were alarmed by secession. Some northern abolitionists thought it was best if the southern states left. However, many Northerners agreed with Lincoln that the southern states could not lawfully leave the Union and that the federal government should not allow them to do it.

Six More States Secede

Many Southerners believed in a state's right to secede. Some, however, wanted to wait and see if the Republicans would really take action in Congress to interfere with slavery.

Within two months, six more states seceded. They were Mississippi, Florida, Alabama, Georgia, Louisiana, and Texas. The process was delayed in Texas by Governor Sam Houston, who refused to call a convention. Delegates to an unofficial convention asked for a popular vote. Texans voted to secede after the state had already been accepted by the Confederacy. Eight other states in the South permitted slavery, but no other states seceded before Lincoln's inauguration.

★ **Which state seceded first from the Union?**

B. Organizing the Confederate States of America

The seven states that had voted to leave the Union knew that they needed to join together. They would be weak unless they stood united against the Union.

The Confederate States of America

In February, the seven states that had seceded sent delegates to a convention in Montgomery, Alabama. There, they created the Confederate States of America, or the Confederacy.

The Confederate states drew up a constitution of their own. In many ways, it was similar to the founding document of the United States—the U.S. Constitution. The new government had an executive branch that included a president. There was also a legislative branch called the congress, made up of a senate and a house of representatives. A judiciary branch, or court system, was provided for but was never fully organized.

While the Confederate constitution resembled the U.S. Constitution, there were some differences. For example, the president could serve only a single, six-year term. The Confederate constitution also did not allow the Confederate congress to spend money within the states for roads or other "internal improvements." The president also had the power of a **line item veto**. This veto meant that he could reject parts of a law without having to reject all of it. Oddly, the new constitution did not include the right to secede. Delegates seemed to take that for granted. A major difference in the constitution of the Confederacy was that it allowed slavery in the territories.

Jefferson Davis, president of the Confederacy, was a graduate of West Point and a former U.S. senator and Secretary of War.

Organizing the Confederate Government

In a meeting, delegates elected Jefferson Davis of Mississippi as the **provisional**, or temporary, president of the Confederacy. They selected Alexander H. Stephens of Georgia as provisional vice president. Both men were elected later by popular vote.

Davis appointed his cabinet immediately. Secretary of War Leroy Walker began organizing an army. Secretary of the Treasury Christopher Memminger worked on a tax system to provide the new government with funds. Secretary of State Robert Toombs worked to get other countries to recognize the Confederacy.

The Confederate government operated in Montgomery, Alabama, until Virginia seceded and joined the Confederacy. Then, the Confederate capital was moved to Richmond in May 1861.

★ **How was the Confederate constitution like the U.S. Constitution?**

C. Attempts at Reunification of the United States

James Buchanan was still President during the first wave of secession. Buchanan did not believe secession was constitutional. However, he did not think that he had the power to stop it. Buchanan decided to wait until Lincoln took office and let him deal with the problem.

Attempts to End Secession

Before Lincoln took office, both houses of Congress appointed committees to consider ways to restore the Union. The group appointed by the House of Representatives was known as the Committee of 33. The Senate group was called the Committee of 13.

The Committee of 33 tried to bargain with the Confederacy. They promised better enforcement of the Fugitive Slave Law. They also proposed a constitutional amendment to stop the government from interfering with slavery.

The Committee of 13 had a different solution. It included extending the Missouri Compromise line of 36°30' north latitude to the Pacific Ocean. Slavery would be permitted south of that line. The Senate committee's plan also promised payment for runaway slaves if the Fugitive Slave Law was not enforced properly. This plan was known as the Crittenden Compromise, named after its author, Senator John J. Crittenden.

A third attempt to find a compromise involved the Washington Peace Conference. Most of the delegates were elderly statesmen, such as former President John Tyler, who were no longer involved in politics. Their ideas were similar to those of Senator Crittenden.

The Point of No Return

Lincoln took office in 1861, believing that it was his duty to preserve the Union. He warned that the southern states did not have the legal right to leave the Union. Unlike Buchanan, Lincoln believed the President had the power to stop them from leaving. At the same time Lincoln talked tough, however, he pledged that there would not be a war unless the South started it. He ended his First Inaugural Address with these words about all the states:

> "... We are not enemies, but friends. We must not be enemies. Though passion [strong feeling] may have strained it must not break our bonds of affection. The mystic chords of memory, stretching from every battlefield and patriot grave to every living heart ... all over this broad land, will yet swell the chorus of the Union. ..."

ANALYZE PRIMARY SOURCES

DOCUMENT-BASED QUESTION According to Lincoln's address, what bonds did all the states share?

Yet all efforts to bring the seceded states back into the Union failed. Confederate officials demanded that federal property within their states be handed over to the Confederate government. Lincoln would not agree to that. Confederate troops began taking over federal property, such as post offices and forts. The President did not want to allow the taking of property, but if he sent troops to prevent it, he might be accused of starting a war.

The bombardment of Fort Sumter signaled the beginning of the Civil War.

By April 1861, the Union held only a few forts in Florida and one in South Carolina. Attention became focused on Fort Sumter, located in a harbor at Charleston, South Carolina. The Confederacy demanded the surrender of the fort, but the Union commander, Major Robert Anderson, refused. On April 12, 1861, Confederate forces opened fire on the fort. The shelling lasted for almost a day and a half and ended when the Union troops ran out of ammunition and Major Anderson surrendered. Many people in Charleston had watched the shelling from their rooftops. The Civil War had begun.

 **How did the U.S. government work to keep the Union together?**

IV Review

Review History

A. How did Lincoln's election affect South Carolina and some other slave states?

B. Why did the states that seceded form their own government?

C. How did the Civil War begin?

Define Terms to Know

Provide a definition for each of the following terms.
Confederacy, line item veto, provisional

Critical Thinking

If Lincoln was willing to keep slavery in order to preserve the Union, why do you think that the South still felt it needed to secede?

Write About History

Write a newspaper editorial about the Confederate decision to fire on Fort Sumter. Use either a northern or a southern point of view.

Get Organized

CAUSE-AND-EFFECT CHAIN

Think about the events that led to the first battle of the Civil War. What events were immediate causes of that battle? What events resulted from that battle? Use your cause-and-effect chain to link these events together.

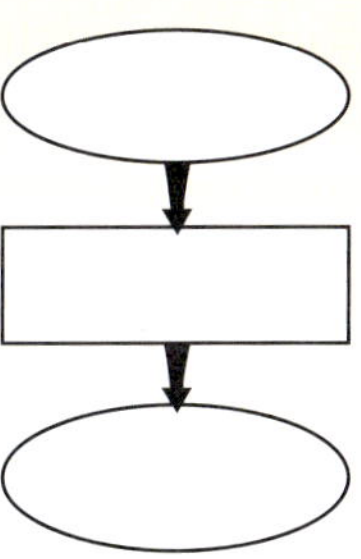

CHAPTER 16 Review

Chapter Summary

In your notebook, complete the following outline. Then, use your outline to write a brief summary of the chapter.

The Road to War

I. The Question of Slavery in the West
   A. Slavery in an Expanding Nation
   B.
   C.

II. Deepening Divisions Over Slavery
   A.
   B.
   C.

III. Challenges to Slavery
   A.
   B.
   C.

IV. Breaking Away From the Union
   A.
   B.
   C.

Interpret the Timeline

Use the timeline on pages 378–379 in order to answer these questions.

1. How long after the Compromise of 1850 did the Civil War start?
2. **Critical Thinking** Which events in the United States and the world show the growth of the antislavery movement?

Use Terms to Know

Select the term that best completes each sentence.

civil war	**fugitive**	**secede**
emancipate	**insurrection**	

1. People who thought slavery was wrong wanted to ________ all slaves.
2. The Underground Railroad was a secret route used by ________ slaves.
3. A ________ occurs when people in the same country fight against each other.
4. South Carolina was the first state to ________, or leave the Union.
5. A slave ________, such as the one John Brown planned, worried many Southerners.

Check Your Understanding

1. **Explain** why westward expansion caused divisions between the North and the South.
2. **Summarize** the main differences between the Missouri Compromise and the Compromise of 1850.
3. **Explain** why there was bloodshed in Kansas in the mid-1850s.
4. **Discuss** how *Uncle Tom's Cabin* changed northern opinions about slavery.
5. **Explain** why a number of southern delegates left the 1860 Democratic convention in Charleston.
6. **Identify** the reason for the formation of the Republican Party.
7. **Describe** the reaction of several southern states to President Lincoln's election.
8. **Explain** the importance of Fort Sumter.

Critical Thinking

1. **Analyze Primary Sources** Do you think that the person who drew the political cartoon on page 382 supported slavery? Explain.
2. **Draw Conclusions** Do you think that resistance to the Fugitive Slave Law surprised people in the national government? Explain.
3. **Make Inferences** How might the presidential election of 1860 eventually affect slavery?
4. **Analyze Primary Sources** Judging by Lincoln's words quoted on page 400, what did he want the states that had seceded to do?

Put Your Skills to Work

CLASSIFY INFORMATION

You have learned that classifying, or sorting, information can help you to understand the relationships between people, events, and ideas.

Copy the chart below. In the first column, write the names of five people from Chapter 16. In the second column, list something each person did. In the third column, write one effect of each person's action.

PERSON	ACTION	EFFECT
Dred Scott	He sued for his freedom.	The Supreme Court judged that the Missouri Compromise was illegal and that Congress could not regulate slavery.

In Your Own Words

JOURNAL WRITING

Harriet Beecher Stowe's book *Uncle Tom's Cabin* changed many people's opinions about slavery. Write a journal entry about a book that you have read. Choose a book that made you change your mind about something. What was the issue? Why did the book have such a strong effect on you?

Net Work

INTERNET ACTIVITY

Work with a group of classmates. Use the Internet as a resource in order to create an illustrated timeline of John Brown's life. Include key events in his life, such as his involvement in Bleeding Kansas and Harpers Ferry. Write a brief description of each event. Then, illustrate your timeline with photographs, artwork, and famous quotations. Share your timeline with the class.

For help in starting this activity, visit the following Web site: www.gfamericanhistory.com.

Look Ahead

In the next chapter, learn how the Civil War divided the nation.

CHAPTER 17

The Civil War 1861–1865

I. The Early Days of the War
II. War and American Life
III. Victory for the North

The Civil War split the country into two warring enemies. Sometimes, families were divided as well. Alexander and James Campbell, two brothers, found themselves on opposite sides of the war. Alexander, who lived in New York, joined the Union army. His brother James lived in South Carolina and joined the Confederate army. After learning that they fought against each other in a battle, Alexander wrote the following letter:

> "I was astonished to hear from the prisoners that you [were the] color Bearer of the Regiment that assaulted the Battery at this point the other day. I was in the [fort] during the whole engagement doing my Best to Beat you but I hope you and I will never again meet face to face bitter enemies on the Battlefield."

The Civil War turned brother against brother and friend against friend. This division resulted in the deadliest conflict ever to occur on American soil.

Hardtack

U.S. Events

- **1860** Lincoln wins election.
- **1861** Eleven states form the Confederate States of America. The First Battle of Bull Run takes place.
- **1862** The Seven Days Battles and the Battle of Antietam occur. Ironclads *Monitor* and *Virginia* clash in a sea battle.

Presidential Term Begins

- 1861 Abraham Lincoln

World Events

- **1861** The czar of Russia frees peasants who had been forced to work for royalty.
- **1862** The International Red Cross is proposed.

VIEW HISTORY The fighting of the Civil War is shown in this painting of General Sherman's "march to the sea." To sustain themselves during the hard days of fighting, soldiers ate hardtack (left), or crackers, and dried salt pork.

★ **What do these images tell you about the life of soldiers during the Civil War?**

Get Organized

CHART

When you read about history, you can classify information to help you find, examine, and remember it. Use a chart to classify two types of information as you read Chapter 17. Fill in headings to describe the information you are classifying. Here is an example of a chart showing Union and Confederate states.

Confederacy	Union	
AL	CA	MN
AR	CT	MO
FL	DE	NH
GA	IA	NJ
LA	IL	NY
MS	IN	OH
NC	KS	OR
SC	KY	PA
TN	MA	RI
TX	MD	VT
VA	ME	WI
	MI	WV

1863
Confederate troops surrender Vicksburg.
The Confederate army is defeated at Gettysburg.
Lincoln formally signs the Emancipation Proclamation.
Lincoln gives the Gettysburg Address.

1864
Sherman begins his "march to the sea."

1865
Lee surrenders to Grant at Appomattox Court House, and the Civil War ends.

1863 **1864** **1865**

1863 **1864** **1865**

1863
French troops capture Mexico City.

1864
French scientist Louis Pasteur develops pasteurization.

1865
Lewis Carroll's *Alice in Wonderland* is published in Britain.

I The Early Days of the War

Terms to Know

border states four slave states located between the Union and the Confederacy that stayed in the Union during the Civil War

strategy a plan

blockade a barrier of ships or troops that prevents goods from entering or leaving an area

Main Ideas

A. The North and the South prepared for war.

B. Both the North and the South had important advantages.

C. The Confederacy won most of the early battles in the East.

Active Reading

EVALUATE
When you evaluate something, you examine it and try to determine its value, or worth. As you read this section, evaluate the plans for victory that the Union and the Confederacy each used.

A. The Buildup to Battle

When Abraham Lincoln was elected President in 1860, many white Southerners became convinced that their rights would no longer be protected. As a result, their thoughts turned to war.

The Confederacy Expands

Six states had seceded by February 1861. Eight other states in the South, however, still hoped that Lincoln would not interfere with slavery where it already existed. Then, the Confederates attacked Fort Sumter, South Carolina, on April 12. President Lincoln asked for 75,000 volunteers to put down the rebellion in the South.

Some of the southern states saw Lincoln's request for militia as a sign of war. So, four more undecided states—Virginia, Arkansas, Tennessee, and North Carolina—seceded from the Union. Nonslaveholding farmers in northwestern Virginia remained loyal to the Union. In 1861, they broke away from Virginia. Two years later, the new state of West Virginia was admitted to the Union.

The last four undecided states did not secede. Missouri, Maryland, Kentucky, and Delaware became known as **border states**—states on the border of the North and the South. These states stayed in the Union, but they sent soldiers to fight for both armies.

The border states were very important to both the North and the South. They had many factories and resources needed by both sides during the war. They could change the balance of power by deciding to join one side or the other. Throughout the war, President Lincoln was very careful not to do anything that might cause the border states to join the Confederacy.

Soldiers wore badges to identify their regiment, or military unit.

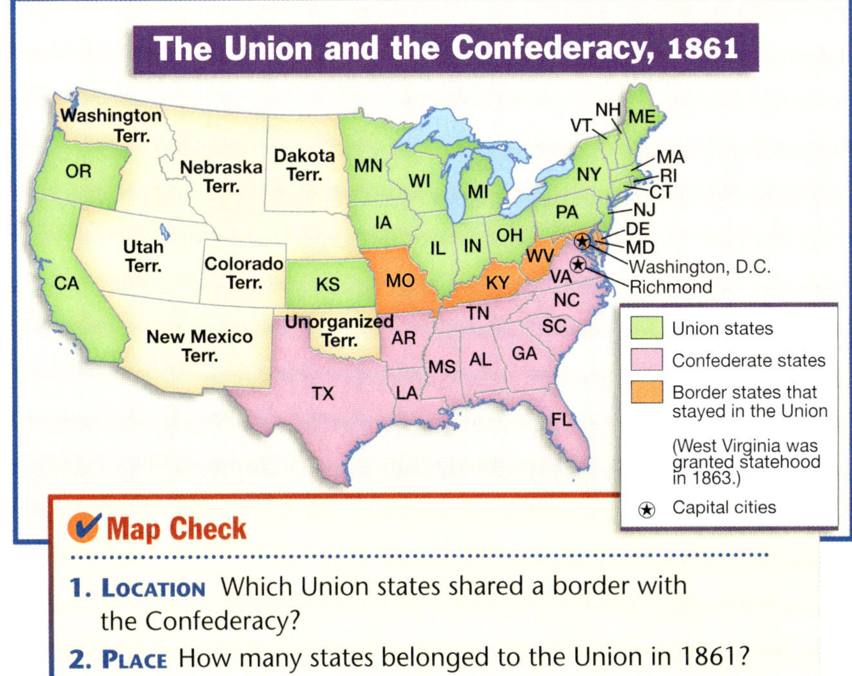

Map Check

1. **Location** Which Union states shared a border with the Confederacy?
2. **Place** How many states belonged to the Union in 1861?

Leadership and Strategy

Each side had its own **strategy**, or plan, to win the war. The Union army had to invade the South and defeat its army. The South would win if it could defend itself and outlast the North.

In 1861, the Union army was commanded by 75-year-old General Winfield Scott. He devised the Anaconda Plan. It was named for the tropical snake that wraps itself around its prey and squeezes the life out of it.

According to the plan, the navy would set up a **blockade**, or a line of ships that would prevent access to southern ports. This blockade would cut off all supply routes to and from the South. Land and naval forces would then seize the Mississippi River valley, cutting the South into two parts. This action would weaken the South by dividing its army and supplies. At the same time, Union soldiers would attack and capture the Confederate capital at Richmond, Virginia.

The Anaconda Plan was a sound one. However, it would take time. People in the North quickly grew impatient for victories. Many wanted to smash the Confederacy instead of slowly squeezing it to death.

The South's strategy was to fight a defensive war. Southern forces would fight only if Union forces attacked them or invaded the South. Except for a few military actions, the Confederate plan was to survive long enough for the North to lose hope and end the war.

What was the Anaconda Plan?

President Abraham Lincoln

B. The Two Sides

The Union and the Confederacy had different goals in the Civil War. Northerners fought to restore the Union and, later in the war, to end slavery. Southerners supported the idea of states' rights. They fought to maintain their way of life, which included owning slaves. Many Southerners also volunteered to fight because the Union army had invaded the Confederacy.

Advantages of the Union

The North had many advantages over the South, including a much larger population. The North had more people to make weapons, provide food, and join the army or navy. About 22 million people lived in the North. Only 9 million lived in the South. Of these, about 3.5 million were enslaved African Americans.

The North had more industry and a better transportation network than the South had. As a result, supplies could be produced and transported more easily. Abraham Lincoln also was a great asset to the North. His leadership and dedication gave the Union troops strength to fight the war.

Advantages of the Confederacy

Even though it was weaker economically, the Confederacy had better military leadership during the early years of the war. Many southern military leaders had trained at West Point, the nation's leading military academy. One southern general, Robert E. Lee, had been offered command of the U.S. Army. He turned the job down because his home state, Virginia, had joined the Confederacy.

The South also had the advantage of fighting on its home soil. To win the war, the South did not have to conquer the North. It had to survive until the North realized it was impossible to defeat the South. Southerners fought bravely because they were defending their land, their homes, and their way of life.

The southern states also had an important crop, cotton. The South hoped that its cotton, needed in Great Britain and other European countries, would lead these countries to support the Confederacy in its battle for independence.

 **How was the population of the North an advantage in the war?**

Spotlight on Culture

Many famous songs are connected with the Civil War. Probably the best-known of all is "Dixie," the favorite marching song of the Confederate army. Surprisingly, the song was written by a Northerner.

In 1859, Daniel Emmett of Mount Vernon, Ohio, wrote the song for a show he was appearing in. He was very upset when he learned his song had become a southern favorite. *Dixie* is a nickname for the South.

C. Early Battles of the War

During the first two years of the war, the South won most of the battles that were fought east of the Appalachian Mountains.

The First Battle of Bull Run

When President Lincoln called for volunteers in 1861, he expected the war to last no more than 90 days. Many Northerners agreed with him. On July 21, 1861, Lincoln ordered 37,000 soldiers under the command of General Irvin McDowell to attack a smaller force of Confederate soldiers at a creek called Bull Run, near Manassas, Virginia. Lincoln hoped they would easily win the battle and move on to capture Richmond. Many spectators from nearby Washington, D.C., followed the Union soldiers. They expected to enjoy a picnic as they watched the skirmish that would bring an end to the rebellion.

As the First Battle of Bull Run began, both sides fought well and held their ground. Then, additional Confederate troops arrived, increasing the number of Confederate soldiers to 35,000. The Confederate soldiers, commanded by General P.G.T. Beauregard, pushed toward the Union forces with a loud, frightening scream, which became known as the rebel yell. The Union soldiers panicked. They fled to Washington, D.C., along with the crowd of spectators who had come to see the fighting.

Map Check

1. **LOCATION** Before which battle did Confederate troops invade the Union?
2. **MOVEMENT** Which battles threatened the capitals of the Union and Confederacy?

Robert E. Lee

Battles in the East, 1862–1863

In the spring of 1862, the Union Army of the Potomac under General George McClellan moved to an area south of Richmond, Virginia. McClellan delayed his attack while he waited for additional troops to arrive. This delay gave the Confederate forces a chance to prepare for the expected Union advance. The new Confederate commander, Robert E. Lee, struck the Union army repeatedly in a series of attacks known as the Seven Days Battles. McClellan was forced to accept defeat.

General Lee believed that the South needed to win the war quickly. He was afraid the North would soon put its great economic advantage to use. Lee planned to invade the North. He advanced into Maryland in September 1862 after defeating the Union army a second time at Bull Run. The two armies clashed on September 17 in the Battle of Antietam. It was the bloodiest day of the war, with more than 23,000 men killed or wounded. Lee lost one third of his army. To Lincoln's dismay, McClellan did not pursue Lee's retreating forces into Virginia, missing a chance to crush the Confederate army.

In December, Confederates defeated the Union army at Fredericksburg, Virginia. Lee won again at the Battle of Chancellorsville in May 1863. This victory was a bitter one, however. Lee's most valuable general, Thomas J. "Stonewall" Jackson, was shot accidentally by his own troops. He died a week later.

Who won the first battle of the Civil War?

Review History

A. How did Union and Confederate plans for victory differ?

B. What advantages did the South possess?

C. What were Lincoln's hopes at the First Battle of Bull Run?

Define Terms to Know

Provide a definition for each of the following terms.
border states, strategy, blockade

Critical Thinking

In what ways did industry in the North help its war effort?

Write About History

Northerners were confident before the Battle of Bull Run that they would win a quick victory over the South. Write a letter to a friend about your feelings after the battle.

Get Organized

CHART

Create a chart to classify the information in this section. For example, classify the battles of the early years of the Civil War as Confederate victories or Union victories.

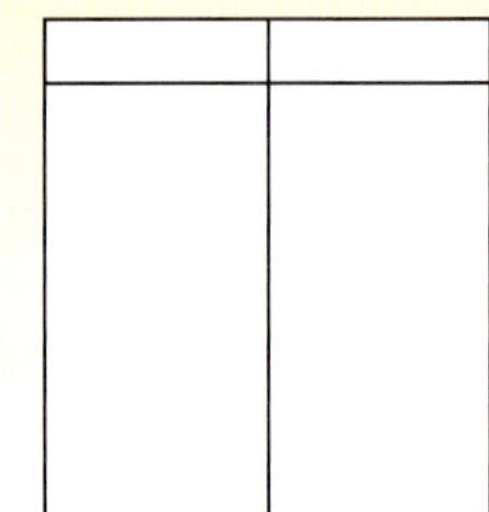

Build Your Skills

Critical Thinking

PREDICT CONSEQUENCES

When you predict consequences, you make an educated guess about something that might happen. You do this by examining what you already know. For example, when you watch a movie you get to know the personalities of the characters. You can use what you know about the characters to predict the end of the movie.

When you read about history, you can predict the consequences of decisions that people made. This helps you to better understand the events you read about. You will also learn how people's decisions have led to consequences, both in the past and today.

Here's How

Follow these steps to predict consequences.

1. Review the information you already have.
2. Look for trends and patterns. Ask yourself the following question: Based on what I already know about this and other situations, what is the most likely consequence?
3. Check your prediction. Were you correct? If not, why?

Here's Why

You have just read about the strengths and weaknesses of the North and the South. Suppose you had to predict the consequences of the North's advantages over the South.

Practice the Skill

Copy the chart on the right on a sheet of paper. In the boxes on top, write three facts from Section I about the North's advantages in the war. Think about how these facts may affect the outcome of the war. In the bottom box, predict a consequence based on this information.

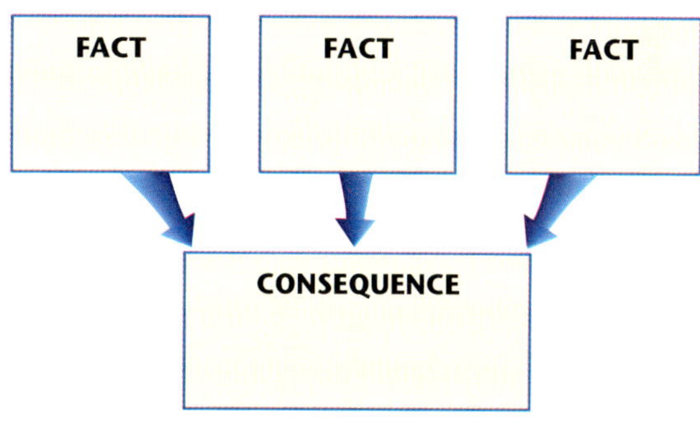

Extend the Skill

Write a paragraph explaining how the information you wrote in the chart led to the consequence you predicted. After you finish reading this chapter, review your prediction to see if it was correct.

Apply the Skill

As you read the remaining sections of this chapter, predict the consequences of the actions taken by the Union and by the Confederacy. For example, in Section III, predict the consequences of General Lee's decision to invade the North again.

II War and American Life

Terms to Know

trench warfare soldiers fighting from long ditches dug in the ground

conscription the act of requiring people to serve in the military

ironclad warship metal or metal-covered steam-driven warship

Main Ideas

A. The Confederacy wanted recognition from other countries, while northern leaders worked to prevent it.

B. Advances in military technology and other developments made the Civil War the first modern war.

C. African Americans played an important role in the Civil War.

SUMMARIZE

When you summarize, you collect and analyze details to make a general statement. As you read this section, summarize the reasons why the Civil War is called the first modern war.

A. The South Looks for Friends

To earn money for the war, the Confederacy needed to sell its products to other countries. Northern leaders worked hard to prevent the South from reaching this goal.

A Search for Allies

Confederate President Jefferson Davis had one important goal in foreign policy. It was to convince other countries, particularly in Europe, that the Confederate States of America was a separate and independent country from the United States of America. Then, these countries might be willing to send troops to help the Confederacy win the war.

For a while, it seemed that Great Britain would formally recognize the Confederacy as a separate nation from the United States. Southern cotton was important to the British textile industry. However, some people in Britain strongly opposed slavery. For that reason they did not want to help the Confederacy. Then, British textile manufacturers discovered new sources of cotton in Egypt and India. Pressure to recognize the Confederacy weakened.

The United States wanted to prevent other countries like Great Britain from recognizing the Confederacy. The United States was represented in Britain by Charles Francis Adams. He was able to convince British leaders to remain neutral. Adams also persuaded British shipyards to stop selling ships to the Confederacy.

The Blockade

As part of the Anaconda Plan, the North's blockade kept the South from shipping cotton to Great Britain. Southerners tried to break the blockade with small, quick ships called blockade runners. These ships could travel faster than the much larger U.S. warships. Yet, the South could not make up for its loss of trade. Food shortages in the South began to reach critical levels.

 **Why did the Confederacy want recognition from other countries?**

B. The First Modern War

The Civil War is called the first modern war. New technological developments and ideas about war shaped the way the war was fought.

New Advances in Technology

The Civil War saw the introduction of several new weapons. Before the war, American soldiers used a weapon called a musket. It had to be reloaded after firing each shot. During the Civil War, the Springfield rifle replaced the musket. It could shoot farther and more accurately. Repeating rifles, which could be loaded with several bullets at a time, were also introduced. The Minié ball, a new bullet invented in France in 1848, could be shot farther than other bullets. With it, a person could hit a target from almost a mile away. Because soldiers could shoot faster, farther, and more accurately, the casualty rate increased greatly during the war.

Trench warfare, or soldiers fighting from long, deep ditches dug in the ground, was used during the Civil War. Trenches played an important role in several battles. Trench warfare became very common 50 years later during World War I.

Soldiers defended their positions from long trenches that often stretched for miles around cities and towns.

Communications and transportation were also improved. Messages were sent by telegraph rather than by riders on horseback. Railroads were widely used to transport soldiers and supplies. Finding enemy positions was made easier by sky views from hot air balloons.

Serving in the Army

Many men were needed to fight the battles of the Civil War. At first, both sides counted on volunteers. However, this system did not produce enough soldiers. In 1862, the South passed a law that called for **conscription**, or requiring people to serve in the military. The North passed its conscription law the following year. These laws were the first national draft laws in U.S. history. A draft is the process by which people are selected for service without their expressed consent. However, the Union's law allowed people to pay a fee of $300 to avoid being drafted. This angered people who could not afford to pay to evade fighting. They felt it favored the wealthy.

Soldiers spent most of their time in temporary camps or traveling to new camps. When they arrived at a new site, soldiers often needed to cut down trees and put up tents. They had to cope with boredom, bad weather, and disease. More than twice as many men died from disease as died in battle. Food was often scarce, unsafe, or unpleasant, as one Union soldier recalled.

ANALYZE PRIMARY SOURCES

DOCUMENT-BASED QUESTION Why do you think Civil War soldiers did not throw out unpleasant food?

> "It was no uncommon occurrence for a man to find the surface of his pot of coffee swimming with weevils [beetles] after breaking up hardtack in it . . . but they were easily skimmed off and left no distinctive flavor behind."

After men left home for battle, many women took over their work. In the South, women learned to run plantations and farms. Others worked in factories or other businesses to support their families. Hundreds of women became wartime nurses. Clara Barton, who became famous as a nurse for the Union army, later founded the American Red Cross. Sally Louisa Tompkins created a hospital for southern soldiers. A few women served as spies, and almost 400 women disguised themselves as men so they could fight.

Women such as Anne Bell helped the war effort in many ways, including serving as nurses for wounded soldiers.

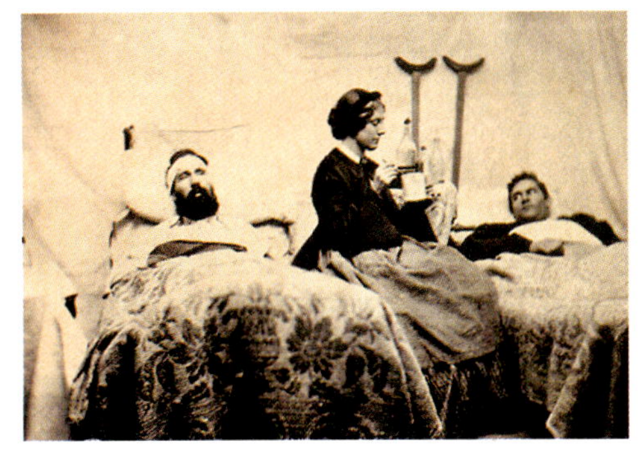

New arrangements were made for prisoners of war. In earlier wars, prisoners were exchanged or released soon after each battle. During the early years of the Civil War, prisoners were allowed to go home if they promised not to fight again. By 1863, however, both sides were keeping prisoners in camps to prevent them from returning to battle.

Most prisoners in camps were treated poorly. They were forced to live in filthy, cramped shelters and were given little food. Almost 50,000 people died in these camps. One much-feared Union camp was located in Elmira, New York. One of the best-known Confederate prison camps was in Andersonville, Georgia. Treatment of Union prisoners was so harsh that Henry Wirz, the commander of Andersonville, was executed after the war for his unjust handling of the prisoners.

The Changing Face of Sea Warfare

A new development in naval warfare was the **ironclad warship**. An ironclad was either a wooden ship covered with iron plates or a ship made mostly out of metal. The Confederates built the first ironclad. They raised a sunken Union ship named the *Merrimack*, covered it with iron plates, and renamed it the *Virginia*. It was described by A. B. Smith, a Union sailor, as a "huge, half submerged crocodile."

On March 8, 1862, the *Virginia* attacked a group of Union ships near Norfolk, Virginia. Shells from the Union ships bounced off the ironclad. After the *Virginia* sank two wooden Union ships, the North sent in its own ironclad, the *Monitor*. The two ships battled for hours, but neither could sink the other. The *Monitor* was forced to withdraw. After this battle, both sides built more ironclads to use in the war.

 **How did policies about prisoners of war change during the war?**

One unusual feature of the *Monitor* (left) was its revolving gun turret. Cannons were rotated within this structure located on top of the ship so that enemy ships such as the *Virginia* (right) could be fired upon easily.

Spotlight on
History

On January 1, 1863, Abraham Lincoln signed the Emancipation Proclamation.

As he began to sign the paper, his hand was shaking so much that he was unable to write. Feeling superstitious, he paused. Lincoln then remembered that, at the New Year's Day reception earlier, he had spent hours shaking hands with several people. That explained the trembling!

Lincoln continued to sign the document—slowly, but firmly. He signed with his full name, which was rare. Then, he said, "I never in my life felt more certain that I was doing right then I do in signing this paper."

You can read the Emancipation Proclamation on page R6.

C. Ending Slavery in the North

An important event in the history of the nation occurred on September 22, 1862. President Lincoln issued an order that would emancipate, or free, enslaved people in areas still controlled by the Confederacy. African Americans played an important part in the Civil War. Their contributions on the battlefield greatly aided the war effort.

The Emancipation Proclamation

President Lincoln had certain goals in mind when he made the decision to issue the Emancipation Proclamation. He felt that once enslaved men and women in the South heard that they had been freed, they might refuse to work. This refusal would harm the Confederacy's war effort. Lincoln also knew that many people in the North would welcome the abolition of slavery and bring renewed energy to the Union war effort.

On January 1, 1863, President Lincoln formally signed the Emancipation Proclamation. Because Lincoln was not the president of the Confederacy, no enslaved people were actually freed until Union forces took control of the southern states. In addition, Lincoln's order did not apply to enslaved people in the border states. However, the Emancipation Proclamation was a promise that slavery would end if the Union won the war. Henry Ward Beecher, a famous abolitionist, said, "The Proclamation may not free a single slave, but it gives liberty a moral recognition."

The Emancipation Proclamation had several other effects. It made the end of slavery a new goal for the North. Before this time, Union soldiers had been fighting primarily to preserve the Union. Now, it became an important goal to fight for the freedom of all enslaved people. In addition, Free Soil Party members believed that white laborers would have more job opportunities when slavery ended. Finally, the Emancipation Proclamation convinced Great Britain and France not to aid the Confederacy. Both countries strongly opposed slavery.

African American Soldiers

Early in the Civil War, Frederick Douglass and others demanded that African Americans in the North be allowed to fight. President Lincoln feared that if African Americans were allowed to join the armed forces, the border states might join the Confederacy. Lincoln eventually became convinced that African American soldiers could be a valuable resource for the Union. In 1863, free African Americans were finally allowed to enlist in the U.S. Army.

Almost 185,000 African Americans served in the Union army. More than half of these soldiers were formerly enslaved and had fled from the South to freedom in the North. About 20,000 African Americans served in the U.S. navy. African American soldiers served in separate regiments, usually commanded by white officers. One of the most famous African American regiments was the 54th Massachusetts Volunteers. The 54th fought with great courage in the attack on Fort Wagner in South Carolina in 1863.

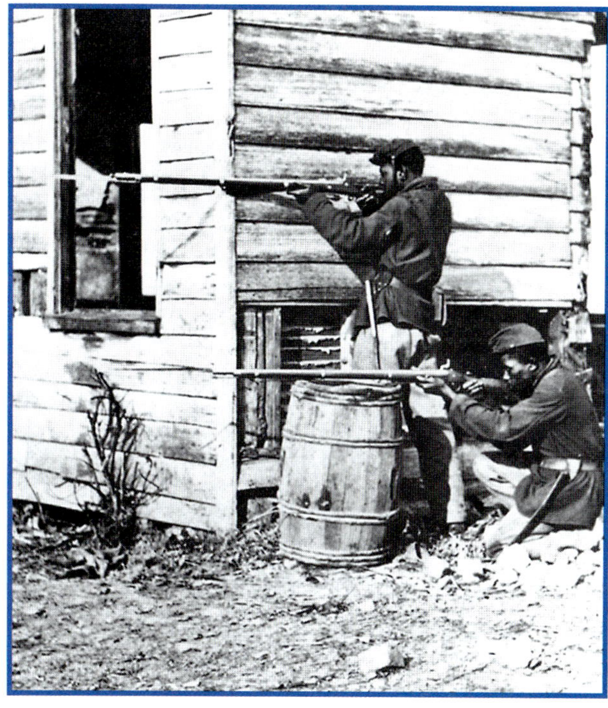

African American sharpshooters

Until June 1864, African American soldiers received lower pay than white soldiers. They had lower-quality supplies and lived in worse conditions. African American soldiers faced an added danger. The Confederacy threatened to kill or sell into slavery any captured African American soldiers and their officers.

By the end of the war, African American troops had fought in nearly 500 engagements, including 39 major battles. About 39,000 African American soldiers died, and 23 were awarded the Medal of Honor for heroism.

 **What special challenges did African American soldiers face?**

Review

Review History

A. How was cotton important to the South's relationships with other nations?

B. What made the Civil War the first modern war?

C. How did African Americans contribute to the war efforts of the North?

Define Terms to Know

Provide a definition for each of the following terms.
trench warfare, conscription, ironclad warship

Critical Thinking

In what ways did advances in technology make fighting more difficult for soldiers?

Write About Citizenship

You are an abolitionist newspaper reporter living in the North. Write an article about the Emancipation Proclamation.

Get Organized

CHART

Create a chart to classify information you read about in this section. For example, classify old and new weapons and technology used before and during the war.

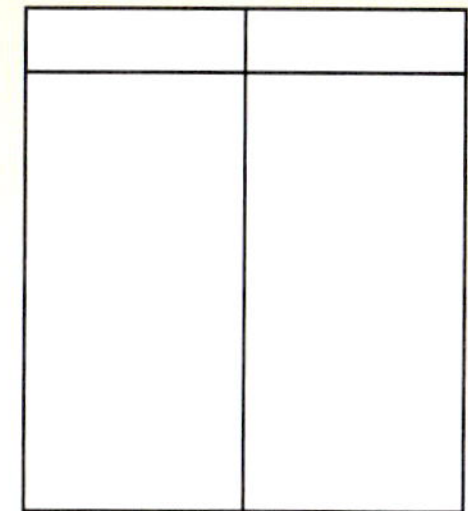

PAST *to* PRESENT

Submarines

During the Civil War, people in the North and the South raced to build a submarine. The Confederates were the first to build one—the *H.L. Hunley*. In February 1864, the *Hunley* rammed a torpedo into the wooden side of a Union ship and sank it. The explosion damaged the *Hunley* and caused it to go down as well.

Some modern submarines are almost as long as two football fields. They are powered by nuclear reactors and can hold more than 150 crew members. Sailors in the U.S. Navy volunteer to live and work in submarines for up to six months at a time.

The *Hunley's* only weapon was a torpedo on a long pole attached to its front. In this painting, the pole appears to the left. The man is standing at the back end of the submarine, near the propeller.

This diagram shows what the inside of the *Hunley* was like. Eight men turned the propeller by hand. A ninth man (not shown) steered the submarine.

4

This view inside the USS *Seawolf* shows sailors working at the main control board.

Modern submarines are much larger than those used in the Civil War. In this photograph of the USS *Seawolf*, contrast its size to the size of the men standing near its top. Now look back at the painting of the *Hunley* and compare the sizes of both submarines.

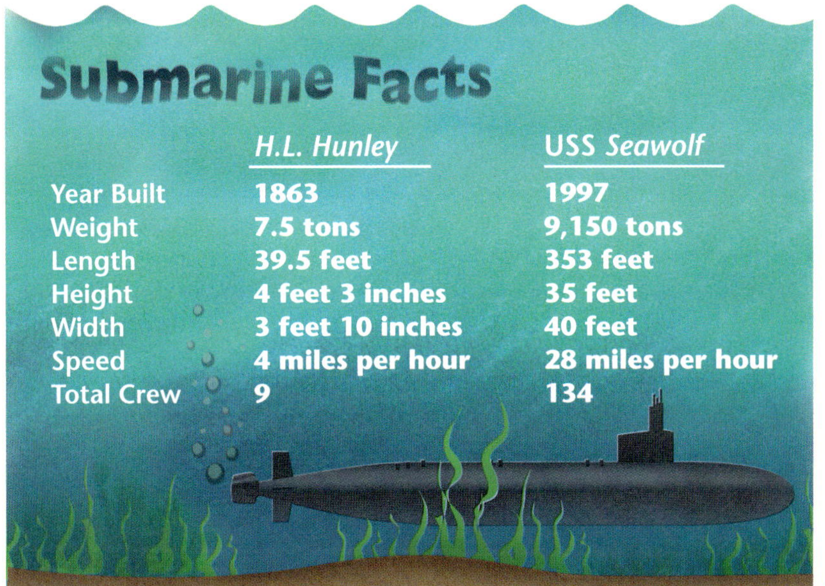

Submarine Facts

	H.L. Hunley	USS *Seawolf*
Year Built	1863	1997
Weight	7.5 tons	9,150 tons
Length	39.5 feet	353 feet
Height	4 feet 3 inches	35 feet
Width	3 feet 10 inches	40 feet
Speed	4 miles per hour	28 miles per hour
Total Crew	9	134

The chart above lists some differences between the *Hunley* and a modern submarine, the *Seawolf*.

Hands-On Activity

What is it like to live and work on a modern submarine? Where do crewmembers sleep? Can they communicate with their families? Using the Internet, "interview" a sailor who has served on a submarine. Make a list of questions, and then answer them by using the information you find. To get started, go to: www.gfamericanhistory.com.

III Victory for the North

Terms to Know

habeas corpus the right of a citizen to ask a court to decide if a prisoner is being held lawfully

censorship control of free expression

total war a war against civilians and resources as well as against armies

Main Ideas

A. The Union army won crucial victories in the West.

B. President Lincoln took some extreme measures during wartime.

C. Campaigns by Union generals Grant and Sherman ended the war.

SEQUENCE OF EVENTS
A sequence of events is the order in which events occur. As you read this chapter, make a timeline of important events to help you understand their sequence.

A. The Turning Point

The Confederate army, battling in the East, had proven to be much stronger than anyone had thought. Yet, Union forces were winning battles in the West. These victories did not, however, cause the Confederacy to collapse. Northerners were asking, How could the Union win the war?

Ulysses S. Grant

Fighting in the West, 1861–1863

In the early years of the war, Union forces fought well west of the Appalachian Mountains. The first important Union victories came in early 1862. A Union general named Ulysses S. Grant captured the Confederate strongholds of Fort Henry and Fort Donelson in Tennessee. Grant defeated the Confederates again at the Battle of Shiloh, also in Tennessee, in April 1862. At the same time, a Union naval force under Admiral David Farragut captured New Orleans, Louisiana.

The Union forces had begun to cut the Confederacy in two. Union troops controlled most of the Mississippi River, which prevented the Confederates from moving troops and supplies. However, the mighty Confederate stronghold at Vicksburg, Mississippi, still stood. It prevented the Union from taking complete control of the river.

The Siege of Vicksburg

In May 1863, General Grant had one goal: to capture the Confederate city of Vicksburg, Mississippi. Control of Vicksburg would give the Union control of the entire Mississippi River and split the Confederacy in two. Grant had wanted to take Vicksburg since the Battle of Shiloh in April 1862. Now, he was ready.

Grant tried five times to capture Vicksburg. The first four attempts failed, but Grant's fifth plan worked. He began a six-week siege, or long attack, of the city while blocking off its supply routes.

With no source of fresh food or water, the people of Vicksburg were forced to eat mules and rats. The lack of food combined with the ongoing siege forced the Confederate troops to give up. On July 4, 1863, about 30,000 Confederate defenders surrendered Vicksburg. Five days later, Union forces took control of Port Hudson, Louisiana. Union troops now had total control of the Mississippi River. The South was now divided completely. They had accomplished one of the goals of the Anaconda Plan.

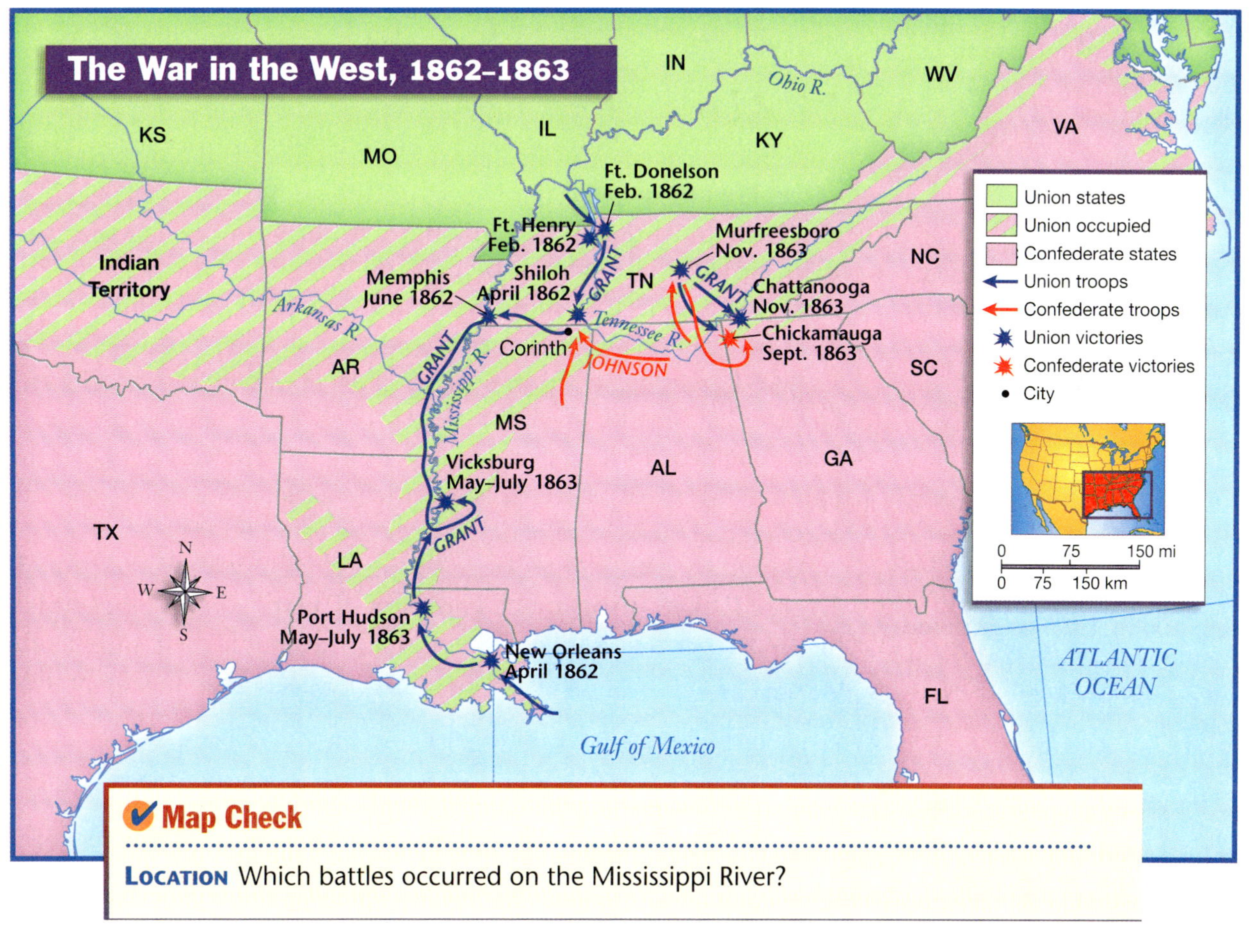

Map Check

LOCATION Which battles occurred on the Mississippi River?

Gettysburg was the Civil War's deadliest battle. Close to 50,000 men were killed or wounded.

Then & Now

The Gettysburg National Cemetery was completed in 1872 to honor the men who had fought at Gettysburg. More than 7,000 veterans are buried there, including soldiers who fought in other major wars involving the United States.

Today, the cemetery is part of a national park, which was created in 1895 as a memorial to the armies that fought there during the Civil War.

Gettysburg

At the same time that Vicksburg was falling to Grant, another battle was taking place in the East. Robert E. Lee believed that it would be necessary to win a great battle to force the North to make peace. He had invaded the Union in 1862 and had been defeated at the Battle of Antietam in Maryland. However, in the late spring of 1863, he decided that it was time to invade the North again. His target was the rich farming region of central Pennsylvania, where he hoped to find supplies for his army.

The Union army in the East, now commanded by General George G. Meade, stayed between Lee's army and Washington, D.C. The two armies met near Gettysburg, Pennsylvania. There, the fighting raged for three days. At first, neither side could gain an advantage. The key moment of the battle came on July 3, 1863.

About 15,000 Confederate soldiers followed their general, George Pickett, in an attack known as Pickett's Charge. Pickett led his soldiers across a mile of open field. Although the Confederate soldiers showed incredible bravery, the attack failed. The open field made the Confederate soldiers perfect targets for the waiting Union troops. Only about one third of the Confederate soldiers made it across the field. Those that succeeded were quickly forced to surrender or retreat. As the fighting broke off, Lee knew he had lost his chance. The Confederates retreated to Virginia. Although Lee and his army continued to battle fiercely against the Union forces, they would never again have the strength to invade the North.

Lincoln's Speech at Gettysburg

In November 1863, President Lincoln was invited to attend a ceremony in Gettysburg. The ceremony was held to honor the men who had died there and to dedicate a cemetery to their memory. The two-minute speech that Lincoln made at Gettysburg is considered one of the greatest speeches in American history.

In his Gettysburg Address, Lincoln reminded the audience of the ideals on which the United States was founded. He stated that the Civil War was being fought to preserve those very ideals. He added that soldiers had fought and died in order to prove that a nation founded on these ideals could survive and prosper. He asked the listeners to make sure that the United States experienced "a new birth of freedom."

You can read the Gettysburg Address on pages R6–R7.

 **What was the key moment at the Battle of Gettysburg?**

B. Lincoln's Leadership

Lincoln's main goal during the war was to restore the Union. Many agreed with his goal, but others disagreed with his methods. Some began to lose faith in Lincoln during the long years of war.

Opposition to the Lincoln Presidency

From the start of his presidency, Abraham Lincoln ran into opposition from people in the North. Some people wanted him to declare the end of slavery immediately rather than move slowly toward emancipation. When Union armies lost battles early in the war, some thought that Lincoln was not managing the war well. Others, mostly Democrats, wanted to make peace with the South and allow it to secede. Some Democrats openly supported the South. These people were known as Copperheads to their enemies because a copperhead is a poisonous snake.

Lincoln felt that criticism of the war weakened the Union. To protect the country, he suspended **habeas corpus**, the constitutional protection against unlawful imprisonment. More than 13,000 opponents of the war were arrested and held in prison without being given trials. The government also closed more than 300 newspapers for criticizing the war. Some people thought this act of **censorship**, or prevention of free expression, violated citizens' First Amendment rights.

Lincoln often visited the Union army camps to discuss strategy with his generals. Here, he meets with two commanders at the Union camp on the battlefield at Antietam Creek.

The Election of 1864

As the 1864 election grew near, not all Republicans thought Abraham Lincoln should run. However, the party nominated him again. The Democrats nominated General George McClellan who had been removed from his command of the Union army.

Many people thought the Democrats would win the election. The war was dragging on with no end in sight. People doubted that President Lincoln could bring the war to a successful end. McClellan promised to end the war quickly if he was elected. Then, events took a turn for the better. News of Union victories lifted spirits in the North. Fortunately for Lincoln, this news arrived just before the election. Lincoln was re-elected by a landslide.

★ **Why did Lincoln suspend habeas corpus?**

C. The End of the War

In March 1864, President Lincoln appointed General Ulysses S. Grant commander of all Union armies. His capture of Vicksburg and his later victories had convinced Lincoln that Grant was the man to beat General Robert E. Lee. After almost three long years of war, the tide finally began to turn in favor of the North.

Grant Moves Toward Richmond

Over the spring and summer of 1864, Grant marched his troops into Virginia. He believed that he could win only by waging **total war**—destroying all food, homes, farms, buildings, and other supplies that could be used by the Confederate army or by civilians. In total war, civilians suffer as much as soldiers.

As Confederates fled Richmond, Virginia, they burned much of the city so that Union forces would not benefit from its capture.

Grant and Lee fought a series of battles near Richmond known as the Wilderness Campaign. Both armies suffered huge losses. However, Grant's philosophy was different from that of earlier Union commanders who let Lee escape. Grant said, "Get at him as soon as you can. Strike at him as hard as you can, and keep moving."

In June 1864, Grant planned a major attack on Petersburg, Virginia. This city was an important railroad center just south of Richmond. Grant and Lee faced off again. As the Union troops began a siege against the city, both sides settled in trenches that stretched for miles. The siege lasted ten months before Lee finally retreated.

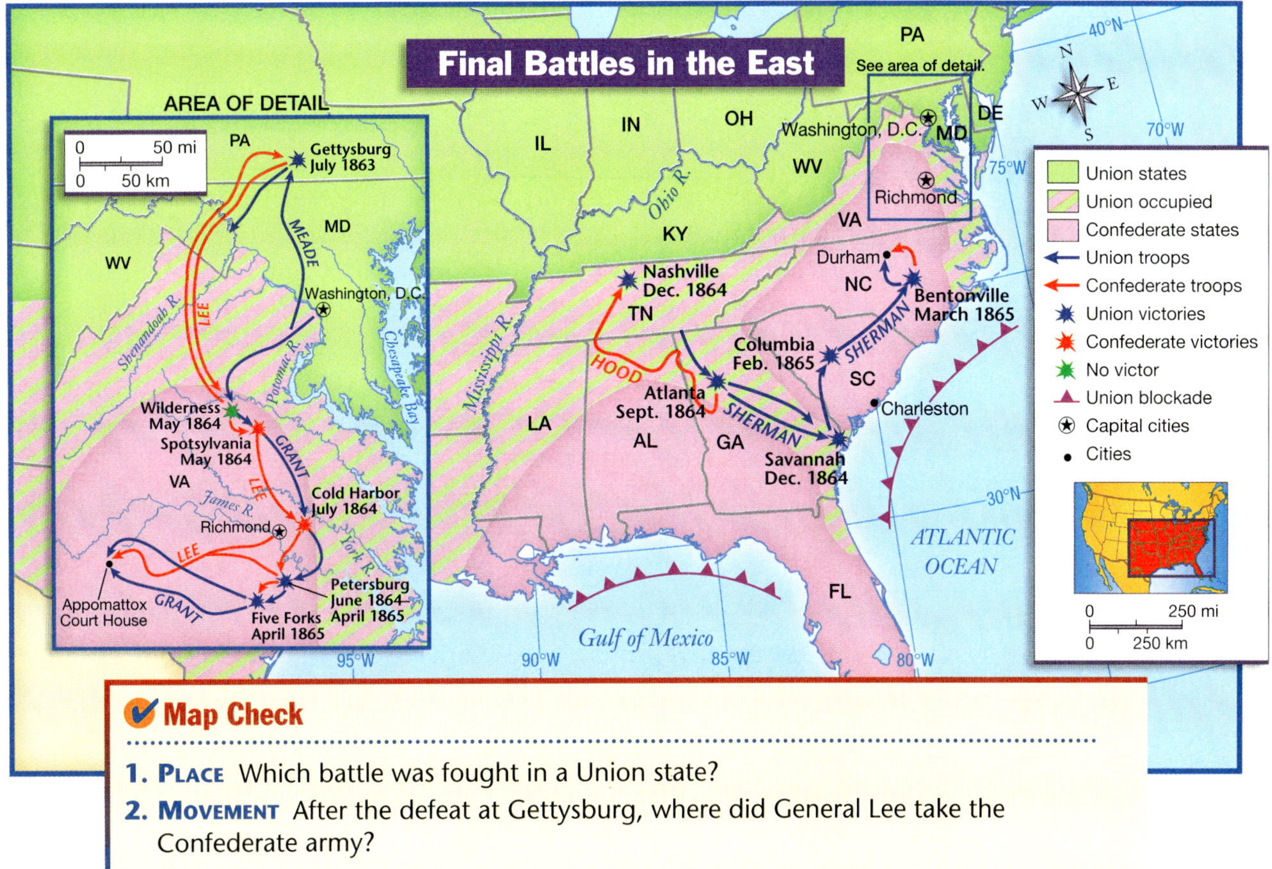

Map Check

1. **PLACE** Which battle was fought in a Union state?
2. **MOVEMENT** After the defeat at Gettysburg, where did General Lee take the Confederate army?

Sherman Marches Across the South

As Grant and Lee battled for Petersburg, General William Tecumseh Sherman took command of Union forces in the Deep South. Like Grant, Sherman also believed in total war as a way of defeating the spirit of the Confederacy. He felt that all people who supported the southern cause were to blame for the war. He wanted them to feel the consequences of their support of the Confederacy's war efforts.

Sherman and 100,000 troops attacked Atlanta, Georgia. The Confederate forces commanded by General John B. Hood were unable to stop Sherman's troops. They captured Atlanta in September 1864. After burning the city, Sherman began his famous "march to the sea." His army sliced a path 60 miles wide through Georgia, destroying everything in its way. The soldiers burned barns and crops, killed livestock, and blew up bridges and railroads. Sherman said his goal was to "make Georgia howl!"

Sherman's army reached the Atlantic Ocean at Savannah, Georgia, in December 1864. The city surrendered without a fight. Next, he turned north, planning to meet Grant's army near Richmond.

The surrender at Appomattox Court House

ANALYZE PRIMARY SOURCES

DOCUMENT-BASED QUESTION What were President Lincoln's goals after the end of the Civil War?

The Collapse of the Confederacy

After losing to Grant at Petersburg, Lee realized that the South's hopes for victory were lost. He knew his desperate army would soon starve. Many of his soldiers had deserted, or run away from, the army. They wanted to protect their families and homes. Lee tried to move his army west, but Grant surrounded it. On April 9, 1865, at Appomattox Court House, a village in Virginia, General Lee finally surrendered. Grant's surrender terms were generous. He even allowed Confederate soldiers to keep their own horses.

The rest of the Confederate commanders quickly surrendered, and Jefferson Davis, president of the Confederacy, was captured. The Civil War had ended. Many Americans had faith that under the wise leadership of Abraham Lincoln, the country could begin to heal. In his second inaugural address, Lincoln shared his hopes for the country's future:

> "With malice [anger] toward none; with charity for all . . . let us strive to finish the work we are in, to bind up the nation's wounds . . . to do all which may achieve and cherish a just and lasting peace."

 **What was Grant's plan to end the Civil War?**

Review History

A. Why were the battles of Gettysburg and Vicksburg the turning point in the Civil War?

B. Who were the Copperheads?

C. Why did General Robert E. Lee surrender?

Define Terms to Know

Provide a definition for each of the following terms.
habeas corpus, censorship, total war

Critical Thinking

Do you think a President is ever justified in restricting civil rights for security reasons in wartime? Why or why not?

Write About History

Write a paragraph explaining what impact total war had on southern soldiers and their families.

Get Organized

CHART

Create a chart to classify the information in this section. For example, classify the military leaders of the war as Union or Confederate.

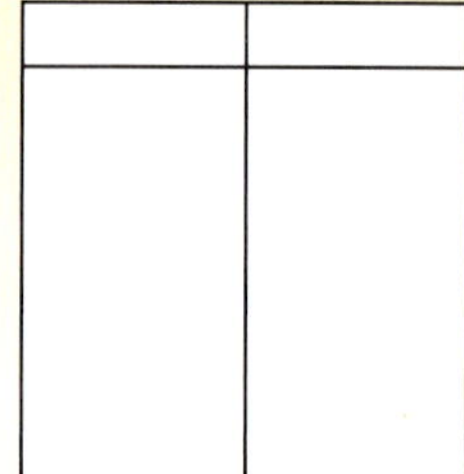

CONNECT History & Technology

The Civil War in Photographs

During the Civil War, photography changed the way history was recorded. For the first time, war was captured in photographs. Portable darkrooms and other advances in technology allowed photographers to record the camps, the aftermath of battles, and the grim realities of the Civil War.

THE PHOTOGRAPHERS Mathew B. Brady was the best-known photographer of the Civil War period. In 1861, he decided to make a complete photographic record of the war. To do so, he hired a number of excellent photographers, including Alexander Gardner and Timothy H. O'Sullivan.

Brady stationed his photographers at various battle sites. Although he took few of the photographs himself, he supervised the operation and may have photographed the most famous battles. He also photographed Abraham Lincoln, Union generals, and Robert E. Lee.

THE TECHNOLOGY During the Civil War, photographs were limited by the technology of the day. Glass negatives were used to print images on paper. Darkroom wagons had to be on hand for developing. Exposure took between 5 and 30 seconds, much improved from the past but still time consuming. This lengthy process made it difficult to take action photos. For this reason, photographers shot mostly still or posed images, such as soldiers standing in front of their tents or wagons and regiments standing in formation.

Critical Thinking

Answer the questions below. Then, complete the activity.

1. Why was it difficult to take photographs of Civil War battles?
2. Brady is believed to have once said, "The camera is the eye of history." Do you think this is still true today? Explain.

Write About It

Use the Internet to learn more about Brady's Civil War photographs. Print out one photo. In a paragraph, describe the photo and explain why it is an important record of history. To get started, go to www.gfamericanhistory.com.

This photograph was taken by Brady after the Battle of Antietam.

CHAPTER 17 Review

Chapter Summary

In your notebook, complete the following outline. Then, use your outline to write a brief summary of the chapter.

The Civil War

I. The Early Days of the War
   A. The Buildup to Battle
   B.
   C.
II. War and American Life
   A.
   B.
   C.
III. Victory for the North
   A.
   B.
   C.

Interpret the Timeline

Use the timeline on pages 404–405 to answer the following questions.

1. How many years separate the First Battle of Bull Run from the end of the Civil War?
2. **Critical Thinking** Which event on the timeline contributed the most to the North's winning of the Civil War? Why?

Use Terms to Know

Select the term that best completes each sentence.

blockade **conscription** **trench warfare**
censorship **strategy**

1. Soldiers in the Civil War engaged in ________ , fighting from long ditches dug in the ground.
2. In wartime ________ has been used to silence criticism of the war.
3. Both sides passed ________ laws to increase the size of their armed forces.
4. The Union created a ________ to cut off supply routes to the South.
5. The Confederacy and the Union each had a different ________ to win the war.

Check Your Understanding

1. **Identify** some of the advantages of the North.
2. **Discuss** the Confederacy's strategy for winning the war.
3. **Describe** the advances made in weapons during the war.
4. **Summarize** ways that women and African Americans contributed to the war efforts of the North and the South.
5. **Explain** the significance of the Battle of Gettysburg.
6. **Describe** the effects of total war.

Critical Thinking

1. **Make Inferences** What advice would you have given to southern leaders planning to fight in the Civil War in 1861? Explain your answer.
2. **Analyze Primary Sources** Judging from the quotation on page 414, what effects did unpleasant food have on soldiers?
3. **Analyze Primary Sources** Reread Lincoln's quotation on page 426. How would you describe Lincoln's attitude toward the South?

Put Your Skills to Work

PREDICT CONSEQUENCES

You have learned how to predict consequences based on information you already know. Predicting consequences helps you to better understand both historical and current events and what kinds of consequences might result.

Copy the following chart on a sheet of paper. Think about the last year of the Civil War. List three events that would have a lasting effect on the nation's recovery from the war. Then, predict a consequence of these events.

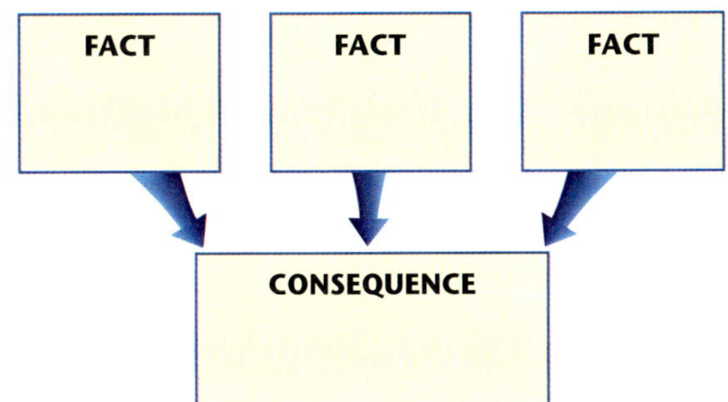

In Your Own Words

JOURNAL WRITING

Although the Civil War was a tragic event, it had some positive effects. For example, one result was the end of slavery in the United States. In your journal, write about a difficult experience you have had that had a positive outcome. Explain how bad things can sometimes have positive results, both intended and unintended.

Net Work

INTERNET ACTIVITY

What was life like for soldiers during the Civil War? What did they eat? What did they wear? What did they do to pass the time between battles? Working with a partner, research and create a short presentation on some part of the life of a soldier in the Union or Confederate army. Include photos, songs, letters, or journal entries—anything that would help show how soldiers lived during the war. Share your presentation with the class.

For help in starting this activity, visit the following Web site: www.gfamericanhistory.com.

Look Ahead

In the next chapter, learn how the nation struggled to rebuild after the Civil War.

CHAPTER 18

Reunion and Reconstruction 1865–1877

I. Reuniting a Nation
II. Conflicts Over Reconstruction
III. The New South

The challenges facing the country after the Civil War were enormous. The federal government needed to reunite the nation. It also had to rebuild the South's ruined cities and shattered economy. Perhaps the greatest challenge was helping millions of newly freed African Americans make new lives. Millie Freeman, who had been enslaved, remembered how difficult it was to move forward when she said,

> "It seemed like it took a long time for freedom to come. Everything just kept on like it was."

The defeated South resisted the North's plans, especially in helping African Americans. Although the nation's wounds were beginning to heal, the scars of war would last for many years.

Primer used in the 1800s

U.S. Events

1865
Civil War ends.
Abraham Lincoln is assassinated.
Freedmen's Bureau is created.
Thirteenth Amendment ends slavery.

1866
Civil Rights Act of 1866 is passed.

1867
Reconstruction Act of 1867 is passed.

1868
Fourteenth Amendment is ratified.
Andrew Johnson is impeached and acquitted.

1870
Fifteenth Amendment is ratified.
Hiram Revels and Blanche Bruce become the first African American senators.

U.S. Events: 1865 — 1868 — 1871

Presidential Term Begins: 1865 Andrew Johnson — 1869 Ulysses S. Grant

World Events: 1865 — 1868 — 1871

World Events

1866
Gregor Mendel begins study of genetics.

1868
Meiji restoration in Japan occurs.

1871
Germany is unified under Prussian leadership.

VIEW HISTORY After the Civil War, newly freed African Americans—from young children to adult men and women—attended schools in the South in order to gain an education. Supplies at these schools often included primers, or early reading books (shown left), that were donated.

★ **For newly freed slaves, what were some possible social and economic advantages in learning how to read and write?**

Get Organized

FLOWCHART

Understanding the order in which events happen can help you to understand the relationship that one event has with another. Create a flowchart as you read Chapter 18. List important events in the correct sequence on the flowchart. Here is an example from this chapter.

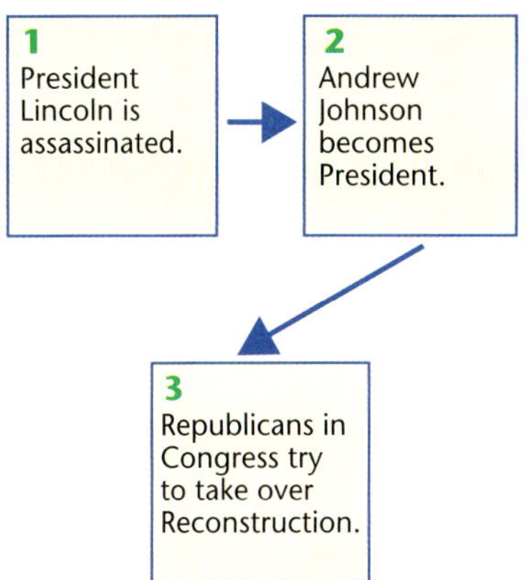

1872 Freedmen's Bureau closes.

1877 Reconstruction ends.

1874 | 1877 | 1880

1877 Rutherford B. Hayes

1874 | 1877 | 1880

1873 Ruins of Troy, in northwestern Turkey, are discovered by archaeologists.

1876 Queen Victoria becomes empress of India.

I Reuniting a Nation

Terms to Know

Reconstruction the period from 1865 to 1877 in which programs were created to reunite the South with the North

amnesty a government pardon for an offense

black codes a series of laws passed in early Reconstruction to limit the freedoms of formerly enslaved African Americans

Main Ideas

A. President Lincoln had hoped to reunite the country, but he was assassinated before he could carry out his plans.

B. Different ideas about how to reunite the nation divided President Andrew Johnson and Congress, while African Americans' rights were being challenged in the South.

POINTS OF VIEW

How do different people feel about important issues? As you read this section, ask yourself the following question: What did President Johnson and the Republicans in Congress think about Reconstruction?

A. Lincoln and Reconstruction

The 12 years after the Civil War are known as **Reconstruction**. During this period, the federal government looked for a way to reunite the former Confederate states with the rest of the country. There were several different plans proposed by government officials for Reconstruction. Like the war itself, Reconstruction caused conflicts between the North and the South.

The Emancipation of Slaves

One of the biggest issues of Reconstruction was the emancipation of slaves. On September 22, 1862, in the midst of the Civil War, President Abraham Lincoln had issued the Emancipation Proclamation. It stated that as of January 1, 1863 all enslaved people in Confederate states would be free. However, Confederate states ignored the Proclamation because they were no longer part of the U.S. government. Instead, Lincoln's Emancipation Proclamation served as a promise to slaves that they would be free when the North won the war.

The process of officially abolishing slavery began in April 1864, when the U.S. Senate, and later the House of Representatives, passed the Thirteenth Amendment to the Constitution. The amendment, however, needed to be ratified, or approved before it could become law. In December 1865, states loyal to the Union ratified the amendment, and slavery was officially abolished throughout the United States.

Spotlight on Culture

Juneteenth is the oldest known celebration of the ending of slavery. It began when General Gordon Granger arrived in Galveston, Texas, on June 19, 1865, and declared the end of the Civil War and slavery. Since that time, Juneteenth has become a celebration of African American freedom.

President Lincoln's Reconstruction Plan

Even before the end of the Civil War, President Lincoln had created a plan to win back the loyalty of the South. This plan was known as the Ten Percent Plan. The Ten Percent Plan would give most former Confederates **amnesty**, or a pardon, for their war actions. To gain amnesty, the states would have to meet the following requirements:

1. Promise their loyalty to the Union
2. Pledge to support the U.S. Constitution and obey laws passed by Congress
3. Accept the end of slavery

When 10 percent of a state's voters promised loyalty to the Union and the U.S. Constitution, that state would be allowed to elect a new state government. Then, the state government would have to approve the Thirteenth Amendment. However, they were not forced to give the same rights to African Americans as were given to white Americans. After approving the amendment, the state could finally re-enter the Union. In Lincoln's plan, the President would be in charge of Reconstruction.

A large reward was offered for the capture of John Wilkes Booth after he assassinated President Lincoln. Booth was shot several days after his attack on the President.

John Wilkes Booth

Death of a Leader

By 1865, most Americans approved of the way President Lincoln had managed the war. They also agreed with his plan for ending slavery and healing the country. The President, however, did not live to see his plan take effect.

On April 14, just five days after Robert E. Lee's surrender at Appomattox Court House, Virginia, Lincoln was assassinated. While watching a play from his presidential box at Ford's Theater in Washington, D.C., the President was shot in the back of the head by a man named John Wilkes Booth. Lincoln died early the next morning.

Booth was both an actor and a southern sympathizer. He hated the Union and its leader. By killing Lincoln, he hoped to gain revenge for the South's defeat.

The President's death caused tremendous grief throughout the North and in the South among African Americans. His body was carried by train from Washington, D.C., back to Springfield, Illinois. As the train passed through cities, towns, and villages, millions of Americans turned out to say goodbye to their wartime President.

Lincoln's Effect on Government

Abraham Lincoln left the federal government stronger than when he first took office. During his term, Lincoln greatly extended the powers of the presidency. He enlarged the army in order to win the war, even though the U.S. Constitution gives this job to Congress.

Lincoln also set a precedent of conduct for a U.S. President during war times. He suspended some constitutional rights for those suspected of disloyalty or those actively opposing the war. At the same time, he introduced the idea that the federal government should protect the civil rights of law-abiding citizens, especially if individual states failed to protect these rights. This idea would grow stronger over the next 100 years.

 **How did Lincoln expand the powers of the federal government and of the presidency?**

B. Different Plans for Reconstruction

Many Republicans in Congress did not support Lincoln's plan for Reconstruction. Some of these Republicans wanted to take strong action to punish the former Confederate leaders.

Congressional Reconstruction Plan

Republicans in Congress were divided over Lincoln's plan for Reconstruction. Some supported Lincoln's plan, whereas others opposed it because they felt the plan made it too easy for the southern states to rejoin the Union.

Some of the Radical Republican leaders included (front, left to right) Benjamin F. Butler, Thaddeus Stevens, Thomas Williams, John A. Bingham, (back, left to right) James F. Wilson, George S. Boutwell, and John A. Logan.

One group, known as Radical Republicans, spoke strongly against the plan. Thaddeus Stevens and Charles Sumner were the leaders of the Radical Republicans. They wished to punish the South for rebelling against the Union. In addition, the Radical Republicans wanted to make sure former slaves gained equal rights. To accomplish their plan, they wanted Congress to control Reconstruction.

The Radical Republicans' plan for reuniting the North and the South was called the Wade-Davis Bill. This plan required that a majority, not just 10 percent, of a state's citizens pledge to support the U.S. Constitution. It also required that citizens swear they had never voluntarily supported the Confederacy. Of course, because most Southerners had sworn allegiance to the Confederacy, this requirement was impossible to meet. Although the Radical Republicans were a minority, or had fewer numbers, in Congress, they gained the support of moderate, or less radical, Republicans in order to pass their plan.

A New President

After Lincoln's death, Vice President Andrew Johnson became the seventeenth President of the United States. Johnson, who was born in North Carolina but later moved to Tennessee, was the only Southerner to remain in Congress during the Civil War. He had refused to join with his state in leaving the Union.

Johnson was nominated as Lincoln's Vice President in 1864 as a way to promote national unity. Throughout his political career, he had been a champion of the common person, standing with poor farmers against rich plantation owners. For this reason, Radical Republicans thought that Johnson would support their plan for Reconstruction.

President Johnson's Plan

President Johnson angered the Radical Republicans by adopting a Reconstruction plan similar to Lincoln's. In addition, he restored property and political rights to most former Confederate leaders. This restoration allowed many of the same people who had led the South before secession to take power again. Both moderate Republicans and Radical Republicans opposed this idea.

The battle over civil rights heated up in 1866. Early in the year, Congress passed the Civil Rights Act of 1866, which gave citizenship to all people born in the United States except Native Americans. President Johnson vetoed the bill. Republicans in Congress voted to override the President's veto.

Meet the President

Andrew Johnson
1808–1875

Years in office 1865–1869

Political Party Democratic

Birthplace
North Carolina

Assumed office at age
57, succeeded Abraham Lincoln

Occupation Tailor

Did you know? Andrew Johnson did not know how to write until his wife Eliza taught him.

Quote "I love my country. Every public act of my life testifies that is so."

Black Codes

Beginning in 1865, southern states formed new governments based on President Johnson's Reconstruction plan. Many former Confederate leaders took positions in the new state governments.

The new governments in the former Confederate states began to find ways to limit the rights of freed African Americans. These laws were known as **black codes**. According to these laws, African Americans were not allowed to vote, hold certain types of jobs, carry weapons, or serve on juries. They also could not own or lease farms. In addition, the black codes allowed authorities to arrest and impose a monetary fine on African Americans who did not work. If a person could not pay the fine, the authorities could rent the person as a laborer to landowners until the fine was paid.

The black codes made life for freed African Americans very similar to life endured under slavery. Radical Republicans were outraged by the new laws. They believed that Southerners were trying to keep slavery in another form. As a result, the Radical and moderate Republicans decided to take control of Reconstruction.

 **Under the black codes, how was life for freed African Americans similar to life under slavery?**

Review History

A. What was President Lincoln's plan for Reconstruction?

B. How did the Radical Republicans' plan for Reconstruction differ from Johnson's plan?

Define Terms to Know

Provide a definition for each of the following terms.
Reconstruction, amnesty, black codes

Critical Thinking

Why might Reconstruction have been frustrating for African Americans who had just received their freedom?

Write About History

Millions of Americans mourned President Lincoln's death. Write a paragraph about the contributions that Abraham Lincoln made to the country.

Get Organized

FLOWCHART

Understanding the order in which events happen helps you understand their relationship with each other. Create a flowchart of events, starting with Johnson's decision to adopt a Reconstruction plan similar to Lincoln's.

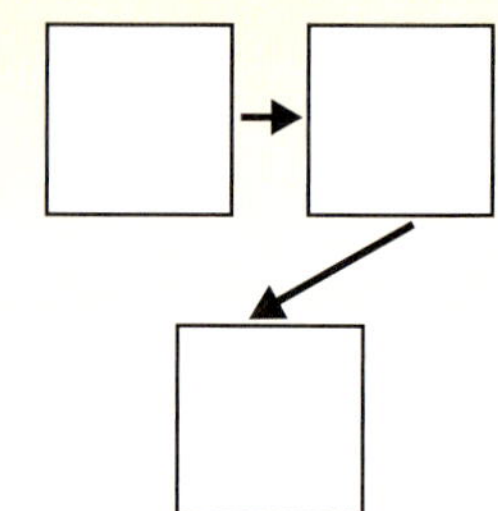

Build Your Skills

Social Studies Skill

COMPARE AND CONTRAST

When you compare and contrast two items, you identify ways they are similar and ways they are different. To compare is to decide how two or more things are alike. To contrast is to find how they are different. A Venn diagram is a special kind of chart that makes it easy to compare and contrast items.

When reading about history, comparing and contrasting places, ideas, policies, or events can help you understand them better.

Here's How

Follow these steps to compare and contrast items using a Venn diagram.

1. Identify important characteristics of items you want to compare and contrast.
2. In the outer sections of the circles, write ways in which the items are different.
3. In the section shared by both circles, write ways in which the two items are alike.
4. Draw conclusions based on your diagram.

Here's Why

You have just read about different plans for Reconstruction proposed by Congress and by Presidents Lincoln and Johnson. Suppose you had to answer an essay question about comparing and contrasting these plans. Using a Venn diagram would help you organize your information and construct your answer.

Practice the Skill

Copy the Venn diagram on a sheet of paper. Review Section I, and fill in the diagram with information from the section about the different plans for Reconstruction.

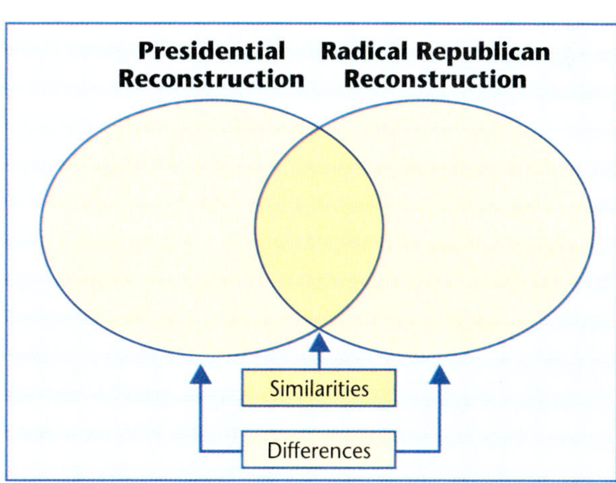

Extend the Skill

Write an essay based on the following direction: Compare and contrast the combined Reconstruction plans of Presidents Lincoln and Johnson with that of the Republicans in Congress.

Apply the Skill

As you read the remaining sections of this chapter, think about ways you can compare and contrast information. For example, you could compare and contrast the lives of white Southerners before and after the Civil War.

II Conflicts Over Reconstruction

Terms to Know

carpetbagger a Northerner who moved to the South after the Civil War for political gain

scalawag a white Southerner who supported the Republicans during Reconstruction

discrimination unjust treatment of someone based on prejudice

impeachment the process of charging a high public official, such as the President, with a crime

Main Ideas

A. Disagreement over the Fourteenth Amendment led to a showdown between the President and Congress.

B. Republicans in Congress took control of Reconstruction and created new governments of southern states.

C. Republicans failed to remove President Johnson from office by a single vote.

Active Reading

CAUSE AND EFFECT
A cause is a person, a thing, or an event that makes something happen. Whatever happens is called a result, or an effect. As you read this section, look for examples of causes and effects.

A. The Struggle for Control

To protect the Civil Rights Act of 1866, Republicans decided to amend the Constitution. Then, by winning most of the seats in Congress, they took control of Reconstruction.

Defining a Citizen

Because Republican leaders were afraid that the Supreme Court would rule the Civil Rights Act of 1866 unconstitutional, they passed the Fourteenth Amendment to the U.S. Constitution, which defined who a citizen was. The following ideas were included in the amendment.

1. Anyone born or naturalized in the United States (except Native Americans) and ruled by its laws is a citizen.
2. States cannot make laws that take away any rights of citizens.
3. States that limit any man's—including any African American man's—right to vote will lose representation in Congress.
4. No former Confederate leaders can hold a government office.

Congress then said that any state wishing to rejoin the Union had to ratify the Fourteenth Amendment. President Johnson, however, discouraged the states from ratifying the amendment. In the end, only Tennessee ratified it. The other 10 states of the former Confederacy refused. This disagreement about ratification of the Fourteenth Amendment set the stage for a final showdown between President Johnson and Congress.

Do You Remember?
In Chapter 16, you read about the Supreme Court's Dred Scott decision. This decision said that Dred Scott was not a citizen and had no rights.

The Election of 1866

The congressional election of 1866 became a contest between President Andrew Johnson's Reconstruction plan and the Reconstruction plan proposed by the Republicans. Johnson urged Americans to elect representatives in the House of Representatives and the Senate who supported his ideas. The voters, however, spoke out clearly for the Republicans. They won enough seats to pass any law over Johnson's veto. When the new Congress assembled in early 1867, the members were in control of Reconstruction.

 **Why did Congress propose the Fourteenth Amendment to the Constitution?**

B. Republicans in Charge of Reconstruction

Republicans went right to work shaping Reconstruction the way they wanted it. As a result, many changes occurred in the South.

New State Governments and Constitutions

To ensure that its Reconstruction measures were carried out, Congress passed the Reconstruction Act of 1867. It placed the 10 southern states that had not ratified the Fourteenth Amendment under military rule. It also gave Congress the right to declare that state governments formed prior to 1867 were illegal. Federal troops were sent into those states to maintain law and order.

The Reconstruction Act of 1867 divided the South into five military regions and placed an army general as military governor in charge of each region. The generals registered male voters, most of whom were freed African Americans and white men who supported the Republicans. Former Confederate leaders and their supporters were not allowed to register.

Next, voters elected delegates to state conventions. Their job was to write new state constitutions supporting voting rights for African American men. Then, the voters in a state had to approve the new constitution and the Fourteenth Amendment. When all of these requirements were met, the state was allowed to be readmitted to the Union. By the end of 1870, all the states had been readmitted.

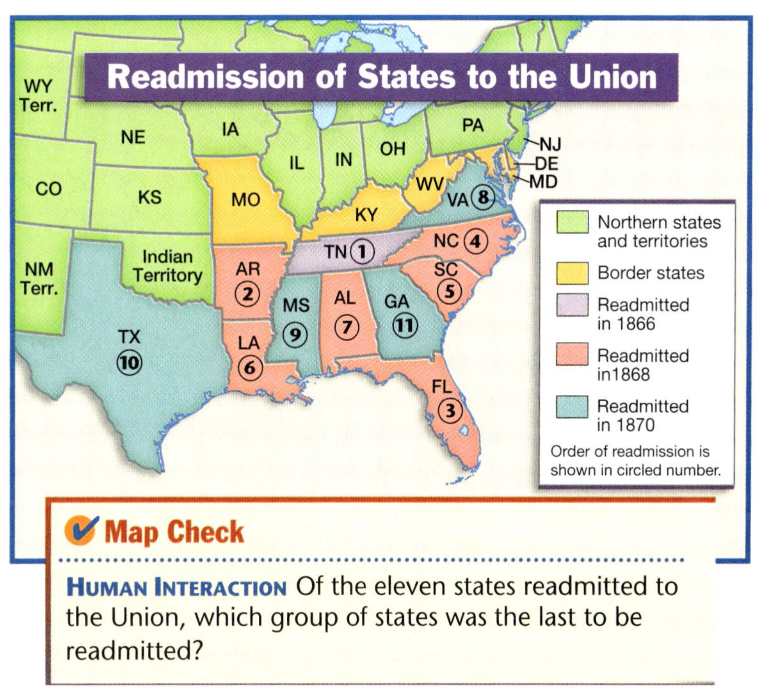

Map Check

Human Interaction Of the eleven states readmitted to the Union, which group of states was the last to be readmitted?

Carpetbaggers were viewed by many Southerners as people who wanted to profit at the South's expense.

A Shift of Power

The new governments in southern states were very different from those of earlier times. They were made up of three groups: African Americans, Northerners who moved to the South, and white Southerners who sided with the Republicans. African Americans provided most of the votes to elect the new governments. However, the Northerners who moved to the South were in charge of most state governments. These Northerners became known as **carpetbaggers** because many of them traveled to the South after the war carrying cloth suitcases called carpetbags.

Most white Southerners disliked the carpetbaggers and accused them of using their government jobs to get rich. White Southerners who sided with the Republicans and the carpetbaggers were called **scalawags.** The word scalawag, used to describe a worthless farm animal, was used in the South as a term to insult people. Most white Southerners thought scalawags were traitors. However, many scalawags were farmers who had always hated slavery. Others were supporters of Republican economic policies.

New Southern Governments and African Americans

The new governments made many changes. They established public schools and built roads, railroads, and hospitals. The governments also reduced the power of wealthy plantation owners. New tax laws required the rich to pay a larger share.

The new governments also eliminated property qualifications for voting and holding office, allowing many poor white men to vote for the first time. Women were not given the right to vote, but they did gain greater rights to own property. Most importantly, the new governments eliminated the black codes. **Discrimination,** or unfair treatment of a person based on race, was outlawed.

Many African Americans were elected to office during Reconstruction. Hiram Revels and Blanche Bruce of Mississippi were the first African Americans to serve as U.S. senators. Other African Americans became representatives to Congress, state officeholders, sheriffs, and mayors. One African American, P.B.S. Pinchback, became the governor of Louisiana.

 **How did Reconstruction change the governments of southern states?**

C. A President on Trial

Although President Johnson could do little to oppose the Republicans, many still viewed him as a threat. They believed that their Reconstruction policies would be safe only if Johnson was removed from office.

Removing a President From Office

The U.S. Constitution provides a way of removing a President from office, but only if that President has committed "treason, bribery, or other high crimes and misdemeanors." Removing a President involves having the House of Representatives vote by a majority to accuse the President of a very serious crime. Then, the Senate puts the President on trial, with senators acting as jurors. It must vote by a two-thirds majority to convict. Only if the Senate convicts a President can he be removed from office. The process in which a U.S. President is accused of a crime is called **impeachment**.

In 1867, Congress passed the Tenure of Office Act, designed to limit President Johnson's power. This law made it illegal for the President to fire a Cabinet member without Senate approval. In February 1868, Johnson fired his Secretary of War, Republican Edwin Stanton, who was working with the Radical Republicans. The House voted to impeach Johnson, claiming that he had broken the Tenure of Office Act. Johnson denied the charge. Republicans, however, wanted to remove Johnson from office so that he could not oppose Reconstruction plans proposed by Congress. The impeachment trial moved to the Senate.

U.S. SENATE
Impeachment of the President
ADMIT THE BEARER
MARCH 13. 1868
Geo. T. Brown
Sergeant-at-Arms.
To be taken up at MAIN ENTRANCE
No.
U. S. SENATE
Philp & Solomons, Wash. D.C.

Tickets for the impeachment trial of President Andrew Johnson in 1868 were eagerly sought.

Impeachment Proceedings

To some observers, the Senate trial was like a circus. Admission tickets were sold. One senator, Edmund Ross of Kansas, described the scene:

> "The galleries were packed. Tickets of admission were at an enormous premium. The House had adjourned and all of its members were in the Senate chamber."

ANALYZE PRIMARY SOURCES

DOCUMENT-BASED QUESTION What does the fact that ticket prices were at a premium, or selling for very high prices, tell you about people's interest in the trial?

Even before the vote took place, all the senators except one had announced how they would vote. Opponents of the President were one vote short of removing him from office. The one undecided senator was Edmund Ross. He was under tremendous pressure to vote against the President. When his name was called to vote, Ross remembered,

ANALYZE PRIMARY SOURCES **DOCUMENT-BASED QUESTION** What do you think Ross meant when he said he could look down into his open grave?

> "Not a foot moved, not the rustle of a garment . . . was heard. . . . Hope and fear seemed blended in every face. . . . It was a tremendous responsibility. . . . I almost literally looked down into my open grave."

Ross said, "Not guilty." With that vote, President Johnson would remain in office. This decision established that only criminal actions by a President, and not political disagreements, justified removal of a President from office.

President Johnson finished his term in office. However, he lacked political influence. As a result, the Republicans continued to control Reconstruction. In 1868, Republicans nominated Ulysses Simpson Grant as their presidential candidate. The popular Civil War hero won the election easily.

What action by President Johnson led to his impeachment?

Review History

A. How did the Fourteenth Amendment protect the rights of citizens?

B. What changes did the new governments make in southern states?

C. Why did Republicans want to remove President Johnson from office?

Define Terms to Know

Provide a definition for each of the following terms.
carpetbagger, scalawag, discrimination, impeachment

Critical Thinking

Why do you think the Republicans wanted to limit the power of former Confederate leaders after the war?

Write About Government

Write a newspaper editorial that reflects your views about the fairness of the impeachment of President Johnson.

Get Organized

FLOWCHART

Understanding the order in which events happen can help you understand their relationship with each other. Create a flowchart listing events, starting with the passage of the Tenure of Office Act by Congress.

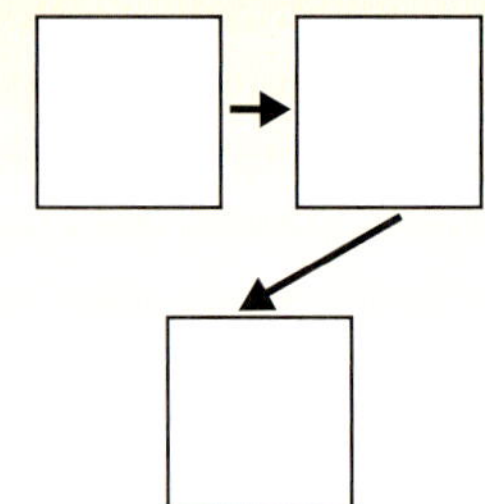

III The New South

Terms to Know

Freedmen's Bureau the federal agency created to help emancipated African Americans adjust to life as free people

sharecropping a system of farming in which farmers work another's land and use part of their crops as rent

segregation separation of the races

Jim Crow laws laws that enforced segregation in the South

Main Ideas

A. Federal programs helped freed African Americans rebuild their lives.

B. Before Reconstruction ended in 1877, white Southerners resisted it through laws that separated races and by violence.

Active Reading

GENERALIZE

When you generalize, you combine details to make an overall statement that describes a situation. As you read this section, generalize about African Americans in the South at the end of Reconstruction.

A. African Americans Build New Lives

All Southerners faced an uncertain future at the end of the Civil War. Reconstruction changed life dramatically in the South. For African Americans, freedom and the end of the war brought new opportunities and challenges.

The Freedmen's Bureau

One of the most successful programs of Reconstruction helped newly emancipated African Americans adjust to life as free people, or "freedmen." In 1865, Congress created the **Freedmen's Bureau**.

Freedmen's Bureau schools, such as this one, were established throughout the South.

This agency, led by Oliver Otis Howard, helped former slaves by finding them jobs that paid fair wages, or pay. It also set up courts to ensure justice for African Americans.

The Freedmen's Bureau had its biggest success in setting up schools. It started 4,300 schools for nearly 250,000 children and adults. The teachers at the schools were volunteers from the North. One of these teachers was Charlotte Forten, who came from a well-known African American family in Philadelphia. Forten described her school in a letter:

ANALYZE PRIMARY SOURCES

DOCUMENT-BASED QUESTION In what ways is Charlotte Forten impressed by the students at her Freedmen's Bureau School?

> "I never before saw children so eager to learn. . . . It is wonderful how a people who have been so long crushed to the earth . . . can have so great a desire for knowledge."

The Bureau also helped establish the South's first colleges for African Americans—Howard University in Washington, D.C., Hampton Institute in Virginia, and Fisk University in Tennessee. The Freedmen's Bureau operated until 1872.

They Made History

Oliver Otis Howard 1830–1909

Oliver Otis Howard was a Union general who fought in several battles during the Civil War. In 1865, President Andrew Johnson appointed Howard to be commissioner of the Freedmen's Bureau. Howard led the Bureau until it closed in 1872. Throughout that time, he was also active in other African American causes. He helped establish Howard University in Washington, D.C., and served as its president from 1869 to 1874. Howard organized a Congregational church in Washington that included both African American and white members. Later in his life, Howard served as a peace commissioner to the Apache people. He also headed the U.S. Military Academy at West Point, New York.

General O. O. Howard led Union troops at several important battles. He was later chosen to lead the Freedmen's Bureau during Reconstruction.

Critical Thinking How does Oliver Howard's work with African Americans in the 1860s and 1870s continue to impact African Americans today?

Life after Slavery

When slavery ended, many African Americans were not prepared for the challenges of planning their own lives. Some left the plantations to make new lives in southern cities. Others used their new freedom to find long-lost family members. During slavery, families were separated and sold to different owners. After emancipation, many African Americans put ads in newspapers trying to find their brothers, sisters, parents, and children.

Sharecroppers were constantly in debt to landowners.

A new system of work, called **sharecropping**, developed during Reconstruction. In this system, many African Americans and poor white people farmed land owned by white landowners. Instead of renting the land with money, sharecroppers gave part of their harvest to the landowner.

The social life of African Americans also changed during Reconstruction. Newly freed African Americans could now openly form their own churches, which quickly became centers of community life.

Another limitation of slavery was also removed. Now, couples could be legally married. To many, legal marriage was an important symbol of freedom and equality.

 **What were the accomplishments of the Freedmen's Bureau?**

B. Opposing Reconstruction

Like African Americans, white Southerners saw changes in the way they lived. Plantation output slowed, Northerners controlled state governments, and African Americans had new rights. Faced with these changes, many white Southerners fought against Reconstruction.

Secret Societies

One way in which some white Southerners opposed Reconstruction was to form secret societies, such as the Ku Klux Klan, or KKK. The Ku Klux Klan was founded in 1866 by Confederate veterans to terrorize African Americans and prevent them from voting. The group also tried to scare away Northerners and those who sympathized with them.

The Klan spread throughout the South. Its members wore white hoods and robes to scare victims and to protect their own identities.

Civil Rights Legislation During Reconstruction

LEGISLATION	PURPOSE
Civil Rights Act of 1866	Gave citizenship to African Americans; protected African American rights
Fourteenth Amendment	Gave citizenship to African Americans; protected the rights of all citizens
Fifteenth Amendment	Protected the voting rights of African American men

Which piece of legislation protected the voting rights of African American men?

The KKK targeted African American leaders and teachers as well as their churches, schools, and homes. Congress responded to KKK violence by passing the Ku Klux Klan Act in 1871. This outlawed the Klan's practices and allowed the government to use military force, if necessary, to stamp them out. As a result, federal troops were sent to the South, and hundreds of Klan members were arrested.

The Fifteenth Amendment

In 1870, the Fifteenth Amendment was adopted. This amendment stated that the right to vote could not be denied to any person based on race or the fact that a person had been a slave.

Although the amendment was meant to protect the voting rights of African American men, enforcement of the Fifteenth Amendment was a problem. After Reconstruction ended in 1877, southern governments found ways to sidestep this amendment. For example, some states denied the vote to people who could not read or write. This excluded many African Americans who had not been able to go to school. In other southern states, people who wanted to vote were required to pay money, called a poll tax, or show that they owned property. These laws applied to all people but affected African Americans most. However, another law, called a grandfather clause, said that if a person's father or grandfather had the right to vote before 1867, then he was now automatically allowed to vote.

Because almost no African Americans could meet this requirement or pay the poll tax, they could not vote. Despite efforts by southern governments to deprive African Americans of the right to vote, the passage of the Fifteenth Amendment made a strong statement of the federal government's position to support African American equality.

Laws to Discriminate

Some southern states wanted to achieve **segregation**, or a separation of the races, in their states. They passed a series of laws that enforced the separation of African Americans and white people in most public places. These laws came to be called **Jim Crow laws**. Jim Crow was an African American character in a popular song—a foolish old dancer who never made any trouble. *Jim Crow* became the name for any law that enforced segregation in schools, restaurants, railroad cars, and other public places.

The End of Reconstruction

After many years of Reconstruction, Americans lost interest in the South's problems. Other issues, such as hard economic times, arose. Many people believed that the government had done enough to help African Americans. They felt Reconstruction should end.

In 1876, Americans turned their attention to the presidential election, which ended up being one of the closest in history. The Democratic candidate, Samuel Tilden, received more popular votes than Republican Rutherford B. Hayes. However, Tilden was one electoral vote short of winning the election. Because the votes of several southern states were in dispute, Congress created a special group to review the election results.

Almost four months after the election, the congressional group made an agreement known as the Compromise of 1877. Rutherford Hayes would be named President. In return, the remaining federal troops in the South would be removed. Without soldiers to protect African Americans' rights, white Southerners quickly took control of their states again. Little time was wasted in returning African Americans to a life that seemed similar to slavery in many ways.

Reconstruction officially ended in 1877, and segregation tightened its grip on the South. Most Americans in the rest of the country turned their attention to other matters.

In the election of 1876, the candidate who won more popular votes did not receive more electoral votes. Tilden did not become President.

This has happened several times in the nation's history, most recently in the 2000 election. Democrat Al Gore won more popular votes, but Republican George W. Bush won more electoral votes. In both elections, disputed votes caused the results of the election to be delayed by more than a month.

 **What was the Compromise of 1877?**

Review History

A. What new freedoms did emancipated African Americans gain under Reconstruction?

B. What was the purpose of the Jim Crow laws?

Define Terms to Know

Provide a definition for each of the following terms.
Freedmen's Bureau, sharecropping, segregation, Jim Crow laws

Critical Thinking

In what ways was Reconstruction successful?

Write About Culture

Volunteer teachers helped educate African Americans. Suppose you were one of these teachers. Write a letter describing your experiences in a Freedmen's Bureau school.

Get Organized

FLOWCHART

Understanding the order in which events happen can help you understand their relationship with each other. Create a flowchart to list a sequence of events, starting with the adoption of the Fifteenth Amendment.

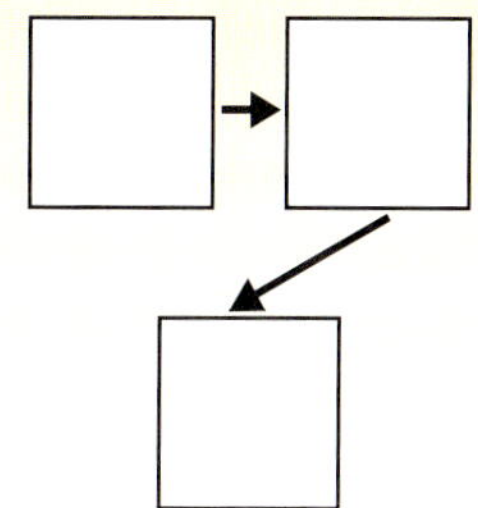

CHAPTER 18 Review

Chapter Summary

In your notebook, complete the following outline. Then, use your outline to write a brief summary of the chapter.

Reunion and Reconstruction

I. Reuniting a Nation
   A. Lincoln and Reconstruction
   B.
II. Conflicts Over Reconstruction
   A.
   B.
   C.
III. The New South
   A.
   B.

Interpret the Timeline

Use the timeline on pages 430–431 to answer the following questions.

1. Which amendment to the Constitution was ratified five years after the Civil War ended?
2. **Critical Thinking** Which events on the timeline promoted civil rights for African Americans?

Use Terms to Know

Select the term that best completes each sentence.

amnesty
discrimination
impeachment
segregation
sharecropping

1. Lincoln wanted to grant ________, or pardon, to Confederates after the war.
2. The unfair treatment of a person based on race or religion is ________.
3. During Reconstruction, many African Americans farmed land through the ________ system.
4. Republicans used ________ to try to remove President Johnson from office.
5. A policy of ________, or separation of the races, grew in the South after the end of Reconstruction.

Check Your Understanding

1. **Explain** how slavery was abolished.
2. **Identify and describe** the ways President Lincoln's death affected the nation.
3. **Summarize** the reasons the Republicans wanted to impeach President Johnson.
4. **Explain** the significance of the Fourteenth and Fifteenth Amendments.
5. **Describe** the role of the Freedmen's Bureau.
6. **Identify** ways that white Southerners showed their resistance to Reconstruction and equal rights for African Americans.

Critical Thinking

1. **Analyze Primary Sources** According to the quote by Edmund Ross on page 442, how was the act of voting for or against impeachment a tremendous responsibility?
2. **Synthesize Information** What new groups of people became involved in the governments of the South during Reconstruction? What factors helped them gain power?
3. **Analyze Primary Sources** Reread the selection from Charlotte Forten's letter on page 444. Why do you think her students were so excited about the chance to go to school and learn?

Put Your Skills to Work

COMPARE AND CONTRAST

You have learned that using a Venn diagram to compare and contrast two items can show you how the items are similar and how they are different.

Copy the following Venn diagram on a sheet of paper. Use it to compare the lives of African Americans in the South before the Civil War and during Reconstruction. In the overlapping area, include characteristics that apply to both time periods.

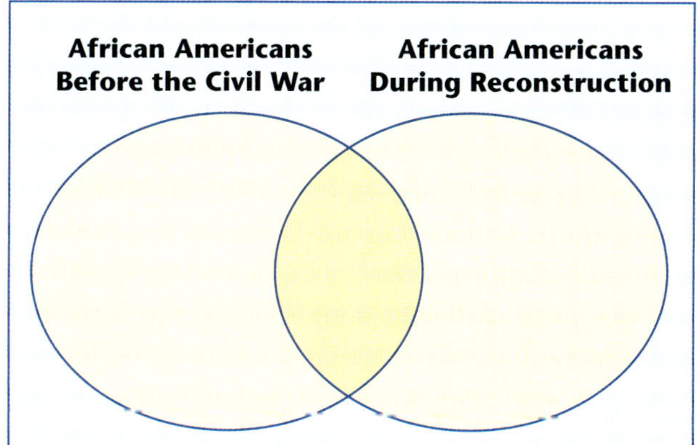

In Your Own Words

JOURNAL WRITING

After the Civil War, freed African Americans faced an uncertain future. Many were excited but probably also apprehensive about their new freedom. Write a journal entry about a time when you were both excited and anxious. Explain what you did in that situation.

Net Work

INTERNET ACTIVITY

Abraham Lincoln is considered one of the greatest U.S. Presidents because of the way he led the country through the crisis of the Civil War. However, he is also considered a great American writer, storyteller, politician, and trial lawyer. Working with a partner, use the Internet as a resource to find sayings, speeches, or stories by the sixteenth President. Use your findings to create a class notebook called "The Wit and Wisdom of Abraham Lincoln."

For help in starting this activity, visit the following Web site: www.gfamericanhistory.com.

Look Ahead

In the next chapter, learn how many Americans joined the rush to the West.

Unit 6 Portfolio Project

Civil War Newspaper

YOUR ASSIGNMENT

It is the summer of 1865. President Lincoln was assassinated a few months ago, and Reconstruction just started. In your class, form five teams of reporters to work on a newspaper. As a class, decide where your newspaper is located. Television, radio, and computers do not exist, so people depend on your newspaper to tell them what is happening in the country and in the world.

THE STAFF MEETING

Choose Your Section Each team of reporters creates one page of the newspaper. As a team, choose one section from each list below to include on your page.

Business	Advertisements
Letters to the Editor	Cartoons and Comics
Inventions	Fashion
U.S. News	Recipes
World Events	Classified Ads

Plan Your Section Plan the articles and pictures for your page. Assign tasks to each team member. Use your textbook to find topics for your page. You may also refer to this Web site for ideas: www.gfamericanhistory.com.

THE NEWSROOM

Research and Write Use encyclopedias, other books, and the Internet to research the material for your page. Create your first draft.

Edit and Proofread Edit and proofread your articles. Make corrections and positive suggestions to your team members.

Design and Layout Paste the articles and artwork onto a large sheet of paper. Combine pages from other teams to construct the class newspaper.

Multimedia Presentation

Now, turn your newspaper into a present-day television documentary that investigates the Lincoln assassination and Reconstruction. Make cue cards that present the main points of each section. Conduct interviews of people who can contribute to the documentary. Practice your script and then rehearse the program in front of another class.

Epilogue: A Look Ahead

Life in the West 1858–1896

Poster advertising western lands for sale

The Big Idea

After the Civil War, Americans again turned their energies toward settling the West. Ranchers, miners, and farmers, all seeking opportunity, traveled west. Settlers came in conflict with the Native American people who lived in the West. The U.S. government forced the Native Americans to move onto land that was far from the land they knew.

Railroads, Ranchers, and Miners

The transcontinental railroad was finished in 1869. Railroads allowed more people to move to the West. Ranchers drove herds of cattle to towns on railroad lines. Trains carried the cattle to cities in the East. Gold strikes in several states brought miners to the West. Silver mining became a big industry, too.

Farming on the Great Plains

Millions of settlers went to farm the Great Plains. Life was hard on the prairie. Rain was scarce. Winters were very cold, and summers extremely hot. For social activity, farmers joined the Grange. They also formed groups to fight unfair pricing by railroad companies. In 1892, farmers began the Populist Party to fight for their interests.

Celebrating the completion of the transcontinental railroad

Native American Struggles

All this settlement was good for the United States. However, it was hard on the Native Americans who lived in the West. Many Native Americans used the buffalo for food and shelter. Yet, settlers and railroad workers killed millions of buffalo to make way for a new way of life. The U.S. government forced Native Americans onto reservations. Once there, they were often mistreated. Some Native Americans fought back. At the Battle of Little Bighorn, 1,200 soldiers were killed. In 1890 in Wounded Knee, South Dakota, soldiers killed about 200 Sioux. This marked the end of the Native American struggle against settlement.

 **How did railroads help the United States grow?**

CHAPTER 20 ★ A Look Ahead

The Rise of Industry 1869–1908

Immigrants looking at the Statue of Liberty

The Big Idea

Americans' way of life changed greatly after the Civil War. New inventions made businesses better able to make industrial products. New kinds of transportation changed the way people traveled. Corporations grew larger, creating wealthy owners. For laborers, however, working conditions worsened. Patterns of immigration changed, too. Millions of people arrived in the United States during the late 1800s. All these people had to adjust to their new home.

Technology, Transportation, and Communication

The oil and steel industries grew quickly in the 1800s. Stronger steel made it possible to build taller buildings and longer bridges. Thomas Edison and other inventors developed electricity. Other inventions included the sewing machine, the phonograph, refrigerators, and barbed wire. Each invention changed Americans' lives. Thousands of miles of railroad track made moving people and products easier. The automobile and airplane came into being. The telephone and the typewriter allowed people to communicate faster.

Big Business and Labor Unions

The growth of industry created great wealth and extreme poverty. Business owners made huge fortunes. John D. Rockefeller controlled the oil refining industry. Andrew Carnegie controlled the steel industry. However, workers' lives worsened during this period. Workers joined labor unions to fight for better conditions. They asked for higher pay and better working conditions. They sometimes went on strike until their demands were met. The government often helped to end these strikes.

Immigration

Between 1890 and 1920, a wave of "new immigrants" arrived on America's shores. They came from southern and eastern Europe. Many could not read or write. Their customs made them stand out from other Americans. Many settled in eastern cities. They lived in neighborhoods with people of similar backgrounds. Many Chinese and Japanese immigrants settled on the West coast. Some native-born Americans were prejudiced against the immigrants. They formed groups to limit immigration.

★ **How did improvements in transportation affect the way people lived?**

Alexander Graham Bell's original telephone

The Progressive Era 1880–1933

Stamp supporting women's right to vote

The Big Idea

By 1880, Americans faced many problems. People in cities lived in run-down housing. Many businesses and city, state, and national governments were corrupt. African Americans and other groups were faced with discrimination and violence. Journalists made these problems public. Some Americans began to work to improve, or reform, conditions. These reformers were called Progressives. The U.S. Presidents of the early twentieth century worked to reform some of these problems as well.

A Troubled Society

As industry grew, so did American cities. However, many workers lived in crowded, unsafe apartment buildings. They worked long hours in unsafe places. In addition, many government officials were corrupt. In national, state, and city governments, some officials lied and cheated. African Americans faced racism. Racism is a feeling against a people because of their skin color.

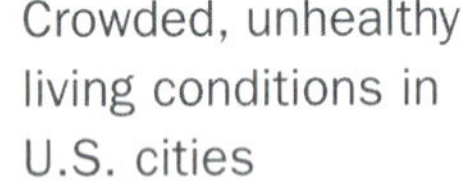

Crowded, unhealthy living conditions in U.S. cities

The Progressive Movement

Journalists helped people see the need for reform. They wrote about inequality and greed. Reformers joined together to form the Progressive movement. They limited the power of big businesses in cities. State governments made factories safer places to work. Other reforms made democracy work better. African Americans organized the National Association for the Advancement of Colored People (NAACP). Women also struggled for the right to vote.

Political Reforms

Theodore Roosevelt became President in 1901. It was the start of a new age in politics. He broke up big businesses and set aside land for national parks. President William Howard Taft continued many of these reforms. He also signed the Sixteenth Amendment to the U.S. Constitution. This amendment gave Congress the power to collect income taxes. Woodrow Wilson became President in 1913. He worked to control how large businesses could grow. The government began to limit the hours workers spent on the job. Women won the right to vote while Wilson was President.

★ **What were some of the problems that the American people were facing by 1880?**

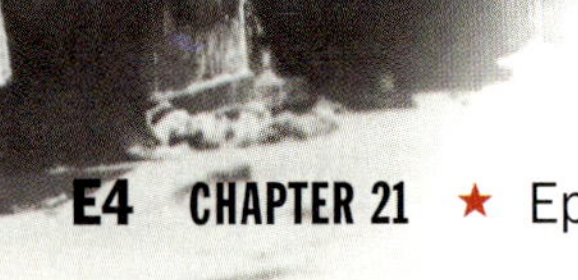

CHAPTER 22 ★ A Look Ahead

Expansion Overseas 1853–1919

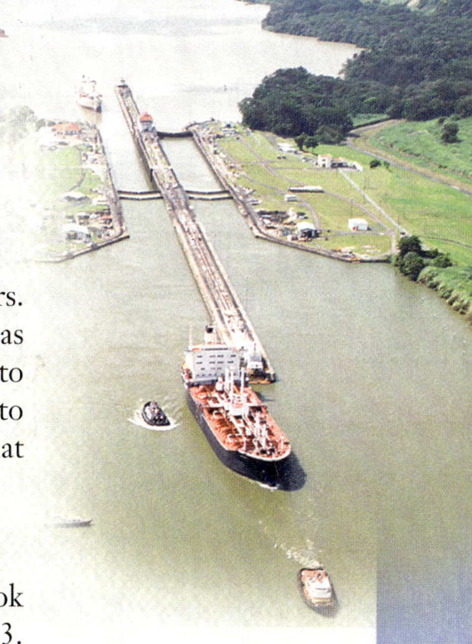

Panama Canal in Central America

The Big Idea

After 1850, the United States began to expand beyond its own borders. Many Americans wanted to see the United States build an overseas empire. One reason the United States sought expansion was to encourage economic growth. In addition, some Americans wanted to take American ways of life to other countries. They believed that people in foreign territories would benefit from American contact.

American Expansion in the Pacific

Even as the West was being settled, the United States began to look outward to other lands. It forced Japan to open trade relations in 1853. It bought Alaska in 1867. The United States expanded its navy. In 1893, it used that navy to force the queen of Hawaii to step down. The United States then took over Hawaii. In 1899, the United States proclaimed that all nations could trade anywhere in China. This proclamation weakened other nations' power in China.

The Spanish-American War

War with Spain broke out in 1898. Cuba was fighting for its independence. The United States sympathized with Cuba. It asked Spain to grant Cuba independence. When Spain refused, the United States declared war. The war lasted only a few months. The United States won. At the war's end, the United States controlled Cuba. It also took Puerto Rico and the Philippine Islands from Spain.

A New Role in Latin America

President Theodore Roosevelt wanted to build a canal across Panama. The canal would connect the Atlantic and Pacific Oceans. The United States bought the land for the canal from Panama. It took seven years to build the canal. Roosevelt also stated a follow-up to the Monroe Doctrine. It said that the United States could interfere in the affairs of countries in the Western Hemisphere. President William Taft used economic power to influence countries in the region. President Woodrow Wilson opposed these policies. Yet, he stepped into Latin American affairs when he thought it was necessary.

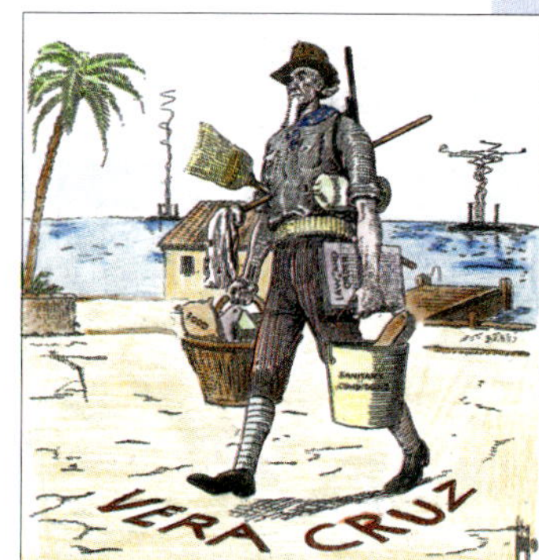

Uncle Sam, a symbol of the U.S. government, in Veracruz, Mexico

 **Why was the United States interested in overseas expansion by the mid- and late 1800s?**

CHAPTER 23 ★ A Look Ahead

World War I 1914–1918

McClure's magazine cover, March 1918

The Big Idea

In 1914, many nations of the world went to war. The war started in Europe, but it spread to almost all parts of the world. The war was called the Great War, or World War I. On one side were the Central Powers. They were led by Germany. On the other side were the Allied Powers, or Allies. France and England led the Allies. The United States kept out of the war at first. It finally entered the war against Germany in 1917. The American effort changed the course of the war. After the war, President Woodrow Wilson proposed a plan for peace called the Fourteen Points.

War in Europe

The stage was set for war in Europe. Nations had begun to build up the number of weapons they had years earlier. They signed alliances, pledging to support each other if attacked. When the Austrian Archduke Franz Ferdinand was assassinated, war broke out. For a time, the war had two fronts. Russian troops fought the Central Powers on the eastern front. French and British soldiers fought on the western front. New technology changed the way people fought. Submarines, airplanes, armored tanks, and poison gas made this a deadlier war than ever before.

The United States Enters the War

For years, the United States kept out of the conflict. In 1917, however, Germany sank five American ships in one month. The U.S. Congress declared war. In time, about 4 million Americans joined the armed services. On the home front, women did men's jobs. Americans bought Liberty Bonds to help pay for the war. Anti-German feelings ran high.

World War I fighter plane

Fighting the War

After the Russian Revolution, Russia withdrew from the war. Americans fought the Germans in France. The German forces were strong. Finally, Germany surrendered on November 11, 1918. The war was over. Planning for peace was almost as hard as winning the war. President Wilson's plan for peace was not well liked by the U.S. Congress. The last point was the creation of a League of Nations, which would settle arguments between nations. The United States never joined the League.

 **What event caused the United States to enter World War I?**

CHAPTER 24 ★ A Look Ahead

Life in the 1920s 1920–1929

Automobiles in the 1920s

The Big Idea

The United States began to recover from World War I in the 1920s. Business boomed. The automobile industry more than doubled. Jazz and the blues became popular music forms. Women gained the right to vote. The 1920s, or Roaring Twenties as the time was called, had its dark side, too. Prejudiced groups, such as the Ku Klux Klan, grew in numbers. Racial tensions ran high.

Business Booms

President Warren Harding offered Americans a return to "normalcy" after the war. This meant a focus on promoting business. However, scandals rocked Harding's administration. Republican Presidents Calvin Coolidge and Herbert Hoover also favored business. Assembly-line production made goods cheaper to buy. The advertising industry urged people to keep buying. People began to buy goods using credit. Yet, American workers struggled to earn a fair wage.

The Roaring Twenties

Americans had more leisure time than ever before. They could turn their attention to culture and entertainment. African American musicians brought jazz and the blues to the nation. Artists and poets flourished too, especially in Harlem, New York. F. Scott Fitzgerald and other writers described the changes in American society. The movie industry was wildly popular. Sports figures such as Babe Ruth became heroes. So did flying aces like Charles Lindbergh. Women gained more freedom and greater rights in the 1920s.

Blues singer Bessie Smith

A Time of Unrest

The 1920s were not all golden, however. Organized crime increased. Groups such as the Ku Klux Klan spread fear. People who were thought to be Communists were jailed. Immigration numbers were set by the government. Groups of people with rigid ideas and ways of life grew in number. In a famous court trial called the Scopes trial, a teacher was prosecuted for teaching about evolution.

 **What kinds of popular entertainment were there in the 1920s?**

The Great Depression and the New Deal 1929–1940

A bushel of apples for sale during the Great Depression

The Big Idea

The Great Depression began with the stock market crash in 1929. Americans lost their jobs and their savings. Business owners, factory workers, and farmers were hit hard. The federal government did not help enough. The election of Franklin D. Roosevelt as President in 1932 gave many Americans new hope. Roosevelt's New Deal called for many kinds of government aid.

The Stock Market Crash

The stock market kept rising through the 1920s. People invested, thinking that there was no limit to the rise. In the autumn of 1929, however, the stock prices began to drop. The stock market crashed for two reasons. First, buyers lost confidence. Second, the economy had been producing too much. After the crash, factories slowed down. Millions lost their jobs. Banks failed. Local and state governments tried to help, but they ran out of money. The federal government did not help much. Drought in the Midwest added to farmers' problems. Farmers' crops were ruined and millions of farmers lost their land.

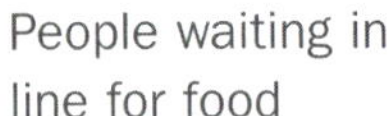

People waiting in line for food

Hard Times at Home

The depression was a hard time in American history. Many people lived in communities of shacks. African Americans were hit even harder. They were the first to lose their jobs. Mexican Americans faced greater discrimination, too. Veteran soldiers formed the Bonus Army. They went to Washington, D.C., to ask for a bonus for their service during World War I. The government refused to talk to them. Then, Franklin Delano Roosevelt was elected President by a landslide. Americans were ready for a change.

The New Deal

President Roosevelt asked Congress to help end the Great Depression by passing new laws. Some laws were about creating jobs. Other laws provided relief for farmers and others. The New Deal programs helped Americans. They led to more power for many groups. The role of the federal government grew as well. Yet, the depression continued to drag on.

What caused the stock market to crash in 1929?

CHAPTER 26 ★ A Look Ahead

World War II 1939–1945

The Big Idea

Less than 20 years after World War I ended, Europe was at war again. Germany, Italy, and Japan made up the Axis Powers. Great Britain and France led the Allies. The United States tried to stay neutral. Then, Japan attacked Pearl Harbor, Hawaii, in 1941. The United States declared war. The United States fought in Europe, in northern Africa, and in the South Pacific. After years of fighting, Germany finally surrendered.

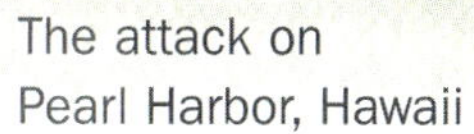

The attack on Pearl Harbor, Hawaii

The Road to War

The 1930s were hard in Europe. Some countries turned to dictators to solve their problems. In Germany, the Nazi Party came into power. Its leader, Adolf Hitler, wanted Germany to be strong again. He formed the Axis Powers with Italy and Japan. Japan invaded China twice in the 1930s. Hitler took control of other countries. Germany invaded Poland in 1939. Finally, Great Britain and France declared war.

The World at War

By 1941, Germany had conquered most of Europe. Only Great Britain remained unbeaten. Then, Hitler attacked the Soviet Union. The Soviet Union joined the Allies. In the Pacific region, the United States stood in the way of further Japanese aggression. So, Japan bombed Pearl Harbor on December 7, 1941. Now, the United States became an Allied Power. Allied troops forced Axis troops out of northern Africa by 1943. The German invasion of the Soviet Union failed. The Allies invaded northern France on D-day—June 6, 1944. It was the largest land-and-sea attack in history.

Winning the War

The American war effort was huge. The war ended the Great Depression. In the Pacific region, the Japanese advance was halted at the Battle of Midway. American troops got closer and closer to Japan. In Europe, Germany was near defeat. Allies discovered the Nazi concentration camps. Millions of people had been murdered in these places. Germany surrendered on May 8, 1945. The United States dropped two atomic bombs on Japan. Japan surrendered on August 15, 1945. The long and terrible war was finally over.

Poster encouraging women to support the war effort

★ **What happened when Japan attacked Pearl Harbor?**

The Cold War 1945–1960

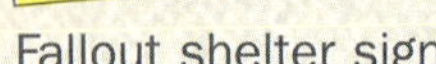
Fallout shelter sign

The Big Idea

After World War II, the world became divided. The United States, Western Europe, and their allies were on one side. The Soviet Union and the nations it controlled were on the other side. The two sides tried to influence other nations. This period of increased tensions lasted for nearly 50 years and was known as the Cold War.

The Cold War Begins

The United Nations was created in 1945 to promote peace among nations. However, tensions increased between Communist countries and those that did not follow communism. Many democratic nations supported the Truman Doctrine, which outlined ways for nations to fight communism. China, however, became a Communist country in 1949. In the Middle East, Israel became an independent nation in 1948. Conflicts began between Israelis and Palestinians.

The United Nations

The Korean War and the Red Scare

North Korea and South Korea were formed after World War II. North Korea was Communist. South Korea was a democracy. In 1950, North Korea invaded South Korea. U.S. troops defended South Korea. The fighting stopped in 1953. On the home front, a Red Scare took hold. Some Americans turned against one another in fear of communism.

The Changing Nation

Dwight Eisenhower became President in 1952. He promised to control government spending and to support social programs. During his presidency, the National Aeronautics and Space Administration (NASA) was created and the space race began. In addition, African Americans started their campaign for civil rights. Many countries in Asia and Africa gained independence at this time.

Life in the Fifties

The population grew after World War II. Many people moved to suburbs because there was not enough housing in the cities. Women worked outside the home more. Television became wildly popular. Rock-and-roll was born. African Americans began to make gains in the fight for equality.

How did the Korean War become an American war?

CHAPTER 28 ★ A Look Ahead

The Kennedy Years 1961–1963

March on Washington, D.C. in 1963

The Big Idea

John F. Kennedy became President in 1961. He was the youngest President ever elected. He led the country through many challenges. Kennedy called his plan for the country the New Frontier. He continued to oppose communism. Kennedy focused on education and workers' health. He supported the civil rights movement.

The Communist Threat

Television was a major factor in the election of 1960. The presidential candidates debated on national television. Once he was elected, Kennedy faced the problem of communism. Cuba was now a Communist country. It was only 90 miles from Florida. Kennedy allowed an invasion of Cuba by U.S. forces to go forward. The Bay of Pigs invasion was defeated, however. Kennedy worked to keep communism out of South Vietnam. In 1962, he found out that Soviet missiles were in Cuba. He insisted that they be removed.

The New Frontier

Kennedy urged the nation to explore new frontiers. His youth and intelligence attracted new advisors to the White House. The Supreme Court expanded people's rights at this time. Kennedy proposed to start the Peace Corps. Volunteers would go to help nations in need. Kennedy continued the space program, too.

The Civil Rights Movement

African Americans began protests for civil rights, called sit-ins, in 1960. Soon, hundreds of sit-ins were taking place at movie theaters, stores, restaurants, libraries, and swimming pools. People watched on television as African Americans were beaten. These sights angered many Americans. Martin Luther King Jr. gave his "I Have a Dream" speech. It is one of the most famous speeches in American history. In 1963, President Kennedy was shot and killed.

John F. Kennedy

★ **In what ways did Kennedy continue to oppose communism?**

CHAPTER 29 ★ A Look Ahead

The Johnson Years 1963–1968

Lyndon Baines Johnson

The Big Idea

President Lyndon Johnson led the country through stormy times. He proposed programs to improve life in America. Head Start, Medicare, and Medicaid began in the Johnson years. Johnson fought to protect the rights of African Americans. Women, Native Americans, and Mexican Americans fought for their rights, as well. The Vietnam War expanded in the Johnson years. The war's unpopularity grew, too.

The Great Society

Lyndon Johnson was Vice President under Kennedy. When Kennedy was killed in 1963, Johnson became President. He promised to continue Kennedy's work. Johnson was elected to office in 1964. He called his social programs the Great Society and the War on Poverty. He and Congress made many changes to help people in America.

Equal Rights

The Civil Rights Act of 1964 and the Voting Rights Act of 1965 are very important civil rights laws. They were both passed during Johnson's administration. They went far to stop segregation in America. However, some African American groups, such as the Black Muslims, wanted to separate totally from white society. Black Panthers wanted African Americans to have pride in themselves. Dr. Martin Luther King Jr.'s assassination was a tragedy for all Americans. During this time, women fought for equal rights, too. They were joined by Mexican Americans and Native Americans.

Conflict in Vietnam

In the 1960s, North Vietnam was a Communist country. South Vietnam was not. The United States was helping South Vietnam fight a Communist takeover. The United States sent more and more troops there. American soldiers and Vietnamese soldiers and civilians were killed each day. At home, people started demonstrations against the war. They were angry with President Johnson's policies. By 1968, Johnson decided not to run for the presidency again. Peace talks between the United States and North Vietnam began that year.

U.S. soldiers in Vietnam

Why were there protests against the war during the Vietnam War?

CHAPTER 30 ★ A Look Ahead

Turbulent Times 1968–1979

President Nixon and Li Shiennian, the Chinese Vice Premier

The Big Idea

Richard Nixon was elected President in 1968. Americans thought he was ending the Vietnam War. However, the war continued. On other issues, President Nixon worked for the environment. He increased civil rights protections. He offered friendship to Communist China. Yet, the poor U.S. economy and a scandal called Watergate caused problems for Nixon. President Gerald Ford gave stability to the country. President Jimmy Carter's leadership suffered from the energy crisis.

The End of the Vietnam War

Richard Nixon promised "peace with honor" in the Vietnam War. He tried to make it possible for South Vietnamese forces to fight the war themselves. This would allow the United States to begin to withdraw its troops. However, his plan did not work. Peace did finally come in 1973. The U.S. Congress then passed the War Powers Act. A President could no longer fight a long war without the approval of Congress. In 1975, South Vietnam surrendered and the war was finally over.

Nixon's Administration

Nixon worked on other issues besides the war. He signed a bill creating the Environmental Protection Agency. Americans celebrated the first Earth Day in 1970. Nixon believed in affirmative action. This policy creates opportunities for minorities. Astronauts walked on the moon in 1969. Nixon did well in relations with the Soviet Union and China. However, he tried to cover up knowledge of illegal acts of his re-election committee. This coverup was called the Watergate scandal. It led to Nixon's resignation in 1974.

Neil Armstrong and Buzz Aldrin on the moon's surface

Domestic Crises

Once again, a Vice President took over for a President. Gerald Ford served until 1977. He ran for election but did not win. Instead, Americans elected Jimmy Carter. He knew Americans wanted a President they could trust. However, rising prices and the energy crisis worsened during his term of office. Iran took Americans hostage during Carter's presidency. Iranians held more than 60 Americans hostage for more than a year. Carter was unable to free them. This caused him to lose the election of 1980.

★ **What happened to the economy while Carter was President?**

New Challenges for the Nation
1980–Present

Ribbon showing support for the country

Clean-up at the World Trade Center after the attacks of September 11, 2001

The Big Idea
Ronald Reagan served as President from 1981 to 1989. He believed in a smaller federal government and lower taxes. He increased military spending. George H. W. Bush's presidency was marked by the Persian Gulf War in 1991. William Clinton became President in 1993. His main issue was the economy. In 2001, George W. Bush became President. The terrorist attacks of September 11, 2001, focused his presidency. He worked to make the country safer from terrorism.

The Reagan Years 1981–1989
President Reagan put conservative policies in place. He cut taxes. He reduced limits on business. The national debt grew in the Reagan years. He also fought communism in Central America. Reagan called the Soviet Union "an evil empire." Later in his presidency, the Soviet Union began to change. Reagan developed a good relationship with the Soviet leader Mikhail Gorbachev.

A Changing World 1987–1993
President George H. W. Bush was forced to focus on a slow national economy during his presidency. He also signed new laws helping Americans. The Americans With Disabilities Act protected people with disabilities. The Clean Air Act helped lessen pollution. In 1991, the Soviet Union broke apart. The Cold War was over. The United States and its Allies began an attack known as Operation Desert Storm in the Middle East. This conflict began when Iraq invaded and seized control of Kuwait. The allied troops claimed victory in the Persian Gulf War and Kuwait was free. In South Africa, people gained rights when the apartheid laws ended.

Americans Respond to Crises 1992–Present
The Cold War was over. Still, conflicts continued around the world. During the Clinton presidency, Americans dealt with troubles in Bosnia and Kosovo. The election of 2000 brought George W. Bush to the presidency. On September 11, 2001, the attacks on the World Trade Towers and the Pentagon changed Americans' lives. President Bush made fighting terrorism the focus of his presidency.

★ **What happened to the Soviet Union in 1991?**

CHAPTER 32 ★ A Look Ahead

Looking to the Future 1990–Present

The Big Idea

Americans of 100 years ago would be amazed at how we live today. People have made great advances in technology and science. Computers have changed our lives. The U.S. economy is more connected to the economy of the world. Jobs will change as the twenty-first century unfolds. One great concern is affordable healthcare. Americans worry about our planet, too. Americans continue to face challenges with hope and strength.

The International Space Station

Advances in Technology and Science

Computers have changed the way people communicate. They have changed the way information is stored and used. Space technology has continued to advance, as well. In addition, technology is allowing people to examine genes. These are the building blocks of living organisms. Scientists are working to cure diseases through genetic research. They have learned to clone, or copy, cells and entire organisms.

Life in the Twenty-First Century

Through globalization, the world economy affects the U.S. economy. The kinds of jobs and the way people work will keep changing as the future unfolds. The people of the United States are changing, too. More immigrants are coming from Latin America and Asia. People are working on how best to educate our new immigrants. Healthcare for all Americans is a great concern. The cost of healthcare keeps rising. People are living longer, too. That makes our population older as time goes on. Housing for seniors will be a challenge in this century.

The Future of Our Planet

Technology can have a negative effect on Earth. Global warming is thought to be caused by the release of harmful gases into the atmosphere. Many people are trying to slow global warming. The U.S. Senate and President George W. Bush have not yet supported these changes. People are also working to find a cure for the disease AIDS. Americans will continue to work for the betterment of our planet and the people on it.

Why is it important for nations to work together in the twenty-first century?

Robot

Reference Section

Primary Source Documents

From The Magna Carta (1215)

This charter, granted by King John of England, limited the powers of a king and protected the basic rights of some individuals. More than 500 years later, American colonists fought against the British for the same rights listed in the Magna Carta.

1. . . . we have granted . . . that the English Church shall be free, and shall have its rights undiminished, and its liberties unimpaired. . . . To all free men of our kingdom, we have also granted, for us and our heirs forever, all the liberties written out below, to have and to keep for them and their heirs, of us and our heirs. . . .

38. In future no official shall place a man on trial upon his own unsupported statement, without producing credible witnesses to the truth of it.

39. No free man shall be seized or imprisoned, or stripped of his rights or possessions, or outlawed or exiled, . . . except by the lawful judgment of his equals or by the law of the land.

40. To no one will we sell, to no one deny or delay, right or justice.

41. All merchants may enter or leave England, unharmed and without fear, and may stay or travel within it, by land or water, for purposes of trade. . . .

42. In future it shall be lawful for any man to leave and return to our kingdom unharmed and without fear, by land or water. . . .

60. All these customs and liberties that we have granted shall be observed in our kingdom in so far as concerns our own relations with our subjects. . . .

63. . . . the English Church be free, and that the men in our kingdom shall have and keep all these liberties, rights, and concessions, well and peaceably, in their fullness and entirety for them and their heirs, of us and our heirs, in all things and all places forever.

From The Mayflower Compact (1620)

The Pilgrims, sailing aboard the Mayflower, *left England behind to begin a new life in North America. The Mayflower Compact was a step toward self-government in the English colonies.*

. . . Having undertaken, for the glory of God, and advancement of the Christian faith, and honor of our King and country, a voyage to plant the first colony in the northern parts of Virginia, do by these presents solemnly and mutually, in the presence of God, and one of another, covenant and combine our selves together into a civil body politic; for our better ordering, and preservation and furtherance of the ends aforesaid; and by virtue hereof to enact, constitute, and frame such just and equal laws, ordinances, acts, constitutions and offices, from time to time, as shall be thought most meet and convenient for the general good of the Colony, unto which we promise all due submission and obedience.

From James Monroe, The Monroe Doctrine (1823)

The Monroe Doctrine stated that the United States would not allow European nations to form new colonies in the Americas. It also declared that the United States would help former colonies to maintain their independence. The doctrine guided U.S. policy in the Western Hemisphere for many years.

. . . the occasion has been judged proper for asserting, as a principle in which the rights and interests of the United States are involved, that the American continents, by the free and independent condition which they have assumed and maintain, are henceforth not to be considered as subjects for future colonization by any European powers. . . .

The citizens of the United States cherish sentiments the most friendly in favor of the liberty and happiness of their fellow-men on that side of the Atlantic. In the wars of the European powers in matters relating to themselves we have never taken any part, nor does it comport with our policy to do so. It is only when our rights are invaded or seriously menaced that we resent injuries or make preparation for our defense. With the movements in this hemisphere we are of necessity more immediately connected, and by causes which must be obvious to all enlightened and impartial observers. . . . We owe it, therefore, to . . . declare that we should consider any attempt on their part to extend their system to any portion of this hemisphere as dangerous to our peace and safety. With the existing colonies or dependencies of any European power we have not interfered and shall not interfere. But with the Governments who have declared their independence and maintain it, and whose independence we have, on great consideration and on just principles, acknowledged, we could not view any interposition for the purpose of oppressing them, or controlling in any other manner their destiny, by any European power in any other light than as the manifestation of an unfriendly disposition toward the United States.

From Appeal of the Cherokee Nation (1830)

In 1830, the U.S. Congress passed the Indian Removal Act. According to this act, Native Americans with homelands in the East would be forced to move to the West. In response, Cherokee leaders wrote this appeal declaring their right to stay on their land. Despite their efforts, most Cherokees were removed to Oklahoma Territory in 1838–1939.

. . . We are aware, that some persons suppose it will be for our advantage to remove beyond the Mississippi. We think otherwise. Our people universally think otherwise. Thinking that it would be fatal to their interests, they have almost to a man sent their memorial to congress, deprecating the necessity of a removal. . . . We are not willing to remove; and if we could be brought to this extremity, it would be not by argument, nor because our judgment was satisfied, not because our condition will be improved; but only because we cannot endure to be deprived of our national and individual rights and subjected to a process of intolerable oppression.

We wish to remain on the land of our fathers. We have a perfect and original right to remain without interruption or molestation. The treaties with us, and laws of the United States made in pursuance of treaties, guaranty our residence and our privileges, and secure us against intruders. Our only request is, that these treaties may be fulfilled, and these laws executed.

But if we are compelled to leave our country, we see nothing but ruin before us. The country west of the Arkansas territory is unknown to us. . . . All the inviting parts of it, as we believe, are preoccupied by various Indian nations, to which it has been assigned. They would regard us as intruders. . . . The far greater part of that region is, beyond all controversy, badly supplied with wood and water; and no Indian tribe can live as agriculturists without these articles.

From The Declaration of Sentiments (1848)

The first women's rights convention was held at Seneca Falls, New York, in 1848. Elizabeth Cady Stanton and other women presented the Declaration of Sentiments to the convention. This document showed that women did not have all the rights listed in the Declaration of Independence.

When, in the course of human events, it becomes necessary for one portion of the family of man to assume among the people of the earth a position different from that which they have hitherto occupied, but one to which the laws of nature and of nature's God entitle them, a decent respect to the opinions of mankind requires that they should declare the causes that impel them to such a course.

We hold these truths to be self-evident: that all men and women are created equal; that they are endowed by their Creator with certain inalienable rights; that among these are life, liberty, and the pursuit of happiness; that to secure these rights governments are instituted, deriving their just powers from the consent of the governed. Whenever any form of government becomes destructive of these ends, it is the right of those who suffer from it to refuse allegiance to it, and to insist upon the institution of a new government, laying its foundation on such principles, and organizing its powers in such form, as to them shall seem most likely to effect their safety and happiness. . . .

He has never permitted her to exercise her inalienable right to the elective franchise.

He has compelled her to submit to laws, in the formation of which she had no voice. . . .

He has made her, if married, in the eye of the law, civilly dead.

He has taken from her all right in property . . .

He has denied her the facilities for obtaining [an] . . . education . . .

He has endeavored, in every way that he could, to destroy her confidence in her own powers, to lessen her self-respect, and to make her willing to lead a dependent and abject life.

Now, in view of this entire disfranchisement of one-half the people of this country, their social and religious degradation—in view of the unjust laws above mentioned, and because women do feel themselves aggrieved, oppressed, and fraudulently deprived of their most sacred rights, we insist that they have immediate admission to all the rights and privileges which belong to them as citizens of the United States.

From Abraham Lincoln, The Emancipation Proclamation (1862)

Abraham Lincoln issued the Emancipation Proclamation during the Civil War. In it, he declared that slaves in areas controlled by the Confederacy were free. Lincoln felt certain that he was doing the right thing when he signed this paper. Although no slaves were freed immediately, the Emancipation Proclamation was a promise that enslaved people in the South would be free when the Union won the war.

. . . I do order and declare that all persons held as slaves within said designated States and parts of States are, and henceforward shall be, free; and that the Executive Government of the United States, including the military and naval authorities thereof, will recognize and maintain the freedom of said persons.

And I hereby enjoin upon the people so declared to be free to abstain from all violence, unless in necessary self-defence; and I recommend to them that, in all case when allowed, they labor faithfully for reasonable wages.

And I further declare and make known that such persons of suitable condition will be received into the armed service of the United States to garrison forts, positions, stations, and other places, and to man vessels of all sorts in said service.

And upon this act, sincerely believed to be an act of justice, warranted by the Constitution upon military necessity, I invoke the considerate judgment of mankind and the gracious favor of Almighty God.

Abraham Lincoln, The Gettysburg Address (1863)

During the Civil War, more than 50,000 soldiers were killed, wounded, or captured at the Battle of Gettysburg. Afterward, Abraham Lincoln went to the battlefield to attend a dedication ceremony for a cemetery. He gave a short speech that lasted just over two minutes. Today the Gettysburg Address is considered one of the greatest speeches in American history.

Four score and seven years ago our fathers brought forth on this continent a new nation, conceived in liberty and dedicated to the proposition that all men are created equal. Now we are engaged in a great civil war, testing whether that nation or any nation so conceived

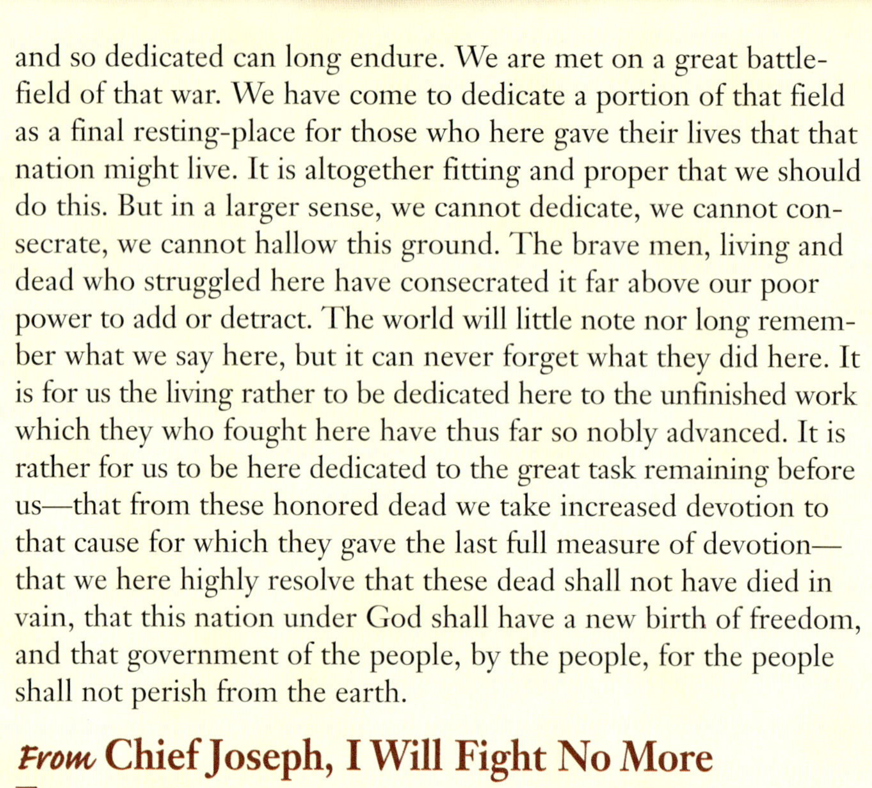

and so dedicated can long endure. We are met on a great battlefield of that war. We have come to dedicate a portion of that field as a final resting-place for those who here gave their lives that that nation might live. It is altogether fitting and proper that we should do this. But in a larger sense, we cannot dedicate, we cannot consecrate, we cannot hallow this ground. The brave men, living and dead who struggled here have consecrated it far above our poor power to add or detract. The world will little note nor long remember what we say here, but it can never forget what they did here. It is for us the living rather to be dedicated here to the unfinished work which they who fought here have thus far so nobly advanced. It is rather for us to be here dedicated to the great task remaining before us—that from these honored dead we take increased devotion to that cause for which they gave the last full measure of devotion—that we here highly resolve that these dead shall not have died in vain, that this nation under God shall have a new birth of freedom, and that government of the people, by the people, for the people shall not perish from the earth.

From Chief Joseph, I Will Fight No More Forever (Speech to the U.S. Army, 1877)

In 1877, the U.S. government ordered the Nez Percé Native Americans to a reservation. Chief Joseph and a group of followers fled toward Canada. U.S. soldiers chased them and fought several battles with them. Finally, Chief Joseph surrendered to the army with these words:

Tell General Howard I know his heart. What he told me before, I have it in my heart. I am tired of fighting. Our chiefs are killed. Looking Glass is dead. Ta Hool Hool Shute is dead. The old men are all dead. It is the young men who say, Yes or No. He who led the young men is dead. It is cold, and we have no blankets. The little children are freezing to death. My people, some of them, have run away to the hills, and have no blankets, no food. No one knows where they are—perhaps freezing to death. I want to have time to look for my children, and see how many of them I can find. Maybe I shall find them among the dead. Hear me, my Chiefs! I am tired. My heart is sick and sad. From where the sun now stands I will fight no more forever.

From Woodrow Wilson, The Fourteen Points (Address to Congress, 1918)

As World War I was coming to an end, President Wilson believed that a peace treaty calling for severe punishment of the Central Powers would only lead to future conflicts. In an effort to maintain world peace, he proposed the following ideas in the Fourteen Points.

Gentlemen of the Congress:

. . . We entered this war because violations of right had occurred which touched us to the quick and made the life of our own people impossible unless they were corrected and the world secure once for all against their recurrence. What we demand in this war . . . is that the world be made fit and safe to live in; and particularly that it be made safe for every peace-loving nation which, like our own, wishes to live its own life, determine its own institutions, be assured of justice and fair dealing by the other peoples of the world as against force and selfish aggression. All the peoples of the world are in effect partners in this interest. . . . The program of the world's peace, . . . as we see it, is this:

I. Open covenants of peace, openly arrived at, after which there shall be no private international understandings of any kind but diplomacy shall proceed always frankly and in the public view.

II. Absolute freedom of navigation upon the seas . . . .

III. The removal, so far as possible, of all economic barriers and the establishment of an equality of trade conditions among all the nations consenting to the peace and associating themselves for its maintenance.

IV. Adequate guarantees given and taken that national armaments will be reduced to the lowest point consistent with domestic safety. . . .

XIV. A general association of nations must be formed under specific covenants for the purpose of affording mutual guarantees of political independence and territorial integrity to great and small states alike. . . .

An evident principle runs through the whole program I have outlined. It is the principle of justice to all peoples and nationalities, and their right to live on equal terms of liberty and safety with one another.

From Martin Luther King Jr., I Have a Dream (Address at the March on Washington, 1963)

On August 28, 1963, Martin Luther King Jr. led a civil rights march on Washington, D.C. On the steps of the Lincoln Memorial, he gave a powerful speech expressing his hopes for the nation's future.

. . . Five score years ago, a great American, in whose symbolic shadow we stand signed the Emancipation Proclamation. . . . But one hundred years later, the Negro is still not free. . . . So we've come here today to dramatize a shameful condition. . . . I say to you today, my friends, so even though we face the difficulties of today and tomorrow, I still have a dream. It is a dream deeply rooted in the American dream.

I have a dream that one day this nation will rise up and live out the true meaning of its creed: "We hold these truths to be self-evident: that all men are created equal." . . . I have a dream that my four little children will one day live in a nation where they will not be judged by the color of their skin but by the content of their character. . . .

This is our hope. This is the faith that I go back to the South with. . . . With this faith, we will be able to work together, to pray together, to struggle together, to go to jail together, to stand up for freedom together, knowing that we will be free one day!

This will be the day when all of God's children will be able to sing with a new meaning, "My country 'tis of thee, sweet land of liberty, of thee I sing. Land where my fathers died, land of the pilgrim's pride, from every mountainside, let freedom ring," and if America is to be a great nation, this must become true. . . .

When we allow freedom to ring, when we let it ring from every village and every hamlet, from every state and every city, we will be able to speed up that day when all of God's children, black men and white men, Jews and Gentiles, Protestants and Catholics, will be able to join hands and sing in the words of the old Negro spiritual, "Free at last! Free at last! Thank God Almighty, we are free at last!"

PRESIDENTS of the United States

		Years in Office	Vice President	State◆
1	**1. George Washington** (1732–1799)	1789–1797	John Adams	Virginia
2	**2. John Adams** (1735–1826)	1797–1801	Thomas Jefferson	Massachusetts
3	**3. Thomas Jefferson** (1743–1826)	1801–1809	Aaron Burr, George Clinton	Virginia
4	**4. James Madison** (1751–1836)	1809–1817	George Clinton, Elbridge Gerry	Virginia
5	**5. James Monroe** (1758–1831)	1817–1825	Daniel D. Tompkins	Virginia
6	**6. John Quincy Adams** (1767–1848)	1825–1829	John C. Calhoun***	Massachusetts
7	**7. Andrew Jackson** (1767–1845)	1829–1837	John C. Calhoun, Martin Van Buren	Tennessee (SC)
8	**8. Martin Van Buren** (1782–1862)	1837–1841	Richard M. Johnson	New York
9	**9. William Henry Harrison*** (1773–1841)	1841	John Tyler	Ohio (VA)
10	**10. John Tyler** (1790–1862)	1841–1845	None	Virginia
11	**11. James K. Polk** (1795–1849)	1845–1849	George M. Dallas	Tennessee (NC)
12	**12. Zachary Taylor*** (1784–1850)	1849–1850	Millard Fillmore	Louisiana (VA)
13	**13. Millard Fillmore** (1800–1874)	1850–1853	None	New York
14	**14. Franklin Pierce** (1804–1869)	1853–1857	William R. King	New Hampshire

◆State of residence at time of election. If state of birth is different, it is shown in parentheses.
*Died while in office **Assassinated while in office ***Resigned while in office

	Years in Office	Vice President	State♦
15. James Buchanan (1791–1868)	1857–1861	John G. Breckinridge	Pennsylvania
16. Abraham Lincoln** (1809–1865)	1861–1865	Hannibal Hamlin, Andrew Johnson	Illinois (KY)
17. Andrew Johnson (1808–1875)	1865–1869	None	Tennessee (NC)
18. Ulysses S. Grant (1822–1885)	1869–1877	Schuyler Colfax, Henry Wilson	Illinois (OH)
19. Rutherford B. Hayes (1822–1893)	1877–1881	William A. Wheeler	Ohio
20. James A. Garfield** (1831–1881)	1881	Chester A. Arthur	Ohio
21. Chester A. Arthur (1830–1886)	1881–1885	None	New York (VT)
22. S. Grover Cleveland (1837–1908)	1885–1889	Thomas A. Hendricks	New York (NJ)
23. Benjamin Harrison (1833–1901)	1889–1893	Levi P. Morton	Indiana (OH)
24. S. Grover Cleveland (1837–1908)	1893–1897	Adlai E. Stevenson	New York (NJ)
25. William McKinley** (1843–1901)	1897–1901	Garret A. Hobart, Theodore Roosevelt	Ohio
26. Theodore Roosevelt (1858–1919)	1901–1909	Charles W. Fairbanks	New York
27. William H. Taft (1857–1930)	1909–1913	James S. Sherman	Ohio
28. T. Woodrow Wilson (1856–1924)	1913–1921	Thomas R. Marshall	New Jersey (VA)
29. Warren G. Harding* (1865–1923)	1921–1923	J. Calvin Coolidge	Ohio

15 16 17 18 19 20 21 22, 24 23 25 26 27 28 29

30 31		Years in Office	Vice President	State◆
30 31	**30. J. Calvin Coolidge** (1872–1933)	1923–1929	Charles G. Dawes	Massachusetts (VT)
	31. Herbert C. Hoover (1874–1964)	1929–1933	Charles Curtis	California (IA)
32 33	**32. Franklin D. Roosevelt*** (1882–1945)	1933–1945	John N. Garner, Henry A. Wallace, Harry S Truman	New York
	33. Harry S Truman (1884–1972)	1945–1953	Alben W. Barkley	Missouri
34 35	**34. Dwight D. Eisenhower** (1890–1969)	1953–1961	Richard M. Nixon	New York (TX)
	35. John F. Kennedy** (1917–1963)	1961–1963	Lyndon B. Johnson	Massachusetts
36 37	**36. Lyndon B. Johnson** (1908–1973)	1963–1969	Hubert H. Humphrey	Texas
	37. Richard M. Nixon*** (1913–1994)	1969–1974	Spiro T. Agnew,*** Gerald R. Ford	New York (CA)
38 39	**38. Gerald R. Ford** (1913–)	1974–1977	Nelson A. Rockefeller	Michigan (NE)
	39. James E. Carter Jr. (1924–)	1977–1981	Walter F. Mondale	Georgia
40 41	**40. Ronald Reagan** (1911–)	1981–1989	George H.W. Bush	California (IL)
	41. George H.W. Bush (1924–)	1989–1993	J. Danforth Quayle	Texas (MA)
42 43	**42. William J. Clinton** (1946–)	1993–2001	Albert Gore Jr.	Arkansas
	43. George W. Bush (1946–)	2001–	Richard B. Cheney	Texas (CT)

Glossary

abolition the elimination of something, in this case slavery (p. 347)

affirmative action programs for reversing the effects of discrimination (p. 713)

agriculture the art or science of raising crops (p. 6)

alliance an agreement between two or more people, groups, or nations to cooperate with one another (p. 257)

ally a nation, group, or people who are friendly with other people for a common goal (p. 119)

ambush a surprise attack from a hidden position (p. 126)

amendment a change or an addition (p. 203)

amnesty a government pardon for an offense (p. 433)

annexation the act of adding to or taking possession of (p. 360)

anthem a song of praise (p. 280)

apartheid a policy in South Africa of complete separation of the races (p. 736)

appeasement an attempt to keep peace with an enemy by giving in to its demands (p. 614)

apprentice a person who works to learn a specific skill (p. 97)

armistice an agreement to stop warfare (p. 555)

arms race a competition to build weapons (p. 542)

arsenal a building used to store weapons and ammunition (p. 196)

assembly an elected group that makes laws (p. 114)

assembly line a row of factory workers who put together a product, part by part, as it passes by on a conveyor belt (p. 566)

assimilate to become absorbed into a main culture (p. 467)

astrolabe an instrument used to calculate the position of the stars (p. 36)

atomic bomb a nuclear weapon that causes large-scale destruction (p. 628)

baby boom the increase in the birthrate after World War II (p. 652)

backcountry an area inhabited by few people and far from more settled areas (p. 82)

barrio a community in which mostly Spanish-speaking people live (p. 594)

barter to exchange one product or service for another (p. 90)

Bessemer process a method for producing a stronger type of steel (p. 476)

bilingual using two languages (p. 761)

black codes a series of laws passed in early Reconstruction to limit the freedoms of formerly enslaved African Americans (p. 436)

Black Power a movement among African Americans to gain political and economic power (p. 688)

blitzkrieg the German method of conducting war with speed and force (p. 616)

blockade a barrier of ships or troops that prevents goods from entering or leaving an area (p. 407)

boomtown a mining camp that grew into a town almost overnight (p. 370)

bootlegger a person who made or transported alcohol illegally (p. 575)

border states four slave states located between the Union and the Confederacy that stayed in the Union during the Civil War (p. 406)

boycott a protest in which people refuse to buy certain goods (p. 139)

Cabinet a group of people chosen by the President to give advice (p. 246)

canal a waterway dug across land for ships to travel through (p. 289)

caravan a group of travelers with pack animals (p. 27)

carpetbagger a Northerner who moved to the South after the Civil War for political gain (p. 440)

cash crop a crop that is grown to be sold rather than used by a farmer (p. 58)

casualty a person wounded, captured, missing, or killed in battle (p. 167)

cede to give up or surrender land (p. 127)

censorship control of free expression (p. 423)

census an official population count (p. 245)

charter an official document in which rights are given by a government to a person or company (p. 56)

checks and balances a system to keep one part of a government from becoming stronger than other parts (p. 201)

civilian a person who is not a member of the military (p. 180)

civilization a well-developed way of life of a people in one place and time (p. 10)

civil war a war between people of the same country (p. 389)

clan a small unit of related Native American families that may be known by a common symbol, such as a bear or turtle (p. 17)

clone to make an exact copy of an organism by duplicating genetic material (p. 756)

Cold War a conflict between countries, with no actual fighting (p. 634)

collective bargaining talks between a union and an employer about working conditions (p. 485)

colony a settlement in a distant land that is governed by another country (p. 39)

commerce the buying and selling of goods (p. 34)

commune a community where people live and work together using shared resources (p. 346)

communism a theory in which the economy is controlled by the government, and property is owned by everyone equally (p. 550)

computer literate having the basic skills needed to operate a computer (p. 753)

concentration camp a place where political prisoners and members of religious and ethnic groups are sent (p. 629)

Confederacy the Confederate States of America, formed in 1861 by southern states that had seceded from the Union (p. 397)

confederation a union of countries or states for a common purpose (p. 188)

conquistador the Spanish term for conqueror, or one who gains control by winning a war (p. 49)

conscription the act of requiring people to serve in the military (p. 414)

conservation protection of natural resources (p. 510)

conservative a person who believes in limited government involvement in the economy (p. 601)

constitution the basic laws and plan of a nation's government (p. 186)

containment a policy of preventing a country from expanding its power (p. 636)

cooperative an organization that is jointly owned by those who use its services (p. 462)

corollary a statement that follows logically from another statement (p. 532)

corporation a large company usually formed by a group of investors (p. 483)

cotton gin a machine that removes seeds from cotton fibers (p. 319)

cowhand a hired person who looks after cattle (p. 457)

culture all of a group's arts, beliefs, and ways of doing things (p. 8)

debtor a person who owes money (p. 84)

declaration a formal statement (p. 151)

deferment a postponement, or a delaying, of having to serve in the armed forces (p. 696)

demilitarized zone an area that military forces cannot enter (p. 642)

deport to force someone to leave a country (p. 577)

depression a long period of economic decline (p. 587)

deregulation the loosening of government controls (p. 727)

détente easing tensions between unfriendly nations (p. 714)

dictator a ruler who has complete power (p. 611)

diplomacy conducting relations with the governments of foreign countries (p. 533)

direct primary an election in which members of a political party vote to choose their candidates (p. 507)

discrimination unjust treatment of someone based on prejudice (p. 440)

doctrine a set of beliefs or principles (p. 292)

domino theory the belief that if one country falls to communism, others nearby will fall, one after the other (p. 692)

downsize lay off or fire workers to cut costs (p. 736)

drought a long period without rainfall (p. 15)

dry farming a method of farming that makes use of all the water available in a dry land (p. 18)

economy the way in which goods and services are produced and consumed in a community (p. 73)

electoral college a group of people from each state who perform the official duty of electing the President and Vice President (p. 201)

emancipate to free (p. 392)

embargo an order stopping trade with another country (p. 273)

emigrate to leave one country to settle in another country (p. 118)

empire a large land area and population controlled by a single ruler or group (p. 11)

empresario a person who received a contract to bring settlers to Texas in the 1800s (p. 356)

encomienda system the system in which Native Americans were forced to work for Spanish landowners (p. 49)

environment the social, cultural, and natural conditions that influence a community (p. 300)

escalation an increasing involvement (p. 693)

ethnic having a common racial, national, or cultural tradition (p. 489)

ethnic cleansing the act of ridding a region or society of one or more ethnic groups (p. 740)

exclusion the act of keeping a person or group out (p. 491)

executive branch the law-enforcing branch of the federal government (p. 200)

exile a person who is forced to live away from his or her home country (p. 662)

Exoduster an African American who moved to the Great Plains in the late 1800s (p. 461)

expedition a journey made for a specific purpose (p. 38)

export to sell goods to another country (p. 93)

extinction the death of a species (p. 466)

extremist a person whose opinions are very different from those of most people (p. 388)

factory a building with workers and machines in which manufacturing takes place (p. 312)

fascism a political system that emphasizes nationalism and is ruled by a dictator (p. 611)

federal deficit the difference produced when the government spends more than it collects during a year (p. 728)

feminism the belief that women's rights should be equal to men's rights (p. 689)

filibuster to give a long speech in order to delay the vote on a bill in Congress (p. 686)

forty-niner a person who went to California in 1849 seeking gold (p. 370)

Freedmen's Bureau the federal agency created to help emancipated African Americans adjust to life as free people (p. 443)

Freedom Ride a protest against segregated buses and bus stations (p. 671)

frontier the region just beyond a settled area (p. 136)

fugitive a person who has run away (p. 383)

fundamentalist a person who believes in a strict interpretation of the Bible or another religious book (p. 578)

garrison a place where troops are stationed and weapons and ammunition are stored (p. 172)

generation gap a difference in tastes and values between young people and their parents (p. 654)

genetic engineering the act of working on genes to change, or copy them (p. 755)

genocide the deliberate destruction of a group of people based on their race, culture, or beliefs (p. 627)

globalization a condition in which countries are members of a world community (p. 758)

global warming the rise in the average temperatures of Earth over time (p. 764)

grand jury a jury that decides if the charges against a person are strong enough for a trial (p. 742)

Great Society President Johnson's goals and programs for the future of the United States (p. 681)

greenhouse effect the process by which Earth is kept warm at all times (p. 764)

guerrilla war fighting involving surprise raids (p. 663)

habeas corpus the right of a citizen to ask a court to decide if a prisoner is being held lawfully (p. 423)

Harlem Renaissance a cultural movement of African American writers, painters, and musicians, many of whom lived in the Harlem area of New York City (p. 570)

Holocaust Hitler's policy of killing European Jews and others considered "unfit to live" during World War II (p. 627)

homesteader a person who received land on which to build a house and farm (p. 460)

hostage a person who is held captive until certain demands are met (p. 721)

human genome the genetic makeup of human beings (p. 755)

human rights the basic freedoms that all people should have (p. 718)

immigrant a person who moves into a country from another country (p. 259)

immigration the act of coming into a country to live there (p. 80)

impeachment the process of charging a high public official, such as the President, with a crime (p. 441)

imperialism the practice of one nation controlling other nations through conquest and colonization (p. 518)

implied power a power that is not stated in the Constitution (p. 251)

import to buy goods from another country (p. 93)

impressment seizing someone and forcing that person into service for a country (p. 255)

inauguration a formal ceremony to induct an elected official into office (p. 244)

indentured servant person who agrees to work for another until a debt is paid (p. 61)

individualism an emphasis on the value, rights, and power of the individual (p. 341)

inflation a sharp increase in the price of goods and services (p. 180)

installment plan the payment for an item in small, regular amounts over a period of time (p. 567)

insurrection a rebellion against established authority (p. 395)

integrate to open to people of all races (p. 672)

interchangeable parts identical parts that can be substituted for each other (p. 314)

internment camp a place in which people are confined, especially during a time of war (p. 619)

ironclad warship metal or metal-covered steam-driven warship (p. 415)

iron curtain a barrier of secrecy that kept Soviet-controlled nations apart from the rest of Europe (p. 635)

irrigate to supply water to dry land for growing crops (p. 15)

isolationism the policy of staying out of the political affairs of other countries (p. 519)

isthmus a narrow strip of land separating two larger land areas (p. 530)

Jazz Age the name given to the 1920s because of the new popularity of jazz music (p. 570)

Jim Crow laws laws that enforced segregation in the South (p. 446)

joint occupation the sharing of an area of land by two or more countries (p. 364)

joint-stock company a group of investors who share both risk and profit (p. 56)

judicial branch the law-interpreting branch of the federal government (p. 200)

judicial review a court review to determine whether a law is constitutional (p. 269)

kamikaze a Japanese pilot who crashes his plane into an enemy ship (p. 626)

kinship family relationships (p. 30)

"kitchen cabinet" unofficial advisors to the President (p. 296)

legislative branch the lawmaking branch of the federal government (p. 200)

libel a false statement made in writing about someone (p. 98)

liberal a person who favors using government resources to bring about social and economic change (p. 601)

line item veto a veto of a portion but not all of a proposed law (p. 399)

Loyalist a person who remained loyal to the British government (p. 164)

Manifest Destiny the idea that the United States had the right to expand from the Atlantic Ocean to the Pacific Ocean (p. 364)

massacre the brutal killing of a large number of people (p. 144)

mass production the making of many items in a short period of time (p. 314)

McCarthyism named after Senator Joseph McCarthy, the practice of publicly accusing people of political disloyalty without regard for evidence (p. 644)

Medicaid public health program that pays medical expenses for low-income people (p. 682)

Medicare national health insurance for older Americans and people with certain disabilities (p. 682)

mercantile system an economic system that stresses increasing national wealth by selling more than buying in foreign trade (p. 93)

mercenary a hired soldier (p. 166)

migrant worker a person who moves from place to place to find work, usually harvesting crops (p. 590)

migrate to move from one place to another (p. 5)

militia a group of citizen-soldiers who volunteer when needed (p. 122)

minuteman a member of the colonial militia (p. 148)

mission a settlement built by a church for religious work (p. 50)

mobilize to organize or prepare, as for war (p. 544)

monarch a ruler (p. 112)

monopoly complete control over a supply, service, or market (p. 483)

mountain man a fur trapper or trader who went west to live in or near the mountains (p. 366)

muckraker a writer who brings attention to problems in society (p. 504)

napalm a sticky gasoline jelly used in bombs (p. 694)

national debt the total amount of money the federal government owes to individuals, institutions, and itself (p. 728)

nationalism pride in one's country (p. 282)

nation-building the support of developing governments in foreign countries (p. 739)

nativism the view that favors people born in a country over immigrants who come to that country (p. 336)

natural resource something provided by nature that is useful to people (p. 6)

navigate to control the direction of a boat or ship (p. 35)

neutral not taking one side or the other (p. 254)

New Frontier President Kennedy's goals and programs for the future of the United States (p. 666)

nomad a person who moves about in search of food (p. 4)

nullify to cancel (p. 259)

ordinance a law (p. 193)

overseer a person who is in charge of enslaved people (p. 103)

pacifist a person who opposes war under any circumstance (p. 543)

Parliament the British law-making branch of government (p. 112)

patent a grant that gives an inventor the sole right to make and sell an invention for a set period of time (p. 477)

Patriot a person who supported independence from Great Britain (p. 149)

patroon a Dutch landowner in the colony of New Netherland (p. 77)

Peace Corps a federal agency that sends trained volunteers to help developing countries (p. 667)

pension an income for retired workers (p. 600)

perjury telling a lie under oath (p. 643)

persecute to punish or mistreat a person because of his or her beliefs (p. 70)

petition a formal written request (p. 147)

Pilgrim a religious traveler to a new land; a founder of Plymouth Colony (p. 71)

plantation a large farm requiring many workers (p. 36)

planter a person who owns and operates a plantation (p. 320)

platform a statement of a political party's policies and beliefs (p. 463)

popular sovereignty control by the people (p. 381)

precedent an example for the future (p. 246)

presidio a Spanish fort (p. 367)

proclamation an official announcement (p. 136)

profit money gained from a business or investment after expenses have been paid (p. 586)

Progressive a person who believes in social progress through reform (p. 505)

Prohibition the ban on the making and sale of alcoholic drinks (p. 506)

propaganda the promotion of certain ideas to influence people's opinions (p. 552)

proprietary colony a colony owned and managed by one or more individuals (p. 78)

prospector a person who looks for gold or other valuable ores (p. 370)

protectorate a small country protected and controlled by a larger one (p. 528)

provisional temporary (p. 399)

public domain land owned by the government (p. 194)

public works projects paid for by the government for public use (p. 588)

pueblo an apartment-like adobe dwelling; Spanish word for village (p. 15)

Puritan a member of a religious group that wanted to simplify the practices of the Church of England (p. 70)

quarantine to isolate (p. 663)

quota a fixed number of a certain group of immigrants admitted to a country (p. 577)

racism feelings against people because of their ethnic background or skin color (p. 501)

radical someone who favors extreme social or economic changes (p. 266)

range the vast public grasslands in the West where cattle graze freely (p. 456)

ratify to approve (p. 189)

ration to limit to small portions in order to make something last (p. 624)

recession a decline in economic activity (p. 718)

Reconstruction the period from 1865 to 1877 in which programs were created to reunite the South with the North (p. 432)

reformer a person who wants to improve society (p. 346)

refugee a person who flees to a foreign country (p. 638)

relief a direct money payment to the unemployed (p. 592)

relocate to move a person or group of people (p. 301)

reparation the payment for damages (p. 557)

repeal to take back or cancel (p. 140)

representative a person selected to act and speak in place of others (p. 125)

republic a government that receives its power from the people, who elect its leaders (p. 181)

reservation public land set aside for special use, as for Native Americans (p. 467)

resolution a formal statement of opinion (p. 143)

revenue money received by a government from taxes and other sources (p. 138)

revival a reawakening (p. 345)

royal colony a colony directly under the rule of a king or queen (p. 81)

rural having to do with the country (p. 334)

sanitation disposal of waste (p. 60)

satellite a nation controlled by another country (p. 635)

scalawag a white Southerner who supported the Republicans during Reconstruction (p. 440)

secede to withdraw from or leave (p. 384)

sectionalism concern for the interests of a certain region or area (p. 296)

segregation separation of the races (p. 446)

self-determination the right of people to decide on their own form of government (p. 557)

Separatist a Puritan who wished to break away, or separate, from the Church of England (p. 70)

sharecropping a system of farming in which farmers work another's land and use part of their crops as rent (p. 445)

siege a long, drawn-out attack (p. 172)

sit-in a protest in which people sit and refuse to leave a place (p. 670)

slave code a set of laws that limited the activities of enslaved people (p. 104)

sovereignty the power of self-government (p. 188)

space race the competition among countries to be the first in exploring space (p. 646)

sphere of influence a region in which one nation has influence or control over other nations (p. 522)

spiritual an expressive religious song (p. 327)

spoils system government appointments of friends by the winning party of an election (p. 295)

stagflation the economic condition of higher prices without economic growth (p. 715)

steerage a large open area beneath a ship's deck (p. 489)

stock a share of ownership in a company (p. 483)

strategy a plan (p. 407)

subsistence farming growing only enough crops to meet the needs of one household (p. 77)

suburb a community at the edge of a city (p. 652)

suffrage the right to vote (p. 508)

summit meeting a meeting between important leaders of nations (p. 649)

superpower one of the most powerful nations in the world (p. 641)

sweatshop an unhealthy workplace where people are overworked (p. 499)

tariff a tax on imported goods (p. 247)

tax money paid to a government (p. 28)

temperance a reform movement that was opposed to drinking alcohol (p. 346)

tenant farmer a person who pays for the right to farm someone else's land (p. 594)

tenement a run-down apartment building (p. 498)

terrorism the use of violence or threats to achieve a goal (p. 741)

textile cloth (p. 312)

totalitarian state a country in which one person or group has complete control (p. 612)

total war a war against civilians and resources as well as against armies (p. 424)

traitor a person who acts against his or her country (p. 150)

transcendentalism the belief that people learn truth and knowledge from their experiences with God and nature (p. 341)

transcontinental across a continent (p. 455)

trench warfare soldiers fighting from long ditches dug in the ground (p. 413)

tribute money paid for protection (p. 272)

truce a temporary agreement to stop fighting (p. 707)

trust a giant corporation made up of a group of companies (p. 510)

unconstitutional something that goes against the U.S. Constitution (p. 247)

Underground Railroad escape routes used by enslaved African Americans to reach freedom in the North (p. 327)

Union the United States of America (p. 254); also, the northern states during the Civil War era (p. 397)

urban describing a city or city life (p. 335)

urban renewal a program to rebuild run-down areas of cities (p. 682)

utopia a perfect society (p. 340)

veto to reject a law (p. 201)

victory garden a garden in which people grow their own food during a war (p. 551)

Vietnamization President Nixon's plan to train the South Vietnamese to fight the Vietnam War (p. 706)

war bond a loan from U.S. citizens to the government meant to be paid back with interest in several years (p. 551)

yellow journalism publishing exaggerated or made-up news stories to attract readers and influence their ideas (p. 524)

Index

An italic *c* indicates a chart or graph; an italic *crt*, a political cartoon; an italic *m*, a map; and an italic *p*, a picture.

C

D

E

K

L

M

Acknowledgments and Photo Credits

All photography © Pearson Education, Inc. (PEI) unless otherwise specifically noted.

Table of Contents iv: © Jonathan Blair/Corbis. v: *t.* The Granger Collection, New York; *b.* © Ted Spiegel. vi: *t.* Photograph Courtesy of the Concord Museum, Concord, MA and the archives of the Lexington Historical Society. David Bohl, photographer; *b.* Mr. and Mrs. John A. Harney Collection/Smithsonian Institution Photographic Service National Museum of American History. vii: *t.* © Bettmann/Corbis; *b.* Courtesy, Library of Congress. viii: *t.* The Granger Collection, New York; *b.* The Charleston Museum.

Geography Handbook and Atlas GH1–GH10: *bkgd.* David Muir/Masterfile. GH1–GH2: *inset* © Bernhard Edmaier/Science Photo Library/Photo Researchers, Inc. GH3: *t.* Bud Freund/Index Stock Imagery, Inc.; *b.* Robert Aschenbrenner/Stock Boston. GH4: *t.* © Andy Sacks/Stone; *m.* Neil Rabinowitz/Corbis; *b.* Robin Hill/Index Stock Inc. A1–A8: *bkgd.* David Muir/Masterfile.

Unit 1 1: © John Elk III/Stock Boston. 2: Jerry Jacka/Jacka Photography. 3: © Richard A. Cooke/Corbis. 4: © Jonathan Blair/Corbis. 6: © Colin Keates/DK Images. 7: Illustration By Rob Wood/Wood Ronsaville Harlin, Inc. 10: Robert Frerck/Odyssey Productions. 11: © Galen Rowell/Corbis. 13: © Alison Wright/Corbis. 14: SuperStock, Inc. 17: British Museum, London, UK/ Bridgeman Art Library. 18: Pictures of Record, Inc. 21: Boltin Picture Library. 24: © Austrian Archives/Corbis. 25: Courtesy, U.S. Naval Academy Museum. 27: © Yann Arthus-Bertrand/Corbis. 29: © Owen Franken/Corbis. 32: The Granger Collection, New York. 33: Correr, Venice, Italy/ Bridgeman Art Library. 35: The Granger Collection, New York. 37: © Bettmann/Corbis. 42: *l.* Digital Vision; *r.* PhotoDisc, Inc. 43: *l.* © Peter Russell; The Military Picture Library/Corbis; *r.* © Onne van der Wal Photography. 46: Ira Block/National Geographic Society. 47: © Hulton Getty/Liaison Agency. 48: Image #: 286838, Amercian Museum of Natural History Library. 49: The Granger Collection, New York. 51: © Hulton Archive. 55: The Granger Collection, New York. 56: The Granger Collection, New York. 57: U.S. Senate Collection. 59: The American Antiquarian Society. 60 Courtesy, Library of Congress. 63: The William Gladstone African American Collection. 66: © Michael Newman/PhotoEdit.

Unit 2 67: Brownie Harris Productions. 68: The American Antiquarian Society. 69: The Granger Collection, New York. 71: © Bettmann/Corbis. 72: Ewing Galloway Inc. 73: © Corbis. 74: Shelburne Museum. 76: New York Historical Society, New York, USA/ The Bridgeman Art Library. 79: © Francis G. Meyer/Corbis. 83: The Granger Collection, New York. 85: Fran Olson/Historic St. Lukes Restoration. 88: © 1999 Musuem of Early Trades and Crafts. 89: The Granger Collection, New York. 91: The Metropolitan Museum of Art, Gift of Edgar William and Bernice Chrysler Garbisch, 1963. (63.201.3) Photograph © 1984 The Metropolitan Museum of Art. 93: The Granger Collection, New York. 94: Courtesy, Library of Congress. 97: © Corbis. 98: © Bettman/Corbis. 99: The Granger Collection, New York. 100: Courtesy, Dartmouth College. 104: Colonial Williamsburg Foundation, Abby Aldrich Rockefeller Folk Art Museum, Williamsburg, VA. 106: *l.* The Granger Collection, New York; *r.* © Bettmann/Corbis. 107: © Stone. 110: © Ted Spiegel. 111: The Granger Collection, New York. 113: The Granger Collection, New York. 115: The Granger Collection, New York. 116: The Granger Collection, New York. 118: © 1997 N. Carter/North Wind Picture Archives. 119: The Granger Collection, New York. 120: © Corbis. 121: © Wolfgang Kaehler/Corbis. 123: Cornelius Krieghoff/ National Archives of Canada. 126: © Bettmann/Corbis. 129: The Granger Collection, New York.

Unit 3 133: © Joseph Nettis/Photo Researchers, Inc. 134: Courtesy, the Concord Museum, Concord, MA. Photo by Chip Fanelli. 135: North Carolina Museum of Art. 138: The Granger Collection, New York. 139: The Granger Collection, New York. 144: The Granger Collection, New York. 145: *t.* The American Antiquarian Society; *b.* Museum of Fine Arts Boston. 148: © Bettmann/Corbis. 149: The Granger Collection, New York. 150: *t.* The Granger Collection, New York; *b.* The Granger Collection, New York. 152: *l.* Custom Medical Stock Photo, Inc.; *r.* The Granger Collection, New York. 153: *l.* © Telegraph Colour Library/FPG International LLC/Getty Images; *r.* © Stone. 156–157 *bkgd.* PhotoDisc, Inc.; *inset* © Tom and Pat Leeson/Photo Researchers, Inc. 162: New-York Historical Society, New York, USA/ Bridgeman Art Gallery. 163: Wells Fargo Bank, Historical Services. 164: Photograph Courtesy of the Concord Museum, Concord, MA and the archives of the Lexington Historical Society. David Bohl, photographer. 165: © David Wagner, 1977. All rights reserved. Courtesy of the collection of the Rhode Island Black Heritage Society. 167: SuperStock, Inc. 168: Nawrocki Stock Photo, Inc. 170: © Corbis. 171: The Granger Collection, New York. 173: *t.* U.S. Naval Academy Museum; *b.* The Granger Collection, New York. 175: The Granger Collection, New York. 178: Winterthur Museum. 179: Lafayette College Art Collection, Easton, PA. 180: Colonial Williamsburg Foundation, Abby Aldrich Rockefeller Folk Art Museum, Williamsburg, VA. 184: Nawrocki Stock Photo, Inc. 185: National Archives. 187: The Granger Collection, New York. 193: The Granger Collection, New York. 196: The Granger Collection, New York. 197: *t.* PhotoDisc, Inc.; *b.* National Postal Museum, Smithsonian Institute. 199: North Wind Picture Archives. 201: The Granger Collection, New York. 206–207 AP/Wide World Photo. 206–239: *bkgd.* PhotoDisc, Inc.

Unit 4 241: National Geographic Society. 242: Courtesy, the Mount Vernon Ladies' Association. 243: National Gallery of Art, Washington. Gift of Edgar Williams and Bernice Chrysler Garbisch. 247: The Granger Collection, New York. 248: The Granger Collection, New York. 251: *l.* The Granger Collection, New York; *r.* © Corbis. 253: The Granger Collection, New York. 256: Hulton/Arichive. 257: © Bettmann/Corbis. 258: The Granger Collection, New York. 260: *l.* Collection of The New-York Historical Society; *r.* © David J. & Janice L. Frent Collection/Corbis. 261: *t.* AP Photo/Eric Draper. 264 *t.* Image #3377 (2) Photo by: P. Hollembeak/American Museum of Natural History; *b.* Image #3378 (2) Photo by: P. Hollembeak/American Museum of Natural History. 265: The Metropolitan Museum of Art, Rogers Fund, 1907. (07.123) Photograph ©1985 The Metropolitan Museum of Art. 266: The Smithsonian Institute. 267: © Corbis. 268: The Granger Collection, New York. 269: The Corcoran Gallery of Art. 270: The Boston Athenaeum. 271: © Bettman/Corbis. 273: The Granger Collection, New York. 274: The Granger Collection, New York. 276: *t.* Courtesy, the Montana Historical Society. 277: Missouri Historical Society. 279: Courtesy, Library of Congress. 280: The Granger Collection, New York. 283: The Granger Collection, New York. 285: Collection of The New-York Historical Society. 286: Independence National Historical Park. 287: Courtesy, the Henry Francis du Pont Winterthur Museum. 289 Thomas Coke Ruckle-Maryland Historical Society. 290: © Corbis. 292: Tom Van Sant/Geosphere Project, Santa Monica/PhotoDisc, Inc. 294: Courtesy, Library of Congress. 296: © Corbis. 297: The Granger Collection, New York. 298: © Bettman/Corbis. 300: © Smithsonian American Art Museum, Washington, D.C./Art Resource, NY. 301: © Smithsonian American Art Museum, Washington, D.C./Art Resource, NY. 303 Woolaroc Museum. 305: © Smithsonian American Art Museum, Washington, D.C./Art Resource, NY.

Unit 5 309: © James L. Amos/Corbis. 310: Courtesy, Library of Congress. 311: © Bettmann/Corbis. 312: © Bohemian Nomad Picturemakers/Corbis. 313: The Granger Collection, New York. 314: © Corbis. 316: © Bettmann/Corbis. 318: © Morton Beebe, S.F./Corbis. 319: *l.* The Granger Collection, New York; *r.* © Bettmann/Corbis. 323: © Bettmann/Corbis. 325–326 © Corbis. 328 © Corbis. 329: The William Gladstone African American Collection. 332: New York City Fire Museum. 333: © Museum of the City of New York/Corbis. 334: © Kevin Fleming/Corbis. 337: North Wind Picture Archives. 338: © Phil Schermeister/Corbis. 341: Courtesy, Library of Congress. 342: The Granger Collection, New York. 343: © Christie's Images. 344: © Geoffrey Clements/ Corbis. 346: The Granger Collection, New York. 347: Courtesy, the Massachusetts Historical Society. 348–349 The Granger Collection, New York. 351: © Bettman/Corbis. 354: Courtesy, Chris Day Collection. 355: The Bancroft Library. 356–357 Texas State Library. 358: *t.* © Sandy Felsenthal/Corbis; *b.* The Daughters of the Republic of Texas Library at the Alamo. 359: Texas State Library. 364: © Corbis. 366: The Granger Collection, New York. 367: © Richard Cummins/Corbis. 368: © Bowers Museum of Cultural Art/Corbis. 369: Archive Photos. 372: William Tylee Ranney/Wood River Gallery. 373: *t.* © Corbis; *b.* © George Hall/Corbis.

Unit 6 377: Kenneth Garrett Photography. 378: The Charleston Museum. 379: Courtesy of The Brooklyn Museum of Art, Gift of Ms. Gwendolyn O. L. Conkling,. 380: Stock Montage, Inc. 382: Courtesy, Library of Congress. 386: The Boston Athenaeum. 387: *l.* The Granger Collection, New York; *r.* Sophia Smith Collection, Smith College. 389: © Corbis. 390: Courtesy, Library of Congress. 391: Collection of The New-York Historical Society. 393: The Granger Collection, New York. 394: Courtesy, Library of Congress. 395: © Corbis. 399: © Corbis. 401: The Granger Collection, New York. 404: © Tria Giovan/Corbis. 405: © Bettmann Archive/Corbis. 406: © Tria Giovan/ Corbis. 408: © Corbis. 410: © Corbis. 414: © Museum of the City of New York/Corbis. 416: © Corbis. 417: © Bettmann Archive/Corbis. 418: *t.* The Museum of the Confederacy, Richmond, VA. Photograph by Katherine Wetzel; *b.* Courtesy of General Dynamics Corp. Electric Boat Div./Naval Historical Center. 419: *l.* The Defense Visual Information Center; *r.* U.S. Navy Photograph. 420: © Corbis. 422: The State Museum of Pennsylvania, Pennsylvania Historicaland Museum Commission. 423: © Corbis. 424: © Bettmann/Corbis. 426: © Bettmann Archive/Corbis. 427: © Corbis. 430: The William Gladstone African American Collection. 431: The Granger Collection, New York. 433: *t.* © Tria Giovan/Corbis; *b.* Getty Images, Inc. 434: Courtesy, Library of Congress. 435: The Granger Collection. 440: © Bettmann/Corbis. 441: © Bettmann/Corbis. 443: The William Gladstone African American Collection. 444: © Medford Historical Society Collection/Corbis. 445: The Granger Collection, New York. 450: PhotoEdit.

Epilogue E2: *t.* Courtesy, Library of Congress; *b.* The Granger Collection, New York. E3: *t.* The Granger Collection, New York; *b.* AT&T Archives. E4: *t.* Sophia Smith Collection, Smith College; *b.* © Bettmann/Corbis. E5: *t.* © Danny Lehman/Corbis; *b.* Courtesy, The Columbus Dispatch. E6: *t.* © Corbis; *b.* © Bettmann/Corbis. E7: *t.* Hirz/Hulton Archive (Archive Photos); *b.* Frank Driggs Collection. E8: *b.* © Corbis. E9: *t.* The Granger Collection, New York; *b.* Courtesy, Library of Congress. E10: *t.* Hulton Archive (Archive Photos); *b.* United Nations. E11: *t.* © Bettmann/Corbis; *b.* AP/Wide World Photo. E12: *t.* Lyndon Baines Johnson Library; *b.* © Bettmann/Corbis. E13: *t.* © Bettmann/Corbis; *b.* Courtesy, NASA. E14: *t.* © David N. Berkwitz; *b.* © AFP PHOTO/Beth A. Keiser/Corbis. E15: *t.* Courtesy, NASA; *b.* Reuters/TimePix.

Reference Section R1–R12 *bkgd.* PhotoDisc, Inc. R10: *l. to r., t. to b.* © Corbis; © Corbis; © Corbis; © Corbis; © Corbis; © Corbis; © Corbis; © Corbis; The Granger Collection, New York; © Corbis; © Corbis; Art Resource, NY; © Corbis; The Granger Collection. R11 *l. to r., t. to b.* © Corbis; The Granger Collection; The Granger Collection; The Granger Collection; © Corbis; © Corbis; The Granger Collection; The Granger Collection; The Granger Collection; © Corbis;The Granger Collection; © Corbis; The Granger Collection; Smithsonian Institution National Portrait Gallery. R12 *l. to r., t. to b.* The Granger Collection; © Corbis; The Granger Collection; The Granger Collection; © Corbis; AP/Wide World Photo; Lyndon Baines Johnson Library; © Corbis; © Corbis; © Corbis; White House Photo Office; White House Photo Office; © Corbis; White House Photo Office.